Communication Yearbook / 18

Communication
Yearbook / 18

edited by
BRANT R. BURLESON

editorial assistant
Tammy Fletcher-Bergland

Published Annually for the
International Communication
Association

SAGE Publications
International Educational and Professional Publisher
Thousand Oaks   London   New Delhi

For information address:

SAGE Publications, Inc.
2455 Teller Road
Thousand Oaks, California 91320

SAGE Publications Ltd.
6 Bonhill Street
London EC2A 4PU
United Kingdom

SAGE Publications India Pvt. Ltd.
M-32 Market
Greater Kailash I
New Delhi 110 048 India

Printed in the United States of America

Library of Congress: 76-45943

ISBN 0-8039-5925-7

ISSN 0147-4642

95 96 97 98 99 10 9 8 7 6 5 4 3 2 1

Sage Production Editor: Astrid Virding

CONTENTS

Introduction   xii
    Brant Burleson

SECTION 1:   COGNITIVE APPROACHES
                 TO COMMUNICATION:
                 PLANNING, PRODUCING,
                 AND PROCESSING MESSAGES

1. **Elaborating the Cognitive Rules Model of
   Interaction Goals: The Problem of Accounting for
   Individual Differences in Goal Formation**
   Steven R. Wilson   3

2. **Production of Messages in Pursuit of Multiple
   Social Goals: Action Assembly Theory Contributions
   to the Study of Cognitive Encoding Processes**
   John O. Greene   26

3. **Managing the Flow of Ideas: A Local Management
   Approach to Message Design**
   Barbara J. O'Keefe and Bruce L. Lambert   54

4. **An Appraisal and Revision of the Constructivist
   Research Program**
   John Gastil   83

5. **Language, Fallacies, and Mindlessness-Mindfulness
   in Social Interaction**
   Judee K. Burgoon and Ellen J. Langer   105

6. **Attention to Television and Some Methods
   for Its Measurement**
   Tom Grimes and Jeanne Meadowcroft   133

   Commentary

7. **Cognitive Interpersonal Communication Research:
   Some Thoughts on Criteria**
   Dean E. Hewes   162

   Commentary

8. **Is the "Golden Age of Cognition" Losing Its Luster?
   Toward a Requirement-Centered Perspective**
   Vincent R. Waldron   180

SECTION 2: COMMUNICATION ABOUT HEALTH
AND ENVIRONMENTAL RISKS:
DEVELOPMENTS
IN THEORY AND RESEARCH

9. **Using the Theory of Reasoned Action to Examine
the Impact of Health Risk Messages**
*Robert J. Griffin, Kurt Neuwirth,
and Sharon Dunwoody*   201

10. **Generating Effective Risk Messages:
How Scary Should Your Risk Communication Be?**
Kim Witte   229

11. **Corporate Environmental Risk Communication:
Cases and Practices Along the Texas Gulf Coast**
Robert L. Heath   255

12. **Attaining a State of Informed Judgments:
Toward a Dialectical Discourse on Risk**
Napoleon K. Juanillo, Jr., and Clifford W. Scherer   278

   Commentary

13. **What Risk Communicators Need to Know:
An Agenda for Research**
Katherine E. Rowan   300

   Commentary

14. **Moving Toward a Framework for the Study of Risk
Communication: Theoretical and Ethical Considerations**
Rajiv Nath Rimal, BJ Fogg, and June A. Flora   320

SECTION 3: MODES OF CONNECTING THROUGH
COMMUNICATION: DISCOURSE,
RELATIONSHIPS, TECHNOLOGY,
AND IDEOLOGY

15. **Micromanaging Expert Talk: Hosts' Contributions
to Televised Computer Product Demonstrations**
Robert E. Nofsinger   345

   Commentary

16. **Studying Conversational Interaction in Institutions**
Robert W. Hopper   371

17. **An Experimental Approach to Social Support Communications: Interactive Coping in Close Relationships**
    Anita P. Barbee and Michael R. Cunningham   381

    Commentary

18. **The Communicative Microdynamics of Support**
    Daena J. Goldsmith   414

19. **Social Impacts of Electronic Mail in Organizations: A Review of the Research Literature**
    Laura Garton and Barry Wellman   434

    Commentary

20. **Don't Blink or You'll Miss It: Issues in Electronic Mail Research**
    Michael E. Holmes   454

21. **A Kinder, Gentler Discipline: Feeling Good About Being Mediocre**
    Michael Burgoon   464

    Commentary

22. **Ideology in Interpersonal Communication: Beyond the Couches, Talk Shows, and Bunkers**
    Malcolm R. Parks   480

Index   498

About the Editor   507

About the Authors   508

THE INTERNATIONAL COMMUNICATION ASSOCIATION

The International Communication Association (ICA) was formed in 1950, bringing together academicians and other professionals whose interests focus on human communication. The Association maintains an active membership of more than 2,400 individuals, of whom some two-thirds are teaching and conducting research in colleges, universities, and schools around the world. Other members are in government, the media, communication technology, business, law, medicine, and other professions. The wide professional and geographic distribution of the membership provides the basic strength of the ICA. The Association is a meeting ground for sharing research and useful dialogue about communication interests.

Through its Divisions and Interest Groups, publications, annual conferences, and relations with other associations around the world, the ICA promotes the systematic study of communication theories, processes, and skills.

In addition to *Communication Yearbook,* the Association publishes the *Journal of Communication, Human Communication Research, Communication Theory, A Guide to Publishing in Scholarly Communication Journals, ICA Newsletter,* and the *ICA Membership Directory.*

For additional information about the ICA and its activities, contact Robert L. Cox, Executive Director, International Communication Association, P.O. Box 9589, Austin, TX 78766; phone (512) 454-8299; fax (512) 454-4221; e-mail UAA513@UTXVM.Bitnet.

Editors of the *Communication Yearbook* series:

Volumes 1 and 2, Brent D. Rubin
Volumes 3 and 4, Dan Nimmo
Volumes 5 and 6, Michael Burgoon
Volumes 7 and 8, Robert N. Bostrom
Volumes 9 and 10, Margaret L. McLaughlin
Volumes 11, 12, 13, and 14, James A. Anderson
Volumes 15, 16, and 17, Stanley A. Deetz
Volumes 18, 19, and 20, Brant R. Burleson

CONSULTING EDITORS

The following individuals helped make possible this volume of the *Communication Yearbook* by providing insightful reviews of papers and proposals. The editor gratefully acknowledges these scholars for the gifts of their time and wisdom.

INTRODUCTION

Communication Yearbook 18 represents a beginning, a continuation, and an ending. *CY18* marks the beginning of my term as editor; this is the first of the three volumes I am slated to edit. The purpose of the *Communication Yearbook,* as I see it, is to help readers think more deeply about human communication, giving insight and perspective on the understandings we have developed thus far. I also believe the *Yearbook* has a mission to stimulate new, creative approaches to communication, especially how it can be conceptualized, studied, and used to improve the human condition.

CY18 represents a continuation in maintaining the practice, initiated by James Anderson with *CY11,* of publishing integrated sets of essays and commentaries that address several different facets of communication scholarship. As with previous volumes of the *Yearbook,* the essays appearing in *CY18* have undergone a rigorous selection and development process. All submissions for *CY18* were subjected to blind review; based on the recommendations of referees, some submissions were selected for further development. Those submissions were then revised and subjected to another round of reviews. Thus all of the essays appearing in this volume have gone through two rounds of reviews, and most were revised extensively to accommodate the advice and criticism of expert referees. These essays represent works of the highest scholarly quality. Once the feature essays were chosen, commentaries were then commissioned from authorities especially able to focus and extend issues raised in the essays. These commentaries constitute major scholarly contributions in their own right.

CY18 is an end, of sorts, in that it will be the last volume to use the essay and commentary format. Beginning with *Communication Yearbook 19,* the *Yearbook* will exclusively publish comprehensive reviews and syntheses of communication literature. I will have more to say about the change in the *Yearbook*'s format later in this introduction. First, however, let's see what this volume has in store.

OVERVIEW OF THE ESSAYS

CY18 contains fourteen feature essays and eight commentaries organized in three sections. Section 1 contains chapters exploring cognitive approaches to the study of communication, Section 2 is concerned with risk communication, and Section 3 looks at some of the diverse ways in which people are connected through communication.

Cognitive Approaches to Communication:
Planning, Producing, and Processing Messages

The cognitive perspective began making significant inroads in the communication discipline during the 1970s and dominated much of the research carried out in the 1980s. Indeed, there was widespread hope in some quarters (e.g., Berger & Chaffee, 1988; Hawkins, Wiemann, & Pingree, 1988) that cognition could become a unifying focus for researchers concerned with communication in interpersonal, group, organizational, mass, and other contexts. The current group of six essays and two commentaries, authored by some of the leading contributors to the cognitive approach, provides an opportunity to evaluate how well the promise of the cognitive approach has been realized.

The first four chapters in Section 1 focus on cognitive accounts of one of the most fundamental aspects of communication: the message production process. Many contemporary models see message production originating in an actor's goals. Steven Wilson overviews his *cognitive rules* (CR) model of interaction goals, which charts how actors form goals as a function of matches between cognitive rules and features of social situations. Wilson notes that empirical tests of an early version of his CR model (Wilson, 1990) indicated it did a good job of accounting for interactional goals formulated by those with sophisticated cognitive systems, but performed less well in accounting for the goals formed by those with simpler cognitive systems. In the current chapter, Wilson proposes and evaluates several revisions of the CR model in an effort to furnish a more general analysis of the goal formation process.

Interaction goals do not immediately translate into message contents; rather, messages must be assembled from various cognitive components—or so says the action assembly theory of John Greene (1984, in press). In many interactional circumstances, people pursue multiple goals simultaneously (see Brown & Levinson, 1978; Clark & Delia, 1979). Rather than just trying to persuade someone, for example, a speaker might engage in persuasion while simultaneously trying to convey a positive evaluation of the other, show respect for the other's autonomy, display a particular social identity, and so on. In his chapter in this volume, Greene shows how action assembly theory can be applied to account for the production of multiple goal messages, and he reviews an extensive body of empirical work demonstrating the value of the action assembly theory framework. Greene's work also shows how temporal qualities of speech (e.g., pause rates and durations) provide important clues about underlying cognitive processes.

Not all analysts of the production process see messages as planned, coherent efforts attempting to achieve predetermined goals. Barbara O'Keefe and Bruce Lambert critique the dominant "holistic-functional" approach to message production and offer as an alternative a *local management approach* to message design. In this approach, message structures are viewed as expressions arising from the movement of an attentional focus through a structure of knowledge, whereas message functions are conceptualized as cognitive mappings relating antecedent conditions, message structures, and outcomes. O'Keefe and Lambert provide a detailed explication of their local management approach and review a computer simulation study suggesting the merit of their analysis.

The constructivist framework of Jesse Delia and his associates (Delia, 1977; Delia, O'Keefe, & O'Keefe, 1982) has generated one of the more popular and empirically fruitful accounts of message production. In his chapter, John Gastil uses criteria derived from Imre Lakatos's (1978) analysis of scientific research programs to carry out a thorough appraisal and critique of the constructivist position. Gastil acknowledges important contributions of constructivist theory and research, but argues that this position needs significant revision if it is to remain a viable framework for the study of message production and related matters.

The other two feature essays in Section 1 focus on cognitive processes implicated in the reception or interpretation of messages. Judee Burgoon and Ellen Langer consider how certain features of language structure and use promote *mindless* functioning, a condition in which "individuals consider available information and alternatives incompletely, rigidly, reflexively, and thoughtlessly." Mindless conduct may often be dysfunctional, resulting in maladaptive psychological and behavioral outcomes. Fortunately, whereas some aspects of language appear to foster mindless functioning, Burgoon and Langer suggest that other features of linguistic structure and use encourage more mindful functioning, and thus may provide a corrective to problems created by mindlessness.

One of the most fundamental aspects of message reception is *attention* to the messages and features of the environment in which messages occur. An increasing number of researchers, especially those concerned with the reception and impacts of televised messages, have begun to study how people attend to the messages bombarding them and how variations in attention influence message effects. Tom Grimes and Jeanne Meadowcroft provide a very useful review of this research, describing some of the common empirical paradigms for the study of attention and critically assessing the adequacy of popular research methods.

The two commentaries on the essays in Section 1 do an excellent job of situating and evaluating the current status of cognitive approaches. Dean Hewes, himself a leading contributor to the cognitive perspective, begins the important task of formulating criteria to be used in evaluating specific cognitive analyses of communication-related phenomena. The framework he develops will help with the appraisal of current theories, as well as with the articulation of more sophisticated positions. Vincent Waldron notes that cognitive positions do a good job of providing detailed and empirically testable accounts of message production and message reception processes. But Waldron argues that these processes are not all there is to communication. A full account of communication must also examine the details of interaction, and few cognitive approaches have done that in any depth. Hence Waldron suggests that cognitive approaches may soon decline in influence unless they "get to the communication part" and account more fully for complex, socially situated actions and interactions.

Communication About Health and Environmental Risks: Developments in Theory and Research

Section 2 explores several areas in the emerging field of risk communication. Interest in risk communication (that is, communication about environmental and health hazards) has grown rapidly over the past two decades, partly fueled by an increasing awareness of how human conduct can imperil health, safety, and well-being (see Covello, 1992). Appreciating that many of our most serious hazards are humanly produced is important, because it means these hazards— whether unsafe sexual practices of individuals or polluting practices of entire industrial sectors—are subject to human control. And communication is one of the chief mechanisms through which people can control these hazards. The four essays and two commentaries in Section 2 explore, at both individual and social levels, the communicative negotiation and management of risks.

Robert Griffin, Kurt Neuwirth, and Sharon Dunwoody apply Ajzen and Fishbein's (1980) theory of reasoned action to explore the effects of risk messages appearing in newspapers on beliefs, attitudes, and behavioral intentions. Significantly, these researchers find that varied features of news stories (headline type, story content, use of personalized leads) can have potent, if complex, effects on what readers believe and feel about risk situations and how they plan to act in those situations. More generally, this study indicates that the powerful and well-supported theory of reasoned action can be successfully applied to the analysis of risk messages and their effects.

Kim Witte is also interested in risk messages, specifically the content of public health appeals intended to curtail risky sexual practices in the face of the AIDS epidemic. Developing effective messages is a complex problem, Witte argues, because how people perceive a risk influences which appeals will be most successful in modifying risky behavior. Witte describes her extended parallel process model (EPPM), which proposes that in the face of risks, people are motivated to control either the danger (when they feel the risk can be managed) or their fear (when they feel the risk cannot be controlled). She also summarizes two pilot studies suggesting how the EPPM can be used to inform the design of messages targeted to specific audience characteristics.

In many cases, appropriate management of risk situations involves far more than effective message design. This is made abundantly clear in Robert Heath's examination of successful and unsuccessful communication efforts by the chemical industry along the Texas gulf coast. Heath's comparative analysis of five case studies, while reinforcing the importance of well-designed messages, clearly demonstrates the value of communicative efforts that create avenues for public involvement, respect the public's desire for control and self-determination, manage uncertainty, disclose information pertaining to both costs and benefits, build trust, and respect all affected groups as equal partners in the decision-making process.

Some of the principles for good communication practice suggested by Heath's analysis are given intense scrutiny by Napoleon Juanillo, Jr., and Clifford Scherer in a chapter devoted to promoting more dialectical discourse on risk situations. Juanillo and Scherer critique classical approaches to risk communication, which they argue privilege scientific and bureaucratic viewpoints while disempowering the public. The dialectical perspective proposed by these theorists strives for the empowerment of all stakeholders in risk situations, attempts to create a sensitivity to the multiple interests and perspectives common in most risk contexts, and works to develop in varied publics the skills required to make informed judgments about risks and alternatives.

In her commentary on the four feature essays in Section 2, Katherine Rowan reminds us that risk communication is fundamentally a pragmatic, applied enterprise: People engage in risk communication to solve practical problems arising from the management of hazards, dangers, and threats. Given this applied focus, Rowan suggests that our approach to theory and research on risk communication should be guided by the question, What do risk communicators need to know to function more effectively? Rowan uses this question as a heuristic to organize and critique existing literature and develop an agenda for future research on risk communication. That agenda includes giving more attention to (a) philosophical analyses of risk management and risk communication, (b) historical and critical studies of policies and regulations governing risk communication, (c) empirical research on the psychological and social factors influencing the perception and interpretation of risks, and (d) empirical research on the communication skills risk communicators need to accomplish the complex obstacles they routinely face. In their commentary, Rajiv Nath Rimal, Brian Fogg, and June Flora also propose a synthetic framework for integrating the risk communication literature. They argue that both theoretical and ethical issues in risk communication need to be examined with a multilevel approach—one that includes individuals, institutions, and whole societies within the same analytic frame. Rimal et al. also articulate an interpretive continuum that arrays risk communication efforts along a descriptive-evaluative-injunctive dimension. The heuristics and syntheses proposed by Rowan and Rimal et al. help considerably with the challenging task of integrating the varied streams constituting the risk communication literature.

Modes of Connecting Through Communication: Discourse, Relationships, Technology, and Ideology

Section 3 consists of essays and commentaries exploring modes of connection achieved through communication. Connecting to others is, of course, one of the most basic functions of communication, and the chapters in Section 3 vividly illustrate the diversity of ways in which this is accomplished.

For example, Robert Nofsinger explores how people connect through the mechanisms of conversational interaction in a particular institutionalized setting, the televised computer product demonstration. The product demonstrations on which Nofsinger focuses are not monological descriptions of product features, but collaborative constructions in which the program host plays a crucial role. Nofsinger details the host's use of multiple conversational devices, some of which are generally available resources and others of which are rooted in the institutional context of the television interview. Nofsinger thus shows how participants use a variety of conversational and institutional resources to connect conversationally with one another, and in the process create a media product. In his commentary on this chapter, Robert Hopper explores additional implications of studying conversational interaction in institutions, pointing out that any theory of communication must both distinguish and describe context-sensitive (institutional) and context-free (mundane) phenomena. Hopper suggests that conversational analysis supplies methods for identifying both mundane and institutionally based features of interaction, and further encourages us to explore how these elements dialectically define and contextualize each other.

One of the most profound ways in which humans connect is through supportive forms of communication. Social support is a basic function of communication that occurs in most relationships (impersonal as well as personal), but is especially characteristic—and constitutive—of intimate relationships. Anita Barbee and Michael Cunningham review their detailed program of research on *interactive coping,* focusing on communication processes through which persons both seek and provide support from others. They also present sensitive interaction systems theory (SIST) as a framework for understanding and explaining the influence of a host of psychological and relationship factors on the seeking and provision of support. In her commentary on this chapter, Daena Goldsmith notes that the theoretical models and rich empirical paradigm developed by Barbee and Cunningham should do much to facilitate even more sophisticated research on social support processes. However, Goldsmith also raises some important questions about the ways in which support-related behaviors have been conceptualized and assessed by Barbee and Cunningham and other researchers in this area. Goldsmith describes procedures for developing approaches to social support that are more fully communication focused, and encourages researchers to examine not only supportive behaviors and their outcomes, but also the interpretive and social processes through which such behaviors and outcomes are generated and apprehended.

Laura Garton and Barry Wellman provide a review of research on electronic mail, a technology whose connective possibilities have lately captured the popular imagination. Focusing specifically on the social implications of e-mail within organizations, Garton and Wellman suggest understanding e-mail as "a communication network operating on a computer network that supports social networks." Although much literature emphasizes how e-mail and related technologies are reshaping the modern organization, Garton and Wellman stress that organizations are not hostages of these technologies; rather, they appropriate innovations in their own ways for their own purposes. Thus a full understanding of e-mail in the organization requires attention to how factors such as organizational power, group relations, and social networks shape the implementation, uses, and abuses of e-mail. In his commentary, Michael Holmes argues that improved understanding of the impacts of e-mail demands further concept development. Exemplifying the creative fashioning of new conceptual tools, Holmes identifies four root metaphors driving e-mail research and describes the contributions and limitations of each.

People are connected not only through conversations, relationships, and technologies, but through beliefs and ideologies, some of which have pernicious effects. In an essay provocative in both content and style, Michael Burgoon asserts that "our research in interpersonal communication, as a whole, is guided by a dominant left-of-center political ideology." Burgoon maintains that many of the social sciences, "and communication in particular, have embraced a Marxist orientation that glorifies the collective while diminishing the importance of the individual." Burgoon's targets include many traditional foci in communication research, and his chapter makes disturbing reading for those of us who have pursued research programs focused on topics such as comforting, conflict management, patient satisfaction, organizational harmony, and communication competence.

Of course, Burgoon is not the first to have analyzed ideologies that infest particular domains of communication research. In a classic essay published more than a dozen years ago, Malcolm Parks (1982) detailed how the *ideology of intimacy* powerfully skewed textbook treatments of and research on interpersonal communication. Parks's analysis appeared in *Communication Yearbook 5,* which, appropriately, was edited by Michael Burgoon. I asked Parks to comment on Burgoon's essay in the current volume of the *Yearbook* and, in the process, revisit his earlier critique of the ideology of intimacy. Parks's chapter does that, and a good deal more. It documents the continuing impact of the ideology of intimacy on communication research and then explores three new ideological influences that unduly constrain discourse about and research on communication. Parks provides a fitting conclusion to this volume by calling for the emergence of an "intellectual commons" where participants with different theoretical and value commitments can meet for good conversations that "get beyond the posturing." Parks initiates such a conversation, engaging in some much-needed plain talk, and invites us to join him in a continuing dialogue about who we are and where we are going. This is an invitation we surely should accept; what could be more appropriate for our discipline than a conversation about communication?

A LOOK AHEAD

This will be the last *Communication Yearbook* to use the essay and commentary format. Beginning with next year's volume, *CY* will exclusively publish articles that survey, critique, and integrate literature on topics of concern to communication scholars. Changing a publication's format is not unusual or a cause for alarm. Virtually all publications undergo evolution during their lives as a way of responding to changing markets, conditions, competition, and a host of related factors. *CY* underwent one major evolutionary change when Jim Anderson instituted the essay and commentary format with *CY11*. It appears to be time for another evolutionary change.

The decision to redefine the mission of *CY* was made in response to the explosion of literature in recent years on communication-related topics. In addition to the growing number of authored and edited books by communication scholars, there is an ever-increasing number of journals publishing more articles on a greater variety of communication topics. For example, *Communication Serials* (Sova & Sova, 1992) lists more than 2,700 communication-related periodicals published at some time between the early 1800s and the present. Clearly, scholars need ways to digest and integrate this literature, and a good review series can facilitate this process.

To this point, the communication discipline has had no outlet exclusively devoted to the publication of major literature reviews. This contrasts with such disciplines as psychology, which has both journals (e.g., *Psychological Bulletin*) and annuals (e.g., *Annual Reviews in Psychology*) that publish literature reviews. These publications have proven to be both valued scholarly resources and commercial successes.

My aim will be to publish comprehensive, integrative literature reviews that not only survey the avenues previously traveled in a research area, but also identify where new roads need to be built. Moreover, every effort will be made to include reviews covering the broad diversity of topics that populate the many specialties and subfields of the communication discipline. To make these aims a reality, I will need advice, assistance, and, most important, contributions of reviews from many of you. To help make *Communication Yearbook* the quality review series it aspires to be, the ICA is developing new procedures for soliciting and reviewing submissions. In particular, ICA's divisions will be more involved in identifying topics and authors for literature reviews and in refereeing proposals. The leadership of each of ICA's divisions and interest groups will be regularly surveyed for ideas about review topics. But it is also vital that individual scholars— those who are often on the cutting edge of important research areas—help with the identification of topics meriting review. I strongly encourage those having ideas about topics and authors for reviews to contact me with suggestions.

You will be hearing more—much more—about the new format for *CY* in forthcoming volumes. But I also hope to be hearing from you about *CY.* Your comments, counsel, contributions, and criticisms are essential for the success of this venture.

ACKNOWLEDGMENTS

This volume would not have been possible without the hard work of many dedicated individuals. I want to recognize and publicly thank a few of those whose efforts were especially noteworthy. First, I wish to acknowledge my editorial assistant, Tammy Fletcher-Bergland, for helping me stay organized and keeping this project on course and on schedule. I must also recognize the Department of Communication and the School of Liberal Arts at Purdue University, which provided me with the time and many of the material resources needed to edit this volume. At Purdue, I called on several of my colleagues for advice, quick reviews, and suggestions about referees, and they all responded with consideration and support. In particular, Kathy Rowan and Glenn Sparks helped out on multiple occasions. Finally, I wish to thank the referees (a list of whom appears elsewhere), who gave thoughtful consideration to the submissions they reviewed, and all those who submitted papers and proposals for sharing their scholarship and themselves with the rest of us.

REFERENCES

Ajzen, I., & Fishbein, M. (1980). *Understanding attitudes and predicting social behavior.* Englewood Cliffs, NJ: Prentice Hall.

Berger, C. R., & Chaffee, S. H. (1988). On bridging the communication gap. *Human Communication Research, 15,* 304-318.

Brown, P., & Levinson, S. (1978). Universals in language usage: Politeness phenomena. In E. N. Goody (Ed.), *Questions and politeness: Strategies in social interaction* (pp. 56-310). Cambridge: Cambridge University Press.

Clark, R. A., & Delia, J. G. (1979). *Topoi* and rhetorical competence. *Quarterly Journal of Speech, 65,* 187-206.

Covello, V. T. (1992). Risk communication: An emerging area of health communication research. In S. A. Deetz (Ed.), *Communication yearbook 15* (pp. 359-373). Newbury Park, CA: Sage.

Delia, J. G. (1977). Constructivism and the study of human communication. *Quarterly Journal of Speech, 63,* 66-83.

Delia, J. G., O'Keefe, B. J., & O'Keefe, D. J. (1982). The constructivist approach to communication. In F. E. X. Dance (Ed.), *Human communication theory: Comparative essays* (pp. 147-191). New York: Harper & Row.

Greene, J. O. (1984). A cognitive approach to human communication: An action assembly theory. *Communication Monographs, 51,* 289-306.

Greene, J. O. (in press). An action assembly perspective on verbal and nonverbal message production: A dancer's message unveiled. In D. E. Hewes (Ed.), *The cognitive bases of interpersonal communication.* Hillsdale, NJ: Lawrence Erlbaum.

Hawkins, R. P., Wiemann, J. M., & Pingree, S. (Eds.). (1988). *Advancing communication science: Merging mass and interpersonal processes.* Newbury Park, CA: Sage.

Lakatos, I. (1978). *The methodology of scientific research programmes.* Cambridge: Cambridge University Press.

Parks, M. R. (1982). Ideology of interpersonal communication: Off the couch and into the world. In M. Burgoon (Ed.), *Communication yearbook 5* (pp. 79-108). New Brunswick, NJ: Transaction.

Sova, H. W., & Sova, P. L. (Eds.). (1992). *Communication serials: An international guide to periodicals in communication, popular culture, and the performing arts.* Virginia Beach, VA: SovaComm.

Wilson, S. R. (1990). Development and test of a cognitive rules model of interaction goals. *Communication Monographs, 81,* 81-103.

SECTION 1

Cognitive Approaches to Communication: Planning, Producing, and Processing Messages

1 Elaborating the Cognitive Rules Model of Interaction Goals: The Problem of Accounting for Individual Differences in Goal Formation

STEVEN R. WILSON
Michigan State University

Current theories of message production typically assume that speakers design messages to accomplish goals, but provide limited detail about how speakers form goals. The cognitive rules (CR) model presents one explicit set of assumptions about how inter-action goals are formed. To date, predictions from the model have fared well for individuals high in interpersonal construct differentiation, but have received little support for less differentiated individuals. This chapter offers two suggestions for how the CR model might be elaborated to accommodate individual differences in goal formation. One possibility is that highly differentiated individuals possess more complex schemata for forming goals than do less differentiated individuals, which allow highly differentiated persons to process evaluatively inconsistent information but also make them prone to perceptual biases. A second possibility is that highly and less differentiated individuals rely on different heuristic principles when forming interaction goals, especially in situations where they lack the ability or motivation to process goal-relevant knowledge systematically. Both possibilities suggest interesting hypotheses for future work on goal formation and message production.

QUESTIONS about message production have captured the attention of a substantial number of communication scholars (e.g., Cody & McLaughlin, 1990; Dillard, 1990). Although researchers are using a variety of concepts and perspectives to investigate message production, their work shares a common interest in explaining how individuals decide what to say in everyday interactions and a common belief that light can be shed on this issue through the examination of the knowledge structures and cognitive processes that underlie message production.

Correspondence and requests for reprints: Steven R. Wilson, Department of Communication, Michigan State University, 470 Communication Arts Building, East Lansing, MI 48824-1212.

The concept of goal has become a centerpiece in theorizing about message production. Consider recent work on the production of interpersonal influence messages. People define and orient to influence situations based on their knowledge of different compliance goals (Canary, Cody, & Marston, 1986; Dillard, 1989; Rule & Bisanz, 1987). Message sources often attempt to reconcile multiple, competing goals when seeking compliance (Tracy, Craig, Smith, & Spisak, 1984), and multiple goals set constraints on how compliance is sought (Dillard, Segrin, & Harden, 1989; Hample & Dallinger, 1987; Kim & Wilson, in press). Variations in the content and paralinguistic features of influence messages can be attributed in part to individual differences in prioritizing influence and interpersonal goals (Cegala & Waldron, 1992; Greene & Lindsey, 1989; O'Keefe & Shepherd, 1987). In turn, priorities assigned to multiple goals often change as interactions unfold (Sanders, 1991; Tracy, 1991; Wilson & Putnam, 1990). Message sources recall or develop plans for achieving influence goals (Berger & DiBattista, 1992; Waldron, 1990) and produce messages in light of anticipated obstacles to achieving goals (Roloff & Janiszewski, 1989; Wilson, Cruz, Marshall, & Rao, 1993). Design logics affect how message sources define influence situations and hence which goals they see as relevant, as well as how they conceive of managing conflicting goals (B. J. O'Keefe, 1988). In sum, theories of message production commonly presume that speakers design messages to accomplish goals. Much less work has examined how speakers form interaction goals.

In earlier work, I offered the cognitive rules (CR) model, which presents one explicit set of assumptions about how interaction goals are formed (Wilson, 1989, 1990). The CR model assumes that individuals possess cognitive rules, or associations, in long-term memory between representations of interaction goals and numerous situational features. An individual forms goals when he or she perceives a sufficient match between cognitive rules and the current situation (this matching process is explicated in detail below). Given these assumptions, an individual should alter his or her interaction goals in response to changes in salient information from the immediate situation, and hence should vary interaction goals across different situations.

I now believe that the CR model, as currently developed, is a better account of goal formation for some individuals than for others. In an initial test (Wilson, 1990), predictions from the model fared well for individuals high in "interpersonal construct differentiation," but received little support for less differentiated individuals. Subsequent research has demonstrated that attributions made by less differentiated individuals also are surprisingly *nonresponsive* to alterations in seemingly relevant situational conditions (Wilson & Kang, 1991; Wilson, Cruz, & Kang, 1992b).

My purpose in this chapter is to discuss how the CR model can be elaborated to accommodate individual differences in goal formation. I pursue this purpose in three sections, the first of which offers a brief overview of the CR model's assumption. The second section reviews recent research about interpersonal construct differentiation suggesting that the CR model fails to describe adequately how less differentiated individuals form interaction goals. In the last section, I propose two ways in which the CR model might be elaborated to explain such individual differences, and then discuss implications for understanding construct differentiation, interaction goals, and message production.

THE COGNITIVE RULES MODEL
OF INTERACTION GOALS

The cognitive rules model assumes that "people possess knowledge about a wide range of instrumental and interpersonal goals, and about *numerous* situational features relevant to each goal" (Wilson, 1990, p. 81; emphasis added). This goal-relevant knowledge is stored in a hierarchical associative network composed of nodes that represent concepts such as people, traits, roles, relational qualities, settings, and desired outcomes (for similar models, see Anderson, 1983; Anderson & Klatzky, 1987; Greene & Geddes, 1988; Srull, Liechtenstein, & Rothbart, 1985). Created through socialization and problem-solving experience, cognitive rules are patterns of association between nodes representing specific outcomes (goals) and nodes representing situational features. As an example, individuals from the United States might associate the goal "obtain a favor" with felicity conditions for making a request, relational qualities such as intimacy and status, and identity concerns about appearing competent and self-sufficient (Craig, Tracy, & Spisak, 1986; Wilson, Aleman, Miller, & Leathem, 1992).

The CR model assumes that a spreading activation process operates on this associative network (Anderson, 1984). A cognitive rule is activated directly by a match between perceived features of the current situation and situational conditions represented in the rule. A cognitive rule also may be activated indirectly, when activation spreads from a directly stimulated node to other nodes that are associatively linked. This activation process is assumed to occur in parallel, so that cognitive rules can be compared with situational perceptions without substantial demand on processing capacity, and situations can simultaneously activate rules for forming multiple goals.

Activation of a cognitive rule is a necessary but not a sufficient condition for goal formation. The CR model assumes that rules have an activation "threshold": A goal is not formed unless a certain level of activation is reached, and once that level is reached a rule is "triggered" and forms a goal (Higgins, Bargh, & Lombardi, 1985). The probability of a rule being triggered is a function of three general criteria: fit, strength, and recency (Anderson, 1983; Greene, 1984).

Based on the *fit criteria,* the probability of goal formation increases when a larger rather than smaller number of situational conditions represented in a rule are perceived in the current situation. Thus a message source is likely to form the goal of "enforcing an obligation" when a target person of equal or lesser status knowingly fails to perform a promised action with tangible consequences for the source, but is less likely to do so when only some of these situational conditions are present (Canary et al., 1986; Wilson & Kang, 1991).

Aside from fit, situations also vary in ambiguity. In the making of attributions about unfulfilled obligations, for example, situations in which the target has a consistent history of violating obligations are clearer than those in which the target's prior behavior is only moderately consistent and extenuating circumstances also are present (see Wilson, 1990). Ambiguous situations are open to multiple interpretations, and hence partially match and activate a larger number of rules than do clear situations. An important assumption of the CR model is that when both degree and clarity of fit are high, situational features are sufficient to trigger rules. When fit is moderate and ambiguity is high, however, strength and recency are more important determinants of goal formation (Srull & Wyer, 1979).

Both the *strength* and *recency criteria* relate to the accessibility of cognitive rules (for differing conceptions of construct accessibility, see Higgins et al., 1985; Smith & Branscombe, 1988; Wyer & Srull, 1986). Within ambiguous situations, cognitive rules are more likely to be triggered as the strength of association between situational conditions and goals increases. Strength is directly related to the frequency of prior activation of the rule; as strength increases, rules become "chronically accessible" (Fazio, Sanbonmatsu, Powell, & Kardes, 1986; Higgins, King, & Marvin, 1982; Markus, 1977). Within ambiguous situations, a cognitive rule also is more likely to be triggered if that rule already has been activated by a recent event (because an activated rule takes time to dissipate). Recency effects have been illustrated in research using a "priming paradigm," in which activation of a cognitive structure by an earlier task affects performance on a subsequent, ostensibly unrelated, task (see Higgins et al., 1985; Wilson, 1990).

In sum, the CR model assumes that goals are formed when cognitive rules are activated past a threshold level, and that the probability of goal formation is a function of fit between rules and perceptions of the situation, rule strength, and recency of rule activation. Strength and recency are inconsequential when the fit between rules and situation features is high and clear, but become important in situations where the degree of fit is moderate and ambiguous. Although the CR model was intended as a general model of interaction goals, recent research suggests that its assumptions must be elaborated to accommodate individual differences in goal formation. I now turn to recent studies of construct differentiation to clarify this claim.

CONSTRUCT DIFFERENTIATION AND GOAL FORMATION

Traditional Conception of Construct Differentiation

Interpersonal construct differentiation refers to the number of dimensions individuals spontaneously utilize when making inferences and judgments about others. Constructivist scholars have argued that personal constructs—bipolar dimensions used to anticipate, interpret, and evaluate actions—are a fundamental social-cognitive element. With maturation, individuals develop systems of constructs that are more differentiated (larger in number), psychologically abstract, and organized (hierarchically integrated). Construct differentiation is domain specific, so that individuals may be differentiated regarding persons but not automobiles. In sum, persons high in interpersonal construct differentiation spontaneously utilize a larger number of dimensions of judgment about people than do their less differentiated counterparts (see Crockett, 1965; Delia, O'Keefe, & O'Keefe, 1982).

Interpersonal construct differentiation influences a wide range of social inferences and communicative functions. Burleson (1987) argues that "individuals with more developmentally advanced systems of interpersonal constructs will possess more sophisticated social perception skills than persons with less developed construct systems" (p. 310). Consistent with his claim, highly differentiated individuals are more likely to take the other's view and to identify another's affective states accurately, and less likely to rely on simple balance schemes when integrating inconsistent information about others (see Delia et al., 1982; O'Keefe & Sypher, 1981). Individuals high in construct differentiation also are more likely to produce "person-centered" or "elaborated" comforting, persuasive, and regulative messages (see Burleson, 1987). As one explanation for these findings, Barbara O'Keefe and her colleagues have argued that highly differentiated message sources are more likely than less differentiated sources to recognize the identity and relational consequences of influence attempts, and hence to address multiple goals in their regulative messages (see, e.g., O'Keefe & Delia 1982; O'Keefe & Shepherd, 1987).

Drawing on this traditional view, I reasoned that construct differentiation would be associated with the chronic accessibility of rules for forming supportive interaction goals. I expected that highly differentiated persons would possess accessible rules for forming goals such as "maintain the relationship" and "protect the other's face," whereas these same rules would be less accessible for less differentiated individuals. I incorporated this reasoning into the initial test of the CR model (Wilson, 1990), which included three experimental factors that corresponded to each of the factors affecting the probability of goal formation. Participants provided open-ended reports of their interaction goals in response to hypothetical persuasive scenarios involving unfulfilled obligations (e.g., a friend fails to repay a loan at the agreed time). To vary degree and clarity of fit, I created attributionally clear versus ambiguous scenarios by manipulating consistency, consensus, and distinctiveness information. In the attributionally clear scenarios, the target's failure to fulfill the obligation was perceived by most pretest participants as either internally caused/intentional or externally caused/unintentional. In the attributionally ambiguous scenarios, both internal and external causes were judged as plausible. Recency of activation was manipulated through a "relational intimacy priming task," because intimacy is a situational

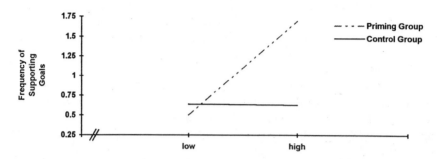

Figure 1.1. Differential Effects of Relational Intimacy Priming Manipulation on Frequencies of Supporting Goals for Two Levels of Construct Differentiation

SOURCE: Data from Wilson (1990), attributionally ambiguous condition.

feature that has been associated with supportive goals (Baxter, 1984; Leichty & Applegate, 1991). Finally, participants completed the Role Category Questionnaire (RCQ) measure of construct differentiation as an indirect measure of rule strength (see Burleson & Waltman, 1988). Based on the CR model's assumptions, both the intimacy priming manipulation and construct differentiation were expected to affect reports of supporting goals in the attributionally ambiguous but not the attributionally clear conditions.

Although many results from this initial test were consistent with the CR model, two unexpected findings are important here. First, the effects of priming and construct differentiation were different from those anticipated. As anticipated, these variables affected reports of supportive goals in the attributionally ambiguous scenarios rather than in the attributionally clear scenarios. Within the attributionally ambiguous condition, however, priming effects were moderated by construct differentiation. The means for this interaction are graphed in Figure 1.1. As is apparent, highly differentiated participants reported substantially more supportive goals in the priming than the control condition, whereas frequencies for less differentiated participants did not differ across conditions. Highly differentiated individuals were affected by the intimacy priming manipulation, and less differentiated individuals were not.

A second unexpected finding was that the attribution main effect also was moderated by construct differentiation. Highly differentiated persons reported significantly more supporting goals when the target's failure to fulfill an obligation clearly was externally caused/unintentional or was attributionally ambiguous rather than when it clearly was internally caused/intentional. This attribution manipulation accounted for 10% of the variance in supporting goal frequencies for highly differentiated participants. In contrast, the same manipulation did not affect reports of supporting goals by less differentiated participants, despite a consistent relationship between attributions and reactions to failure events in prior research (see Martinko & Gardner, 1987; Sillars, 1982; Weiner, 1986).

Indeed, mean scores for supporting goal frequencies by less differentiated individuals did not differ across any experimental condition.

These unexpected findings are difficult to reconcile with my original thinking that construct differentiation could simply be equated with possessing chronically accessible rules for forming supportive goals. As I noted in previous work:

Such a position assumes that all message sources have the same kind of rules, but that some people have rules which simply are more accessible. However, less differentiated people failed to report more supporting goals even when the fit between rules and situational features should have been high and clear, that is, in situations where most pretest participants attributed the target's noncompliance only to extenuating circumstances. (Wilson, 1990, p. 98)

These findings suggest more dramatic differences between highly and less differentiated persons, which in turn may require elaborating the assumptions of the CR model. In the next subsection I propose a somewhat different conception of construct differentiation and review two studies that evaluate this conception.

An Alternative Conception of Construct Differentiation

Recently, several colleagues and I have suggested that interpersonal construct differentiation may be usefully conceived as tapping the degree to which individuals' social judgments are responsive to information from the immediate situation (Wilson, 1991; Wilson et al., 1992b; Wilson & Kang, 1991). Highly differentiated individuals are influenced by a range of features in the immediate situation and display more variable judgments across different situations. Less differentiated persons appear less responsive to features of the immediate situation and make more consistent judgments across situations. This view of construct differentiation contains less implicit evaluation than does the traditional conception, because highly differentiated individuals are characterized as more "variable" but not necessarily as more "sophisticated" (this point is developed in detail below).

We have investigated this alternative view by assessing people's attributions in compliance-gaining situations involving unfulfilled obligations, where message sources have to seek compliance from a target who already should have performed the requested behavior. If a target fails to repay a loan from a friend on time, for example, either party may attribute late repayment to qualities of the target (e.g., irresponsibility), the source (e.g., passivity), their relationship (e.g., a history of living up to the "spirit" but not the letter of agreements), and/or external circumstances (e.g., busy schedule).

When assessing the relative importance of these four causes, one might expect that both parties would be influenced by situational features such as each party's perspective, their intimacy, and the benefits of compliance to each party. Jones and Nisbett's (1972) classic work on actor/observer differences suggests that message sources, because they focus perceptually on the target, should be more likely than targets to attribute unfulfilled obligations internally to the target. Message targets, who focus perceptually on the environment, should be more likely to attribute unfulfilled obligations to circumstances. In his balance analysis, Heider (1958) suggests that message sources should be less likely to make internal attributions for unfulfilled obligations when they like rather than dislike the target. Finally, Jones and Davis's (1965) concept of hedonic relevance implies that sources should be more likely to make internal attributions when they have suffered personally from the target's failure to fulfill the obligation rather than when source benefits for compliance are low. Based on our alternative view, we expected that attributions made by highly differentiated persons would be influenced by these features, whereas attributions by less differentiated persons would not.

We have conducted two studies examining whether construct differentiation moderates the effects of situational features on attributions for unfulfilled obligations. Although both studies explore the process of attribution rather than goal formation, the findings also have implications for the cognitive rules model (see below).

In the first study (Wilson & Kang, 1991), we reasoned that perspective, intimacy, and source and target benefits should account for significantly more variance in attributions for unfulfilled obligations as construct differentiation increased. In a between-groups design, participants recalled a "real-life" obligation situation in which a message source had to ask a target to do something that the target already had agreed to do. One-half of the participants provided open-ended descriptions of situations in which they had been the message sources; the other half described situations where they had been the targets. Participants indicated the degree to which they had attributed the unfulfilled obligation to the message target, provided ratings for intimacy and benefits to the source and target, and completed the RCQ measure of construct differentiation.

We used hierarchical multiple regression analyses to evaluate the prediction that construct differentiation would moderate the effects of situational features on attributions to the target. Two findings are pertinent here. First, there was a significant interaction between construct differentiation and recall perspective. To interpret this interaction, we trichotomized construct differentiation into low, moderate, and high levels. Figure 1.2 displays message sources' and message targets' mean levels of attribution to the target at each level of differentiation. As is apparent, the typical actor/observer pattern occurred only for highly differentiated participants. Recalling an obligation episode from the message source (observer) versus target (actor) perspective accounted for 19% of the variance in target attributions made by highly differentiated participants. In contrast, recall perspective was not a significant predictor of target attributions for either moderately or less differentiated participants.

Aside from this two-way interaction, a construct differentiation × role × intimacy × source benefits interaction also emerged. This four-way interaction reflected that the situational features of recall perspective, intimacy, and source

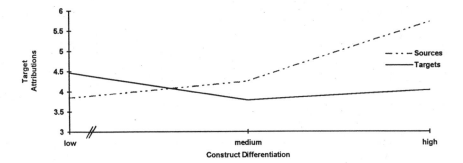

Figure 1.2. Differential Effects of Memory Recall Perspective on Ratings of Attributions to the Message Target for Three Levels of Construct Differentiation

SOURCE: Data from Wilson and Kang (1991).

benefits jointly accounted for significantly more variance in attributions to the target made by highly differentiated participants ($R = .57$) than in those made by moderately ($R = .32$, $z = 1.83$, $p < .04$) or less differentiated participants ($R = .36$, $z = 1.59$, $p = .055$). Although promising, we wanted to replicate and extend these findings employing a different research design.

In the second study (Wilson et al., 1992b), we reasoned that construct differentiation should be positively associated with making variable attributions when participants viewed situations from different psychological perspectives. To assess this claim, we collected repeated-measures data on people's attributions across three situations involving unfulfilled obligations. Using a procedure modified from Howe (1987), we videotaped three role-play interactions in which a message source sought a target's compliance with an obligation. Experimental participants viewed these videotapes from different psychological perspectives. Specifically, one-third of the sample watched each videotape from the perspective of the message source, one-third from the perspective of the message target, and one-third from the perspective of a third-party observer. Participants assigned to the message target condition in the repay loan situation, for example, were instructed to "watch the video from Mike's [the target's] perspective; so you should try to take Mike's role, see things as Mike would see them, and get an idea of how Mike would think and feel in the situation." After observing each videotape, participants rated the degree to which they attributed the target's noncompliance to four causes: the message source, the message target, the source and target's relationship, and/or external circumstances. They also rated the degree to which the target's noncompliance was intentional. Participants finished by completing the RCQ measure of construct differentiation.

As expected, construct differentiation was positively associated with intrapersonal attributional variability. To assess attributional variability, we computed a "sums of squares" index. For attributions to circumstances, for example, we computed each participant's mean rating across the three viewing roles (source,

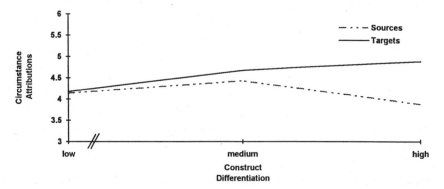

Figure 1.3. Differential Effects of Psychological Viewing Perspective on Ratings of Attributions to Circumstances for Three Levels of Construct Differentiation

SOURCE: Data from Wilson et al. (1992b).

target, third party). We then calculated a variability index by summing the squared differences between each participant's rating of attributions to circumstances in each of the three viewing roles and his or her overall mean rating across roles. Large variability scores indicated that participants' attributions depended on their assigned viewing perspective. Construct differentiation was significantly correlated with this "sums of squares" variability index for three causes (attributions to the message source, relationship, and circumstances) as well as for perceived intent. Construct differentiation accounted for 3-5% of the variance in these indices of "attributional variability" across psychological perspectives.

Aside from attributional variability, we also examined mean levels of attributions. Separate 2×3 ANOVAs crossing the within-groups variable of psychological perspective (message source versus target) and the between-groups variable of construct differentiation (trichotomized into high, medium, and low groups) were conducted for attributions to circumstances and to the message target. As in the first study (Wilson & Kang, 1991), construct differentiation mediated actor/observer differences. Regarding attributions to circumstances, Figure 1.3 displays mean scores when participants at three levels of differentiation took the perspective of the message target (actor) versus the source (observer). As is apparent, the typical actor/observer pattern occurred only for highly differentiated participants. Psychological perspective accounted for 12% of the variance in circumstance attributions for highly differentiated participants, but was not a significant predictor of circumstance attributions for either moderately or less differentiated participants.

A similar but weaker pattern occurred for attributions to the message target. Figure 1.4 graphs mean target attributions when participants at each level of differentiation took the perspective of the message source versus target. As is apparent, actor/observer differences were largest for highly differentiated participants. Psychological perspective accounted for 11% of the variance in target

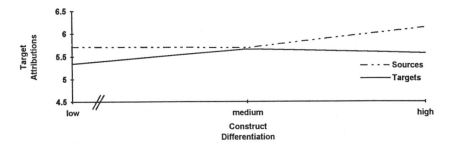

Figure 1.4. Differential Effects of Psychological Viewing Perspective on Ratings of Attributions to the Message Target for Three Levels of Construct Differentiation

SOURCE: Data from Wilson et al. (1992b).

attributions for highly differentiated participants. The same effect approached significance for less differentiated participants, but accounted for almost three times less variance. Perspective did not exert significant effects on target attributions for the moderately differentiated group.

In sum, I have proposed in this section an alternative conception of interpersonal construct differentiation and reviewed findings from three studies consistent with this view (Wilson, 1990; Wilson et al., 1992b; Wilson & Kang, 1991). Taken together, these studies paint a picture in which highly differentiated individuals are responsive to information from the immediate situation when making social inferences, whereas less differentiated individuals are not. My colleagues and I have confidence in this pattern because it has been detected in studies that have (a) investigated two different outcomes (attributions and interaction goals), (b) gathered those outcomes in response to three different stimuli (reactions to hypothetical scenarios, recall of natural episodes, and responses to videotaped interactions), (c) measured those outcomes using two different techniques (open- and closed-ended) as part of two different designs (between and within groups), and (d) manipulated multiple situational features associated with those outcomes (perspective, intimacy, benefits) using two different procedures (priming and variation in scenarios).

This alternative view of construct differentiation has important consequences for the CR model of interaction goals. As noted earlier, the model initially assumed (a) that all persons associate interaction goals such as "enforce an obligation" and "protect the other's face" with a substantial number of situational features, (b) that persons from the same culture will associate each goal with about the same set of features, and (c) that persons differ simply in terms of the strength or chronic accessibility of rules for forming goals. These assumptions now appear problematic because individuals low in construct differentiation may not form goals even when a clear match exists between features they perceive in the current situation and those thought to be represented in their cognitive rules (i.e., in situations where the degree of match should be sufficient to trigger the rule regardless of its prior accessibility).[1] In the following section I suggest that the assumptions of the CR model must be elaborated in greater detail to account for the effects of construct differentiation.[2]

DIRECTIONS FOR ELABORATING
THE COGNITIVE RULES MODEL

In this section I explore two ways in which construct differentiation could affect the structure or selection of cognitive rules. Interpersonal construct differentiation could be associated with differences in the development of schemata organized around various compliance goals or with differences in the types of heuristics individuals employ as they form goals.

Cognitive Rules and Schema Development

One candidate explanation for why highly differentiated individuals are more responsive to situational features than are less differentiated persons is that construct differentiation may be associated with differences in the "complexity" of other cognitive structures. Rather than simply possessing more accessible rules, highly differentiated individuals may possess more "complex" modular rule structures that associate desired end states with a larger number of interconnected situational features.

Several scholars have argued that people represent their knowledge about compliance gaining as "schemata" that associate situational dimensions, targets, and strategies with specific compliance goals such as "enforcing obligations" and "asking favors" (Canary et al., 1986; Dillard, 1989; Meyer, 1990; Rule & Bisanz, 1987). Information pertinent to attributions, such as typical motives and constraints, also may be represented in such structures. Given this, Fiske and Taylor's (1991) analysis of schema development may provide insight about the effects of construct differentiation.

Complex or well-developed schemata differ from simple schemata based on limited experience in several respects. First, complex schemata contain more concepts or nodes (Fiske, Kinder, & Larter, 1983); for example, the goal "protect the other person's face" may be associated with a larger number of situational dimensions (e.g., the target's intent, relational intimacy) within complex schemata. Second, general categories are divided into a larger number of subtypes within complex schemata; for instance, the goal of "giving advice" might be associated with more specific goals such as "giving advice to friends" versus "to parents" (Canary et al., 1986) or "giving advice about consumer products" and "about health" (Dillard, 1990). Specific compliance goals also may become associated with particular "supporting" goals, such as "advice about health" and "don't embarrass either party" versus "advice to parents" and "avoid making the other defensive" (Wilson et al., 1992). Associations between general and specific compliance goals may take the form of a "tangled web," in which each compliance goal shares connections with some but not all of the situational features and interpersonal goals associated with other compliance goals (Anderson & Klatzky, 1987; Cantor & Kihlstrom, 1987).

Third, and finally, complex schemata contain nodes interconnected by a large number of strong associative links. Such schemata become increasingly "compact" or "unitized" so that they are activated in an all-or-nothing fashion (Fiske & Dyer, 1985; Greene, 1984; Hayes-Roth, 1977). Because of unitization, individuals can retain information in short-term memory with greater ease and hence have more capacity to process schema-inconsistent information. Complex schemata therefore are more likely than simple ones to contain associations between evaluatively inconsistent attributes (Fiske et al., 1983; Linville, 1982). Within the CR model, then, individuals may differ in the size, specificity, and compactness of their cognitive rules.

If construct differentiation leads to more developed goal schemata, then highly differentiated individuals should be more responsive to situational features for at least three reasons. Highly differentiated persons should be more likely, on average, to associate goals with any situational feature; hence manipulating attributions or priming relational intimacy might not affect reports of supporting goals by less differentiated individuals because they do not associate supporting goals with those features (Wilson, 1990). Highly differentiated individuals also should be more likely to develop more subcategories for global goals; hence construct differentiation may be associated with making variable attributions across scenarios involving unfulfilled obligations because those scenarios activate different schemata in highly differentiated individuals but the same schemata in less differentiated individuals (Wilson et al., 1992b). Finally, highly differentiated individuals should have greater capacity to process schema-inconsistent information; hence both highly and less differentiated individuals may expect that message targets will be the primary cause of unfulfilled obligations but only the former group may have sufficient capacity to attend to inconsistent circumstance information when taking the perspective of the target (Wilson et al., 1992b; Wilson & Kang, 1991).

Consistent with this first account, constructivist scholars have suggested that highly differentiated individuals possess more complex schemata for traits, persons, roles, relationships, and other forms of social knowledge (see O'Keefe & Delia, 1982; Sypher & Applegate, 1984). Shepherd and Trank (1986) provide the most direct evidence for these claims to date. Students in their study rated instructors on course evaluation items designed to assess the dimensions of teacher competence, sociability, and communicative skill. Construct differentiation was inversely associated with the degree to which ratings of instructors along these three dimensions were intercorrelated. That is, highly differentiated students were more likely than less differentiated students to make evaluatively inconsistent ratings on the three dimensions (for a review of similar findings from studies employing other measures of construct differentiation, see O'Keefe & Sypher, 1981, pp. 80-81).

Unfortunately, data bearing on this first explanation are limited and indirect. To test hypotheses about cognitive structures more precisely, measures tapping the content of attributions, goals, and messages should be supplemented with measures tapping the processes underlying this content (Greene, 1988; Srull, 1984). For example, Shepherd and Trank's (1986) results also are consistent with the position that both highly and less differentiated individuals possess complex schema regarding instructors, but that the latter group feels more pressure to maintain balance by adjusting their initial ratings along multiple dimensions to regain evaluative consistency. This seems possible in light of evidence that less differentiated individuals are more likely to cling to balance schemes than are highly differentiated persons after both groups have encountered evidence contradicting those schemes (Delia & Crockett, 1973; Press, Crockett, & Rosenkrantz, 1969).

The proposition that construct differentiation leads to complex goal schemata does suggest several testable hypotheses involving indices of cognitive process. After thinking about an influence goal such as asking a favor, for example, highly differentiated individuals should display quicker response times than less differentiated persons to questions about associated situational features or supporting goals if the former group's nodes representing those features are more likely to be activated as a unit along with the influence goal (Fazio et al., 1986; Markus, 1977). In addition, highly and less differentiated individuals should display different patterns of intrusions when given a recall test about hypothetical "enforce obligation" scenarios if the two groups possess different structural representations of that class of situations (for an example, see Greene, Smith, & Lindsey, 1990). Prior research has found that highly and less differentiated individuals do recall different information from conversation (Daly, Vangelisti, & Daughton, 1987; Neuliep & Hazelton, 1986).

This first explanation also has implications for message production. Several scholars argue that knowledge about message strategies and tactics also is associated with knowledge about influence goals (Canary et al., 1986; Dillard, 1989; Meyer, 1990; Rule & Bisanz, 1987). Like the CR model, these views of message production may need to be elaborated to explain individual differences in the variability of people's message strategies and tactics across situations defined by the "same" influence goal. Consistent with this implication, D. J. O'Keefe (1980; O'Keefe & Delia, 1981) found that construct differentiation was positively related to variation in behavioral intentions across nine situations involving the same target.

Cognitive Rules and Heuristic Processing

A second candidate explanation for why highly differentiated individuals are more responsive than less differentiated persons to features of the immediate situation is that the two groups differ in their use of specific heuristics. Heuristics are simple decision rules or rules of thumb that typically lead to reasonable decisions with minimal effort (see Chaiken, 1987; Chaiken, Liberman, & Eagly, 1989; Eagly & Chaiken, 1993; Sherman & Corty, 1984).

People who use heuristics simplify complex decision-making tasks by relying on only one of several sources of diagnostic information. When making a causal judgment about an unfulfilled obligation, for example, Sherman and Corty (1984) argue that people potentially could rely on three types of information. The first of these is information about base rates or population parameters— What typically is the reason obligations are not fulfilled? How often is the target the primary cause? The second type is information about outcomes from other occurrences involving either party—Has this target consistently failed to fulfill obligations in the past? Has this source had difficulty enforcing obligations with other targets? The final type is individuating information—How intimate is the relationship between this particular source and target? Who would have bene-fited from compliance in this situation? Heuristic processing entails considera-tion of only one of these types of information, whereas more systematic processing entails consideration of all three types.

Within the CR model, heuristic processing can be conceptualized as setting a low minimum threshold for triggering cognitive rules. Goals are formed when "sufficient" match exists between features perceived in the current situation and those represented in the relevant rules. Of course, the match between rules and perceptions never will be perfect, because situations typically contain some novel configuration of relevant features. Hence the degree of match sufficient to trigger rules could vary from high to low (Greene, 1988). Individuals engaged in careful (systematic) processing can be thought of as setting a high threshold for forming goals, so that almost all features represented in a rule must be perceived in the current situation before that rule will be triggered and a goal will be formed. As Chaiken et al. (1989) note, systematic processing is "a compre-hensive, analytic orientation in which perceivers access and scrutinize all in-formational input for its relevance and importance to their judgment task, and integrate all useful information in forming their judgments" (p. 212). Thus individuals engaged in systematic processing during goal formation would carefully scrutinize whether nearly all of the features represented in a cognitive rule are present in the current situation, rather than just a few features made salient by their prior expectations or psychological perspective. By setting a high threshold, individuals engaged in systematic processing could achieve greater confidence that their goals would be appropriate for the current situation (see Chaiken et al., 1989, for a similar analysis of systematic processing and confidence in the accuracy of attitudinal judgments following persuasive mes-sage exposure). This greater confidence, however, could be attained only by placing greater demands on processing capacity, because systematic pro-cessing is assumed "to require more than marginal levels of effort and cognitive capacity" (Chaiken et al., 1989, p. 212).

In contrast, individuals engaged in heuristic processing can be thought of as setting a low threshold for forming goals, so that rules will be triggered when only a small percentage of relevant features are perceived. By using heuristics, individuals could avoid making heavy demands on processing capacity when forming goals. Processing heuristically, however, also would increase the chance that people's rules would be triggered by small amounts of information made salient by their prior expectations or psychological perspectives. Chaiken et al. (1989) describe heuristic processing as "more exclusively theory driven because recipients utilize minimal informational input in conjunction with simple (declarative or procedural) knowledge structures" (p. 216).

Given this analysis, construct differentiation may moderate responsiveness to situational features because both highly and less differentiated persons in prior research have been engaging in heuristic processing, but the two groups have relied on different heuristics. Individuals low in construct differentiation may not have varied their goals across obligation situations because they overemphasize base-rate data, relying on heuristics such as "People generally are responsible when they miss a deadline" or "People usually keep their promises unless circumstances prevent them from doing so." Put differently, base-rate heuristics may be chronically accessible for less differentiated individuals. When processing heuristically, almost any mention of a missed deadline or a broken promise may be sufficient to trigger these heuristics and the associated goals in less differentiated individuals.

Highly differentiated individuals may have varied their goals across obligation situations because they overemphasize individuating information, such as information made salient by their current visual perspectives. In making causal judgments, salient information for message sources might be the target or the tangible consequences of noncompliance, whereas for targets it might be extenuating circumstances. According to Jones and Nisbett (1972), actor/observer differences in attribution reflect the use of an "availability" heuristic in which the immediate focus of attention is assigned as the cause. In heuristic processing, then, a small amount of salient individuating information may be sufficient to trigger the associated goals in highly differentiated individuals.[3]

Aside from actor/observer differences, heuristic processing also suggests an explanation for why the effects of priming are limited to attributionally ambiguous situations (Wilson, 1990). Attributionally ambiguous situations by definition are those that partially activate multiple cognitive rules; hence the use of different heuristics accompanied by a low triggering threshold for cognitive rules would be especially evident in ambiguous situations.

This heuristic processing explanation differs from the schema development explanation by focusing on the process of rule selection rather than on the structure of cognitive rules. Although it does not deny that highly and less differentiated individuals may possess different representations of goal-relevant knowledge, this second explanation assumes that the key factor distinguishing the two groups is their differential reliance on base-rate versus individuating information as they form goals under heuristic processing conditions (i.e., when they set a low minimum triggering threshold for rules).

To date there is scant evidence relevant to this second candidate explanation. Although a good deal of research indicates that individuals differ in their preferences for and likelihood of using heuristics of any type (e.g., Axsom, Yates, & Chaiken, 1987; Cacioppo, Petty, & Morris, 1983), I am aware of no research that has examined stable individual differences in people's preferences for particular heuristics. Chaiken and her colleagues have demonstrated that people are more likely to rely on a particular heuristic after that rule has been made "temporarily accessible" via a priming manipulation, or after situational features associated with that rule have been made salient (for a review, see Chaiken, 1987).

Although this second explanation has not been evaluated in prior research, it does suggest several testable hypotheses. One important implication is that differences between highly and less differentiated individuals ought to be reduced or eliminated when people process systematically rather than heuristically. Regarding attributions, highly differentiated individuals should display smaller actor/observer attribution differences and less differentiated individuals should display greater variability across situations when there is sufficient ability and motivation to process systematically (i.e., as both groups rely on multiple sources of information). In a research program investigating stable individual differences in "attribution complexity" (i.e., differences in the complexity of attributional schemata), Fletcher and his colleagues have shown that highly versus less complex individuals indeed are more likely to make disparate causal judgments under conditions that promote heuristic rather than systematic processing of situational information (Fletcher, Reeder, & Bull, 1990; Fletcher, Rosanowski, Rhodes, & Lange, 1992).

Regarding interaction goals, this second explanation also suggests that construct differentiation, attributions, and ability/motivation to process systematically will interact in their effects on people's likelihood of forming multiple goals. When regulating misbehavior, for example, less differentiated individuals should vary their likelihood of forming supporting goals across different attribution conditions when both their ability and motivation to process systematically are high, but not when either is low (because less differentiated persons would rely primarily on base-rate information to make attributions in the latter condition). To test this hypothesis, one must identify the determinants of ability and motivation to process systematically during goal formation. Fortunately, several determinants of both ability and motivation to process persuasive messages systematically are known (for a review, see Eagly & Chaiken, 1993), and these may be translatable into factors relevant to goal formation.

This second explanation also may offer new insight into the relationship between construct differentiation and use of person-centered or multifunctional messages (see Burleson, 1987). Highly differentiated individuals may be more likely than less differentiated individuals to use (or to vary their use) of persuasive messages that coordinate multiple goals when processing heuristically, but differences between the two groups may be reduced under systematic processing conditions. Beatty and Payne (1985) have shown that people in general form more complex impressions of others as motivation to do so increases, but no research to date has examined whether the effects of construct differentiation on person-centered communication are moderated by motivation to process systematically.

CONCLUSION

In this chapter I have argued that the cognitive rules model needs to be elaborated to account for individual differences in goal formation. After reviewing assumptions of the CR model, I highlighted a pattern of results present in three studies of interpersonal construct differentiation that illustrate this need (Wilson, 1990; Wilson et al., 1992b; Wilson & Kang, 1991). In particular, these studies all suggest that highly differentiated individuals are responsive to features of the immediate situation when forming goals or making attributions, and less differentiated individuals are not. In light of these results, I now believe that simply equating construct differentiation with the chronic accessibility of rules for forming interaction goals is not sufficient to account for individual differences in goal formation.

To account for individual differences, I have explored assumptions regarding the structure and selection of cognitive rules in greater detail. In doing so, I have proposed two ways in which the CR model might be elaborated. One possibility is that highly differentiated individuals may possess more complex schemata for forming goals than do less differentiated persons, which associate desired end states with a larger number of interconnected situational features in a more compact fashion. According to this possibility, highly differentiated individuals possess more elaborated and unitized representations of goal-relevant knowledge, which allow them to process inconsistent information evaluatively but also make them prone to particular biases, such as actor/observer differences (Wilson et al., 1992b).

A second possibility is that highly and less differentiated individuals may rely on different heuristic principles to form interaction goals, especially in situations where they lack the ability or motivation to process goal-relevant information systematically. According to this possibility, highly and less differentiated persons rely on different information-processing shortcuts in some situations. Both possibilities seem capable of accounting for prior findings, and both suggest testable hypotheses about goal formation and message production.

Since its inception, the literature on message production has provided a good deal of insight about how communicators utilize pragmatic and strategic knowledge to pursue and coordinate interaction goals. By also continuing to explore how people form goals, we should gain complementary insights about why people say what they do in everyday interactions.

NOTES

1. The initial version of the CR model also cannot be rescued by arguing that highly and less differentiated persons possess the same set of cognitive rules but differ in their perceptions of the immediate situation and hence in the data matched against those rules. Construct differentiation undoubtedly does affect perceptions of situational features; for example, Delia and Clark (1977) show that children are more likely to recognize communication-relevant differences in listeners spontaneously as construct differentiation increases. But differences in perceptual acuity are not sufficient to explain the findings reviewed above. For example, how would this explanation account for the finding that within attributionally ambiguous situations an intimacy priming manipulation affected reports of supporting goals by highly but not by less differentiated individuals (Wilson, 1990; see Figure 1.1)? This finding cannot be explained by differences in perceptual acuity, because the situational feature of intimacy was activated outside of awareness for all participants. In addition, perceptual acuity also is not a plausible explanation for why individuals low in construct differentiation were not affected by the attribution manipulation, because the vast majority of pretest participants did perceive differences among the three attribution conditions (see Wilson, 1990).

2. Aside from construct differentiation, these elaborations of the CR model also may be useful in accounting for other individual differences in goal formation. As an example, we have presented two reports demonstrating that individuals high in "attributional complexity" (Fletcher, Danilovics, Fernandez, Peterson, & Reeder, 1986) display patterns of actor/observer attribution differences very similar to those displayed by highly differentiated persons (see Wilson, Cruz, & Kang, 1992a; Wilson, Levine, & Humphreys, 1994). If attribution complexity also moderates the effects of situational features on goals, then the proposed elaborations also may help explain the effects of this variable.

3. An alternative possibility is that construct differentiation relates to one's propensity to engage in systematic rather than heuristic processing during goal formation. This possibility seems less plausible on several grounds. For example, in two studies, Hines (1991) found only very small correlations ($r = .13$ and .16) between construct differentiation and Cacioppo and Petty's (1982) "need for cognition" scale, a variable known to affect propensity for systematic processing. In addition, in a subsidiary analysis of the recall data from naturalistic situations, Wilson and Kang (1989) found no significant relationships between construct differentiation and three different indices of the likelihood of making complicated attributions for the target's noncompliance (i.e., judgments involving multiple causes). One might argue that these variables should have correlated at least moderately if highly differentiated individuals were more likely to engage in systematic processing, because consideration of multiple sources of information should have made multiple causes plausible in at least some situations.

REFERENCES

Anderson, J. R. (1983). *The architecture of cognition.* Cambridge, MA: Harvard University Press.

Anderson, J. R. (1984). Spreading activation. In J. R. Anderson & S. M. Kosslyn (Eds.), *Essays in learning and memory* (pp. 61-89). New York: Freeman.

Anderson, S. M., & Klatzky, R. L. (1987). Traits and social stereotypes: Levels of categorization in person perception. *Journal of Personality and Social Psychology, 53,* 235-246.

Axsom, D., Yates, S. M., & Chaiken, S. (1987). Audience response as a heuristic cue in persuasion. *Journal of Personality and Social Psychology, 53,* 30-40.

Baxter, L. A. (1984). An investigation of compliance-gaining as politeness. *Human Communication Research, 10,* 427-456.

Beatty, M. J., & Payne, S. K. (1985). Is construct differentiation loquacity? A motivational perspective. *Human Communication Research, 11,* 605-612.

Berger, C. R., & DiBattista, P. (1992). Information seeking and plan elaboration: What do you need to know to know what to do? *Communication Monographs, 59,* 368-387.

Burleson, B. R. (1987). Cognitive complexity. In J. C. McCroskey & J. A. Daly (Eds.), *Personality and interpersonal communication* (pp. 305-349). Newbury Park, CA: Sage.

Burleson, B. R., & Waltman, M. S. (1988). Cognitive complexity: Using the Role Category Questionnaire measure. In C. H. Tardy (Ed.), *A handbook for the study of human communication: Methods and instruments for observing, measuring, and assessing communication processes* (pp. 1-35). Norwood, NJ: Ablex.

Cacioppo, J. T., & Petty, R. E. (1982). The need for cognition. *Journal of Personality and Social Psychology, 42,* 116-131.

Cacioppo, J. T., Petty, R. E., & Morris, K. J. (1983). Effects of need for cognition on message evaluation, recall, and persuasion. *Journal of Personality and Social Psychology, 45,* 805-818.

Canary, D. J., Cody, M. J., & Marston, P. J. (1986). Goal types, compliance-gaining and locus of control. *Journal of Language and Social Psychology, 5,* 249-269.

Cantor, N., & Kihlstrom, J. F. (1987). *Personality and social intelligence.* Englewood Cliffs, NJ: Prentice Hall.

Cegala, D. J., & Waldron, V. R. (1992). A study of the relationship between communicative performance and conversation participants' thoughts. *Communication Studies, 43,* 105-123.

Chaiken, S. (1987). The heuristic model of persuasion. In M. P. Zanna, J. M. Olson, & C. P. Herman (Eds.), *Social influence: The Ontario Symposium* (Vol. 5, pp. 3-40). Hillsdale, NJ: Lawrence Erlbaum.

Chaiken, S., Liberman, A., & Eagly, A. (1989). Heuristic and systematic information processing with and beyond the persuasion context. In J. S. Uleman & J. A. Bargh (Eds.), *Unintended thought* (pp. 212-252). New York: Guilford.

Cody, M. J., & McLaughlin, M. L. (Eds.). (1990). *The psychology of tactical communication.* Clevedon: Multilingual Matters.

Craig, R. T., Tracy, K., & Spisak, F. (1986). The discourse of requests: Assessment of a politeness approach. *Human Communication Research, 12,* 437-468.

Crockett, W. H. (1965). Cognitive complexity and impression formation. In B. A. Mahler (Ed.), *Progress in experimental personality research* (Vol. 2, pp. 47-90). New York: Academic Press.

Daly, J. A., Vangelisti, A. L., & Daughton, S. M. (1987). The nature and correlates of conversational sensitivity. *Human Communication Research, 14,* 167-202.

Delia, J. G., & Clark, R. A. (1977). Cognitive complexity, social perception, and the development of listener-adapted communication in six-, eight-, ten-, and twelve-year old boys. *Communication Monographs, 44,* 326-345.

Delia, J. G., & Crockett, W. H. (1973). Social schemas, cognitive complexity, and the learning of social structures. *Journal of Personality, 41,* 413-429.

Delia, J. G., O'Keefe, B. J., & O'Keefe, D. J. (1982). The constructivist approach to communication. In F. E. X. Dance (Ed.), *Human communication theory: Comparative essays* (pp. 147-191). New York: Harper & Row.

Dillard, J. P. (1989). Types of influence goals in personal relationships. *Journal of Social and Personal Relationships, 6,* 293-308.

Dillard, J. P. (Ed.). (1990). *Seeking compliance: The production of interpersonal influence messages.* Scottsdale, AZ: Gorsuch Scarisbrick.

Dillard, J. P., Segrin, C., & Harden, J. M. (1989). Primary and secondary goals in the production of interpersonal influence messages. *Communication Monographs, 56,* 19-38.

Eagly, A. H., & Chaiken, S. (1993). *The psychology of attitudes.* Fort Worth, TX: Harcourt Brace Jovanovich.

Fazio, R. H., Sanbonmatsu, D., Powell, M. C., & Kardes, F. R. (1986). On the automatic activation of attitudes. *Journal of Personality and Social Psychology, 50,* 229-238.

Fiske, S. T., & Dyer, L. M. (1985). Structure and development of social schemata: Evidence from positive and negative transfer effects. *Journal of Personality and Social Psychology, 48,* 839-852.

Fiske, S. T., Kinder, D. R., & Larter, W. M. (1983). The novice and the expert: Knowledge-based strategies in political cognition. *Journal of Experimental Social Psychology, 19,* 381-400.

Fiske, S. T., & Taylor, S. E. (1991). *Social cognition* (2nd ed.). Reading, MA: Addison-Wesley.

Fletcher, G. J. O., Danilovics, P., Fernandez, G., Peterson, D., & Reeder, G. D. (1986). Attributional complexity: An individual difference measure. *Journal of Personality and Social Psychology, 51,* 875-884.

Fletcher, G. J. O., Reeder, G. D., & Bull, V. (1990). Bias and accuracy in attitude attribution: The role of attribution complexity. *Journal of Experimental Social Psychology, 26,* 275-288.

Fletcher, G. J. O., Rosanowski, J., Rhodes, G., & Lange, C. (1992). Accuracy and speed of causal processing: Experts versus novices in social judgment. *Journal of Experimental Social Psychology, 28,* 320-338.

Greene, J. O. (1984). A cognitive approach to human communication: An action assembly theory. *Communication Monographs, 51,* 289-306.

Greene, J. O. (1988). Cognitive processes: Methods for probing the black box. In C. H. Tardy (Ed.), *A handbook for the study of human communication: Methods and instruments for observing, measuring, and assessing communication processes* (pp. 37-66). Norwood, NJ: Ablex.

Greene, J. O., & Geddes, D. (1988). Representation and processing in the self-system: An action-oriented approach to self and self-relevant phenomena. *Communication Monographs, 55,* 287-314.

Greene, J. O., & Lindsey, A. E. (1989). Encoding processes in the production of multiple-goal messages. *Human Communication Research, 16,* 120-140.

Greene, J. O., Smith, S. W., & Lindsey, A. E. (1990). Memory representations of compliance-gaining strategies and tactics. *Human Communication Research, 17,* 195-231.

Hample, D., & Dallinger, J. M. (1987). Individual differences in cognitive editing standards. *Human Communication Research, 14,* 123-144.

Hayes-Roth, B. (1977). Evolution of cognitive structure and processes. *Psychological Review, 84,* 260-278.

Heider, F. (1958). *The psychology of interpersonal relations.* New York: John Wiley.

Higgins, E. T., Bargh, J. A., & Lombardi, W. (1985). Nature of priming effects on categorization. *Journal of Experimental Psychology: Learning, Memory, and Cognition, 11,* 59-69.

Higgins, E. T., King, G. A., & Marvin, G. H. (1982). Individual construct accessibility and subjective impressions of recall. *Journal of Personality and Social Psychology, 43,* 35-47.

Hines, S. C. (1991, November). *Cognitive complexity, attribution complexity, need for cognition, and the understanding of friends: A comparison of measures.* Paper presented at the annual meeting of the Speech Communication Association, Chicago.

Howe, G. W. (1987). Attributions of complex cause and the perception of marital conflict. *Journal of Personality and Social Psychology, 53,* 1119-1128.

Jones, E. E., & Davis, K. E. (1965). From acts to dispositions: The attribution process in person perception. In L. Berkowitz (Ed.), *Advances in experimental social psychology* (Vol. 2, pp. 219-266). New York: Academic Press.

Jones, E. E., & Nisbett, R. E. (1972). The actor and the observer: Divergent perceptions of the causes of behavior. In E. E. Jones, D. E. Kanouse, H. H. Kelley, R. E. Nisbett, S. Valins, & B. Weiner (Eds.), *Attribution: Perceiving the causes of behavior* (pp. 78-94). Morristown, NJ: General Learning.

Kim, M. S., & Wilson, S. R. (in press). A cross-cultural comparison of implicit theories of requesting. *Communication Monographs.*

Leichty, G., & Applegate, J. L. (1991). Social-cognitive and situational influences on the use of face-saving persuasive strategies. *Human Communication Research, 17,* 451-483.

Linville, P. W. (1982). The complexity-extremity effect and age-based stereotyping. *Journal of Personality and Social Psychology, 42,* 193-211.

Markus, H. (1977). Self-schemata and processing information about the self. *Journal of Personality and Social Psychology, 35,* 63-78.

Martinko, M. J., & Gardner, W. L. (1987). The leader/member attribution process. *Academy of Management Review, 12,* 235-249.

Meyer, J. R. (1990). Cognitive processes underlying the retrieval of compliance-gaining strategies: An implicit rules model. In J. P. Dillard (Ed.), *Seeking compliance: The production of interpersonal influence messages* (pp. 57-74). Scottsdale, AZ: Gorsuch Scarisbrick.

Neuliep, J. W., & Hazelton, V. (1986). Enhanced conversational recall and reduced conversational interference as a function of cognitive complexity. *Human Communication Research, 13,* 211-224.

O'Keefe, B. J. (1988). The logic of message design: Individual differences in reasoning about communication. *Communication Monographs, 55,* 80-103.

O'Keefe, B. J., & Delia, J. G. (1982). Impression formation and message production. In M. E. Roloff & C. R. Berger (Eds.), *Social cognition and communication* (pp. 37-72). Beverly Hills, CA: Sage.

O'Keefe, B. J., & Shepherd, G. J. (1987). The pursuit of multiple objectives in face-to-face persuasive interactions: Effects of construct differentiation on message organization. *Communication Monographs, 54,* 396-419.

O'Keefe, D. J. (1980). The relationship between attitudes and behavior: A constructivist analysis. In D. P. Cushman & R. D. McPhee (Eds.), *Message-attitude-behavior relationships: Theory, methodology, and application* (pp. 117-148). New York: Academic Press.

O'Keefe, D. J., & Delia, J. G. (1981). Construct differentiation and the relationship of attitudes and behavioral intentions. *Communication Monographs, 48,* 146-157.

O'Keefe, D. J., & Sypher, H. E. (1981). Cognitive complexity measures and the relationship of cognitive complexity to communication: A critical review. *Human Communication Research, 8,* 72-92.

Press, A. N., Crockett, W. H., & Rosenkrantz, P. S. (1969). Cognitive complexity and the learning of balanced and unbalanced social structures. *Journal of Personality, 37,* 541-553.

Roloff, M. E., & Janiszewski, C. A. (1989). Overcoming obstacles to compliance: A principle of message construction. *Human Communication Research, 16,* 33-61.

Rule, B. G., & Bisanz, G. L. (1987). Goals and strategies of persuasion: A cognitive schema for understanding social events. In M. P. Zanna, J. M. Olson, & C. P. Herman (Eds.), *Social influence: The Ontario Symposium* (Vol. 5, pp. 185-206). Hillsdale, NJ: Lawrence Erlbaum.

Sanders, R. E. (1991). The two-way relationship between talk in social interactions and actors' goals and plans. In K. Tracy (Ed.), *Understanding face-to-face interaction: Issues linking goals and discourse* (pp. 167-188). Hillsdale, NJ: Lawrence Erlbaum.

Shepherd, G. J., & Trank, D. M. (1986, November). *Construct system development and dimensions of judgment.* Paper presented at the annual meeting of the Speech Communication Association, Chicago.

Sherman, S. J., & Corty, E. (1984). Cognitive heuristics. In R. S. Wyer & T. K. Srull (Eds.), *Handbook of social cognition* (Vol. 1, pp. 189-286). Hillsdale, NJ: Lawrence Erlbaum.

Sillars, A. L. (1982). Attribution and communication: Are people "naive scientists" or just naive? In M. E. Roloff & C. R. Berger (Eds.), *Social cognition and communication* (pp. 9-32). Beverly Hills, CA: Sage.

Smith, E. R., & Branscombe, N. R. (1988). Category accessibility as implicit memory. *Journal of Experimental Social Psychology, 24,* 490-504.

Srull, T. K. (1984). Methodological techniques for the study of person memory and social cognition. In R. S. Wyer & T. K. Srull (Eds.), *Handbook of social cognition* (Vol. 2, pp. 2-72). Hillsdale, NJ: Lawrence Erlbaum.

Srull, T. K., Liechtenstein, M., & Rothbart, M. (1985). Associative storage and retrieval processes in person memory. *Journal of Experimental Psychology: Learning, Memory, and Cognition, 11,* 316-345.

Srull, T. K., & Wyer, R. S. (1979). The role of category accessibility in the interpretation of information about persons: Some determinants and implications. *Journal of Personality and Social Psychology, 37,* 1660-1672.

Sypher, H. E., & Applegate, J. L. (1984). Organizing communication behavior: The role of schemas and constructs. In R. N. Bostrom (Ed.), *Communication yearbook 8* (pp. 310-329). Beverly Hills, CA: Sage.

Tracy, K. (1991). Introduction: Linking communicator goals with discourse. In K. Tracy (Ed.), *Understanding face-to-face interaction: Issues linking goals and discourse* (pp. 1-20). Hillsdale, NJ: Lawrence Erlbaum.

Tracy, K., Craig, R. T., Smith, M., & Spisak, F. (1984). The discourse of requests: Assessment of a compliance-gaining approach. *Human Communication Research, 10,* 513-538.

Waldron, V. R. (1990). Constrained rationality: Situational influences on information acquisition plans and tactics. *Communication Monographs, 57,* 184-201.

Weiner, B. (1986). *An attributional theory of motivation and emotion.* New York: Springer-Verlag.

Wilson, S. R. (1989). *Coordinating compliance and face goals within persuasive messages: A cognitive rules model of communicative goals and strategies.* Unpublished doctoral dissertation, Purdue University.

Wilson, S. R. (1990). Development and test of a cognitive rules model of interaction goals. *Communication Monographs, 57,* 81-103.

Wilson, S. R. (1991, May). *Modeling individual differences in social inferences and interaction goals.* Paper presented at the annual meeting of the International Communication Association, Chicago.

Wilson, S. R., Aleman, C. G., Miller, L., & Leathem, G. B. (1992, November). *Systematic relationships among compliance and face goals: I. Asking favors, giving advice, and enforcing obligations.* Paper presented at the annual meeting of the Speech Communication Association, Chicago.

Wilson, S. R., Cruz, M. G., & Kang, K. H. (1992a, April). *Evaluating the predictive and external validity of the Attribution Complexity Scale.* Paper presented at the annual meeting of the Central States Communication Association, Chicago.

Wilson, S. R., Cruz, M. G., & Kang, K. H. (1992b). Is it always a matter of perspective? Construct differentiation and variability in attributions about compliance gaining. *Communication Monographs, 59,* 350-367.

Wilson, S. R., Cruz, M. G., Marshall, L. J., & Rao, N. (1993). An attributional analysis of compliance-gaining interactions. *Communication Monographs, 60,* 352-372.

Wilson, S. R., & Kang, K. H. (1989, May). *Attributions of complex cause in compliance-gaining situations involving obligations.* Paper presented at the annual meeting of the International Communication Association, San Francisco.

Wilson, S. R., & Kang, K. H. (1991). Communication and unfulfilled obligations: Individual differences in causal judgments. *Communication Research, 18,* 799-824.

Wilson, S. R., Levine, K., & Humphreys, L. (1994, April). *Individual differences in attribution: What does the Attribution Complexity Scale really measure?* Paper presented at the annual meeting of the Central States Communication Association, Oklahoma City.

Wilson, S. R., & Putnam, L. L. (1990). Interaction goals in negotiation. In J. A. Anderson (Ed.), *Communication yearbook 13* (pp. 374-406). Newbury Park, CA: Sage.

Wyer, R. S., & Srull, T. K. (1986). Human cognition in its social context. *Psychological Review, 93,* 322-359.

2 Production of Messages in Pursuit of Multiple Social Goals: Action Assembly Theory Contributions to the Study of Cognitive Encoding Processes

JOHN O. GREENE
Purdue University

This chapter reviews the program of research on multiple-goal message production conducted within the action assembly theory framework. Action assembly theory has served to direct attention to the temporal characteristics of multiple-goal messages. These message features are seen not only to have social significance by virtue of the fact that they are related to social perception and attributions, but also to provide a window on cognitive encoding processes. From the perspective of action assembly theory, messages aimed at accomplishing multiple social objectives are formulated through the same processes of activation and assembly that are held to underlie all behavioral production. The specific characteristics of these processes have been used to derive a number of hypotheses concerning the temporal features of messages produced under various goal instruction sets. The bulk of this chapter reviews the experimental tests of these hypotheses, summarizes the pattern of empirical findings across multiple studies, and traces the theoretical implications of these findings.

T HIS chapter reviews the program of research on production of multiple-goal messages conducted within the framework of action assembly theory (Greene, 1984a, 1989, in press-a; Greene & Geddes, 1993). Amid the constellation of phenomena that constitute human symbolic activity, few, if any, are more ubiquitous than the multifunctionality of message behavior. It is not surprising, then, that a substantial literature addressing the multifunctional character of messages has emerged. As examples, one can point to various attempts to develop typologies of social goals (e.g., Clark & Delia, 1979; Dillard, Segrin, & Harden, 1989; Pervin, 1983), research on social and individual factors that

Correspondence and requests for reprints: John O. Greene, Department of Communication, Purdue University, West Lafayette, IN 47907.

influence the production of multiple-goal messages (e.g., Baxter, 1984; Hale, 1986; O'Keefe & Shepherd, 1987; Tracy, Van Dusen, & Robinson, 1987), and investigations of message resources for accommodating and/or reconciling competing goals (e.g., Bavelas, Black, Chovil, & Mullett, 1990; Brown & Levinson, 1978; McCornack, 1992; O'Keefe, 1988; Tracy, 1984).

In this expansive and varied research landscape, the work on multiple-goal messages prompted by action assembly theory occupies a relatively distinct position defined by the configuration of assumptions and commitments it reflects. Some mention of these attributes, then, is of value in establishing a foundation for the discussion to follow and in locating research in the action assembly tradition within the broader context of work on multifunctional messages. Although far from exhaustive, certain key characteristics of the action assembly work in this area can be listed under general headings of "conceptual/theoretical attributes" and "empirical/methodological attributes."

Conceptual/Theoretical Attributes

A focus on message encoding processes. Drawing as it does on action assembly theory, the work reviewed here is concerned with illuminating the psychological encoding processes that give rise to multiple-goal messages. The focus, then, is on the output, or behavioral production, system of the individual social actor, and not upon input processing of multifunctional messages produced by others.

A commitment to a human information-processing approach to message encoding. The particular approach to the psychological processes of message production reflected in this program of study is that of human information processing (see Greene, 1984b, 1988). From this perspective, behavioral phenomena are seen to arise from cognitive processes operating over information structures that preserve or represent specific content. The particular emphasis of the research conducted within the action assembly framework has been upon specification of structures and processes underlying multiple-goal messages; less attention has been focused on attempting to describe specific cognitive content that might be employed in producing such messages. In part, this decision to emphasize the study of structure and process over content stems from the problematic nature of attempts to specify relevant cognitive content on the basis of observed behavior (see Greene, 1990). That is, having observed utilization of some strategy or other abstractly characterized act type by an individual, ascribing particular corresponding memorial content to that person in not necessarily warranted. Beyond this, an emphasis on cognitive structure and process reflects a desire to illuminate properties of the output system that apply over individuals, time, and cultures (see Greene, 1984b, 1989). Whereas cognitive content is viewed as the product of the individual's experiences and personal dispositions, conceptions of structures and processes afford a vehicle for advancing general, powerful claims that apply across people.

A hybrid intentional/functional stance. Intentional-stance approaches, which involve explanation by recourse to the actor's goals and knowledge, are limited by the fact that they are predicated on an assumption of rationality and optimal design such that they yield accurate predictions only when the individual acts in a manner consistent with his or her goals and the information at his or her disposal (Dennett, 1971). In the face of the sort of imperfect rationality that characterizes human communicative behavior (see Greene & Geddes, 1993), Dennett (1971) argues that it is necessary to pursue functional-stance accounts where explanation and prediction follow from description of the mental structures and processes that give rise to the phenomena of interest. A key characteristic of the action assembly approach is that it incorporates elements of the intentional stance while embedding these elements in a functional architecture that is capable of accommodating deviations from rationality and optimal design (see Greene, in press-b; Greene & Geddes, 1993).

An effort to locate multiple-goal message production within a more encompassing theoretical framework. Rather than a piecemeal, phenomenon-specific approach to theory building, action assembly work reflects a commitment to broad, encompassing theory capable of addressing a range of distinct phenomena from a single, coherent perspective. Thus the purview of action assembly theory is not limited to the production of multiple-goal messages, but instead is intended to extend to a much broader range of behavioral phenomena. To illustrate, the nature of the self and its role in social interaction (Greene & Geddes, 1988), the sources of cross-situational consistency and discriminativeness (Greene, 1989), and social skill deficits (Greene & Geddes, 1993) are but a few of the areas besides multiple-goal message production where action assembly theory has found application.

An alternative conception of messages. The conception of message behavior suggested by action assembly theory is a marked departure from our commonsense notions of human action (see Greene, 1990, in press-b). Briefly, behavior is seen as a dense, hierarchically organized collocation of elemental features where these features are represented in a number of distinct symbolic codes ranging from the sort of abstract act specifications that constitute our phenomenal experience of our own behavior to low-level sensorimotor codes.

Empirical/Methodological Attributes

A focus on temporal characteristics of messages. The studies of multiple-goal messages prompted by action assembly theory have focused on a set of message features that, although conceptually and practically important, are often neglected by researchers in the field of communication (although these variables do have a long history of investigation by scholars in cognate disciplines). The temporal characteristics of messages are particularly appealing from the standpoint of communication science because they have both social and cognitive significance. Thus they play a role in social perception and attribution while at the same time providing a window on cognitive encoding processes (see Brown, Warner, & Williams, 1985; Butterworth, 1980; Greene, 1988; Siegman, 1987; Siegman & Feldstein, 1979).

The pursuit of incremental, programmatic investigations. Far too often, progress in understanding communication processes is limited by the fact that researchers simply do not conduct enough careful studies to illuminate the nature of the phenomena of interest. It is not unusual for a researcher to conduct two or three studies in an area and then move on to some new topic. As a result, the sorts of insights that come from a "critical mass" of focused studies are sacrificed. Assuming requisite care, the value of an additional study in an area is exponential rather than additive. For this reason, a key aim in the studies reviewed here has been the systematic and incremental extension of research on the production of multiple-goal messages.

ACTION ASSEMBLY THEORY AS
AN APPROACH TO MESSAGE PRODUCTION

Central to action assembly theory's depiction of the behavioral production system is the conception of a long-term memory store of modular units termed *procedural records*. Each procedural record is an associative network structure consisting of associative links connecting three types of symbolic nodes: features of action, outcomes or functional ends, and situations. These features are represented in a number of different code systems that reflect a range of levels of abstraction. Thus some procedural records are cast in abstract propositional formats such as might be used to represent the ideational content of talk, others represent the sort of lower-level information used to specify words and syntactic order, and still others contain motor-control codes for executing articulatory production.

Action assembly theory specifies two processes involved in using the content of procedural records to produce behavior. The first of these, *activation,* serves to retrieve particular memory content and bring it to bear on behavioral production. Procedural records are activated by the occurrence of goals and situational conditions that correspond to the outcomes and situational features held in each record. This activation process is held to operate in parallel and is not restricted by a limited processing-capacity mechanism; as a result, a very large number of procedural records may be activated at any moment. In contrast, the second process, *assembly,* is capacity limited and operates serially. Assembly serves to integrate various activated behavioral features to form a coherent output representation. This output representation specifies the content, order, and timing of the entire complex of behavioral features that make up a person's behavior at any instant. This output structure itself is hierarchically organized in the sense that more abstract behavioral specifications typically function to constrain the content of lower-level specifications.

A key aspect of action assembly theory lies in its specification of means for partially overcoming the time and processing-capacity demands associated with assembly. First, although procedural records are conceived as modular entities that are structurally independent, in practice, repeated concurrent activation and assembly of a particular subset of procedural records will result in the development of unitized assemblies that can be retrieved and implemented as a whole. Second, the theory suggests that it is possible to alleviate cognitive load stemming from assembly by assembling parts of the output representation in advance of actual use, as in cases where the content of one's talk is planned in advance.

From the perspective of action assembly theory, the encoding of messages aimed at accomplishing multiple social objectives involves the same processes of activation and assembly that underlie all behavioral production. In simplest terms, an individual's goals serve to activate relevant behavioral features that are then assembled to form a message representation that incorporates those features. However, the general effect of attempting to accomplish multiple social ends is to increase the complexity of the assembly process by making it more difficult to formulate an output representation that accommodates the behavioral features associated with each goal. When the behavioral features associated with one goal are incompatible with those associated with a second objective, it may be necessary to rely on less readily available, but more mutually compatible, behavioral features or to formulate a more complex output representation that permits either simultaneous or sequential accommodation of the incompatible features (see Greene & Lindsey, 1989).

METHODOLOGICAL CONSIDERATIONS

Drawing on this theoretical foundation, the general research strategy underlying the studies of multiple-goal message production developed within the action assembly framework has been to contrast the temporal characteristics of messages produced by people assigned one social objective with that of their counterparts charged with accomplishing multiple social ends. More specifically, although it certainly would have been possible to contrast other types of interaction goals, following Brown and Levinson (1978), we have sought to contrast the performance of people attempting to communicate a body of information in a clear and direct fashion with that of people who were charged not only with communicating this information but also with being sensitive to the face concerns of the message recipient.

Beyond this general research strategy, these studies have employed a number of procedures pertaining to assessment and analysis of temporal characteristics of speech that merit explicit mention. The first of these concerns the fact that temporal speech variables tend to be characterized by an individual-difference component that accounts for a substantial portion of the variance across different speaking tasks (see Greene, 1989). For this reason, all of the studies reviewed here have employed analysis of covariance designs in which an initial message task is used to establish baseline covariates for the temporal measures under investigation. With few exceptions, these covariate terms are statistically significant and typically account for 10%-20% of the variance, although in some cases this figure ranges as high as 50%-60%.

A second methodological issue in studies such as those under examination here concerns how large an observational unit should be employed in the assessment of pausal phenomena. Our initial studies in this area employed a lower bound of 250 milliseconds in identifying silent pauses during speech (Greene & Lindsey, 1989; Greene, Lindsey, & Hawn, 1990; Greene, McDaniel, Buksa, & Ravizza, 1993). An observational unit of this size is generally consistent with previous studies of such phenomena (see Greene, 1989). More recently, however, we have adopted a cutoff of 125 milliseconds in assessing periods of silent pausing in light of arguments that even pauses of this duration are systematically related to psychological, as opposed to strictly articulatory, phenomena (Hieke, Kowal, & O'Connell, 1983).

One final point concerns methods for measuring periods of silence and phonation employed in these studies. Speech-onset latency, that period between completion of message instructions and onset of the first substantive vocalization, was assessed to hundredths of a second using a digital stopwatch. This method routinely yields intercoder reliabilities on the order of .99 or higher. Periods of silence and phonation after the initial onset of speech were assessed using a series of computer programs written for this purpose. These programs sample the amplitude of the speech signal at a user-specified rate (in the case of the studies reported here, 40 or 80 times per second), smooth this output by averaging over groups of 10 data points, and, finally, compare this mean amplitude with a threshold value to identify periods of silence or phonation. Pause/phonation ratio (the total duration of silence over the total duration of phonation) and average pause duration (total duration of silence over the total number of pause events) are then computed from this output. Reliabilities for these variables established by multiple passes through this computerized system are on the order of .95.

STUDIES OF MULTIPLE-GOAL MESSAGE PRODUCTION

Our initial investigation in this area (Greene et al., 1990) was prompted by the general working hypothesis that people charged with addressing two social objectives would exhibit less fluent speech than their counterparts presented with just one of those goals. Of course, numerous previous investigations of a variety of cognitive and motoric tasks have indicated that as the number or complexity of those tasks increases, so does the time required to initiate and/or execute them (see Kahneman, 1973; Navon, 1984; Norman & Bobrow, 1975; Schneider & Shiffrin, 1977; Shiffrin & Schneider, 1977). It was important, then, to establish whether and under what conditions this general pattern might extend to the production of interpersonal messages. Toward this end, this study contrasted the speech fluency of participants given the task of communicating a negative performance appraisal in a clear and direct fashion with that of people who were not only to communicate this information but also to show concern for the recipient's feelings and self-esteem.

Some discussion of experimental procedures is in order here, because although no two studies reviewed in this chapter have employed the same stimulus materials and task instructions, the general techniques for administering materials and data collection developed for this first study have provided the framework for each of the subsequent investigations. In order to establish baseline covariates for the dependent measures of interest in this study, we presented all subjects initially with a message task involving an issue unrelated to the subsequent experimental message tasks. To prevent prior planning, the instructions for this monologue were not made known to the participant in advance. On a signal from the experimenter, the participant was to reveal the message instructions, read them aloud, and proceed with his or her message.

Following this initial message, each participant was given a file containing a job-performance review for a fictitious person that indicated that his work over the past year had been deficient. This file was removed only after the participant had studied it to his or her satisfaction. The participant was then presented with a second set of monologue instructions, again, without opportunity for advance preparation. For those in the "single-goal" condition, this second set of instructions indicated that they should be "as clear and direct as possible" in reporting on the worker's job performance to his superiors.[1] The designation of a third party as a recipient of this message was intended to suppress the spontaneous generation of face goals that might arise in the communication of this information to the employee. In contrast, people in the "multiple-goals" condition were instructed to deliver their message to the worker himself, with the dual goals of being "clear and direct" while also "showing concern for his feelings and self-esteem."

The effectiveness of the number-of-goals manipulation in this study was assessed in two different ways. At the conclusion of the second message task, each participant completed a short inventory designed to assess his or her concern with goals of conveying the performance evaluation in a clear fashion and with providing face support for the employee. Analysis of these responses indicated that although participants in the single-goal and multiple-goals conditions were equally concerned with being clear and direct in delivering their evaluations, those in the multiple-goals conditions indicated significantly more concern with the employee's feelings. In order to determine whether the instructions to provide support for the employee had actually had an influence on message content, six coders blind to the experimental manipulation rated transcripts of each message according to the degree to which it reflected "a concern for the feelings and self-esteem of the message recipient." Analysis of these ratings revealed that not only did people charged with pursuing multiple goals indicate more concern for providing face support, their messages actually reflected efforts to accomplish this end.

Consistent with expectations, analysis of speech-onset latency indicated that people in the single-goal condition were significantly faster to initiate their responses (adjusted $M = 3.28$ seconds) than those in the multiple-goals condition (adjusted $M = 5.86$ seconds). Further, there was a marginally significant effect ($p = .064$) on pause/phonation ratio stemming from the tendency for people in the single-goal condition to exhibit more fluent speech (adjusted $M = .229$) than their counterparts in the multiple-goals condition (adjusted $M = .350$). These results, then, indicate that the general finding of an inverse relationship between task complexity and speed of execution established in other sorts of information-processing domains does extend to the production of messages such as that under examination in this study.

This study also produced a number of other noteworthy differences between the single-goal and multiple-goal messages. A finding that we originally took to be unremarkable but that has come to assume more significance as our understanding grows is that people addressing multiple goals spoke longer (adjusted $M = 56.38$ seconds) than those given a single goal (adjusted $M = 40.78$ seconds). Beyond this, the multiple-goal messages reflected significantly greater use of sociocentric sequences (e.g., "you know," "well," "okay," "or whatever") and repetition than did the single-goal messages. These latter two results we take to be further evidence of increased time and processing-capacity demands associated with the attempt to address multiple goals. As one final note, and perhaps counter to expectations, this study produced no difference in filled-pause rate (e.g., "er," "um," "uh") between the two message conditions. In fact, however, this finding is generally consistent with other research involving monologue message tasks and may reflect the fact that filled pauses serve functions beyond simply delaying speech production while message assembly is being executed (see Greene, 1988).

The results of our initial experiment (Greene et al., 1990), then, are consistent with the idea that multiple goals serve to increase the difficulty of the assembly process and, as a result, tend to be associated with slower message production. We next sought to replicate these findings with a different set of stimulus materials and to ascertain whether the opportunity for advance planning might be used to reduce time and processing-capacity demands associated with pursuit of multiple social objectives. Recall that according to action assembly theory, assembly of components of the output representation in advance of actual production should be expected to result in more fluent speech.

This second study (Greene & Lindsey, 1989) again contrasted single- and multiple-goal messages, but in this case the number-of-goals manipulation was crossed with presence or absence of opportunity for advance planning. As in the first study, the number-of-goals manipulation pitted pursuit of the task goal of delivering information in a clear and direct fashion against the dual goals of

TABLE 2.1
Adjusted Speech-Onset Latencies (seconds)

| | Message Preparation | |
	Spontaneous	Advance Planning
Single goal	4.04	2.58
Multiple goals	6.26	2.99

SOURCE: Greene and Lindsey (1989).

being clear and direct in communicating this information while also showing concern for the recipient of that information. In this study, participants first reviewed the credentials of a scholarship applicant. Following this, those in the single-goal condition were instructed to communicate to a third party that they had decided not to award a scholarship to the applicant and the reasons behind this decision. In contrast, those in the multiple-goals condition were to communicate this same information to the applicant herself, while also showing concern for her feelings. Again, this manipulation was crossed with a planning manipulation in which half the participants in each condition were given 60 seconds after presentation of the instructions to plan their messages. The remaining participants in each condition proceeded with their messages immediately after reading the task instructions.

As in the earlier study by Greene et al. (1990), the number-of-goals manipulation in this experiment had a significant effect on speech-onset latency arising from the fact that people given a single objective were faster to begin their messages (see Table 2.1). In addition, there was a main effect for the planning manipulation reflecting the fact that those given the opportunity for advance planning exhibited shorter response latencies. The interaction term in this case approached, but did not reach, conventional levels of significance ($p = .088$). Analysis of pause/phonation ratio produced a significant effect for the number-of-goals manipulation, but not for planning or the interaction term. In contrast to the first study, then, where the number-of-goals manipulation had produced only a marginally significant effect on pause/phonation ratio ($p = .064$), the effect in this case was highly significant ($p = .007$), again because people charged with accomplishing multiple ends had higher pause/phonation ratios (adjusted $M = .490$ versus adjusted $M = .375$). As in the earlier study, analysis of filled-pause rate produced no effect for number of goals, advance planning, or their interaction.

In summary, this second study indicated that, relative to messages aimed at accomplishing a single social goal, those directed toward multiple ends were characterized by longer onset latencies and higher pause/phonation ratios. Additionally, the opportunity for advance planning significantly reduced onset latencies, even when a person was attempting to address multiple goals. Advance planning did not, however, significantly improve fluency after the onset of speech as indexed by pause/phonation ratio.

The results for the planning manipulation in this study are interesting because they indicate that opportunity for advance message preparation significantly reduced onset latency but had little effect on pause/phonation ratio. Greene et al. (1990) suggest that this pattern of results may have arisen because participants in the advance-planning condition used this period for formulating global components of their messages such as general ideational content and organization, but once they began speaking were still faced with specification of local features such as word choice, syntax, and so on. As a result, they may not have enjoyed a large advantage over their counterparts who had not been given the opportunity for advance planning.

Based on this line of reasoning, Greene and Lindsey (1989) performed a follow-up analysis, examining the proportion of silent pausing after the onset of speech that was taken up by long pauses (i.e., those 1.5 seconds duration or greater). Previous research has indicated that longer pauses such as this may reflect different underlying processes than shorter pauses (see Siegman, 1987), and that they may be related to formation of major conceptual or strategic moves in a message (see Chafe, 1980; Gee & Grosjean, 1984; Greene & Cappella, 1986; Grosjean, Grosjean, & Lane, 1979). As a result, an advance-planning period devoted to specifying global features of one's message might be expected to reduce the incidence of such long pauses. Consistent with this rationale, Greene and Lindsey (1989) found that the advance-planning manipulation had a significant effect in reducing long-pause ratio. Thus, although advance planning did not have a significant effect on pause/phonation ratio, it did significantly reduce the amount of a person's silent pausing taken up by long pauses.

The results of our first two studies in this area are generally consistent with hypotheses derived from action assembly theory and indicate that pursuit of multiple objectives is associated with slower message production and that this tendency can be at least partially offset (particularly with respect to speed of message onset) under conditions of advance planning. Additionally, the analysis of long pauses reported in Greene and Lindsey (1989) is consistent with conceptions of hierarchical message specifications such as that given in action assembly theory.

SOCIAL VERSUS COGNITIVELY BASED PAUSES

The studies reviewed to this point are limited by the fact that they are characterized by a potential confounding factor associated with the number-of-goals manipulations that could have contributed to the observed results. In these studies people in the multiple-goal conditions were to provide personally relevant information to an individual him- or herself. People in the single-goal conditions, on the other hand, were to convey their messages to third parties. As noted above, this difference in message targets was adopted in order to suppress the spontaneous generation of face goals that might arise if people in the single-goal conditions were asked to speak to the individuals who were the focus of the messages. The potential problem is that people addressing multiple goals may have exhibited less fluent speech not as a result of cognitive load, but for social reasons. That is, they may have used pauses strategically to convey their reluctance to deliver the message.

We undertook to examine this possibility in a pair of studies designed to eliminate the increased cognitive load associated with formulating multiple-goal messages without removing the potential for socially based pauses (Lindsey, Greene, & Parker, 1993; Lindsey, Greene, Parker, & Sassi, 1994). In the first of these studies, we again employed a single- versus multiple-goals manipulation, this time involving a fictitious applicant for an internship position. Participants were given either the single goal of informing a third party of the decision to reject the applicant or the dual goals of delivering this information to the applicant while showing concern for her face needs. This manipulation was crossed with a second manipulation designed to reduce the cognitive load associated with pursuit of multiple goals. In this case, half the participants were allowed time to write down their messages prior to recording them. The remaining participants produced spontaneous messages, as in the previous studies. The purpose of the opportunity for writing one's message in advance was to alleviate the cognitive load associated with assembling a message "on-line," while leaving unchanged the potential for social pauses. (In fact, it is possible that the opportunity to write the message in advance would actually *increase* pausing for social reasons because processing capacity previously devoted to assembling a message addressing both goals might now be allocated to other aspects of performance.)

This experiment produced no evidence that previously observed effects were caused by strategic use of pauses to convey reluctance. A priori pairwise contrasts on speech-onset latency indicated that when speaking spontaneously, people assigned a single goal were significantly faster to initiate their messages (adjusted $M = 2.50$ seconds) than were those given multiple goals (adjusted $M = 3.87$ seconds). Under conditions of advance preparation, however, there was no such pairwise difference (single goal, adjusted $M = 1.60$ seconds; multiple goals, adjusted $M = 1.77$ seconds). This same pattern emerged for pause/phonation ratio. Again, under conditions of spontaneous speech, those pursuing single goals were more fluent (adjusted $M = .307$) than those given multiple goals (adjusted $M = .425$). When given the chance to prepare in advance, however, pause/phonation ratios were virtually equal (single goal, adjusted $M = .194$; multiple goals, adjusted $M = .210$). Examination of average pause duration indicated that those in the spontaneous-message conditions addressing a single goal exhibited pauses that were not significantly different (adjusted $M = .319$ seconds) from those of people addressing two goals (adjusted $M = .366$ seconds) ($p = .10$). Likewise, for the advance-preparation conditions, there was no difference between groups addressing single (adjusted $M = .220$) versus multiple goals (adjusted $M = .253$).

In a second study we again undertook to determine whether the reduced fluency associated with multiple-goal messages truly reflects a cognitive component and is not caused simply by social factors (Lindsey et al., 1994). In this case, people in the single-goal condition were to report to a third party that a senior drama student had not been cast in the final theater production of the year. In contrast, those in the multiple-goals condition were to inform the student herself that she had not been cast in the play and also to support her confidence and self-esteem. In this study, once people had recorded their messages they were given a second monologue task in which they were to convey the same casting decision about another student. Thus each person in this study produced two messages, one spontaneous and one that was essentially a repetition of a previously prepared message. Our hypothesis was that if the reduced fluency characteristic of multiple-goal messages reflects a cognitive component, then we should find that when giving the first, spontaneous, message, people attempting to accomplish multiple goals would be less fluent than their counterparts charged with accomplishing a single end. In contrast, once such a message had been worked out, the cognitive load associated with producing it a second time should be reduced, thereby attenuating differences in speech fluency. On the other hand, if observed differences in the temporal characteristics of speech arise from strategic social considerations, people delivering bad news to the student herself should continue to make use of pauses when repeating their messages to the second student.

The results of this study again confirm that there is indeed a heavier cognitive burden associated with the production of multiple-goal messages, and that differences in the speech fluency of people addressing single versus multiple goals is not caused solely by social factors. A priori contrasts indicated that when producing the first, spontaneous, message, people pursuing a single goal had significantly shorter onset latencies (adjusted $M = 1.45$ seconds) than those given the task of addressing multiple goals (adjusted $M = 2.06$ seconds). In contrast, there was no difference in onset latencies for the single-goal (adjusted $M = 1.51$ seconds) and multiple-goal groups (adjusted $M = 1.74$ seconds) when they were allowed to rely on a previously formulated message in addressing the case of the second student. A similar pattern emerged in the analysis of pause/phonation ratio. Again, when speaking spontaneously, those in the single-goal condition were more fluent (adjusted $M = .259$) than their multiple-goal counterparts (adjusted $M = .449$). This difference did not emerge in the delivery of the second message (single goal, adjusted $M = .219$; multiple goals, adjusted $M = .233$). Analysis of average pause duration indicated that although there was some tendency for people pursuing multiple goals in the first message to be less fluent (adjusted $M = .545$ seconds) than people in the single-goal condition (adjusted $M = .365$ seconds), this difference did not reach conventional levels of significance ($p = .085$). There was no difference in average pause duration for the single-goal (adjusted $M = .385$ seconds) and multiple-goal groups (adjusted $M = .426$) for the second message.

The results of these two studies, then, generally parallel those of the earlier studies in indicating that under conditions of spontaneous message production, pursuit of multiple goals is associated with slower output than pursuit of a single end, although this difference was not statistically significant in the case of average pause duration. Perhaps even more important, these data indicate that there is indeed a cognitive component that contributes to slower speech production when an individual is pursuing multiple social goals. It is also noteworthy that these experiments provide little evidence that the patterns observed in previous studies are the result of strategic use of pauses to convey one's reluctance to deliver bad news. When people were given the opportunity to prepare their messages in advance, so that much of the cognitive work of message assembly "on-line" was eliminated, no differences between single- and multiple-goal conditions were observed for any variable in either study. This is not to say, of course, that people do not pause for the sort of social reasons of interest here. But it does not appear likely that such social pauses are a major contributor to the patterns observed in these studies.

ASSEMBLY OF COMPATIBLE
VERSUS INCOMPATIBLE MESSAGE FEATURES

We next sought to undertake a pair of more stringent tests of the action assembly formulation (Greene et al., 1993). More specifically, we wished to ascertain whether the increased time and processing-capacity demands characteristic of multiple-goal messages arise solely from difficulties in assembling an output representation capable of accommodating incompatible behavioral features. The implication of this question is that it may not be the pursuit of multiple goals, per se, that results in reduced fluency. If assembly of incompatible features is the source of increased cognitive load, then when the message features associated with multiple goals are easily integrated there should be little evidence of increased cognitive demands despite the attempt to accomplish multiple ends. It is only when the individual's goals result in activation of incompatible features and subsequent difficulties in assembly that speech fluency should be reduced. Seen in this light, all of the previous studies involved multiple-goal manipulations likely to require assembly of incompatible features. Our general hypothesis for the next two studies was that evidence of increased time and processing-capacity demands would emerge only when the individual's objectives were incompatible.

In the first of these studies (Greene et al., 1993, Experiment 1) we contrasted the performance of people given two compatible goals with that of their counterparts given two corresponding, but incompatible, goals. In this case, participants first examined a background file for a fictitious scholarship applicant. Unlike in any of the other studies reviewed here, participants were allowed to keep this file open before them for subsequent reference. After studying this background information, participants were presented with monologue instructions indicating that they should inform the applicant whether or not she would receive the scholarship and the reasons for this decision while also showing concern for the applicant's feelings and self-esteem. People in the compatible-goals condition were instructed to inform the applicant that she would receive the scholarship, and those in the incompatible-goals condition were to tell her that her application had been denied. Our assumption was that it would be more difficult for subjects to assemble messages supporting the applicant while also reviewing the reasons for denying her application.

Analysis of speech-onset latency in this experiment indicated that although people in the compatible-goals condition were almost a full second faster in initiating their messages (adjusted $M = 6.32$ seconds versus 7.26 seconds), this difference did not approach significance ($p = .479$). In contrast, goal compatibility did have a significant effect on pause/phonation ratio, with those in the compatible-goals condition exhibiting more fluent speech (adjusted $M = .448$) than people in the incompatible goals condition (adjusted $M = .588$). Similarly, average pause duration was significantly shorter for those pursuing compatible goals (adjusted $M = .621$ seconds) than for those attempting to accomplish incompatible goals (adjusted $M = .804$ seconds).

The analysis of pause/phonation ratio and average pause duration in this experiment thus produced results in line with our expectation that pursuit of two incompatible goals would be more cognitively demanding than pursuit of two corresponding, but compatible, objectives. On the other hand, despite means in the predicted direction, the analysis of speech-onset latency did not reveal a significant effect owing to goal compatibility. This latter result may have arisen from the fact that participants were allowed to keep the background file open before them while recording their messages. The availability of this information may have prompted some participants to begin their messages when they were only minimally specified and then to scan the information sheet for specific message-relevant content after they had already begun. As a result, speech-onset latency in this case may not have been a particularly good index of cognitive processing involved in initial message formulation.

Taken together, the results of this study are useful because they indicate that pursuit of two compatible goals is less cognitively demanding than pursuit of two incompatible goals. This study is limited, however, in that it does not indicate whether pursuit of two compatible objectives is more demanding than pursuit of a single end. If the sole source of increased load associated with multiple goals consists of difficulties in assembling incompatible message features, then we might expect that two compatible goals will impose no more demand on time and processing capacity than pursuit of a single goal. Alternatively, it is possible that although multiple-compatible-goals messages are less demanding than pursuit of multiple-incompatible goals, they still impose a heavier cognitive load than single-goal messages.

TABLE 2.2
Adjusted Speech-Onset Latencies (seconds)

| | Evaluation | |
	Positive	Negative
Single goal	3.60[a,b]	3.02[a]
Multiple goals	3.57[a,b]	5.95[b]

SOURCE: Greene et al. (1993, Experiment 2).
NOTE: Common superscripts indicate a lack of significant pairwise difference in means using Scheffé's criterion with $\alpha = .05$.

To examine this possibility, we undertook a second experiment that served to cross number of goals with goal compatibility (Greene et al., 1993, Experiment 2). In this study, participants first familiarized themselves with an employee's performance record. Half of the participants saw a report that indicated that the employee's performance had been very good; for the other half, the employee's record indicated substandard work. This manipulation was then crossed with a number-of-goals manipulation in which participants were given either the single goal of reporting on the employee's performance to a third party or the dual goals of conveying the performance evaluation to the employee himself while also bolstering his self-esteem and morale.

The results of this study proved to be particularly important in advancing our thinking about message-production processes. Analysis of speech-onset latency revealed no effect for the communication of positive versus negative information, but there was a main effect for the number-of-goals manipulation. More important, there was also a significant interaction effect that resulted from the fact that onset latencies for both single-goal groups and the multiple-compatible-goals group were very similar, whereas that of the multiple-incompatible-goals group was considerably longer (see Table 2.2). This result, then, is consistent with the notion that the reduced fluency previously found to characterize multiple-goal messages was the result of difficulties in assembling incompatible message features.

The picture suggested by analysis of pausing after the onset of speech, however, is rather different. Rather than an interaction effect, analysis of pause/phonation ratio produced only a main effect for number of goals that was caused by the fact that people attempting to accomplish multiple goals were less fluent (adjusted $M = .877$) than those presented with a single goal (adjusted $M = .593$). Average pause duration was characterized by a similar pattern in which those assigned multiple objectives exhibited longer pauses ($M = .823$ seconds) than their counterparts given a single goal ($M = .632$ seconds). These latter findings, then, are inconsistent with the idea that the cognitive load associated with multiple-goal messages stems solely from difficulties in assembling incompatible message features. Instead, there must be some factor that contributes to reduced fluency even when one's goals are compatible, and the behavioral features associated with those goals are, presumably, easily integrated.

If the increased time and processing-capacity demands associated with multiple-goal messages are not solely the result of assembly of incompatible features, then what is the nature of this additional source of cognitive load? Drawing upon our original extension of action assembly theory into the domain of multiple-goal message production (Greene & Lindsey, 1989), we advanced a speculative proposal centering on increased load stemming from the maintenance of more complex message representations (Greene et al., 1993). More recently, we have refined the complexity account to suggest that the formulation and maintenance of more complex message-relevant specifications prior to and during their execution constitutes a source of heightened temporal and processing-capacity demands (Greene & Ravizza, 1993). Thus, even when message features are easily integrated, increasing the complexity of the output representation should serve to reduce speech fluency.

This complexity account is useful in addressing an apparent inconsistency in the results of Experiments 1 and 2 reported by Greene et al. (1993). In Experiment 1, both pause/phonation ratio and average pause duration were characterized by main effects for goal compatibility. In contrast, goal compatibility had no significant effect on either of these variables in Experiment 2. Instead, the analysis of both pause/phonation ratio and average pause duration produced only a main effect for the number-of-goals manipulation. The complexity hypothesis suggests that the significant effect on fluency after the onset of speech in Experiment 1 may have been a result of the fact that people attempting to address incompatible goals formulated more complex message representations than their compatible-goals counterparts. In Experiment 2, in contrast, it is possible that there was no difference in the complexity of the message representations for the compatible-goals and incompatible-goals groups. The plausibility of this speculative account is supported by examination of message duration in these experiments. In Experiment 1, where there was a significant effect for the compatibility manipulation, there was also a significant difference in message duration between the compatible-goals condition (adjusted $M = 40.8$ seconds) and the incompatible-goals condition (adjusted $M = 53.2$ seconds). In contrast, in Experiment 2, where there was no effect for goal compatibility, there also was no difference in message duration between the compatible-goals (adjusted $M = 31.1$ seconds) and incompatible-goals groups (adjusted $M = 35.9$ seconds). Although far from conclusive, this pattern is consistent with the complexity account and suggests that the discrepancy in results for these experiments can be traced to differences in the complexity of the message representations formulated by participants in each study.

Elements of the complexity account are also useful in addressing the different patterns of results observed in Experiment 2 for speech-onset latency and the measures of pausing after the onset of speech. Recall that speech-onset latency in this case was characterized by an interaction between number of goals and goal compatibility such that only those attempting to address multiple, incompatible goals exhibited longer speech-onset latencies. Pause/phonation ratio and average pause duration, on the other hand, produced no corresponding interaction effect, but, again, only main effects for the number-of-goals manipulation. We took the observed interaction effect for speech-onset latency to be indicative of difficulties associated with integrating incompatible message features. On the other hand, the main effects found to characterize pause/phonation ratio and average pause duration may indicate that once a portion of a message representation is assembled, more complex representations, such as those associated with pursuit of multiple goals, are more difficult to maintain.

TESTS OF THE COMPLEXITY ACCOUNT

In the next phase of this program of research we set out to subject the complexity account to more direct test. Several previous studies have indicated that when people are provided with prespecified letter strings, word lists, or sentences for subsequent recitation, speech-onset latency is a function of the length of the string to be output (Ferreira, 1991; Henderson, Chard, & Clark, 1981; Sternberg, Monsell, Knoll, & Wright, 1980; Sternberg, Wright, Knoll, & Monsell, 1980). Although suggestive, such studies do not indicate whether such effects might extend beyond prespecified strings to the realm of spontaneous message production or whether representational complexity has any impact on measures of fluency after the onset of speech. To investigate these issues, we undertook a series of four studies on the effects of complexity on temporal characteristics of speech (Greene & Ravizza, 1993; Ravizza, 1992; Ravizza & Greene, 1993).

In the first of these studies (Ravizza & Greene, 1993, Experiment 1), we followed previous research in this area by operationalizing complexity as the amount of information to be communicated in a message. Our assumption was that as the amount of information to be communicated in a message increased, so too would the complexity of the underlying cognitive representation of that message. A second aim of this investigation was to determine whether any effects of representational complexity on speech fluency might be offset by the opportunity for advance planning. This experiment thus involved crossing an amount-of-information manipulation (in which participants were presented with either four or seven pieces of information to be used in a subsequent message) with a planning manipulation (in which participants spoke either immediately upon presentation of the message instructions or after being permitted to take as long as they wished in planning their responses). In this case, participants reviewed background information on a scholarship applicant and then were instructed to employ all of this information in arguing that the individual should receive the scholarship. A manipulation check involving examination of the messages produced in this study indicated that those in the high-information condition made mention of significantly more pieces of background information ($M = 5.47$) than did those in the low-information condition ($M = 3.68$).

Analysis of speech-onset latency in this experiment produced a significant effect for the planning manipulation but no effect for amount of information or the interaction of the two independent variables. The main effect for planning arose from the fact that those given the opportunity to plan their messages in advance were considerably faster in initiating their responses (adjusted $M = 2.43$ seconds) than their counterparts who spoke spontaneously (adjusted $M = 4.16$). It is worthy of note that although amount of information did not have a significant impact on onset latency ($p = .136$), the means were in the expected direction, with those in the high-information condition exhibiting longer latencies (adjusted $M = 3.73$ seconds versus 3.00 seconds).

Unlike the results for speech-onset latency, analysis of pause/phonation ratio produced a main effect for amount of information. Neither the planning manipulation nor the interaction term was significant in this case. As hypothesized, the effect for amount of information was a result of the fact that those charged with communicating more information had higher pause/phonation ratios (adjusted $M = .57$) than those who were to convey fewer pieces of information (adjusted $M = .45$). Analysis of average pause duration produced no effect for planning, amount of information, or their interaction.

These results, then, indicate mixed support for the complexity account. The results for pause/phonation ratio are in line with expectations and indicate that increasing the amount of information to be communicated in a message will result in reduced fluency. On the other hand, neither speech-onset latency nor average pause duration was characterized by a main effect for the amount-of-information manipulation. The failure to find an effect for speech-onset latency is particularly interesting in light of previous studies that have shown that complexity, operationalized as the length of prespecified strings, does have an impact on onset latency (e.g., Ferreira, 1991; Henderson et al., 1981; Sternberg, Monsell, et al., 1980; Sternberg, Wright, et al., 1980). It is possible that such complexity effects do not extend to longer, spontaneous message tasks such as that employed in this experiment. In the case of relatively short, prespecified strings, it may well be possible to formulate the output representation in advance of overt production. In such cases, onset latency may be a relatively sensitive index of the complexity of output specifications. In contrast, it is unlikely that participants in this study formulated the entire output representation for their message before beginning to speak. Instead, the work of formulating and maintaining elements of the output representation for the monologues in this study was doubtless distributed over the course of participants' responses. As a result, although there was some tendency for increased complexity to be associated with longer onset latencies, this effect is less clear-cut for spontaneous, extended messages than for short, prespecified utterances.

With respect to the second aim of this study, investigating possible effects of advance planning, opportunity for prior message preparation was shown to reduce onset latency, but planning had no effect on pause/phonation ratio or average pause duration. This pattern is, of course, consistent with that produced in our original study of the effects of advance planning on production of multiple-goal messages (Greene & Lindsey, 1989). Again, this pattern may indicate that although planning affords an initial advantage, the need to specify local features for later parts of the message may lead to less of an advantage after message onset. Alternatively, the fact that planning did not afford a significant advantage after the onset of speech may indicate that once the message representation was formulated, the need to maintain this representation while it was executed constituted an additional source of cognitive load. People given the opportunity for advance planning, then, may still have been subjected to cognitive demands associated with maintaining the output representation and, as a result, were not significantly more fluent than those who spoke spontaneously.

Our second investigation of complexity effects (Ravizza & Greene, 1993, Experiment 2) again involved manipulating the amount of information to be conveyed in a message. In this case, however, we employed three levels of this factor. Participants in this second study were instructed to produce messages in which they conveyed seven, five, or three pieces of information about a fictitious scholarship applicant. Additionally, we sought to determine whether any possible effects of complexity might be offset when the person was communicating familiar, rather than unfamiliar, information. Information was assumed to be familiar to the participant when it was similar to his or her own experiences (see Greene, Smith, Smith, & Cashion, 1987; Langer & Weinman, 1981). In contrast, participants in the unfamiliar-information conditions were charged with reporting on the educational background of a student whose experiences were quite different from their own.

Consistent with the first study in this series, the amount-of-information manipulation had no significant effect on speech-onset latency. Nor were there any effects on onset latency owing to familiarity or the interaction of familiarity and amount of information. Analysis of pause/phonation ratio, however, did produce a significant effect for the amount-of-information manipulation, just as in the first experiment. Additionally, pause/phonation ratio was characterized by a significant main effect for the familiarity manipulation. This same pattern emerged in the analysis of average pause duration, where there were significant main effects for both amount of information and familiarity. As can be seen in Tables 2.3 and 2.4, increasing the amount of information to be conveyed in a message had the effect of raising pause/phonation ratios and average pause durations. This tendency toward less fluent speech was exacerbated when the participant was communicating unfamiliar information.

Taken together, the results of these two studies indicate that complexity, operationalized as the amount of information to be communicated in a message, does influence the speed of message production after the onset of speech. In both experiments, amount of information had a significant effect on pause/phonation ratio. In addition, Experiment 2 revealed a significant main effect for the amount-

TABLE 2.3
Adjusted Pause/Phonation Ratios

	Amount of Information		
	Low	*Moderate*	*High*
Familiar information	$.32^a$	$.33^a$	$.45^{a,b}$
Unfamiliar information	$.35^a$	$.48^{a,b}$	$.65^b$

SOURCE: Ravizza and Greene (1993, Experiment 2).
NOTE: Common superscripts indicate a lack of significant pairwise difference in means using Scheffé's criterion with $\alpha = .05$.

TABLE 2.4
Adjusted Average Pause Durations (seconds)

	Amount of Information		
	Low	*Moderate*	*High*
Familiar information	$.23^a$	$.28^{a,b}$	$.32^{a,b,c}$
Unfamiliar information	$.25^{a,b}$	$.35^{b,c}$	$.40^c$

SOURCE: Ravizza and Greene (1993, Experiment 2).
NOTE: Common superscripts indicate a lack of significant pairwise difference in means using Scheffé's criterion with $\alpha = .05$.

of-information manipulation on average pause duration. These results are in line with the complexity hypothesis that the formulation and maintenance of more complex message representations constitutes a source of cognitive load. They are limited, however, by the fact that both studies employed a single operationalization of complexity: the amount of information to be conveyed in a message. We next sought to expand our understanding of complexity effects by employing a very different sort of operationalization. Our use of amount of information as a means of manipulating complexity had grown out of our observations about message length in Greene et al. (1993) and previous research on the length of prespecified utterances. Our next two studies attempted to manipulate complexity while holding amount of information constant. More specifically, we manipulated the coherence of the information to be conveyed in a message on the assumption that complexity would be greater for participants charged with delivering seemingly disjointed propositions than for people attempting to convey the same information but for whom the propositions formed a coherent whole.

Toward this end, our next experiment in this series (Greene & Ravizza, 1993, Experiment 3) involved a situation in which participants first studied a brief (61-word) paragraph, adapted from Bransford and Johnson (1972), describing a sequence of steps for washing clothes. This paragraph was carefully constructed so that the process being described was not readily apparent. For participants in the coherent-message condition, the title "Washing Clothes" was given at the top of the paragraph. In contrast, those in the incoherent-message condition saw no such heading, and, in the absence of a clear theme, were faced with what appeared to be a series of unrelated propositions. After studying this paragraph for as long as they wished, participants received a monologue instruction card indicating that they should convey this information to another person.

As has often been true in our study of temporal characteristics of speech, the results of this experiment proved to be particularly valuable in advancing our thinking, because our hypotheses about the effects of the coherence manipulation were not supported. In fact, the coherence manipulation had no significant effect on speech-onset latency, pause/phonation ratio, or average pause duration. An examination of the time spent studying the stimulus paragraph indicated that those in the incoherent condition took much longer ($M = 53.5$ seconds) than those in the coherent condition ($M = 34.5$ seconds) ($p = .016$). Thus, although no one reported being able to discern the topic of the paragraph and thereby impose some coherence on the content, we believe that coherence was established through sheer rote repetition, much as when the unrelated items making up the alphabet become a coherent string through repeated practice.

We thus undertook yet another experiment (Greene & Ravizza, 1993, Experiment 4) in light of these results. Once again we manipulated coherence of information to be conveyed in a subsequent message. In this case, however, rather than presenting all of the stimulus sentences simultaneously in paragraph form, we presented sentences one at a time through a computer program written for this purpose. Each sentence was displayed for 10 seconds or until the participant pushed a key to move on to the next item. Participants were free to go through the entire series of sentences as many times as they wished. Beyond this, half of the subjects received the stimulus items in the same order on each pass, whereas for the other half the order of items was randomized each time through the series.

The manipulation of coherence in this case involved presentation to half the participants of a line drawing accompanying the stimulus sentences. This drawing provided a context for the six stimulus items and made the interrelations among six otherwise unrelated sentences apparent. After studying the sentences to their satisfaction, participants received message instructions to convey this information to another person.

Unlike in the other studies in this series, analysis of speech-onset latency in this case produced a significant effect for the complexity (i.e., coherence) manipulation. Further, there was also a marginally significant effect ($p = .061$) for the random-versus-fixed-order manipulation and a significant interaction effect. As can be seen in Table 2.5, this pattern of effects stems from the fact that although there was some slight tendency for people in the incoherent conditions to exhibit longer onset latencies, this pattern was particularly pronounced when the stimulus sentences were presented in fixed order. The longer onset latencies for those in the incoherent, fixed-order condition may indicate

TABLE 2.5
Adjusted Speech-Onset Latencies (seconds)

| | Stimulus Coherence | |
	Coherent	Incoherent
Fixed order	2.63[a]	4.13[b]
Random order	2.66[a,b]	2.74[a,b]

SOURCE: Greene and Ravizza (1993, Experiment 4).
NOTE: Common superscripts indicate a lack of significant pairwise difference in means using Scheffé's criterion with $\alpha = .05$.

an attempt to produce the stimulus sentences in the order they were presented, even though the instructions did not require that this be done.

Pause/phonation ratio in this study was characterized by a main effect for coherence stemming from the fact that the mean for the incoherent conditions was considerably higher ($M = 1.24$) than for coherent conditions ($M = .65$). Neither the effect for fixed versus random order nor the interaction term was significant. A similar pattern emerged for average pause duration, where those in the incoherent conditions exhibited markedly longer pauses (adjusted $M = 1.29$ seconds) than did people in the coherent conditions (adjusted $M = .70$ seconds).

To summarize, these four experiments examining complexity effects on temporal characteristics of speech were prompted by the pattern of results observed in Greene et al. (1993, Experiment 2). Whereas we had originally hypothesized that the reduced fluency associated with pursuit of multiple social ends was a result of difficulties in assembling incompatible behavioral features, the results of that study indicated that there was some factor contributing to slower production speeds even when the message features should have been easily integrated. In the face of this finding we advanced the speculative hypothesis that in addition to capacity and temporal demands stemming from difficulties in integrating incompatible features, the formation and maintenance of more complex message representations constitutes a source of cognitive load even when behavioral features are easily integrated. The studies reviewed here have operationalized complexity both in terms of amount of information to be conveyed in a message and as the coherence of message information. Although not entirely uniform, the results of these experiments do tend to support the idea that complexity has some impact on the temporal characteristics of message production.

CONCLUSION

From the perspective of action assembly theory (Greene, 1984a, 1989, in press-a; Greene & Geddes, 1993), behavior at any moment is seen to consist of a hierarchical collocation of a very large number of elemental behavioral features that are specified in a variety of different code systems. These behavioral features are activated and brought to bear on output production when goals and functional ends arise that correspond to symbolic representations of outcomes linked through associative pathways to the behavioral features in question. At the very heart of this perspective, then, is its emphasis on the multifunctional character of behavior (see Greene, 1984a, in press-b). At every instant, behavioral production is seen to involve efforts to satisfy numerous goals and functional requirements, some abstract, (more or less) enduring, and available to introspection, others related to routinized processes of verbal production, and still others pertaining to physiological processes and biomechanical control.

Action assembly theory, then, treats pursuit of the sorts of social objectives traditionally of concern to communication scholars in terms of the same processes of activation and assembly that are held to underlie all behavioral production. The particular properties ascribed to the activation and assembly processes have been used to derive the hypotheses that have driven the studies reviewed here. At the same time, the temporal message characteristics observed in these experiments have suggested refinements in our understanding of the mechanisms of message production. It is useful, then, to summarize key aspects of the characterization of these message-production processes that has emerged from the interplay of theory and data.

We began with the relatively straightforward question of whether the sort of multitasking effects on time and processing capacity established in other domains would extend to the realm of social message production. The studies reviewed here indicate that increasing the number of goals people are instructed to pursue is, indeed, related to speech-onset latency and to pausing after the onset of speech. Our view is that these effects result from two distinct factors. First, multiple goals may increase the complexity of the assembly process because the particular content of the activated features makes it difficult to formulate an output representation capable of accommodating those features. Thus particular features may be incompatible, or they may impose constraints on lower levels of the output representation that are difficult to satisfy. In such cases, we have suggested that it may be necessary to retrieve other, less readily available procedural information that *can* be used in formulating the output representation or to assemble a more complex output representation that permits either sequential or simultaneous accommodation of the incompatible features (Greene & Lindsey, 1989).

Again, in addition to the tendency for multiple goals to increase the complexity of the assembly process, there is a second factor that we believe contributes to the decreased fluency associated with such messages. This is the demand on processing capacity associated with retention of message representations once they are partially or completely formulated. That is, quite aside from the tendency for multiple goals to increase the difficulties associated with assembly, maintaining more complex message representations prior to and during their execution also constitutes a source of load.

No less important than these considerations is the fact that the studies reviewed in this chapter indicate that the effects of the number-of-goals manipulations can be offset under conditions of advance planning and repetition, and that this is particularly true for speech-onset latency. This effect, of course, is consistent with the general conception of assembly in advance of actual production (see Greene, 1984c).

Finally, these studies indicate differential patterns of results for speech-onset latency and measures of pausing after the onset of speech (i.e., pause/phonation ratio, average pause duration, and incidence of pauses 1.5 seconds in duration or greater). Additionally, there is evidence that complexity effects on speech-onset latency observed for short, prespecified strings do not apply in the case of longer, spontaneous messages. As indicated in the body of the chapter, we take these results to implicate the sort of hierarchical, componential approach to message generation reflected in standard treatments of action assembly theory.

As a final comment, and in view of the title of this chapter, I want to conclude with a brief note on the contributions of action assembly theory to the study of multiple-goal message production. I would suggest the following four primary points in this regard.

An explanatory account. Action assembly theory provides a specification of relevant mechanisms. Further, the explanation lends coherence and synthesis to the experimental findings reviewed here by simultaneously accommodating all the empirical results (with minimal stretching and pulling). Finally, the theory serves to link the phenomena of interest here to a much broader constellation of behavioral phenomena.

Now, having said this, I would hasten to add that the explanation of these results given in action assembly theory certainly is not the only possible account. Indeed, it is a fundamental tenet of cognitivism that it is always possible to formulate multiple alternative models capable of accounting for the same results (see Churchland, 1988; Flanagan, 1984; Greene, 1984b). Moreover, the specification of explanatory mechanisms given in action assembly theory is certainly subject to refinement (see Greene, 1984a). Thus, although action assembly theory provides an explanation, I think it is essential that we continue to pursue development of alternative models that afford more adequate characterizations of relevant mechanisms and/or greater ranges of application.

Heurism. Action assembly theory has served to direct attention to a set of features (i.e., temporal characteristics) associated with multiple-goal messages that was previously unexplored. Moreover, the experiments reviewed here, the hypotheses and methods, arose directly from action assembly theory. Too often we pay lip service to heurism while overlooking its value. It is important to keep in mind that developing an alternative perspective to account for a body of results after the fact is not at all the same as employing a theory to generate that set of experiments and findings in the first place.

A body of empirical findings. One of the attributes of temporal measures of speech production that I personally find most satisfying is that they are among the least time- and space-bound of all attributes of human communication. The situation is much like that for reaction-time studies in psychology, where data collected a century ago still constitute an important part of the corpus of empirical regularities that current theories must address. Long after the conceptual framework that gave rise to these studies has been surpassed by more sophisticated treatments, the data will remain to inform and guide the theorizing and empirical endeavors of communication scientists.

An analogy. The three points I have touched upon so far are the standard stuff of science. I want to conclude by mentioning one other little insight my colleagues and I have gleaned along the way. An analogy that has come to guide our thinking is that of pursuit of multiple goals as solving a puzzle. In one sense, the presentation of studies developed in this chapter is misleading, because the reader might get the idea that the process is much cleaner than in fact it is. In one sense, the studies reviewed here are but the tip of an iceberg. We have conducted several pilot studies that simply did not work. In some cases, studies failed to produce differences between single-goal and multiple-goals conditions because it was relatively easy to reconcile the multiple goals. In other cases, it proved so difficult to address dual goals that people simply gave up. Thus part of the art of designing these studies is to present people with a puzzle that is just hard enough. By the same token, some individuals solve the puzzle much more readily than do others. Some people are able to address multiple goals with succinct messages that are quite fluent; for others, the solution to the puzzle is much less obvious, and they struggle to assemble a message. In the end, this research program has been driven by the desire to arrive at a fine-grained understanding of the mechanisms of message production, but this little analogy, too, captures a part of what we have heard, and measured, along the way.

NOTE

1. An essential claim of action assembly theory is that all behavior is directed toward multiple goals and functional ends. The terms *single goal* and *multiple goals* are used here to refer to the number of social objectives that participants were explicitly assigned in the monologue instructions, and the use of these terms should not be taken to imply that these were the only goals and functional ends influencing the behavior of the participants.

REFERENCES

Bavelas, J. B., Black, A., Chovil, N., & Mullett, J. (1990). *Equivocal communication.* Newbury Park, CA: Sage.
Baxter, L. A. (1984). An investigation of compliance-gaining as politeness. *Human Communication Research, 10,* 427-456.
Bransford, J. D., & Johnson, M. K. (1972). Contextual prerequisites for understanding: Some investigations of comprehension and recall. *Journal of Verbal Learning and Verbal Behavior, 11,* 717-726.

Brown, B. L., Warner, C. T., & Williams, R. N. (1985). Vocal paralanguage without unconscious processes. In A. W. Siegman & S. Feldstein (Eds.), *Multichannel integrations of nonverbal behavior* (pp. 149-193). Hillsdale, NJ: Lawrence Erlbaum.

Brown, P., & Levinson, S. (1978). Universals in language usage: Politeness phenomena. In E. N. Goody (Ed.), *Questions and politeness: Strategies in social interaction* (pp. 56-310). Cambridge: Cambridge University Press.

Butterworth, B. (Ed.). (1980). *Language production: Vol. 1. Speech and talk.* London: Academic Press.

Chafe, W. L. (1980). The development of consciousness in the production of narrative. In W. L. Chafe (Ed.), *The pear stories: Cognitive, cultural, and linguistic aspects of narrative production* (pp. 9-50). Norwood, NJ: Ablex.

Churchland, P. M. (1988). *Matter and consciousness: A contemporary introduction to the philosophy of mind* (rev. ed.). Cambridge: MIT Press.

Clark, R. A., & Delia, J. G. (1979). Topoi and rhetorical competence. *Quarterly Journal of Speech, 65,* 187-206.

Dennett, D. C. (1971). Intentional systems. *Journal of Philosophy, 68,* 87-106.

Dillard, J. P., Segrin, C., & Harden, J. M. (1989). Primary and secondary goals in the production of interpersonal influence messages. *Communication Monographs, 56,* 19-38.

Ferreira, F. (1991). Effects of language and syntactic complexity on initiation times for prepared utterances. *Journal of Memory and Language, 30,* 210-233.

Flanagan, O. J., Jr. (1984). *The science of the mind.* Cambridge: MIT Press.

Gee, J. P., & Grosjean, F. (1984). Empirical evidence for narrative structure. *Cognitive Science, 8,* 59-85.

Greene, J. O. (1984a). A cognitive approach to human communication: An action assembly theory. *Communication Monographs, 51,* 289-306.

Greene, J. O. (1984b). Evaluating cognitive explanations of communicative phenomena. *Quarterly Journal of Speech, 70,* 241-254.

Greene, J. O. (1984c). Speech preparation processes and verbal fluency. *Human Communication Research, 11,* 61-84.

Greene, J. O. (1988). Cognitive processes: Methods for probing the black box. In C. H. Tardy (Ed.), *A handbook for the study of human communication: Methods and instruments for observing, measuring, and assessing communication processes* (pp. 37-66). Norwood, NJ: Ablex.

Greene, J. O. (1989). The stability of nonverbal behaviour: An action-production approach to problems of cross-situational consistency and discriminativeness. *Journal of Language and Social Psychology, 8,* 193-220.

Greene, J. O. (1990). Tactical social action: Towards some strategies for theory. In M. J. Cody & M. L. McLaughlin (Eds.), *The psychology of tactical communication* (pp. 31-47). Clevedon: Multilingual Matters.

Greene, J. O. (in press-a). An action assembly perspective on verbal and nonverbal message production: A dancer's message unveiled. In D. E. Hewes (Ed.), *The cognitive bases of interpersonal communication.* Hillsdale, NJ: Lawrence Erlbaum.

Greene, J. O. (in press-b). What sort of terms ought theories of human action incorporate? *Communication Studies.*

Greene, J. O., & Cappella, J. N. (1986). Cognition and talk: The relationship of semantic units to temporal patterns of fluency in spontaneous speech. *Language and Speech, 29,* 141-157.

Greene, J. O., & Geddes, D. (1988). Representation and processing in the self-system: An action-oriented approach to self and self-relevant phenomena. *Communication Monographs, 55,* 287-314.

Greene, J. O., & Geddes, D. (1993). An action assembly perspective on social skill. *Communication Theory, 3,* 26-49.

Greene, J. O., & Lindsey, A. E. (1989). Encoding processes in the production of multiple-goal messages. *Human Communication Research, 16,* 120-140.

Greene, J. O., Lindsey, A. E., & Hawn, J. J. (1990). Social goals and speech production: Effects of multiple goals on pausal phenomena. *Journal of Language and Social Psychology, 9,* 119-134.

Greene, J. O., McDaniel, T. L., Buksa, K., & Ravizza, S. M. (1993). Cognitive processes in the production of multiple-goal messages: Evidence from the temporal characteristics of speech. *Western Journal of Communication, 57,* 65-86.

Greene, J. O., & Ravizza, S. M. (1993). *Complexity effects on temporal characteristics of speech.* Unpublished manuscript, Purdue University.

Greene, J. O., Smith, S. W., Smith, R. C., & Cashion, J. L. (1987). The sound of one mind working: Memory retrieval and response preparation as components of pausing in spontaneous speech. In M. L. McLaughlin (Ed.), *Communication yearbook 10* (pp. 241-258). Newbury Park, CA: Sage.

Grosjean, F., Grosjean, L., & Lane, H. (1979). The patterns of silence: Performance structures in sentence production. *Cognitive Psychology, 11,* 58-81.

Hale, C. L. (1986). Impact of cognitive complexity in a face-threatening context. *Journal of Language and Social Psychology, 5,* 135-143.

Henderson, L., Chard, J., & Clark, A. (1981). Initiation latency and advanced planning in rapid recitation and oral reading. *Canadian Journal of Psychology, 35,* 224-243.

Hieke, A. E., Kowal, S., & O'Connell, D. C. (1983). The trouble with "articulatory" pauses. *Language and Speech, 26,* 203-214.

Kahneman, D. (1973). *Attention and effort.* Englewood Cliffs, NJ: Prentice Hall.

Langer, E. J., & Weinman, C. (1981). When thinking disrupts intellectual performance: Mindfulness on an overlearned task. *Personality and Social Psychology Bulletin, 7,* 240-243.

Lindsey, A. E., Greene, J. O., & Parker, R. (1993, May). *The effects of advance preparation on message encoding: Distinguishing social and cognitively based hesitation in the production of multiple-goal messages.* Paper presented at the annual meeting of the International Communication Association, Washington, DC.

Lindsey, A. E., Greene, J. O., Parker, R., & Sassi, M. (1994, May). *Effects of advance message formulation on message encoding: Evidence of cognitively based hesitation in the production of multiple-goal messages.* Paper presented at the annual meeting of the International Communication Association, Sydney, Australia.

McCornack, S. A. (1992). Information manipulation theory. *Communication Monographs, 59,* 1-16.

Navon, D. (1984). Resources: A theoretical soup stone? *Psychological Review, 91,* 216-234.

Norman, D. A., & Bobrow, D. G. (1975). On data-limited and resource-limited processes. *Cognitive Psychology, 7,* 44-64.

O'Keefe, B. J. (1988). The logic of message design: Individual differences in reasoning about communication. *Communication Monographs, 55,* 80-103.

O'Keefe, B. J., & Shepherd, G. J. (1987). The pursuit of multiple objectives in face-to-face interaction: Effects of construct differentiation on message organization. *Communication Monographs, 54,* 396-419.

Pervin, L. A. (1983). The stasis and flow of behavior: Toward a theory of goals. In M. M. Page (Ed.), *Nebraska symposium on motivation: Personality—current theory and research* (pp. 1-53). Lincoln: University of Nebraska Press.

Ravizza, S. (1992). *The effects of representational complexity on speech fluency.* Unpublished master's thesis, Purdue University.

Ravizza, S., & Greene, J. O. (1993, May). *The effects of representational complexity on speech fluency.* Paper presented at the annual meeting of the International Communication Association, Washington, DC.

Schneider, W., & Shiffrin, R. M. (1977). Controlled and automatic human information processing: I. Detection, search, and attention. *Psychological Review, 84,* 1-66.

Shiffrin, R. M., & Schneider, W. (1977). Controlled and automatic human information processing: II. Perceptual learning, automatic attending, and a general theory. *Psychological Review, 84,* 127-190.

Siegman, A. W. (1987). The telltale voice: Nonverbal messages of verbal communication. In A. W. Siegman & S. Feldstein (Eds.), *Nonverbal behavior and communication* (2nd ed., pp. 351-434). Hillsdale, NJ: Lawrence Erlbaum.

Siegman, A. W., & Feldstein, S. (Eds.). (1979). *Of speech and time: Temporal speech patterns in interpersonal contexts.* Hillsdale, NJ: Lawrence Erlbaum.

Sternberg, S., Monsell, S., Knoll, R. L., & Wright, C. E. (1980). The latency and duration of rapid movement sequences: Comparisons of speech and typewriting. In R. A. Cole (Ed.), *Perception and production of fluent speech* (pp. 469-505). Hillsdale, NJ: Lawrence Erlbaum.

Sternberg, S., Wright, C. E., Knoll, R. L., & Monsell, S. (1980). Motor programs in rapid speech: Additional evidence. In R. A. Cole (Ed.), *Perception and production of fluent speech* (pp. 507-534). Hillsdale, NJ: Lawrence Erlbaum.

Tracy, K. (1984). The effect of multiple goals on conversational relevance and topic shift. *Communication Monographs, 51,* 274-287.

Tracy, K., Van Dusen, D., & Robinson, S. (1987). "Good" and "bad" criticism: A descriptive analysis. *Journal of Communication, 37,* 46-59.

3 Managing the Flow of Ideas: A Local Management Approach to Message Design

BARBARA J. O'KEEFE
University of Illinois, Urbana-Champaign

BRUCE L. LAMBERT
University of Illinois, Chicago

This chapter develops the case for a local management model of message design. In contrast to other current approaches, in which message structure is understood in terms of holistic-functional categories, a local management approach separates the analysis of message structure and message function. Message structure is understood as patterns of expressed thoughts. Message function is understood in terms of context-sensitive mappings between antecedent conditions and message structure and between message structure and message effects. After making the case for a local management approach, the authors introduce an initial model of the message design process that offers an integrated treatment of message production, adaptation, and effects.

O UR objective is to develop a theory of message design, a systematic theory of the relationship between message structure and message function. *Message structure* refers to the substance, organization, and placement of discourse. *Message function* involves both the antecedent conditions of message generation (especially the goals of the message producer) and the intended and unintended effects of the message.

Most current theories of message design are based on a view of messages that is both holistic and functional. In such holistic-functional analysis, units in the stream of discourse are identified and then labeled, as wholes, in terms of their discourse function. In different holistic-functional approaches, the nature of the unit may vary (it may be a turn, it may be a text) and the kind of functional characterization may vary (illocutionary force, perlocutionary effect, type of adjacency pair, type of compliance-gaining strategy, and so on). Examples of holistic

Correspondence and requests for reprints: Barbara J. O'Keefe, 702 South Wright Street, No. 244, Urbana, IL 61801.

Communication Yearbook 18, pp. 54-82

functional categories include illocutionary and perlocutionary acts (Searle, 1969), taxonomies of communicative strategies (e.g., Marwell & Schmitt, 1967a, 1967b), and first and second pair parts (Schegloff, 1968). Once a functional terminology has been constructed, it can be used in research on the conditions that influence the type of message produced and the consequences of using different types of messages.

This approach, in which functional theory is based on functional categorizations of discourse, has been fruitful in a variety of very different research traditions, including research on the development, deployment, and effects of interpersonal message strategies (for reviews, see McLaughlin, 1984; O'Keefe & Delia, 1988; Seibold, Cantrill, & Meyers, 1985); research on the organization of face-to-face interaction (for reviews, see McLaughlin, 1984; Roger & Bull, 1989; Taylor & Cameron, 1987); and research on message comprehension and generation (for examples, see Cohen, Morgan, & Pollack, 1990; Levelt, 1989). However, although this approach has been helpful in generating information about the general pattern, distribution, and effects of messages, it is limited in its ability to address a set of important basic questions about message production, variation, and outcomes.

In this chapter we describe an alternative to the standard holistic-functional approach to message analysis, one that treats message design as the local management of situated beliefs. Rather than viewing messages as coherent instantiations of globally defined actions, this approach views messages as collations of thoughts. Message design, then, is conceptualized as the local management of the flow of thought—both the management of own thoughts by the message producer and the management of the other's thoughts in the service of communicative goals. The question we address is how patterns of thoughts and ways of managing thought can give rise to message structure and message functions.

We begin by describing current problem-solving models of message generation and their limitations in accounting for message design. We then describe a set of phenomena that present special difficulties for a problem-solving approach and suggest the value of a local management approach. Next, we provide a general characterization of the local management approach. We then present a detailed model of message design as the management of thought, and summarize our work to date developing models of message generation. We go on to show how this model can account for message adaptation and effects. We close with a discussion of the broader implications of this work for theories of discourse and communication.

THE PROBLEM-SOLVING MODEL

The most popular current models of message generation, which we call *problem-solving models,* are generally based on a holistic-functional view of messages. In this section, we discuss models based on artificial intelligence (AI) conceptions of planning as problem solving (Fikes & Nilsson, 1971; Miller, Galanter, & Pribram, 1960; Newell & Simon, 1972; Sacerdoti, 1974) and the role of functional categories in such models. This approach has stimulated a great deal of research and is exemplified in the impressive computer models of Cohen and Perrault (1979) and Appelt (1982). In what follows, we describe the problem-solving approach and discuss its limitations.

In a problem-solving model, goals are presented to the system; subgoals are identified by comparing the current state to the goal state, and actions are chosen to eliminate existing differences between current and goal states (see Levelt, 1989). For example, if the goal state specifies "H believes that S believes p," and the current state specifies "H believes that S believes not p," then the task is to select an action that changes H's beliefs. The choice of an appropriate action is made possible by indexing actions by the differences they eliminate.

A problem-solving model will have a repertoire of actions at its disposal, each indexed by the type of difference it eliminates. Within different models, these action repertoires will be represented a bit differently. For purposes of discussion, assume they take the form of if-then rules: "IF the intention is to commit oneself to the truth of p, THEN assert p" (Levelt, 1989, p. 10). This is unobjectionable if one grants that asserting p, by definition, has the desired effect on H's beliefs (Cohen & Perrault, 1979; Searle, 1969).

From the standpoint of a theory of message design, a key weakness of a problem-solving approach derives precisely from the fact that problems are represented and solved abstractly, that is, in terms of types of situations and actions rather than in terms of specific situations and the field of thoughts that accompany them. A plan derived from an abstract problem-solving process will always be a sequence of act types. To move from a sequence of act types to a message, each act type must be *instantiated* as a particular utterance.

Hence these models must somehow solve the problem of instantiation: They must show how a system moves from a high-level act category (e.g., request H to do A) to a string of produced sounds. A common solution is to posit a hierarchy of linguistic structures in which a structure at one level is instantiated from choices at the next level down. For example, in Appelt's (1982, 1985) model, the system is endowed with a repertoire of choices at each of a number of levels. Having selected a speech act to instantiate (e.g., an assertion), the system's next task is to select a sentence type. At the level of sentence type, the system can choose among declarative, interrogative, and imperative sentence types. The choice is made possible through an indexing of each sentence type by the speech acts it instantiates. Thus declaratives instantiate assertions, interrogatives instantiate requests, and imperatives instantiate commands. Needing to instantiate an assertion, the system's choice of a declarative sentence is simple.

Essentially the same approach is taken at levels below the sentence (see Garrett, 1975, and the critique of Garrett by Dell & Juliano, 1993). Once a sentence type is chosen, words must be chosen to fill the slots in the sentence frame. The system has a lexicon of words, and each word is indexed by its grammatical function (noun, verb, determiner) and by its meaning. Once words are chosen, morphemes and phonemes must be chosen to fill in the slots in the words' representations. Once phonemes are chosen, articulatory patterns must be chosen to produce the relevant sounds. At each level there is a choice to be made, and the dilemma of choice is always resolved in the same way, by indexing choices in terms available at the highest adjacent level of abstraction.

These abstract representations with slots to be filled are called *functional representations* (Garrett, 1988), and we refer to this way of solving the instantiation problem as a *functional indexing scheme*. The use of functional indexing schemes is a definitive characteristic of standard, problem-solving models of message production.

However, there are difficulties with functional indexing schemes as they have been implemented in computer models of message production. The indexing that is required in order to enable rational choice among forms depends on there being a decontextualized relationship between form and function. But, to put it bluntly, decontextualized linguistic forms have no functional significance. It is a truism to say that the meaning of a form depends on the context of its use. At the level of discourse acts or message features, the evidence shows that the form-function relationship is mediated by reasoning from context-specific beliefs (Levinson, 1982; Tannen, 1993). At the level of words, the analogous phenomenon is known as polysemy (Green, 1989). Similar context dependencies are apparent at lower levels of abstraction as well (Levelt, 1989).

Notice that the instantiation problem arises, in the very beginning, from assuming that the materials of planning—communicative acts—are represented, selected, and ordered independently from some specific context. Not surprisingly, this problem has been recognized by researchers working within the problem-solving approach, and various solutions have been proposed. For example, Hovy (1990) offers a model that assumes a particular input representation rather than generating the input through problem solving. However, his approach, because it involves reasoning with abstract message features rather than concrete situated message contents, still faces the instantiation problem. Even though Hovy's model offers a richer array of functional indices (e.g., he includes rhetorical indices that permit choice among instantiations based on situational features), it nonetheless must ultimately rest on a view of form-function relations as decontextualized and fixed.

We have focused on the difficulties that arise from assuming an invariant, decontextualized relationship between message forms and message functions, regardless of the sophistication of the planning model being constructed. But different views of planning differ in the way functional units are used in planning. Thus one legitimate question concerns whether the problems we have discussed might be attributable to the planning model itself as opposed to the way communicative action is represented within the model.

For example, limitations in strictly top-down planning systems have been recognized for years (Agre & Chapman, 1987; Miller, 1990), and dissatisfaction with so-called classical approaches to planning has led to several modifications in the basic planning approach. To grasp these changes, it is important to appreciate the distinction made in planning theories between plan construction (done by the planner) and plan execution (done by the executive). Plan construction involves assembling a sequence of abstract actions. Plan execution involves implementing abstract actions by selecting concrete options and monitoring the consequences of selected options.

Classical planning systems place most of the control and intelligence in the plan construction module. A plan is carefully constructed and then passed to the executive. If the plan fails during execution, a classical planner has little recourse except to begin again from scratch. In their summary of recent research, Agre and Chapman (1987) note that some modelers have experimented with relocating the center of control in a plan from the planner to the executive. With an intelligent executive, it is possible to monitor plan execution and return control to the planner when execution fails or hits an obstacle. Planning systems that invest most of their resources in plan construction are known as classical or top-down planners. Bottom-up, reactive planning systems have a repertoire of preformulated plans and place more emphasis on plan selection and execution monitoring. So there is a continuum between classical, top-down planners and newer, reactive planners. Between the extremes are the so-called interleaved or limited-commitment planners, which pass control back and forth between the planner and the executive, based on careful monitoring of plan execution (see Agre & Chapman, 1987; Hovy, 1990; Miller, 1990).

One might suggest that the problems highlighted in a model like Appelt's (1985) are solved in an interleaved or reactive planning framework. This is not the case. In both Appelt's classical planning framework and Hovy's interleaved planner, the function of a form is still an explicit part of the representation of the form itself. Hovy (1990), for example, uses top-down planning (what he calls "prescriptive" planning) to collect and assemble topics for expression. Prescriptive planning is formative; it is used to "act over and give shape to long ranges of text" (p. 167). Bottom-up planning (what Hovy calls "restrictive" planning) selects from an available set of options the concrete linguistic realization of the planned topics (i.e., the actual words and phrases).

But this is a difference only in the grain-size at which planning takes place. Prescriptive planning involves selection from functionally indexed high-level forms, and restrictive planning involves selection from functionally indexed low-level forms. In both cases, at both high and low levels of abstraction, a given option is selected only if it achieves a stated goal. In both cases, options are indexed by the goals they help to satisfy—part of the explicit representation of each and every form is its functional index, a list of the goals achieved by selecting that form. So even in the context of an interleaved planning framework, function is an integral part of the form's representation from the moment it is introduced into the system.

It is precisely this practice—representing communicative action in terms of functions—that leads to difficulties. In the investigation of message design (i.e., the relationship between forms and functions), form and function must be representationally distinct. Moreover, it is the use of functional representation that gives rise to the instantiation problem. Finally, even though no problem-solving model makes the explicit assumption that there is an invariant form-function relationship, mechanisms for modeling variability are conspicuously absent from problem-solving models.

SPEECH AND THE FLOW OF THOUGHT

In the preceding section we discussed the difficulties faced by holistic-functional models that result from the assumption of a context-invariant relationship between message forms and message functions. In this section we discuss a second problem facing holistic-functional approaches, namely, that message structure and function are not holistic, but rather reflect the grounding of messages in an ongoing stream of thought and action. We illustrate the grounding of speech in the flow of thought by considering two distinct classes of messages: descriptions and complex interpersonal tasks. We show how features of these classes of messages point toward a very different image of message design, namely, a view of messages as the local management of thought.

The Structure of Descriptions

A good deal of thought and research has been devoted to understanding descriptions, although what is meant by *description* can vary quite widely from one investigation to another. For example, one tradition examines relatively short characterizations of objects or states of affairs (e.g., "the dog with the brown spots") and analyzes their properties and use in acts of referring (e.g., Grosz, 1981). Other lines of research focus on extended speech acts in which description is used not simply in the service of reference, but to offer information about a referent to a hearer. Although all this research on descriptions clearly connects to important underlying theoretical issues, the kinds of texts, discourse structures, and communicative functions under examination vary widely across this topic area.

However, one consistent theme throughout the study of descriptions is the close relationship between message structure and the substance and organization of knowledge in the topic domain. For example, Grosz (1981) studied instructions provided for the assembly of a mechanical device; to explain the structure of the instructions, she developed a model of describing as the movement of focus of attention through a knowledge structure. A similar model was developed in very different research contexts by Chafe (1979), who studied descriptions of events; Levy (1979), who analyzed descriptions of student class schedules; and Sibun (1990, in press), who modeled descriptions of houses and family trees.

Examples of a highly detailed analysis of discourse structure as reflecting the movement of attention through a structure of knowledge can be found in studies of descriptions of spatial layouts. Beginning with Linde and Labov's (1975) study of apartment descriptions, considerable research has shown that the structure of such descriptions, whether they describe a room (e.g., Ullmer-Ehrich, 1982), a residence (e.g., Linde & Labov, 1975), or a route between points in a city (e.g., Wunderlich & Reinelt, 1982), generally exhibit a pattern in which hypothetical movement through a space provides the organizing principle for a linearized recounting of spatial information. So, for example, descriptions of both apartments and rooms commonly take the form of "tours" in which the hypothetical gaze of the hearer is guided through the space and led to focus on key features of interest.

As Ullmer-Ehrich (1982) argues, one should not assume that explaining the structure of descriptions is therefore simply a matter of developing a model of the representation of spatial information, because there are three problems that must be solved in moving from a spatial representation to a verbal message. The first problem, the selection problem, arises from the fact that much more spatial information is stored than can or should be expressed. Hence the speaker must select just those elements of the representation that are relevant for the purpose at hand. The second problem, the transformation problem, arises from the fact that in order to be expressed, elements of the representation must be temporalized, placed in a one-dimensional order. The third problem, the symbolization problem, arises from the fact that spatial information must be verbally formulated.

All three of these issues can be addressed within a theory of focus. As Groscz (1981) envisions it, "Focusing is the active process, engaged in by the participants in a dialogue, of concentrating attention on, or highlighting, a subset of their shared reality" (p. 101). A focus involves not simply attention given to cognitive elements, but a perspective on those elements, a perspective that is implicit in the terms of a description. By specifying the perspective, a theory of focus contributes to an analysis of symbolization; by modeling the restriction on relevance that comes with focusing attention, a theory of focus contributes to an analysis of selection; and by explaining the movement of focus through a knowledge structure, a theory of focus contributes to an analysis of the linearization of knowledge as text.

In the case of descriptions, much of the substance and organization of messages can be seen as reflecting the substance and organization of knowledge in the topic domain. This knowledge is represented, selected, and ordered for expression as focus follows a route (e.g., a tour) through the spatial representation. Hence descriptions originate as content that becomes focal as attention is directed by a specific communicative task; utterances result from expression of focal elements.

This general picture of message production is also exemplified in work by Kellermann and her associates (for a review, see Kellermann & Lim, 1989) on a very different problem: exchanges of information in initial interactions. These researchers have shown how the problem of becoming acquainted leads individuals to move systematically through an agenda of knowledge exchanges; the talk produced in discussing a topic reflects a standard agenda of points of focus within the topic. Although their work is presented in a framework very different from ours, it nonetheless provides yet another example of how talk is generated by the movement of focus through knowledge structures.

Complex Interpersonal Tasks and Message Design

Description is a domain in which performance is generally uniform across individuals—different people produce messages that are extremely similar in structure and content. By contrast, complex interpersonal situations (regulating, comforting, and so on) elicit highly variable performance from different individuals.

Because of this, performance on complex communication tasks provides a useful point of contrast for a local management theory of message design. It might be argued, for example, that descriptions are one of the domains (initial interactions being another) in which behavior is highly routinized (indeed, Linde & Labov, 1975, make this claim), and therefore speakers make no detectable strategic choices. With tasks that elicit greater functional variation, high-level choices among distinct strategies might be more apparent.

But in this section we argue that responses to complex communication tasks offer yet another compelling example of the grounding of talk in the ongoing stream of thought. We have conducted several recent investigations in which we have addressed the question of whether messages consist of relatively distinct and unified "strategies" or relatively inchoate and fragmented collations of thoughts. To address this question, we required a different type of message analysis than had previously been employed in research on message structure and effects; the standard approach, holistic-functional classification, obviously begs the very question we wanted to answer.

Our method is based on the identification of relatively fine-grained discourse units. Adapting techniques used by Chafe (1979) in studies of oral discourse and by Hunt, Matsuhashi, and others in studies of written communication (for a review, see Hillocks, 1986), we segmented messages into thought units, which essentially correspond to independent clauses. These thought units are then grouped based on synonymy into categories that reflect the basic ideas expressed in the thoughts, independent of specific wording. The criteria for synonymy are quite conservative, and generally require that alternative members of a category be similar except for grammatical transformation or substitution of synonymous terms or phrases.

For example, Lambert (1992) studied messages elicited by a hypothetical interpersonal conflict situation in which a friend repeatedly breaks dates with the speaker. He analyzed 320 messages, and found that their content could be

TABLE 3.1

Ideas Appearing in Interpersonal Conflict Messages

Idea Type	Frequency[a]	Idea Type	Frequency[a]
You have broken our dates a lot lately.	.362	Our friendship may end.	.056
Sorry, I can't go tomorrow.	.325	Friendship takes mutual effort.	.056
Call me when you have more time.	.272	Let's talk tomorrow about the date.	.056
Okay, I can go tomorrow.	.266	Understand my perspective.	.053
I'm tired of your behavior.	.203	If you don't want dates, don't make dates.	.050
Your behavior is bothering me.	.193	You don't have time for me.	.050
What is going on?	.191	I want to remain your friend.	.047
I understand your constraints.	.184	I have tried to set up dates with you.	.047
We have been good friends for some time.	.173	You have not been a good friend lately.	.047
You've been busy.	.159	I've made sacrifices to be with you.	.047
If you don't want to see me, just say so.	.150	If you called sooner I could have replaced you.	.047
I want to get together.	.147	If you cancel again, I'll be angry.	.047
Is there a problem?	.134	I miss you.	.041
Check with me another time.	.116	I think/believe/feel that. . . .	.041
When we make dates make sure you are free.	.113	I make time for you.	.036
Tomorrow is fine if we can make it.	.113	I'm not angry.	.034
Your behavior is unacceptable.	.109	Our friendship is important to me.	.034
Since you cancel, I won't make plans with you.	.109	We haven't been together for a while.	.034
I expect you to cancel tomorrow, too.	.109	We have done so much together.	.028
If our friendship is important, then make time.	.109	If our friendship isn't important, then forget it.	.028
Goodbye.	.094	Skip the meeting and keep our date.	.028
Forget it, Terry.	.094	I care for you.	.025
I'll find alternatives.	.094	We had a date.	.025
I have a busy life, too.	.084	Be more organized.	.025
You leave me with nothing to do.	.084	I want to have an honest talk.	.022
Keep our date tomorrow.	.081	I'll stop bothering you.	.022
We need to talk.	.081	You take me for granted.	.022
You have made me a low priority.	.081	Friends are important.	.019
I want to see the movie tonight.	.078	I can't count on you.	.019
I suspect that you are avoiding me.	.075	I hope we get together tomorrow.	.019
What is the story on the meeting?	.075	You need to make choices.	.016
Our friendship is suffering.	.066	Maybe I'm overreacting.	.016
You should consider your priorities.	.063	We can solve this problem.	.016
Okay, go ahead and cancel.	.063	Do not feel obliged to me.	.016
Let's find a compromise plan.	.059	You should make some compromises.	.013
		I don't know what to think.	.013
		I'm sorry for my behavior.	.006

SOURCE: Lambert (1992).
a. Proportion of messages in which a given unit appeared.

characterized as subsets drawn from a list of 72 basic types of thought units (see Table 3.1). In subsequent studies, we have further classified thought units into

TABLE 3.2
Themes Identified in Rejection Messages

Theme		Idea Types
Report rejection	(2)	The selection process is over.
	(3)	You were not selected.
Supportive account	(4)	The competition was intense.
	(5)	You were well qualified.
	(6)	You would be good for the club.
Critical account	(7)	You were poorly qualified.
Encourage candidate	(8)	Improve and try again.
	(9)	Next time you will succeed.
	(10)	Thanks for applying.
Impersonal decision	(11)	The criteria were rigorous.
	(12)	The decision was impersonal.
	(13)	Please understand our decision.
Deflect anger	(14)	I wanted to choose you.
	(15)	We are good friends.
	(16)	Do not be upset.
	(17)	I did what I could to help you.
Minimize rejection	(18)	The rejection is not important.
	(19)	Do not be discouraged.
Offer consolation	(20)	I feel bad about the rejection.
	(21)	Let's do something together.

SOURCE: Saeki and O'Keefe (in press).

larger categories—for example, Saeki and O'Keefe (in press) and Lambert and Lee (in press) grouped types of thoughts into themes based on similarity in meaning, commonality of topic, and co-occurrence.

Using these methods, we have observed that the expression of thought units is not strongly constrained by the functional "type" of a message. In Lambert's (1992) investigation, there were some tendencies for particular types of thoughts to co-occur, but in general the thoughts did not cluster strongly. Some kinds of thought units were very common, and appeared in up to a third of the messages; other thought units occurred much less commonly.

In their similar investigation, Saeki and O'Keefe (in press) studied messages elicited by a hypothetical situation in which a student must tell another student that he or she has been rejected for admission to an honor society. The situation was varied in terms of the relationship between speaker and hearer (friend versus stranger) and the hearer's qualifications (well versus poorly qualified). Saeki and O'Keefe analyzed 228 messages produced by American and Japanese students and found that the messages could be characterized as subsets drawn from 21 basic types of thought units. They further grouped the 21 thought units into eight content themes (see Table 3.2). Their results show that elaboration of each of the eight themes was influenced by a distinctive set of situation features and associated with a distinctive set of goals. They conclude that this pattern of findings suggests that, rather than being composed of unitary and coherent strategies, messages are composed of "many independent parts" (p. 28).

Lambert and Lee (in press) investigated messages produced by pharmacy students for a hypothetical patient compliance situation. They analyzed 85 messages and found that the messages could be characterized as subsets drawn from a set of 61 idea types. Using procedures similar to those of Saeki and O'Keefe (in press), they grouped the idea types into 11 distinct content themes (see Table 3.3). The degree of elaboration of each theme within a message was calculated by summing the number of idea types associated with a given theme in the message. The degree of elaboration of a theme was not in general associated with the elaboration of other themes; only 7 of 55 correlations were significant, and even these were relatively small effects (i.e., $r < .30$). In addition, Lambert and Lee found that only 3 of the 11 content themes played significant roles in influencing perceptions of effectiveness in meeting task and interpersonal goals.

Finally, Lambert (1993) used a similar method to analyze messages produced by pharmacy students for a hypothetical situation in which they were to tell a physician that a patient was allergic to a drug the physician had prescribed. Lambert reasoned that, given the structure of pharmacist and physician roles, reporting the allergy and recommending an alternative treatment would be differentially face-threatening, and consequently these two themes would be expressed with differing degrees of politeness. His results support his hypotheses, which suggests that just as distinct message themes can have distinctive effects, contextual conditions such as power and solidarity can have distinctive effects on the elaboration of themes within messages.

In general, then, the distribution of content themes within messages is relatively unconstrained by the functional type of the message. Any theory of message design must account for (a) the fact that messages with very different points and effects can nonetheless share a good deal of content and that messages with similar points or effects can be very different in content and (b) the observation that message antecedents and effects are associated with specific message contents rather than messages taken as wholes.

Conclusion: The Flow of Thought and the Flow of Talk

In short, then, the holistic-functional approach is confronted by two different problems. First, the relationship between message forms and message functions is context specific. A theory that offers no independent account of message structure and function will consequently face difficulty in explaining why people say what they do or in providing anything but a circular account of message effects. Second, messages are sometimes not functionally unified. A theory that offers only a global characterization of message structure will face difficulty in explaining variability in the mapping of message forms to message functions.

TABLE 3.3

Themes Identified in Compliance-Gaining Messages

Theme	Idea Types
Take medication	The medication only works when taken as directed.
	It is important to take the medication as directed.
	If you do not take the medication as directed, it will not work.
	Take the medication as directed.
	Don't stop taking the medication.
	It's up to you to take your medication.
Dangerous disease	It is important to control your hypertension.
	Uncontrolled hypertension has dangerous consequences.
	High blood pressure has no symptoms.
	Hypertension is a serious disease.
	You feel fine without the medication.
	This medication is for your high blood pressure.
Doctor communication	If there are problems, the doctor should be notified.
	You/I should contact your doctor.
	Tell your doctor how you feel about the side effects.
	Have you contacted your doctor lately?
	The doctor will follow up with your care.
	Get your blood pressure checked.
Express understanding	I understand the medication has some unpleasant side effects.
	I understand your feelings.
	Taking the medication makes you feel bad/worse.
	You do not like taking your medicine.
	Your situation is not unusual.
	The medication may not work well for you.
Express concern	The medication will make you healthier in the long run.
	I am concerned about your health and well-being.
	I want to help you.
	We need to work together.
	You are a regular customer.
Describe alternatives	A more effective alternative can be found.
	There are alternative drugs.
	A proper diet can help control your blood pressure.
	The regimen can be made easier.
Be patient	Be patient so the medicine has a chance to work.
	The medication make take some time to work.
	You may not feel the medicine working.
	The side effects go away eventually.
	You'll see your blood pressure go down.
	Let's see how it works.
Cost-benefit	The medication is effective/is not ineffective.
	The medication is worth the cost.
	The medication is expensive.
	You may be wasting your money.
Describe experience	Tell me how you feel when you take the medication.
	Tell me how you take your medication.

(Continued)

TABLE 3.3
Continued

Theme	Idea Types
Patient problems	You are noncompliant/overdue for a refill.
	Your blood pressure is not controlled.
Gather information	Why aren't you taking your medication?
	Do you have any questions?
	What do you think?

SOURCE: Lambert and Lee (in press). Published by permission of Lawrence Erlbaum Associates, Inc.

This reasoning has led us to seek an alternative to the standard image of communication as beginning with abstractly represented goals and realized through a process of planning with functional representations. We found such an alternative in an image of communication situations as organized fields of thoughts, and messages as the result of thought selection and expression. Message structures arise as focus moves through the field of thoughts. Focus is driven by goals and guided by the route that the speaker formulates to move through the field. In the case of descriptions, a route is envisioned only in relationship to a particular spatial representation; similarly, in the case of refusals, compliance-gaining messages, regulative messages, and the like, a route is formulated in relationship to a particular field of thoughts. The resulting message, rather than being a functionally unified act, is a collation of thoughts, each of which may have distinctive consequences and effects.

The diversity of messages in complex situations arises from the fact that communicators can have different goals and different "routes" associated with those goals. When this is true, it will naturally lead to a diversity in focusing; where there is diversity in focusing, there will be diversity in the thoughts selected for expression and differences in the resulting message.

Whether a message domain is characterized by low or high functional diversity, unity or fragmentation, message structure reflects the intimate relationship between knowledge and expression. Specifically, message structure results from the movement of a focus of attention through a structure of knowledge. A local management model thus offers a particular view of message planning as involving the imposition of a focus or perspective on a representation of the situation.

One key advantage of a local management view of planning is that it faces no instantiation problem—the route is traced in the space to be negotiated, not a generic representation of spaces; the actions are specific thoughts to be uttered, not a generic representation of actions that might be undertaken. Because planning occurs with the materials provided within the context and not with decontextualized functional categories, the problem of connecting an abstract representation of action with expressions appropriate to the context simply disappears.

A second key advantage of a local management view is that it does not presume message coherence. A problem-solving model can generate only messages that conform to a plan and cohere around a set of goals. But real messages often contain functionally distinct or even dysfunctional themes. A local management approach can easily accommodate this fact, because the field of thoughts may or may not be functional and coherent. To the extent that an individual has conflicting or dysfunctional thoughts, he or she may produce a relatively incoherent or fragmented message.

LOCAL MANAGEMENT AND MESSAGE DESIGN

In the two previous sections we highlighted the need for an approach to message design that avoids holistic-functional analysis and instead treats message structure as the movement of focus of attention through knowledge structures. We also argued for a view of planning as a process of local management rather than problem solving. In this section we outline an approach to message design that meets these requirements.

First, we describe our general image of planning. Second, because any model of message generation is predicated on some particular image of cognitive architecture, we explain why our model assumes a connectionist architecture.

Planning as Local Management

Local management conceptions of planning (Agre & Chapman, 1987, 1990) and language production (Sibun, 1991a) derive from an ethnomethodological and activity-theoretic understanding of everyday action (see, e.g., Garfinkel, 1967; Lave, 1988; Suchman, 1987). Agre and Chapman (1990) execute a classic "ethnomethodological inversion" when they claim that planning is based on communication rather than vice versa: "Our ability to make and use plans is built on our ability to use language during activities we share with others" (p. 25). Planning itself is made possible only by our abilities to improvise and interpret sequentially unfolding, situated activities. As improvisational skills are what make planning possible, they themselves cannot be explained in terms of planning. Rather, an independent theory must be offered to explain what allows people to reason through each moment's action by a fresh reasoning-through of that moment's situation (Agre & Chapman, 1990, p. 21). Although the models we propose differ to some extent from the kind of cognitive machinery Agre and Chapman suggest, our perspective, like theirs, reflects an effort to explain the cognitive substrate that supports improvisation during situated activity (for a detailed exploration of these issues, see Greeno, 1993).

The model we propose also shares design principles and theoretical commitments with Sibun's (1991a, 1991b) Salix, a system for generating natural language descriptions of houses and families. Salix generates coherent text without using abstract structural representations and without reference to functional act types or global plans. Instead, text is generated through the exploitation of the existing structure of the content domain being described. Global planning and organizational processes are supplanted by strategies for choosing what to say next from among a small set of locally available alternatives. In a similar vein, our model explains message design (generation and effects) without reference to act types or hierarchical plans. Instead, message structure is explained in terms of the organization of situated beliefs and the movement of focus through belief structures.

The Organization of Knowledge

There is substantial controversy in cognitive science concerning the fundamental design of the architecture of cognition. Our model assumes a connectionist (parallel distributed processing, or PDP) architecture. We outline the basis for this preference below.

Since the 1950s, it has been widely agreed that the mind is a "physical symbol system." The physical symbol system hypothesis, derived primarily from the work of Newell and Simon (Newell, 1980), asserts that cognition is the creation, destruction, manipulation, and transformation of symbols and complex symbol structures.

A symbol is a physically realizable atomic (primitive) element with no internal structure, occupying a discrete location in memory. Symbolic structures are collections of symbols that stand in rule-governed, formally specified, syntactic relations to one another. Physical symbol systems consist of processes that act on symbols and symbol structures. A unique symbol designates each unique process. A process can act according to a symbol, manipulate a symbol, or execute a process designated by a symbol. Symbol systems evolve over time as they move through different symbolic states or spaces. Intelligent action, according to this account, involves heuristic selective search through symbolic structures. Aspects of a wide variety of human abilities, including problem solving, learning, language production and comprehension, and vision have been simulated using this method of "symbols and search." The approach is frequently, but not necessarily, associated with serial computing and the von Neumann computer architecture.

During the past decade or so, this view has been challenged by a community of researchers who view cognitive architecture as being constituted by distributed representations and parallel processes (Hinton & Anderson, 1981; McClelland, Rumelhart, & the PDP Research Group, 1986; Rumelhart, McClelland, & the PDP Research Group, 1986; Smolensky, 1988). Instead of symbols and search, the primitives here are units and connections. In this view, the mind consists of a highly interconnected network of simple computing elements functioning in parallel.

In a PDP representation, each element or unit has a numeric state of activation. Units are connected to one another by modifiable, weighted connections. In most connectionist models, the effect of a unit i on a unit j is the product of i's activation with the numeric strength of the weight connecting i to j. Information is represented in the network as vectors of activation values across input and output units. The activation of a given unit is typically interpreted as the degree of presence or absence of some concept or (micro-) feature of the input or output. The inputs effect the outputs by propagating their activations through the network of weighted connections. The network's knowledge is contained in the matrix of weights that connects units to one another.

Several attractive computational properties emerge naturally from parallel distributed processing models. Among those frequently cited are (a) content-addressable memory; (b) graded, continuous processing; (c) context sensitivity; and (d) learning (Anderson & Hinton, 1981; Clark, 1989; McClelland, Rumelhart, & Hinton, 1986; Mikkulainen, 1993). Many of these properties result from the use of distributed, rather than local or discrete, representations of items in memory and from storing knowledge in connections between units rather than at discrete locations in memory. In a standard symbolic model, an item in memory is represented by an atomic symbolic token residing at a specific address in memory. In a PDP model, by contrast, an item is represented by a pattern of activation over many units. Where a standard model might represent a communicative goal as a discrete symbol, a PDP model can represent a goal as a pattern of activation over many units, where each unit represents the degree of presence or absence of a specific thought.

This mode of representation and processing allows items in memory to be content addressed. One can retrieve a memory simply by activating parts of the memory. The knowledge associated with an item is not stored at any discrete location, but rather in the connections between units that represent microfeatures of the item being remembered.

In standard symbolic AI, a symbol is either present or absent in an all-or-nothing manner. Actions are either taken or not taken based on the presence or absence of discrete symbols. This all-or-nothing mode of response leads symbolic models to manifest brittle performance in the face of exceptional or novel input. However, continuous shadings of meaning and response are possible in a PDP framework. Units representing microfeatures of a stimulus object may take on a range of continuous values representing degrees of presence or absence. In addition, because meaningful objects (e.g., goals) are represented by patterns of activation over many units, slightly different goals may be represented by slightly different patterns of activation. Thus graded, continuous processing is manifest at the level of individual units and at the level of patterns of activation.

An appealing form of context sensitivity also emerges from this type of graded, distributed processing. As Smolensky (1988) puts it, the context of a symbol in a standard cognitivist model is provided by other symbols, whereas the context of a PDP "symbol" is part of the internal structure, the distributed pattern of activation, which is the representation of the symbol itself. Thus the "same" symbol is represented in different contexts by slightly different patterns of activation across the subsymbols or microfeatures that constitute it.

Finally, PDP models are able to learn from examples and generalize their knowledge to novel inputs. There are procedures for adjusting the connection weights such that they come to approximate the function embodied in a set of correct input-output pairs. Most learning procedures follow the same general pattern (Hinton, 1990). First, a vector of input activations is presented to the input units, and activation is propagated forward to the output units. Next, the desired output value (from the correct example) is compared with the actual value produced by the training example, and the difference is computed. Finally, each of the weights is modified in proportion to the error it caused. The process is repeated until the weights reach a state that minimizes the square of the errors across all of the units and examples. A simple procedure with only input and output units has principled limitations (Minsky & Papert, 1969), but there are now learning rules for networks with hidden units that can approximate any input-output function.

In sum, several important computational properties emerge naturally out of PDP-style representations and processes, and these properties are difficult if not impossible to implement with standard symbolic AI methods. There are other equally attractive features of PDP models (such as automatic default assignment and spontaneous generalization; see Clark, 1989), but our choice of PDP over traditional models is motivated in large part by the properties just described.

A MODEL OF MESSAGE GENERATION

In this section, we propose a specific model of message generation as local management of situated beliefs. We describe the antecedents of the model in work by the Mannheim group on speech and situation, sketch a view of relevance as a function of focus, and discuss development of a computer simulation by Lambert (1992) that provides a concrete demonstration of a key process in our model.

Antecedents of the Model

Our model is influenced by the basic model of speech production created by Herrmann (1983) and his colleagues at the Research Group in Language and Cognition at the University of Mannheim, Germany (Hoppe-Graff, Herrmann, Winterhoff-Spurk, & Mangold, 1985). Although Herrmann's (1983) model seems the most useful starting point for this project, it should be noted that many of the central features of the model are similar to other models reviewed by Levelt (1989). For the present purposes, the key feature of all these models is that they posit a selection process in which a subset of available knowledge about a topic is organized for expression during a given turn at talk.

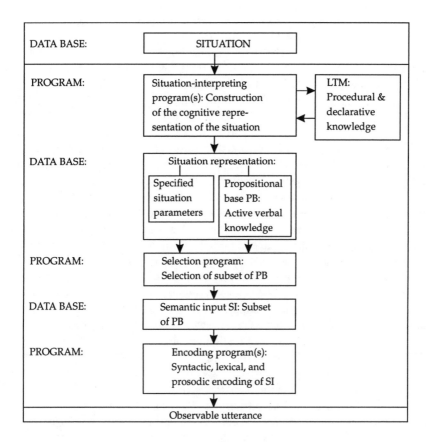

Figure 3.1. Herrmann's Speech Production Model
SOURCE: Herrmann (1983). Used by permission of Springer-Verlag New York, Inc.

Herrmann's (1983) model is a multistep cognitive model of language production in which message generation is seen as originating in the construction of a
situation representation by a situation-interpreting program (see Figure 3.1).
The situation representation contains information about relevant situation parameters as well as procedural and declarative knowledge retrieved by the
situation-interpreting program. Situation parameters are features of the immediate context that will shape the choice of appropriate utterance (e.g., in a
request situation: hearer's ability to perform the requested action, hearer's
willingness to perform, speaker's legitimate right to make the request). The
remaining knowledge retrieved from long-term memory by the interpretation
program consists of situation-specific scripts and more loosely organized facts
that embody knowledge about the constraints on and procedures appropriate to

the current situation. The declarative portion of this accumulated store of knowledge is referred to as the *propositional base* (PB) of the utterance.

According to Herrmann (1983), the propositional base of an utterance is "the foundation of what is meant . . . [including] all that the speaker has perceived, recollected, imagined, inferred, presumed, planned, etc. in connection with the process of speaking. . . . [It is] the activated data base of the utterance" (p. 25). The PB consists of those "elements of knowledge" relevant to achieving the speaker's current goal. The PB comprises both what the speaker means (his or her intention) and what the hearer must reconstruct in order to comprehend a given utterance. The PB does not always come in neat, preformed chunks from memory, but may require active construction processes for its on-line elaboration.

If the PB is the foundation of what is meant, the *semantic input* (SI) is the foundation of what is said (Herrmann, 1983). According to Hoppe-Graff et al. (1985), "What is meant is always 'more' than what is said. The cognitive content that directly underlies the speaker's verbal expression is the semantic input" (p. 84). This observation leads to the positing of the *pars pro toto* (the part from the whole) principle. People verbalize in *pars pro toto* fashion, explicitly saying only part of what they "mean." Conversely, comprehension obeys the *totum ex parte* (the whole from the part) principle. Acknowledgment of the *totum ex parte* nature of comprehension is just another way of recognizing the familiar point that people can go beyond the information given (see, e.g., Jacobs, 1985).

Because the PB is always more than the SI, it is plausible to suggest that the PB is transformed into the SI by some sort of selection process. Ideally, this selection will result in a semantic input that is relevant, informative, instrumental, sufficient, truthful, and so on (Grice, 1975). These are abstract, general constraints on the selection process, but "which part of the PB will fulfill these criteria in the case of a concrete utterance depends on the specific features of a situation" (Hoppe-Graff et al., 1985, p. 85).

In summary, the Mannheim group's model of message production posits three steps: (a) the execution of a situation-interpreting program to construct a situation representation embodying both the propositional base of the utterance and specified, situation-specific parameters; (b) *pars pro toto* selection of semantic input from the propositional base; and (c) low-level encoding of semantic input.

Message Generation and Relevance

It is not possible for a message producer to utter every proposition in his or her currently active propositional base. Consequently, a mechanism is needed to select the subset of propositions that are relevant for expression.

Like Sperber and Wilson (1986), we view the problem of relevance as a matter of explaining what is manifest to speaker and made manifest to hearer; the fundamental principle of message design is, Say what's relevant. However, whereas Sperber and Wilson attempt to account for relevance purely in terms of relationships between propositions, we see relevance as a function of focus. And focus originates either in external inputs (which lead to the activation of a unit or pattern of units) or in internal connections between units (when the activation of one unit spreads to an associated unit or pattern of units).

In this view, goals are patterns of thoughts about the situation and messages are collations of selected and expressed thoughts. What is most distinctive about this image of message design is the absence of explicit reference to abstract goals or abstract strategies. The question, How do communicators reason from goals to strategies to message contents? is replaced with, In a given situation, why and how do message producers see different thoughts about the situation as relevant for expression? And part of the answer is to be found in the connection between patterns of thoughts that represent goals and patterns of message elements.

A Computer Simulation of Message Generation

We have begun to test this model by writing a computer program to simulate the mapping of goals onto messages (Lambert, 1992), an objective shared with standard plan-based models. However, there are important differences in how the relationship between goals and messages is implemented in our model. In the proposed model (a) no explicit logic of action intervenes between goals and messages, (b) message types play no explicit role in processing, (c) goals are represented as distributed patterns of thoughts, and (d) messages are represented as distributed patterns of elemental clauses. Implementing these design features in a PDP framework has enabled us to avoid some of the problems that confront problem-solving models.

PDP networks learn their connection weights by being trained on correct examples of input-output pairs. Thus, to train the model, we developed a method for constructing pairings of activated thoughts and expressed thought units. We asked undergraduate students to respond to a hypothetical broken-date situation, in which an old friend (named Terry) repeatedly cancels dates with the message producer. The message producer is asked to respond to the old friend when he or she calls and asks to reschedule yet another date.

Each subject also completed a Thought Checklist task (Lambert, 1992; B. J. O'Keefe, 1992; O'Keefe & Lambert, 1989; Waldron & Cegala, 1992) for this scenario. Responses to the checklist produced a pattern of thoughts represented as a vector of binary values on the 121 variables constituted by the thoughts on the checklist. Each element of each message was classified as representing 1 of 72 types of thoughts. Based on these codings, messages were represented as vectors of binary values on the 72 variables constituted by the possible content categories.

Lambert (1992) used the example set to train a network using the Quickprop learning algorithm (Fahlman, 1988). Once the network was trained, Lambert examined its knowledge by inspecting patterns of excitation and inhibition between thoughts and message elements. Analysis of the network showed that message elements appear to be serving different functions for different message producers. Substantively different (if not completely contradictory) thoughts could strongly influence the same message elements in the same direction (positively or negatively). For example, the message element "Call me when you have more time" was excited both by negative characterizations of Terry (e.g., "Terry is rude," "Terry knows too many people") and by positive characterizations of Terry (e.g., "Terry feels bad about canceling the date," "Terry is highly motivated," "Terry thinks it is important to keep commitments"). It was excited both by thoughts that express disaffection (e.g., "I'm tired of being patient with Terry," "It would be better if Terry weren't so sure of my friendship") and by thoughts that express concern for the friendship (e.g., "If I criticize Terry it will hurt our friendship"). This finding is puzzling if one believes that messages are planned as unifunctional types that are straightforwardly and statically associated with goals. In such a view, message elements should be strongly excited only by a conceptually coherent set of thoughts. That this is not the case implies that message elements are neither unifunctional nor determinate in meaning. Given a set of training examples drawn from a diverse group of communicators, multiple (possibly contradictory) coalitions of thoughts may excite the same message element because that element is embedded in functionally different webs of meaning for different people.

Summary

We have described a model of situated message design, in which situated message design is conceived as the movement of focus through an organized network of thoughts. The model was designed to avoid the two central problems facing problem-solving models: (a) instantiating abstract act types as concrete message elements and (b) reifying a single functional description of messages. In our model, the instantiation problem never arises, because it employs no abstract act types for computation; instead, thoughts map directly onto concrete message elements. Similarly, it was not necessary to reify a single functional description of messages, because the model needed no explicit logic of action to guide selection of message contents and the goal-message mapping is induced from empirical examples.

A MODEL OF ADAPTATION AND EFFECTS

In the preceding section we provided a view of message structures as expressed thoughts. But a theory of message design connects message structures to message antecedents and message effects. We think of this second component as the theory of adaptation that accompanies the theory of message structure. In this section we develop a model of adaptation in which adaptation is equated with the control of focus by the functional requirements of the current activity, specifically, by an internalized model of the effects of utterance. Our model of adaptation and effects is a developmental one. It reflects the application and extension of ideas first articulated by Rumelhart and Jordan (Jordan, 1989; Jordan & Rumelhart, 1992; Rumelhart, Smolensky, McClelland, & Hinton, 1986).

We first discuss a view of focus as a product of socialization within activities. We then offer a specific model of the processes through which models of activity are internalized and used to guide adaptation. Finally, we discuss the developmental dimension of the model.

Activity, Relevance, and Focus

Lambert's (1992) model was designed to simulate only one aspect of the process of focusing, the activation of one set of units (message elements) by another set of units (goals, as distributed in patterns of thoughts). Focus, however, depends not only on patterns of connection between units, but also on the way input guides focus.

From the standpoint of a theory of communication, one of the most critical ways in which input shapes focus is through transition relevance—that is, through the way antecedent and projected contributions shape what is relevant to say at any particular juncture. Most current treatments of this issue reflect an essentially Gricean view, in which some form of perspective taking is seen as driving the calculation of what will be a cooperative contribution (Grice, 1975). For example, in Grice's view, conversationalists are thought to abide by a "quantity" maxim, in which they try to say just what is required and no more in order to meet the listener's needs for information.

Many theorists have attempted to explain cooperation in terms of recipient design, the selection and adaptation of what is said to the requirements of the listener (see, e.g., Clark & Marshall, 1981). Such models assume that speakers base linguistic choices on a model of the hearer's current beliefs. However, we see focus as guided primarily by a model of the activity and only secondarily, if at all, by a model of the specific addressee. A study of instruction giving by Burke (1986) provides a useful illustration of the difference. Burke studied the design of instructions given in four media: face-to-face, telephone, audiotape (asynchronous oral), and writing. Students in one group, the "experts," were trained to assemble a toy water pump. Students in a second group, the "apprentices," received instructions from the experts in how to assemble the pump. Each expert-apprentice pair gave and received instructions in one of the four media. The task thus resembled the one studied by Grosz (1981).

Burke analyzed both the instructions and the behavior of the apprentice in following the instructions. Using an early version of the method we have employed in our recent studies of message organization, Burke segmented the instructions into units that reflected the key steps to be performed in assembling the pump. She then classified these units as to the degree of elaboration of two key themes (specification of the parts to be assembled, specification of the action to be performed in assembly). She found that across media, experts at

first organized their instructions in terms of a characteristic pattern of elaboration in which both the designation of the parts and the action description were
quite elaborate and detailed. This finding is consistent with research on descriptions summarized earlier; Burke's experts employed a systematic method of
navigation through their information about the pump.

However, analysis of the messages in the face-to-face condition showed that,
in fact, the messages given by the experts were overly informative. In a variety
of ways, apprentices signaled that the expert model was not well adapted (for
example, they would commonly finish a step before the expert had completed
the instructions for it). Over the course of the interaction, experts revised their
models and ultimately provided much less detailed directions. In the other three
media, where the expert had little access to feedback from the apprentice, no
such adaptation of the activity model was observed.

What Burke's findings suggest is that, rather than relying on a model of the
hearer to compute the informativeness, relevance, or clarity of a contribution,
speakers have induced models of particular activities. These models are based
on past experience with the activities, as opposed to past experience with a
specific hearer and inferences about the specific hearer's beliefs. Because of
this, there is no guarantee that a given activity model will in fact embody a
correct assessment of any given hearer's needs for information. Moreover, as
in Burke's study, strong and direct feedback from recipients can be required to
induce speakers to modify their activity models.

In summary, then, we see focus as shaped by interactional placement as well
as patterns of connection within the field of thoughts that represents a situation.
But whereas transition relevance is generally understood as being structured
either by sequencing rules that connect types of acts or by recipient design, we
see transition relevance as deriving from models of activity that are induced
from experience with particular communicative tasks. We provide a more
detailed discussion of activity, adaptation, and message effects below.

Focus, Adaptation, and Effects

The simulation developed by Lambert (1992) represented an attempt to map
from current and desired state (represented as a single pattern of thoughts) to a
message. Theoretically, a message is chosen because its utterance is expected
to transform the current intentional state into the goal state. In symbolic terms:

$$S(I_c, I_g) \rightarrow U_{c,g} \qquad [1]$$

The selection function $S(\ )$ maps the current state I_c and the goal state I_g onto
some contextually appropriate utterance $U_{c,g}$. But there is a hidden step here:
Why does $S(I_c, I_g)$ map to $U_{c,g}$ and not to some other utterance? The answer is
obviously that $U_{c,g}$, when uttered, is expected to transform I_c into I_g. Again

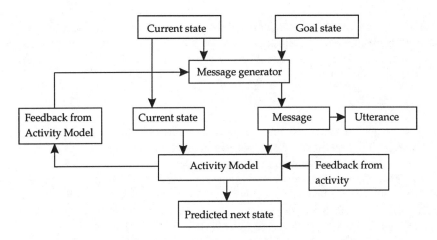

Figure 3.2. Relationships Among Message Generator, Activity Model, and Activity

SOURCE: Framework patterned after Jordan and Rumelhart (1992). Reprinted by permission of Lawrence Erlbaum Associates, Inc.

symbolically, the hidden step involves passing candidate utterances through a model of effects on the world (E), which we call a model of activity:

$$E_c(I_c, U_{c,g}) = I_g \qquad [2]$$

That is, $E(\ )$ takes a message and the current state as input, and then outputs a description of its effect. With Equations 1 and 2 in mind, a fairly specific account of message generation and its development can be given.

Equation 1 models the message generator; Equation 2 models the activity. A complete model of message adaptation and development includes both (see Figure 3.2). In theory they are connected, with the output of the message generator being the input to the activity model.

$$S(I_c, I_g) \rightarrow U_{c,g} \rightarrow E_c(I_c, U_{c,g}) = I_g \qquad [3]$$

If the current state I_c is factored out, the message generator maps a goal onto an utterance, and the activity model maps a message onto its expected effects:

$$S(I_g) \rightarrow U_g \rightarrow E(U_g) = I_g \qquad [4]$$

It might be noted that this model of message adaptation preserves some of the most important features of problem-solving models (discussed earlier). In particular, the current model accords with the intuition that goals play a key role in message planning and adaptation. But whereas in a problem-solving model goals are seen as discrete and abstract, within this approach goals are viewed as situated and distributed in patterns of thoughts. Moreover, a problem-solving approach gives a central role to anticipated effects in the generation process, whereas we conceptualize effects as being primarily involved in processes of reflection and evaluation.

Learning and Growth

Finally, it is important to note that within this model of adaptation, two key developmental phenomena can be neatly conceptualized: short-term practice effects and long-term acquisition of competence.

Practice effects. It is well known that as individuals become more experienced in an activity, their behavior becomes more practiced and automatic. We recognize the need to account for such practice effects. In terms of the present model, these effects are accounted for in terms of the feedback provided to the message generator by the activity model (Jordan & Rumelhart, 1992).

Message design begins with a pattern of activated thoughts that corresponds to a goal. Activation of the goal state initiates message generation, the selection and transformation of situated knowledge; the goal maps to a message by way of the message generator. Output of the message generator is evaluated by the activity model to determine whether its utterance would bring about the desired effect; if so, the message is uttered. If not, the activity model propagates an error message back through the message generator, changing the weights in that network. The process is repeated until the system is satisfied with the chosen message (perhaps because no more time is available).

Over time, the weights in the message generator will be trained to meet the expectations of the activity model. Hence reflection and practice should lead to quicker message planning, because fewer iterations should be required to satisfy the activity model.

Acquisition of competence. It is also well established that as individuals mature they develop generally improved skills at message design and adaptation (for a review, see O'Keefe & Delia, 1988). Hence we also see the need to explain the acquisition of competence over the long term. In the present model, these processes are accounted for in terms of the feedback provided to the activity model by direct experience with the activity. As individuals mature, they accumulate observations of actual effects of their messages; these message-effect pairings are the examples from which the activity model generalizes its knowledge of relations between messages and effects in context.

As B. J. O'Keefe (1988; O'Keefe & Delia, 1988) has argued, many classic progressions in the development of listener-adapted communication can be accounted for in this way, in terms of the acquisition of an increasingly accurate model of communicative activity. As the activity model becomes more accurate, it embodies a better understanding of effects and how to achieve them. To do so requires that the activity model become sensitive to those features of the situation that are objectively, rather than subjectively, relevant. These changes, of course, give rise to observed differences in the logic of message design (B. J. O'Keefe, 1988).

CONCLUSION

The study of message structures has been characterized by a de facto commitment to holism—that is, by an approach in which messages are treated as instances of acts or strategies. Although holism is essential to *descriptive* models of message meaning, it offers an inadequate approach to *causal* explanation of message production and effects. A superior causal account can be found in local management approaches to message design (for a more extended discussion of this issue, see Clark, 1989; Lambert, 1992; B. J. O'Keefe, 1992).

The approach we have suggested in this chapter has the advantage of simultaneously acknowledging the utility of holistic-functional analysis and recognizing that any given description of a message is only one of indefinitely many possible true descriptions (D. J. O'Keefe, 1987). Any message can be given multiple functional characterizations, some of them mutually incompatible, and all of them equally justified. As can be seen in Brown and Levinson's (1987) analysis of politeness, such a functional description can provide an important and useful perspective on a discourse system.

However, a model that takes such holistic-functional descriptions to play a causal role in message generation will necessarily confront not only the instantiation problem described earlier but also the task of providing a consistent and exhaustive representation of a text. Given the open-endedness and indeterminacy of meaning, such a quest would seem to be bootless.

The local management approach we have developed has given us a distinctive analysis of message structure, one that avoids functional description of message structure in favor of a content-based description of the ideas expressed in the message. In this review we have attempted to show how such a content-based description of message structure, elaborated within a local management view of message planning, can address the enduring problem of explaining message organization and adaptation. By providing independent analyses of message structures and message functions, we make it possible to ask, rather than beg, questions about message design.

REFERENCES

Agre, P. E., & Chapman, D. (1987). Pengi: An implementation of a theory of activity. In P. Langley (Ed.), *Proceedings of AAAI-87* (pp. 196-201). Los Altos, CA: Morgan Kaufmann.

Agre, P. E., & Chapman, D. (1990). What are plans for? *Robotics and Autonomous Systems, 6,* 17-34.

Anderson, J. A. , & Hinton, G. E. (1981). Models of information processing in the brain. In G. E. Hinton & J. A. Anderson (Eds.), *Parallel models of associative memory* (pp. 9-48). Hillsdale, NJ: Lawrence Erlbaum.

Appelt, D. E. (1982). Planning natural-language utterances. In *Proceedings of the National Conference on Artificial Intelligence* (pp. 59-62). Menlo Park, CA: American Association for Artificial Intelligence.

Appelt, D. E. (1985). *Planning English sentences.* Cambridge: Cambridge University Press.

Brown, P., & Levinson, S. C. (1987). *Politeness: Some universals in language usage.* London: Cambridge University Press.

Burke, J. A. (1986). Interacting plans in the accomplishment of a practical activity. In D. G. Ellis & W. A. Donahue (Eds.), *Contemporary issues in language and discourse processes* (pp. 203-222). Hillsdale, NJ: Lawrence Erlbaum.

Chafe, W. L. (1979). The flow of thought and the flow of language. In T. Givon (Ed.), *Syntax and semantics: Vol. 12. Discourse and syntax* (pp. 159-182). New York: Academic.

Clark, A. (1989). *Microcognition: Philosophy, cognitive science, and parallel distributed processing.* Cambridge: MIT Press.

Clark, H., & Marshall, C. R. (1981). Definite reference and mutual knowledge. In A. K. Joshi, B. L. Webber, & I. A. Sag (Eds.), *Elements of discourse understanding* (pp. 10-63). Cambridge: Cambridge University Press.

Cohen, P. R., Morgan, J. P., & Pollack, M. E. (Eds.). (1990). *Intentions in communication.* Cambridge: MIT Press.

Cohen, P. R., & Perrault, C. R. (1979). Elements of a plan-based theory of speech acts. *Cognitive Science, 3,* 177-212.

Dell, G., & Juliano, C. (1993). Structure and content in language production: A theory of frame constraints in phonological speech errors. *Cognitive Science, 17,* 149-195.

Fahlman, S. E. (1988). *An empirical study of learning speed in back-propagation networks* (Tech. Rep. No. CMU-CS-88-162). Pittsburgh, PA: Carnegie Mellon University.

Fikes, R. E., & Nilsson, N. J. (1971). STRIPS: A new approach to the application of theorem proving to problem solving. *Artificial Intelligence, 2,* 189-208.

Garfinkel, H. (1967). *Studies in ethnomethodology.* Cambridge: Polity.

Garrett, M. F. (1975). The analysis of sentence production. In G. Bower (Ed.), *Psychology of learning and motivation* (pp. 133-177). New York: Academic Press.

Garrett, M. F. (1988). Processes in language production. In F. J. Newmeyer (Ed.), *Linguistics: The Cambridge survey: Vol. 3. Language: Psychological and sociological aspects* (pp. 69-96). Cambridge: Cambridge University Press.

Green, G. (1989). *Pragmatics and natural language understanding.* Hillsdale, NJ: Lawrence Erlbaum.

Greeno, J. (Ed.). (1993). Situated action [Special issue]. *Cognitive Science, 17*(1).

Grice, H. P. (1975). Logic and conversation. In P. Cole & J. L. Morgan (Eds.), *Syntax and semantics: Vol. 3. Speech acts* (pp. 41-58). New York: Academic Press.

Grosz, B. J. (1981). Focusing and description in natural language dialogues. In A. K. Joshi, B. L. Webber, & I. A. Sag (Eds.), *Elements of discourse understanding* (pp. 84-105). Cambridge: Cambridge University Press.

Hermann, T. (1983). *Speech and situation: A psychological conception of situated speaking.* Berlin: Springer-Verlag.

Hillocks, G. (1986). *Research on written composition: New directions for teaching.* Urbana, IL: National Council of Teachers of English.

Hinton, G. E. (1990). Connectionist learning procedures. In J. Carbonell (Ed.), *Machine learning: Paradigms and methods* (pp. 185-234). Cambridge: MIT Press.

Hinton, G. E., & Anderson, J. A. (Eds.). (1981). *Parallel models of associative memory.* Hillsdale, NJ: Lawrence Erlbaum.

Hoppe-Graff, S., Herrmann, T., Winterhoff-Spurk, P., & Mangold, R. (1985). Speech and situation: A general model for the process of speech production. In J. Forgas (Ed.), *Language and social situations* (pp. 81-95). New York: Springer-Verlag.

Hovy, E. (1990). Pragmatics and natural language generation. *Artificial Intelligence, 43,* 153-197.

Jacobs, S. (1985). Language. In M. L. Knapp & G. R. Miller (Eds.), *Handbook of interpersonal communication* (pp. 313-343). Beverly Hills, CA: Sage.

Jordan, M. (1989). Action. In M. I. Posner (Ed.), *Foundations of cognitive science* (pp. 727-767). Cambridge: MIT Press.

Jordan, M., & Rumelhart, D. E. (1992). Forward models: Supervised learning with a distal teacher. *Cognitive Science, 16,* 307-354.

Kellermann, K., & Lim, T.-S. (1989). Conversational acquaintance: The flexibility of routinized behaviors. In B. Dervin, L. Grossberg, B. J. O'Keefe, & E. Wartella (Eds.), *Rethinking communication: Vol. 2. Paradigm exemplars* (pp. 172-187). Newbury Park, CA: Sage.

Lambert, B. L. (1992). *A connectionist model of message design.* Unpublished doctoral dissertation, University of Illinois, Urbana-Champaign.

Lambert, B. L. (1993, November). *Reporting allergies and recommending alternatives: Directness and deference in pharmacy students' messages to physicians.* Paper presented at the 79th Annual Meeting of the Speech Communication Association, Miami, FL.

Lambert, B. L., & Lee, J. Y. (in press). Patient perceptions of pharmacy students' hypertension compliance gaining messages: Effects of message design logic and content themes. *Health Communication.*

Lave, J. (1988). *Cognition in practice: Mind, mathematics and culture in everyday life.* Cambridge: Cambridge University Press.

Levelt, W. J. M. (1989). *Speaking: From intention to articulation.* Cambridge: MIT Press.

Levinson, S. C. (1982). *Pragmatics.* Cambridge: Cambridge University Press.

Levy, D. M. (1979). Communicative goals and strategies: Between discourse and syntax. In T. Givon (Ed.), *Syntax and semantics: Vol. 12. Discourse and syntax* (pp. 183-212). New York: Academic Press.

Linde, C., & Labov, W. (1975). Spatial networks as a site for the study of language and thought. *Language, 51,* 924-929.

Marwell, G., & Schmitt, D. R. (1967a). Compliance-gaining behavior: A synthesis and model. *Sociological Quarterly, 8,* 317-328.

Marwell, G., & Schmitt, D. R. (1967b). Dimensions of compliance-gaining behavior: An empirical analysis. *Sociometry, 30,* 352-364.

McLaughlin, M. (1984). *Conversation.* Beverly Hills, CA: Sage.

McClelland, J. L., Rumelhart, D. E., & the PDP Research Group. (Eds.). (1986). *Parallel distributed processing: Explorations in the microstructure of cognition: Vol. 2. Psychological and biological models.* Cambridge: MIT Press.

McClelland, J. L., Rumelhart, D. E., & Hinton, G. E. (1986). The appeal of PDP. In D. E. Rumelhart, J. L. McClelland, & the PDP Research Group (Eds.), *Parallel distributed processing: Explorations in the microstructure of cognition: Vol. 1. Foundations* (pp. 3-44). Cambridge: MIT Press.

Mikkulainen, R. (1993). *Subsymbolic natural language processing: An integrated model of scripts, lexicon, and memory.* Cambridge: MIT Press.

Miller, D. P. (1990). Towards a believable theory of planning. *Journal of Mathematical Psychology, 34,* 489-498.

Miller, G., Galanter, E., & Pribram, K. (1960). *Plans and the structure of behavior.* New York: Holt, Rinehart & Winston.

Minsky, M., & Papert, S. (1969). *Perceptrons.* Cambridge: MIT Press.

Newell, A. (1980). Physical symbol systems. *Cognitive Science, 4,* 135-183.

Newell, A., & Simon, H. (1972). *Human problem solving.* Englewood Cliffs, NJ: Prentice Hall.

O'Keefe, B. J. (1988). The logic of message design. *Communication Monographs, 55,* 80-103.

O'Keefe, B. J. (1992). Developing and testing rational models of message design. *Human Communication Research, 18,* 637-649.

O'Keefe, B. J., & Delia, J. G. (1988). Communicative tasks and communicative practices: The development of audience-centered message production. In B. A. Rafoth & D. L. Rubin (Eds.), *The social construction of written communication* (pp. 70-98). Norwood, NJ: Ablex.

O'Keefe, B. J., & Lambert, B. L. (1989, November). *Effects of message design logic on the communication of intention.* Paper presented at the annual meeting of the Speech Communication Association, San Francisco.

O'Keefe, D. J. (1987). *Describing messages.* Paper presented at the annual meeting of the Speech Communication Association, Boston.

Roger, D., & Bull, P. (1989). *Conversation: An interdisciplinary perspective.* Clevedon: Multilingual Matters.

Rumelhart, D. E., Smolensky, P., McClelland, J. L., & Hinton, G. (1986). Schemata and sequential thought processes in PDP models. In J. L. McClelland, D. E. Rumelhart, & the PDP Research Group (Eds.), *Parallel distributed processing: Explorations in the microstructure of cognition: Vol. 2. Psychological and biological models* (pp. 7-57). Cambridge: MIT Press.

Rumelhart, D. E., McClelland, J. L., & the PDP Research Group. (Eds.). (1986). *Parallel distributed processing: Explorations in the microstructure of cognition: Vol. 1. Foundations.* Cambridge: MIT Press.

Sacerdoti, E. (1974). Planning in a hierarchy of abstraction spaces. *Artificial Intelligence, 5,* 115-135.

Saeki, M., & O'Keefe, B. J. (in press). Refusals and rejections: Designing messages to serve multiple goals. *Human Communication Research.*

Schegloff, E. (1968). Sequencing in conversational openings. *American Anthropologist, 70*(6).

Searle, J. R. (1969). *Speech acts.* Cambridge: Cambridge University Press.

Seibold, D. R., Cantrill, J. G., & Meyers, R. A. (1985). Communication and interpersonal influence. In M. L. Knapp & G. R. Miller (Eds.), *Handbook of interpersonal communication* (pp. 551-611). Beverly Hills, CA: Sage.

Sibun, P. (1990). The local organization of text. In *Proceedings of the Fifth International Workshop on Natural Language Generation* (pp. 120-127). Dawson, PA: Linden Hall.

Sibun, P. (1991a). *Locally organized text generation.* Unpublished doctoral dissertation, University of Massachusetts, Amherst.

Sibun, P. (1991b). *Salix: A strategy-based architecture for text organization.* Unpublished manuscript, Xerox Palo Alto Research Center, Palo Alto, CA.

Sibun, P. (in press). Generating text without trees. *Computational Intelligence, 8.*

Smolensky, P. (1988). On the proper treatment of connectionism. *Behavioral and Brain Sciences, 11,* 1-59.

Sperber, D., & Wilson, D. (1986). *Relevance: Communication and cognition.* Cambridge, MA: Harvard University Press.

Suchman, L. (1987). *Plans and situated actions: The problem of man-machine communication.* Cambridge: Cambridge University Press.

Tannen, D. (1993). The relativity of linguistic strategies: Rethinking power and solidarity in gender and dominance. In D. Tannen (Ed.), *Gender and conversational interaction* (pp. 165-188). Oxford: Oxford University Press.

Taylor, T. J., & Cameron, D. (1987). *Analysing conversation: Rules and units in the structure of talk.* Oxford: Pergamon.

Ullmer-Ehrich, V. (1982). The structure of living space descriptions. In R. J. Jarvella & W. Klein (Eds.), *Speech, place, and action: Studies in deixis and related topics* (pp. 219-249). New York: John Wiley.

Waldron, V., & Cegala, D. (1992). Assessing conversational cognition: Levels of cognitive theory and associated methodological requirements. *Human Communication Research, 18,* 599-622.

Wunderlich, D., & Reinelt, R. (1982). How to get there from here. In R. J. Jarvella & W. Klein (Eds.), *Speech, place, and action: Studies in deixis and related topics* (pp. 183-201). New York: John Wiley.

4 An Appraisal and Revision of the Constructivist Research Program

JOHN GASTIL
University of Wisconsin—Madison

This essay uses Imre Lakatos's methodology of scientific research programs to assess and revise the constructivist approach to communication. Constructivism is evaluated as a series of changing theories that share common assumptions. A review of constructivist theory and research scrutinizes the program's main methodological innovations and its insights into cognitive development, social perception, and person-centered communication. Revisions are then suggested: Constructivism needs a more advanced explication of knowledge structures, cognitive processing, cognitive development, and self-perception. Constructivist research should also employ more precise hypotheses, maintain methodological diversity, and vigorously examine anomalous findings. The conclusion briefly estimates the program's longevity and highlights ethical imperatives that could fuel future constructivist research.

ONSTRUCTIVISM entered the field of communication in the 1970s and offered a new perspective on cognitive development, social perception, and communication (Delia & Crockett, 1973; Swanson & Delia, 1976). Before the end of the decade, constructivists had studied the cognitive and communicative development of children and adolescents (Delia & Clark, 1977), perspective taking (Hale & Delia, 1976), interpersonal evaluations (Delia, Crockett, Press, & O'Keefe, 1975), conversation (Delia, Clark, & Switzer, 1979), and persuasion (B. J. O'Keefe & Delia, 1979). Although individual theorists have branched in different directions, the central tenets of constructivism continued to shape research throughout the 1980s and into the present decade (e.g., Burleson & Denton, 1992; Martin, 1992; B. J. O'Keefe, 1992; Zimmerman & Applegate, 1992).

Periodic reviews have summarized and organized constructivist research (e.g., Applegate, 1990; Burleson & Waltman, 1988; Delia, O'Keefe, & O'Keefe,

AUTHOR'S NOTE: I would like to acknowledge the assistance of James Dillard, Mary Anne Fitzpatrick, Brant Burleson, and anonymous reviewers in the revision of this manuscript.

Send correspondence to: John Gastil, Department of Political Science, University of New Mexico, Albuquerque, NM 87131-1121.

Communication Yearbook 18, pp. 83-104

1982); however, as this body of research continues to grow, it becomes increasingly important to conduct an overall appraisal, rather than a summary or review. Therefore, in this essay I aim to identify the successes and failures of the past 20 years of constructivist theory and research. Using Imre Lakatos's (1978a, 1978b) methodology of scientific research programs, I will identify and evaluate the constructivist research program and then suggest strategies for its future development.

THE METHODOLOGY OF
SCIENTIFIC RESEARCH PROGRAMS

The 1978 collection of Lakatos's philosophical papers provides an excellent summary of his views on the nature of science (Lakatos, 1978a, 1978b; for praise, elaborations, and criticism, see Cohen, Feyerabend, & Wartofsky, 1976; Gavroglu, Goudaroulis, & Nicolacopoulos, 1989). Therein, Lakatos (1978b) writes, "The history of science has been and should be a history of competing research programmes (or, if you wish, 'paradigms')" (p. 69). For Lakatos (1978b), research programs, as opposed to isolated hypotheses or theories, are the "typical descriptive unit of great scientific achievements" (p. 4). Although some authors, including Lakatos (Dar, 1987), might object to applying the methodology of scientific research programs to social science, doing so is consistent with more inclusive views of the scientific enterprise (Gholson & Barker, 1985; Serlin & Lapsley, 1984; more generally, see Nagel, 1979).

There are four essential features of any research program: the hard core, the protective belt, and the positive and negative heuristics. Lakatos (1978b) illustrates these components with the case of Newtonian physics:

> Newtonian science . . . is not simply a set of four conjectures—the three laws of mechanics and the law of gravitation. These four laws constitute only the "hard core" of the Newtonian programme. But this hard core is tenaciously protected from refutation by a vast "protective belt" of auxiliary hypotheses [or theories]. And, even more importantly, the research programme also has a "heuristic," that is, a powerful problem-solving machinery, which . . . digests anomalies and even turns them into positive evidence. For instance, if a planet does not move exactly as it should, the Newtonian scientist checks his conjectures. . . . He may even invent a hitherto unknown planet and calculate its position, mass and velocity in order to explain the anomaly. (p. 4)

Later, Lakatos (1978b) distinguishes between the positive and negative heuristics. The positive heuristic is a planned alteration of the protective belt that focuses on new phenomena and generates new predictions. The negative heuristic, by contrast, is used to respond to external pressures, such as the accumulation of anomalies (see pp. 47-52, 112-113).

To compare competing research programs, one cannot apply falsificationist logic to the hard core of the program, because the core can never be directly tested. A belt of surrounding theories "protects the hard core from refutations: anomalies are not taken as refutations of the hard core but of some hypothesis in the protective belt." The protective belt is regularly altered through the use of the positive and negative heuristics, "while the hard core remains intact" (Lakatos, 1978b, p. 179).

Moreover, every program "has unsolved problems and undigested anomalies. All theories, in this sense, are born refuted and die refuted." The difference between a "progressive" program and a "degenerating" one is that the former is able to anticipate or "predict novel facts, facts which had been either undreamt of, or have indeed been contradicted by previous or rival programmes." Striking examples include the Newtonian prediction of the return of Haley's comet or the Einsteinian prediction of astral light bending. By contrast, "in degenerating programmes . . . theories are fabricated only in order to accommodate known facts" (Lakatos, 1978b, p. 5).

To judge whether a research program is progressing or degenerating, one must examine the "series of theories" surrounding the hard core (Lakatos, 1978b, p. 34). This evolving belt of theories can be construed as progressive in two respects. First, the belt is "theoretically progressive if each modification leads to new unexpected predictions." Second, "it is empirically progressive if at least some of these novel predictions are corroborated. . . . What matters is a few dramatic signs of empirical progress" (Lakatos, 1978b, p. 179).

This second form of progress reveals Lakatos's intention to complement the falsificationist emphasis on deductive refutation with a verificationist search for inductive verisimilitude (see Lakatos, 1978a, chap. 8; 1978b, chap. 3). "Within a research programme," Lakatos (1978b) writes, "a theory can only be eliminated by a better theory," one that makes predictions that go beyond its predecessors and has some subsequent confirmations of these predictions. The original theory "does not even have to be 'falsified' in Popper's sense of the term. Thus, progress is marked . . . [by verification] rather than by falsifying instances" (pp. 112-113; see also Lakatos, 1978a, p. 176).

Research programs are judged similarly, but scientific juries must be more cautious and forgiving with programs, arriving at many uncomfortable acquittals and only a few, painstaking convictions. Lakatos (1978b) writes:

> It is very difficult to decide, especially if one does not demand progress at every single step, when a research programme has degenerated hopelessly; or when one of two rival programmes has achieved a decisive advantage over the other. There can be no "instant rationality." *Neither the logician's proof of inconsistency nor the experimental scientist's verdict of anomaly can defeat a research programme at one blow.* . . . But when should a particular theory, or a whole research programme, be rejected? I claim, only if there is a better one to replace it. (pp. 149-150)

Because we can judge research programs only "from the vantage point of our present theories," this assessment is always fallible because our present theories are fallible. Moreover, "we cannot grade our best available theories . . . even tentatively, for they are our ultimate standards for the moment" (Lakatos, 1978a, p. 185). In sum, a research program must ultimately be judged tentatively and only in relation to its rivals.

APPRAISING THE
CONSTRUCTIVIST RESEARCH PROGRAM

Having established an epistemological standpoint, I turn now to an evaluation of the constructivist research program. This evaluation begins with an explication of constructivism's hard core and protective belt of theories. I then present an examination of these theories, looking at predictions, corroborations, explanations, scope, and parsimony. Finally, I undertake an appraisal of the overall program to determine whether constructivism is currently progressing or degenerating.

The Hard Core of Constructivism

In an early discussion of constructivism, Delia (1977) posits that the centerpiece or "root metaphor" of constructivism is that humans are living, active organisms. The essence of their being is purposeful and interpretive activity. "The person is conceived as an active agent who reconstructs his environment and who is a source of acts" (Delia, 1977, p. 69; see also Delia et al., 1982, p. 149; Swanson & Delia, 1976, p. 9).

"Within the framework of constructivism," Delia (1977) continues, "interpretive processes are conceived as central to individual and social behavior" (p. 75). Constructivists presume that "persons approach the world with an ordering attitude. . . . In human perception, an ordered, organized interpretation of events is achieved . . . within a system of personal interpretive constructs or categories." The social world is understood "only through the application of personal constructs—individual classification and interpretation schemes" (Swanson & Delia, 1976, pp. 13-14). A scheme is defined as "any classification device persons use to make sense of their world." As a consequence, constructivists "recognize that a variety of schemes and beliefs serve the process of interpretation" (Delia et al., 1982, p. 152).

The interpretive schemes constructivists focus upon are interpersonal constructs. These constructs are "employed in construing persons," generating "a variety of interpersonal judgments." They help us categorize "the behavior, roles, personality characteristics, habits, attitudes, values, intentions, beliefs, and emotions of others" (Delia et al., 1982, p. 160).

All of an individual's constructs develop "as a consequence of the interaction between the individual's structure at a given time and the demands of the world he is experiencing." The individual's cognitive system goes through "a series of stages, the order of which is invariant" (Delia, 1977, p. 70).

Through social experience, "the normal individual can be expected to develop . . . an increasingly large number of interpersonal constructs, and . . . the patterns of relationship among constructs can be expected to become increasingly complex and organized" (Delia & O'Keefe, 1979, p. 164; see also Samter, Burleson, & Basden-Murphy, 1989, pp. 615-616, 624-625). Although development may continue throughout the entire life span of the individual, the individual's construct system becomes a relatively stable trait after adolescence (Delia, 1977, p. 78; Delia & Clark, 1977, p. 344; Delia & O'Keefe, 1979, pp. 162-166; Hale & Delia, 1976, pp. 196-199; Swanson & Delia, 1976, pp. 29-31).

During and after development, the qualities of an individual's interpersonal construct system have a profound effect on social perception: "The nature of a person's impression of another or of a social situation will be a function of the complexity, content, and implicit rules of use characterizing his interpersonal construct system" (Delia, 1977, p. 71).

Individuals' strategic communication is also profoundly influenced by their cognitive frames. People equipped with a greater variety, depth, and integration of constructs and an understanding of how to use them effectively will communicate in a more sophisticated manner (Delia et al., 1982, pp. 162-163). The constructivist hard core broadly defines sophisticated speech as that which can simultaneously accommodate a speaker's task and social goals, anticipate situational contingencies, and adapt to the characteristics and needs of different listeners. Over the years, this general definition has encompassed research on messages that are "listener adapted" (Delia & Clark, 1977), "person centered" (Applegate, 1990), or reflective of a "rhetorical design logic" (B. J. O'Keefe, 1988).

Defining the Protective Belt

Around this hard core orbits a thick belt of concepts and theories. Much of the protective belt consists of relatively precise theoretical definitions and operationalizations. Of these, the Role Category Questionnaire (RCQ) and a variety of constructivist coding schemes have played central roles in the development (and criticism) of the research program.

Although there have been variations and alterations, the current form of the RCQ is essentially similar to that used in early constructivist research. Whether answers are written or spoken, coders transform the respondents' words into measures of construct differentiation (number of constructs listed), abstraction (descriptions of specific attitudes or behaviors versus abstract dispositions), and organization or integration (comprehensiveness of constructs) (Burleson & Waltman, 1988, pp. 6-9; Crockett, Press, Delia, & Kenny, 1974).

Constructivists have produced favorable test results demonstrating the reliability and validity of the RCQ (e.g., O'Keefe, Shepherd, & Streeter, 1982; for reviews, see Burleson, Applegate, & Delia, 1991; Burleson & Waltman, 1988). Nevertheless, some scholars have gone so far as to suggest that problems surrounding the RCQ bring the entire constructivist research program into question (Allen, Mabry, Banski, & Preiss, 1991; Allen, Mabry, Banski, Stoneman, & Carter, 1990; Beatty & Payne, 1985; Bonk, 1990; Miller & Wilson, 1979; Powers, Jordan, & Street, 1979).

Two questions have been raised about the measure: (a) What is it *supposed to be* measuring? and (b) What is it *actually* measuring? As for the first of these questions, the RCQ has suffered from conceptual imprecision and terminological inconsistency. Cognitive complexity was originally conceptualized as the combination of differentiation, abstraction, and integration, yet constructivist research has often construed differentiation measures as adequate indicators of overall cognitive complexity (Burleson & Waltman, 1987; Hale & Delia, 1976; Kline, Hennen-Floyd, & Farrell, 1990; O'Keefe et al., 1982; for a notable exception, see Babrow, O'Keefe, Swanson, Meyers, & Murphy, 1988). Delia et al.'s (1982) review does this repeatedly, and frequent citations of this landmark essay have compounded the error. Further complicating matters, some authors treat *differentiation* and *complexity* as synonyms and use *construct system quality* to encompass differentiation, abstractness, and integration (e.g., Applegate, 1990). (Herein, I use *cognitive complexity* to denote overall construct system quality.)

Regardless of its name, differentiation has an inadequate theoretical definition. For instance, Beatty and Payne (1985) ask whether *differentiation* refers to the number of interpersonal constructs in a person's cognitive system, the number of constructs available for use, or the number of constructs the person is able to retrieve in an allotted period of time.

Another conceptual issue surrounding the RCQ is the breadth of the construct domain it measures (see Freeman & Barnes, 1982). The most common view among constructivists is that the RCQ measures only the system of constructs associated with interpersonal perception and communication (Burleson & Waltman, 1988; Crockett, 1965; B. J. O'Keefe, 1984; D. J. O'Keefe, 1980; Shepherd & Condra, 1988), as opposed to construct systems regarding politics (Swanson, 1981), religion (D. J. O'Keefe & Shepherd, 1982), and so on. However, research suggests the need to specify the location and permeability of the boundaries of the "interpersonal" construct system (see Babrow et al., 1988; Burleson, Applegate, & Neuwirth, 1981; Daly, Bell, Glenn, & Lawrence, 1985; Freeman & Barnes, 1982).

Critics have not only questioned the theoretical definition of cognitive complexity, they have also asked whether the RCQ is an adequate operational definition of construct system quality. According to critics, the prevailing interpretation of the RCQ is unable to account for significant variations in differentiation scores caused by different wordings of the RCQ (Allen et al., 1990), liked versus disliked peer descriptions (Dallinger & Hample, 1989, 1991), and observer and participant codings (Allen et al., 1991). In addition, critics have argued that the RCQ is actually measuring verbal ability or "loquacity" (e.g., Beatty, 1987). The most powerful response to these criticisms of the RCQ is that alternative understandings of what it measures must explain all of its previous correlations. Why would a measure of loquacity correlate with other, methodologically distinct measures of social cognition, not to mention a vast array of sophisticated communication strategies? Talkative people are not necessarily more cognitively or communicatively sophisticated (Delia et al., 1982, p. 176; see also Samter et al., 1989, pp. 626-627, n. 4). If rival interpretations of the RCQ are unable to subsume available data, they are not satisfactory alternatives.

The second most prominent set of constructivist operationalizations is an array of hierarchical message typologies. These distinguish messages by the social-cognitive processes that underlie them (Clark & Delia, 1979; B. J. O'Keefe, 1988). Constructivists have created coding schemes for distinguishing different levels of regulative and comforting parent-child communication (Applegate, Burke, Burleson, Delia, & Kline, 1985), persuasive strategies (Delia, Kline, & Burleson, 1979), request strategy and request support (Clark & Delia, 1976), refusal messages (Kline & Hennen-Floyd, 1990), relationship-enhancing messages (Applegate, 1980a), conflict and goal management strategies (B. J. O'Keefe & Shepherd, 1987), messages reconciling instrumental goals with face needs (Hale, 1986) or identity (Shepherd & Condra, 1988), and positive face support and autonomy-granting strategies (Applegate & Woods, 1991).

The most serious criticism lodged against existing coding schemes is that they often lack representational validity. Social scientific researchers routinely impose meanings upon communication, and sometimes these interpretations contradict those of the communicators (and listeners) involved in the observed interaction. It is precisely this problem, along with unitizing reliability (Folger & Poole, 1982; O'Donnell-Trujillo, 1981), that has brought the Rogers and Farace (1975) relational coding scheme into question.

A few researchers have directly and indirectly addressed this issue, and their studies have produced mixed results (Burleson & Samter, 1985a, 1985b; Kline & Hennen-Floyd, 1990; Samter et al., 1989). Because constructivists explicitly state that messages at the top of their coding hierarchies are more socially sophisticated (e.g., B. J. O'Keefe, 1988), if it turns out that social actors disagree with the theorists, these hierarchies will need to be reinterpreted.

Prediction, Corroboration, Explanation

Using these coding schemes, the RCQ, and other measures, constructivists have advanced three sets of theories. First of all, constructivists have tried to clarify the process whereby cognitive complexity develops in children and adolescents (for reviews of early research on development, see Delia & O'Keefe, 1979; Delia et al., 1982; O'Keefe & H. Sypher, 1981). Constructivists have also conducted extensive research on the development of the ability to produce listener-adapted messages. As children grow older, they become more sophisticated in their comforting (Clinton & Hancock, 1991), compromising (Clark, O'Dell, & Willihnganz, 1986), and persuasion (Clark & Delia, 1976; Delia, Kline, & Burleson, 1979).

The second set of constructivist theories concerns the effects of cognitive complexity on interpersonal perceptions. In the constructivist framework, perspective taking is considered "the basic social cognitive process in interpersonal communication" (Hale & Delia, 1976, p. 196; see also Swanson & Delia, 1976). A series of related studies has tried to show that construct differentiation is predictive of perspective taking (e.g., Hale & Delia, 1976; Ritter, 1979) and the detail of the psychological portraits people create (e.g., Delia et al., 1975; Sypher & Applegate, 1982).

The third and most prominent set of constructivist theories moves from perception to communication (for reviews, see Applegate, 1990; Burleson & Waltman, 1988; Delia et al., 1982). As Zorn (1991) recently wrote, "The major conclusion from constructivist research is that there is a moderate correlational relationship between interpersonal construct system development . . . and the ability to produce person-centered messages" (p. 183).

Typically, these studies correlate one or more of the dimensions of the RCQ with listener-adapted communication strategies (e.g., Delia & O'Keefe, 1979). For example, B. J. O'Keefe and Delia (1979) found moderate to high correlations between level of construct differentiation and the sophistication of persuasive strategies, as measured by the number of appeals and the degree of adaptation to the listener. Related studies have found that persons with higher levels of construct differentiation (and sometimes construct abstractness) use more person-centered messages (e.g., Delia, Clark, & Switzer, 1979), internally focused messages (Kline et al., 1990), listener-adapted messages (e.g., Applegate, 1982; Delia & Clark, 1977; Rowan, 1990), face-saving messages (Applegate & Woods, 1991), sensitive refusal messages (Kline & Hennen-Floyd, 1990), rhetorical messages (B. J. O'Keefe, 1988), flexible self-disclosure (Neimeyer & Banikiotes, 1980), and comforting communication (e.g., Samter & Burleson, 1984; Zimmerman & Applegate, 1992). Going just a step further, construct differentiation has been found to be associated, through sophisticated communication, with interpersonal success in face-to-face interactions (B. J. O'Keefe & Shepherd, 1987) and upward mobility in organizational hierarchies (Sypher & Zorn, 1986).

Constructivists have also developed theories that address traditional issues in social science, rather than concerns that emanate from the constructivist hard core. For example, constructivists have contributed to the literature on attitude-behavior inconsistency (Babrow & O'Keefe, 1984; Shepherd, 1987) and relationship formation and satisfaction (Burleson & Denton, 1992; Neimeyer & Mitchell, 1988; Neimeyer & Neimeyer, 1983).

Taken together, the past 20 years of constructivist research have produced a steady stream of predictions regarding the development of cognitive complexity and its influence on interpersonal perception and communication. Usually these predictions have proved accurate, but their explanatory depth may be somewhat shallow. The theoretical models tested frequently involve simple bivariate relationships. Too little attention has been devoted to direct tests of the cognitive processes mediating construct systems and communication strategies (e.g., Greene, Lindsey, & Hawn, 1990) and the variables moderating the cognition-communication relationship (e.g., Applegate et al., 1985; Delia, Kline, & Burleson, 1979).

Scope and Parsimony

The theoretical scope of constructivism is more impressive than its depth because constructivists hope to generalize many of their findings across wide stretches of time and space. Their theories are intended to apply to "human behavior" (Swanson & Delia, 1976; Delia et al., 1982), and this is broadly construed to encompass diverse cultures and historical eras. To their credit, some constructivist researchers have respected this scope and moved beyond the college classroom to collect data (e.g., Applegate, Coyle, Seibert, & Church, 1989). Nonetheless, it is indisputable that relative to the diversity of human beings, constructivists have only tested their theories in a small corner of the social world.

As for parsimony, individual pieces of constructivist research almost always frame themselves within the larger context of the research program. Each research report restates the broader tenets of the program and ties itself to previous research and broad theoretical questions (e.g., B. J. O'Keefe & Shepherd, 1987; Zorn, 1991). In addition, the theoretical writings by constructivists effectively illustrate how these areas of research are interconnected and related to the hard core (e.g., Applegate, 1990; Delia et al., 1982). These connections between single studies and larger issues give the protective belt of theories a remarkable coherence.

Progression Versus Degeneration

In the methodology of scientific research programs, all of the above considerations are important, but the fundamental issue is whether or not the program is progressive. Are changes in the progressive belt producing new predictions, and are these predictions receiving empirical support?

On balance, the constructivist program may be progressive. A clear indication is the recent use of the positive heuristic, which alters the protective belt through creative theorizing, rather than a defensive response to anomalies. These alterations have generated novel hypotheses, most of which have received modest empirical support.

For instance, recent research has probed the conceptual and empirical boundaries of interpersonal constructs. Martin (1991, 1992) recently developed and successfully applied the Relational Cognition Complexity Instrument to extend constructivist ideas to perception and communication in ongoing personal relationships. Similarly, Daly et al. (1985) have distinguished interpersonal from conversational cognitive complexity, arguing that people employ a separate construct system for producing, interpreting, and remembering conversations. By contrast, Babrow et al. (1988) have shown that the original measure of interpersonal cognitive complexity can be applied to perceptions of both real and televised peers.

The most striking use of the positive heuristic may be recent research on "message design logics" (B. J. O'Keefe, 1988, 1990, 1992). B. J. O'Keefe (1992) and other researchers have become dissatisfied with the limited theoretical link between cognitive complexity and strategic communication, and they are trying to create a more precise portrait of the knowledge structures and cognitive processes that generate sophisticated messages. Toward this end, O'Keefe (1988) has identified expressive, conventional, and rhetorical message design logics, each of which is a distinct set of beliefs about communication. Differences in design logics partially explain differences in message production: Because cognitively complex individuals have a greater propensity to use the most advanced design logic (B. J. O'Keefe, 1988), their messages are more sophisticated and are interpreted more favorably by peers (Bingham & Burleson, 1989; B. J. O'Keefe & McCornack, 1987).

According to its proponents, this new theoretical framework "can subsume and reinterpret the findings of the constructivist program" (B. J. O'Keefe, 1988, p. 98). To do so, however, it will be necessary to (a) show the role of construct differentiation, abstractness, and integration within message design logics and (b) superimpose the three levels of design logic upon preexisting constructivist message typologies.

REVISING THE
CONSTRUCTIVIST RESEARCH PROGRAM

Strengthening Theories Through the Positive Heuristic

The most important changes in constructivism must take place within the protective belt. Above all else, constructivist theories need to move beyond a simple cognitive trait approach and provide richer descriptions of the cognitive process (Burleson, 1987; B. J. O'Keefe, 1988), particularly in light of the failures of other trait theories (see Hewes & Planalp, 1987; Knapp & Miller, 1985). This move toward a more cognitively rich research program should draw upon previous theory and research, a process characteristic of the development of research programs in the social sciences (Pouncy, 1988).

First, constructivism needs to clarify the features of the knowledge structures central to its theories. It is unclear how constructs differ from "schemas" (Sypher & Applegate, 1984), or how social perception through the use of constructs differs from the attribution process (Wilson, Cruz, & Kang, 1992; Wilson & Kang, 1991). In addition, it is unclear whether individuals scoring higher in cognitive differentiation have more constructs, more motivation to use them (Beatty & Payne, 1985; Allen et al., 1990), greater recall speed, or more accessible constructs (Burleson & Waltman, 1988; Sypher & Applegate, 1982). If the last of these interpretations is chosen, expectations, activation recency, and construct salience are likely to affect construct accessibility (Higgins & Wells, 1986; Wilson, 1990; see also Fazio, 1989).

Constructivism also needs an "adequate specification of . . . the nature of the information transformation" that occurs when constructs are developed and used. Ultimately, the use of constructs needs to be defined in terms of parallel versus serial processing, allowing predictions about the time and cognitive effort required in using constructs (Greene, 1984, pp. 246-247; Greene et al., 1990).

Regarding the social perception process, constructivists might argue that cognitive complexity aids perceivers by enhancing the decoding and interpretation of messages; this, in turn, creates richer psychological portraits of message senders (Samter et al., 1989). Cognitive differentiation permits the development and/or retrieval of more detailed attributions (Leichty, 1989; Wilson et al., 1992), whereas construct abstractness may aid in the production of more elaborate, motivational attributions (see Delia, 1974). Cognitive integration may be necessary for organizing these attributions into a coherent and accurate understanding of messages received and the persons sending them.

As for the boundaries of construct systems, the sets of constructs used for perceiving and remembering messages may be different from those used for remembering people. For example, conversational cognitive complexity would have the largest effect on conversational memory, but interpersonal cognitive complexity would be used in remembering person-centered or trait-related conversational features (Daly et al., 1985; Higgins, King, & Mavin, 1982; Neuliep & Hazelton, 1986).

A richer model of memory may also distinguish between working and long-term memory. Theoretically, an individual may have a highly sophisticated storage system, but an average processing capacity. Differentiation, abstraction, and integration may all be properties of long-term memory, necessitating the inclusion of an additional variable to account for differences in working memory ability.

The final and most important issue is the communication process. Constructivists have long recognized that individuals have "implicit rules of use" in their construct systems regarding when and how to use different communication strategies (Delia, 1977, p. 71; B. J. O'Keefe, 1988). Along these lines, Wilson (1990) posits that cognitive complexity aids in the development and use of rules linking different strategies to situations and outcomes. In this view, individuals with the same goals and behavioral repertoires might make different decisions because they have different systems of "cognitive rules" linking strategies to possible situations and likely outcomes. Greater cognitive differentiation will allow finer distinctions among different social settings, whereas abstraction will facilitate adaptation to novel situations. Integration may shorten one's response time by allowing more rapid movement among the cognitive rules in one's system.

In addition to clarifying theories of knowledge structures and cognitive processes, constructivist research also needs to provide a richer account of cognitive development. When cognitive complexity or communication is construed as a dependent variable, the independent variable is usually just chronological age or grade level (Babrow et al., 1988; Clark et al., 1986; Clinton & Hancock, 1991; Delia & Clark, 1977). It may be more fruitful to measure cognitive development in relation to individuals' "life phases" (Higgins & Wells, 1986). Previous research has suggested that development proceeds in spurts during adolescence (e.g., Clark & Delia, 1976), but there has been no attempt to determine what internal or social changes engender these developmental transitions.

Other, nonphasic, properties of children's social worlds also need to be taken into account. Parents, teachers, and peers influence an individual's development by encouraging, discouraging, and modeling detailed analysis of the social world (Applegate, 1980a). Children's cognitive development is also surely influenced by the degree to which they enjoy frequent and rich social interaction owing to a diversity of social situations, cultural and subcultural communication norms, and individuals (Delia, 1974; Delia & Clark, 1977; Neimeyer & Banikiotes, 1980). Children's development may be aided by the need to use social skills to satisfy needs or wants. All other things being equal, people who are more dependent upon tact or persuasiveness for satisfaction may develop higher levels of cognitive complexity (see Hale, 1986). However, all other things are not equal, and the people in such situations are more likely to occupy subordinate social positions (Henley, 1977; Scott, 1990), which may deny them commensurate educational opportunities.

Constructivists should also clarify whether or not there is a tail end to a person's development. Initially, constructivists argued that people who fail to reach the highest developmental level of cognitive complexity during adolescence will not develop further during adulthood (Delia & Clark, 1977). Recent writings, however, imply the malleability of adult construct system differentiation and abstractness (Applegate, 1990; Applegate et al., 1989). Researchers need to determine when and how adult cognitive complexity develops, or they must produce evidence that such development cannot occur.

An even more ambitious approach to developmental theory would explore the dynamic relationships among cognitive variables over time. If more cognitively complex children are better able to comprehend deviations from conversational expectations and experiment with their own behavior (Reardon, 1982), they should be able to learn more from each of their interactions and, consequently, continue their development at a more rapid pace. Research on this process could prove fruitful, but it would require careful measurement of on-line processing, communication strategy selection, and microscopic changes in construct system quality.

The preceding recommendations concern increasing the depth or complexity of constructivist theories. By contrast, the breadth of these theories is already quite impressive, and I have only one additional area of investigation to suggest. In an early presentation of constructivist theory, Swanson and Delia (1976) emphasized the role of cognitive complexity in self-perception. They argued that the "self" consists of the individual's personal repertoire of interpretive constructs. "The modes of thought by which the person constitutes his unique perceptual field is the essence of his personality." Hence one's "self-concept" is the way in which one construes oneself—"the organized totality of . . . self-relevant beliefs or inferences." Moreover, it is through communication with others that one forms this self-concept. "It is by imagining and construing how others see and judge us that we come to form basic primitive ideas about ourselves" (pp. 17-18). To my knowledge, constructivists have neither refined nor tested these ideas. Doing so would significantly expand the constructivist understanding of cognition and interpersonal perception.

Regardless of the breadth of constructivist research, individual studies should make precise predictions and identify rival hypotheses. First, researchers might strengthen predictions by speaking in terms of magnitudes. If constructivists are confident of the existence of statistical associations among variables, they should conduct meta-analyses on frequently tested associations and begin to make arguments about average effect sizes. Specifically, they could try using ranged null hypotheses, wedding minimum levels of substantive significance with critical values for statistical significance (Meehl, 1978, 1986; on the relation of this to Lakatos's philosophy of science, see Serlin & Lapsley, 1984).

With or without a prediction of magnitude, constructivist hypotheses should be directional. Researchers continue to overuse nondirectional hypotheses (e.g., Martin, 1992), research questions instead of hypotheses (e.g., Clark et al., 1986; Sypher & Zorn, 1986; Zorn, 1991), and research questions in conjunction with hypotheses (e.g., Burleson & Denton, 1992; Wilson, 1990; Wilson et al., 1992). Research questions and vague hypotheses make it difficult to test theories in the protective belt and limit the progress of the research program.

Relatedly, constructivist research must pay greater attention to statistical power (Cohen, 1988), especially when predicting nonsignificance (e.g., Hale, 1980). Otherwise, it is easy to overinterpret nonsignificant findings (e.g., Zimmerman & Applegate, 1992). To their credit, a few constructivist studies have reported levels of power (e.g., D. J. O'Keefe & Shepherd, 1982; Shepherd & Condra, 1988; Wilson et al., 1992), but these reports sometimes reveal that only large effect sizes have sufficient statistical power (e.g., Babrow & O'Keefe, 1984; Burleson et al., 1981).

In addition, constructivist research should specify plausible alternative hypotheses, preferably ones connected with rival theories (Clark, 1979, pp. 54-55).

Pitting one hypothesis against another makes findings more revealing, even if the competing hypotheses have the same basic theoretical orientation (e.g., Gastil, 1992). At the very least, studies should specify what statistical findings will support or contradict initial hypotheses. Otherwise, statistical analysis might proceed through various modes until researchers find a result that supports their hypotheses (e.g., Delia, Kline, & Burleson, 1979, pp. 253-254).

Finally, if the theoretical scope of constructivism is as broad as it appears, then empirical research must begin to spread itself out within this scope. The generalizability of findings can be ascertained only through the measurement and analysis of the effects of potential limiting variables (see Clark, 1979, pp. 57-63). Applegate and Woods (1991) suggest that researchers examine social factors systematically. Instead of treating these variables as nuisances that need to be shown as nonsignificant or partialed out, they can be linked to theory in interesting ways (e.g., Hale, 1986; Leichty & Applegate, 1991).

A full test of constructivism's theoretical scope requires more than demographically diverse samples. It also entails the use of more varied and ecologically valid communication situations (e.g., Applegate et al., 1989). As Burleson (1987) has noted, tests of constructivist theories have relied primarily upon hypothetical communication (i.e., asking people what they would say in hypothetical situations). Some research has used recollections of actual communication (Zorn, 1991) or directly observed behaviors with confederates (Samter & Burleson, 1984) or other study participants (Kline et al., 1990). The strongest tests of constructivism will come outside of the laboratory, where researchers observe spontaneous communication among a wide range of people in natural settings. Such studies require twice the time and resources of the average study, but they are worth the effort.

Engaging the Negative
Heuristic and Cataloging Anomalies

For constructivism to move forward, however, it must do more than generate new theories and predictions. The negative heuristic must begin to respond to the limitations and problems associated with the RCQ. If constructivists began to measure linguistic ability regularly and to treat it as a moderating variable (rather than a nuisance), they would make excellent use of the negative heuristic. They would respond to external pressures (i.e., criticisms of the RCQ) by returning to the core of the program—the original notion of an interplay between cognitive and linguistic ability. Constructivists would then reformulate the protective belt in a way that not only addresses the original concerns of critics, but generates new predictions and, potentially, additional support for the program.

Constructivist researchers should also reembrace the principle of methodological diversity (e.g., Applegate, 1980b). Although some studies have used oral versions of the RCQ through interviews (Burleson & Waltman, 1988), no study has used both written and oral versions and compared their results. Similarly, constructivists have used both the RCQ (e.g., Delia, Kline, & Burleson, 1979) and the Role Construct Repertory Test (e.g., Applegate et al., 1989) to measure construct abstractness, but a successful juxtaposition of these measures could show their convergent validity. In general, it may be more important to develop a repertoire of valid measures (e.g., O'Keefe et al., 1982) than to reject alternative measures (e.g., Applegate, Kline, & Delia, 1991).

If the RCQ remains the preferred measure of cognitive complexity, researchers should change how they analyze its results. If construct differentiation is conceptualized as a continuous variable and abstraction and integration are at least rank-order variables (Miller & Wilson, 1979, p. 26), scores on the RCQ or an alternative measure should never be dichotomized. Dichotomization via a median split was more common in early research (e.g., Delia & Clark, 1977), but the practice continues today (e.g., Greene et al., 1990). The potential benefits of this process are limited (e.g., graphic representation of an interaction in ANOVA), and its costs are high. Dichotomization essentially amounts to discarding meaningful variance and increasing unreliability (Hunter & Schmidt, 1989).

In addition, it might be more appropriate to use a root transformation of RCQ differentiation scores, as opposed to using raw scores. The redundancy problem in coding similar words as different constructs (Beatty, 1987) might be addressed through this transformation. Moreover, this procedure would reduce the potential distortions caused by outliers, many of which may be artificially low or high. At a minimum, a theoretical justification should be provided for the use of raw scores (Swanson, 1981), rank orderings (Crockett, 1965), dichotomies (Greene et al., 1990), trichotomies (Bingham & Burleson, 1989), or quartiles (Burleson & Samter, 1990).

If one is interested in the overall effects of cognitive complexity, one could code all three (or more) different dimensions and enter them into a regression as a set of variables (Cohen & Cohen, 1983). If one is more concerned with their independent effects (e.g., Applegate, 1982; Delia, Kline, & Burleson, 1979), one would need to establish conceptually whether these dimensions are hierarchically ordered. If they are, one could enter them sequentially into a regression; if they are not, one could obtain their semipartial correlations. Researchers' failure to use these methods of analysis makes results more difficult to interpret (see D. J. O'Keefe & Delia, 1981, pp. 155-157).

Beyond the RCQ and the controversies surrounding it, constructivist researchers have not attempted to catalog and address systematically the anomalous findings past research has produced. This is partly the result of imprecise hypotheses, which make it more difficult to identify anomalous findings, but many predictions have been clear enough to produce contradictory results. When a surprising finding appears (e.g., Applegate, 1980a; Greene et al., 1990; Martin, 1992), researchers must go beyond explaining it in the discussion section.

A research program should not become obsessed with explaining contradictory findings. So long as it is progressive, a program can thrive in an "ocean of anomalies" (Lakatos, 1978b, p. 53). But anomalies should be viewed as opportunities for further research. If recurrent, they should trigger the negative heuristic to produce theoretical revisions that both explain the anomalies and generate fruitful hypotheses for future research.

CONCLUSION

Criticisms such as those I have presented here may be signs of the health of constructivism, rather than symptoms of its decline. If scholars had begun to abandon or ignore constructivism, an extended evaluation and critique would be of little consequence. The research program is worth scrutinizing because it has generated valuable scholarship and has the potential to raise and address important research questions in the future.

Constructivism will maintain its prominence in the field of communication until it is either replaced or abandoned. Critics who argue that constructivism has become a hopelessly degenerating program are charged with the task of replacing it with an alternative research program capable of explaining constructivist research findings (see Lakatos, 1978b, pp. 149-150; Metaxopoulos, 1989; see also D. J. O'Keefe, 1975, pp. 177-179). A critic would be unwise to suggest abandoning a ship that has taken on water if there are no other seaworthy vessels in sight.

However, constructivism's ultimate demise may come from within: Constructivists themselves may decide to reject portions of the hard core. B. J. O'Keefe's (1992) message design logics may move further away from the hard core's emphasis upon cognitive complexity and person perception. The hard-core assumption that construct systems solidify by adulthood is also being questioned by constructivist scholars who discuss the possible effects of adult training programs (Applegate, 1990) and adult socialization (Applegate et al., 1989). Through moves such as these, constructivism may be replaced by a research program that shares a similar, but distinct, hard core.

Nonetheless, it is likely that constructivism—or something close to it—will remain a prominent research program in the near future. This likelihood makes it necessary for me to conclude this evaluation by moving outside of Lakatos's epistemology. Like any sustained program of research, constructivism raises important ethical questions. Should society view a high level of cognitive complexity as a valuable resource? If so, it is important to know who has it and who does not because a democratic society relies upon a broad distribution of both material and social resources, including cognitive and communication competencies (Barber, 1984; Fishkin, 1991; Gastil, 1993). If cognitive complexity is not evenly distributed, researchers need to learn how it is acquired. How does it develop during childhood, and does it solidify by adulthood? What social conditions or public education programs are conducive to its development in children and adults?

Although they originate from ethical concerns, all of these questions require empirical research. Consequently, if these questions are deemed important, there is an ethical imperative for continued research within either the constructivist research program or a viable alternative. Communication scholars should continue to study the social advantages, distribution, and development of communication competence and its cognitive origins.

REFERENCES

Allen, M., Mabry, E., Banski, M., & Preiss, R. (1991). Valid and constructive thoughts: Continuing the dialog about the RCQ. *Communication Reports, 4,* 120-125.

Allen, M., Mabry, E., Banski, M., Stoneman, M., & Carter, P. (1990). A thoughtful appraisal of measuring cognition using the Role Category Questionnaire. *Communication Reports, 3,* 49-57.

Applegate, J. L. (1980a). Adaptive communication in educational contexts: A study of teachers' communicative strategies. *Communication Education, 29,* 158-170.

Applegate, J. L. (1980b). Person- and position-centered teacher communication in a day care center: A case study triangulating interview and naturalistic methods. In N. K. Denzin (Ed.), *Studies in symbolic interaction* (Vol. 3, pp. 59-96). Greenwich, CT: JAI.

Applegate, J. L. (1982). The impact of construct system development on communication and impression formation in persuasive contexts. *Communication Monographs, 49,* 277-289.

Applegate, J. L. (1990). Constructs and communication: A pragmatic integration. In R. Neimeyer & G. Neimeyer (Eds.), *Advances in personal construct psychology* (Vol. 1, pp. 197-224). Greenwich, CT: JAI.

Applegate, J. L., Burke, J. A., Burleson, B. R., Delia, J. G., & Kline, S. L. (1985). Reflection-enhancing parental communication. In I. E. Sigel (Ed.), *Parental belief systems* (pp. 107-142). Hillsdale, NJ: Lawrence Erlbaum.

Applegate, J. L., Coyle, K., Seibert, J. H., & Church, S. M. (1989). Interpersonal constructs and communicative ability in a police environment: A preliminary investigation. *International Journal of Personal Construct Psychology, 2,* 385-399.

Applegate, J. L., Kline, S. L., & Delia, J. G. (1991). Alternative measures of cognitive complexity as predictors of communication performance. *International Journal of Personal Construct Psychology, 4,* 193-213.

Applegate, J. L., & Woods, E. (1991). Construct system development and attention to face wants in persuasive situations. *Southern Communication Journal, 56,* 194-204.

Babrow, A. S., O'Keefe, B. J., Swanson, D. L., Meyers, R., & Murphy, M. (1988). Person perception and children's impressions of television and real peers. *Communication Research, 15,* 680-698.

Babrow, A. S., & O'Keefe, D. J. (1984). Construct differentiation as a moderator of attitude-behavior consistency: A failure to confirm. *Central States Speech Journal, 35,* 160-165.

Barber, B. (1984). *Strong democracy.* Berkeley: University of California Press.

Beatty, M. J. (1987). Erroneous assumptions underlying Burleson's critique. *Communication Quarterly, 35,* 329-333.

Beatty, M. J., & Payne, S. K. (1985). Is construct differentiation loquacity? A motivational perspective. *Human Communication Research, 11,* 605-612.

Bingham, S. G., & Burleson, B. R. (1989). Multiple effects of messages with multiple goals: Some perceived outcomes of responses to sexual harassment. *Human Communication Research, 16,* 184-216.

Bonk, C. J. (1990). A synthesis of social cognition and writing research. *Written Communication, 7,* 136-163.

Burleson, B. R. (1987). Cognitive complexity. In J. C. McCroskey & J. A. Daly (Eds.), *Personality and interpersonal communication* (pp. 305-349). Newbury Park, CA: Sage.

Burleson, B. R., Applegate, J. L., & Delia, J. G. (1991). On validly assessing the validity of the Role Category Questionnaire: A reply to Allen et al. *Communication Reports, 4,* 113-119.

Burleson, B. R., Applegate, J. L., & Neuwirth, C. M. (1981). Is cognitive complexity loquacity? A reply to Powers, Jordan, & Street. *Human Communication Research, 7,* 212-225.

Burleson, B. R., & Denton, W. H. (1992). A new look at similarity and attraction in marriage: Similarities in social-cognitive and communication skills as predictors of attraction and satisfaction. *Communication Monographs, 59,* 268-287.

Burleson, B. R., & Samter, W. E. (1985a). Consistencies in theoretical and naive evaluations of comforting messages. *Communication Monographs, 52,* 103-123.

Burleson, B. R., & Samter, W. E. (1985b). Individual differences in the perception of comforting messages: An exploratory investigation. *Central States Speech Journal, 36,* 39-50.

Burleson, B. R., & Samter, W. E. (1990). Effects of cognitive complexity on the perceived importance of communication skills in friends. *Communication Research, 17,* 165-182.

Burleson, B. R., & Waltman, M. S. (1987). Popular, rejected, and supportive preadolescents: Social-cognitive and communicative characteristics. In M. L. McLaughlin (Ed.), *Communication yearbook 10* (pp. 533-552). Newbury Park, CA: Sage.

Burleson, B. R., & Waltman, M. S. (1988). Cognitive complexity: Using the Role Category Questionnaire measure. In C. H. Tardy (Ed.), *A handbook for the study of human communication: Methods and instruments for observing, measuring, and assessing communication processes* (pp. 1-35). Norwood, NJ: Ablex.

Clark, R. A. (1979). Suggestions for the design of empirical communication studies. *Central States Speech Journal, 30,* 51-66.

Clark, R. A., & Delia, J. G. (1976). The development of functional persuasive skills in childhood and early adolescence. *Child Development, 47,* 1008-1014.

Clark, R. A., & Delia, J. G. (1979). *Topoi* and rhetorical competence. *Quarterly Journal of Speech, 65,* 187-206.

Clark, R. A., O'Dell, L. L., & Willihnganz, S. (1986). The development of compromising as an alternative to persuasion. *Central States Speech Journal, 37,* 220-224.

Clinton, B. L., & Hancock, G. R. (1991). The development of an understanding of comforting messages. *Communication Reports, 4,* 55-63.

Cohen, J. (1988). *Statistical power analysis for the behavioral sciences.* Hillsdale, NJ: Lawrence Erlbaum.

Cohen, J., & Cohen, P. (1983). *Applied multiple regression/correlation analysis for the behavioral sciences.* Hillsdale, NJ: Lawrence Erlbaum.

Cohen, R. S., Feyerabend, P. K., & Wartofsky, M. W. (Eds.). (1976). *Essays in memory of Imre Lakatos.* Boston: D. Reidel.

Crockett, W. H. (1965). Cognitive complexity and impression formation. In B. Mather (Ed.), *Progress in experimental personality research* (Vol. 2, pp. 47-90). New York: Academic Press.

Crockett, W. H., Press, A. N., Delia, J., & Kenny, C. T. (1974). *Structural analysis of the organization of written impressions.* Unpublished manuscript, University of Kansas.

Dallinger, J. M., & Hample, D. (1989, May). *Cognitive editing of arguments and interpersonal construct differentiation.* Paper presented at the annual meeting of the International Communication Association, San Francisco.

Dallinger, J. M., & Hample, D. (1991). Cognitive editing of arguments and interpersonal construct differentiation: Refining the relationship. In F. H. van Eemeren, R. Grootendorst, J. A. Blair, & C. A. Willard (Eds.), *Proceedings of the Second International Conference on Argumentation* (pp. 567-574). Amsterdam: International Society for the Study of Argumentation.

Daly, J. A., Bell, R. A., Glenn, P. J., & Lawrence, S. (1985). Conceptualizing conversational complexity. *Human Communication Research, 12,* 30-53.

Dar, R. (1987). Another look at Meehl, Lakatos, and the scientific practices of psychologists. *American Psychologist, 42,* 145-151.

Delia, J. G. (1974). Attitude toward the disclosure of self-attributions and the complexity of interpersonal constructs. *Speech Monographs, 41,* 119-126.

Delia, J. G. (1977). Constructivism and the study of human communication. *Quarterly Journal of Speech, 63,* 66-83.

Delia, J. G., & Clark, R. A. (1977). Cognitive complexity, social perception, and the development of listener-adapted communication in six-, eight-, ten-, and twelve-year-old boys. *Communication Monographs, 44,* 326-345.

Delia, J. G., Clark, R. A., & Switzer, D. E. (1979). The content of informal conversations as a function of interactants' interpersonal cognitive complexity. *Communication Monographs, 46,* 274-281.

Delia, J. G., & Crockett, W. H. (1973). Social schemas, cognitive complexity, and the learning of social structures. *Journal of Personality, 41,* 413-429.

Delia, J. G., Crockett, W. H., Press, A. N., & O'Keefe, D. J. (1975). The dependency of interpersonal evaluations on context-relevant beliefs about the other. *Speech Monographs, 42,* 10-19.

Delia, J. G., Kline, S. L., & Burleson, B. R. (1979). The development of persuasive communication strategies in kindergartners through twelfth-graders. *Communication Monographs, 46,* 241-256.

Delia, J. G., & O'Keefe, B. J. (1979). Constructivism: The development of communication in children. In E. Wartella (Ed.), *Children communicating* (pp. 157-185). Beverly Hills, CA: Sage.

Delia, J. G., O'Keefe, B. J., & O'Keefe, D. J. (1982). The constructivist approach to communication. In F. E. X. Dance (Ed.), *Human communication theory: Comparative essays* (pp. 147-191). New York: Harper & Row.

Fazio, R. (1989). On the power and functionality of attitudes: The role of attitude accessibility. In A. R. Pratkanis, S. J. Breckler, & A. G. Greenwald (Eds.), *Attitude structure and function* (pp. 153-180). Hillsdale, NJ: Lawrence Erlbaum.

Fishkin, J. (1991). *Democracy and deliberation.* New Haven, CT: Yale University Press.

Folger, J. P., & Poole, M. S. (1982). Relational coding schemes: The question of validity. In R. Burgoon (Ed.), *Communication yearbook 5* (pp. 235-247). New Brunswick, NJ: Transaction.

Freeman, D. N., & Barnes, R. D. (1982). Generalizability of cognitive complexity in the political domain. *Perceptual and Motor Skills, 55,* 1151-1157.

Gastil, J. (1992). Why we believe in democracy: Testing theories of attitude functions and democracy. *Journal of Applied Social Psychology, 22,* 423-450.

Gastil, J. (1993). *Democracy in small groups: Participation, decision making, and communication.* Philadelphia: New South.

Gavroglu, K., Goudaroulis, Y., & Nicolacopoulos, P. (Eds.). (1989). *Imre Lakatos and theories of scientific change.* Boston: Kluwer Academic.

Gholson, B., & Barker, P. (1985). Kuhn, Lakatos, and Laudan: Applications in the history of physics and psychology. *American Psychologist, 40,* 755-769.

Greene, J. O. (1984). Evaluating cognitive explanations of communicative phenomena. *Quarterly Journal of Speech, 70,* 241-254.

Greene, J. O., Lindsey, A. E., & Hawn, J. J. (1990). Social goals and speech production: Effects of multiple goals on pausal phenomena. *Journal of Language and Social Psychology, 9,* 119-134.

Hale, C. L. (1980). Cognitive complexity-simplicity as a determinant of communication effectiveness. *Communication Monographs, 47,* 304-311.

Hale, C. L. (1986). Impact of cognitive complexity on message structure in a face-threatening context. *Journal of Language and Social Psychology, 5,* 135-143.

Hale, C. L., & Delia, J. G. (1976). Cognitive complexity and social perspective-taking. *Communication Monographs, 43,* 195-203.

Henley, N. (1977). *Body politics.* Englewood Cliffs, NJ: Prentice Hall.

Hewes, D., & Planalp, S. (1987). The individual's place in communication science. In C. R. Berger & S. H. Chaffee (Eds.), *Handbook of communication science* (pp. 146-183). Newbury Park, CA: Sage.

Higgins, E. T., King, G. A., & Mavin, G. H. (1982). Individual construct accessibility and subjective impressions and recall. *Journal of Personality and Social Psychology, 43,* 35-47.

Higgins, E. T., & Wells, R. S. (1986). Social construct availability and accessibility as a function of social life phase: Emphasizing the "how" versus the "can" of social cognition. *Social Cognition, 4,* 201-226.

Hunter, J. E., & Schmidt, F. L. (1989). *Methods of meta-analysis.* Newbury Park, CA: Sage.

Kline, S. L., & Hennen-Floyd, C. (1990). On the art of saying no: The influence of social cognitive development on messages of refusal. *Western Journal of Speech Communication, 54,* 454-472.

Kline, S. L., Hennen-Floyd, C., & Farrell, K. M. (1990). Cognitive complexity and verbal response mode use in discussion. *Communication Quarterly, 38,* 350-360.

Knapp, M. L., & Miller, G. R. (1985). Introduction: Background and current trends in the study of interpersonal communication. In M. L. Knapp & G. R. Miller (Eds.), *Handbook of interpersonal communication* (pp. 7-24). Beverly Hills, CA: Sage.

Lakatos, I. (1978a). *Mathematics, science, and epistemology.* Cambridge: Cambridge University Press.

Lakatos, I. (1978b). *The methodology of scientific research programmes.* Cambridge: Cambridge University Press.

Leichty, G. (1989). Interpersonal constructs and friendship form and structure. *International Journal of Personal Construct Psychology, 2,* 401-415.

Leichty, G., & Applegate, J. L. (1991). Social-cognitive and situational influences on the use of face-saving persuasive strategies. *Human Communication Research, 17,* 451-484.

Martin, R. W. (1991). Examining personal relationship thinking: The relational cognition complexity instrument. *Journal of Personal and Social Relationships, 8,* 467-480.

Martin, R. W. (1992). Relational cognition complexity and relational communication in personal relationships. *Communication Monographs, 59,* 150-163.

Meehl, P. E. (1978). Theoretical risks and tabular asterisks: Sir Karl, Sir Ronald, and the slow progress of soft psychology. *Journal of Consulting and Clinical Psychology, 46,* 806-834.

Meehl, P. E. (1986). What social scientists don't understand. In D. W. Fiske & R. A. Shweder (Eds.), *Metatheory in social science* (pp. 315-338). Chicago: University of Chicago Press.

Metaxopoulos, E. (1989). A critical consideration of the Lakatosian concepts: "Mature" and "immature" science. In K. Gavroglu, Y. Goudaroulis, & P. Nicolacopoulos (Eds.), *Imre Lakatos and theories of scientific change* (pp. 203-214). Boston: Kluwer Academic.

Miller, A., & Wilson, P. (1979). Cognitive differentiation and integration: A conceptual analysis. *Genetic Psychology Monographs, 99,* 3-40.

Nagel, E. (1979). *The structure of science.* Indianapolis: Hackett.

Neimeyer, G. J., & Banikiotes, P. G. (1980). Flexibility of disclosure and measures of cognitive integration and differentiation. *Perceptual and Motor Skills, 50,* 907-910.

Neimeyer, R. A., & Mitchell, K. A. (1988). Similarity and attraction: A longitudinal study. *Journal of Social and Personal Relationships, 5,* 131-148.

Neimeyer, R. A., & Neimeyer, G. J. (1983). Structural similarity in the acquaintance process. *Journal of Social and Clinical Psychology, 1,* 146-154.

Neuliep, J. W., & Hazelton, V. (1986). Enhanced conversational recall and reduced conversational interference as a function of cognitive complexity. *Human Communication Research, 13,* 211-224.

O'Donnell-Trujillo, N. (1981). Relational communication: A comparison of coding systems. *Communication Monographs, 48,* 91-105.

O'Keefe, B. J. (1984). The evolution of impressions in small working groups: Effects of construct differentiation. In H. E. Sypher & J. L. Applegate (Eds.), *Communication by children and adults* (pp. 262-291). Beverly Hills, CA: Sage.

O'Keefe, B. J. (1988). The logic of message design: Individual differences in reasoning about communication. *Communication Monographs, 55,* 80-103.

O'Keefe, B. J. (1990). The logic of regulative communication: Understanding the rationality of message designs. In J. P. Dillard (Ed.), *Seeking compliance: The production of interpersonal influence messages* (pp. 87-104). Scottsdale, AZ: Gorsuch Scarisbrick.

O'Keefe, B. J. (1992). Developing and testing rational models of message design. *Human Communication Research, 18,* 637-649.

O'Keefe, B. J., & Delia, J. G. (1979). Construct comprehensiveness and cognitive complexity as predictors of the number and strategic adaptation of arguments and appeals in a persuasive message. *Communication Monographs, 46,* 231-240.

O'Keefe, B. J., & McCornack, S. A. (1987). Message design logic and message goal structure: Effects on perceptions of message. *Human Communication Research, 14,* 68-92.

O'Keefe, B. J., & Shepherd, G. J. (1987). The pursuit of multiple objectives in face-to-face persuasive interactions: Effects of construct differentiation on message organization. *Communication Monographs, 54,* 396-419.

O'Keefe, D. J. (1975). Logical empiricism and the study of human communication. *Speech Monographs, 42,* 169-183.

O'Keefe, D. J. (1980). The relationship between attitudes and behavior: A constructivist analysis. In D. P. Cushman & R. D. McPhee (Eds.), *Message-attitude-behavior relationship: Theory, methodology, and application* (pp. 117-148). New York: Academic Press.

O'Keefe, D. J., & Delia, J. G. (1981). Construct differentiation and the relationship of attitudes and behavioral intentions. *Communication Monographs, 48,* 146-157.

O'Keefe, D. J., & Shepherd, G. J. (1982). Interpersonal construct differentiation, attitudinal confidence, and the attitude-behavior relationship. *Central States Speech Journal, 33,* 416-423.

O'Keefe, D. J., Shepherd, G. J., & Streeter, T. (1982). Role Category Questionnaire measures of cognitive complexity: Reliability and comparability of alternative forms. *Central States Speech Journal, 33,* 333-338.

O'Keefe, D. J., & Sypher, H. E. (1981). Cognitive complexity measures and the relationship of cognitive complexity to communication: A critical review. *Human Communication Research, 8,* 72-92.

Pouncy, H. (1988). Terms of agreement: Evaluating the theory of symbolic politics' impact on the pluralist research program. *American Journal of Political Science, 32,* 781-795.

Powers, W. G., Jordan, W. J., & Street, R. L. (1979). Language indices in the measurement of cognitive complexity: Is complexity loquacity? *Human Communication Research, 6,* 69-73.

Reardon, K. K. (1982). Conversational deviance: A structural model. *Human Communication Research, 9,* 59-74.

Ritter, E. M. (1979). Social perspective-taking ability, cognitive complexity and listener-adapted communication in early and late adolescence. *Communication Monographs, 46,* 40-51.

Rogers, L. E., & Farace, R. V. (1975). Analysis· of relational communication in dyads: New measurement procedures. *Human Communication Research, 1,* 222-239.

Rowan, K. E. (1990). Cognitive correlates of explanatory writing skill. *Written Communication, 7,* 316-341.

Samter, W. E., & Burleson, B. R. (1984). Cognitive and motivational influences on spontaneous comforting behavior. *Human Communication Research, 11,* 231-260.

Samter, W. E., Burleson, B. R., & Basden-Murphy, L. (1989). Behavioral complexity is in the eye of the beholder: Effects of cognitive complexity and message complexity on impressions of the source of comforting messages. *Human Communication Research, 15,* 612-629.

Scott, J. C. (1990). *Domination and the arts of resistance.* New Haven, CT: Yale University Press.

Serlin, R. C., & Lapsley, D. K. (1984). Rationality in psychological research: The good-enough principle. *American Psychologist, 40,* 73-83.

Shepherd, G. J. (1987). Individual differences in the relationship between attitudinal and normative determinants of behavioral intent. *Communication Monographs, 54,* 221-231.

Shepherd, G. J., & Condra, M. B. (1988). Anxiety, construct differentiation, and message production. *Central States Speech Journal, 39,* 177-189.

Swanson, D. L. (1981). A constructivist approach. In D. D. Nimmo & K. R. Sanders (Eds.), *Handbook of political communication* (pp. 169-191). Beverly Hills, CA: Sage.

Swanson, D. L., & Delia, J. G. (1976). *The nature of human communication.* Chicago: Social Research Associates.

Sypher, B. D., & Zorn, T. E. (1986). Communication-related abilities and upward mobility: A longitudinal investigation. *Human Communication Research, 12,* 420-431.

Sypher, H. E., & Applegate, J. L. (1982). Cognitive differentiation and verbal intelligence: Clarifying relationships. *Educational and Psychological Measurement, 42,* 437-543.

Sypher, H. E., & Applegate, J. L. (1984). Organizing communication behavior: The role of schemas and constructs. In R. N. Bostrom (Ed.), *Communication yearbook 8* (pp. 310-329). Beverly Hills, CA: Sage.

Wilson, S. R. (1990). Development and test of a cognitive rules model of interaction goals. *Communication Monographs, 57,* 81-103.

Wilson, S. R., Cruz, M. G., & Kang, K. H. (1992). Is it always a matter of perspective? Construct differentiation and variability in attributions about compliance gaining. *Communication Monographs, 59,* 350-367.

Wilson, S. R., & Kang, K. H. (1991). Communication and unfulfilled obligations: Individual differences in causal judgments. *Communication Research, 18,* 799-824.

Zimmerman, S., & Applegate, J. L. (1992). Person-centered comforting in the hospice interdisciplinary team. *Communication Research, 19,* 240-263.

Zorn, T. E. (1991). Construct system development, transformational leadership and leadership messages. *Southern Communication Journal, 56,* 178-193.

5 Language, Fallacies, and Mindlessness-Mindfulness in Social Interaction

JUDEE K. BURGOON
University of Arizona

ELLEN J. LANGER
Harvard University

Much communication research invokes the concept of mindlessness-mindfulness under various guises. *Mindlessness* refers to both chronic and state conditions in which individuals consider available information and alternatives incompletely, rigidly, reflexively, and thoughtlessly. To the extent that communicators behave mindlessly and mindlessness contributes to maladaptive physical, psychological, and behavioral states, it becomes useful to determine what triggers or reinforces mindless and/or mindful behavior. The position forwarded in this essay is that one neglected factor in understanding mindlessness-mindfulness is language, which by its very nature may encourage mindless or mindful behavior. Although it does not inherently demand misuse, routine language use, by virtue of its abstracting properties and reliance on identities and categorization, can create a false appearance of completeness, promote stimulus generalization rather than discrimination, encourage word-object confusions, and abet heuristic reasoning rather than ratiocination. By functioning to hold things still so that they may be considered, described, or discussed, language may contribute to a lack of awareness of mutability, variation, or creative use of what is described. Through semantic and syntactic constructions that mimic sound argumentative discourse, language may also structure responses and prompt fallacious reasoning. However, language may also mitigate mindlessness. Novel use of language and linguistic markers of conditionals, context, and multiple perspectives in everyday speech are among the mechanisms posited to engender more mindful thoughts and behavior.

IMPLICIT in theories of human communication and behavior are assumptions about how conscious, thoughtful, and rational people are. Work on cognitive planning and strategic communication has promulgated a view of social

AUTHORS' NOTE: We wish to thank Roger Brown, BenZion Chanowitz, Scott Jacobs, Michael Burgoon, Tim Barefield, and Renee Oatway for their helpful comments on this essay.

Correspondence and requests for reprints: Judee K. Burgoon, Department of Communication, University of Arizona, Tucson, AZ 85721.

Communication Yearbook 18, pp. 105-132

actors and observers as engaged in active cognition and deliberation (e.g., Berger, 1987; Hobbs & Evans, 1980; Lachman, Lachman, & Butterfield, 1979; Miller, Galanter, & Pribram, 1960; Seibold, Cantrill, & Meyers, 1985), that is, as typically "mindful." Yet much social interaction has also been characterized as reflexive and lacking forethought (e.g., Bargh, 1989; Bavelas & Coates, 1992; Kellermann, 1992; Langer, 1978a, 1989a, 1989b, 1992; Waldron, 1990), that is, as "mindless."[1] Some have gone so far as to claim that mindlessness is the default condition of social interaction. Given these alternative characterizations, it becomes useful to reexamine what is meant by *mindlessness-mindfulness* and to determine the circumstances under which people might become more or less mindful.

We believe a useful analysis of the antecedents of mindless and mindful states can be advanced by examining the role that communication itself, and specifically language, plays in the process. Our thesis is that routine language practices may promote or reinforce mindlessness both directly—through semantic, syntactic, and pragmatic relationships—and indirectly—through the cuing of fallacious reasoning. This is not to say that language inherently causes mindlessness. Indeed, we believe that certain language practices can just as easily instigate mindfulness, a prospect we take up at the conclusion of this essay. But we contend that ordinary language use often encourages mindlessness and that many of the so-called causes of mindlessness devolve to a matter of language. Moreover, we believe that the relationship is a reciprocal or nonrecursive one, in which certain kinds of language use beget mindlessness and mindlessness begets certain kinds of language use.

That language shapes thought and action may be considered a commonplace among communication scholars. As Hample (1992) argues quite cogently, even the way we write about mindlessness itself reflects and shapes our understanding of it and of related communication and cognitive processes. Yet much social cognition and cognitive processing work, by focusing on internal processes, overlooks the important role that social phenomena such as language play in instigating or reinforcing mindlessness. (As one indicator of this neglect, subject indexes in social cognition books typically have no key words related to language phenomena; see, e.g., Fiske & Taylor, 1991; Uleman & Bargh, 1989; Zebrowitz, 1990.) That people frequently fail to attend to, comprehend, access, and/or analyze much of the relevant information when making judgments or decisions is also well documented in the extensive research on cognitive schemata, expectancies, scripts, prototypes, stereotypes, and heuristics (see, e.g., Burgoon & Walther, 1990; Fiske & Taylor, 1991; Taylor & Crocker, 1981; Tversky & Kahneman, 1974), all of which facilitate selective (and often biased or error laden) information processing. Our contention is that such mental shortcuts can be triggered by fallacies in argumentative discourse. Yet the role of language as the external stimulus cuing these shortcuts has also been largely overlooked. Two purposes of this essay, then, are to analyze those features of mindlessness that are especially susceptible to the influence of language and to examine characteristics of language and fallacies that can be linked to mindlessness.

Another purpose is to consider how mindlessness can be inhibited or reversed through the same mechanisms of language. To the extent that mindless processing is controlled by language and reasoning capacities, it is likely to be deeply ingrained and thus resistant to change. Nevertheless, there appear to be a number of ways that language can be adapted and deployed to encourage more mindfulness. Our speculations have implications not only for circumstances that are likely to elicit more mindful processing but also for the development of intervention strategies that may engender more persistent mindfulness where advantageous.

THE NATURE OF MINDLESSNESS AND MINDFULNESS

Defining Characteristics

At the outset, it is important that we define mindlessness and distinguish it from other concepts, such as unconsciousness and automaticity, that are often erroneously treated as synonymous to it. Originally, mindlessness was defined as limited information processing, where the individual responds on the basis of a few general cues in the environment and is essentially oblivious to particular context cues that might suggest even an opposite course of action (Langer, 1978a, 1978b). By contrast, mindfulness was construed as thoughtful action and awareness, as active information processing characterized by differentiation (see Langer, Blank, & Chanowitz, 1978).

Subsequent treatments have modified and amplified the relevant features of mindlessness (Langer, 1989a, 1989c). Mindlessness entails *limited information processing, rigid categorical thinking, single perspectives,* and *failure to recognize context.* By failing to make use of information relevant to the situation or misreading such information, an individual behaves rigidly, like an automaton, unaware of alternative choices and interpretations. Inflexibility occurs by default rather than by design. When mindless, individuals unwittingly treat information in a single-minded way, that is, as *context-free.* Mindlessness holds the world still and prevents an awareness that things could be otherwise. It is behavior that is *rule governed* rather than *rule guided,* frozen rather than fluid. In this state of mind, individuals are caught in a single perspective focused on unconditional conceptualization. Conversely, when mindful, individuals actively construct their environments, draw distinctions, and create categories. Mindfulness is being sensitive to changes in context, to being situated in the present and thus being aware of (creating) multiple perspectives. This is what is meant by *active information processing*: the creation of categories and distinctions (Langer, 1989a, 1989c). It is the state of mind characterized as fluid, where conditional conceptualizations rather than absolutes dominate. Mindfulness is hypothesized to be both a state and a trait variable. It may be induced as a state and enhanced as a trait.

This characterization should make clear that mindlessness is not to be treated as isomorphic with all manner of automated or routinized communication. Normal discourse is typified by a fair degree of habituated but adaptive behavior requiring low levels of awareness. Such automated behavior, which falls somewhere between mindful and mindless (Bavelas & Coates, 1992), is not only cognitively efficient but also often essential to skilled performance and smooth interaction (see, e.g., Csikszentmihalyi, 1990; Sperber & Wilson, 1986). To the degree that such communicative activity is intentional, guided by goals and plans that reflect choice making and flexible thinking, it can be characterized as mindful. Thus what Bargh (1989) calls "goal-directed automaticity" and Kellermann (1992) refers to as "strategic automatic communication" may still entail mindfulness. Moreover, mindfulness need not be cognitively effortful once ingrained, and it may prevent the need for more effortful responses when novel stimuli present themselves (Langer, 1989b).[2] This distinction is important, because our later claims regarding deleterious consequences of mindlessness derive from the more narrow construal of it that we have offered here than from the popularized use of the term that includes all unconscious and automatic responding. We are concerned here with the kind of inflexible, reflexive, thoughtless activity that undermines rather than facilitates individual information processing and successful behavioral functioning.

Antecedents of Mindlessness-Mindfulness

The factors that have been identified as contributing to mindless or mindful behavior are several. As we shall see, many of those believed to cause mindlessness are thought processes that become manifested through, or fostered by, routine language use. That is, language may reflect mindless encoding and/or be the stimulus cuing mindless decoding.

One factor is *certainty*. Certainty breeds mindlessness (Langer, 1989a). Conviction in one's beliefs and actions minimizes the need to evaluate alternatives or to reflect on new information. As Abelson (1981) astutely observes, beliefs are treated like objects. As such, they should stay fixed and constant. To the extent that facts can be boiled down to truths or lies and behavioral options to choices between good and bad, there is little need for deliberation. Moreover, when people believe that context-free answers are possible, they become uncomfortable with their own uncertainty. Certainty means that the many ways the target information could be framed are reduced to a single way. Thus certainty encourages mindless action rather than conscious analysis and choice making.

A second cause of mindlessness is *dichotomization*. To take action and justify that action, one presumably needs clear choices. The need for action predicated on well-defined alternatives leads us to dichotomize. For instance, antonyms such as *good/bad, true/false, up/down,* and *black/white* illustrate the common tendency to think in terms of bipolar opposites. These dichotomous labels hide the underlying ambiguity and allow people to proceed straightforwardly: "Do it or don't do it"; "Come or go"; "Take it or leave it." It is almost inevitable that people with enough practice deciding on the basis of dichotomized data will fail to consider the information that falls in between the clear, concise categories. Dichotomization, then, can lead to mindlessness.

Overlearning and habitual responding also predispose one to the rigid use of information characteristic of mindlessness. In theory, one could engage in "repeated" behavior where each "repetition" was considered anew, noticing different aspects of the situation either with respect to the perception and labeling of the stimulus (stimuli) or in the selection of a response(s). In practice, few people recognize benefits accruing from such mindful consideration, and the overlearning that results from repeated exposure to what is taken to be the same given situation makes it possible to respond on subsequent occasions without processing much information or deliberating on a course of action. Habitual responding is often mindless responding.

In contrast to mindlessness that derives from repetition (the hallmark of both habitual responding and automatic processing), the rigid use of information also may come about on single exposure to information, producing *premature cognitive commitment* (Chanowitz & Langer, 1981). Single exposure to information results in mindlessness when it leads to uncritical acceptance of that information. This may occur when the information is given by an authority, is given authoritatively, obfuscates alternatives, or, in a psychodynamic sense, is egocentonic. When individuals are presented with information that they have no motivation to question, they may form a premature cognitive commitment to using that information in the predetermined way. Later, if creative (or simply other) use of that information is required, it will not occur to them to reconsider it. The information, in essence, exists only in the single, rigid form in which it was initially encoded. Although this commitment may have certain advantages, it often can limit novel future use of the information. Without flexibility in the future use of information, the potential value of the information is minimized because other possible uses or applications are not fully explored; alternative understandings of the information are not available even when such reconsideration could prevent decrements in performance. In a sense, when individuals initially process information mindlessly, they also make a premature cognitive commitment to that mode of processing in the future.

Because they occur on a single exposure to information, premature cognitive commitments help distinguish mindlessness from similar concepts such as habit, functional fixedness, and overlearning, all of which involve multiple exposures and are concerned primarily with responses rather than with the state of the organism. Habits and overlearning often result in mindlessness, and functional fixedness is a result of mindlessness.

Each of these tendencies—the pursuit of certainty, dichotomization, overlearning or habitual responding, and premature cognitive commitments—can lead to chronic mindlessness as well as follow from it in a mutually reciprocal and interactive fashion. The result is that people may believe they are engaged in thoughtful action but in reality are regularly following well-learned and general scripts. Beyond this traitlike mindless condition, various circumstances can trigger mindless or mindful states. Langer (1978b), in her original articulation of the nature of mindlessness, conjectured that mindlessness is pervasive but that people will become more thoughtful under the following conditions:

1. when encountering a novel situation (which, of course, has no script)
2. when engaging in scripted behavior becomes effortful (perhaps because the new situation demands more of the behavior than was demanded by the original script)
3. when enacting scripted behavior is interrupted by external factors that disrupt its completion
4. when experiencing a negative or positive consequence that is markedly discrepant from the consequences of prior enactments of the same behavior
5. when the situation does not allow for sufficient involvement

It follows, then, that mindlessness should be more common when situations are familiar and uninvolving, when little effort is required, when consequences are similar to previous ones, and when behavioral routines are not disrupted. These features parallel or presage other conditions that have been identified as ones likely to evoke limited cognitive elaboration, peripheral information processing, reliance on mental heuristics, and scripted behavior, all of which contribute to mindlessness. These include information complexity and overload, multiple goals, heavy cognitive demands imposed by speech production, heavy behavioral demands imposed by interaction management, inadequate or excessive environmental stimulation, stimulus familiarity, physical stress, fatigue, boredom, low motivation, low involvement or vested interest, and other forms of distraction (see, e.g., Buller, 1986; Burgoon, Buller, Dillman, & Walther, 1993; Cialdini, 1988; Crano, 1992; Gilbert, 1989; Kruglanski, 1989; Petty & Cacioppo, 1986; Schroder, Driver, & Struefert, 1967; Stiff, 1986; Waldron, 1990; Webster, in press).

Consequences of Mindlessness-Mindfulness

Research has demonstrated many psychological, physical, and behavioral consequences of being mindless or mindful. An overall summary of the work may be found in Langer (1989a, 1989b). Therefore, we make only brief mention of some beneficial properties of mindfulness (and by implication, the absence of these benefits when mindless) in order to suggest the breadth of implications for effective functioning. Psychologically, mindfulness has been found to increase memory (Langer & Imber, 1980; Langer, Rodin, Beck, Weinman, & Spitzer, 1979), perceptual performance (Chanowitz & Langer, 1981; Langer et al., 1990), positive affect (Alexander, Langer, Newman, Chandler, & Davies, 1989; Langer, Field,

Paches, & Abrams, 1989; Langer, Heffernan, & Keister, 1988), creativity (Langer & Piper, 1987), recovery from alcoholism (Langer, Perlmuter, Chanowitz, & Rubin, 1988; Margolis & Langer, 1991), and perceived control (Alexander et al., 1989). It has also been found to decrease self-induced dependence (Avorn & Langer, 1982; Langer & Imber, 1979) and prejudice (Langer, Bashner, & Chanowitz, 1985; Langer, Taylor, Fiske, & Chanowitz, 1976). The psychological consequences, then, are obviously wide-ranging.

The physical consequences found to date include decreased arthritis, increased SIGA (a measure of immunocompetence), and improved general health and longevity (Alexander et al., 1989; Langer, Beck, Janoff-Bulman, & Timko, 1984; Langer, Field, et al., 1989; Langer et al., 1990; Langer & Rodin, 1976; Rodin & Langer, 1977). As an illustration, in a recent experiment hospitalized patients suffering from rheumatoid arthritis, osteoarthritis, and hip fractures participated in a two-week (eight-session) mindfulness program (Langer, Field, et al., 1989). The high mindful group was told that research suggests keeping one's mind active is likely to be good for one's health. The low mindful group was told that research suggests keeping the mind focused on the familiar can prevent stress and accrue health benefits. Both groups were told that keeping their minds active (relatively inactive) might be difficult, so they were given specific things to think about during the researchers' visits and between the visits. The low mindful group was given common sayings, such as "A bird in the hand is worth two in the bush." To ensure novelty, for the high mindful group these sayings were inverted, for example, "A bird in the bush is worth two in the hand." Psychological and physical measures revealed a significant improvement for the high mindful group on the major measure of disease activity, lower erythrocyte sedimentation rate (a measure of joint inflammation); the high mindful group also became less stressed and happier. There was no improvement for the low mindful and no treatment groups. Research with animals also indirectly corroborates the conclusion that mindful activity is beneficial and the lack of it harmful, in showing that under repetitive conditioning, synapses die and are not replaced during the process (Fuchs, Montemayor, & Greenough, 1990).

Possible educational consequences are evident in early research by Chanowitz and Langer (1981), who found that when subjects were given information they seemingly had no reason to question, they made a premature cognitive commitment to it (i.e., they formed a single understanding of the information without considering alternatives). When subjects later needed an alternative use of that information, they were unable to provide it.

THE ROLE OF LANGUAGE
IN FOSTERING MINDLESSNESS

We now turn to a consideration of the role of language in instigating mindless behavior. It has long been hypothesized that language shapes thought. The

Sapir-Whorf hypothesis of linguistic relativity (Carroll, 1956; Sapir, 1921), for example, posits a reciprocal relationship between a culture's language and that culture's thoughts and behaviors: "Reality" is constructed upon the language habits of a given culture or group, and those language habits predispose it to certain interpretations. The result is that language habitually covaries with and constrains meaning and interpretive processes. As expressed by Whorf, "Thinking . . . follows a network of tracks laid down in the given language, an organization which may concentrate on certain phases of reality, certain aspects of intelligence, and may systematically discard others featured by other languages" (in Carroll, 1956, p. 256). Language does not determine thought, but it makes certain lines of thought more probable.

We recognize that the linguistic relativity hypothesis has not won unanimous endorsement. Contrary views about linguistic universality, coupled with current controversies about reality as a social construction created through the vehicle of language, pose challenges and qualifications to a deterministic view of language molding thought (see, e.g., Bates, Benigni, Bretherton, Camaioni, & Volterra, 1977; Clark & Clark, 1977; Shepard & Cooper, 1982; see also the 1992 forum in *Communication Theory* on social approaches to the study of communication). Nevertheless, the notion that language *is capable of* influencing and channeling thought remains largely uncontested. Moreover, empirical evidence confirms that labels and speech acts affect cognition (e.g., Lakoff, 1987), often through activating scripts (e.g., Abelson, 1981; Langer & Abelson, 1972, 1974; Schank & Abelson, 1977).

To analyze the relationship of language to mindlessness, we turn first to concepts originating in the general semantics movement of 50 years ago (Hayakawa, 1939, 1943; Johnson, 1946; Korzybski, 1941; Lee, 1941), concepts that have been revived in various psychotherapeutic contexts (e.g., Watzlawick, Beavin, & Jackson, 1967), in contemporary work on general semantics (e.g., Kellogg & Bourland, 1990), and most recently in cognitive psychology and information-processing work, although not under the same labels.

Language and Aristotelian Logic

According to Korzybski (1941), language syntax and semantics are modeled after Aristotelian logic. There are three principles to which Western logic adheres and that are reflected in our language system. The first is the *law of identity*: A is A. Whatever is on the left-hand side of the equation must form an identity with whatever is on the right-hand side: "Jane is a professor." Language routinely creates these definitional identities syntactically through the use of the *to be* verb (used as either a copulative or transitive verb). Children's first forays into language learning are predominantly centered on learning these identifying labels and descriptors: "This is a dog"; "That is hot." This principle leads people to equate the predicate descriptors with the object being described, that is, as forming an identity with it. The *to be* verb implies a state of permanence, such that the qualities attributed to the subject of the sentence are taken as stable and dispositional rather than transitory and situational. The law of identity obscures the fact that whereas "Jane is a professor," for example, from another perspective Jane may also be a student. Consider another example: "A bachelor is a person who is unmarried." Given this identity, how does one categorize a person who has been living in an intimate relationship with someone for 20 years or someone "married" who has been separated from a spouse for 20 years? The law of identity leads to "neat" classifications into which the real world does not so neatly fit.

The second principle is the *law of the excluded middle*: Everything is A or not A. Linguistically, this translates into creating mutually exclusive and collectively exhaustive categories, such as in versus out or up versus down. Among the earliest language concepts introduced to children are these basic oppositions. Even when gradations are to be represented, they are still typically created categorically, as in large, medium, and small. Categories provide the superordinate organizing structures for processing the particulars of our world. Although linguistic categorization in itself may be essential to the conduct of our daily lives, and the law of the excluded middle is *logically* true, these classifications encourage us to think in terms of nominal categories rather than dimensions or degrees. As such, they may pose *psychological* problems. The Tibetan Buddhists call this phenomenon the "Lord of Speech":

> We adopt sets of categories which serve as ways of managing phenomena. The most fully developed products of this tendency are ideologies, the systems of ideas that rationalize, justify and sanctify our lives. Nationalism, communism, existentialism, Christianity, Buddhism—all provide us with identities, rules of action, and interpretations of how and why things happen as they do. (Trungpa, 1973)

As in the above example, large groups of people may be separated into categories that underscore in-group/out-group differences even though members of the different groups share more properties in common than differences. Entire genres of social psychological research on social categorization, stereotyping, in-group/out-group relations, and minority/majority influence attest to the importance of this categorization process. The risk is that setting up discrete categories reifies assumptions about people and objects fitting into one and only one category, such as male/masculine or female/feminine, ignoring all the ways one may be both masculine and feminine (as Bem's, 1985, work on gender roles has confirmed and attempted to ameliorate, but by producing two new categories —androgynous and undifferentiated). Hermaphrodites, people who have the sex organs and many of the secondary sex characteristics of both male and female, or others who do not neatly fall into specific categories, become problematic in ways they otherwise would not. Although we may recognize that maleness and femaleness should be treated as points on a continuum rather than as discrete categories, standard language usage does not encourage that.

We wish to clarify that we view language as a tool, which does not inexorably force us to misuse it. Indeed, often we do not. Nevertheless, the way language is typically used may subtly lead people away from perceiving dimensionally. Language is not a blunt instrument, but often it is used as though it were.

The third principle is the *law of noncontradiction*: Something cannot be both A and not-A. If it is "easy," it cannot be "not-easy." If it is a wave, it cannot be a quantum. Many, if not most, apparent contradictions are not contradictions at all. For example, something can be simultaneously "easy" and "not-easy" as soon as we consider the difficulty of boredom. But our language masks the ambiguities that would make this evident by creating what seem to be clear, logically independent categories. Traits such as "consistent" and "inconsistent" on the surface appear completely incompatible until one equates "consistent" with "rigid," a quality that may not seem the opposite of "inconsistent." We know that psychologic is different from logic. Studies on dissonance (Festinger, 1964), for example, reveal that when these inconsistencies become apparent, there is motivation to remove them.

In short, we abide by language and logic for information-processing and communication shortcuts, but doing so may foster mindlessness, because the shortcuts gloss over the fact that much of what can be said, is not.

The Process of Abstracting

This "glossing" property can be understood as part of the process of abstracting: By its very nature, language represents a small sampling of reality. Just as a map represents only some features of the territory it covers, language represents only selective features of what it symbolizes. To the extent that people believe in the "allness" of language, they may be deluded into regarding it as a comprehensive mirror of reality.

Take, for example, the common object we call a "chair." The label as an abstraction for a collection of associated qualities—a four-legged piece of furniture on which we sit—leaves out an immense amount of detail—whether the object is large or small; wooden, upholstered, or wrought iron; new or old; expensive or inexpensive; for indoor or outdoor use; and so on. Even adding descriptors such as "an old, wooden rocking chair with arms" still omits a great deal of information. Semantically, then, language distills the massive amount of potential stimuli in our environment into increasingly abstract concepts that minimize differences and focus on commonalities. The result is incompleteness and stimulus generalization rather than stimulus discrimination. Moreover, as language moves away from the "fact" or description level, it becomes increasingly inferential, which further simplifies and focuses attention on only a few properties.

The problem may be exacerbated by the pragmatics of language (language-in-use, or connotations as separate from denotations), in that certain words and expressions come to be associated through repeated use with particular referents. So, for example, until recently the label *leader* was associated in most First

World countries with men. For many, *abortion* means "death for fetuses," whereas for others it connotes "privacy or personal autonomy for women."

A related problem is that although reality is in a constant state of flux, language in everyday usage fails to index these changes because it references static or constant features rather than variability and differentiation. The word *river* belies Heraclitus's injunction that you cannot step in the same river twice. Thus language can obscure dynamic processes, creating instead a sense of immutability and permanence. Nouns might be understood as the main "culprits" in perpetrating this sense of constancy, but a moment's reflection should make it evident that adjectives, adverbs, and verbs can be equally responsible. Consider these propositions: "Saving is good"; "Hard work pays"; "Traffic runs smoothly." The denotative and connotative meanings of *saving, good, hard, work, pays, runs,* and *smoothly* are readily subject to change across time and context, even though the terminology remains the same.

The lack of awareness of the abstracting feature of language, combined with the law of identity, leads people into word-object confusions: treating words as if they were the thing itself (see Abelson, 1981). This confusion between the word and the object is evident when people cringe at the word *snake* or become ill after being told that the peanut butter cookies they have eaten were made from grasshoppers. That words can become imbued with such potency as to elicit the same response as would be elicited by the referent itself is illustrated in Bailey and Dileo's (1990) work on language as magic. They found that many people could not bring themselves to utter expressions such as, "I hope that X [the person they love most] dies a terrible death next week," for fear that saying it aloud might actually bring tragedy to the loved one; many of those who did utter the expression reported feelings of guilt and anxiety. Similarly, "in *Chaplinski v. New Hampshire* (1942), the Supreme Court recognized a class of 'fighting words' that are considered too efficacious (too powerful) to receive First Amendment protection" (Bailey & Dileo, 1990, p. 20).

Avoiding the difficulties associated with the abstracting nature of language does not require that one mention all attributes, but merely that people, in principle, become more aware of what is not spoken. There are potentials of a chair, for example, that may go beyond any individualizing inventory of the attributes of a chair. Using a chair as a weapon or a fortress uses no property of the category or the individual case, but rather awareness of properties that do not belong to the definition of chairs either in a strict or fuzzy way. Use of a chair as a weapon depends on its weight and heftability; use of a chair as a fortress depends on its impermeability.

Mindfulness and mindlessness (which may be viewed as points on a continuum or discrete categories, with relative advantages and disadvantages to each view), then, are not isomorphic with concrete and abstract (which, of course, also may be viewed as continuous or discrete). Indeed, abstractness can lead to mindfulness, and concrete examples that are treated as more representative than they truly are may lead to mindless overlooking of other relevant examples. But because a major function of language is abstraction, it is always less than the thing it is describing. If this "deceitful" character of language is not recognized, then language may foster mindlessness.

Links to Mindlessness

General semanticists have identified a number of practical consequences of these properties of language, all of which parallel the characteristics of mindlessness and can be seen as precursors of it.

First, although language can be a vehicle for differentiation, by emphasizing similarities rather than differences it readily promotes stereotyping and disregard for differentiating information that might warrant a new response. The apparent familiarity that language breeds by labeling disparate situations in the same way begets an automated response because one has "seen it all before." Consider: How different is fear of a bear from the fear of being betrayed? By labeling both experiences with the same umbrella term, *fear,* we may miss a good deal of information about emotions. As another example, consider the label *alcoholics.* Used to describe a large number of individuals with highly varying attributes, the single label encourages viewing all alcoholics as alike, such that all the attributes associated with one can be projected onto another through the identity principle (commonly addressed under the rubric of expectancy or halo effects). Thus stereotyping can be understood in part as a mindless response to language that fails to index the distinguishing features of members of the stereotyped category.

One investigation tried to reverse this process (Langer et al., 1985). Children were invited to a picnic where, for different activities, they had to select partners. Children who had been given mindfulness training, which essentially consisted of noting the many ways they were similar to and different from various target people, selected as partners differently abled children when that could be advantageous (e.g., a blind child as a partner to play pin the tail on the donkey). Children in the control groups, on the other hand, systematically avoided "disabled" children to their own disadvantage.

Second, by emphasizing constancy rather than change, language may encourage fixed responses and frozen evaluations. The existence of parking spaces for the "handicapped" obscures the variability in how disabled or abled an individual is at any particular moment. The "disabled" individual may feel well enough today to make the walk, and the "abled" individual with a brand-new broken leg may not. In the former case, the label may encourage mindless acceptance of the disability rather than recognition that one's state of health or ability changes. Similarly, Ruesch (1951) offers an example of mindlessly frozen evaluation in a teacher's observation that "Johnny is a liar." Even though the statement may have originated as a description of a single incident, the language places Johnny in a particular class of individuals and so comes to represent a generalization about Johnny's past and future proclivities. The surface structure of the language not only transforms the description from a situational to a dispositional one, but, by leaving out other relevant information about Johnny's previous or future character and behavior, gives the appearance of being a summary statement. Johnny may now be seen as a chronic liar and reactions to him based accordingly. The tendency of certain language choices to foster dispositional rather than situational attributions for behavior encourages mindlessness. In the same way, social scientists may overlook novel aspects of topics they study once they accept prior labels for the phenomena.

Third, the similarities and constancies of language, coupled with the law of the excluded middle and the law of noncontradiction, produce the rigidity associated with mindlessness rather than the adaptability associated with mindfulness. The language activates schematic thinking and people become trapped by categories: "Mindlessness sets in when we rely too heavily on categories and distinctions created in the past (masculine/feminine, old/young, success/failure). Once distinctions are created, they take on a life of their own" (Langer, 1989a, p. 11).

Rigidly adhering to preexisting categories rather than modifying them in light of new information or creating new categories leads to routinization of behavior. Even though contemporary Japan is markedly different in its relations with the United States than it was during World War II, many Westerners remain suspicious of anyone or anything Japanese; their reactions are enmeshed in old understandings, old categories. Because the label has not changed, neither has their thinking.

Such categorical thinking also results in problem solvers' inability to overcome "functional fixedness" (Duncker, 1945). Work by Langer and Piper (1987) clearly demonstrates this. Students were taught the names of items either absolutely or conditionally; for example, some were shown an item and told, "This is a dog's chew toy," whereas those in the conditional group were told, "This could be a dog's chew toy." Subsequently, when an eraser was needed, 40% of those in the conditional group thought to use the dog's chew toy in a novel way, as an eraser, whereas none of those in the other group did. A second study requiring another novel use determined if subjects were responding to uncertainty or conditionality. If it were the former, then there should be no advantage for conditional instruction with respect to the second use because the first use would have cleared up the uncertainty. So, for example, if the target were now considered an eraser, there would be no uncertainty regarding that use but no advantage over the "dog's chew toy" for some third altogether different use. If it were tagged as conditional, on the other hand, then it would still be conditional even after the first creative use. Conditionally taught subjects were able to generate a second novel use for the object in question.

In a similar study, students were taught a more complex lesson in one of three ways: The language of the lesson was (a) conditional, (b) absolute, or (c) conditional in form and absolute in content (Langer, Hatem, Joss, & Howell, 1989). The last group was taught about a *theory* of neighborhood evolution as one possible model for viewing neighborhood growth, in *absolute* language. After learning the lesson, students were asked to list the stages of neighborhood development they learned, to verify the assumption that all groups took in the same information. Next they were given descriptions of two neighborhoods, one that clearly fit the scheme and one that did not, and asked to outline the evolution of the neighborhoods. Students responded mindlessly when taught absolutely even when the absolute language described a model that by definition is conditional. That is, they used the neighborhood structure they learned even when it was inappropriate. The conditional group did not. When the information did not fit into the given scheme, the mindful group created a new one.

It should be noted that it is not language per se that produces categorical and rigid thinking, but particular types of language use. In fact, labeling can prompt more rather than less creative thinking. Using the classic functional fixedness problem, in which people given a box of tacks, a candle, and some matches must figure out how to attach the lighted candle to the wall so that the candle will not drip (see Duncker, 1945), Glucksberg and Weisberg (1966) conducted an experiment in which the box, candle, tacks, and matches were either labeled or not labeled. Ironically, it was those subjects who had the box and tacks labeled separately who were able to solve the problem most rapidly—by using the box as a candle holder. The subjects who were not given labels tended to see the box only as a receptacle for the tacks. If we infer that the latter subjects tacitly labeled it "a box of tacks," then the experiment exemplifies how language can either promote or inhibit novel thinking and problem solving.

Fourth, confusing words with their referents leads to the kind of automatic, nondeliberative behavior that often characterizes mindlessness (Chanowitz & Langer, 1980). This is what has been described as engaging in a signal rather than a symbol response (Johnson, 1946; Mead, 1934). The word-object associations are so strong that the word is able to invoke reflexively the responses associated with the object. For a political liberal, for example, labeling a proposal as "conservative" may be sufficient to cause the individual to dismiss it automatically rather than to weigh its merits. Labeling a prospective employee as "lighthearted" and "spontaneous" may prompt positive evaluations; labeling the same person as "silly" and "impulsive" may trigger negative ones that close off further consideration. These kinds of "hair-trigger" reactions contravene careful ratiocination in which words are recognized as symbols and the meanings behind the symbols are potential targets of analysis.

The syntax of language may likewise produce automatic mindless responding. Adjacency pairs in conversation, such as question/answer, are one mechanism whereby language can structure responses. The typical pattern is to follow a question with an answer, in which case any superficially plausible declarative statement may satisfy structural conversational requirements (see Grice's, 1975, maxims, e.g., "Be informative") and hence escape careful scrutiny. In one study, subjects were approached when about to use a copying machine and were asked if the experimenter could use it first (Langer et al., 1978). Subjects were asked (a) "May I use the Xerox machine"; (b) "May I use the Xerox machine because

I need copies"; or (c) "May I use the Xerox machine because I am in a rush." The first two requests say the same thing; each of the last two includes a reason for the request. If subjects are considering the information and not just moved by the structure, then the first two requests should be responded to similarly. They were not. Subjects may have listened to the request, but they did not think about it. That is to say, they did not consider anything about the information, but instead mindlessly complied with the request that included the bogus "reason." In a second study in that series, secretaries were sent a memo that simply asked them to return the memo. It said nothing else. Unless the memo was structured in an unfamiliar way, almost all of the secretaries seemingly unquestioningly complied with the request and returned the memo. (In another study, physicians behaved similarly.)

Other research demonstrates the same kind of mindless response to the way language is structured. In a study by Newman (1982), subjects witnessed a conversation that for half of them actually consisted of parallel monologues written by two individuals to tell each individual's story in whole. For half of each group, the pauses between statements were long; for the other half they were not. Results suggested that all that mattered in the judging of the quality of the conversation was the timing of the words spoken. Statements were not examined, so the fact that it was a noninteractive monologue instead of a true dialogue did not matter. Similarly, in studies by Langer and Abelson (1972), subjects all heard the same request for help, but the order of the words varied. Behavior depended on when the words were heard rather than what the words meant (see Bruner & Potter, 1963). As soon as people believed they had heard a message, they stopped listening.

Fifth, owing to the process of abstracting, much language-in-use operates at the level of inference rather than fact. Higher-order linguistic abstractions elicit corresponding cognitive schemata, scripts, expectancies, prototypes, and stereo-types that govern thought and behavior. Although use of scripts and schemata are doubtless essential to efficient information processing and routine behav-ioral functioning, scripted or schema-driven behavior may be mindless, causing the individual to ignore or discount concrete data. In a provocative experiment, von Hippel (1990) showed that schematic processing (which involves taking in semantic abstractions) facilitates cognitive or inferential processing but hinders encoding of instances, or data-driven memory. His research revealed that the process of abstraction leads us to "lose" the specific data. Other research demon-strates the strong persistence of expectancies even in the face of disconfirming evidence (see, e.g., Snyder, 1984; Snyder & Swann, 1978). For example, in an experiment in which perceivers were induced to hold preinteraction expectan-cies about a target through favorable or unfavorable verbal descriptions, Burgoon and Le Poire (1993) found a strong proclivity for people to cling to those descriptions even though the target's actual subsequent behavior contradicted the expectancies in half the cases.

Finally, language in its abstracted form regularly masks personalization. Instead of saying, "Stars look white to me," a child says, "Stars are white." What begins as personal opinion, observation, or inference becomes "fact" because of the omission of any personalization "tags." Such "facts" do not invite further discussion or scrutiny.

MINDLESSNESS AND FALLACIOUS REASONING

So far, we have considered the ways in which the properties of language and language-in-everyday-use can elicit mindlessness. Another way to examine language's role in mindlessness is to view it as the external stimulus that prompts fallacious reasoning. By mimicking the semantics and syntax of valid arguments, language in the form of discursive argument fallacies can short-circuit the thought process. Fallacies give the appearance of valid inference and reasoning while actually oversimplifying or relying on false premises that are nevertheless widely accepted (see, e.g., Nolt & Rohatyn, 1988; Toulmin, Rieke, & Janik, 1984). Many of the mental shortcuts described as heuristics operate on the same principles (see Tversky & Kahneman, 1974); it is the connection between language and the activation of such heuristics that has been overlooked. That such faulty reasoning is pervasive is evident from a recent investigation that found only 33% of respondents were able to detect faulty sign reasoning and only 13% were able to recognize faulty causal reasoning (Mineo, 1991). Although fallacious reasoning may at times paradoxically lead to "right" answers and may be viewed as cognitively efficient, our point is that mindless language use can also result in inadequate or inappropriate use of information.

Faulty reasoning can arise from language encouraging us to attend to larger, abstract categories rather than the specific data that would disabuse us of our faulty intuitions. It can also result from linguistic structure itself. Illustrative of this point is one experiment on mindlessness-mindfulness described earlier. Langer et al. (1978) hypothesized that mindless behavior occurs unless the transmitted message is structurally (rather than semantically) novel and the interaction between the participants requires an effortful response: "With repeated exposure [to an activity] and emerging structure, the person pays less and less attention to the semantics of the activity. . . . If the structure of the situation is novel, the indications are that this activity is not representative of earlier occurrences of this activity. The novel structure indicates a novel semantics" (p. 47). This experiment showed that when a request involved minimal effort (making five Xerox copies), people complied, even when given a meaningless reason, to the same extent that they complied when a legitimate reason was given. The authors argue that the mindless compliance was the result of subjects' invoking a script: favor X + reason Y leads to compliance. Cast in communication terms, the syntax of the request mimicked a legitimate one, thereby producing the same kind of response: "If the *structure* is congruent with the earlier encounter with the activity, the individual assumes the *semantics* are congruent with the earlier encounters and will consequently process a minimal amount of the information available" (p. 52). True to the hypothesis, when the request required greater effort on the part of subjects, and presumably shifted them into a more mindful response mode, they were less likely to comply with the placebic (or uninformative) request.

Consider some sample forms of argumentative fallacies that may trigger heuristic processing. *Missing grounds (petitio principii,* or begging the question) fallacies are statements that structurally look like a claim plus evidence, but the evidence is actually reassertion. Because the last part of the request "May I use the Xerox machine because I need to make copies" masquerades as a reason, people politely comply. This form of fallacy works especially well in connection with preexisting predispositions to behave in certain ways, in this case, with polite deference to the request (see Brown & Levinson, 1987).

Fallacies entailing *irrelevant grounds* are non sequiturs—such as straw man arguments; *ad hominem* attacks; bandwagon appeals *(ad populem)*, appeals to authority, pity, ignorance, or force *(argumentum ad verecundiam, ad misericordiam, ad ignorantiam, ad baculum)*; guilt by association; and red herrings—that employ premises that have no bearing on the conclusion (Nolt & Rohatyn, 1988). Many of Cialdini's (1988) categories of effective influence appeals—liking, authority, scarcity, and social proof—depend on invocation of irrelevant grounds. For example, use of authority appeals such as "This [next] question has to do with an important research project at _ University" in compliance-gaining studies has succeeded in keeping desk clerks on hold during telephone calls (see Burger, 1986; Brock, 1992). Similarly, Gilovitch (1981) found that an individual given an award that had the *name* of a more famous individual was rated more highly than one whose award bore the name of a less well known individual.

A third class of fallacies relies on *defective grounds.* These include inductive fallacies such as hasty generalizations (often based on inadequate, atypical, or biased samples), premature instance reification, and false dichotomies. Hasty generalizations are what cognitive scientists call insensitivity to sample size. They are also what is responsible for premature cognitive commitments. Faulty premises likewise explain such phenomena as the just world hypothesis ("People get what they deserve") (Lerner & Miller, 1978) and use of a representativeness heuristic in lieu of actual probability or sample size information ("Similarity evidence is more relevant than other evidence") (Kahneman, Slovic, & Tversky, 1982). False dichotomies produce the "trapped in categories" problem. This is well illustrated by such distinctions as central versus peripheral information processing, top-down versus bottom-up processing, and logic versus emotion. Even those who argue that both can be operative (e.g., that there is parallel processing) are still seeing the situation as a case of categories, not of degrees.

A fourth relevant category includes *semantic fallacies,* which introduce multiple meanings or vagueness through ambiguity, equivocation, amphiboly, figures of speech, doublespeak, loaded words, and structured responses. An example of the last of these is an argument in which the framing of successive questions makes only one choice in each juncture along a decision tree seem reasonable or plausible: "We either have to use up our natural resources, like coal, or develop nuclear energy; and given that nuclear energy is "cleaner" than coal, it is the only way to go." (The first decision point leaves out other alternatives—conservation, windmills, and so on—and the second decision point focuses on only one criterion for choosing among alternatives, rather than recognizing other factors such as safety or cost.) In such a case, the sequencing of language encourages the listener to avoid careful analysis and deliberation. Other semantic fallacies may invite mindless acceptance because of ambiguity associated with how words are used, as illustrated by this fallacy from Nolt and Rohatyn (1988): "It is silly to fight over mere words; Apartheid is just a word; therefore, it is silly to fight over apartheid" (p. 175). In this instance, "apartheid" is being used to refer to both the practice and the label for the practice, thereby allowing the meaning to shift during the argument and to give the appearance of validity. Similar examples can be found in Higginbotham (1990), some of which are the result of language falsely creating the appearance of strict identity between two nonidentical objects.

These illustrative classes of fallacies, which by no means exhaust all the possibilities, are meant to show how these problematic thought processes can be instigated by the language used; that is, language is the immediately proximal factor eliciting such mindlessness. Thus, whereas cognitive scientists might point to cognitive economy as the reason people engage in such mindlessness, communication scholars might point to the discourse itself as also playing a crucial role.

ACHIEVING MINDFULNESS THROUGH LANGUAGE

The foregoing illustrations, which by no means exhaust all the possible fallacies, are meant to show how language, through its semantics, pragmatics, and syntactic arrangements, can beget mindless information processing and behavior. Of course, mindlessness can be partly ameliorated through the reorientation of thinking processes themselves, so that individuals view the world dimensionally rather than categorically, multidimensionally rather than unidimensionally, and as dynamic rather than constant—essentially taking a more cognitively complex stance toward information processing. Mindlessness can also be partly attenuated by routine awareness of the polysemic, connotative, and context-bound nature of language—something that is frequently taught in basic communication courses.

The language-behavior connections are so well ingrained, however, that disrupting them often requires novel and marked changes in stimulus conditions, context, or language use itself before individuals will shift to more mindful states. It will be recalled that two of the conditions that are postulated to heighten mindfulness are novel situations and unexpectedly positive or negative consequences for a given behavior. These match tenets of expectancy violations theory (Burgoon, 1978, 1993), which posits that novel stimuli and violations of communication expectations heighten awareness of the violative act, and the valence assigned to it (positive or negative) influences information processing, decision making, and behavior (see Burgoon & Le Poire, 1993; Burgoon & Walther, 1990; Langer & Imber, 1980). Thus unexpected communication behavior and strongly valenced consequences should cause a shift from mindlessness to greater mindfulness. For example, using familiar expressions in a novel way (e.g., "Gentlemen and ladies") and following a question with a question are atypical conversational moves that, by calling attention to themselves, may encourage more mindful processing of what is said. Engaging in positively or negatively valued communicative acts may likewise draw greater attention to their meanings. (Of course, there are occasions when such violations may produce unwanted mindfulness, as when one is attempting to persuade another and wishes unquestioning acceptance.)

Other linguistic devices and tactics can also promote mindfulness. We close by considering a sampling of these. First, the preceding arguments imply that more mindfulness can accrue if there is a shift from discrete category descriptors to continua, so as to reduce false dichotomization and polarization. Continua can be denoted through the use of hyphens (e.g., warm-cold) (see Johnson, 1946) or through explicit reference to given continua. Merely moving from dichotomies to continua, however, may still cause people to think of something as an A or a B or a C (i.e., on the A, B, C continuum) and does not allow for something to be both A and B (e.g., work and play). This may be overcome through the use of composite descriptors (e.g., "serious but playful," "biopsychosocial").

Second, an alternative that may remind language users of its incompleteness or the potential for multiple completions and that follows most directly from research is increased conditionalism. Changing language explicitly to reflect conditionality through the use of qualifying expressions such as "could be," "perhaps," "it would seem," "from one perspective," "considering this point of view," and "I believe" immediately signals the listener that there are alternative "readings."

Third, mindfulness should be heightened by the inclusion of context in everyday speech, whether context is denoted by space or time qualifiers. Moving from facts or certainties that seemed context-free to an awareness of their context dependence may be accomplished by the inclusion of the relevant context explicitly in the speech act (e.g., stating that something is "from the male point of view" or "as understood by Eurocentric cultures" or "at this time in history"). This may transform "facts" into "inferences." Explicit identification of context may also unfreeze orientations toward unidimensionality and constancy to multidimensionality and change. Although it can be cumbersome to add the specificity that reference to context entails, much of the same effect may be achieved with the addition of quotation marks, as illustrated above (noting to ourselves that in an important way "all" language should be in quotes).

Fourth, a further linguistic tactic that acknowledges context dependency is a shift from evaluative and connotative to descriptive and denotative language. If we start with the assumption that evaluation is context dependent, such that what is good within one frame of reference may be bad or neutral within another, then use of descriptive rather than evaluative language may reduce lapses into mindless acceptance of the evaluative connotations attached to references in one context that are inapplicable in others. The shift from asking, "Is estrogen good or bad?" to "In which sorts of circumstances are the effects of estrogen positive and in which sorts are they negative?" can be seen as moving to a more descriptive, lower level of abstraction. Instead of "I made a horrible mistake today," one could say, "I put detergent in the dishwasher and it overflowed all over the kitchen floor." This view recognizes that it may have been a mistake from one perspective but, whether intended or not, the floor may be cleaner as a result.

Fifth, language may promote greater mindfulness as it moves from aggregation to individuation (from similarities to differences). The language already marks the difference between "the" and "this" or "that." Recognizing that "this" flower, for example, is different from "the" flower directs our attention to the particularities of the flower. It suggests that previous knowledge about flowers is not enough to understand "this" flower. To understand why the target is this flower one must look at it in the present. In the early years of education at home and in school, emphasis is on generalization within class and discrimination between classes. Through the contrasting of within and between, elements within a class come to be taken as more similar than not. Simply adding an additional instruction to find differences between things thought similar and similarities between things thought different should encourage mindfulness.

Sixth, another linguistic maneuver that may reduce mindlessness and heighten attentiveness to multiple perspectives is reduced use of anaphoric expressions, replacing "this," "that," and "it" with the thoughts to which they refer. The idea of reducing anaphora by increasing specificity suggests consideration of the larger relationship between specificity and mindfulness and mindlessness. Without an awareness of multiple perspectives, there is little need to mark speech. A hallmark of the presumption of one shared perspective is the use of anaphoric expressions. It would not be important to state the referent of a communication if there were only one possible referent or if everyone knew which one of many is under consideration. Given the implicit presumption of multiple perspectives, explicitly stating the referent would clarify the target perspective and open discussion to the possibility of disagreement.

The relationship between specificity and mindfulness is complex. If the communication is too specific, it may not lead the listener to generalize; if it is too abstract, it may lead the speaker to overgeneralize or not to know what an appropriate response is. Consider a request for help with varying degrees of specificity.

The more specific the request, the more likely there will be compliance. But Langer (1989a) describes a study that shows the downside of this strategy. A person purporting to have a sprained ankle asked subjects to request assistance from a pharmacist. When the victim asked specifically for an Ace bandage and the pharmacist had previously agreed to say that he had none, not one subject thought to ask for an alternative for the victim. Thus specificity may overdirect behavior. The lack of specificity, as we have said, may likewise obscure alternative perspectives. Who is speaking and for whom the message is intended may be an appropriate moderate level of specificity that limits these costs and the cost of mindlessness. For example, consider "Smoking is hazardous to your health" versus "The surgeon general believes smoking is hazardous to the health of those with many years of living in them." The latter message suggests that old people and people with diseases such as AIDS who find smoking rewarding perhaps should not be encouraged to resist their temptation mindlessly. To say the "U.S. surgeon general" is even more specific and as such suggests that experts in other countries may disagree, giving people more food for thought and more control over their own behavior.

On the other hand, the above degree of specificity may lead some mindlessly to assume the opposite of the intended communication rather than mindfully question the alternative understandings of the information. Research is needed to discern the parameters of the trade-off between specificity and mindlessness. Along these lines, one may compare less specific languages with those that are more specific. For example, Japanese is less specific than English in many ways (see, e.g., Ting-Toomey, 1989). There is no singular/plural distinction for most nouns, no count/mass distinction, and the ubiquitous politeness system further drives the language away from the specific and direct to the ambiguous and indirect. Japanese speakers, however, are not thought to view the overt message passed through the verbal communication as possessing the degree of importance English speakers accord it. For them, the words are not the important thing and are treated accordingly.

Seventh, mindfulness might also be increased through the intentional switching of levels of analysis. Intentionally becoming more abstract and broader or reversing the direction helps to put remarks in a context by suggesting alternative contexts. Metaphor is designed to do just this—the more novel, the more thought-provoking.

There are many other devices one may use to increase mindfulness, such as avoidance of allness terms or absolutisms (*all, none, never, everybody,* and the like; see Read, 1985), use of multiple descriptors (e.g., "One of the properties of this is . . . "), and use of plurals ("The good things about this are . . . " instead of "The good thing about this is . . . "). Some have even proposed eradicating the verb *to be* from our language, because it tends to promote dispositional attributions, and replacing it with something called E-Prime (e.g., Bourland, 1965-1966; Kellogg, 1987; Kellogg & Bourland, 1990; Korzybski, 1941). Some of these suggestions are more practical than others. Regardless of their feasibility, the larger point is that language practices may also enable mindfulness.

This sampling of linguistic practices that can stimulate mindfulness is not meant to suggest that only language can accomplish such changes. As we have already alluded to, thought processes themselves, which are the basis for chronic mindlessness-mindfulness, can be altered through educational practices. And various situational factors, such as motivation, stress, cognitive load, novelty, and strong affect, can influence degree of state mindlessness-mindfulness. We also do not mean to imply that language changes alone will always succeed in stimulating mindfulness. Obviously, "politically correct" language and euphemisms are insufficient to overcome deep-seated prejudices; consumers recognize that proposed "price adjustments" are price increases, regardless of what they are called. Still, the strong social pressures to use "appropriate," value-neutral, or affirming language are testament to a fundamental faith in language's ability to shape beliefs.

Before closing, we wish to acknowledge that increased "mindful" language use may have some sociopolitical ramifications. If language use tends to obscure context and perspective, as we have argued it does, then exposing perspective may have the effect of changing the status quo and, as such, may meet with resistance. What were taken as unqualified truths may now come up for questioning. In a recent article, Erev, Wallsten, and Neal (1991) contend that vagueness may be useful to a society where resources are limited. That way, the path to those resources would be found by only a few, and certain problems of doling out those resources would be avoided. These researchers are saying that specificity will lead all to the same path. Their conclusion is at first glance the same as ours: Specificity may lead people to recognize options they now do not notice. Our views differ in that we see advantages to increasing options for more people, one result of which can be the voicing of alternative viewpoints and creative problem solving. Thus contextualizing may lead to power equalization.

Teaching our children to act like scientists by operationalizing their communications may train them to see how conditional their assumptions really are. Language supports and teaches the norms of the culture. Currently, conditionalizing speech is often tantamount to weakness; it is equated with powerless speech (Bradac, 1992; Liska, 1992; O'Barr & Atkins, 1980). It is not surprising, then, that in a culture where women are seen as less powerful, it is they who are more likely to qualify their speech with hedges, disclaimers, hyperformality, tag questions, and the like. Children start off in most families as less powerful members and, if this reasoning is correct, they learn early on to accept what is said by those in positions of authority rather than to notice alternative views and engage in friendly questioning. Multiple perspectives set the stage for uncertainty. Progress may come, then, through a healthier respect for uncertainty and a resultant severing of the link between conditional (uncertain or qualified) language and power. Until that time, social barriers inhibit this route to increased mindfulness.

CONCLUSION

Our purposes in this essay have been to clarify the nature of mindlessness-mindfulness and to examine it through a communication lens. In contrast to the emphasis on mental constructs and heuristics so popular in some social and cognitive psychology circles, we have attempted to call attention to the ways in which the communication process itself—through routine language use and use of fallacious arguments that masquerade as rational discourse—promotes uncritical, automatic thought and behavior patterns. At the same time, we have speculated on the ways in which these mindless processes could be impeded or reversed through language. Our goal has been not only to offer a counterpoint to what may be a misplaced emphasis on mentalisms and a neglect of communicative phenomena in inducing various thought processes and behavioral patterns, but also to propose greater attention to the interventionist role that communication mechanisms might play. Because we are convinced that mindlessness is often counterproductive, our arguments at time may sound like social commentary. For that we make no apologies. Social science redeems itself with its critics to the extent that it contributes to the social good by unmasking dysfunctional actions and proffering communicative routes to greater personal and societal efficacy. This essay is a modest offering toward that end.

NOTES

1. It should be noted that the construct of mindlessness-mindfulness is not fully embraced by all (see, for example, Benoit & Benoit, 1986). However, the plethora of literature explicitly on mindlessness-mindfulness, as well as the frequent use of the concept in discussions of communication processes (see, for example, "Chautauqua," 1992; Nofsinger, 1986), warrants, in our estimation, a closer examination of the construct.

2. The misconceptions about the disadvantages of mindfulness and the advantages of mindlessness are discussed in detail in Langer (1989b).

REFERENCES

Abelson, R. (1981). Psychological status of the script concept. *American Psychologist, 36,* 715-729.

Alexander, C., Langer, E., Newman, R., Chandler, H., & Davies, J. (1989). Aging, mindfulness and meditation. *Journal of Personality and Social Psychology, 57,* 950-964.

Avorn, J., & Langer, E. (1982). Induced disability in nursing home patients: A controlled trial. *Journal of the American Geriatric Society, 30,* 397-400.

Bailey, W., & Dileo, D. (1990). *Magic, magical behavior, and communication.* Unpublished manuscript, University of Arizona, Department of Communication.

Bargh, J. A. (1989). Conditional automaticity: Varieties of automatic influence in social perception and cognition. In J. S. Uleman & J. A. Bargh (Eds.), *Unintended thought* (pp. 3-51). New York: Guilford.

Bates, E., Benigni, L., Bretherton, I., Camaioni, L., & Volterra, V. (1977). From gesture to the first word: On cognitive and social prerequisites. In M. Lewis & L. Rosenblum (Eds.), *Interaction, conversation, and the development of language* (pp. 247-307). New York: John Wiley.

Bavelas, J. B., & Coates, L. (1992). How do we account for the mindfulness of face-to-face dialogue? *Communication Monographs, 59,* 301-305.

Bem, S. L. (1985). Androgyny and gender schema theory: A conceptual and empirical integration. In T. B. Sonderegger (Ed.), *Nebraska Symposium on Motivation 1984: Psychology and gender* (pp. 179-226). Lincoln: University of Nebraska Press.

Benoit, P. J., & Benoit, W. L. (1986). Consciousness: The mindlessness/mindfulness and verbal report controversies. *Western Journal of Speech Communication, 50,* 41-63.

Berger, C. R. (1987). Planning and scheming: Strategies for initiating relationships. In R. Burnett, P. McGhee, & D. Clarke (Eds.), *Accounting for relationships: Social representations of interpersonal links* (pp. 158-174). London: Methuen.

Bourland, D. D., Jr. (1965-1966). A linguistic note: Writing in E-Prime. *General Semantics Bulletin, 32-33,* 11-114.

Bradac, J. J. (1992). Thoughts about floors not eaten, lungs ripped, and breathless dogs: Issues in language and dominance. In S. A. Deetz (Ed.), *Communication yearbook 15* (pp. 457-468). Newbury Park, CA: Sage.

Brock, T. C. (1992, February). *Relative efficacy of influence tactics.* Colloquium presented at the University of Arizona, Department of Communication.

Brown, P., & Levinson, S. C. (1987). *Politeness: Some universals in language usage.* London: Cambridge University Press.

Bruner, J., & Potter, M. C. (1963). Interference in visual recognition. *Science, 144,* 3617, 424-425.

Buller, D. B. (1986). Distraction during persuasive communication: A meta-analytic review. *Communication Monographs, 53,* 91-114.

Burger, J. M. (1986). Increasing compliance by improving the deal: The that's-not-all technique. *Journal of Personality and Social Psychology, 51,* 277-283.

Burgoon, J. K. (1978). A communication model of personal space violations: Explication and an initial test. *Human Communication Research, 4,* 129-142.

Burgoon, J. K. (1993). Interpersonal expectations, expectancy violations, and emotional communication. *Journal of Language and Social Psychology, 12,* 13-21.

Burgoon, J. K., Buller, D. B., Dillman, L., & Walther, J. (1993). *Interpersonal deception: III. Effects of suspicion on perceived communication and nonverbal behavior dynamics.* Manuscript submitted for publication.

Burgoon, J. K., & Le Poire, B. A. (1993). Effects of communication expectancies, actual communication, and expectancy disconfirmation on evaluations of communicators and their communication behavior. *Human Communication Research, 20,* 75-107.

Burgoon, J. K., & Walther, J. B. (1990). Nonverbal expectancies and the evaluative consequences of violations. *Human Communication Research, 17,* 232-265.

Carroll, J. B. (Ed.). (1956). *Language, thought, and reality: Selected writings of Benjamin Lee Whorf.* New York: John Wiley.

Chanowitz, B., & Langer, E. (1980). Knowing more (or less) than you can show: Understanding control through the mindlessness/mindfulness distinction. In M. E. P. Seligman & J. Garger (Eds.), *Human helplessness* (pp. 97-130). New York: Academic Press.

Chanowitz, B., & Langer, E. (1981). Premature cognitive commitment. *Journal of Personality and Social Psychology, 41,* 1051-1063.

Chautauqua: Mindlessness-mindfulness and communication [Special section]. (1992). *Communication Monographs, 59*(3).

Cialdini, R. B. (1988). *Influence: Science and practice.* Glenview, IL: Scott, Foresman.

Clark, H. H., & Clark, E. V. (1977). *Psychology and language: An introduction to psycholinguistics.* New York: Harcourt Brace Jovanovich.

Crano, W. D. (1992, October). *Vested interest: Alternate formulations.* Paper presented at the annual meeting of the Society for Experimental Social Psychology, San Antonio, TX.

Csikszentmihalyi, M. (1990). *Flow: The psychology of optimal experience.* New York: HarperCollins.

Duncker, K. (1945). On problem-solving. *Psychological Monographs, 58* (5, Whole No. 270).

Erev, I., Wallsten, T., & Neal, M. (1991). Vagueness, ambiguity, and the cost of mutual understanding. *Psychological Science, 2,* 321-330.

Festinger, L. (1964). *Conflict, decision, and dissonance.* Stanford, CA: Stanford University Press.

Fiske, S. T., & Taylor, S. E. (1991). *Social cognition* (2nd ed.). New York: McGraw-Hill.

Fuchs, J., Montemayor, M., & Greenough, W. (1990). Effect of environmental complexity on size of superior colliculus. *Behavior and Neural Biology, 54,* 198-203.

Gilbert, D. T. (1989). Thinking lightly about others: Automatic components of the social inference process. In J. S. Uleman & J. A. Bargh (Eds.), *Unintended thought* (pp. 189-211). New York: Guilford.

Gilovitch, T. (1981). Seeing the past in the present: The effect of associations to familiar events on judgements and decisions. *Journal of Personality and Social Psychology, 40,* 797-808.

Glucksberg, S., & Weisberg, R. W. (1966). Verbal behavior and problem-solving: Some effects of labelling in a functional fixedness problem. *Journal of Experimental Psychology, 71,* 659-664.

Grice, H. P. (1975). Logic and conversation. In P. Cole & J. L. Morgan (Eds.), *Syntax and semantics: Vol. 3. Speech acts* (pp. 41-58). New York: Seminar.

Hample, D. (1992). Writing mindlessly. *Communication Monographs, 59,* 315-323.

Hayakawa, S. I. (1939). The meaning of semantics. *New Republic, 99,* 354-357.

Hayakawa, S. I. (1943). *Language in action.* New York: Harcourt Brace.

Higginbotham, J. (1990). Philosophical issues in the study of language. In D. N. Osherson & H. Lasnik (Eds.), *Language: An invitation to cognitive science* (Vol. 1, pp. 253-257). Cambridge: MIT Press.

Hobbs, J. R., & Evans, D. A. (1980). Conversation as planned behavior. *Cognitive Science, 3,* 275-310.

Johnson, W. (1946). *People in quandaries: The semantics of personal adjustment.* New York: Harper & Row.

Kahneman, D., Slovic, P., & Tversky, A. (Eds.). (1982). *Judgement under uncertainty: Heuristics and biases.* New York: Cambridge University Press.

Kellermann, K. (1992). Communication: Inherently strategic and primarily automatic. *Communication Monographs, 59,* 288-300.

Kellogg, E. W., III. (1987). Speaking in E-Prime: An experimental method for integrating general semantics into daily life. *Et Cetera, 44,* 118-128.

Kellogg, E. W., III, & Bourland, D. D., Jr. (1990). Working with E-Prime: Some practical notes. *Etc.: A Review of General Semantics, 47,* 376-393.

Korzybski, A. (1941). *Science and sanity: An introduction to non-Aristotelian systems and general semantics* (2nd ed.). Lancaster, PA: Science.

Kruglanksi, A. (1989). *Lay epistemics and human knowledge: Cognitive and motivational bases.* New York: Plenum.

Lachman, R., Lachman, J. L., & Butterfield, W. C. (1979). *Cognitive psychology and information processing: An introduction.* Hillsdale, NJ: Lawrence Erlbaum.

Lakoff, G. (1987). *Women, fire, and dangerous things.* Chicago: University of Chicago Press.

Langer, E. (1978a). The psychology of chance. *Journal for the Theory of Social Behaviour, 7,* 185-207.

Langer, E. (1978b). Rethinking the role of thought in social interaction. In J. Harvey, W. Ickes, & R. Kidd (Eds.), *New directions in attribution research* (pp. 35-58). Hillsdale, NJ: Lawrence Erlbaum.

Langer, E. (1989a). *Mindfulness.* Reading, MA: Addison-Wesley.

Langer, E. (1989b). Minding matters: The consequences of mindlessness/mindfulness. In L. Berkowitz (Ed.), *Advances in experimental social psychology* (Vol. 22, pp. 137-173). New York: Academic Press.

Langer, E. (1989c, August). *Mindlessness: Hardening of the categories*. Paper presented at the 97th Annual Meeting of the American Psychological Association, New Orleans.

Langer, E. (1992). Interpersonal mindlessness and language. *Communication Monographs, 59*, 324-327.

Langer, E., & Abelson, R. (1972). The semantics of asking a favor: How to succeed in getting help without really trying. *Journal of Personality and Social Psychology, 24*, 26-32.

Langer, E., & Abelson, R. (1974). A patient by any other name . . . : Clinician group differences in labelling bias. *Journal of Consulting and Clinical Psychology, 42*, 4-9.

Langer, E., Bashner, R., & Chanowitz, B. (1985). Decreasing prejudice by increasing discrimination. *Journal of Personality and Social Psychology, 49*, 113-120.

Langer, E., Beck, P., Janoff-Bulman, R., & Timko, C. (1984). The relationship between cognitive deprivation and longevity in senile and non-senile elderly populations. *Academic Psychology Bulletin, 6*, 211-226.

Langer, E., Blank, A., & Chanowitz, B. (1978). The mindlessness of ostensibly thoughtful action: The role of placebic information in interpersonal interaction. *Journal of Personality and Social Psychology, 36*, 635-642.

Langer, E., Chanowitz, B., Jacobs, S., Rhodes, M., Palmerino, M., & Thayer, P. (1990). Nonsequential development and aging. In C. Alexander & E. Langer (Eds.), *Higher stages of human development* (pp. 114-138). New York: Oxford University Press.

Langer, E., Field, S., Paches, W., & Abrams, E. (1989). *A mindful treatment for arthritis*. Unpublished manuscript, Harvard University.

Langer, E., Hatem, M., Joss, J., & Howell, M. (1989). Conditional teaching and mindful learning: The role of uncertainty in education. *Creativity Research Journal, 2*, 139-150.

Langer, E., Heffernan, D., & Keister, M. (1988). *Reducing burnout in an institutional setting: An experimental investigation*. Unpublished manuscript, Harvard University.

Langer, E., & Imber, L. (1979). When practice makes imperfect: The debilitating effects of overlearning. *Journal of Personality and Social Psychology, 37*, 2014-2025.

Langer, E., & Imber, L. (1980). The role of mindlessness in the perception of deviance. *Journal of Personality and Social Psychology, 39*, 360-367.

Langer, E., Perlmuter, L., Chanowitz, B., & Rubin, R. (1988). Two new applications of mindlessness theory: Aging and alcoholism. *Journal of Aging Studies, 2*, 289-299.

Langer, E., & Piper, P. (1987). The prevention of mindlessness. *Journal of Personality and Social Psychology, 53*, 280-287.

Langer, E., & Rodin, J. (1976). The effects of enhanced personal responsibility for the aged: A field experiment in an institutional setting. *Journal of Personality and Social Psychology, 33*, 117-122.

Langer, E., Rodin, J., Beck, P., Weinman, C., & Spitzer, L. (1979). Environmental determinants of memory improvement in late adulthood. *Journal of Personality and Social Psychology, 37*, 2003-2013.

Langer, E., Taylor, S., Fiske, S., & Chanowitz, B. (1976). Stigma, staring and discomfort: A novel-stimulus hypothesis. *Journal of Personality and Social Psychology, 12*, 451-463.

Lee, I. J. (1941). *Language habits in human affairs*. New York: Harper.

Lerner, M., & Miller, D. (1978). Just world research and the attribution process: Looking back and ahead. *Psychological Bulletin, 85*, 1031-1051.

Liska, J. (1992). Dominance-seeking language strategies: Please eat the floor, dogbreath, or I'll rip your lungs out, okay? In S. A. Deetz (Ed.), *Communication yearbook 15* (pp. 427-456). Newbury Park, CA: Sage.

Margolis, J., & Langer, E. (1991). An analysis of addiction from a mindlessness/mindfulness perspective. *Psychology of Addictive Behavior, 4*, 107-115.

Mead, G. H. (1934). *Mind, self and society: From the standpoint of a social behaviorist.* Chicago: University of Chicago Press.

Miller, G. A., Galanter, E., & Pribram, K. H. (1960). *Plans and the structure of behavior.* New York: Holt, Rinehart & Winston.

Mineo, P. (1991). *Argumentative subsumption: A test of a cognitive schema for argumentative discourse.* Unpublished doctoral dissertation, Michigan State University.

Newman, H. (1982). The sounds of silence. *Communication Quarterly, 30,* 142-149.

Nofsinger, R. E. (Ed.). (1986). Communication and consciousness [Special issue]. *Western Journal of Speech Communication, 50*(1).

Nolt, J., & Rohatyn, D. (1988). *Theory and problems of logic.* New York: McGraw-Hill.

O'Barr, W. M., & Atkins, B. K. (1980). "Women's language" or "powerless speech"? In S. McConnell-Ginnet, R. Borker, & N. Furnam (Eds.), *Women and language in literature and society* (pp. 93-110). New York: Praeger.

Petty, R. E., & Cacioppo, J. T. (1986). *Communication and persuasion: Central and peripheral routes to attitude change.* New York: Springer-Verlag.

Read, A. W. (1985). Language revision by deletion of absolutisms. *Et Cetera, 42,* 7-12.

Rodin, J., & Langer, E. (1977). Long-tern effects of a control-relevant intervention among the institutionalized aged. *Journal of Personality and Social Psychology, 35,* 897-902.

Ruesch, J. (1951). Communication and mental illness: A psychiatric approach. In J. Ruesch & G. Bateson (Eds.), *Communication: The social matrix of psychiatry* (pp. 50-93). New York: W. W. Norton.

Sapir, E. (1921). *Language: An introduction to the study of speech.* New York: Harcourt, Brace & World.

Schank, R., & Abelson, R. (1977). *Scripts, plans, goals, and understanding: An inquiry into human knowledge structures.* Hillsdale, NJ: Lawrence Erlbaum.

Schroder, H. M., Driver, M. J., & Struefert, S. (1967). *Human information processing.* New York: Holt, Rinehart & Winston.

Seibold, D. R., Cantrill, J. G., & Meyers, R. A. (1985). Communication and interpersonal influence. In M. L. Knapp & G. R. Miller (Eds.), *Handbook of interpersonal communication* (pp. 551-611). Beverly Hills, CA: Sage.

Shepard, R. N., & Cooper, L. A. (1982). *Mental images and their transformations.* Cambridge: MIT Press.

Snyder, M. (1984). When belief creates reality. In L. Berkowitz (Ed.), *Advances in experimental social psychology* (Vol. 18, pp. 248-305). New York: Academic Press.

Snyder, M., & Swann, W. B., Jr. (1978). Behavioral confirmation in social interaction: From social perception to social reality. *Journal of Experimental Social Psychology, 14,* 148-162.

Sperber, D., & Wilson, D. (1986). *Relevance: Communication and cognition.* Cambridge, MA: Harvard University Press.

Stiff, J. (1986). Cognitive processing of persuasive messages: A meta-analytic review of the effects of supporting information on attitudes. *Communication Monographs, 53,* 75-89.

Taylor, S. E., & Crocker, J. (1981). Schematic bases of social information processing. in E. T. Higgins, C. P. Herman, & M. P. Zanna (Eds.), *Social cognition: The Ontario Symposium* (Vol. 1, pp. 89-134). Hillsdale, NJ: Lawrence Erlbaum.

Ting-Toomey, S. (1989). Identity and interpersonal bonding. In M. K. Asante & W. B. Gudykunst (Eds.), *Handbook of international and intercultural communication* (pp. 351-373). Newbury Park, CA: Sage.

Toulmin, S., Rieke, R., & Janik, A. (1984). *An introduction to reasoning* (2nd ed.). New York: Macmillan.

Trungpa, C. (1973). *Cutting through spiritual materialism.* Boulder, CO: Shambhala.

Tversky, A., & Kahneman, D. (1974). Judgment under uncertainty: Heuristics and biases. *Science, 185,* 1124-1131.

Uleman, J. S., & Bargh, J. A. (Eds.). (1989). *Unintended thought.* New York: Guilford.

von Hippel, W. (1990). *The effect of schemata on memory for instances.* Unpublished doctoral dissertation, University of Michigan.

Waldron, V. R. (1990). Constrained rationality: Situational influences on information acquisition plans and tactics. *Communication Monographs, 57,* 184-201.

Watzlawick, P., Beavin, J. H., & Jackson, D. D. (1967). *Pragmatics of human communication: A study of interaction patterns, pathologies, and paradoxes.* New York: W. W. Norton.

Webster, D. M. (in press). Motivated augmentation and reduction of the overattribution bias. *Journal of Personality and Social Psychology.*

Zebrowitz, L. A. (1990). *Social perception.* Pacific Grove, CA: Brooks/Cole.

6   Attention to Television and
Some Methods for Its Measurement

TOM GRIMES
Kansas State University

JEANNE MEADOWCROFT
University of Wisconsin—Madison

This chapter examines the role of attention in television comprehension and memory
research. Attention is an often neglected, or improperly operationalized, variable in
television research. The authors define attention in the context of television viewing,
examine ways in which it can be operationalized, and then review some methods for
measuring it.

MEASURING attention is difficult because attention processes often cannot be observed directly. So researchers, primarily experimental psychologists, have developed indirect observation and measurement
techniques to give them a window into the "black box" of cognition. It is not surprising that measuring attention can seem to be a highly specialized endeavor,
one that could prompt a researcher in communication to wonder whether attention
is a useful communication variable. We will offer an explanation of why attention
should be isolated and studied as an independent variable, as well as provide an
overview of some of the methods used to measure attention to television.
Finally, we will review selected communication studies to illustrate the range
of research on attention. Let us begin by answering some commonly asked
questions about attention and its role in communication research.

AUTHORS' NOTE: We gratefully acknowledge the advice and recommendations of Mr. Brian Deith,
School of Journalism and Mass Communication, and Dr. Arthur Glenberg, Department of Psychology, both at the University of Wisconsin—Madison; Dr. Annie Lang, Murrow School of Communication, Washington State University; Dr. James Shanteau, Department of Psychology, Kansas State
University; Dr. Joan Schleuder, Austin, Texas; and two anonymous reviewers.

Correspondence and requests for reprints: Tom Grimes, Miller School of Journalism and Mass
Communications, Kansas State University, Manhattan, KS 66506.

Communication Yearbook 18, pp. 133-161

IS ATTENTION A USEFUL
COMMUNICATION VARIABLE?

Is attention more useful as a "psychology variable," best left to the study of cognitive psychologists? We have heard colleagues assert that psychologists are better equipped to handle the attention variable because of the difficulty involved in isolating and measuring it. In addition, so the argument goes, media messages are sufficiently chaotic and complex that the subtleties of attention are often lost. But if attention is not a communication variable, why are other equally finicky cognitive variables, such as attitudes, source credibility, and affective variables, considered useful communication variables? Anyone who has worked with these variables would be reluctant, to put it mildly, to describe them as easy to isolate and measure. Indeed, these other cognitive variables have a long tradition of use in mass media research, and their inclusion in communication studies is seldom questioned as appropriate. Yet the idea that attention is somehow uniquely a subject for psychological study persists.

Traditionally, attention measures, when they have been used, have been included in mass media research to strengthen the predictability of media exposure variables. Chaffee and Schleuder (1986), for example, found that the ability to predict media effects was greater if survey respondents were asked not only how much time they spent with a medium, but also how much attention they paid to media content. These researchers, then, felt that it was important to know something about attention. Further, questions estimating attention allocated to media content are frequently included in survey research.

In the mid-1970s, however, a few researchers started to study attention to television in a dramatically different way (e.g., Anderson, Alwitt, Lorch, & Levin, 1979; Poulis, Rubinstein & Liebert, 1975). Rather than using survey items to ask people to estimate how much attention they allocated to various media content, these researchers made use of computer technology and brought the study of attention into the laboratory, where they developed methods to observe attention on-line, while viewers watched the television screen.

These studies represent the beginnings of a revolutionary shift in our study of attention to television because they were the first indicators of a paradigm shift. The term *paradigm* refers to a common set of ideas scientists bring to their research. Paradigm shifts not only indicate dramatic changes in those ideas and in assumptions made about focal variables, but also shifts in the ways scientists frame questions, the theories employed, and the methods used to gather evidence (Lachman, Lachman, & Butterfield, 1979).

Carter, Ruggles, Jackson, and Heffner (1973) describe this shift as a move away from the traditional sender-message-receiver paradigm toward an information-processing paradigm. As a result, the research undertaken with this new paradigm in mind focuses on questions about what happens while messages are being processed, in an attempt to understand how messages and the human mind interact. In this effort, the attention variable often becomes the focus of media research rather than simply being viewed as a measure that will strengthen the predictive power of media exposure variables. In addition, experimental methods are often needed that will allow observation of mental processes that would otherwise be hidden, bringing the study of attention into the laboratory. As a result, attention studies that follow this new paradigm have much in common with attention research in psychology, at least in terms of theory addressed and methods used to explore research questions.

These changes, we believe, have contributed to the misunderstanding that attention is a psychology variable. Indeed, mass media researchers who study attention are often asked if they would not feel more comfortable in psychology departments (Reeves & Anderson, 1991). However, the following section specifies three reasons that mass media researchers should study attention.

WHY SHOULD COMMUNICATION RESEARCHERS STUDY ATTENTION?

One reason communication researchers should study attention is that attention research in psychology differs in two important ways from attention research in the mass media literature. First, mass media researchers tend to have very different questions about attention from those addressed by psychologists. And psychologists tend to employ simplistic stimuli when they study attention, so that it is not at all certain that results of psychologists' studies will generalize to more complex information-processing tasks, such as those posed by television.

For example, the psychology literature offers studies of "spans of apprehension," seeking to discover how much information a subject can attend to and remember after exposure to brief (100-200 milliseconds), simplistic visual displays (e.g., McIntyre, Blackwell, & Denton, 1978). In these studies, psychologists are interested mainly in discovering the limitations of attentional processes, as were the British psychologists who proposed "bottleneck" theories of attention (e.g., Cherry, 1953; Deutsch & Deutsch, 1963; Treisman, 1960).

In contrast, rather than studying attention as an isolated process, mass media researchers tend to ask questions about how attention and communication processes interact. We want to know how message design variables influence attention and how viewers sort through the complex stream of incoming information, selecting some ideas for thought and ignoring others. How are these decisions made? Are they based on superficial stimulus characteristics, or are decisions based on semantics or meaning analysis?

We also want to know how attention is related to other cognitive activity. How direct is the relationship between attention and memory? Do different cognitive tasks posed by messages use attentional resources differently? As children mature and develop different ways of thinking, do the ways they attend to television change?

In other words, mass media researchers ask questions concerning the inter-action between a message and the human mind, seeking to discover how attention and other cognitive processes mediate between message exposure and reaction to messages. So, although communication researchers have found it useful to import theory and methods from psychology, it is clear that media researchers are in a unique position to ask questions that are relevant to the communication field. This is one important reason the mass media literature should include studies of attention.

Another reason is that knowing something about the interaction between messages and the human mind enhances our understanding of communication processes. An example of this is the way our thinking about what it means to watch television has changed in recent years. Not too long ago, most people—including popular writers and media researchers—assumed that watching tele-vision was a rather passive activity (Anderson & Lorch, 1983; Mander, 1978; Singer, 1980; Winn, 1977). Because of the results of early attention studies grounded in the information-processing paradigm, however, we have come to understand that television viewing is far from a simple task. In fact, it has been suggested that television messages are processed at both local (micro) and global levels (e.g., Huston & Wright, 1983; Thorson, Reeves & Schleuder, 1987). According to this view, local analysis involves rapid and frequent sampling of television stimuli as sensory events, as well as program features, such as pacing and action levels. At the global level, attention involves semantic analysis, for instance, using schemata to relate program events to one another and to make inferences that help viewers construct meaning out of television content. Sam-pling at both levels involves answering questions viewers pose: Is this content interesting, important, comprehensible? The answers to these questions are used to direct subsequent attention and information selection. The evidence, then, clearly indicates that watching television involves much cognitive activity, and psychology studies that employ overly simplistic stimuli simply would not allow observation of this type of multilevel message analysis.

Although the study of attention to television is in its infancy, it has already given us a better appreciation for what it means to watch television. The literature also offers implications for message design. Knowing what stimuli tend to elicit attention, for example, implies that eliciting stimuli can be placed strategically throughout a message to help direct a viewer's attention to important content (e.g., Bryant, Zillmann, & Brown, 1983). Similarly, knowing something about the kinds of strategies people use in selecting and organizing incoming infor-mation has led to the idea that television forms (e.g., pacing, camera techniques) can be viewed as analogous to punctuation in print, and can be similarly used to help structure the way incoming information is processed (Huston & Wright, 1983). For example, important information might be presented in both auditory and visual channels to increase the likelihood viewers will pick up key content. Program pacing might slow down during presentation of some content to allow viewers more time to rehearse (i.e., think about) and store that information. And background auditory and visual events might be minimized when complex information is being presented to allow viewers to focus more on global-level analyses without being distracted by incidental stimulus events (Huston & Wright, 1983).

In short, attention studies have enhanced our understanding of communication processes, casting light on what happens between message reception and message comprehension. Such findings are not incidental to the communication literature; they offer information critical to understanding how communication processes work. Findings tell us that television viewers do not simply react to program stimuli and content. Instead, they actively pose questions and sort through incoming information in efforts to make sense of program content. This is an important reason for mass media researchers to study attention: more than any other literature, these studies are beginning to sketch a picture of what it is people do with message content.

A final reason the attention variable should hold a place in the mass media literature is an extension of our first point. It does not make sense to exclude study of a phenomenon simply because that study involves importing theory and methods from other disciplines. There is a strong multidisciplinary tradition in communication research that not only invites importation of theory and methods from other fields, but actively encourages it. Just a glance through the literature provides evidence of how significant such importation has been to our understanding of communication processes (e.g., Lowery & DeFleur, 1983); media researchers have adopted methods from other fields as a part of the literature's maturation (Meadowcroft & McDonald, 1986). Excluding such importation would stunt development of theory in our field and limit our potential to understand communication processes.

SOME COMMON MISCONCEPTIONS ABOUT ATTENTION

Are media messages too complex to allow researchers to isolate message traits that influence attention? Is it not a mistake to try to chase down unseen attention processes that even psychologists often have a difficult time locating and measuring? These questions, we believe, are based on some misconceptions about attention research that are worth our time to address here.

Are Media Stimuli Too Chaotic
to Measure Subtle Attention Processes?

Some communication researchers are concerned that media stimuli are too chaotic to allow valid interpretation of attention data. Of the arguments asserting the futility of including the attention variable in communication research, this is probably the most understandable, because the concern is based on the fact that television stimuli are very complex, offering a simultaneous array of auditory and visual events. It seems, then, that the complexity of media stimuli is both a blessing and a burden for communication researchers. On the one hand, as we have already noted, the complexity of media stimuli is comparable to typical information-processing situations faced by people in everyday life. As a result, findings from media attention studies potentially are more reflective of what most people encounter every day, and less like what they encounter in psychology labs, where stimuli are simplistic and contrived. On the other hand, the complexity of media stimuli forces media researchers to be on the lookout for possible confounds. And it is the problem of confounds—two or more difficult-to-separate causes for a particular effect—that often worries communication researchers when they try to manipulate the attention variable.

Anderson et al. (1979) acknowledged this problem more than a decade ago. Their early research tried to determine the influence of various audio and visual events on the television screen (e.g., movement) on viewer attention. They noted that because television messages often involve simultaneous presentation of several audio and visual effects, it is difficult to isolate the influence of any one stimulus event. They found, for example, that although the presence of male voices was associated with depressed attention levels, male voices were also associated with little on-screen movement, a variable also found to depress attention. In other words, correlations between male voices on-screen and attention could be confounded by the presence of other stimulus events that could contribute to, or even wholly explain, those correlations.

Although the possibility of such confounds exists, the problem is not so great that it renders all attention studies uninterpretable. Indeed, several tools are available for dealing with the problem of confounds. It is necessary, for instance, to exercise great care in identifying independent variables for measurement—or for control. And the careful use of experimental design procedures can help tease out confounds (e.g., Shaughnessy & Zechmeister, 1985). For example, both variables (adult men on-screen and activity on-screen) could be manipulated as separate factors in an experimental design, allowing the separate contribution of each variable on attention to be assessed, as well as any interactions between variables.

There are also statistical techniques that can be used to partial out the effect of different independent variables on a dependent variable. Hierarchical regression is one such technique. By entering into the regression equation the different independent variables, a researcher can measure the magnitude of the effect each independent variable has had on the dependent variable by looking at the increment in R^2, or by looking at the statistical significance of such an increment. Note that more than one variable may account for the same portion of the variance. In this case, the variable that is more important from a theoretical standpoint is entered first, and the portion of the shared variance is customarily attributed to that one variable. For example, if one were to conduct a study investigating the effects of age and weight on biochemicals in the blood, and the subjects were adolescents, we would expect age and weight to be correlated, and therefore to explain a certain portion of shared variance. Thus we would enter first the variable we believe is of most interest theoretically (for instance, weight). Then we would attribute all of the shared variance between age and weight to weight only, the theoretically most important of the two variables.

Finally, what would be considered confounds in some research contexts might actually be considered message characteristics for television. There are, in television, multicollinear relationships among variables that, as a whole, define a particular genre. Who is to say, for instance, that "action television," often conceptualized as one independent variable, is not inextricably bound with other independent variables such as camera movement, quick scene changes, and loud, fast-paced musical accompaniment? These variables may be inseparable attributes of action television, with none taking theoretical precedence over the others. Thus, in studies that focus on attention and action television, it is not difficult to imagine situations where it would be meaningless to isolate each variable and study its impact independently (e.g., Meadowcroft & Zillmann, 1987). The art, then, is knowing when to accept one of these multicollinear relationships as a single message attribute and when to view such relationships as posing a potential confound. The point is that the challenge of confounds is not sufficient to warrant the dismissal of attention as a communication variable.

Isn't the Viewer's Presence at the Time a Message Is Delivered a Good Enough Estimate of Attention?

McLeod, Rucinski, Pan, and Kosicki (1988) argue that mere exposure to a newspaper or to a television program is often confused with attention to that medium. Estimates of exposure to a message can give researchers only a valid estimate of the opportunity media consumers have to attend to a message. Such an estimate can be useful if the researcher means to infer opportunity to attend rather than attention itself. The problem comes when the researcher infers the magnitude of a viewer's attention, or the focus of the viewer's attention on any given message component, based on exposure data alone.

For instance, because viewers scored better on an audio recall exam than on a video recall exam, Drew and Grimes (1987) inferred that the viewers paid more attention to the audio track than to the accompanying video of television news stories. Later research, however, showed that viewers probably pay about equal attention to the audio and video, and that better memory for auditory facts may have been an artifact of the auditory recall task Drew and Grimes used in their study (Grimes, 1990, 1991). Thus mere exposure to both message channels —audio and video—appears not to be an adequate measure for purposes of inferring attentional focus.

Isn't Attention to a Message a Function of the Comprehensibility or Clarity of the Message Itself?

The idea that media researchers are better off when they are concerned with things they can see, such as message traits (e.g., comprehensibility of message), rather than with unseen cognitive processes such as attention is appealing. After all, the argument goes, research has shown that attention is influenced by these variables (e.g., Grimes, 1991), so why not focus on variables that define the message itself—variables that can be more readily observed and measured?

The problem with this view is that it is based on the "magic bullet" effects model, which has lost support because it is not consistent with contemporary research findings that show media effects are not universal. Instead, it is now widely accepted that mass media effects vary from one receiver to another, in part because different receivers do different things with incoming information. So, although message traits such as comprehensibility influence attention, this is only a part of the picture. Attention is also influenced by what the viewer contributes to message interpretation, such as prior knowledge and cultural and schematic biases.

To understand message effects fully, therefore, we must know something about these "unseen" cognitive processes as well as something about message traits. As we stated earlier, attention patterns arise from the interaction between the message and the human mind; to understand communication processes it is important to understand this interaction, not just one piece of the process, namely, the message itself.

Isn't It Sufficient to Study Memory of a Message If
You Want to Know What a Media Consumer Has Attended To?

Based on our review of 21 communication and related journals published between January 1974 and June 1993, we suspect that the equation of attention with memory is one of the most common mistakes made in communication research.[1] Recent studies in communication have demonstrated that the relationship between attention and memory is not always direct (e.g., Collins, 1983; Meadowcroft & Reeves, 1989). In other words, information attended to most is not always the information that will be remembered best.

In addition, it is clear that some components of memory may be systematically distorted or entirely fabricated (e.g., Britton, Meyer, Simpson, Holdredge, & Curry, 1979; Collins, 1983). Bartlett's (1932) classic studies of British subjects' interpretation of an American Indian folktale leave little doubt about this. Bartlett found that memory of narratives is shaped by a receiver's cultural biases, cognitive schemata, and tendency to fill in missing information with stereotypical explanations, regardless of whether or not these expectations are consistent with story content.

Similar forces are at work when receivers process media content as well. Collins (1983), for example, reports that social and schema-based biases influence children's interpretation of television stories. Similarly, Grimes and Drechsel (1994) found that adult television news viewers' cultural biases were the controlling factor in memory for television news stories featuring blacks and women, so that cultural biases were better predictors of memory than was attention to news story content. The shaping of memory by schemata is especially noticeable with the passage of time (see discussion of the dissociative-cue hypothesis in Gruder et al., 1978).

It is clear that, although it is necessary for receivers to attend to information if they are to remember it, the correlation between attention and memory is not always so straightforward as to allow memory to be used as a valid surrogate measure of attention. Inclusion of attention variables in communication research, therefore, is necessary if we hope to obtain reliable information concerning attention processes.

In summary, there are some who argue that attention is not a communication variable or that it is too messy or not even necessary to measure in mass media research. When the logic behind such arguments is examined, however, the arguments fail to be convincing. Instead, discussion of these issues tends to lead to the conclusion that it is important to include the attention variable in communication research. The study of attention has led not only to a better understanding of what it means to attend to television, but to an understanding of how to design communication messages in ways that help direct attention and information-processing activity so that messages will be processed successfully. To illustrate these points further, we now turn to a discussion of attention measures and a review of studies that illustrate the wide range of research in this literature.

TWO POPULAR STRATEGIES FOR MEASURING ATTENTION

It would be impossible, not to mention foolish, to try to abstract each of the different conceptualizations of attention that may have some bearing on communication. We will, however, abstract the two that have most often been used by communication researchers since the paradigm shift mentioned earlier, using the PsychLit database (American Psychological Association, 1993) as a reference. The measures we review below are grounded in experimental methodology. These two conceptualizations view attention as either a covert process that must be measured indirectly or an overt behavior that can be measured directly.

Overt attention processes involve a behavioral component, such as eye movement, that can be observed directly. In contrast, covert attentional processes do not bring with them behavioral manifestations. Indeed, *covert* is a term used by psychologists to refer to mental processes that have no behavioral manifestations whatever (Kinchla, 1992; Posner & Petersen, 1990). Kinchla (1992) calls these processes "choices." Choices, in this context, are changes in a state of mind. They may ultimately manifest themselves through behavior, but in their initial stages they are not observable by outsiders. Such choices may involve deciding which voice to listen to in a roomful of voices or which part of a message to think about—including changes that may occur without the individual's moving his or her head or eyes.

In the following subsections, we give an overview of attention models and procedures used to measure both overt and covert attentional processes. We also review selected studies to show the diversity of research addressed in this literature.

Before considering measures, however, it is always a good idea to offer a conceptual definition of the variable being measured. We offer the following definition, which is consistent with research evidence from the mass media and psychology literatures. *Attention* is an integral component of all mental activity, something that both directs thought and provides the fuel for cognition. Like some other types of fuel, attention is a limited resource, so that attention is inherently selective, focusing mental effort toward processing a subset of available information. Evidence suggests selection is directed by salient stimulus characteristics (such as motion and loud noises) and by an individual's knowledge, goals, and schemata (Anderson & Lorch, 1983; Lang, 1992; Neisser, 1976). In addition, once selection occurs, attention continues to play an important role in cognition, providing the fuel for thought that defines the intensity of mental effort allocated toward thinking about selected stimuli.

From this definition, it is clear that the term *attention* has many meanings. Indeed, it is an umbrella term for different cognitive processes that act in concert and enable a person to select something to think about, listen to, or look at (Kahneman, 1973; Kinchla, 1992; Posner & Snyder, 1975; Schneider & Shiffrin, 1977). In fact, cognitive psychologists often use the expression *to process* rather than *to attend,* because the notion of processing better fits the multidimensional nature of attention (e.g., Pezdek & Stevens, 1984; Shiffrin & Dumais, 1981). As we will see, some attentional processes are easier to observe than others.

Covert Attentional Processes and Their Measurement

When there is no behavioral manifestation of attention, that does not mean that attention is not being paid, that Kinchla's "choices" are not being made. Something is happening, albeit covertly. In describing what that something is, social scientists usually construct a model of attention. A model is a hypothesis, hypothetical because a researcher is unable, of course, to see the covert processes taking place. It is a researcher's "best guess" at what is happening, based on the evidence available. In any event, a model provides a researcher with a set of rules that cognitive processes are assumed to follow.

Most of the formal models of attention that communication researchers use were developed by cognitive psychologists. With these models come inferential measures, also developed by psychologists, that are designed to test the models. So in order to understand how to infer covert attentional processes properly with these inferential measures, a communication researcher must first understand the model from which the measures are derived. We will abstract one of the most frequently used models of attention in communication research, the capacity model, and describe some inferential methods used to test it.

The Capacity Model

The capacity model is based on Kahneman's (1973) attention allocation model. According to Kahneman, attending to something requires mental effort, a resource limited by available capacity.[2] As a result, the amount of mental effort available to an individual to invest in attending to different tasks or messages is limited, making it necessary for him or her to select some information from the environment and ignore the rest (Neisser, 1976). Kahneman's model also suggests a positive relationship between the amount of mental effort allocated to a task and task performance.

Kahneman's model does not rule out the idea that people can process information from more than one source simultaneously. As long as the concurrent tasks do not exceed available capacity, a person may perform simultaneous tasks adequately. However, when a difficult task demands greater investment of mental effort, this necessarily implies that fewer attentional resources are available to be allocated to other tasks. As a result, performance on other tasks will suffer. This can happen, for example, when a student is reading a textbook while watching television. When the student comes across a difficult passage in the text that requires a great deal of mental effort to process, the amount of attention allocated to the television viewing task will diminish until the reading task demands less effort or the student decides to watch television instead of reading the difficult passage.

The capacity model has generally shown that the number of different messages is less important than the difficulty of each message in determining attention overload. For instance, Armstrong and Greenberg (1990) suggest that a student doing homework can probably attend to both the homework and TV messages if both tasks are making simple demands on the student. In other words, a viewer can handle several tasks as long as, in the aggregate, the tasks do not overload the viewer's total attentional capacity (see Norman & Bobrow, 1975, for further discussion of this phenomenon).

By virtue of the fact that television conveys both audio and video simultaneously, the viewer is faced with competing or complementary messages from those two channels. Thus researchers who study comprehension issues in television are almost always faced, at some level, with an attentional issue as well. The capacity model offers an investigator a "format" for conceptualizing the competing attention demands imposed by television viewing.

So, by conceptualizing attention as (a) a limited resource (b) that is capable of fielding multiple inputs simultaneously and (c) is governed by the number of inputs and/or the magnitude of demand each input makes on attention, the capacity model offers strategies for observing covert attentional processes. One such strategy is found in secondary task methodology.

Secondary Task Methodologies:
Ways to Infer Covert Attention Processes

The secondary task method measures a covert component of attention: attention allocation. The method is used in experimental settings where subjects are engaged in performing two simultaneous tasks. The primary task is the ongoing task of attending to mass media content (e.g., print, television). The secondary task is periodic; typically, subjects are asked to depress a button in response to reaction-time (RT) probes. RT probes can be auditory (tone), visual (a flash of light), or tactile (a bump periodically felt by the finger, for example). RT probes can be placed randomly throughout a message or placed strategically to ensure they occur when subjects are processing media content of particular interest to the experimenter. In either case, a computer keeps a record of when RT cues were presented during message presentation so that researchers can go back and match RT performance with specific program events. Reaction time to RT probes is also recorded by computers and is typically measured in milliseconds.

How does the secondary task allow attention to be measured? Just as a driver becomes less articulate in conversation with a passenger when traffic picks up, subjects in the laboratory become less able to handle a secondary RT task when more attention is allocated to the primary televiewing task. As a result, attention to the primary task is measured indirectly, by noting variance in secondary task performance. When RTs are very fast, it is assumed less attention is being allocated to the primary television viewing task, compared with points in the program when RTs slow, indicating a decline in secondary task performance.

The secondary task method has been used to examine the impact of program events on attention allocation. Typically, these studies use experimental designs that involve systematic manipulation of a particular stimulus characteristic (such as complexity), and research questions concern the influence of those manipulations on attention allocation. Thorson et al. (1987), for example, examined the relationship between audio and visual complexity as subjects watched television ads. They found that, compared with processing ads in an audio-only or a video-only condition, more attention was allocated in an audiovisual condition. Other studies have examined attention allocation as a function of time compression in televised advertisements (Hausnecht & Moore, 1986), propositional structure (Thorson, 1983), and camera cuts (Geiger & Reeves, in press; Lang, Geiger, Strickwerda & Sumner, 1993).

The secondary task literature also addresses questions about how program structure influences attention allocation. Schleuder and White (1989), for example, asked if bumpers and teasers used in television news stories have a priming effect. They predicted such devices are associated with the allocation of more mental effort to news stories and better memory of news story content. In general, their findings confirm these hypotheses.

Secondary task studies have also contributed to what we know about the relationship between cognition and attention allocation. Meadowcroft and Reeves (1989), for example, studied the influence of story schema development on children's attention to a television story. They found that, compared with other children, those who had well-developed story schemata (a) allocated less attention to processing the story, (b) showed better correspondence between content attended to and content remembered, and (c) allocated attention based on the meaning of content to the story, rather than on more superficial components, such as program stimulus characteristics.

Meadowcroft and Watt (1989) also looked at the relationship between attention and cognition. Consistent with the researchers' hypotheses, the findings indicate that attending to television involves a number of cognitive tasks. And, as predicted, different tasks were found to produce distinct attention patterns, many of which were found to be cyclical. Meadowcroft and Watt call these cyclical or repeating attention patterns "attention spans," and they define each attention span in terms of cycle length, intensity, and frequency. In addition, their findings suggest that in an effort to deal with capacity limitations, television viewers execute cognitive tasks that require little effort in parallel, freeing-up capacity to allocate to more demanding tasks that peak in intensity in opposition to the less demanding tasks, suggesting serial processing.

Taken as a whole, the secondary task literature has added much to our understanding of what it means to attend to television. The method has been used to discover the relationship between message attributes and attention, having clear implications for message design. In addition, the method has been used as a window to identify and observe cognitive processing that occurs as viewers watch television, leaving no doubt that watching television is not always the simple cognitive task some have claimed.

The Nature of Reaction Times

In our own research, we have seen subjects respond to probes in as few as 130 milliseconds owing to the simplicity of the primary task, a finding that suggests that the subject has a large amount of residual attention available to devote to performing the secondary task. On the other hand, we have seen some subjects take 4,000 milliseconds to respond to probes—or fail to respond to probes at all—because attending to the primary task left little residual attention to be applied to performing the secondary RT task.

These numbers are not meaningless units of measure. Sternberg (1969) has shown that the time it takes for a subject to respond to a probe is proportionate to the amount of mental effort the subject devotes to detecting a probe and deciding to respond to it. Sternberg presents what he calls a "reaction time equation," which looks something like this:

$$RT = Detection_{t1} + Recognition_{t2} + Decision_{t3} + Response_{t4}$$

Here, the act of probe detection takes a certain amount of time, represented by t1. Then, the probe must be identified in memory as that to which the subject is to respond (t2). The subject must then decide what to do. That is, the subject must decide to push a button as instructed by the experimenter (t3). Finally, the subject must give the command to the finger and push the button (t4).

Whatever amount of time is required to go through this multistep process, that amount of time is dependent on the residual attention capacity available for probe detection and response. The more residual attention, the less time consumed by t1 through t4. So when Grimes (1991) found that one subject's averaged RT to a probe was 130 milliseconds, that meant that the subject had enough residual processing capacity to enable him to run through these stages in a split second, literally.[3]

Collecting RT data is not easy. The software and hardware requirements are stringent. First, the internal clock of the average personal computer must be recalibrated to measure in milliseconds with software that is difficult to write properly. Second, the computer must be fitted with a lot of equipment—videotape playback machines, a TV monitor, a response button, various connectors and cables, and sometimes a tone generator. In addition, RT data are most often collected one subject at a time, so such experiments require large investments of time to run the needed number of subjects through the laboratory.

On the other hand, if an investigator can manage the hardware and software demands of the method, the advantages of RT-based secondary task methodology are considerable. If an investigator desires, he or she can place probes in the message precisely where he or she wants to measure attention, just as Schleuder and White (1989) were able to do. In any case, RT data can be matched with specific program events to allow study of moment-to-moment fluctuations of attention, or RT data can be averaged across program segments or across entire programs to give estimates of overall attention levels. Meadowcroft and Reeves (1989), for example, placed RT cues randomly throughout a television program, about four probes for every minute of program time. Later, they went back and averaged RT across selected program segments so they could compare the average amount of attention allocated to central versus incidental story segments.

Given that the hardware and software requirements are exacting and that data collection is particularly labor-intensive, RT collection is not a practical option for many communication researchers. Furthermore, RTs may provide more precision than the researcher needs. Often, a researcher might need only a summary measure of attention allocation, something RTs can provide, but something that can be collected more efficiently with other methods. This is where a second type of secondary task methodology, preload task methodology, is useful.

Preload Task Methodology

Like RT secondary task methods, preloads require subjects to perform two simultaneous tasks, an ongoing primary task (attending to a televised message) and a secondary task, referred to as the preload task. The preload serves the same function as the RT. The preload measures residual attention capacity, but it does so without the paraphernalia attendant to RT collection. It is a simple pencil-and-paper test that offers an estimate of attention invested in messages as a whole. Unlike RTs, which can assess moment-to-moment fluctuations in attention, preloads can give the researcher only a summary measure of the viewer's attention to the message. As long as the researcher does not need information about moment-to-moment changes in attention, preloads can be useful in measuring attention allocation.

Preload methodology was first described by Baddeley and Hitch (1974) as they were attempting to differentiate working memory (the memory component that contains working capacity and storage capacity) from short-term memory (which contains only storage capacity). They were attempting to develop a technique for occupying working memory so that they could measure its capacity. They did this by asking subjects to hold certain letter-number combinations in memory while the subjects attended to a message about which they would be tested. Assuming that attending to the message was the subjects' primary task, the accuracy with which the subjects reproduced the alphanumeric material could give a clue as to the amount of working memory consumed by the primary task. In the process, Baddeley and Hitch discovered a method for measuring residual attention. That is, the ability to rehearse (i.e., to think about) an alphanumeric string in working memory while attending to a message is a function of the individual's ability to split attention between the message and the string. And that attention can be split only if there is enough capacity to go around. If the primary task requires too much attention (or working memory space, as Baddeley and Hitch conceptualize it), then the subject will not be able to reproduce the contents of the alphanumeric string accurately. Baddeley and Hitch's experiments, as well as those of others (Luce, Feustel, & Pisoni, 1983; Martin, Mullennix, Pisoni, & Summers, 1989), have dealt only with auditory preloads, but additional research in cognitive psychology has used visual preloads (e.g., Kruley, Sciama, & Glenberg, in press). Preload methodology for use in communication research also assumes that there is both auditory and visual working memory, and that the two can be differentiated in testing (e.g., Shiffrin, 1993).

Mechanically, the preload method works this way. Subjects are told to attend to a TV news story, commercial, or other target message. Prior to doing so, subjects are asked to memorize a visual pattern described by several blackened cells within a multicell matrix (see Figure 6.1 for an example). They are shown the matrix long enough so that they can grasp the pattern within it, but for a short enough time that they are not able to memorize it (i.e., to store it in long-term memory where it would lie inert, not interacting with attention). Next, subjects

Figure 6.1. Example of a Visual Preload

SOURCE: Grimes, Broholm, Pounds, Vogl, and Hoekstra (1993).

NOTE: Subjects were shown this matrix, then were shown a television news story. Afterward, subjects were shown a blank matrix and were asked to fill in the cells they remembered were blackened. The percentage of correctly blackened cells was considered a measure of the amount of residual visual attention that the television news story did not consume.

are shown the target message. After the message is finished, subjects are asked to use a blank matrix to recall the cell pattern they were shown before message presentation. The reasoning here is that, if watching the TV news story requires a lot of attention, then there will be very little attention capacity in reserve to rehearse the preload, which requires attentional capacity to rehearse. Consequently, the subject should exhibit poor preload recall. Thus, by comparing the accuracy of preload recall between or among differing visual conditions in the televised message subjects are presented, an investigator can make inferences as to which condition required the most visual attention. Messages that require more visual attention capacity will produce more errors in the preload recall task.

The same principle holds true for auditory attentional tests. In this instance, subjects are presented with an alphanumeric string (e.g., N3L5H7P), then presented with a news story, and then are asked to recall the alphanumeric string.

Although the string is presented visually, it is encoded by the phonological/articulatory loop (Conrad, 1964; also see the review of the literature on this phenomenon in Penney, 1989). Much as in the memorization of a phone number, it is not usually the visual image that a person remembers; rather, it is the auditory rehearsal of a number that helps a person remember it. This rehearsal usually takes place until the person can write the number down for future reference. What is presumably happening is that the phonological/articulatory working memory buffer is attending to both the television narration and the alphanumeric string.

This method is not without problems. The researcher must perform extensive pretesting to find just the right visual or auditory preload to accompany the primary task. This pretesting must include measures that guarantee that the preloads are not shunted to short-term memory, where they do not require secondary task effort to remember while the primary task is engaged. The pretests should also guarantee that the preloads are not so difficult that they cannot be remembered at all, regardless of the amount of secondary task effort applied.[4] In any event, if the correct "ratio of difficulty" is not struck between the primary task and the secondary task, then the secondary task (the preload) will not measure residual attention allocation.

Preload task methodology requires careful choice of suitable preloads, but it is still a useful low-tech, easy-to-interpret method for measuring attention capacity. To date, very little communication research has used the preload method —indeed, we are aware only of work done by the first author. However, it is widely used in experimental psychology, where it is considered to provide a highly reliable measure of residual attention capacity; we believe it represents a low-risk method of collecting attention data for communication research as well.

Psychophysiological Measures:
Another Way to Infer Covert Attention Processes

A few media researchers have attempted to measure covert attention processes using psychophysiological responses to televised messages. Reeves et al. (1985), for example, measured brain wave activity as their subjects watched television. Brain wave measures of attention to television are rare in the literature, so we will not dwell on them here. Instead, we will focus on a more frequently used psychophysiological measure of attention to television: heart rate.

Lang (1987) introduced heart rate as a measure of attention to television. "To collect heart rate data that is time locked to television messages," she explains, "you need a system that can pick up the electrical or blood volume changes associated with heart rate. This system must be able to record either the heart rate (usually as beats per minute) or the heart period (milliseconds between beats) time locked to the frame in the videotape" (personal communication, 1994). A real strength of this measure, she notes, is that it provides several types of information. To understand this, we need to examine how heart rate patterns can be used to indicate attention processes.[5]

According to Thorson and Lang (1992), there are two distinct dimensions of attention that can be measured with heart rate data: phasic and tonic. The former describes short-term or moment-to-moment changes in attention that are characterized (but not limited to) orienting responses that occur as an automatic reaction to salient television stimuli. In psychology, the orienting response (OR) has been labeled the "what is it? reflex" (Pavlov, 1927), the "investigatory reflex" (Sokolov, 1963), and the "orienting reaction" (Lynn, 1966). It is an involuntary response to certain types of stimulus characteristics, such as novelty, intensity, color, complexity, surprise, and conflict (Berlyne, 1960). The OR is a selection process that disrupts other processing activity so that a person can focus attention on the eliciting stimulus, interpret its meaning, and determine what action should be taken (Lynn, 1966; Shiffrin & Schneider, 1977). The OR is accompanied by physiological changes, including photochemical changes in the eye, increases in electroencephalogram (brain wave) activity, contraction of the blood vessels in the limbs and expansion of those in the head, increased galvanic skin response, and varied changes in cardiac and respiratory systems (Berlyne, 1960). All these physiological changes are, among other things, thought to facilitate information-processing activity. Sokolov (1963), for example, has shown that sensory thresholds are lowered following the OR, making the individual more sensitive to information from the environment.

Two distinct phasic attention patterns associated with the OR have been identified in the literature. The first is the monophasic pattern characterized by an inverted U-shaped function that occurs in the 10 heartbeats immediately following the OR. The second is a biphasic pattern characterized by a "heart rate [that] slows initially for about two beats, then accelerates to a peak by the seventh beat and then recovers to baseline level" (Thorson & Lang, 1992, p. 355).

In contrast, the second dimension of attention that can be measured by heart rate data, tonic attention, measures long-term investments of cognitive effort, processes generally directed by the television viewer (Thorson & Lang, 1992). As with the RT studies, tonic attention is related to the amount of capacity allocated to an information-processing task. Tonic attention processes are analyzed through examination of the long-term variance in the baseline heart rate level (Thorson & Lang, 1992).

Lang (1992) notes that television viewers' conscious attention-related decisions play a larger role in their deciding what to attend to than do involuntary ORs. However, she explains that the role of the OR is not unimportant. This is because the short-term phasic attention responses associated with ORs help shape subsequent attention patterns. Thorson and Lang (1992), for example, found that orienting responses to complex television stimuli are likely to exhaust attentional capacity to the extent there is not enough capacity left to process effectively and store other incoming information. As a result, ORs not only play a role in determining attention selection, but continue to influence subsequent information-processing activity in other ways as well.

The use of heart rate (and other psychophysiological) methods to measure attention is in its infancy in communication research, although there is a rich body of theory and research in psychology that communication researchers have used as a foundation for media research in this area (e.g., Bull & Lang, 1972; Lacey, Kagan, Lacey, & Moss, 1963; Ohman, 1979). One feature of this method that we particularly like is that it allows observation of both voluntary and involuntary attention processes, so that the researcher can examine the relationship between the two to understand their joint influence on communication processes.

Measuring Covert Attention Processes: A Summary

In summary, our review of the PsychLit database for the past 19 years shows that attention to television has been measured using secondary task methods and psychophysiological measures. RT secondary task methods and heart rate data collection involve the use of elaborate computerized laboratories and labor-intensive data-collection efforts, which pay off when researchers are interested in studying moment-to-moment fluctuations in attention allocated to television. Otherwise, pencil-and-paper measures that capture overall or aggregate levels of attention allocated to an entire message are available and useful for answering many questions about attention to television. One such method we have reviewed in some detail is the preload task method, which is based on a capacity model of attention.

As a whole, this literature has contributed a great deal to what we know about what it means to watch television, as the studies reviewed demonstrate. However, this literature owes a great debt not only to psychologists who first developed theories and methods for measuring covert attention processes, but also to the literature on attention to television that employs an overt measure of attention, eyes-on-screen. This literature came first, offering the benefits of programmatic research: a variety of key questions about attention, often answered through a series of multiple studies; elaborate empirically based theoretical development; and true innovation in the literature. It is to this literature that we now turn.

OVERT BEHAVIOR AS
A DIRECT MEASURE OF ATTENTION

The "eyes-on-screen" method of measuring attention—the most common behavioral conceptualization of attention in the communication literature—was popularized by Daniel Anderson and his colleagues (Anderson et al., 1979; Anderson & Levin, 1976). The eyes-on-screen method involves the study of an overt component of attention: visual selection.

The method often requires the use of computer equipment and a laboratory setup consisting of two rooms joined by a wall with a one-way mirror. In one room, subjects watch television; the other room houses computer equipment. Subjects are seated facing the one-way mirror, so that their eye movements are visible to experimenters looking through that mirror from the other room. As subjects watch television, experimenters record visual selection, for example, by pushing a key on the computer key board whenever the subject is looking at the television screen and releasing the key when subject looks away. The computer also keeps a record of elapsed program time, so that researchers can later determine exactly when during the program a subject was looking or not looking at the television. In order to avoid ceiling effects—a constant gaze at the screen that might mask variance—subjects are often presented with other options, such as magazines, toys, and even changing slides shown on a projection screen next to the TV set (Alwitt, Anderson, Lorch, & Levin, 1980; Hawkins, Tapper, Bruce, & Pingree, 1994; Mielke, 1983; Palmer, 1974). The presence of these alternate activities can also increase ecological validity, as viewing television in the lab becomes more like viewing television at home, where viewers often engage in other activities while watching television.

Eyes-on-screen data can be used to summarize visual selection patterns. For example, the data can be used to tell what proportion of the program was visually selected for attention, and exactly which program segments were selected. In addition, the method allows researchers to correlate specific stimulus events occurring on-screen (e.g., complexity, puppets) with visual selection.

A variety of research questions have been addressed using the eyes-on-screen measure, and even the earliest research in this area yielded a theoretically rich discussion in the literature. Anderson and Levin (1976), for example, studied visual selection for children 1 to 4 years of age. They found that few stimulus characteristics have an effect on visual selection until a child is about 2.5 years old. It is about this time, too, when a child develops a "viewing schema," understanding that watching television is "something to do" and orienting him- or herself toward the TV set while playing with toys or engaging in other activities (Anderson & Lorch, 1983, p. 12). From 3 to 5 years of age, children's visual selection was found to be based in part on response to program attributes, although only a few attributes have systematic influence for this age group (Krull, 1983). By 7 or 8 years of age, children's visual selection is more sophisticated; they "react based on what they have seen, what they are seeing, and what they expect to see" (p. 118). Anderson and Lorch (1983) suggest this more sophisticated viewing style "reflects cognitive development, increased world knowledge, and understanding of the cinematic codes and format structures of television" (p. 13). With age, then, visual selection appears to be increasingly under control of the child viewer, guided not only by program attributes, but also increasingly by the viewer's ability to anticipate content, distinguish important from incidental material, and use schemata to help select, organize, and make meaningful the incoming information (Anderson & Lorch, 1983; Collins, 1983; Krull, 1983; Meadowcroft & Reeves, 1989).

Visual selection studies have also identified general television viewing strategies. In a study by Lorch, Anderson, and Levin (1979), for instance, 5-year-old children watched television either in a room with toys or in a room without toys. Although visual selection in the no-toys group was nearly double that in the toys condition (44% and 87%, respectively), there were no significant differences between conditions in terms of information acquisition. Based on these findings, the researchers described children's visual selection as strategic—how else could one group look at the television screen during only 44% of the program, yet pick up as much program content as children who looked at the screen twice as much? Clearly, children have developed ways of dividing attention between television viewing and other activities that do not also diminish program comprehension. In using this strategy, Lorch et al. (1979) assert that children do not continuously look at the television screen. Instead, they divide attention between television viewing and other activities, and they monitor the audio track for cues they have learned are associated with the presentation of comprehensible, interesting, or central program content. Once they pick up such cues, their visual orientation is toward the television screen and will be maintained there until program content becomes incomprehensible, redundant, or otherwise uninteresting.

Similarly, Zhao (1989) describes viewer strategies for looking at television commercial clusters. He wanted to know whether viewers actually watch commercials if they are left to their own devices. To answer this question, he had subjects watch television in a laboratory set up to mimic a home environment, complete with TV, sofa, chairs, kitchen, magazines, newspapers, drinks, snacks, and an adjacent bathroom. A video camera was placed behind a one-way mirror so that it recorded looks at the television screen during commercial breaks. Zhao discovered that when the viewers were exposed to a commercial cluster, they glanced at the TV screen at intervals that varied between 60 and 65 seconds. Zhao hypothesizes that practiced TV viewers have developed an automatic "scanning behavior" for monitoring commercial clusters. They do this as they go about other things, waiting for commercials to end. He also found that placing a product name within those intervals significantly increased subjects' memory of the product brand.

Using visual selection data, Hawkins et al. (1994) have identified four different general strategies for watching television: monitoring, orienting, engaged, and stares. Some viewers, for example, tend to look at television frequently, but for very brief periods of time (1.5 seconds or less); Hawkins et al. refer to these viewers as "monitors," reflecting their conclusion that these viewers only monitor content while viewing television. In contrast, engaged viewers appear more involved in program content, looking at television for longer periods of time (6-15 seconds). Hawkins et al. suggest these different viewing styles exist because viewers have different goals, and thus process content in different ways that produce different visual selection strategies.

In summary, the eyes-on-screen method allows observation of visual selection, a behavioral manifestation of attention. Studies employing this method have contributed a great deal to what we know about what it means to attend to television. These studies show us the variety of visual selection strategies people use to divide attention between television viewing and other activities. In fact, it is these studies that led Anderson and his colleagues to reject the idea that television viewing is a passive activity. Instead, Anderson and his colleagues found that TV viewing is an activity in which viewers exert a considerable amount of mental effort as they pose questions about incoming content and make decisions about what to do with selected information (Anderson & Lorch, 1983).

Knowing something about the interaction between the human mind and messages also has implications for message design. The program *Sesame Street,* for example, often uses rhyming, animation, and alliteration in its educational segments, as well as other devices found to elicit children's visual selection. The knowledge that visual selection is influenced by a program's comprehensibility has implications for program design. Lorch et al. (1979), for example, suggest that the relationship between visual selection and program comprehension is described by an inverted U-shaped function; they note, "If a TV segment is moderately comprehensible, it challenges the viewer to further attention" (p. 723). Given this, one would predict that moderately comprehensible program content has a greater chance of visual selection than do other types of content.

CONCLUSION

For the chief question is always simply this: what and how much can the understanding and reason know apart from all experience? (Kant, 1781/1965, p. 12)

The German philosopher Immanuel Kant wrote those words in 1781. In a sense, we are still asking the question today: How do we know what we know? Attention studies can help us understand how we come to select particular messages from the myriad messages bombarding us. Those messages we retain help construct our view of the world as we know it (Lippmann, 1922).

What a viewer learns, as far as television messages are concerned, derives from the interaction between the message and the human information-processing system. Communication researchers long ago put to rest the notion of the magic bullet theory of message reception, in which a reality that exists apart from us directly enters our minds. We now understand that complex media messages are rarely entered and stored unaltered in long-term memory. And it is, in part, the many different cognitive processes we collectively call "attention" that help alter those messages. The proof that these processes are an important object of study can be seen in what communication researchers have recently learned about message traits and their influence on attention to television.

For instance, consider visual selection and orienting response studies, some of which we have reviewed in this chapter. We know that salient stimuli elicit attention and increase the likelihood that content presented at that moment will be remembered by the viewer. On the other hand, we also know that salient features should be used sparingly when messages are complex. Otherwise, orienting responses may exhaust available attention capacity to the extent viewers will fail to process messages in a meaningful way.

We also know that there is a certain rhythm to television viewing, a rhythm that arises from interactions among viewer goals, information-processing activity, and program structure. Zhao's work tells us that viewers may be most attentive to a commercial message at the very beginning and at the end, given the viewer's propensity to glance at the TV screen every 60 to 65 seconds. In addition, many researchers have noted that visual selection occurs most frequently at content boundaries, as viewers sample new content and decide if they want to continue viewing the new segment (e.g., Anderson & Lorch, 1983; Anderson & Smith, 1984; Burns & Anderson, in press; Hawkins et al., 1994). Using a secondary RT task to measure attention allocation, Meadowcroft (in press) also reports that most attention span cycles produced by environmental monitoring and dramatic sampling last between 60 and 90 seconds before the cycles begin repeating themselves. Cognitive processing associated with integration of program content, however, was longer in duration (e.g., the attention span cycle produced by the use of story schema was about 3.5 minutes in duration).

Attention studies have also given us a better understanding of what it means to watch television. We know that viewers have different goals and that the way they attend to information is a function of those goals, as well as of the more automatic reactions to program stimuli characterized by the orienting response. We also know that watching television can involve a sophisticated analysis of incoming information at several levels, the results of which are quickly integrated as viewers assign meaning to program content.

As a whole, the research on attention to television forces us to consider more seriously the idea that *attention* is an umbrella term for a number of different cognitive processes. This is one reason so many different methods of measuring attention are in use: Different measures tap different cognitive processes associated with attention. The eyes-on-screen method measures visual selection, for example, whereas secondary task methods measure allocation of mental effort. The idea that these different methods measure different components of attention is supported by the fact that measures are not always correlated. Lang (personal communication, 1993) reports that she has measured attention with RT, heart rate, and self-report measures in a single study and found that although the different measures sometimes covary, they often diverge, suggesting that they are not all measuring the same concept. Meadowcroft and Olson (1993) have noted a similar lack of correlation between self-report and RT data in her study of attention to televised and print narratives, and has also found the two measures are related differently to memory. The lack of covariance among methods makes it clear that these measures are not all indicators of the same processes, suggesting that the theoretical development in these literatures may not be interchangeable.

We have also argued the importance of including attention variables in mass media research. Inferring attention from memory data, for instance, can lead to inaccurate conclusions about attention processes. In addition, most psychology studies of attention fall far short of examining everyday attention processes because the stimuli typical of psychology experiments tend to be contrived, wholly unlike what people encounter in a stimulus-rich processing task like that presented by television. It is unlikely, therefore, that findings from this kind of psychology study will generalize to a television viewing context.

Finally, mass media researchers tend to ask questions that are very different from those psychologists ask. Psychologists tend to ask questions that focus on attention process limitations; mass media researchers ask questions that focus on the interaction between the television viewer and the message, or, as Lang (1992) puts it, "the interaction between the television and the human brain" (p. 4). The psychology literature, therefore, does not always have answers to the questions communicators are likely to ask.

Why study attention? By adding attention to the list of independent variables, communication researchers can better discover the ways in which messages are transformed by human perception. Communication researchers are qualified—indeed, obligated—to study any variable, in whatever manner they see fit, if doing so will help them better understand communication processes and effects.

NOTES

1. We used the American Psychological Association's (1993) PsychLit database to select for further examination pertinent communication and related studies that used attention, memory, recall, recognition, comprehension, learning, or processing as a measured variable. We did not perform a formal content analysis of the pertinent studies in these publications, but we did read them carefully and take their content into consideration as we prepared this chapter. The journals we examined are as follows: *American Behavioral Scientist, Child Development, Communication, Communication & Cognition, Communication Education, Communication Monographs, Communication Research, Communications, Educational Communication & Technology Journal, Human Communication Research, Human Factors, Journal of Advertising, Journal of Advertising Research, Journal of Broadcasting & Electronic Media, Journal of Communication, Journal of Consumer Research, Journalism Quarterly, Public Opinion Quarterly, Quarterly Journal of Speech, Signs,* and *Visual Arts Research.*

2. Attentional capacity can change; it is not static. An increase in capacity usually comes with the message consumer's level of arousal (Kahneman, 1973, pp. 17-24). Messages that arouse can include violent messages, sexually explicit messages, messages that intimidate or anger the message receiver, and messages that are simply interesting to look at and listen to. If variation in capacity is not an independent variable, an investigator would want to control for capacity variation by pretesting and then adopting messages of approximately the same magnitude of arousal. A pretest might include, among several options available, the use of a Likert scale such as the one used by Zaichkowsky (1985) or Nowak and Salmon (1987).

3. There is experimental evidence to suggest that attentional processing is not serial, as described by Sternberg (1969), but parallel, meaning that different processes occur simultaneously (Rumelhart, McClelland, & the PDP Research Group, 1986). Thus varying expenditures of time, as explained by the parallel processing model, are accounted for by the time it takes to accomplish all cognitive tasks simultaneously. In addition, Sternberg's RT equation does not address the physiological component of RT responses: the motor skills involved in physically responding to RT cues. This is important, because it is reasonable to expect variance in motor skills, particularly when comparisons are made between children at various levels of cognitive and motor development. In this case, it is wise to control for such variance by taking a baseline RT and using it as a covariate (Meadowcroft & Reeves, 1989). When subjects are randomly assigned to experimental conditions, however, this type of individual variance should be minimized.

4. Pretesting visual and auditory preloads is complicated enough to make outlining the process in more detail here impractical. Those interested in a more in-depth explanation of preload pretesting should contact Tom Grimes at the address given on the first page of this chapter.

5. There has been quite a bit of debate recently concerning validation of heart rate measures. Those interested in the issue are referred to Lang (1992), who describes replicating results of earlier attention research that used different measures of attention in an effort to validate the use of heart rate as a measure of attention.

REFERENCES

Alwitt, L. F., Anderson, D. R., Lorch, E. P., & Levin, S. R. (1980). Preschool children's visual attention to attributes of television. *Human Communication Research, 7,* 52-67.

American Psychological Association. (1993). *PsychLit* [database]. Washington, DC: Author.

Anderson, D. R., Alwitt, L. F., Lorch, E. P., Levin, S. R. (1979). Watching children watch television. In G. A. Hale & M. Lewis (Eds.), *Attention in cognitive development* (pp. 331-361). New York: Plenum.

Anderson, D. R., & Levin, S. R. (1976). Young children's attention to Sesame Street. *Child Development, 47,* 866-911.

Anderson, D. R., & Lorch, E. P. (1983). Looking at television: Action or reaction? In J. Bryant & D. R. Anderson (Eds.), *Children's understanding of television: Research on attention and comprehension* (pp. 1-33). New York: Academic Press.

Anderson, D. R., & Smith, R. N. (1984). Young children's TV viewing: The problem of cognitive continuity. In F. J. Morrison, C. Lord, & D. F. Keting (Eds.), *Advances in applied developmental psychology* (Vol. 1, pp. 115-163). New York: Academic Press.

Armstrong, G. B., & Greenberg, B. S. (1990). Background television as an inhibitor of cognitive processing. *Human Communication Research, 16,* 355-386.

Baddeley, A. D., & Hitch, G. (1974). Working memory. In G. Bower (Ed.), *Recent advances in learning and motivation* (Vol. 8, pp. 47-87). New York: Academic Press.

Bartlett, F. C. (1932). *Remembering: A study in experimental and social psychology.* London: Cambridge University Press.

Berlyne, D. E. (1960). *Conflict, arousal, and curiosity.* New York: McGraw-Hill.

Britton, B. K., Meyer, B. J., Simpson, R., Holdredge, T. S., & Curry, C. (1979). Effects of the organization of text on memory: Tests of two implications of selective attention hypotheses. *Journal of Experimental Psychology: Human Learning & Memory, 5,* 496-506.

Bryant, J., Zillmann, D., & Brown, D. (1983). Entertainment features in children's educational television: Effects on attention and information acquisition. In J. Bryant & D. R. Anderson (Eds.), *Children's understanding of television: Research on attention and comprehension* (pp. 221-240). New York: Academic Press.

Bull, K., & Lang, P. J. (1972). Intensity judgments and physiological response amplitude. *Psychophysiology, 9*, 428-436.

Burns, J., & Anderson, D. R. (in press). Paying attention to television. In J. Bryant & D. Zillmann (Eds.), *Responding to the screen*. Hillsdale, NJ: Lawrence Erlbaum.

Carter, R. F., Ruggles, W. L., Jackson, K. M., & Heffner, M. B. (1973). Application of signaled stopping technique to communication research. In P. Clark (Ed.), *New models for mass communication research* (pp. 15-43). Beverly Hills, CA: Sage.

Chaffee, S. H., & Schleuder, J. (1986). Measurement and effects of attention to media news. *Human Communication Research, 13*, 76-107.

Cherry, E. C. (1953). Some experiments on the recognition of speech, with one and with two ears. *Journal of the Acoustical Society of America, 25*, 975-979.

Collins, W. A. (1983). Interpretation and inference in children's television viewing. In J. Bryant & D. R. Anderson (Eds.), *Children's understanding of television: Research on attention and comprehension* (pp. 125-150). New York: Academic Press.

Conrad, R. (1964). Acoustic confusions in immediate memory. *British Journal of Psychology, 55*, 75-84.

Deutsch, J. A., & Deutsch, D. (1963). Attention: Some theoretical considerations. *Psychological Review, 70*, 80-90.

Drew, D. G., & Grimes, T. (1987). Audio-visual redundancy and TV news recall. *Communication Research, 14*, 452-461.

Geiger, S., & Reeves, B. (in press). The effect of cuts and semantic relatedness on attention to television. *Communication Research.*

Grimes, T. (1990). Audio-video correspondence and its role in attention and memory. *Educational Technology Research and Development, 38*(3), 15-25.

Grimes, T. (1991). Mild auditory-visual dissonance in television news may exceed viewer attentional capacity. *Human Communication Research, 18*, 268-298.

Grimes, T., Broholm, J., Pounds, J. C. S., Vogl, R., & Hoekstra, S. (1993). *Visual and auditory preload methodology.* Unpublished manuscript.

Grimes, T., & Drechsel, B. (1994). *How race and gender schemata can create defamatory meaning in television news.* Manuscript submitted for publication.

Gruder, C. L., Cook, T. D., Hennigan, K. M., Flay, B. R., Alessis, C., & Halamaj, J. (1978). Empirical tests of the absolute sleeper effect predicted from the discounting cue hypothesis. *Journal of Personality and Social Psychology, 36*, 1061-1074.

Hausnecht, D. R., & Moore, D. L. (1986). The effects of time compressed advertising on brand attitude judgments. In R. J. Lutz (Ed.), *Advances in consumer research* (Vol. 13, pp. 105-110). Provo, UT: Association for Consumer Research.

Hawkins, R. P., Tapper, J., Bruce, L., & Pingree, S. (1994). *Strategy, inertia, and style in television viewing.* Unpublished manuscript.

Huston, A. C., & Wright, J. C. (1983). Children's processing of television: Informative functions of formal features. In J. Bryant & D. R. Anderson (Eds.), *Children's understanding of television: Research on attention and comprehension* (pp. 35-68). New York: Academic Press.

Kahneman, D. (1973). *Attention and effort.* New York: Holt, Rinehart & Winston.

Kant, I. (1965). *Critique of pure reason* (N. K. Smith, Trans.). New York: St. Martin's. (Original work published 1781)

Kinchla, R. A. (1992). Attention. In M. R. Rosenzweig & L. W. Porter (Eds.), *Annual review of psychology* (Vol. 43, pp. 711-742). Palo Alto, CA: Annual Reviews.

Kruley, P., Sciama, S. C., & Glenberg, A. M. (in press). On-line processing of textual illustrations in the visuo-spatial sketchpad: Evidence from dual-task studies. *Memory & Cognition.*

Krull, R. (1983). Children learning to watch television. In J. Bryant & D. R. Anderson (Eds.), *Children's understanding of television: Research on attention and comprehension* (pp. 103-123). New York: Academic Press.

Lacey, J. I., Kagan, J., Lacey, B. C., & Moss, H. A. (1963). The visceral level: Situational determinants and behavioral correlates of autonomic response patterns. In P. H. Knapp (Ed.), *Expression of the emotions in man.* New York: International University Press.

Lachman, R., Lachman, J. L., & Butterfield, E. C. (1979). *Cognitive psychology and information processing: An introduction.* Hillsdale, NJ: Lawrence Erlbaum.

Lang, A. (1987). *The effects of the formal features of television on viewers' attention and arousal: Cardiac responses, attention, and arousal.* Unpublished doctoral dissertation, University of Wisconsin—Madison.

Lang, A. (1992). *A limited capacity approach to television viewing.* Unpublished manuscript.

Lang, A., Geiger, S., Strickwerda, M., & Sumner, J. (1993). The effects of related and unrelated cuts on viewers' attention, capacity, and memory. *Communication Research, 20,* 4-29.

Lippmann, W. (1922). *Public opinion.* New York: Macmillan.

Lorch, E. P., Anderson, D. R., & Levin, S. R. (1979). The relationship of visual attention to children's comprehension of television. *Child Development, 50,* 722-727.

Lowery, S., & DeFleur, M. L. (1983). *Milestones in mass communication research: Media effects.* New York: Longman.

Luce, P. A., Feustel, T. C., & Pisoni, D. B. (1983). Capacity demands in short-term memory for synthetic and natural speech. *Human Factors, 25,* 17-32.

Lynn, R. (1966). *Attention, arousal and the orienting reaction.* Oxford: Pergamon.

Mander, J. (1978). *Four arguments for the elimination of television.* New York: William Morrow.

Martin, C. S., Mullennix, J. W., Pisoni, D. B., & Summers, W. V. (1989). Effects of talker variability on recall of spoken word lists. *Journal of Experimental Psychology: Learning, Memory, and Cognition, 15,* 676-684.

McIntyre, C. W., Blackwell, S. L., & Denton, C. L. (1978). Effects of noise distractibility on the spans of apprehension of hyperactive boys. *Journal of Abnormal Child Psychology, 6,* 483-492.

McLeod, J. M., Rucinski, D. M., Pan, Z., & Kosicki, G. M. (1988, May). *Attention to television news: An empirical explication.* Paper presented at the annual meeting of the International Communication Association, New Orleans.

Meadowcroft, J. M. (in press). Attention span cycles. In J. H. Watt & A. Van Lear, Jr. (Eds.), *Cycles and dynamic patterns in communication processes.* Thousand Oaks, CA: Sage.

Meadowcroft, J. M., & Olson, B. (1993). *Attention to televised vs. print messages.* Unpublished manuscript.

Meadowcroft, J. M., & McDonald, D. G. (1986). Meta-analysis of research on children and the mass media: An atypical history of theoretical development? *Journalism Quarterly, 63,* 474-480.

Meadowcroft, J. M., & Reeves, B. (1989). Influence of story schema development on children's attention to television. *Communication Research, 16,* 352-374.

Meadowcroft, J. M., & Watt, J. H. (1989, May). *A multi-component theory of children's attention spans.* Paper presented to the Mass Communication Division at the annual meeting of the International Communication Association, San Francisco.

Meadowcroft, J. M., & Zillmann, D. (1987). Women's comedy preferences during the menstrual cycle. *Communication Research, 14,* 204-218.

Mielke, K. W. (1983). Formative research on appeal and comprehension in *3-2-1 Contact.* In J. Bryant & D. R. Anderson (Eds.), *Children's understanding of television: Research on attention and comprehension* (pp. 241-263). New York: Academic Press.

Neisser, U. (1976). *Cognitive reality: Principles and implications of cognitive psychology.* San Francisco: W. H. Freeman.

Norman, D. A., & Bobrow, D. G. (1975). On data-limited and resource-limited processes. *Cognitive Psychology, 7*(1), 44-64.

Nowak, G., & Salmon, C. T. (1987). *Measuring involvement with social issues.* Paper presented at the annual meeting of the Association for Education in Journalism and Mass Communication, San Antonio, TX.

Ohman, A. (1979). The orienting response, attention, and learning: An information-processing perspective. In H. D. Kimmel, E. H. van Olst, & J. F. Orlbeke (Eds.), *The orienting reflex in humans.* Hillsdale, NJ: Lawrence Erlbaum.

Palmer, E. L. (1974). Formative research in the production of television for children. In D. E. Olson (Ed.), *Media and symbols: The forms of expression, communication, and education.* Chicago: University of Chicago Press.

Pavlov, I. P. (1927). *Conditional reflexes.* Oxford: Oxford University Press.

Penney, C. G. (1989). Modality effects and the structure of short-term verbal memory. *Memory & Cognition, 17,* 398-422.

Pezdek, K., & Stevens, E. (1984). Children's memory for auditory and visual information on television. *Developmental Psychology, 20,* 212-218.

Posner, M. I., & Petersen, S. E. (1990). The attention system of the human brain. In W. M. Cowan, E. M. Shooter, C. F. Stevens, & R. F. Thompson (Eds.), *Annual review of neuroscience* (Vol. 13. pp. 25-42). Palo Alto, CA: Annual Reviews.

Posner, M. I., & Snyder, C. R. R. (1975). Attention and cognitive control. In R. L. Solso (Ed.), *Information processing and cognition: The Loyola Symposium.* Hillsdale, NJ: Lawrence Erlbaum.

Poulis, R. W., Rubenstein, E. A., & Liebert, R. M. (1975). Positive social learning. *Journal of Communication, 25,* 90-97.

Reeves, B., & Anderson, D. R. (1991). Media studies and psychology. *Communication Research, 18,* 597-600.

Reeves, B., Thorson, E., Rothschild, M., McDonald, D., Hirsch, J., & Goldstein, R. (1985). Attention to television: Intrastimulus effects of movement and scene changes on alpha variation over time. *International Journal of Neuroscience, 25,* 241-255.

Rumelhart, D. E., McClelland, J. L., & the PDP Research Group. (Eds.). (1986). *Parallel distributed processing: Explorations in the microstructure of cognition: Vol. 1. Foundations.* Cambridge: MIT Press.

Schleuder, J., & White, A. V. (1989, May). *Priming effects of television news bumpers and teasers on attention and memory.* Paper presented to the Information Systems Division at the annual meeting of the International Communication Association, San Francisco.

Schneider, W., & Shiffrin, R. M. (1977). Controlled and automatic human information processing: I. Detection, search, and attention. *Psychological Review, 84,* 1-66.

Shaughnessy, J. J., & Zechmeister, E. B. (1985). *Research methods in psychology.* New York: Knopf.

Shiffrin, R. M. (1993). Short-term memory: A brief commentary. *Memory & Cognition, 21,* 193-197.

Shiffrin, R. M., & Dumais, S. T. (1981). The development of automatism. In J. R. Anderson (Ed.), *Cognitive skills and their acquisition* (pp. 111-140). Hillsdale, NJ: Lawrence Erlbaum.

Shiffrin, R. M., & Schneider, W. (1977). Controlled and automatic human information processing: II. Perceptual learning, automatic attending, and a general theory. *Psychological Review, 84,* 127-190.

Singer, J. L. (1980). The power and limitations of television: A cognitive-affective analysis. In P. H. Tannenbaum (Ed.), *Entertainment functions of television* (pp. 31-65). Hillsdale, NJ: Lawrence Erlbaum.

Sokolov, E. N. (1963). *Perception and the conditioned reflex.* New York: Pergamon.

Sternberg, S. (1969). The discovery of processing stages: Extensions of Donders' method. *Acta Psychologica, 30,* 276-315.

Thorson, E. (1983). Propositional determinants of memory for television commercials. In R. Martin & H. Leigh (Eds.), *Current issues and research in advertising.* Ann Arbor: University of Michigan Press.

Thorson, E., & Lang, A. (1992). The effects of television videographics and lecture familiarity on adult cardiac orienting responses and memory. *Communication Research, 19,* 346-369.

Thorson, E., Reeves, B., & Schleuder, J. (1987). Attention to local and global complexity in television messages. In M. L. McLaughlin (Ed.), *Communication yearbook 10* (pp. 366-383). Newbury Park, CA: Sage.

Treisman, A. M. (1960). Contextual cues in selective listening. *Quarterly Journal of Experimental Psychology, 12,* 242-248.

Winn, M. (1977). *The plug-in drug.* New York: Viking.

Zaichkowsky, J. L. (1985). Measuring the involvement construct. *Journal of Consumer Research, 12,* 341-352.

Zhao, X. (1989). *Effects of commercial position in television programming.* Unpublished doctoral dissertation, University of Wisconsin—Madison.

7 Cognitive Interpersonal Communication Research: Some Thoughts on Criteria

DEAN E. HEWES
University of Minnesota

THE cognitive explanations of the causes and consequences of human communication are as old as communication theory itself, and probably older. For instance, the scientific study of persuasion (the premier component of communication theory) was derived primarily from mass communication research focusing on the human psyche (see Delia, 1987). Newer components, such as interpersonal communication, were grounded, in part, in cognitive consistency theories (Newcombe, 1953), mentalist social learning theories (Miller & Steinberg, 1975), and humanistic psychology, with its clinical interest in the workings of the human mind (Jourard, 1971). The prevalence of cognitive theories of human communication continues to this day (see Hewes, in press-a).

Modern cognitive theories of interpersonal communication, although retaining an emphasis on mental processes, differ in quality and, to some extent, in kind from those earlier theories. I can think of no better way to explore the special attributes and requirements of modern cognitive theories than in a critical review of the chapters in this volume by Wilson, Greene, O'Keefe and Lambert, Burgoon and Langer, and Grimes and Meadowcroft.[1]

Each of these chapters is worthy of considerable attention and thought; however, rather than critique each separately, I looked for common issues, issues that provide answers to three questions: What are the ingredients of fully realized modern cognitive theories? What are the special responsibilities of modern cognitive theories of interpersonal communication? What issues may guide future efforts at theorizing? Answers to these questions serve as the basis of my criticisms. It is my hope that, even if controversial, they may also trigger debate on desiderata for cognitive approaches to communication theorizing.

Correspondence and requests for reprints: Dean E. Hewes, Department of Speech Communication, University of Minnesota, Minneapolis, MN 55455.

Communication Yearbook 18, pp. 162-179

MODERN COGNITIVE THEORIES

What are the ingredients of fully realized modern cognitive theories? The answer to this question is to be found in weltanschauungs of the cognitive approach. Modern cognitive theories, despite their diversity in content and form, share certain assumptions.[2] In earlier work I have summarized these assumptions (Hewes & Planalp, 1987; Planalp & Hewes, 1982), as have many others before and since (see Greene, 1984b; Littlejohn, 1992; Newell, 1980; Newell, Rosenbloom, & Laird, 1989). I have compressed these assumptions into the three I discuss below.

The Assumptions of Cognitive Theories

The unit of analysis for cognitive theories is the "actor" or an "active organism." "Actors" (a) respond to their environments, (b) initiate actions with respect to their environments (i.e., they can create their own stimulation), (c) construct and pursue goals, and (d) reflect on their cognitive representations, processes, and relationships among their actions, goals, and environments (i.e., they are "conscious"), although they do not always do so (Bargh, 1984; Posner & Snyder, 1975; Schneider & Shiffrin, 1977; Shiffrin & Schneider, 1977).

The alternative to this assumption is that people are either too much or too little influenced by their environments. Too much, and they are merely reacting to the environment as in behaviorist or "transindividual" theories (organismic theories of social aggregates—groups, organizations, cultures, and so on). Too little, and they are clockwork mechanisms passing through, but not acting on or reacting to, their environment as in many personality trait explanations of human communication (Hewes & Planalp, 1987).

An actor's interactions with his or her environment will be moderated by computations performed on mental representations of that environment, under specifiable conditions. This assumption implies, first, that the interplay between mental representations and processes may alter the effects of environmental stimuli such that, at least sometimes, one can predict a response only if one knows *both* the stimuli *and* the relevant mental representations and processes that are operating on those stimuli. To be complete, then, cognitive theories must specify the representations and processes necessary for predicting actors' responses, the content of those representations, their organization, and the ways in which they interact with specific cognitive processes (Anderson, 1984; Greene, 1984b; Hewes & Planalp, 1982, 1987; Wyer & Srull, 1984).

Second, in those cases where cognitive representations and processes need not be considered in predicting actors' responses (i.e., when bridge laws can connect stimuli directly with responses), cognitive explanations must specify the conditions and the cognitive mechanisms that incline actors to respond directly, consistently, and automatically to environmental stimuli (Bargh, 1984; Langer,

1978; Planalp & Hewes, 1982). Without such, cognitive theories would lead to predictions that are inconsistently accurate.

Cognitive representations and processes are driven by actor goals, design goals, and the complex interactions among them. As noted in the first assumption, people are assumed to be actors and thus to have goals. In the second assumption, these actors are endowed with complex mental machinery. The machinery is deployed in the pursuit of those goals. To understand how the machinery grinds out responses in reaction to stimuli, we must understand how the pursuit of goals is implemented in the machinery (see Hewes & Planalp, 1982; Newell, 1990).

This task would be simpler were it not for three factors. First, at least two, often inconsistent, kinds of goals (actor goals and design goals) are typically involved in the determination of any response. *Actor goals* are simply the conscious or nonconscious wishes of the actor—to gain some reward or to avoid some punishment. *Design goals,* in contrast, are hypothetical constructs attributed to biological systems. For example, the human brain is simply too limited in its capacity to be ideally rational, although such rationality would greatly aid in the pursuit of actors' goals (Cherniak, 1986). Because the human brain has limited capacity to process information, we can treat it as if it had a wired-in goal to protect that capacity under task demands through (a) principles of "cognitive economics" (Hewes, in press-b; Hewes & Graham, 1988) and (b) the use of heuristics to reduce processing load (Hewes & Planalp, 1987). Design goals such as this cannot be said to belong *to* actors, although they are *in* actors. They are, instead, the result of evolution. Moreover, individual actor goals may conflict with design goals, complicating cognitive theories. As an illustration, my theory of problematic message processors notes the potential conflict among three goals: the need for accurate information (actor goal), the need to protect cognitive capacity (design goal), and the desire to conserve social effort (perhaps a combination of the two other goals or a separate one in its own right) (Hewes, in press-b).

Besides the potential conflict between actor and design goals, the relationship between goals and action is complicated further because two or more potentially inconsistent actor goals may be active simultaneously, resulting in creative interference, synthesis, compromise, or the formation of hierarchies of priorities (Greene, 1984a; Tracy, 1984). Finally, when actors are responding automatically to the environment, though they still have goals, they probably do not have conscious access to those goals. The goals have become embedded in their automatic responses by means of socialization. Thus measuring these goals becomes difficult, especially in routinized communication.

Applying the Assumptions
of Modern Cognitive Theories

Now let us apply these assumptions to the chapters under review. The first assumption is that the unit of analysis for cognitive theories is the "actor" or "active organism." Do these chapters reflect that assumption and all that it implies? Most do somewhat, but none fully capitalizes on all the attributes. For example, consider the actor attribute of "responsiveness to the environment." Burgoon and Langer posit a direct link between messages and a cognitive syndrome ("mindlessness"), thus recognizing this aspect of actors. Grimes and Meadowcroft reflect responsiveness of a cognitive process or processes (attention) to media displays. Greene emphasizes responsiveness through the encoding of messages, whereas Wilson looks at situational influences on goal production. Only O'Keefe and Lambert start their analysis "in the head" with what they call "thoughts" and proceed outward to message production.

Purely production-oriented theories such as O'Keefe and Lambert's (see Littlejohn, 1992, chap. 6), although impressive in many regards, face difficult theoretical extensions to capture the adaptability of human communicators. For instance, in O'Keefe and Lambert's theory, how are thoughts affected by environmental stimuli? If they are a simple, direct result of such stimuli, then stimuli lead directly to thoughts, thence to messages. Where lies the value of their cognitive explanation if one can predict from environmental stimuli directly to messages? If the connection between the two is more complex, what form might it take? Given that O'Keefe and Lambert reduce goals to connections between thoughts and the production of discourse, does their theory suggest that environmental stimuli, such as those studied by Wilson, do not affect goals directly, as Wilson's theory suggests, or must the effects on goals pass through the vague concept of "thoughts"? None of these questions should be taken to imply that O'Keefe and Lambert's work is without merit. Quite the contrary, I view it as the most innovative of the chapters under discussion here. I merely wish to point out that the assumptions of cognitive theory must be taken seriously, because they set an agenda of issues that need to be addressed eventually by all cognitive theories.

The assumption that the actor is the unit of analysis in cognitive theories also implies that actors can create goals, initiate action, and reflect on their cognitive representations, processes, and goal-path linkages. Most of the chapters under review here are weak in addressing these issues. The strongest of them are Wilson's and O'Keefe and Lambert's. O'Keefe and Lambert's strength is their focus on message production. Wilson's chapter has implications, but no direct explanations, for action. His implications come via two routes: (a) His individual difference variable, cognitive differentiation, is known to have many and varied implications for message selection; and (b) interpersonal goals *may* have implications for action. The connection between goals and action is highly complex and contingent (Greene, 1984a; von Wright, 1971), and it is ill specified in Wilson's account to date.

The other chapters do less with cognitive assumptions concerning the initiation of action, construction of goals, and reflection on mental states and processes. Focusing for a moment on the initiation of action, consider the example of Grimes and Meadowcroft's chapter. These authors present a methodologically motivated case for the study of attention to the mass media. They suggest only that attention may affect the degree and kind of impact that mediated messages have on behavior, but provide no clear description of how their various, orthogonal indices of attention are linked to specific cognitive processes that have known connections to behavior. In a different vein, Greene's theory, despite an excellent elaboration of the cognitive processing of messages during multiple-goal situations, never explains the production of communicative action. His dependent variables, although measured lexically, have no apparent relevance to communicative activity. They are, instead, indices of cognitive processing.

Finally, concerning the first assumption, none of the chapters, save Burgoon and Langer's, addresses actors' abilities to reflect on mental states and processes. This is surprising, because most of the authors recognize the importance of goals at some point during their treatment of communication. How do actors *learn* how to forge connections among mental representations, processes, goals, and communicative activity? What facets of face-to-face or mediated communication prompt this learning? By what mechanisms does this learning take place?

Learning is the least understood element of social cognition (see Fiske & Taylor, 1991; but see O'Keefe & Lambert, Chapter 3, this volume, for an interesting use of connectionist learning theories);[3] yet, without it, there can be no rhetorically effective response to changing social situations. Burgoon and Langer offer hints concerning the role of communication in impeding or facilitating a reflective orientation that promotes effective functioning in a social environment. Unfortunately, the cognitive processes linking communication and reflection are not well explained (though there is considerable evidence for their existence). We know what a mindless or mindful mental orientation is; we know what its cognitive outcomes are (limited information processing, categorical thinking, single perspectives, and failure to recognize context); we know nothing about the cognitive mechanisms that lead to either a mindful or a mindless state. We do not know what common mechanisms produce this set of outcomes in a mindless state. Actors may learn effective behavior during a mindful state, but we do not know why or how.

In subsequent work, Burgoon and Langer might want to explore (a) the cognitive mechanisms that explain their findings and (b) actors' capacities to reflect on their own mental states. An actor, in the sense promoted by most commentators on cognition, should be able under some conditions to identify and correct a mindless state. In general, the theories presented in these chapters would benefit from an exploration of the general capacities of actors—the focus of cognitive theories. Careful reflection on those capacities should make it clear that, if any of them are not accounted for in cognitive theories, those theories are no longer cognitive. They become behaviorist, trait, or "transindividual" theories (a) that do not need cognitive mechanisms for explanation and (b) that, therefore, may not be adequate to explain human communication (Hewes & Planalp, 1987).

Now let us move on to the second assumption. Cognitive theories necessarily assume that cognitive representations and processes can, but do not always, moderate the connection between stimuli and responses. Do these chapters address this critical assumption that separates cognitive theories from trait, transindividual, and behaviorist theories (Hewes & Planalp, 1987)? Most do. For example, Greene recognizes the importance of goals (single versus multiple) in moderating the cognitive mechanisms that process messages. Wilson's chapter is also explicit in this regard. Grimes and Meadowcroft support this requirement of cognitive theories.

Obviously, theories that do not explore the impacts of messages or environmental features cannot do so. Thus O'Keefe and Lambert's chapter is lacking in this area—odd, given O'Keefe's leadership in exploring individual difference variables that moderate the relation between contextual stimuli and message production (see, e.g., O'Keefe, 1988). Still, O'Keefe and Lambert's work reflects a concern for the status of cognitive mechanisms as moderators between environment and behavior. They employ a connectionist cognitive architecture to demonstrate their claim that there is not a one-to-one correspondence between global interpersonal goals and specific reflections of those goals in discourse. This claim to the "multifunctionality" of messages is well taken (Hewes, 1979). In fact, their theory highlights the fact that there cannot be a simple, mediating relationship between environmental manipulation of goals and the production of real messages. All cognitive theories need to make this claim. If they do not, then the discussion of cognitive mechanisms is an unnecessary elaboration of processes that simply pass on the impact of environmental stimuli to message production. Cognitive mechanisms must have the capacity to alter the impact of environmental stimuli to be worthy of study.

Finally, let us turn to the third assumption of cognitive theories. Cognitive representations and processes are driven by complex interactions between and among goals of similar and different kinds. Wilson and Greene both acknowledge this assumption explicitly. Grimes and Meadowcroft recognize the importance of this assumption for measuring cognitive processes, although they only sketch the cognitive mechanisms that might be involved in managing these interactions. O'Keefe and Lambert challenge it explicitly, but provide a detailed rationale for doing so that deserves careful attention.[4] Only Burgoon and Langer fail to address this assumption directly.

This becomes problematic for Burgoon and Langer's central claim. They speculate without direct evidence that broad, diffuse classes of communicative behaviors trigger or suppress mindlessness. What the evidence from the research on mindlessness suggests is that a certain amount of novelty has positive effects on people, both psychologically and physiologically (Langer, 1989). Burgoon and Langer suggest that certain kinds of language may produce or suppress novelty. This claim rings true, but attention to the goals of communication, cognition, and their interplay suggests modifications in this claim.

Consider the simplest possible case involving the effects of reinforcing, not competing, design and actor goals on the relationship between language and the positive outcomes of mindfulness. The chief design goal of cognitive systems is to protect cognitive capacity within the limitations set by the actor's goal performance. That is, cognitive systems conserve as much capacity as they can, given what the actor is trying to accomplish. This leads to cognitive shortcuts, such as heuristic processing of messages (Hewes & Planalp, 1982; Petty & Cacioppo, 1986).

The chief actor goal in communicative exchanges is the ability to comprehend messages (Planalp & Tracy, 1980; Tracy, 1985). Moreover, research on comprehension shows that (a) it is quite sensitive to message characteristics that reflect novelty in structure or content (Clark, 1985; Hewes & Planalp, 1987), and (b) messages that make comprehension difficult often lead to serious negative judgments concerning the social competence of the sender (Planalp & Tracy, 1980). Consequently, too much novelty, and especially sustained novelty, although arousing uncertainty and, thus, provoking mindfulness, should also lead to increased demands on cognitive capacity and heuristic processing. Heuristic processing is precisely what mindfulness is supposed to avoid, according to Burgoon and Langer.

Is this apparent contradiction likely to occur in real communicative exchanges within normal ranges of uncertainty? Apparently so. My theory of the processing of problematic messages presents evidence that a mindful, reflective orientation to the interpretation of messages leads to results quite different from those hypothesized by Burgoon and Langer (Hewes, in press-b). My theory implies that the higher the need for accuracy, the more vigilant social actors should be in identifying sources of biased information that might prevent them from taking appropriate social action to attain their goals; however, increased vigilance does not necessarily have the obvious effect of increasing a social actor's sensitivity to the occurrence of cues to biased information. Increasing the need for accuracy could decrease the detection rate for cues.

The need for accuracy can be pursued (a) by increasing the social actor's awareness of cues otherwise undetected (increasing sensitivity) or (b) by decreasing the ambiguity of cues used in judgments (discounting normally observed but less diagnostic cues). Social actors tend to prefer the latter alternative. The rate for cue detection for very simple objective cues decreases as motivation to identify those cues increases (Davenport, 1968, 1969; Levine, 1966). The explanation for this finding is that under conditions in which the task is open-ended and rewarding in its own right, increases in motivation lead social actors to report having detected cues more conservatively than they normally would (Eysenck, 1982; McGraw, 1978). Thus, as the need for accurate information increases, the perceived number of cues decreases.

Preliminary evidence obtained in a study by Hewes, Monsour, and Rutherford (1989) provides some support for this prediction. We obtained a small, but significant, negative correlation between need for accurate information and the number of cues identified. A regression of the need for accurate information on the use of 18 kinds of cues to biases in messages determined that an increase in the need for accurate information resulted in a near significant multiple R of .50 ($p = .064$) for the whole model. Of the 18 cues, only 1, background consistency cues, had an unstandardized regression coefficient (positive) significantly different from zero. Thus, as the need for accurate information increased, the number of perceived cues to bias decreased. In high need situations, social actors tended to ignore cues, suggesting that the message was biased, and assumed that what they already knew to be true was still true despite information to the contrary. In contradiction to Burgoon and Langer, messages that can increase uncertainty/novelty can lead to decreases in mindful, questioning activity.

My point here is not to suggest that Burgoon and Langer are wrong. They may be correct up to some threshold level of novelty, after which novelty is problematic. Instead, I am trying to show that even in the simple case where actor and design goals operate in concert, failure to understand how these goals figure in processing can mask important complications for cognitive theories. Where design and actor goals contradict, or where two or more actor goals are in conflict, the complications can become severe. More generally, I am suggesting that cognitive theorists would be well advised to take all three of the assumptions of cognitive theory seriously. To do otherwise is either to oversimplify cognitive theories so that they are indistinguishable from other, less useful, theoretical forms or to leave unaddressed issues that can greatly enhance the heuristic value of cognitive theories.

COGNITIVE INTERPERSONAL
COMMUNICATION THEORIES

At the beginning of this essay, I asked three questions. The second and third, as yet unanswered, questions are, What are the special responsibilities of modern cognitive theories of interpersonal communication? and What issues may guide future efforts at theorizing? To answer these questions, I propose some properties of interpersonal communication that can be ignored by cognitive theorists only at the risk of distorting the phenomena they purport to study. Note, however, that I am not suggesting that all cognitive theories of interpersonal communication must address these properties at this point in their development. In fact, it would be unfair to do so given how little we know about cognition in interpersonal exchanges. At minimum, cognitive interpersonal communication theories should be pursued in such a way as to allow extensions to encompass these properties at some future date.

Like cognitive theories, interpersonal communication theories are the work of many hands. Interpersonal communication is communication (a) in a particular context (i.e., face-to-face interaction between or among two or more individuals), (b) with rapid and unmediated feedback, (c) in which personal (i.e., psychological, individuating) information is acquired about another person (see Miller & Steinberg, 1975), and in which the relationship between the people is both affected by and reflected in communication (see Knapp & Vangelisti, 1992). Behind these and all other properties of interpersonal communication are the basic abilities of individuals that make communication possible.

The Assumptions of Cognitive
Interpersonal Communication Theories

Poole, Folger, and Hewes (1986), Hewes and Planalp (1987), and Hewes, Roloff, Planalp, and Seibold (1990) have explored those properties and abilities that have direct implications for cognitive interpersonal communication theories. Hewes et al. (1990) point to "impact," "influence," and "coordination skills" as the cognitive essentials for effective interpersonal communicators. Hewes and Planalp (1987) and Poole et al. (1986) see "impact" and "intersubjectivity" as key markers of interpersonal communication that reflect those three skills. My two criteria for cognitive interpersonal communication flow from these abilities and skills.

An adequate account of interpersonal communication must, at minimum, (a) identify the cognitive mechanisms that generate one person's behavior and (b) determine the degree, and kind, of impact that behavior has on another's behavior and/or on another's emotional and/or cognitive states. In other words, for there to be interpersonal communication, one person must affect, have impact on, another. Further, because the cognitive mechanisms of sender and receiver must play not simply a mediating but a moderating role in this impact, the cognitive processes must alter the connection between stimulus and response such that one cannot predict the response from the stimulus without knowledge of the cognitive processes linking them.

This is a necessary assumption for cognitive interpersonal communication theories for two reasons. First, it flows directly from most standard "effects" definitions of communication. Communication cannot be said to have occurred unless behavior by person A changes the odds of person B's behavior (see Hewes, 1986; Hewes, Planalp, & Streibel, 1980; Stevens, 1950), although there are additional complexities in a definition of communication (see, e.g., Hewes, 1986; Littlejohn, 1992; Miller & Steinberg, 1975). Without this assumption, communication is not social; it does not connect people. And given that we are discussing cognitive theories, at minimum, the units of analysis for a cognitive interpersonal communication theory must be the message production system of one actor affecting the message reception system of another.

Second, this assumption prevents cognitive theorists from getting "lost in the head" (Hewes & Planalp, 1987). Cognitive theorizing all too frequently leads to explanations only of phenomena (attention, attribution, interpretation, memory, choice, and so on) that are located entirely within one person's cognitive system rather than in social influence between people (Fiske & Taylor, 1991;

Hewes & Planalp, 1987). Interpersonal communication theory ultimately must explain interpersonal influence. Let me go a step further in this direction.

Cognitive explanations of interpersonal communication must trace the impact of messages received to messages sent, and so on interactionally. It is not enough merely to trace the production of person A's message through person B's cognitive system to B's behavior, cognition, and/or emotion. The impact needs to be traced through to person B's behavior so that that behavior can serve as a potential message to person A, and so on through patterns of social interaction between them. Ultimately, cognitive interpersonal communication theories should explain the reciprocal connections between people. If they do not, they miss the essential character of all communication, and especially interpersonal communication—that it is a process (Berlo, 1960).

The above two criteria are not met yet in any theory of interpersonal communication. Such a theory would simply be too complex for our current understanding of either cognition or communication processes. Thus it would not be fair to evaluate any current theories by these criteria and find them wanting. These two criteria are indices of the adequacy of the *goals* of research programs and theories: Are the authors simultaneously mindful of the requirements of cognitive theory and of the phenomena of interpersonal communication—or are they "lost in the head"?

Applying the Assumptions of Cognitive Interpersonal Communication Theories

The first assumption is that an adequate account of interpersonal communication must, at minimum, identify the cognitive mechanisms that determine the degree, and kind, of impact that one person's behavior has on another's behavior and/or on another's emotional and/or cognitive states. This assumption may sound redundant with the three assumptions of cognitive theories, but it is not. Whereas the assumptions of cognitive theories presuppose elaboration of one cognitive system, the assumptions of cognitive interpersonal communication require the elaboration of at least two, as well as the communicative processes that link them.

No current theories of interpersonal communication do this, though several have starts in the right direction. For instance, the theory of the processing of problematic messages mentioned earlier (Hewes, in press-b) traces the impact of messages from one person through the cognitive system of another to the production of messages from that other person. This is a step in the right direction, as are many of the chapters under review here, but it is incomplete. How might those chapters be made more complete? Consider the following examples.

Theories by Greene and by Wilson, as well as the methodological chapter by Grimes and Meadowcroft, recognize the importance of goals in structuring social situations. For Greene, a sender's goals are properties of messages to be processed by a receiver; for Wilson, goals exist in a receiver before message production; for Grimes and Meadowcroft, goals structure a receiver's message processing. Note that (a) none of these chapters includes *both* a sender's and a receiver's goals in its formulations, and (b) none of these chapters recognizes that, when both a sender and a receiver interact and their goals are initially seen to be inconsistent, each person's goal may alter the other's—whether to achieve compromise or to polarize the exchange (Cappella & Greene, 1982; Giles & Street, 1985; see also most research on formal negotiation, e.g., Putnam & Roloff, 1992; and most Goffmanesque, symbolic interactionist, and dramatistic formulations of communication theory, e.g., Littlejohn, 1992). In the future, cognitive interpersonal communication theories that focus on goals will need to consider goals, and environmental factors that support or inhibit them, to be dynamic. Goals in interpersonal communication are not only the causes of processing, or only the result of processing; they are *dynamically interrelated* with the cognitive processing of two actors.

The importance of locating the relationships between two cognitive systems to the understanding of communication is not limited to the issue of goals. In fact, it probably applies to all aspects of cognition. As an illustration, Zajonc (1960) showed that the degree of overlap in the cognitive systems of two actors directly influenced the effectiveness of their communication, an issue that also arises in the study of small group decision making (see Poole & Doelger, 1986, on "group task representations") and conflict management (see Brehmer & Hammond, 1977). The point is simply that future cognitive theorizing in interpersonal communication research should be extended to cover at least the production mechanisms of one person as they impact on the decoding mechanisms of another. To do less is to miss phenomena that are already known to be of importance to understanding interpersonal communication.

But our theorizing should not stop there, as my second assumption of cognitive interpersonal communication theories emphasizes. In it, I proposed that cognitive explanations of interpersonal communication must trace the impact of messages received to messages sent, and so on interactionally. In a sense, this second assumption is a reflection of Cappella's (1976) proposal for framing interpersonal communication research and many of my own methodological and theoretical efforts (Hewes, 1979, 1986). Drawing from Ashby's (1963) seminal work in cybernetics, Cappella (1976) argues that we should conceive of dyads as "a pair of machines coupled through feedback." That is, we should conceive of people as machines with describable inner workings that are connected to each other through a feedback system (interpersonal communication). With an understanding of both the machinery and the feedback system, global properties of the system, such as subsequent states of the system, its equilibrium, and its channel capacity, could be computed where the appropriate mathematical conditions obtained. In other words, one could potentially trace out the dynamics of social interaction far into the future, even without knowing initial conditions that triggered the interaction.

Cappella's insight continues to offer a useful framework for interpersonal communication (see, e.g., Cappella, 1987); however, it does have limitations in practice (though not necessarily in principle) that are instructive for the study of cognitive interpersonal communication theories. To translate this insight into research, Cappella, and I, and all the rest, followed Ashby (1963) in choosing linear mathematical models to capture dynamic patterns of social interaction that result from *both* the feedback system *and* the cognitive machinery of the individual actors.[5] If the feedback system, the cognitive machinery, or both are not linear, then the models (Markov processes, linear difference, and differential equations) used to describe dyads, or any larger aggregation of people, are probably inaccurate, perhaps devastatingly so.

Do we have reason to worry? As my neighbors here in Minneapolis would say, You betcha! For example, three of the chapters under review here (Greene, O'Keefe and Lambert, and Wilson) make good cases for connectionist cognitive architectures. These architectures, also called "parallel distributed processes" or "neural networks" (Rumelhart, 1989), must be described, at least partially, in nonlinear terms (a) to square with known neurological properties of the brain (Anderson & Silverstein, 1978; Hopfield, 1982) and (b) to make the architectures do the kind of theoretical work claimed for them by Wilson, Greene, and, especially, O'Keefe and Lambert (see Quinlan, 1991; Rumelhart, McClelland, & the PDP Research Group, 1986).

If these communication scholars are correct, then at least some interpersonal communication theories that predict ongoing interaction processes will be anchored in connectionist architectures. Models of social interaction based on these architectures must be described with nonlinear, rather than linear, dynamic models. This conclusion suggests two others. First, budding interpersonal communication theorists need to familiarize themselves with a variety of nonlinear calculi, and the programming languages that support them. Connectionist models and, perhaps, cellular automata, complex game theories, catastrophe theory, chaos theories, and a number of simulation languages currently used by researchers in "artificial life" are potential theoretical calculi for the future (see Abraham & Shaw, 1992; Casti, 1989; Kosko, 1992; Langton, 1989; Langton, Taylor, Farmer, & Rasmussen, 1992; Peitgen, Jurgens, & Saupe, 1992).

Second, if we do need nonlinear calculi to model cognitively driven social interaction processes, they may afford us the opportunity to address an emerging issue for the field of communication. Hewes et al. (1990) contend (a) that our field should be responsible for studying the processes by which individual human minds combine into larger social structures, and (b) that we, and researchers in all other domains of scholarship, have as yet done a poor job of it. The underlying difficulty with this project is that we tend to think in terms of irreducible levels of social organization—the individual, the dyad, the group, the organization, the culture, and so on.

Communication theories and research are pitched at each of these separate levels, with associated arguments justifying the distinct "reality" of each level

(Berger & Chaffee, 1987). Even attempts to cross levels, such as those made by Doise (1986) and Hewes et al. (1990), only show the relevance of theories at one level for theories at another level. These attempts do not explain how the particular character of a relationship (the dyadic level) can emerge from two individual minds (the individual level), for example. Instead, we get stopgap methodological solutions, such as making the dyad (or the group, or whatever) the unit of analysis (see Kenny & LaVoi, 1984), that only beg the problem of emergent properties. What we need, instead, is to be able to explain emergent structure. I see this as an up-and-coming issue in interpersonal communication, and in communication theory generally.

Although I can only speculate on how we will address this issue, the previous discussion of nonlinear calculi provides some direction. Many nonlinear calculi, such as connectionist models, produce emergent structures (Casti, 1989; Forrest, 1991; Hopfield, 1982; Langton, 1989; Langton et al., 1992). That is, descriptions of simple lower-level structures combine to form more complex, diverse, higher-level structures. The cognitive interpersonal communication theory project may well lead us to the kinds of models we need to study emergence. Nonlinear cognitive architectures, when linked into cognitive interpersonal theories as defined by the second assumption, produce models of communication that can generate emergence at a higher level (the dyad, the group, and so on). Whether they will generate the types of emergence that have parallels in the social processes connecting levels of communication phenomena remains to be seen.[6] Still, they are a place to start—the first one I have had any faith in since I began investigating this issue.

REFLECTIONS AND PREDICTIONS

What can be said about current attempts at building cognitive theories of interpersonal communication? First, all of the examples reviewed here offer intriguing insights into such important aspects of communication theory as the formation of goals, the enactment of plans, the processing of multiple-goal messages, and the relationship between messages and attention. These theories represent good-faith efforts to expand our knowledge of human communication by means of a productive theoretical approach. Although the cognitive perspective is hardly the only useful approach to the study of human communication, it has been heuristic and will continue to be so (Littlejohn, 1992).

Second, these assumptions are all necessary for the building of adequate cognitive theory: (a) that people are "actors" (with all that implies), (b) that cognitive representations and process moderate the connection between the environment and behavior, and (c) that cognitive processes are driven by both the goals of the actors themselves and those intrinsic to the cognitive systems they utilize. The more fully any cognitive theory utilizes these three basic assumptions of cognition, the richer and more complete it becomes. Thus these three assumptions can be applied as topoi to evaluate and extend cognitive theories.

Third, although most cognitive theories of communication are good cognitive theories, they are not yet good cognitive interpersonal communication theories. To understand interpersonal communication, we must understand the dynamics of social interaction. To understand interpersonal communication cognitively is to understand the interplay of two or more cognitive systems connected through feedback. Our understanding of cognitive systems and the dynamics of social feedback is not up to the task of developing cognitive interpersonal theories. The next decade of research will need to be devoted to acquiring this understanding.

Cognitive theories are complex because they treat people as complex beings; theories become much simpler if you assume away conditional adaptability, or individuality, or the importance of interpretation, or the emergence of social structure. A cognitive approach to building communication theories points down a long, winding, arduous path. I respect Burgoon, Greene, Grimes, Lambert, Langer, Meadowcroft, O'Keefe, and Wilson for starting down it. They believe that easier pathways are less rewarding in the long run. I agree.

NOTES

1. In order to narrow my focus to cognitively oriented interpersonal communication theories, I will not discuss Gastil's interesting chapter. His emphasis is on the philosophical evaluation of a research program that is incidentally cognitive. Grimes and Meadowcroft focus on mass media studies, but their discussion of attention is relevant to interpersonal communication. My comments on their chapter would be the same regardless of their area of application.

2. In "modern cognitive theory" I include those theories that separate conceptual processing and representation, and that discuss the relationship. Further, modern cognitive theories point to aspects of processing that are seen to generalize beyond the representation to which they are hypothesized to operate. This means, for instance, that balance and consistency theories are not modern cognitive theories, whereas information processing, most artificial intelligence theories, and parallel distributed processing theories are.

3. It is not entirely clear what function these learning theories serve in O'Keefe and Lambert's chapter. They enter into a "simulation" of mental processing, but close inspection indicates that this simulation is really only a data reduction technique that demonstrates that even contradictory goals may be instantiated in the same message.

4. I am unclear exactly what O'Keefe and Lambert have in mind, but two of their claims seem to me to be problematic. First, it looks like they are positing a massively parallel cognitive architecture for message production that should make the system resilient to pressures on the design goal—that is, parallel systems should have little trouble preserving capacity limitations compared with the serial processing systems typical in most artificial intelligence and cognitive psychological theories. If so, why do Wilson, Greene, and Grimes and Meadowcroft seem to find so many instances best explained by capacity limitations? Second, O'Keefe and Lambert appear to be stating that a parallel distributed processing architecture is sufficient to represent the connection between "thoughts" and messages. This ignores some of the limitations of these architectures for representing symbolic processes, for instance, the ability to represent complex hierarchical structures effectively and to structure sensitive operations on those representations (Hinton, 1990). Most researchers employing these connectionist architectures are aware (a) that no available example of these architectures is

capable of handling complex learning, representation of complex phenomena, or complex problem solving of the order found in the social context; and (b) that important breakthroughs in connectionist architectures are essential before they will be able to do so (Hinton, 1990; Quinlan, 1991).

5. Ashby's (1963) models of coupled machines (a dyad, for instance) could be described in terms of three separate components (machinery describing the inner workings of each actor plus the feedback system linking them) or "unfolded" into a single linear mechanism. Thus, for example, a "transition matrix" in a Markov chain model of social interaction is a linear representation of the dynamics of events and is an "unfolded" model of what must be assumed to be linear feedback systems and cognitive machinery.

6. For example, emergence may be generated by particular types of nonlinearity in the feedback systems that are not the result of cognitive processes.

REFERENCES

Abraham, R. H., & Shaw, C. D. (1992). *Dynamics: The geometry of behavior* (2nd ed.). Redwood City, CA: Addison-Wesley.

Anderson, J. R. (1984). Spreading activation. In J. R. Anderson & S. M. Kosslyn (Eds.), *Essays in learning and memory* (pp. 61-89). New York: Freeman.

Anderson, J. R., & Silverstein, J. W. (1978). Reply to Grossberg. *Psychological Review, 85,* 597-603.

Ashby, W. R. (1963). *An introduction to cybernetics.* New York: John Wiley.

Bargh, J. A. (1984). Automatic and conscious processing of social information. In R. S. Wyer & T. K. Srull (Eds.), *Handbook of social cognition* (Vol. 3, pp. 1-44). Hillsdale, NJ: Lawrence Erlbaum.

Berger, C. R., & Chaffee, S. H. (1987). The study of communication as a science. In C. R. Berger & S. H. Chaffee (Eds.), *Handbook of communication science* (pp. 15-19). Newbury Park, CA: Sage.

Berlo, D. K. (1960). *The process of communication.* New York: Holt, Rinehart & Winston.

Brehmer, B., & Hammond, K. R. (1977). Cognitive factors in interpersonal conflict. In D. Druckman (Ed.), *Negotiations: Social-psychological perspectives* (pp. 79-104). Beverly Hills, CA: Sage.

Cappella, J. N. (1976). Modeling interpersonal communication systems as a pair of machines coupled through feedback. In G. R. Miller (Ed.), *Explorations in interpersonal communication* (pp. 59-86). Beverly Hills, CA: Sage.

Cappella, J. N. (1987). Interpersonal communication: Definitions and fundamental questions. In C. R. Berger & S. H. Chaffee (Eds.), *Handbook of communication science* (pp. 184-238). Newbury Park, CA: Sage.

Cappella, J. N., & Greene, J. O. (1982). A discrepancy-arousal explanation of mutual influence in expressive behavior for adult-adult and infant-adult interaction. *Communication Monographs, 49,* 89-114.

Casti, J. L. (1989). *Alternate realities: Mathematical models of nature and man.* New York: John Wiley.

Cherniak, C. (1986). *Minimal rationality.* Cambridge: MIT Press.

Clark, H. H. (1985). Language use and language users. In G. Lindzey & E. Aronson (Eds.), *Handbook of social psychology* (3rd ed., Vol. 2, pp. 179-232). New York: Random House.

Davenport, W. G. (1968). Auditory vigilance: The effects of costs and values on signals. *Australian Journal of Psychology, 20,* 213-218.

Davenport, W. G. (1969). Vibrotactile vigilance: The effects of costs and values on signals. *Perception and Psychophysiology, 5,* 25-28.

Delia, J. G. (1987). Communication research: A history. In C. R. Berger & S. H. Chaffee (Eds.), *Handbook of communication science* (pp. 20-98). Newbury Park, CA: Sage.

Doise, W. (1986). *Levels of explanation in social psychology* (E. Mapstone, Trans.). Cambridge: Cambridge University Press.

Eysenck, M. W. (1982). *Attention and arousal.* Berlin: Springer-Verlag.

Fiske, S. T., & Taylor, S. E. (1991). *Social cognition* (2nd ed.). Reading, MA: Addison-Wesley.

Forrest, S. (Ed.). (1991). *Emergent computation.* Cambridge: MIT Press.

Giles, H., & Street, R. L. (1985). Communicator characteristics and behavior. In M. L. Knapp & G. R. Miller (Eds.), *Handbook of interpersonal communication* (pp. 205-262). Beverly Hills, CA: Sage.

Greene, J. O. (1984a). A cognitive approach to human communication: An action assembly theory. *Communication Monographs, 51,* 289-306.

Greene, J. O. (1984b). Evaluating cognitive explanations of communicative phenomena. *Quarterly Journal of Speech, 70,* 241-254.

Hewes, D. E. (1979). The sequential analysis of social interaction. *Quarterly Journal of Speech, 65,* 56-73.

Hewes, D. E. (1986). A socio-egocentric model of group decision-making. In R. Y. Hirokawa & M. S. Poole (Eds.), *Communication and group decision-making* (pp. 265-292). Beverly Hills, CA: Sage.

Hewes, D. E. (Ed.). (in press-a). *The cognitive bases of interpersonal communication.* Hillsdale, NJ: Lawrence Erlbaum.

Hewes, D. E. (in press-b). Cognitive processing of problematic messages: Reinterpreting to "unbias" messages. In D. E. Hewes (Ed.), *The cognitive bases of interpersonal communication.* Hillsdale, NJ: Lawrence Erlbaum.

Hewes, D. E., & Graham, M. L. (1988). Second-guessing theory: Review and extension. In J. A. Anderson (Ed.), *Communication yearbook 12* (pp. 213-248). Newbury Park, CA: Sage.

Hewes, D. E., Monsour, M., & Rutherford, D. K. (1989). *Second-guessing: The effects of need for accuracy on cue extraction, doubt, and normative adequacy.* Unpublished manuscript, University of Minnesota, Minneapolis.

Hewes, D. E., & Planalp, S. (1982). There is nothing as useful as a good theory . . . : The influence of social knowledge on interpersonal communication. In M. E. Roloff & C. R. Berger (Eds.), *Social cognition and communication* (pp. 49-77). Beverly Hills, CA: Sage.

Hewes, D. E., & Planalp, S. (1987). The individual's place in communication science. In C. R. Berger & S. H. Chaffee (Eds.), *Handbook of communication science* (pp. 146-183). Newbury Park, CA: Sage.

Hewes, D. E., Planalp, S., & Streibel, S. (1980). Analyzing social interaction: Some excruciating models and some exhilarating results. In D. Nimmo (Ed.), *Communication yearbook 4* (pp. 123-142). New Brunswick, NJ: Transaction.

Hewes, D. E., Roloff, M. R., Planalp, S., & Seibold, D. R. (1990). Interpersonal communication research: What should we know? In G. M. Phillips & J. T. Wood (Eds.), *Speech communication: Essays to commemorate the 75th anniversary of the Speech Communication Association* (pp. 130-180). Carbondale: Southern Illinois University Press.

Hinton, G. (1990). Preface to the special issue on connectionist symbolic processing. In G. Hinton (Ed.), *Connectionist symbol processing.* Cambridge, MA: MIT Press.

Hopfield, J. J. (1982). Neural networks and physical systems with emergent collective computational abilities. *Proceedings of the National Academy of Science, 79,* 2554-2558.

Jourard, S. M. (1971). *The transparent self* (rev. ed.). New York: Van Nostrand.

Kenny, D. A., & LaVoi, L. (1984). The social relations model. In L. Berkowitz (Ed.), *Advances in experimental social psychology* (Vol. 18, pp. 141-182). New York: Academic Press.

Knapp, M. L., & Vangelisti, A. L. (1992). *Interpersonal communication and human relationships* (2nd ed.). Boston: Allyn & Bacon.

Kosko, B. (1992). *Neural networks and fuzzy systems: A dynamical systems approach to machine intelligence.* Englewood Cliffs, NJ: Prentice Hall.

Langer, E. J. (1978). Rethinking the role of thought in social interaction. In J. Harvey, W. Ickes, & R. Kidd (Eds.), *New directions in attribution research* (Vol. 2, pp. 35-58). Hillsdale, NJ: Lawrence Erlbaum.

Langer, E. J. (1989). *Mindfulness.* Reading, MA: Addison-Wesley.

Langton, C. G. (Ed.). (1989). *Artificial life.* Redwood City, CA: Addison-Wesley.

Langton, C. G., Taylor, C., Farmer, J. D., & Rasmussen, S. (Eds.). (1992). *Artificial life II*. Redwood City, CA: Addison-Wesley.

Levine, J. M. (1966). The effects of values and costs in the detection and identification of signals in auditory vigilance. *Human Factors, 8,* 525-537.

Littlejohn, S. W. (1992). *Theories of human communication* (4th ed.). Belmont, CA: Wadsworth.

McGraw, K. O. (1978). The detrimental effects of reward on performance: A literature review and a prediction model. In M. R. Lepper & D. Greene (Eds.), *The hidden costs of reward* (pp. 102-134). Hillsdale, NJ: Lawrence Erlbaum.

Miller, G. R., & Steinberg, M. (1975). *Between people: A new analysis of interpersonal communication*. Chicago: Scientific Research Associates.

Newcombe, T. M. (1953). An approach to the study of communicative acts. *Psychological Review, 60,* 393-404.

Newell, A. (1980). Physical symbol systems. *Cognitive Science, 45,* 135-183.

Newell, A. (1990). *Unified theories of cognition*. Cambridge, MA: Harvard University Press.

Newell, A., Rosenbloom, P. S., & Laird, J. E. (1989). Symbolic architectures for cognition. In M. I. Posner (Ed.), *Foundations of cognitive science* (pp. 93-132). Cambridge: MIT Press.

O'Keefe, B. J. (1988). The logic of message design. *Communication Monographs, 55,* 80-103.

Peitgen, H., Jurgens, H., & Saupe, D. (1992). *Chaos and fractals: New frontiers of science*. New York: Springer-Verlag.

Petty, R. E., & Cacioppo, J. T. (1986). *Communication and persuasion: Central and peripheral routes to attitude change*. New York: Springer-Verlag.

Planalp, S., & Hewes, D. E. (1982). A cognitive approach to communication theory: *Cogito ergo dico?* In M. Burgoon (Ed.), *Communication yearbook 5* (pp. 49-77). New Brunswick, NJ: Transaction.

Planalp, S., & Tracy, K. (1980). Not to change the topic but . . . : A cognitive approach to the management of conversation. In D. Nimmo (Ed.), *Communication yearbook 4* (pp. 237-260). New Brunswick, NJ: Transaction.

Poole, M. S., & Doelger, J. A. (1986). Developmental processes in group decision-making. In R. Y. Hirokawa & M. S. Poole (Eds.), *Communication and group decision-making* (pp. 35-62). Beverly Hills, CA: Sage.

Poole, M. S., & Folger, J. P., & Hewes, D. E. (1986). Analyzing interpersonal interaction. In M. E. Roloff & G. R. Miller (Eds.), *Interpersonal processes: New directions in communication research* (pp. 123-154). Beverly Hills, CA: Sage.

Posner, M. I., & Snyder, C. R. R. (1975). Attention and cognitive control. In R. L. Solso (Ed.), *Information processing and cognition: The Loyola Symposium.* Hillsdale, NJ: Lawrence Erlbaum.

Putnam, L. L., & Roloff, M. E. (Eds.). (1992). *Communication and negotiation*. Newbury Park, CA: Sage.

Quinlan, P. (1991). *Connectionism and psychology*. Chicago: University of Chicago Press.

Rumelhart, D. E. (1989). The architecture of mind: A connectionist approach. In M. I. Posner (Ed.), *Foundations of cognitive science* (pp. 133-160). Cambridge: MIT Press.

Rumelhart, D. E., McClelland, J. L., & the PDP Research Group. (Eds.). (1986). *Parallel distributed processing: Explorations in the microstructure of cognition: Vol. 1. Foundations.* Cambridge: MIT Press.

Schneider, W., & Shiffrin, R. M. (1977). Controlled and automatic human information processing: I. Detection, search, and attention. *Psychological Review, 84,* 1-66.

Shiffrin, R. M., & Schneider, W. (1977). Controlled and automatic human information processing: II. Perceptual learning, automatic attending, and a general theory. *Psychological Review, 84,* 127-190.

Stevens, S. S. (1950). Introduction: A definition of communication. *Journal of the Acoustical Society of America, 22,* 689.

Tracy, K. (1984). The effect of multiple goals on conversational relevance and topic shift. *Communication Monographs, 51,* 274-287.

Tracy, K. (1985). Regulating conversational coherence: A cognitively grounded rules approach. In R. L. Street & J. N. Cappella (Eds.), *Sequence and pattern in communicative behavior* (pp. 30-49). Baltimore: Edward Arnold.

von Wright, G. H. (1971). *Explanation and understanding.* Ithaca, NY: Cornell University Press.

Wyer, R. S., & Srull, T. K. (1984a). *Handbook of social cognition* (Vols. 1-3). Hillsdale, NJ: Lawrence Erlbaum.

Zajonc, R. F. (1960). The process of cognitive tuning in communication. *Journal of Abnormal and Social Psychology, 61,* 159-167.

8 Is the "Golden Age of Cognition" Losing Its Luster? Toward a Requirement-Centered Perspective

VINCENT R. WALDRON
Arizona State University West

FACED with the daunting task of bridging the widening conceptual gap that separated mass and interpersonal communication scholars, Berger and Chaffee (1988) saw promise in what they labeled an emerging "Golden Age of Cognition." Looking back to the 1950s and 1960s (the "Golden Age of Persuasion"), these authors hoped the discipline could be unified once more by the emergence of a common research problem. Berger and Chaffee warned that the study of cognition was "no panacea" for the discipline as a whole, but the increased attention afforded cognitive concepts in the 1980s was for them a sign that communication researchers might begin theorizing with a common purpose.

As a doctoral candidate busy with a dissertation on the topic of conversational cognition, I felt an optimistic glow upon reading this assessment. In the years since, like a number of other researchers who "came of age" during the Golden Age of Cognition, I have typically ignored Berger and Chaffee's warning, preferring to focus instead on their endorsement of cognition-based theorizing. Accordingly, much of my research has been driven (at least implicitly) by the belief that communication would be better explained if researchers would just (a) construct more accurate models of how communicators think, (b) be guided by the best theories available in the cognitive sciences, and (c) use more careful methods for probing the mind. Unfortunately, there are some tentative signs that the Golden Age of Cognition is losing its luster—that the theoretical appeal of cognitive approaches has been actually a kind of fool's gold, appealing on the surface, but of limited value in explaining the complexities of human communication.

Of course, even in 1988 my excitement over the prospect of a continued Golden Age of Cognition was tempered by nagging doubts about why the disci-

Correspondence and requests for reprints: Vincent R. Waldron, Department of Communication Studies, Arizona State University West, 4701 West Thunderbird Road, Phoenix, AZ 85069.

Communication Yearbook 18, pp. 180-197

pline would rally around *cognition*. I could see why communication researchers of all types in the 1950s and 1960s might place persuasion at the top of their research agenda. After all, despite its obvious psychological and sociological implications, persuasion is a process that centrally involves messages. And messages, particularly the features of persuasive messages, have been a central concern of communication scholars for centuries. In contrast, my reading of the increasingly cognition-oriented studies filling communication journals during the 1980s left me with some basic and uncomfortable questions, such as, When do we get to the *communication* part?

It's 1994 now and that question still leaves me feeling uncomfortable. For this reason, I find the extended treatment of cognitive approaches to communication in this *Communication Yearbook* timely and, to some extent, reassuring. Though diverse in their individual objectives, the preceding essays, as a package, convince me that communication researchers are no longer content simply to dress up cognitive research in communicative clothes. The reassurance comes less from the systematic and theory-driven nature of the research programs described here (although this is particularly noteworthy in the essays by Greene and Wilson) than from the fact that *communication* itself is central in these essays. That statement belies my primary thesis: that the influence of cognitively oriented scholarship will decline if we cannot improve our capacity to account for what most of us recognize as "real" communication and if we continue to ignore the hard questions about the role of cognition as an ongoing process of communication.

In this essay, I will comment on what I believe are signs of a possible decline in influence of cognitive approaches and argue that cognitive theorists must do a better job of getting to the "communication part." I submit that the primary justification for studying cognitive concepts is to account better for how people meet (or fail to meet) the communicative requirements of the situations in which they find themselves. In proposing a "requirement-centered" approach, I urge researchers to ground their work in a communication theory-based analysis of the requirements of social situations and specify the cognitive operations inferred from the requirements. Because my own expertise lies primarily in the area of interpersonal communication, my comments apply most directly to that part of the discipline (with apologies to Grimes and Meadowcroft). I assume that strategic interpersonal interactions are primary sites for the interplay of cognition and communication, though many of my comments apply to other sites as well. I conclude the essay by describing briefly a study of strategic interaction that illustrates a requirement-centered approach and demonstrates its potential for unifying cognitive perspectives that have traditionally been compartmentalized in our discipline.

The six preceding essays are the catalyst for this effort, and I am indebted to the authors as I make a case for what I consider to be the problematic present and the potentially productive future of cognitive perspectives. Burgoon and Langer, in their wide-ranging discussion of mindlessness, make a point that is too often lost in the interpersonal communication literature: Cognitive states can be conceptualized not only as antecedents of functional or dysfunctional communication behavior, but also as the outcomes of such behavior. Gastil deserves credit for his well-organized critique of the constructivist program and for pointing to some of the key methodological and theoretical extensions that could be added to this framework. Wilson's essay goes further by documenting the considerable progress he has made in linking individual differences in social perception to the communication process. O'Keefe and Lambert stake out new and welcome theoretical ground by situating the study of thought and talk in the complex and continuous flow of interaction. Grimes and Meadowcroft provide a useful discussion of the methods available for studying attention processes as they operate on the similarly complex and continuous flow of television messages. Finally, Greene's essay adds to his already extensive program of research on the production of communicative action and demonstrates that considerable tenacity and experimental creativity are required of researchers seeking convincing tests of cognitive models.

IS THE GOLDEN AGE OF
COGNITION LOSING ITS LUSTER?

One need not be a committed devil's advocate to conclude that the influence of cognitive perspectives is declining within the communication discipline. Given the enormous, some would say undue, influence of cognitive perspectives across the social sciences in the past 15 years or so, this decline is neither unexpected nor particularly troubling. But there are at least four signs indicating the scholarly audience for cognitively oriented research is (or should be) becoming increasingly skeptical about the relevance of such work in the study of communication.

Disenchantment With the
"Psychologization" of Communication

One indicator of potential decline is the growing influence of "social approaches" to interpersonal communication (e.g., Leeds-Hurwitz, 1992). Although this label implies many things, the most obvious is a disenchantment with "nonsocial" approaches. Given the prominence in the 1980s of cognitive approaches, nonsocial can all too easily be associated with "cognitive." This seems to be the case with Baxter (1992), who, in reacting in part to the cognitive turn in interpersonal communication research, proposes that a dialogic approach to cognition would focus on how cognitions are socially constructed through interaction. She cites Middleton and Edwards's (1990) volume on collective remembering as an example of how social conceptions of cognition might replace the traditional view of cognition as an internal property of individual minds.

The growth of subdivisions in our professional organizations around issues of "language and social interaction" is a similar sign. The increasing psychologization of interpersonal communication has left many scholars looking for a new label for their scholarship, one that makes salient the process that a considerable amount of cognitive research simply ignores: social interaction. Of course, some cognitive researchers are actively theorizing about uniquely communicative aspects of cognition (e.g., Sanders, 1992). In their essay in this volume, Burgoon and Langer show in myriad ways how patterns of social interaction can account for mindlessness and related cognitive states. This is a welcome development, because communication researchers have been much enamored of the mindlessness concept (for a recent example, see "Chautauqua," 1992), but only recently has the role of interaction in managing this psychological state been a central part of the discussion. Increasingly, cognitive researchers are being asked to move communication from the periphery to the center of their work.

The Rise of Emotion as a Communication Variable

Another sign of decline is evident in the rise of emotion as a variable in communication research. The renewed interest in emotion may be more a reflection of the inability of social scientists generally to allocate their attention in a sustained manner to any one aspect of social life (e.g., the cognitive revolution in the 1980s; the emotion revolution in the 1990s) than of the inadequacy of cognitive research. Perhaps a saturation point has been reached, where communication scholars have been scripted, schema'd, and construct-differentiated to the limits of their endurance, and a certain refocusing of research attention is inevitable. Yet even relational (Planalp, 1993) and persuasion (Dillard, 1993) scholars with impeccable cognitive credentials are placing emotion at the top of their research agendas. I have noted in a previous essay a similar trend among some organizational communication scholars (Waldron, 1993). Obviously, emotion and cognition are intimately related psychological processes. The rise in the fortunes of emotion theories need not correspond with a fall in the fortunes of cognitive theories. Theoretical integration is more likely. But, in addition to guaranteeing a new round of theory importation from relatively untapped branches of psychology, the renewed interest in emotion signals a recognition by communication scholars that affect is an integral part of communicative life, one that has been too long ignored in a literature that has privileged cognitive theories.

Compartmentalization of Research Programs

I interpret as another sign of weakness the continued compartmentalization of cognitively oriented research programs. As Greene notes in his essay in this volume, an essential tenet of cognitivism is that alternate models can always be proposed to account for experimental results. Thus it is possible for cognitive researchers to labor in relative isolation, believing their models are as plausible as any other, feeling no pressure to test their frameworks aggressively against others. But healthy research programs integrate concepts and findings from programs other than their own (Pouncy, 1988). That is why Gastil, in his chapter, advises constructivist researchers to draw more freely from existing cognitive theory and test rival hypotheses. (Wilson's essay is a notable attempt to extend constructivist thought with concepts drawn from the cognitive science literature.) The same recommendation could be offered to most cognitive research programs.

The advantages of scholars working methodically within a theoretical framework are obvious. Yet it seems quite clear that cognitive researchers have studied similar processes and knowledge structures in relative intellectual isolation. Peruse the reference list of any cognitively-oriented study (including my own) published in our major journals, and you are likely to find (a) a set of references that establish that the authors' key explanatory constructs are drawn from psychological studies only marginally relevant to communication as we would define it; (b) a smattering of superficial references to a broad variety of communication studies, apparently to establish that other researchers find cognitive approaches to be legitimate; and (c) references to previous work by the author and a committed band of followers. Often missing are an acknowledgment that communication researchers have used apparently similar cognitive constructs under different names and an attempt to reconcile or integrate that previous conceptual work with the researcher's own. Within my own limited area of expertise, I am struck by the large number of researchers who use the term *communication plan* (Berger, in press; Berger & Jordan, 1992; Dillard, 1990; Waldron, 1990; see also Greene's essay in this volume) with approximately similar meaning (the *goal* concept is used similarly). Yet, despite the accumulating body of solid research around the planning concept, there is precious little theoretical cross-fertilization evident in the literature thus far. Laboring in separate camps to reinvent similar constructs, cognitive researchers have been unusually inclined (it seems to me) to ignore opportunities for conceptual integration and aggregation of research findings.

Failure to Address the Hard Questions

Finally, the potential decline of cognitive perspectives is foreshadowed by a continued willingness to avoid the hard questions. For me at least, the hard questions have to do with cognition as it is situated in interaction. It would be unfair to criticize theorists for failing to study cognitive processes clearly outside the scope of their theories. Yet much cognitively oriented theory and research on "strategic communication" is clearly intended to generalize to the interactive realm. In the case of constructivism, Gastil notes in his essay that one area of theoretical interest has evolved around the relationship of perception to communication. Comforting, persuasion, self-disclosure, and the other types of communication that have interested constructivists all get played out (typically) in interactive contexts. Apparently because of an assumption that individual differences affecting self-reported messages will have similar effects on interactive behavior, few constructivist researchers have specified how differentiated construct systems (for example) might facilitate interactive behavior. Very little empirical work has tested this assumption (Burleson, 1987), and the work that has been done has yielded apparently small statistical effects (O'Keefe & Shepherd, 1987; Waldron & Applegate, in press). For constructivists, the hard questions require theory extensions and new methods that explain how (and whether) individual differences in cognitive development translate into patterns of interaction.

One might argue sensibly that questions about the role of cognition in interaction are not central to the constructivist program, which is, after all, primarily about individual differences in social perception (see Gastil's discussion of the constructivist core). My point is simply that questions about individual social perception (and other individual differences in cognition) are becoming less important in a discipline increasingly concerned with social processes; the challenge now is to relocate constructivist research to interactive sites, where social perceptions are negotiated. The safe course would be simply to extend the impressive body of studies linking construct differentiation with self-reported messages to relatively understudied message types (say, information acquisition strategies). But the authors of several of these six essays are pushing beyond this. Gastil proposes that greater attention to the "communication process" is the most important of his proposed revisions to the constructivist program. Wilson makes an incremental extension to the constructivist literature by linking individual differences in Role Category Questionnaire (RCQ) scores to his cognitive rules model. As Wilson explores how rules are activated under conversational conditions, he will help constructivists make the conceptual leap from perception to interaction. The essay authored by O'Keefe and Lambert stands out in this collection because it makes that leap most boldly, by directing theoretical attention to the flow of thought during interaction.

Greene's essay also exhibits a willingness to tackle some of the hard cognitive questions with creative experimental manipulations. Action assembly theory (Greene, 1984) is strengthened considerably as it is extended to account for action production under increasingly communication-like conditions. Multi-tasking and the need to "maintain the output representation" over time, as Greene puts it, are certainly two of those conditions. Greene proceeds with the conviction that the cognitive machinery underlying the production of all action, including communicative action, is similar. Working from that premise, it is easy to see how the temporal message features of monologues might form a window through which cognitive encoding processes could be examined. Presumably, temporal features of other tasks of about the same level of complexity, including noncommunicative tasks (driving a car down an uncrowded highway? responding to a warning light on an instrument panel?), would be similarly useful in probing the action assembly process. Although sympathetic to Greene's project, I am uncertain about how his dependent variables (e.g., speech onset latency) or independent variables (e.g., one interaction goal or two) relate to the production of action under interactive conditions (I am not sure that Greene intends them to). Imagine the complexity experienced by Greene's participants if they faced not just two experimenter-defined goals, but the numerous task, identity, and relational goals that become more or less relevant as conversations unfold (for a recent analysis, see Tracy & Baratz, 1993). Imagine the cognitive demands of "maintaining the output representation" not just through the course of a short monologue, but through multiple turns in demanding conversation.

I suspect that Greene will show in a future series of studies that his significant results not only generalize to, but are actually magnified by, these more demanding interactive conditions. My optimism, which clearly identifies me as an experimental researcher, is tempered a bit by difficulties cognitive scientists have had in accounting for the production of complex, situated action (see, for example, the recent special issue of *Cognitive Science* edited by Greeno, 1993). It is possible that the kind of cognitive improvisation required in complex conversation is not just more demanding, but also just plain different from the cognitive operations used in monologic tasks. Interestingly, the very thing Greene finds useful about the temporal features of speech production (they are context-free indicators of cognitive functioning) clearly distinguishes his perspective from that of O'Keefe and Lambert. The latter see message production as a process of improvising messages from *context-dependent* thought patterns. By making "patterns of thought" their focus, O'Keefe and Lambert find explanatory power in the level of the cognitive system most likely to vary across communication tasks. By making the architecture of action assembly his focus, Greene finds explanatory power in the level of the cognitive system least likely to vary across communication tasks.

In sum, what I have suggested thus far is that despite the signs of progress evident in the essays featured in this section of *Communication Yearbook,* there are signs that the influence of cognitive perspectives will decline, partially because cognitive programs of research have insufficiently addressed the hardest questions: those that link cognition to the production of interactive message behavior. In other words, we have not yet gotten to the "communication part."

GETTING TO THE COMMUNICATION PART: A REQUIREMENT-CENTERED APPROACH

I have contributed previously to the discussion of what ought to be the appropriate level of theorizing and the methodological requirements for an invigorated study of cognition and strategic communication (Waldron & Cegala, 1992). The gist of that argument is this: Studies of cognitive operations are most useful when they explain how interactants meet the communicative requirements of the situations in which they find themselves. The communicative requirements are derived from communication theories (see the exemplar provided below) and depend in part on the nature of the communicative task (e.g., small talk versus conflict; monologic versus dialogic).

I offer this "requirement-centered" approach as an alternative to what I view to be the prevailing architecture-centered assumptions guiding cognitively oriented communication research. Regarding the latter, cognitive researchers have recently complained that compelling evidence exists in support of vastly different cognitive architectures (e.g., Anderson, 1990). This is no reason to abandon the search for feasible cognitive models of communication processes, but it should give communication researchers pause as we argue the merits of various architectures (e.g., serial versus parallel) in the pages of our journals. Perhaps our efforts would be better spent specifying the abstract cognitive functions or operations that must be completed by the cognitive system (Anderson, 1990; Waldron & Cegala, 1992) during communicative tasks. This perspective allows that the cognitive system could "output" these operations through any number of configurations, and directs attention to the role of these outputs in the communication process.

At the operational level, at least, strategic interactions have characteristics that distinguish them from the noninteractive tasks cognitive researchers have studied so often. Waldron and Cegala (1992) present a partial list of distinguishing characteristics that includes the following:

> (1) processing of large amounts of information, (2) performance of multiple cognitive tasks simultaneously (or at least in rapid succession), (3) processing of ambiguous or conflicting verbal or nonverbal information, (4) processing information within variable but relatively restrictive time limits (e.g., imposed by normative limits on pause length), (5) projection of future events from current information (e.g., anticipating partner moves), and (6) selection or construction of highly complex behavior sequences. (p. 603)

Beyond these general concerns, researchers can specify the detectable cognitive operations that ought to (given the application of a reasonable theory of communication) facilitate or hinder communication in certain types of interactions. Depending on the nature of the communication event being studied, the production of certain patterns of thought (i.e., cognitive content; see O'Keefe & Lambert, this volume), the application of certain cognitive processes (e.g., attention), or the use of knowledge structures (e.g., plans) with certain characteristics ought to account for variation in communication activity. Theorists specify which of these cognitive operations their cognitive framework concerns (and which it does not) and the role that the operation plays in producing the messages required by the situation. Subsequent empirical tests could be used to (a) demonstrate that the cognitive operations do in fact occur as the communication theory implies they should, and/or (b) verify that these detectable cognitive operations account for *meaningful* variation in interactants' success in the communication situation.

In the first case, researchers collect data about cognitive phenomena primarily to gauge support for communication theories. This of course reverses the common practice of collecting data that are minimally communicative to support strong inferences about what is happening inside the head. The second approach (with communication measures in the more familiar dependent variable role) is used to good effect by Greene to account for variation in structural features of messages. But is this *meaningful* variation? In the case of Greene's experimental task (delivering an evaluation in a face-saving manner), the temporal message features he uses as data no doubt have some communicative impact. But one is left wondering if the *strategic* qualities and content of the evaluative messages would not weigh more heavily than their *structural* qualities in a theory of evaluative communication (or a more general theory of strategic communication applied to evaluation situations). If structural message features were relatively unimportant theoretically (or demonstrated to be so empirically), this would be no argument against Greene's theory of action assembly, nor would it be reason to doubt the usefulness of structural message features as evidence of what are otherwise impenetrable cognitive processes. It *would* prompt skeptics to question whether cognitive theories such as Greene's account for how people meet their communication objectives in evaluative communication situations (the situation he has chosen to scrutinize in this series of experiments).

The question of meaningful effects requires an answer if cognitive theories are to remain influential. Cognitive researchers can do a better job of establishing the relative contribution of cognitive variables (and associated theories) in explaining communication behavior. As is obvious from the six essays collected here, cognitive theories used in communication lay claim to different components of the information-processing continuum (see the useful discussion by Grimes and Meadowcroft of attentional processes), but sometimes make similar predictions about communication. For example, researchers operating from both constructivist (O'Keefe & Shepherd, 1987) and planning theory perspectives (e.g., Waldron, 1990) claim to account for the production of multifunctional behavior. Both claims may be supportable, because the cognitive operations on which these theoretical claims rest (social perception, action production) arguably have important (if somewhat different) effects on communication in multiple-goal situations. What cognitive researchers have yet to determine is the relative amount of variance in communication behavior accounted for by these two operations individually or jointly.

One could hardly argue with Grimes and Meadowcroft's assertion that attentional processes can be important communication variables, but in interpersonal communication tasks (as in television viewing) there is great variety in the nature and magnitude of the effects of attentional processes (see Burgoon and Langer's extended discussion of mindlessness). For example, interactants are often required to behave *as if* they were paying attention, even though they need not be cognitively engaged. The attentional processes needed to appear attentive (e.g., activating a scripted sequence of head nods and back channels) in a small-talk exchange are obviously quite different from those needed to comprehend a set of directions fully and repeat them back to the sender. The relative contribution of various attentional subprocesses ought to be specified by theories that articulate the communicative requirements of small talk and informative communication, respectively, and the data gathered about them should be interpreted in light of these requirements. Grimes and Meadowcroft lament the tendency of mass communication researchers to study memory rather than attention processes. From a requirement-centered perspective, mass communication researchers should study attention not just because it is a potentially interesting psychological variable that can be measured with new and refined techniques, but because attentional processes facilitate the performance of TV viewing tasks. Media researchers' preference for measures of memory might be an indication that their theories (implicitly or explicitly) specify that remembering the message is more important in viewing performance than simply attending to it.

If requirement-centered analyses were conducted systematically, they might yield data not only about the relative importance of various cognitive operations (and associated theories) in specific communication contexts, but also about the importance of cognition processes generally in meeting the requirements of communication situations. Arguably, constructs informed by theories that assume a strategic, engaged cognitive system will account for relatively small amounts of variance in some situations (compared with emotion factors, behavioral skill deficits). If the relative importance of cognitive constructs can be established empirically, cognitive frameworks will stand a better chance of retaining influence in the changing milieu of interpersonal communication research.

REFOCUSING COGNITIVE RESEARCH:
A BRIEF RESEARCH AGENDA

In advocating a requirement-centered view, I have argued for a renewed emphasis on the uniquely communicative aspects of cognition. If cognitive researchers were to put the communicative horse before the cognitive cart, how would the research agenda change? The six essays included in this section of *Communication Yearbook* give some clear indications of where cognitive researchers should be looking.

Cognition During Communication

Arguably, we would spend less effort studying cognition *about* communication and more effort studying cognition *during* communication. Interaction can be conceptualized as a stream of loosely integrated and somewhat redundant cognitive operations. As conversation unfolds, each operation reinforces and modifies previous operations. When study participants construct written messages in response to hypothetical communication scenarios, or produce cognitive assessments of transcripted conversations, they engage in cognitive operations that may have only superficial resemblance to those required during strategic communication.

As Gastil notes, constructivist research has been successful in establishing the importance of individual differences in perceptions of persons and social situations. Yet during strategic interaction initial social perceptions can be updated and modified in myriad ways, as new information is discovered and integrated. From constructivist theorizing about person-centered communication (Applegate, 1990), one can infer that success in complex interaction *requires* updating of perceptions of the partner and situation. Yet the updating process, how and if it occurs during conversation, and individual differences in on-line perceptual adjustment—presumably the essential "stuff" of person-centered communication—have yet to be studied thoroughly.

Wilson's discussion of heuristic processing is relevant here because conversation, particularly strategic conversation, is likely to make greater demands on cognitive resources (than, say, responses to written scenarios), and thus is likely to require heuristic, rather than systematic, processing. The suggestion that individuals high and low in construct differentiation use different heuristics offers a particularly promising conceptual route through which constructivist theorizing about individual differences might be extended to interaction.

Success on some conversational tasks (e.g., acquiring socially sensitive information) requires interactants to think several steps into the conversational future as they construct behavior sequences that approach conversational topics indirectly. Waldron (1990) reported evidence that, as communicative demands (the priority and number of communication objectives that needed to be obtained) increased, interactants used more efficient (direct) plans and tactics. Using Wilson's terms, participants may have abandoned systematic processing and "lowered the threshold" for rule firing, such that even minimal progress in protecting the partner's face was perceived as sufficient reason to activate direct questions about the sensitive topic.

The study of cognition during communication is methodologically challenging, requiring communication researchers to abandon measurement tools that are familiar but insensitive to the dynamics of situated cognition. Methods that produce data about a single cognitive operation (e.g., forming an initial impression) may encourage us to overestimate its importance in the larger interaction. An alternative is to examine cognitive activities across whole conversations, looking for patterns and tracing changes. This requires the collection of multiple indicators of cognitive functioning over the course of the conversation. The use of such composite measures also increases reliability of measurement, an important consideration given the incomplete data yielded by nearly any measure of cognitive functioning (Ericsson & Simon, 1980).

A central contribution of Grimes and Meadowcroft's essay is their discussion of techniques for measuring attention as it is allocated *during* message reception (in place of self-reports taken after the fact). An analysis of the advantages and disadvantages of methods potentially useful in studying conversational cognition has been presented elsewhere (Waldron & Cegala, 1992).

Conversational Content:
What Do Communicators Think About?

O'Keefe and Lambert's essay reminds us that, although theories of strategic communication typically rest on assumptions about what is happening inside the heads of communicators, surprisingly little research examines what interactants actually think about. For example, politeness theory (Brown & Levinson, 1978) and its descendants (Lim & Bowers, 1991) posit that interactants will consider face wants (for autonomy, competence, solidarity) in constructing and interpreting potentially face-threatening messages. Support for the theory is typically inferred from the messages people generate or choose in various situations. A more direct test, one that might explain why message behavior might not be accounted for by the theory (as is sometimes the case; Baxter, 1984), might examine what interactants actually think about in those situations. This is the kind of work that O'Keefe and Lambert find supportive of their theoretical position, although they have apparently not extended it to interactive contexts.

Berger's (1988, in press) planning theory assumes that interactants engage in considerable strategic thought during interaction, an assumption that would be bolstered by empirical examination of interactive thought patterns. In fact, studies of self-reported cognition indicate that as much as 40% of self-reported thoughts are plan related in some strategic tasks (Waldron, 1990, 1993). Interestingly, however, interactants also report a variety of apparently nonstrategic thought types, including preoccupations, daydreams, assessments of emotional states, and confusions (Cegala et al., 1988; Waldron, Cegala, Sharkey, & Teboul, 1990). Other evidence indicates that competent interactants have more thoughts about conversational goals and fewer about themselves than do less competent interactants (Cegala & Waldron, 1992).

Communication theorists have developed any number of individual difference measures that imply people will think differently in social interaction. Few have been validated with cognitive data drawn from interactive settings, although Cegala's (1981) interaction involvement measure has been shown to predict conversational thought patterns (Cegala, Bayer, Waldron, & Ludlum, 1994). In sum, the individual differences and constructs invoked by communication theorists have testable implications at the level of cognitive content.

Cognitive Interdependence

The traditional view of cognition as a strictly individual concept is being questioned as researchers come to view knowledge as a social construction

(Baxter, 1992) and relationships as defined by mutual knowledge (Planalp, 1993). Interactants share their perceptions, anticipate the other's reactions, coordinate conversational plans, and jointly reconstruct memories. The dyadic nature of thought is acknowledged by O'Keefe and Lambert, who see message production as a process of managing thoughts, not just of the self, but also of the partner. Similarly, the cognitive states of interactants are partially a function of the interactive behaviors of the partner, as Burgoon and Langer make clear in their essay on mindlessness.

Conversation is a prominent site for the mutual shaping of thought. Studies of the shaping process must incorporate two important features of conversation: time and interaction. Methodologies that reveal data about the similarities and differences in partners' conversational thought patterns, the correspondence of self thoughts with partner behavior, and the changing representations of the other in self thoughts and plans will be particularly useful in stimulating theoretical developments that better account for the communication-cognition relationship.

AN EXEMPLAR: COGNITIVE BASES
OF INTEGRATIVE CONFLICT TACTICS

In this section I describe a study that, though cognitive in nature, advances from an analysis of the communicative requirements of strategic interaction. The details of the study are reported elsewhere (Waldron & Applegate, in press); I summarize it here because it represents an application of a requirement-centered approach and yields data that bear on the three issues described above (cognition during interaction, patterns of content, cognitive interdependence). By articulating the communicative requirements of integrative conflict behavior and then the cognitive operations implied by those requirements, we realized that two different cognitive concepts (planning, construct differentiation) might separately or jointly account for the behavior produced by interactants. Consistent with the recommendation made by Gastil, we tested rival cognitive accounts and, more important, considered how theories that address different requirements of the conflict process (social perception, planning) might be complementary.

We chose to study verbal disagreement because it is a relatively demanding form of strategic interaction, defined by incompatible goals, negotiation, and coordination of self and other actions (Canary & Spitzberg, 1989). This is the type of communication activity that requires strategic thought (Berger, 1988), so cognitive theories should be helpful in accounting for conflict behavior.

Analysis of Communication Requirements

There exists general agreement in the conflict literature that successful outcomes require integrative behavior instead of avoidant or distributive tactics (for recent discussions of conflict tactics, see Canary & Spitzberg, 1989; Conrad, 1991). Integration tactics are responsive to requirements of effectiveness and social appropriateness (Canary & Spitzberg, 1989; Spitzberg & Cupach, 1984); they are typically protective of the partner's need for autonomy (Brown & Levinson, 1978). Integrative approaches imply joint construction of solutions, rather than "forcing" of existing positions or simple acquiescence. They imply coordination of tactics and sometimes redefinition of the situation so that goals appear compatible (O'Keefe & Shepherd, 1987).

Analysis of Cognitive Requirements

From the analysis above we speculated that integration of one's own behavior and objectives with that of the other would require these operations (among others):

> *perceiving* conflict situations in a manner which recognizes the possible existence of multiple perspectives, motives, and interpretations; cognitively *representing* the partner's perspective and goals; and *anticipating* likely partner actions. Obviously, the competent interactant is required to offer persuasive arguments. Therefore, the cognitive requirements of competent performance should include *retrieving* from memory multiple, specific, and effective arguments; *constructing on-line* new arguments which accommodate and integrate previously voiced partner concerns; *developing contingency plans* for instances when primary arguments are rejected by the partner; and *editing* planned actions when changes in the situation make them inappropriate. (Waldron & Applegate, in press)

This list of cognitive requirements is obviously not exhaustive, but we reasoned that cognitive approaches that incorporated these operations should be at least partially successful in accounting for the production of integrative tactics. We examined two such accounts: constructivism and planning theory.

Two Cognitive Accounts

Constructivist communication theory associates variation in communication behavior with individual differences in social-cognitive development. Construct differentiation, as operationalized by the Role Category Questionnaire, remains the most central cognitive construct in constructivist research. Given that the RCQ is a measure of an individual's capacity to represent others and situations in a complex fashion, it is reasonable to expect cognitively differentiated individuals to be advantaged in situations that require a complex analysis of the partner (such as verbal disagreement) as a precondition to the production of competent messages.

Recognizing that complex social perceptions help interactants meet only certain of the cognitive requirements of verbal disagreement, we turned our attention to the other cognitive operations described above—on-line construction of argument sequences that accommodate and integrate previously voiced partner concerns, anticipating future conversational states, and editing actions that might be offensive to the partner. We reasoned that these are better addressed by cognitive theories of action production in general, and theories of conversational planning in particular.

To summarize the more extended argument, we hypothesized that plans that were more specific, complex, and adapted to the partner's previous utterances would facilitate the production of integrative conflict behavior. Similarly, we expected plan editing operations to be associated meaningfully with tactics.

Method

We measured RCQ using the traditional paper-and-pencil procedure (Burleson & Waltman, 1988). Several weeks later, participants engaged in dyadic discussions regarding a topic about which they were known to disagree. Planning measures were taken using a stimulated recall method adapted for this purpose (Waldron, 1990). Tactics were coded for their integrativeness. Both the cognitive measures and tactic measures were taken at 1-minute intervals during the 8-minute conversation. Regression procedures were used to estimate the variance accounted for in tactic integrativeness during the last half of the conversation by RCQ, planning measures (during the first half of the conversation), and the interaction terms.

Results

Results indicated that the RCQ score by itself accounted for only small amounts of tactic variance (less than 1%). Planning measures accounted for up to an additional 19% of variance and the interaction terms an additional 3%. Although not strongly associated with interactive behavior, the RCQ score was strongly correlated with some planning measures, with r values as high as .59.

Discussion

We found these results interesting for a number of reasons, all of which relate to the discussion above. First, it appeared that interactant's patterns of thought *during* the early minutes of conversation facilitated (or inhibited) success in meeting the behavioral requirements of this task later in the conversation. We found that the self-reported cognitive content of interactants using integrative tactics included more complex, specific, and partner-adapted plans. Cognitive interdependence was evidenced in "accommodative" plans that explicitly incorporated the thoughts of the partner (as evidenced in previous utterances) and the associated plan editing process. At least in this study of verbal disagreement, it appears that the effects of construct differentiation on interactive behavior are not direct. Instead, construct differentiation appears to influence planning processes, which then affect the production of integrative tactics. This study allowed us to test the adequacy of two distinct theoretical accounts for the use verbal disagreement tactics. More important in terms of theoretical progress, the results stimulated us to consider a more comprehensive and integrated model of the cognitive processes undergirding this form of strategic communication.

CONCLUSION

I began by referencing Berger and Chaffee's (1988) hope that a Golden Age of Cognition might unify the discipline. It is only appropriate that I end with another sentiment similar to one they expressed six years ago: that the overall health of the discipline will be enhanced as researchers develop and test "homegrown" theories of communication. The essays presented in this section of the *Communication Yearbook* are evidence that cognitive researchers are beginning to take that charge seriously. Continued progress will require a willingness to ask the hard questions about communication and strategic interaction and the use of creative methods to answer them. Testing of rival theories and the integration of constructs that are complementary will be signs that the cognitivist perspective is maturing.

In the coming years, researchers will increasingly feel pressured to demonstrate how their work is meaningful, not just in refining theories of cognition, but in extending theories of communication. The most persuasive tonic for the symptoms of skepticism emerging in the field is to establish clearly the link between the mind and the message. No doubt, given the challenging requirements of this more advanced stage of cognitive inquiry, researchers who have merely dabbled in cognition will prospect for new topics. But as the preceding essays illustrate, cognitive concepts have been and will remain rich conceptual resources for those motivated to dig deeply in their search for improved explanations for the variety in communication activity.

REFERENCES

Anderson, J. R. (1990). *The adaptive character of thought*. Hillsdale, NJ: Lawrence Erlbaum.

Applegate, J. L. (1990). Constructs and communication: A pragmatic integration. In G. Neimeyer & R. Neimeyer (Eds.), *Advances in personal construct psychology* (Vol. 1, pp. 203-230). Greenwich, CT: JAI.

Baxter, L. (1984). An investigation of compliance gaining as politeness. *Human Communication Research, 10*, 427-456.

Baxter, L. (1992). Interpersonal communication as dialogue: A response to the "social approaches" forum. *Communication Theory, 2*, 330-336.

Berger, C. R. (1988). Planning, affect, and social action generation. In L. Donohew, H. E. Sypher, & E. T. Higgins (Eds.), *Communication, social cognition, and affect* (pp. 93-115). Hillsdale, NJ: Lawrence Erlbaum.

Berger, C. R. (in press). A plan-based approach to strategic communication. In D. E. Hewes (Ed.), *The cognitive bases of interpersonal communication*. Hillsdale, NJ: Lawrence Erlbaum.

Berger, C. R., & Chaffee, S. H. (1988). On bridging the communication gap. *Human Communication Research, 15,* 304-318.

Berger, C. R., & Jordan, J. M. (1992). Planning sources, planning difficulty, and verbal fluency. *Communication Monographs, 59,* 130-149.

Brown, P., & Levinson, S. (1978). Universals in language usage: Politeness phenomena. In E. N. Goody (Ed.), *Questions and politeness: Strategies in social interaction* (pp. 56-310). Cambridge: Cambridge University Press.

Burleson, B. R. (1987). Cognitive complexity. In J. C. McCroskey & J. A. Daly (Eds.), *Personality and interpersonal communication* (pp. 305-349). Newbury Park, CA: Sage.

Burleson, B. R., & Waltman, M. S. (1988). Cognitive complexity: Using the Role Category Question-naire measure. In C. H. Tardy (Ed.), *A handbook for the study of human communication: Methods and instruments for observing, measuring, and assessing communication processes* (pp. 1-35). Norwood, NJ: Ablex.

Canary, D. J., & Spitzberg, B. H. (1989). A model of the perceived competence of conflict strategies. *Human Communication Research, 15,* 630-649.

Cegala, D. J. (1981). Interaction involvement: A cognitive dimension of communication compe-tence. *Communication Education, 30,* 109-121.

Cegala, D. J., Bayer, C., Waldron, V., & Ludlum, J. (1994). *Cognitive dynamics of interaction involvement.* Manuscript submitted for publication.

Cegala, D. J., & Waldron, V. R. (1992). A study of the relationship between communicative performance and conversation participants' thoughts. *Communication Studies, 43,* 105-123.

Cegala, D. J., Waldron, V. R., Ludlum, J., McCabe, B., Yost, S., & Teboul, B. (1988, March). *A study of interactants' thoughts and feelings during conversation.* Paper presented at the Ninth Annual Conference on Discourse Analysis, Philadelphia.

Chautauqua: Mindfulness-mindlessness and communication [Special section]. (1992). *Communication Monographs, 59*(3).

Conrad, C. (1991). Communication in conflict: Style-strategy relationships. *Communication Mono-graphs, 58,* 135-155.

Dillard, J. P. (1990). A goal-driven model of interpersonal influence. In J. P. Dillard (Ed.), *Seeking compliance: The production of interpersonal influence messages* (pp. 41-56). Scottsdale, AZ: Gorsuch Scarisbrick.

Dillard, J. P. (1993). Persuasion past and present: Attitudes aren't what they used to be. *Communi-cation Monographs, 60,* 90-97.

Ericsson, K. A., & Simon, H. A. (1980). Verbal reports as data. *Psychological Review, 87,* 215-257.

Greene, J. O. (1984). A cognitive approach to human communication: An action assembly theory. *Communication Monographs, 51,* 289-306.

Greeno, J. (Ed.). (1993). Situated action [Special issue]. *Cognitive Science, 17*(1).

Leeds-Hurwitz, W. (1992). Forum introduction: Social approaches to interpersonal communication. *Communication Theory, 2,* 131-139.

Lim, T., & Bowers, J. W. (1991). Facework: Solidarity, approbation, and tact. *Human Communica-tion Research, 17,* 415-450.

Middleton, D., & Edwards, D. (Eds.). (1990). *Collective remembering.* Newbury Park, CA: Sage.

O'Keefe, B. J., & Shepherd, G. J. (1987). The pursuit of multiple objectives in face-to-face persuasive interactions: Effects of construct differentiation on message organization. *Communi-cation Monographs, 54,* 396-419.

Planalp, S. (1993). Communication, cognition, and emotion. *Communication Monographs, 60,* 3-9.

Pouncy, H. (1988). Terms of agreement: Evaluating the theory of symbolic politic's impact on the pluralist research program. *American Journal of Political Science, 32,* 781-795.

Sanders, R. E. (1992). Conversation, computation, and the human factor. *Human Communication Research, 18,* 623-636.

Spitzberg, B. H., & Cupach, W. R. (1984). *Interpersonal communication competence.* Beverly Hills, CA: Sage.

Tracy, K., & Baratz, S. (1993). Intellectual discussion in the academy as situated discourse. *Communication Monographs, 60,* 300-320.

Waldron, V. R. (1990). Constrained rationality: Situational influences on information acquisition plans and tactics. *Communication Monographs, 57,* 184-201.

Waldron, V. R. (1993, February). *Does planning pay off? Information acquisition success in peer conversations about AIDS.* Paper presented at the annual meeting of the Western Communication Association, Albuquerque, NM.

Waldron, V. R., & Applegate, J. A. (in press). Interpersonal construct differentiation and conversational planning: An examination of two cognitive accounts for the production of competent verbal disagreement tactics. *Human Communication Research.*

Waldron, V. R., & Cegala, D. J. (1992). Assessing conversational cognition: Levels of cognitive theory and associated methodological requirements. *Human Communication Research, 18,* 599-622.

Waldron, V. R., Cegala, D. J., Sharkey, W. F., & Teboul, B. (1990). Cognitive and tactical dimensions of goal management. *Journal of Language and Social Psychology, 9,* 101-118.

SECTION 2

Communication About Health and
Environmental Risks:
Developments in Theory
and Research

9 Using the Theory of Reasoned Action to Examine the Impact of Health Risk Messages

ROBERT J. GRIFFIN
Marquette University

KURT NEUWIRTH
SHARON DUNWOODY
University of Wisconsin—Madison

Results from a laboratory experiment indicate that information about risk probability affects the belief that drinking parasite-infested tap water leads to personal illness. In line with Fishbein and Ajzen's theory of reasoned action, this behavioral belief combined with other components of cognitive structure to affect subjects' attitudes toward the act of drinking the water. These attitudes, along with subjective norms and perceived behavioral control, then affected behavioral intention to drink the water. Message stylistic variables interacted with information about the characteristics of the hazard to affect personal belief about risk from the contamination. In general, key concepts regarding risk-related behavior are accommodated well by Fishbein and Ajzen's theory, which appears to be very useful for exploring the effects of risk communication.

COMMUNICATION scholars have long wrestled with the question of how messages influence behavior. That question has been addressed recently—and with renewed intensity—by researchers and professionals concerned with risk communication. A spate of recent books illustrates this concern, driven in part by the perceived bad fit between scientists' and lay audiences' risk judgments (see, e.g., Leiss, 1989; National Research Council, 1989; Sandman, Sachsman, Greenberg, & Gochfeld, 1987).

In the study reported in this chapter, we applied one of the more successful social psychological models to the task of understanding the influence of health risk messages on individuals. Specifically, we used Fishbein and Ajzen's (1975; Ajzen & Fishbein, 1980) theory of reasoned action to investigate some effects of communication on beliefs people have about actions they might take to

Correspondence and requests for reprints: Robert J. Griffin, Center for Mass Media Research, College of Communication, Marquette University, Milwaukee, WI 53233.

Communication Yearbook 18, pp. 201-228

reduce health risks caused by an environmental hazard—in this case, a parasite lurking in the local tap water. Waterborne disease is a problem that has produced increasing concern among health professionals, government agencies, and members of the public.

THEORY OF REASONED ACTION

The theory of reasoned action deals with the causal antecedents of actions people take that are voluntary—that is, behaviors that are under the individual's own control. The theory has generated a lot of research attention and activity, and has been applied to a wide range of human activities, including communication as a behavior (e.g., Loken, 1983; Palmgreen & Rayburn, 1985; Warshaw & Davis, 1985) and a variety of health-related behaviors, including actions taken in the face of health risks (e.g., Boyd & Wandersman, 1991; Fishbein & Middlestadt, 1989; Henning & Knowles, 1990; Montano & Taplin, 1991; Stasson & Fishbein, 1990).[1] Ajzen (1988) notes that the theory of reasoned action "is based on the assumption that human beings usually behave in a sensible manner; that they take account of available information and implicitly or explicitly consider the implications of their actions" (p. 117).

Behavior, Attitude, Norms

The theory proposes that a voluntary behavior (B) will be predicted by behavioral intention (BI). Behavioral intention, in turn, is determined by two variables: attitude toward the behavior ($AAct$), which is the person's positive or negative evaluation of performing the particular behavior; and subjective norms (SN), which is the person's perception of social normative pressures, that is, that relevant others believe he or she should (or should not) perform the particular behavior (Ajzen & Fishbein, 1980; Fishbein & Ajzen, 1975).[2] The main equation is as follows:

$$B \sim BI = f(AAct_{w1} + SN_{w2})$$

For some behaviors, attitudinal ($AAct$) matters may be more important considerations than normative (SN) matters; for other behaviors, the opposite may be true. Thus the weights (w1 and w2) for each component may vary, and are empirically derived (usually as standardized regression coefficients) in tests of the theory. Overall, people are expected to be more likely to perform a given behavior when they evaluate their performance of it positively, and when they believe that others important to them want them to perform the behavior (Ajzen, 1988). In a meta-analysis of 87 studies that tested the theory of reasoned action, Sheppard, Hartwick, and Warshaw (1988) found that the relationship of $AAct$

and *SN* to behavioral intention was usually strong (average correlation = .66). Therefore, we expected to find positive relationships between *BI* and the components *AAct* and *SN* in our study.

Practical constraints did not allow us to measure actual behavior in our study. Past research has found, however, that *BI* predicts volitional behavior rather well. In their meta-analysis, Sheppard et al. (1988) discovered an average correlation of .53 between behavioral intention and performance. They conclude that the theory "has strong predictive utility, even when utilized to investigate situations and activities that do not fall within the boundary conditions originally specified for the model" (p. 338).

Cognitive Structure

The theory also states that attitudes toward performing a behavior are determined by salient behavioral beliefs (*b*) a person has about the behavior. According to Fishbein and Ajzen (1975), salient beliefs are those a person retrieves from memory and "considers" when deciding how to behave in a given situation. Beliefs are formed from personal experience, from information a person receives from other sources, such as the mass media, and from inferences a person draws from other beliefs.

In the Fishbein and Ajzen formulation, a behavioral belief associates performance of the behavior with a certain outcome (e.g., someone may believe that "taking a vacation trip" will "make me relax") or with some attribute related to performing the behavior (e.g., that the trip "will be costly"). The strength of a behavioral belief is usually measured on a scale that indicates how likely it is that a particular outcome or attribute will be associated with performing the behavior, as perceived by the person completing the scale. Scale values typically range from –3 (*very unlikely*) to +3 (*very likely*).

Using an expectancy-value formulation, each behavioral belief is multiplied by a measure of evaluation (*e*) of the outcome or attribute. The valence of an evaluation is commonly measured on a semantic differential scale ranging from –3 for *bad* to +3 for *good* (e.g., a person would indicate on the scale whether, for him or her, doing something to relax would be bad or good or somewhere in between). The resulting product term is usually referred to as a belief-evaluation compound (*be*). The compound yields positive values when the person perceives that good outcomes (attributes) are likely to result from performing the behavior, or that bad outcomes (attributes) are unlikely to result. It yields negative values when the person perceives that bad outcomes (attributes) are likely or that good outcomes (attributes) are unlikely. Compounds for all beliefs are then summed to produce a measure of cognitive structure (our notation *CSbe*) designed to predict attitude toward the behavior (*AAct*):[3]

$$AAct = f\left(\sum_n b_i\, e_i\right)$$

Because our study concerned cognitive structure and the chain of relationships between it and behavioral intention, we included subjective norms in our analysis only at the component level (*SN*), because it is essential to control the relationship of subjective norms to behavioral intention. We did not consider in this study the subcomponent or communication antecedents of subjective norms.[4]

Applying the Theory to Health Behaviors

Generally, the theory of reasoned action has been supported when applied to health-related behavior in a wide variety of contexts (Carter, 1990). In a handful of recent health-related studies that provide comparable correlation coefficients between *AAct* and cognitive structure (Brubaker, Prue, & Rychtarik, 1987; Godin, Colantonio, Davis, Shephard, & Simard, 1986; McCaul, O'Neill, & Glasgow, 1988; Toneatto & Binik, 1987; Tuorila, 1987), we found a raw average correlation of .50 between these components of the model. Thus we expected to find somewhat strong positive relationships between cognitive structure and *AAct* in our study, which involved an environmental health risk.

Some researchers who have applied Fishbein and Ajzen's theory to health contexts have found only partial support for the model (e.g., Godin et al., 1986; Mullen, Hersey, & Iverson, 1987). Various researchers have found "crossover effects" (i.e., relationships among what are supposed to be uncorrelated variables, such as *AAct* and *SN*) or have otherwise found the structure of the model to be more complex than originally formulated (e.g., Beck, 1979; Grube, Morgan, & McGree, 1986; Oliver & Bearden, 1985; Toneatto & Binik, 1987).[5]

Some studies have found better prediction of behavior or behavioral intention by adding other variables (e.g., Hill, Gardner, & Rassaby, 1985; Montano & Taplin, 1991; Pender & Pender, 1986). The single most common addition to the model that seems to increase prediction of health-related behavioral intention is some aspect of self-efficacy (McCaul et al., 1988) or perceived control over one's own behavior (Ajzen, 1988; Ajzen & Timko, 1986; Godin & Gionet, 1991; Schifter & Ajzen, 1985). Ajzen (1988) proposes an extension of the Fishbein-Ajzen formulation so that it covers behaviors over which the person has incomplete volitional control. The new version adds a measure of perceived behavioral control (*PBC*), which is an additional component designed, along with *SN* and *AAct,* to predict *BI* directly. Perceived behavioral control, according to Ajzen (1988), is the perceived ease of performing the behavior, and reflects past experience as well as anticipated impediments and obstacles. We included *PBC* primarily as a control variable in our study.

RISK COMMUNICATION AND
THE THEORY OF REASONED ACTION

Although studies of the influence of risk information on lay audiences' risk judgments or on their risk-related behaviors have proliferated in recent years, we were unable to find any that empirically explored the effects of risk communication by applying the Fishbein-Ajzen theory. In fact, relatively few studies overall that have tested the Fishbein-Ajzen theory have measured or manipulated communication variables, even though the theory lends itself to examinations and assessments of communication processes and effects in the area of health risk behavior (see Fishbein & Middlestadt, 1989) and other behavioral domains. Variations in measurement and conceptual schemes also make it difficult to synthesize findings across those studies that do look at the effects of communication.[6] However, the results that have emerged are useful in revealing some communication influences on beliefs and other components of the model.

Communication, Lutz (1977) suggests, can alter the structure of beliefs by creating a new salient belief, by altering the strength or salience of a belief, or by modifying the evaluation of a belief. In the risk communication literature, studies of the relationship between use of mass media channels and judgments about the risk of AIDS (Dunwoody & Neuwirth, 1991) and the risk of crime (Sparks & Ogles, 1990) have found that mediated channel use is related to cognitive dimensions of risk judgment (knowledge of the level of risk) but not to affective dimensions (level of worry about the risk). Such a pattern is consistent with the proposition that messages can rather directly influence the structure of beliefs.

However, some risk communication research suggests that cognitive changes can be by-products of communication effects on affective states such as worry or happiness (e.g., Dunwoody, Friestad, & Shapiro, 1987; Johnson & Tversky, 1983). In a study testing the Fishbein-Ajzen theory outside of a risk context, Ryan (1982) found that booklets containing cognitive and normative information about a toothpaste brand affected cognitive structure only through effects on subjective norms, a pattern Ryan attributes to his use of an expert's endorsement in the booklets and to behavioral belief inferences drawn by his experimental subjects. Thus it would appear that communication could affect components other than cognitive structure, and that changes in these other components could influence cognition indirectly.

Other communication studies that involve the Fishbein-Ajzen theory suggest that information that is more focused on a specific behavior affects components of the model more strongly than information that is more general or that concerns a whole class of behaviors (e.g., Lutz, 1977; Stutzman & Green, 1982). Fishbein and Middlestadt (1989) observe that "many educational campaigns and interventions have been unsuccessful because they have not focused directly on the appropriate intentions" (p. 101).

In undertaking the study described below, we proposed that communication about the likelihood of harm from a specific behavior that exposes one to a specific environmental contaminant and about the severity of the harm that could result from the behavior would create a risk-related behavioral belief (b) and affect the risk-related outcome evaluation (e) in regard to that specific behavior. We also suggested that some stylistic presentation characteristics used by the media might amplify these effects.

We also proposed that communication influences on risk-related beliefs would indirectly influence behavioral intention (*BI*) through effects on cognitive structure (*CSbe*) and attitude toward the behavior (*AAct*). This proposition is consistent with the theory of reasoned action and with research that indicates that behavioral beliefs about risk influence individual behavior in the face of a potential health hazard, at least indirectly (e.g., Boyd & Wandersman, 1991; Stasson & Fishbein, 1990).

Also consistent with the theory, perceived social pressures might also influence how people deal behaviorally with risky situations. For example, Stasson and Fishbein (1990) found in an experiment that subjects' intentions to wear auto seat belts were affected by their perceptions that important others would want them to wear seat belts under risky conditions. Future research should examine communication influences on such subjective norms, but in our study we employed *SN* as a control variable and remained alert to the possibility of crossover relationships. Similarly, we used perceived behavioral control as a control variable, although communication effects on *PBC* are also worthy of future research. Because we could not measure behavior in this study, we relied on the past performance of *BI* in predicting behavior.

The Manipulated Variables

Many people rely on the mass media for information about hazards in their environments (Freimuth, Edgar, & Hammond, 1987; McCallum, Hammond, Morris, & Covello, 1990). A typical news story employs conventional journalistic techniques to convey information about a hazard and may contain information about what people might do, either individually or collectively, to deal with the problem. In this study we addressed two dimensions of risk messages. The first dimension, here called *hazard characteristics,* was operationalized as level of risk and severity of outcome, perceptions of the risk situation itself that may be, to some extent, independent of the message structure. The second dimension, labeled *stylistic structure,* was

examined here as vividness of lead and headline as frame of reference; this dimension deals with writing conventions of news accounts that typically appear in the news media and are, to some extent, independent of content.[7]

Hazard Characteristics

One would expect individuals to vary in their reactions to risks that themselves vary in likelihood of occurrence and severity of outcome. Indeed, research coincident with health information campaigns has shown that the probability of exposure to health risks, the unpleasantness of the outcome, and the individual's perception of his or her ability to achieve recommended behavioral changes are all important message factors leading to behavioral modification (Beck, 1984; Beck & Lund, 1981; Maddux & Rogers, 1983; Rippetoe & Rogers, 1987).

Studies of the types of information that journalists include in stories have suggested that information about behavioral options—something Lemert, Mitzman, Seither, Cook, and Hackett (1977) call "tactical mobilizing information"—is often omitted. Such information could affect the efficacy a person feels in regard to changing his or her own behavior, or what Ajzen (1988) has termed perceived behavioral control in the context of the model we are using. Our study did not test this possible communication effect on *PBC*, but it does seem to be a promising path for future research.

In this particular experiment we decided to manipulate types of information that would be more common to risk stories: level of risk and severity of outcome. Based on the robustness of the studies cited above, we would expect information about level of risk to influence assessments of personal risk (i.e., how likely one is to be afflicted), whereas varying information about the severity of outcome should affect perceptions of how bad or unpleasant such affliction would be.

Stylistic Structure

Kasperson (1992) argues that media coverage of risks plays a major role in what he and colleagues term the "social amplification of risks." That is, notes Kasperson, "the processing of risk events by the media, cultural and social groups, institutions, and individuals profoundly shapes the societal experience with risk and plays a crucial role in determining the overall societal impacts of particular hazard events" (p. 168).

How risk stories have such effects, however, remains very much a mystery. A number of researchers have begun, through both experiments and surveys, to explore the ability of media accounts to influence the ways in which audience members make judgments about issues (see, e.g., Iyengar, 1991; Iyengar & Kinder, 1987; Iyengar & Simon, 1993), but these studies have failed to isolate and measure the effects of individual attributes of media texts, as we have in this study. We selected two attributes of media story structure that we thought could reasonably influence risk perceptions: the presence of risk in a story headline and the use of vivid information in the story body.

Risk in the headline. Headlines have long been identified as establishing "frames of reference" within which stories may subsequently be interpreted (Tannenbaum, 1953). More recently, discourse analysts who have turned their attention to news accounts, such as van Dijk (1988), have agreed, arguing that "topics may be expressed and signaled by headlines, which apparently act as summaries of the news text" (pp. 35-36).

In an earlier study, Dunwoody et al. (1987) found that headlines that mentioned risk made the topics of those stories seem more worrisome to respondents than did headlines that did not mention risk. In general, such "risk" headlines could sensitize readers to the risk-related information in the text of the accompanying story and thereby encourage them to interpret the story in terms of a danger (Dunwoody, Neuwirth, Griffin, & Long, 1992). In an aroused state, such as worry, readers might process risk information more deeply.[8] Repetition of risk content in the headline and in the story might also deepen the memory trace for the risk-related information.[9] Either process could make the risk information more accessible in memory (i.e., enhance "top-of-the-mind" awareness) and thereby make risk-related beliefs stronger, more salient, and more likely to be considered by individuals who might need to respond behaviorally to a potential health hazard.

Vivid information in the story. Personalization is a strategy employed by communicators of all kinds. The assumption is that telling a story about an individual to illustrate a pattern will make information more vivid, more colorful, and thus more memorable. This view is embraced by scholars as well as practitioners. As Nisbett and Ross (1980) note, vivid information is "likely to attract and hold our attention and to excite the imagination to the extent it is (a) emotionally interesting, (b) concrete and imagery-producing and (c) proximate in a sensory, temporal or spatial way" (p. 45). Vividly presented information indeed has been found to result in greater recall than pallid information (D'Agostino & Small, 1980; Holmes & Langford, 1976; Paivio, 1973), perhaps in part because of the redundant (sensory image and semantic) memory traces that vivid information can create in human memory (Paivio, 1973).

Within the field of mass communication, however, vividness has received relatively little research attention.[10] The limited number of studies that have been conducted, although providing some mixed results, generally suggest that mass media presentation of concrete, vivid information could affect cognition and behavior. Yagade and Dozier (1990) found that the mass media influenced the salience of concrete issues more than that of abstract issues. Respondents in their study considered concrete issues to be easier to visualize and thus, according to the researchers, more vivid. On the other hand, Iyengar and Kinder (1987) found that vividness, operationalized as a personalized narrative in television news stories, had no impact on issue salience. And a study by Spencer, Seydlitz, Laska, and Triche (1992) suggests that differences in content across media channels produce differential behavioral effects; visual material presented on television newscasts, more than visual material appearing in newspapers, influenced the purchase of bottled water. The authors cite differential modeling behaviors as the most likely explanation for these results.

Kennamer (1988) is concerned that making some information in journalistic accounts more vivid than other information can cause audiences to misinterpret what they read or see. Dunwoody et al. (1987) found that risk stories that began with personal narratives rather than with straightforward informational leads made the risks discussed seem more worrisome to respondents, even when the level of risk was held constant. Again, we would expect that worry-based arousal could result in better memory for risk information, as could redundant memory traces for that information in long-term memory.

Researchers have operationalized vividness in a number of ways, but the central aspects of manipulating vividness involve concreteness and the use of detail. Consistent with the work of other researchers (Nisbett & Ross, 1980; Iyengar & Kinder, 1987), in this study we operationalized vividness as the use of a personalized narrative lead in a news story. In general, we expected that a "risk" headline and use of vivid information in the body of the story (here operationalized as personalized lead) would influence the accessibility of the risk information in memory and thereby strengthen risk-related behavioral beliefs.

The Dependent Variables

Our dependent variables were some components of the theory of reasoned action as applied to the context of an environmental health risk. In particular, we investigated the effects of print communication on some cognitions related to actions that students would take if a parasite were infesting the campus water supply. At this stage, we were particularly interested in the way that a perception of risk can be embodied in the behavioral belief (b) that performing an action could lead to an illness outcome with a certain probability, and how this belief could be affected by risk communication, especially a risk estimate. We were also interested in the extent to which the valence of the evaluation of becoming ill (e) could be affected by information about the severity of the outcome of becoming ill with a particular malady. In this way, the expectancy-value compound (be) regarding illness contains two important aspects of an individual's risk judgment: How likely am I to become ill? and How bad will it be?

We also investigated relationships among some of the components of the model. In particular, we related cognitive structure ($CSbe$) to attitude ($AAct$) regarding drinking this water, and $AAct$ to behavioral intention (BI).

The behavior we investigated was whether or not a student decreased his or her drinking of campus-area tap water. Because subjects in the experiment could be thinking in terms of substituting other liquids for the tap water, we also asked them to evaluate drinking the tap water along other dimensions of behavioral beliefs that represent benefits (i.e., tastiness, and whether the liquid would be thirst quenching) and costs (i.e., monetary costs, convenience, and whether the liquid would be time-consuming to use). A pilot study indicated that these dimensions could have some influence on a person's judgment about drinking the tap water.

RESEARCH QUESTIONS AND HYPOTHESES

Figure 9.1 illustrates the components of the model and highlights the relationships of primary interest in this study. Based on this model, our first research question was, What are the effects of stylistic structure of a risk news story, and the hazard characteristics as presented in that story, on some components of the Fishbein-Ajzen model, in particular on components of cognitive structure (behavioral belief and outcome evaluation) in regard to that risk?

Our first hypotheses were as follows:

- *Hypothesis 1a:* The higher the level of risk of illness presented in the story, the stronger the behavioral belief that drinking the water will make one ill.
- *Hypothesis 1b:* The higher the severity of outcome as presented in the story, the stronger the negative (i.e., bad) valence of the evaluation regarding drinking things that make one ill.

Including risk information in a headline could result in deeper processing of risk information in the headline and story and therefore strengthen risk-related behavioral beliefs, thus:

- *Hypothesis 1c:* Referring to a health hazard in a headline ("risky" headline) will increase the strength of the behavioral belief that drinking the water will likely make one ill.

Personalizing the lead of the story could also affect the strength of behavioral beliefs by influencing memory storage structure and recall of risk information in the story. Therefore:

- *Hypothesis 1d:* A personalized lead will strengthen the behavioral belief that drinking the water will make one ill.

Our second research question was, What are the relationships among cognitive structure, attitude toward the act, subjective norms, perceived behavioral control, and behavioral intention in regard to response to a hazard posing a risk to human health? We tested the patterns of relationships among some of these components that are specified by the model, being most sensitive to relationships among *CSbe, AAct,* and *BI*:

- *Hypothesis 2a:* Cognitive structure (*CSbe*) will correlate positively with attitude toward the behavior (*AAct*).
- *Hypothesis 2b: AAct* will correlate positively with behavioral intention (*BI*).

METHOD

Subjects and Design

The research participants were 252 students in introductory journalism and mass communication classes who were awarded extra course credit for their participation. A $2 \times 2 \times 2 \times 2$ factorial design was used to assess the effects of the four manipulated variables on the dependent variables of interest. Two levels of outcome severity (high and low), two levels of risk level (high and low), two

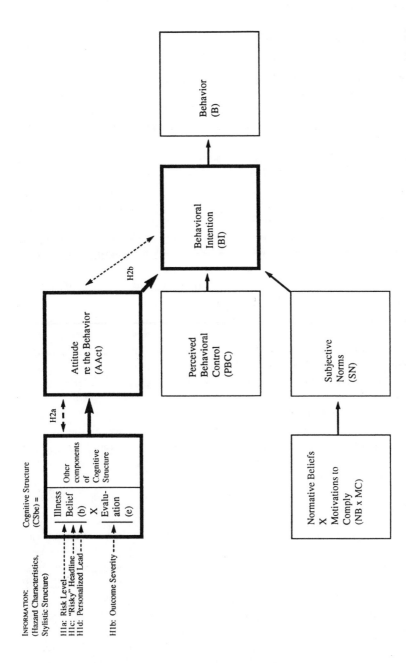

Figure 9.1. Fishbein-Ajzen Theory of Reasoned Action, Including Perceived Behavioral Control, as Applied to Communication About a Health Risk

NOTE: Components of primary interest in this study—illness belief (*b*) and evaluation (*e*), cognitive structure (*CSbe*), attitude toward the behavior (*AAct*), and behavioral intention (*BI*)—are represented by the bold lines in this figure. Dotted lines represent hypothesized relationships.

levels of personalization (personalized and nonpersonalized), and two levels of headline (risky and nonrisky) were manipulated.

Procedure and Stimulus Materials

Subjects met in small groups ranging in size from 2 to 16. Individuals were assigned randomly to 1 of the 16 experimental conditions. The study was presented as an effort to gauge reactions to the use of videotext news stories from the university news service. Subjects were told that all the stories they would see were excerpted from the videotext news service. Each subject worked individually at a computer terminal.

After verbal instructions were given, subjects viewed a screen containing a menu of six news stories especially created for the experiment. Three of the stories were of general interest to students (on time use, apartment hunting, and academic standards) and three stories were about hazards (fluorescent lighting affecting GPA, an illness caused by chemically treated library books, and a parasite in the campus water supply). After selecting and reading the stories, subjects answered detailed questions about each potential threat. Data from the parasite story are the focus of this report.

Subjects in the experiment received different versions of the parasite story consisting of (a) high or low outcome severity (severe diarrhea lasting for more than two weeks or slight stomach cramps lasting less than 45 minutes), (b) high or low risk level (odds of 1 in 12 or 1 in 3,100 of becoming ill),[11] (c) personalized or nonpersonalized presentation ("When pharmacy major Jack Snyder experienced stomach cramps last month, he immediately recognized . . . " or "A parasite has found its way into Madison's water supply and is making students sick."), and (d) risky or nonrisky headlines ("Water parasite afflicts students" or "New type of wildlife on campus").

When all subjects had completed their sessions at the computer, they participated in a debriefing session that consisted of a full explanation of the purpose of the study. At this time they were alerted to the deception involved and were informed that the hazards mentioned in the experiment did not exist.

Dependent Measures

After reading the stimulus materials, subjects rated the six behavioral belief (b) items on a 9-point scale to indicate the likelihood (+4 = *very likely,* −4 = *very unlikely*) that their campus-area tap water would be associated with each outcome, including that of becoming ill. Subjects also rated the prospect of becoming ill from drinking the tap water, and the other outcomes, on a 9-point scale that ranged from *extremely bad* (−4) to *extremely good* (+4), as a measure of evaluation (e) of each outcome. Because evaluations of illness were expected to cluster on the negative (*bad*) end of the scale, 9-point (rather than 7-point) scales were used, to allow for a wider range of responses to all belief and evaluation items.

We derived the belief-by-evaluation (*be*) compound for each behavioral belief by multiplying the belief and evaluation scales for that belief, and we computed cognitive structure indexes by summing the six compounds. The compounds and the cognitive structure index are scored such that higher positive values represent more favorable orientations toward using campus-area tap water for drinking. Reliability (alpha) for the cognitive structure variable (*CSbe*) is .66.

We derived attitude toward the act (*AAct*) of drinking campus-area tap water by summing semantic differential scales of foolish/wise, good/bad (reversed), harmful/beneficial, and rewarding/punishing (reversed). *AAct* is scored such that higher values represent more favorable attitudes toward drinking this tap water. Reliability (alpha) is .94.

We measured behavioral intention (*BI*) by summing standardized scores of two measures: the subject's estimated future likelihood that he or she would use campus-area tap water for drinking (based on the standard Fishbein and Ajzen measure) and the subject's estimate of the average number of times per day he or she would drink campus-area tap water. Higher scores represent greater likelihood. Reliability (alpha) is .73.[12]

Control Variables

Based on work by Ajzen (1988) and others, our index of perceived behavioral control (*PBC*) is the sum of two measures: the amount of control the subject believes he or she has in regard to drinking this tap water and the extent to which not using campus-area tap water for drinking would be difficult or easy. Habits, for example, might be hard for some people to change, even in the face of a health risk. Higher scores represent greater perceived control. Reliability (alpha) is .58.

We assessed subjective norms (*SN*) with the usual single item that measured the extent to which the subject believed "most people who are important to me" would think he or she should or should not use the tap water for drinking. The *SN* measure is scored such that higher values represent perceptions that important others expect the subject to drink the tap water. Appropriately, this item correlates negatively ($r = -.72, p < .001$) with subjects' beliefs that these others would expect the subject to drink other liquids instead of the tap water.

Because we were studying this model in an experimental setting, we also wanted to control for the believability of the stimulus materials. To do so, we asked subjects near the end of the session to rate the parasite story on a scale of 1 to 9 according to the level of doubt they had about its accuracy. Higher scores represent stronger doubts. The mean score for all subjects was 4.9, about the midpoint of the scale. Controlling for believability should enhance the internal and especially external validity of the results of our experiment.[13]

Statistical Analysis

We employed hierarchical multiple regression to test the relationships (main effects and interactions) between independent variables and dependent variables of primary interest. Independent variables representing the experimental conditions were contrast coded prior to entry. We created variables representing two-way, three-way, and four-way interactions among the independent variables by multiplying independent variables (e.g., we represented a two-way interaction between level of risk and severity of outcome by multiplying these two variables) (see Cohen & Cohen, 1975).

Perceived accuracy of the story was entered as the first block in each analysis. The four manipulated (main effect) variables were entered as the second block. The six two-way interaction variables were the third block. They were followed in each analysis by the block of four three-way interaction variables, and these in turn were followed by the four-way interaction variable.

We performed a series of hierarchical multiple regression analyses to determine the mitigating roles of each successive component in the model. Subjective norms (SN) and perceived behavioral control (PBC) were entered in the same final block as AAct in the regression of behavioral intention (BI).

RESULTS

Effects of Hazard and Style Characteristics

Illness Belief and Evaluation

Our first set of hypotheses (1a through 1d) concerned the effects that stylistic structure of a news story and the hazard characteristics presented in that story have on components of cognitive structure, in this case the behavioral belief that drinking campus-area tap water will make one ill and the evaluation of that outcome. As Table 9.1 shows, we found support only for Hypothesis 1a: The higher the level of risk of illness presented in the story, the stronger the behavioral belief (b) that drinking the water will make one ill (beta = .19, $p = .001$). The level of risk also affected the illness belief-evaluation (be) compound (beta = $-.18$, $p = .01$) such that those who read that the level of risk is higher were more likely to perceive that illness is a bad outcome that would probably result if they drank campus-area tap water. None of the other hazard characteristic or stylistic structural variables had the hypothesized main effects on belief or evaluation. Generally, however, it appears that information about the level of risk from an environmental hazard, expressed in this study as a risk estimate, does have some influence on the amount of personal risk people believe they face from that hazard.

Table 9.1 shows that the level of risk, severity of outcome, and use of a risk-related headline interact to affect the belief (b) that drinking the water will likely lead to illness (beta = .17, $p = .01$). This three-way interaction is illustrated in Figure 9.2. A comparable three-way interaction occurs with the illness belief-evaluation (be) compound as the dependent variable (beta = $-.14$, $p = .05$ in Table 9.1; interaction not shown in a figure). Table 9.1 also shows that using a

TABLE 9.1
Drinking Contaminated Tap Water: Illness-Related Behavioral Belief and
Evaluation With Control and Independent Variables ($N = 252$)

Variable	Illness-Related Dependent Variable		
	Belief (b)	*Evaluation (e)*	*Compound (be)*
Story accuracy	.03	.06	−.04
adjusted R^2	.00	.00	.00
Hazard characteristics			
risk level (R)	.19***	−.08	−.18**
severity of outcome (S)	.05	.09	−.05
Stylistic structure			
risk in headline (H)	.07	.04	−.08
personalized lead (P)	−.07	−.04	.07
adjusted R^2	.03	.00	.03
Interactions			
$R \times S$	.07	−.01	−.05
$R \times H$	−.11	−.02	.10
$R \times P$	.09	.09	−.10
$S \times H$	−.06	.06	.03
$S \times P$	−.07	.12	.05
$H \times P$	.01	−.08	−.01
adjusted R^2	.04	.01	.03
$R \times S \times H$	.17**	−.06	−.14*
$R \times S \times P$	−.02	−.03	.01
$R \times H \times P$	−.02	.01	.01
$S \times H \times P$	.04	−.06	−.02
adjusted R^2	.06	.00	.04
$R \times S \times H \times P$	−.13*	.04	.11
adjusted R^2	.07	.00	.05
Multiple R	.36**	.25	.33*

NOTE: Belief is the perceived likelihood that illness will result from drinking the contaminated tap water. Evaluation is the perceived "goodness" of that outcome. The compound is the product of belief times evaluation.
$*p = .05; **p = .01; ***p = .001$.

personalized lead lessens the effect of the headline-risk level-severity interaction on the behavioral belief (b) that drinking the water will produce illness (beta = −.13, $p = .05$), as illustrated in the four-way interaction in Figure 9.2. The four-way interaction in regard to the illness compound (be) is comparable, but does not reach statistical significance (beta = .11, $p = .08$; interaction not shown in a figure). Our analysis of the interaction will proceed in regard to the illness belief (b) dependent variable.

When both hazard characteristics (risk level and outcome severity) are high, stylistic factors have little or no effect on this perception of personal risk (see four-way illustrations in Figure 9.2). However, when both risk level and outcome severity are low, a risky headline has a relatively strong impact on this belief, as illustrated most clearly in the three-way interaction in Figure 9.2. In

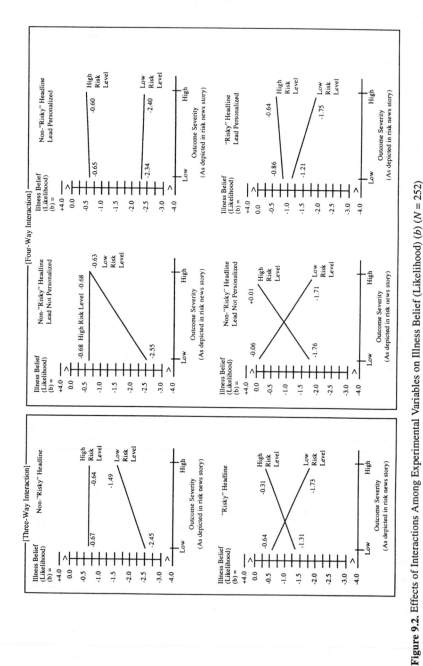

Figure 9.2. Effects of Interactions Among Experimental Variables on Illness Belief (Likelihood) (*b*) (*N* = 252)

NOTE: Higher illness belief values represent greater perceived likelihood of becoming ill from drinking the tap water. Means in the figure are adjusted by the control variable of perceived story accuracy.

this case, the headline amplifies the perceived personal risk from the hazard when the hazard is less dangerous.

Also noteworthy is that information about the severity of outcome has a contingent influence on subjects' personal risk estimates. We expected severity information to affect evaluation (e) but not perceived likelihood of affliction (b). Perhaps outcome severity has side effects on personal risk estimates owing to affective responses to outcome severity or through some related inferential processes.

The relationships from the three-way interaction, in particular the effect of a risky headline on risk perception among those reading the low-severity and low-risk message, are stronger when the lead is not personalized (Figure 9.2, four-way interaction). Personalizing the lead reduces or eliminates the influence of the interactions among risk level, severity, and a risky headline, while the main effect of the risk estimate on perceived risk remains apparent.

This interaction suggests that, when risk and severity are low, a risky headline can give readers a perception of greater risk than the story information itself would produce. In most cases, we found that subjects' perceptions of personal risk were more consistent with the relative level of risk when a risky headline was not used. The most direct relationship of risk level to perceived risk occurred when subjects read a personalized lead and did not encounter a risky headline.

The reasons for these interaction patterns are not clear, but there are a few possible explanations worth exploring. One possibility is that, consistent with findings reported by Kennamer (1988), the vividness of the personalized lead attracted the subjects' attentional and memory organizational resources. This process may have, as a by-product, interfered with cognitive processing of headline and illness severity information in semantic memory, making that information relatively unavailable in the memories of subjects who were forming their risk perceptions under those conditions. The reason that information about the risk level remained relevant to subjects reading personalized stories is not clear. Perhaps identification processes are also involved when the case used to personalize the story is from the same group of people (e.g., students at the same university) as the reader. Under these circumstances, a risk estimate may in effect suggest to the reader how likely it is that he or she will suffer the same fate (in this case, illness from drinking the tap water) and therefore is attended to as pertinent information.

Another explanation is that the vivid, personalized lead induced some fear that, in turn, produced some cognitive discounting of information about the threat. This result would be consistent with the reverse curvilinear (i.e., inverted U-shaped) relationship McGuire (1969) posits between fear appeals and their effectiveness.

A third possibility is that people might apply a sort of probability folklore (i.e., a naive probability theory) when told about someone else nearby who has been affected by such an illness. Some may believe that "lightning doesn't strike twice in the same place," and discount all but the most direct information (e.g., a risk estimate) about the threat to themselves. Overall, it is apparent that when a personalized lead is used, headline risk information and information about the severity of the illness become much less relevant to a person's risk judgment. These relationships are worthy of future research.

Cognitive Structure and Attitude

Personalization also has a statistically significant and, unexpectedly, positive relationship (beta = .20, p = .01) with cognitive structure (*CSbe*), as shown in Table 9.2. In weighing all the costs and benefits of drinking the tap water, including that of illness, that make up cognitive structure, those who read personalized leads were somewhat more likely to perceive positive outcomes for themselves from drinking the tap water. Conversely, those who did not read personalized leads were less likely to see positive outcomes from drinking the water. This result could also be based on the discounting process suggested previously. It also indicates that the various components of cognitive structure operate as inter-dependent systems that respond somewhat differentially to the introduction of informational and inferential beliefs. These relationships should also be considered in future research.

Information about the level of risk from this environmental hazard had a negative impact (beta = −.23, p = .001) on subjects' attitudes (*AAct*) toward drinking the tap water, as shown in Table 9.2. The higher the risk level, the more unfavorable the feelings they had about their drinking the water. This relationship, of course, makes some sense, especially because the illness belief compound (*be*) was also affected negatively by information about the level of risk. However, we expected that cognitive structure would have mitigated any direct effects of information on attitude. This relationship requires further investigation, but one explanation that is consistent with the model is that the cognitive structure compounds we used did not exhaust the number of salient beliefs relevant to the students' consideration of whether or not to drink the tap water. Future research should seek to identify even more of these beliefs.

The level of risk also interacts with the use of a risky headline (Table 9.2) to affect cognitive structure (beta = .14, p = .01) and, to a lesser extent, attitude toward the act of drinking the tap water (beta = .11, p = .05). The illustrations in Figure 9.3 show that, among those who did not read a risky headline, higher risk levels led to cognitive structures (*CSbe*) and attitudes (*AAct*) that were more aversive toward drinking the tap water. This result, in which higher risks produced greater aversion, is about what might be expected regardless of the kind of headline read. When the level of risk was low, those who read a risky headline were more likely to perceive bad outcomes for themselves if they drink the tap water (*CSbe*) and more likely to feel unfavorable toward drinking this water (*AAct*) than were those who did not read a risky headline. This result, in which a risky headline amplified aversive reactions to the hazard, is about what we might expect to find regardless of risk level. Thus we might expect to find that

TABLE 9.2
Drinking Contaminated Tap Water: Hazard Characteristics, Stylistic
Structure, and Components of the Fishbein-Ajzen Model ($N = 252$)

	Dependent Variables		
Variable	Cognitive Structure (CSbe)	Attitude Toward Act (AAct)	Behavioral Intention (BI)
Story accuracy	−.03	.07	.08
adjusted R^2	.00	.00	.01
Hazard characteristics			
risk level (R)	.02	−.23***	.02
severity of outcome (S)	−.08	.00	−.01
Stylistic structure			
risk in headline (H)	−.03	.00	.05
personalized lead (P)	.20**	−.02	−.04
adjusted R^2	.03	.06	.01
Interactions			
R × S	−.03	−.02	−.01
R × H	.14**	.11*	−.02
R × P	−.05	−.04	.05
S × H	.05	−.02	−.04
S × P	−.03	.07	.02
H × P	−.02	.02	.04
adjusted R^2	.03	.08	.00
R × S × H	−.08	−.03	−.02
R × S × P	.00	.08	−.01
R × H × P	−.03	−.05	−.08
S × H × P	−.07	.04	.02
adjusted R^2	.03	.08	.00
R × S × H × P	.05	.01	−.04
adjusted R^2	.03	.07	.00
Model components			
cognitive structure (CSbe)		.55***	.15*
adjusted R^2		.37	.21
attitude toward act (AAct)			.36***
subjective norms (SN)			.22**
perceived behavioral control (PBC)			−.12*
adjusted R^2			.43
Multiple R	.30	.64***	.69***

NOTE: *CSbe* is the summation of all belief-evaluation compounds related to drinking the contaminated tap water. *AAct* is attitude toward oneself drinking the contaminated tap water, and *BI* is the intention to do so.
*$p = .05$; **$p = .01$; ***$p = .001$.

the high-risk, risky headline group would have the lowest means for *CSbe* and *AAct*. Instead, the surprising result was that, when risk was high, reading a risky headline reduced aversion to the hazard, at least in terms of cognitive structure and attitude toward the act of drinking the infested tap water.

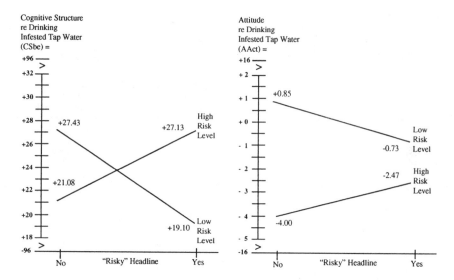

Figure 9.3. Effects of Two-Way Interactions Between Risk Level and Use of Risky Headline on Cognitive Structure and Attitude Toward the Behavior of Drinking Infested Tap Water ($N = 252$)

NOTE: For the left side of the figure, higher cognitive structure (*CSbe*) values represent stronger beliefs that, on balance across the six elements of cognitive structure (e.g., health risk, cost, convenience), more good than bad is likely to result from drinking the tap water. Means in this part of the figure are adjusted by the control variable of perceived story accuracy. For the right side of the figure, higher attitude (*AAct*) values represent more favorable feelings toward drinking tap water, whereas lower values represent greater aversion. Means in this part of the figure are adjusted by the control variable of perceived story accuracy and by cognitive structure (*CSbe*).

Although the reason for this turnabout is not clear, it is possible that some discounting of the hazardous situation may again have taken place when subjects encountered a risky headline over the necessarily brief story that contained information about a high-risk hazard. Many subjects might have considered such a headline to be overkill.

Relationships Among Model Components

Our second set of hypotheses (2a and 2b) concerned relationships among some of the components of the theory of reasoned action. Table 9.2 shows that Hypothesis 2a, that cognitive structure will relate positively to attitude (*AAct*), is supported (beta = .55, $p = .001$). This relationship is relatively strong, and about of the magnitude expected, based on comparable coefficients we found in other studies that related this model to health behaviors. The relationship indicates that those who believe that a behavior, in this case drinking the tap water, will lead to mostly positive outcomes for themselves have a more favorable attitude toward performing that behavior. Those who believe that their performing this behavior will lead to mostly negative outcomes have a less favorable attitude toward performing that behavior.

Hypothesis 2b, that behavioral intention (*BI*) will correlate positively with attitude toward the behavior (*AAct*), is also supported. *AAct* is the strongest correlate of *BI* (beta = .36, *p* = .001), as indicated in Table 9.2. Subjective norms (*SN*) also relate positively to *BI* (beta = .22, *p* = .01). There is, however, a crossover relationship (*r* = .75, *p* = .001) between *AAct* and *SN,* two components of the model that were expected to be relatively unrelated. The relationship of *AAct* with *BI* is much stronger (beta = .53, *p* = .001) with *SN* removed from the regression equation, and is closer to the magnitude expected from past studies. Similarly, the relationship of *SN* to *BI* is stronger (beta = .44, *p* = .001) with *AAct* removed from the regression equation.

Perceived behavioral control (*PBC*) has a slight negative relationship (beta = −.12, *p* = .05) with behavioral intention, such that those who sense more control over their use of this tap water are less likely to intend to drink it in the future. The direction of this result, and its magnitude, are about as expected.

It also appears that cognitive structure can affect behavioral intention (beta = .15, *p* = .05 in Table 9.2), quite apart from working through *AAct*. However, cognitive structure has a weaker relationship with behavioral intention than do either attitudes or subjective norms. Generally, in the chain of relationships from cognitive structure to attitude to behavioral intention, the components of the model that are directly adjacent to one another have stronger relationships with each other than do components that are not adjoining. These results tend to support the structure of the model. Crossover effects between *SN* and *AAct* tend to complicate the model, and require further examination.[14] The effects of information on cognitive structure, and on other components of the model, also warrant further research.

Although we tried to compensate for the experimental situation as much as possible through design and statistical control, two factors could affect the external validity of the findings. First, because our subjects were university students, it is possible that they were more sensitive to the implications of probabilistic risk estimates than would be most other members of the public. Second, the crossover relationship between *SN* and *AAct* could be a by-product of temporary judgments, because the subjects were not able to verify for themselves what others would expect them to do. They simply may have inferred *SN* from other information in the cognitive/attitudinal chain of components, thus producing the strong correlation we found.[15]

CONCLUSION

Our first research question concerned the effects of hazard characteristics and stylistic structure, as presented in a message, on various components of the Fishbein-Ajzen model. As we expected, the level of risk presented in a news story, formulated as a probabilistic risk estimate, strengthened the belief that, in this case, drinking infested tap water would lead to illness. This risk information also affected the illness belief-evaluation compound and attitude toward the act of drinking the infested tap water in the direction of greater aversion to that behavior. Therefore, such a risk estimate can have some effect on subjective appraisals of personal risk from such a hazard.

When the story indicated that this hazard is high risk and severe in its effects, the stylistic factors we investigated produced almost no adjustment of subjects' beliefs that drinking the tap water would make them ill. Thus information that the hazard is risky and severe seems to override stylistic influences on subjective risk estimates. However, when the hazard was depicted as less dangerous (i.e., lower in risk level and/or severity of outcome), stylistic factors interacted with hazard characteristics to affect subjective risk estimates.

Generally, subjects' processing of risk information contained in headlines and in personalized leads was more complex than expected. The use of risk information in headlines often played a role in distorting cognitive and attitudinal aspects of subjects' risk judgments. It appears in this study that readers' subjective perceptions of risk usually correlated better with the relative levels of risk when risk information was not highlighted in headlines. Those who read personalized leads were more likely to ignore or discount headline risk information and information about the severity of the illness when forming their personal estimates of risk, and tended to have cognitive structures more favorable toward performing the hazardous behavior. It is noteworthy that perception of personal risk from the hazard correlated most directly with relative level of risk when subjects read personalized leads and were not given headlines that stressed the risk. More research should be conducted into the cognitive (e.g., information processing, subjective risk estimation) and affective (e.g., identification, fear reaction) processes that could have produced such results.

Overall, effects of communication tended to be more common among the earlier and primary components of the model (e.g., beliefs), and had no direct influence on behavioral intention. Therefore, it appears that behavioral intention, and presumably behavior, would be affected only indirectly through the cognitive/ affective and normative chains of components, as would be consistent with the theory.

Our second research question concerned the relationships among cognitive structure (*CSbe*), attitude toward the act (*AAct*), subjective norms (*SN*), perceived behavioral control (*PBC*), and behavioral intention (*BI*) in our application of the model to responses to a health risk. Generally, the model performed as expected. The rather strong crossover relationship between *AAct* and *SN*, two elements that are supposed to be independent, might have been caused by subjects' using their own attitudes toward the behavior to infer how important others would view that behavior.

Future research that applies this model to risk communication should further identify salient behavioral beliefs relevant to risk-related behavior. As Fishbein and Middlestadt (1989) note, this research would be important for theory building as well as to guide risk information and education programs. It may be important, for example, for such programs to target entire families of specific beliefs in risk-related cognitive structures (Stasson & Fishbein, 1990) and perhaps to stress the benefits (positive outcomes) of specific behaviors people might perform in the face of health risks, especially if those beliefs are less well established (Henning & Knowles, 1990). Even with expected advances in medicine and technology, the informed behavioral responses that people make to water-borne diseases, AIDS, and other health risks will continue to be an essential component of public health programs (see Fishbein & Middlestadt, 1989), and therefore critical to assess.

In general, key concepts in risk-related behavior, such as perceived risk, outcome severity, and personal control over exposure to the hazard, seem to be accommodated well by the theory of reasoned action, as amended to include *PBC*. In addition, the model allows for personal risk judgments to be weighed amid a set of costs and benefits associated with the risk-related behavior and specifies effects for social normative forces often overlooked in studies of this type of behavior.

The theory also specifies roles for communication, personal experience, and mental operations (e.g., beliefs formed from inference) as part of the process of behavioral change. Future communication research should also examine informational effects on perceived behavioral control, the normative chain of components, and the relative salience of beliefs (e.g., the creation of salient beliefs). It is possible that media agenda-setting and priming effects (see, for example, Iyengar & Kinder, 1987) could be extended to the health risk context through effects on belief salience. In fact, many key variables in communication research—cognitive, attitudinal, normative—are embodied in the structure of the theory of reasoned action. Overall, this theory is very useful for exploring risk communication, and promises to be quite applicable to studies of communication in other contexts as well.

NOTES

1. See Sheppard, Hartwick, and Warshaw (1988) for a more comprehensive enumeration of the applications of this theory.

2. Ajzen and Fishbein (1980) caution that a measure of behavioral intention will predict volitional behavior provided that the intention measure corresponds to the behavior in terms of context and specific action, that intentions do not change prior to performance of the behavior, and that unforeseen events do not occur. Similarly, measures of attitude tend to predict volitional behavior more strongly when the attitude measure is more relevant and specific to the behavior. (See Kim & Hunter, 1993, for a meta-analytic review.) In general, the theory of reasoned action demands that all of its components be conceptualized and measured in terms of specific behavior.

3. Studies involving the theory of reasoned action are not consistent in their use of the belief-by-evaluation compounds. Many ignore them. In some cases, the expectancy-value formulas are used to represent attitude or perceived social norms directly, rather than as antecedents to these components.

4. The theory predicts subjective norms (*SN*) from an expectancy-value combination of two concepts: normative beliefs (*NB*), which are the person's beliefs that specified others (e.g., parents or groups such as coworkers) approve or disapprove of the behavior; and motivation to comply (*MC*), which is the extent to which the person wants to do the same as, or the opposite of, what he or she believes the referent would like the person to do.

5. A number of researchers have raised concerns over crossover effects in the Fishbein-Ajzen formulation, in part because these relationships can produce multicollinearity problems in multiple regression analysis (e.g., Liska, 1984; Miniard & Cohen, 1981; Oliver & Bearden, 1985; Ryan, 1982).

6. Various other studies have found communication relationships with salient beliefs in the Fishbein-Ajzen tradition, but have operationally defined beliefs in ways other than as beliefs about individual behavior (e.g., Cronen, 1973; Jeffres, Dobos, & Sweeney, 1987; Kantola, Syme, & Nesdale, 1983; Mitchell & Olson, 1981).

7. We recognize that, at some level, stylistic and content elements do interact. The pertinent question here is the relative influence of each component.

8. Negative mood states have been found to lead to deeper processing of information than positive mood states. See Martin, Ward, Achee, and Wyer (1993).

9. In their work on the "availability heuristic," Tversky and Kahneman (1973) state that people tend to judge events as more likely to happen if the events are easier to recall. Newspaper coverage of rare events might be one factor contributing to public overestimation of risk from those events (Combs & Slovic, 1979), by making those events easier to recall. Similarly, risk headlines might reinforce memory for a hazardous event and subsequent recall, making the event seem riskier.

10. The question of a vividness effect with respect to persuasion is disputed by some researchers (see Collins, Taylor, Wood, & Thompson, 1988; Taylor & Thompson, 1982). We distinguish our research on several grounds. First, Taylor and Thompson (1982) note that personalized histories, an operationalization akin to our use of a personalized narrative lead, consistently have been found to produce an effect. Second, the experimental stimulus materials used in studies disputing the existence of any vividness effect (e.g., Collins et al., 1988) are restricted to concrete and colorful language. Third, the terms of the debate so far have been limited to persuasive effects—attitude change—whereas we are interested not so much in the influence of persuasive messages, but in the cognitive, affective, and conative effects of information as it typically is produced by media professionals and used by audience members.

11. We established high and low risk levels in a pilot study by showing students the risky situations designed for this study and asking them to volunteer risk levels that they thought corresponded to "high" and "low" risks.

12. Sheppard et al. (1988) found that the best predictions of performance from behavioral intention (averaging .59) occurred in studies that used likelihood estimates of *BI* (i.e., the person's estimate of the likelihood he or she would perform a behavior) to predict volitional behavior.

13. The experimental subject's awareness of being observed as part of an artificial experimental setting is the most commonly encountered threat to the external validity (generalizability) of the results of experiments (Campbell & Stanley, 1963). In a methodological review of 68 published experiments in communication, Rossiter (1976) found that "communication scholars generally do little about reactive aspects of their experiments" (p. 203). Our design sought to reduce the effects of subject reactivity by (a) giving subjects a thorough rationale for the collection of the data (see Harris & Lahey, 1982) and (b) measuring subject doubt about the reality of the stimulus materials in a nonsensitizing way (by asking the subject how "accurate" the story seemed to be), and then using that measure as a covariate in the analysis.

14. Multiple regression of behavioral intention on the manipulated variables, their interactions, and the "accuracy" control variable found no statistically significant relationships between these variables and *BI*. That is, the experimental manipulations had no direct effect on *BI*, but rather operated indirectly through elements of cognitive structure.

15. The process of creating inferential beliefs, Ryan (1982) notes, can produce an interplay between behavioral beliefs and normative beliefs, and thus opens a channel of influence between

the chain of attitudinal components and the chain of normative components in the model. Cognitive consistency (e.g., Heider, 1958) might create the assumption among some experimental subjects that friends, for example, would approve of actions that the subject also finds desirable, and thereby produce what McLeod and Chaffee (1973) term "congruency" (a perceived similarity in attitude between oneself and relevant others).

REFERENCES

Ajzen, I. (1988). *Attitudes, personality, and behavior.* Milton Keynes, UK: Open University Press.

Ajzen, I., & Fishbein, M. (1980). *Understanding attitudes and predicting social behavior.* Englewood Cliffs, NJ: Prentice Hall.

Ajzen, I., & Timko, C. (1986). Correspondence between health attitudes and behavior. *Journal of Basic and Applied Social Psychology, 7,* 259-276.

Beck, K. H. (1979). The effects of positive and negative arousal upon attitudes, belief acceptance, behavioral intention, and behavior. *Journal of Social Psychology, 107,* 239-251.

Beck, K. H. (1984). The effects of risk probability, outcome severity, efficacy protection and access to protection on decision making: A further test of protection motivation theory. *Social Behavior and Personality, 11*(5), 121-125.

Beck, K. H., & Lund, A. K. (1981). The effects of health threat seriousness and personal efficacy upon intentions and behavior. *Journal of Applied Social Psychology, 11,* 401-415.

Boyd, B., & Wandersman, A. (1991). Predicting undergraduate condom use with the Fishbein and Ajzen and the Triandis attitude-behavior models: Implications for public health interventions. *Journal of Applied Social Psychology, 21,* 1810-1830.

Brubaker, R. G., Prue, D. M., & Rychtarik, R. G. (1987). Determinants of disulfiram acceptance among alcohol patients: A test of the theory of reasoned action. *Addictive Behaviors, 12,* 43-51.

Campbell, D. T., & Stanley, J. C. (1963). *Experimental and quasi-experimental designs for research.* Chicago: Rand McNally.

Carter, W. (1990). Health behavior as a rational process: Theory of reasoned action and multiattribute utility theory. In K. Glanz, F. M. Louis, & A. A. Reimer (Eds.), *Health behavior and health education: Theory, research, and practice* (pp. 63-91). San Francisco: Jossey-Bass.

Cohen, J., & Cohen, P. (1975). *Applied multiple regression/correlation analysis for the behavioral sciences.* Hillsdale, NJ: Lawrence Erlbaum.

Collins, R. L., Taylor, S. E., Wood, J. V., & Thompson, S. C. (1988). The vividness effect: Elusive or illusory? *Journal of Experimental Social Psychology, 24,* 1-18.

Combs, B., & Slovic, P. (1979). Newspaper coverage of causes of death. *Journalism Quarterly 56,* 837-843, 849.

Cronen, V. E. (1973). Belief, salience, media exposure, and summation theory. *Journal of Communication, 23*(1), 86-94.

D'Agostino, P. R., & Small, K. G. (1980). Cross modality transfer between pictures and their names. *Canadian Journal of Psychology, 34*(2), 113-118.

Dunwoody, S., Friestad, M., & Shapiro, M. (1987, May). *Conveying risk information in the mass media.* Paper presented at the annual meeting of the International Communication Association, Montreal.

Dunwoody, S., & Neuwirth, K. (1991). Coming to terms with the impact of communication on scientific and technological risk judgments. In L. Wilkins & P. Patterson (Eds.), *Risky business* (pp. 11-30). Westport, CT: Greenwood.

Dunwoody, S., Neuwirth, K., Griffin, R. J., & Long, M. (1992). The impact of risk message content and construction on comments about risks embedded in "letters to friends." *Journal of Language and Social Psychology, 11,* 9-33.

Fishbein, M., & Ajzen, I. (1975). *Belief, attitude, intention, and behavior: An introduction to theory and research.* Reading, MA: Addison-Wesley.

Fishbein, M., & Middlestadt, S. E. (1989). Using the theory of reasoned action as a framework for understanding and changing AIDS-related behaviors. In V. M. Mays, G. W. Albee, & S. F. Schneider (Eds.), *Primary prevention of AIDS: Psychological approaches* (pp. 93-110). Newbury Park, CA: Sage.

Freimuth, V. S., Edgar, T., & Hammond, S. L. (1987). College students' awareness and interpretation of the AIDS risk. *Science, Technology and Human Values, 12,* 37-40.

Godin, G., Colantonio, A., Davis, G. M., Shephard, R., & Simard, C. (1986). Prediction of leisure time exercise behavior among a group of lower-limb disabled adults. *Journal of Clinical Psychology, 42,* 272-279.

Godin, G., & Gionet, N. J. (19
91). Determinants of an intention to exercise of an electric power commission's employees. *Ergonomics, 34,* 1221-1230.

Grube, J. W., Morgan, M., & McGree, S. T. (1986). Attitudes and normative beliefs as predictors of smoking intentions and behaviours: A test of three models. *British Journal of Social Psychology, 25,* 81-93.

Harris, F. C., & Lahey, B. (1982). Subject reactivity in direct observational assessment: A review and critical analysis. *Clinical Psychology Review, 2,* 523-538.

Heider, F. (1958). *The psychology of interpersonal relations.* New York: John Wiley.

Henning, P., & Knowles, A. (1990). Factors influencing women over 40 years to take precautions against cervical cancer. *Journal of Applied Social Psychology, 20,* 1612-1621.

Hill, D., Gardner, G., & Rassaby, J. (1985). Factors predisposing women to take precautions against breast and cervix cancer. *Journal of Applied Social Psychology, 15,* 59-79.

Holmes, V. M., & Langford, J. (1976). Comprehension and recall of abstract and concrete sentences. *Journal of Verbal Learning and Verbal Behavior, 15,* 559-566.

Iyengar, S. (1991). *Is anyone responsible?* Chicago: University of Chicago Press.

Iyengar, S., & Kinder, D. R. (1987). *News that matters.* Chicago: University of Chicago Press.

Iyengar, S., & Simon, A. (1993). News coverage of the gulf crisis and public opinion. *Communication Research, 20,* 365-383.

Jeffres, L. W., Dobos, J., & Sweeney, M. (1987). Communication and commitment to community. *Communication Research, 14,* 619-643.

Johnson, E. J., & Tversky, A. (1983). Affect, generalization, and the perception of risk. *Journal of Personality and Social Psychology, 45,* 20-31.

Kantola, S. J., Syme, G. J., & Nesdale, A. R. (1983). The effects of appraised severity and efficacy in promoting water conservation: An informational analysis. *Journal of Applied Social Psychology, 13,* 164-182.

Kasperson, R. (1992). The social amplification of risk: Progress in developing an integrative framework. In S. Krimsky & D. Golding (Eds.), *Social theories of risk* (pp. 153-178). New York: Praeger.

Kennamer, J. D. (1988). News values and the vividness of information. *Written Communication, 5,* 108-123.

Kim, M., & Hunter, J. E. (1993). Attitude-behavior relations: A meta-analysis of attitudinal relevance and topic. *Journal of Communication, 43*(1), 101-142.

Leiss, W. (Ed.). (1989). *Prospects and problems in risk communication.* Waterloo, ON: University of Waterloo Press.

Lemert, J. L., Mitzman, B., Seither, M., Cook, R., & Hackett, R. (1977). Journalists and mobilizing information. *Journalism Quarterly, 54,* 721-726.

Liska, A. E. (1984). A critical examination of the causal structure of the Fishbein/Ajzen attitude-behavior model. *Social Psychology Quarterly, 47,* 61-74.

Loken, B. (1983). The theory of reasoned action: Examination of the sufficiency assumption for a television viewing behavior. In R. P. Bagozzi & A. M. Tybout (Eds.), *Advances in consumer research* (Vol. 10, pp. 100-105). Provo, UT: Association for Consumer Research.

Lutz, R. J. (1977). An experimental investigation of causal relations among cognitions, affect, and behavioral intention. *Journal of Consumer Research, 3,* 197-208.

Maddux, J. E., & Rogers, R. W. (1983). Protection motivation and self-efficacy: A revised theory of fear appeals and attitude change. *Journal of Experimental Social Psychology, 19,* 469-479.

Martin, L. L., Ward, D. W., Achee, J. W., & Wyer, R. S., Jr. (1993). Mood as input: People have to interpret the motivational implications of their moods. *Journal of Personality and Social Psychology, 64,* 317-326.

McCallum, D. E., Hammond, S. L., Morris, L. A., & Covello, V. T. (1990). *Public knowledge and perceptions of chemical risks in six communities: Analysis of a baseline survey.* Washington, DC: Environmental Protection Agency.

McCaul, K. D., O'Neill, K., & Glasgow, R. E. (1988). Predicting the performance of dental hygiene behaviors: An examination of the Fishbein and Ajzen model and self-efficacy expectations. *Journal of Applied Social Psychology, 18,* 114-128.

McGuire, W. (1969). The nature of attitudes and attitude change. In G. Lindzey & E. Aronson (Eds.), *Handbook of social psychology* (2nd ed., Vol. 3, pp. 177-199). Reading, MA: Addison-Wesley.

McLeod, J., & Chaffee, S. H. (1973). Interpersonal approaches to communication research. *American Behavioral Scientist, 16,* 469-499.

Miniard, P. W., & Cohen, J. (1981). An examination of the Fishbein-Ajzen behavioral-intentions model's concepts and measures. *Journal of Experimental Social Psychology, 17,* 309-339.

Mitchell, A., & Olson, J. C. (1981). Are product attribute beliefs the only mediator of advertising effects on brand attitude? *Journal of Marketing Research, 18,* 318-332.

Montano, D. E., & Taplin, S. H. (1991). A test of an expanded theory of reasoned action to predict mammography participation. *Social Science and Medicine, 32,* 733-741.

Mullen, P. D., Hersey, J. C., & Iverson, D. C. (1987). Health behavior models compared. *Social Science and Medicine, 24,* 973-981.

National Research Council. (1989). *Improving risk communication.* Washington, DC: National Academy Press.

Nisbett, R. E., & Ross, L. (1980). *Human inference: Strategies and shortcomings of social judgment.* Englewood Cliffs, NJ: Prentice Hall.

Oliver, R. L., & Bearden, W. O. (1985). Crossover effects in the theory of reasoned action: A moderating influence attempt. *Journal of Consumer Research, 12,* 324-340.

Paivio, A. (1973). Picture superiority in free recall: Imagery or dual coding? *Cognitive Psychology, 5,* 176-206.

Palmgreen, P., & Rayburn, J. D. (1985). An expectancy-value approach to media gratifications. In K. E. Rosengren, L. A. Wenner, & P. Palmgreen (Eds.), *Media gratifications research: Current perspectives* (pp. 61-72). Beverly Hills, CA: Sage.

Pender, N. J., & Pender, A. R. (1986). Attitudes, subjective norms, and intentions to engage in health behaviors. *Nursing Research, 35,* 15-18.

Rippetoe, P. A., & Rogers, R. W. (1987). Effects of components of protection-motivation theory and adaptive and maladaptive coping with a health threat. *Journal of Personality and Social Psychology, 52,* 596-604.

Rossiter, C. M. (1976). The validity of communication experiments using human subjects: A review. *Human Communication Research, 2,* 197-206.

Ryan, M. J. (1982). Behavioral intention formation: The interdependency of attitudinal and social influence variables. *Journal of Consumer Research, 9,* 263-278.

Sandman, P. M., Sachsman, D., Greenberg, M. R., & Gochfeld, M. (1987). *Environmental risk and the press.* New Brunswick, NJ: Transaction.

Schifter, D. E., & Ajzen, I. (1985). Intention, perceived control, and weight loss: An application of the theory of planned behavior. *Journal of Personality and Social Psychology, 49,* 843-851.

Sheppard, B. H., Hartwick, J., & Warshaw, P. R. (1988). The theory of reasoned action: A meta-analysis with recommendations for modifications and future research. *Journal of Consumer Research, 15,* 325-343.

Sparks, G. G., & Ogles, R. M. (1990). The difference between fear of victimization and the probability of being victimized: Implication for cultivation. *Journal of Broadcasting and Electronic Media, 34*, 351-358.

Spencer, J. W., Seydlitz, R., Laska, S., & Triche, E. (1992). The different influences of newspaper and television news reports of a natural hazard on response behavior. *Communication Research, 19*, 299-325.

Stasson, M., & Fishbein, M. (1990). The relation between perceived risk and preventive action: A within-subject analysis of perceived driving risk and intentions to wear seatbelts. *Journal of Applied Social Psychology, 20*, 1541-1557.

Stutzman, T. M., & Green, S. (1982). Factors affecting energy consumption: Two field tests of the Fishbein-Ajzen model. *Journal of Social Psychology, 117*, 183-201.

Tannenbaum, P. (1953). The effect of headlines on the interpretation of news stories. *Journalism Quarterly, 30*, 189-197.

Taylor, S. E., & Thompson, S. C. (1982). Stalking the elusive vividness effect. *Psychological Review, 89*, 155-181.

Toneatto, T., & Binik, Y. (1987). The role of intentions, social norms, and attitudes in the performance of dental flossing: A test of the theory of reasoned action. *Journal of Applied Social Psychology, 17*, 593-603.

Tuorila, H. (1987). Selection of milks with varying fat contents and related overall liking, attitudes, norms and intentions. *Appetite, 8*, 1-14.

Tversky, A., & Kahneman, D. (1973). Availability: A heuristic for judging frequency and probability. *Cognitive Psychology, 5*, 207-232.

van Dijk, T. A. (1988). *News as discourse.* Hillsdale, NJ: Lawrence Erlbaum.

Warshaw, P. R., & Davis, F. D. (1985). Disentangling behavioral intention and behavioral expectation. *Journal of Experimental Social Psychology, 21*, 213-228.

Yagade, A., & Dozier, D. (1990). The media agenda-setting effect of concrete versus abstract issues. *Journalism Quarterly, 67*, 3-10.

10 Generating Effective Risk Messages: How Scary Should Your Risk Communication Be?

KIM WITTE
Michigan State University

No consensus exists on how to develop effective risk messages that motivate appropriate action yet do not unduly frighten people. A useful framework for developing risk messages is the extended parallel process model (EPPM). The EPPM suggests that when people are faced with health or environmental risks, they are motivated to either control the danger or control their fear. This chapter offers a description of how the EPPM can explain public responses to risk messages, and then reports on two pilot studies that illustrate how existing audience perceptions can be used in the design and generation of effective risk management messages.

R ISK managers continually search for effective ways to disseminate risk information to the public. Unfortunately, "despite agreement that the way information is presented matters, there is no clear consensus in the literature about what specific features communicate risk concepts well" (Johnson, Fisher, Smith, & Desvousges, 1988, p. 30). Further, "while risk communication among technical people may be more or less straightforward (for example, interagency dialogue), risk communication with the public remains quite elusive" (Devgun, 1991, p. 7).

Much research has gone into establishing how individuals perceive risks, how people make decisions regarding risks, and how risks are quantified by experts (e.g., Douglas, 1985; Kishchuk, 1987; Slovic, 1987). However, little has been done to develop a theory of how to communicate risks effectively to the public in a manner that (a) motivates appropriate risk reduction behaviors, as well as (b) prevents panic and/or outrage among those faced with environmental and/or

AUTHOR'S NOTE: The comments and suggestions of Tim Levine, Beth Le Poire, Abran Salazar, and Mike Basil improved this chapter substantially. An earlier version of this chapter was presented at the May 1993 meeting of the International Communication Association, Washington, DC.

Correspondence and requests for reprints: Kim Witte, Department of Communication, Michigan State University, East Lansing, MI 48824-1212.

Communication Yearbook 18, pp. 229-254

technological risks. The goal of the present work is to provide theoretical and methodological guidelines for developing effective risk management messages that result in appropriate public action. This chapter is intended to help both risk managers, who must inform and educate the public about environmental and technological risks, and public health practitioners, who must persuade people either to reduce or to engage in certain behaviors in order to decrease health risks.

A useful framework for conceptualizing and developing messages aimed at managing risks is offered by the extended parallel process model (EPPM), a recently developed fear appeal theory based on 40 years of empirical research, that integrates previous theoretical approaches. In the following section I describe how the EPPM can be used to explain public responses to risk messages. I then present two pilot studies that illustrate how existing audience perceptions can be used in the design and generation of effective risk management messages.

USING FEAR APPEAL THEORY
TO DEVELOP RISK MESSAGES

Fear Appeals and Risk Communication

The EPPM is a "fear appeal" theory. Fear appeals are defined as messages that evoke fear by focusing on severe and probable threats in order to induce adherence to recommended courses of action. Typically, fear appeals contain two sections. The first attempts to increase *perceived threat* by emphasizing the *severity* of the threat (i.e., its magnitude of harm) and the *probability* of the threat's occurrence (i.e., the audience's likelihood of experiencing that threat). Fear is aroused when a threat is perceived as likely and severe. The second section of a typical fear appeal attempts to increase *perceived efficacy* about the recommended response by (a) outlining specific feasible and easy steps to avert the threat (*self-efficacy*) and (b) emphasizing the effectiveness of the recommended response in averting or minimizing the threat (*response efficacy*).

By definition, risk messages appear to be fear appeals. For example, risk experts define risk as the quantitative estimate of P (probability of an outcome) $\times S$ (severity of consequences) (Douglas, 1985). Thus both risk messages and fear appeals focus on (a) how likely it is that a hazard or threat will occur, and (b) how severe the hazard will be if it does occur. As in fear appeals, risk messages sometimes offer specific solutions or recommended responses (efficacy messages) to avert or minimize harm from the threat. Unfortunately, this portion of a risk message is often missing and may be a key reason for negative responses to risk mes- sages. By focusing on the risk or threat of a hazard, communications about risk tend to evoke fear in audiences. Because risk messages can arouse fear in audiences, the processes underlying responses to fear appeals may be identical to the processes underlying responses to risk messages. By applying what we know from fear appeal research to risk communication research, we may

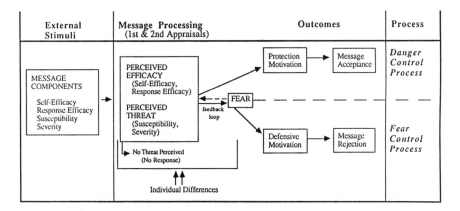

Figure 10.1. The Extended Parallel Process Model

improve our ability to produce effective risk management messages as well as to understand why some risk communications backfire.

The EPPM

Recent fear appeal research has focused on explaining the mechanisms and processes underlying individuals' rejection and/or acceptance of fear-arousing messages (Witte, 1994). The extended parallel process model (Witte, 1992a) is based on Leventhal's (1970) danger control/fear control framework and is an expansion and integration of previous fear appeal theories (e.g., Hovland, Janis, & Kelly, 1953; Janis, 1967; Rogers, 1975, 1983). According to the EPPM, the evaluation of a fear appeal (or, in this case, risk message) initiates two appraisals of the message, which result in the domination of either danger control or fear control processes (see Figure 10.1). First, individuals appraise the threat of the hazard. The more they believe themselves to be threatened by a serious danger, the more motivated they are to begin the second appraisal, which is an evaluation of the efficacy of the recommended response. If the threat is perceived as irrelevant or insignificant, there is no motivation to process the message further, and the fear appear elicits no response. When threat is perceived as high, the appraisal of efficacy determines whether danger control or fear control processes will dominate. Thus perceived threat determines the *extent* of a response (i.e., how strong the danger or fear control responses are), whereas perceived efficacy determines the *nature* of the response (i.e., whether danger or fear control responses are elicited). If no information regarding the efficacy of the recommended response is given, individuals will rely on past experiences and prior beliefs to determine their level of perceived efficacy.

When people realize they are susceptible to a serious threat and believe they can successfully avert it (i.e., high perceived threat/*high* perceived efficacy; e.g., "I'm at risk for skin cancer, but am able to use sunscreen to successfully prevent it"), they become motivated to protect themselves and think of strategies to control the danger or threat. These cognitive *danger control processes* generate protection motivation, which stimulates actions, such as attitude, intention, or behavior changes, that reduce or diminish the threat (e.g., "I'm going to wear sunscreen the next time I'm at the beach to prevent skin cancer"). However, at some critical point, when persons realize they cannot prevent a serious threat from occurring—because they believe the response to be futile, they had no prior efficacy-related thoughts or beliefs, or they believe they are incapable of carrying out the recommended response (i.e., high perceived threat/*low* perceived efficacy; e.g., "I'm at risk for skin cancer, and there's nothing I can do to effectively prevent it—it's too late for me")—fear control processes will begin to dominate over danger control processes. *Fear control processes* are primarily emotional processes through which people respond to and cope with their fear, not the danger. Defensive motivation is elicited by heightened fear arousal, which occurs when perceived threat is high and perceived efficacy is low and produces defensive avoidant or reactant responses that control the individual's fear (e.g., "I'm just not going to think about skin cancer, it scares me too much"). In earlier work, it has been shown that fear control processes interfere with danger control processes such that there is an inverse relation between fear control responses (e.g., defensive avoidance, reactance) and danger control responses (e.g., attitudes, intentions, behaviors) (Witte, 1992b). For example, when a person is denying the threat of AIDS (controlling one's fear), he or she is not asking a partner to use condoms (controlling the danger). In short, message recommendations are accepted when danger control dominates and rejected when fear control dominates. Thus message acceptance is defined as attitude, intention, and behavior change, and message rejection is defined as defensive avoidance, minimization (denial), and perceived manipulation (reactance). Much research has shown that perceived threat and perceived efficacy interact in the manner just described to influence behavioral or psychological outcomes (e.g., Kleinot & Rogers, 1982; Maddux & Rogers, 1983; Witte, 1992c).

The Critical Point

The notion that perceived threat and perceived efficacy are compared in some subjective manner by the individual is implied in the appraisal processes. For example, even though the second appraisal process is said to focus on efficacy, it is more accurate to state that this appraisal is really an *appraisal of efficacy in light of perceived threat*. That is, if the threat is perceived as significant and/or relevant enough, then efficacy is appraised. In this second appraisal, individuals are believed to weigh (either deliberately or automatically) perceived efficacy against perceived threat in a *joint appraisal process* to determine whether anything can be done to prevent the threat. As long as perceived efficacy is greater than perceived threat (e.g., "I know that AIDS is a terrible threat, but if I use condoms correctly, I can protect myself"), danger control processes will dominate. But when perceived threat outweighs perceived efficacy (e.g., "I'm at risk for this terrible disease and there's no way I can effectively prevent it"), fear control processes will dominate. This point, where perceived threat begins to outweigh perceived efficacy, is when fear control processes begin to dominate over danger control processes; this is the *critical point.*

The two parts of Figure 10.2 show that the critical point (where threat exceeds efficacy) is never reached when perceived efficacy is high. Because perceived efficacy always exceeds perceived threat in the top lines of both parts of the figure, message acceptance is positive and linear. For example, people always feel able to cope successfully with the threat and become increasingly motivated to accept the message as threat increases. However, in the low-efficacy condition, the critical point occurs immediately (top part of Figure 10.2), because individuals believe there is no effective response that would feasibly avert the threat. Thus the message is rejected because individuals defensively avoid or react against the threat. Finally, in the moderate-efficacy condition, the critical point is reached when threat is at a moderate level (bottom part of Figure 10.2). In this case, people feel able to cope successfully with a threat up to a point, but as threat continues to increase—and efficacy remains constant—the threat suddenly seems insurmountable and they give up any danger control actions and begin to cope with their fear. The critical point is a key construct in the EPPM that heretofore has not been explored. Later, I will return to this construct and expand on it.

Parallels Between
the EPPM and the Risk Literature

There are several parallels between the risk perception literature and the constructs outlined by the EPPM. First, it is important to note that members of the general public (i.e., nonexperts) do not estimate risks in the same manner as experts (Kishchuk, 1987). For example, objective estimates of risk (generated by the Probability × Severity formula) may occur at "acceptable" levels for risk managers (e.g., 1 out of 1 million) but still be perceived as too risky by the general public (Slovic, 1987). Subjective factors such as whether a hazard is perceived as controllable, familiar, voluntary, necessary, catastrophic, personally relevant, or representative are more likely to influence nonexperts' risk perceptions (Kishchuk, 1987; Slovic, 1987). Slovic and others (1987; Fischhoff, Slovic, Lichtenstein, Read, & Combs, 1978; Slovic, Fischhoff, & Lichtenstein, 1982) have demonstrated that these and other qualitative risk dimensions cluster into two main factors: (a) dreaded-common and (b) unknown-known.[1] Dreaded risks are characterized by "perceived lack of control, dread, catastrophic potential, fatal consequences, and the inequitable distribution of risks and benefits" (Slovic, 1987, p. 283). Unknown risks are those perceived to be "unobservable, unknown, new, and delayed in their manifestation of harm" (Slovic, 1987, p. 283).

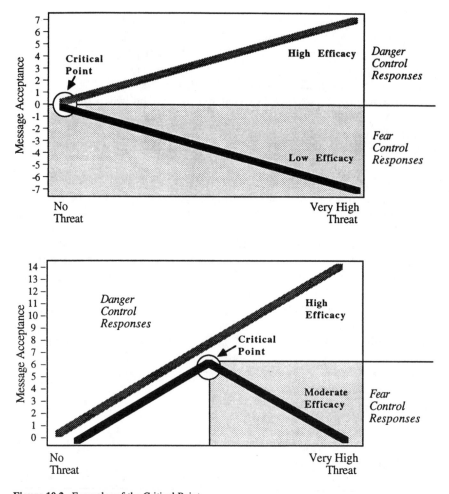

Figure 10.2. Examples of the Critical Point

Figure 10.3 shows the kinds of hazards that fall into each quadrant for the various combinations of the dreaded and unknown dimensions.

There appear to be many similarities between how people perceive risks and how the EPPM explains reactions to fear-arousing messages. Specifically, consider the possibility that the four quadrants of risk can be conceptualized in terms of perceived threat and perceived efficacy levels (see Figure 10.3). Although they do not fit perfectly, it appears that perceived threat is similar to the dreaded-common dimension, and perceived efficacy is related to the known-unknown dimension. For example, perceptions of threat appear to vary along the dreaded-common dimension, with dreaded risks producing the strongest perceptions of threat and common risks producing the weakest perceptions of threat. Similarly, perceptions of efficacy appear to vary along the unknown-

Common/Unknown Risks	Dreaded/Unknown Risks
Water Fluoridation	DNA Technology
Saccharin	Radioactive Waste
Water Chlorination	Nuclear Reactor Accidents
Oral Contraceptives	Nuclear Weapons Fallout
Low Perceived Threat/	*High Perceived Threat/*
Low Perceived Efficacy 1	2 *Low Perceived Efficacy*
Common/Known Risks 4	3 **Dreaded/Known Risks**
Bicycles	Coal Mining Accidents
Home Swimming Pools	Handguns
Downhill Skiing	High Construction
Recreational Boating	Aviation
Low Perceived Threat/	*High Perceived Threat/*
High Perceived Efficacy	*High Perceived Efficacy*

Figure 10.3. Hazards Associated With the Dimensions of Risk and Perceived Threat/Perceived Efficacy Levels

NOTE: See Slovic (1987) for further information on where hazards fall in multidimensional space.

known dimension, with unknown risks producing the weakest levels of perceived efficacy (e.g., people don't know or think they can't do anything to diminish their risk of harm because not much is known about the hazard) and known risks producing the strongest levels of perceived efficacy (e.g., people know what to do to reduce risks). An analysis of the hazards listed in the quadrants of Figure 10.3 adds further support to this analysis, in that laypersons seem to be motivated to respond to risks (in either a danger control or fear control manner) for some quadrants and not motivated to respond to other risks because of lack of perceived relevance or importance for other quadrants. The level of perceived threat and perceived efficacy that characterizes each quadrant offers an explanation for public responses to these hazards.

For example, those hazards that laypersons have deemed the most dreaded and most unknown also appear to be the same hazards for which there is high perceived threat and low perceived efficacy (quadrant 2). According to the EPPM, great fear would be associated with these hazards (given the high-threat/low-efficacy condition), and as a means of coping individuals would engage in fear control strategies. For instance, those living next door to a nuclear reactor may minimize or deny any chances of an accident, engage in reactance through angry protests, or simply ignore the fact that they live next door to the reactor (defensive avoidance). A message that tries to minimize a perceived serious and catastrophic threat while neglecting the efficacy of recommended responses in averting harm from the threat can inadvertently produce fear control responses. For example:

> In the wake of the Chernobyl accident there was a tendency for the authorities in European states to respond with what they thought were reassuring messages about the safety of nuclear reactors in their own countries. But in the circumstances this may not have been appropriate. An opinion poll carried out in France near the nuclear power stations at Chinon and Civaux showed that on average 11% of people wanted information relating to accident risks against 40% wanting information on measures to protect the public if an accident took place. A further 43% wanted information on measures to prevent accidents and on the consequences of radioactivity exposure. (Cannell & Otway, 1988, p. 524)

To increase perceptions of control (and thereby increase perceptions of efficacy in dealing with the threat), clear and specific information should have been given to the public about what to do in the event of an accident, as well as what to do currently to minimize potential harms from the hazard. Note that in this example, experts focused on reducing perceptions about the severity of the hazard (thereby attempting to reduce perceptions of threat), but did not address efficacy issues. People wanted to increase their perceptions of control (i.e., efficacy) and wanted to know what to do in the event of an accident. Thus risk management messages must address not only perceived threat issues (i.e., likelihood and severity of threat issues), but perceived efficacy issues (i.e., What are the recommended responses should the hazard occur, and what do I do?) in order to avert negative reactions to risk messages.

In contrast, when hazards are viewed as common (quadrants 1 and 4 of Figure 10.3), they appear to be seen as low in threat. That is, people either do not believe they are susceptible to harm from these hazards or do not believe the hazards to be severe. When perceived threat is low, regardless of efficacy level, the EPPM would predict little motivation to reduce any risk (neither danger nor fear control processes would be initiated). The risk is seen as somewhat trivial and/or irrelevant. An example of a perceived threat that was so low it did not provoke any response—either danger or fear control—was the case of geological radon. Geological radon is a severe enough threat (typically leading to lung cancer) that in 1988, the "Environmental Protection Agency and the Office of the Surgeon General jointly announced that 80 million U.S. households (everyone not in an apartment above the second floor) should test their homes for radon. . . . [Radon] kills lots of people" (Sandman, 1988, pp. 2, 6). Perceived efficacy for solving any threat of radon should have been high. As Sandman (1988) notes, "[Radon] is fairly easy to solve. It offends no industry and costs no jobs. And it requires individual rather than government action" (p. 6). He also points out that radon tests are simple and inexpensive. Even though experts viewed radon as a high-threat/high-efficacy condition (which should have initiated danger control responses), public response was minimal. The main reason for this lack of response was that the public did not perceive geological radon as a significant or relevant threat. Thus, regardless of how easy it was to test for radon (i.e., high efficacy), it did not matter because the threat was perceived as negligible and/or irrelevant. For example, besides "downplaying their own risk" by believing "their radon levels to be lower than average," the general public "also greatly underestimated the seriousness of radon" (Sandman, 1988, p. 7). Apathetic responses by the public to certain risks, such as that of geological radon, appear to result from lack of perceived threat of the hazard (i.e., "It's not really a severe threat; I'm not really vulnerable to it").

Finally, those hazards that are perceived as dreaded and known also appear to be the same hazards that produce high perceived threat *and* high perceived efficacy, resulting in danger control responses. Thus the hazards in quadrant 3 of Figure 10.3 may be perceived as dangerous, yet individuals are motivated to take appropriate precautions because they believe they can easily do so. For example, elaborate safety procedures and training are promoted for hazards considered high in perceived threat and efficacy, such as construction work or aviation practices. Additionally, in the case of geological radon, those individuals who did view radon as a significant and relevant threat engaged in danger control responses and took steps to avert the threat (recall that efficacy was high too). Specifically, "people who believed that radon was likely to be a serious problem in their own home were more inclined to test" (Sandman, 1988, p. 8). Thus, consistent with the EPPM, when perceived threat and perceived efficacy were high, people were motivated to control the danger.

In sum, the EPPM suggests that people respond to fear-arousing or risky messages in one of three ways. First, if the threat is perceived as irrelevant or trivial, people ignore it and do nothing to protect themselves against health, environmental (i.e., natural disaster warnings), or technological risks. Second, if the threat is perceived to be high, and individuals believe they can effectively minimize their chances of being harmed by the threat, they engage in behaviors that control the danger. Third, if a threat is perceived as very high, and individuals believe it is uncontrollable and they must be exposed to it involuntarily, they engage in fear control responses. They do not cognitively consider the threat; instead, they react emotionally (overwhelmed with fear) and lash out at those perceived as producing the threat (reactance).

By knowing which of the four quadrants a hazard falls into, we can predict whether danger control or fear control responses will be produced. Additionally, we can diagnose what it is about a certain hazard that produces unanticipated outcomes and then generate messages designed to counteract any needlessly high or low threat or efficacy perceptions.

Using the EPPM to Generate Risk Messages

As suggested by the preceding analysis, it is probable that individuals engage in either fear control or danger control *prior* to the evaluation of any risk message.

For instance, most people already have a great deal of knowledge about AIDS and, because of this, have existing perceptions of threat and existing perceptions of efficacy. Similarly, many in the risk field have noted that "new information is evaluated in terms of people's existing values and beliefs" (Cannell & Otway, 1988, p. 524). According to the EPPM, it is likely, therefore, that those with high perceptions of threat and high perceptions of efficacy are already engaging in danger control processes, whereas those with high perceived threat and low perceived efficacy are already engaging in fear control processes.

Consider the case of AIDS. If people believe themselves to be at risk for the disease and also believe they can easily and effectively use condoms to prevent contraction of HIV (i.e., existing high-threat/high-efficacy perceptions), then they would be likely to control the danger (i.e., AIDS) by performing self-protective behaviors (i.e., using condoms). Conversely, if people believe themselves to be at risk for AIDS, but they believe either that recommended responses like condoms are ineffective in preventing HIV contraction or that they are incapable of successfully using condoms to prevent HIV transmission, then they would be likely to control their fear by denying or defensively avoiding the threat of AIDS.

From a public health or risk manager's standpoint, discovering *prior* to a campaign or the release of risk messages whether individuals are engaging in danger control or fear control is of great importance if the messages are to have the intended effect. Specifically:

1. If one's targeted audience is currently engaging in fear control processes, then the messages developed should focus on the efficacy of the recommended response in order to counteract the already high levels of perceived threat.
2. Conversely, if a targeted audience is currently engaging in danger control processes, the messages should encourage the continuation of danger control responses by focusing on the persistent threat (to keep protection motivation at a high level) as well as the efficacy of the recommended response.

One purpose of this chapter is to offer a predictive formula that identifies whether a targeted audience is engaging in fear control or danger control processes. This predictive formula acts as a diagnostic tool and offers an easy method for determining existing audience beliefs within the EPPM theoretical framework. Once practitioners or risk managers discover which parallel process is dominating in a given audience, they can devise effective and theoretically guided messages.

Below, I develop the discriminating value formula derived from the EPPM that can be used to predict audience reactions to risk messages. I will then report on two pilot studies that tested the formula's predictive ability.

Predicting the Parallel Process:
The Discriminating Value Formula

Overall, the point at which perceived threat surpasses perceived efficacy is likely to be dependent on the study topic, population, or individual differences in the subjects. However, predictions concerning whether a given person or population will engage in fear control or danger control processes are possible utilizing the following equation, which will be tested in the reported studies:

$$\frac{\begin{array}{r}(Z\text{-Perceived Efficacy}) \\ -\quad (Z\text{-Perceived Threat})\end{array}}{\text{Discriminating Value}}$$

This equation attempts to quantify the joint appraisal process—the implicit or explicit "weighing" of perceived threat against perceived efficacy by an individual—by summing separately items measuring perceived threat (susceptibility and severity) and items measuring perceived efficacy (response and self-efficacy) to create perceived threat and perceived efficacy variables. The robust interactions between threat and efficacy found in the empirical fear appeal literature justify "weighing" threat and efficacy against each other in a joint appraisal (e.g., see reviews by Witte, 1992a, 1992b). Thus it makes sense that, given this interaction, there is some sort of weighing process taking place.

First, the threat and efficacy items are standardized, to create comparable scales. Then the threat and efficacy items are summed. Next, the perceived threat sum is assigned a negative value, because we are interested in weighing perceived threat *against* perceived efficacy. Finally, negative threat and positive efficacy are summed to yield a "discriminating" value. This discriminating value will indicate whether fear control or danger control processes dominate. A positive discriminating value indicates that perceived efficacy exceeds perceived threat and that danger control processes dominate. Thus a positive score would predict danger control outcomes (i.e., message acceptance) such as attitude, intention, or behavior change. Conversely, a negative discriminating value would indicate that perceived threat exceeds perceived efficacy, and fear control responses (i.e., message rejection)—fear control outcomes such as defensive avoidance or reactance, for example—would be expected. *Zero* is the turning point in the discriminating value equation where perceived threat begins to exceed perceived efficacy (i.e., the critical point; see Figure 10.2).

For instance, following is a hypothetical example of one person's discriminating value. The items measuring threat and efficacy in the following example range from 1 to 7 (e.g., *not at all susceptible to AIDS* to *highly susceptible to AIDS*; *condoms do not work at all* to *condoms completely prevent AIDS*).

Item Scores for Perceived Threat		*Item Scores for Perceived Efficacy*	
susceptibility item 1:	6	response efficacy item 1:	2
susceptibility item 2:	5	response efficacy item 2:	1
severity item 1:	7	self-efficacy item 1:	3
severity item 2:	4	self-efficacy item 2:	1
(assign negative value)	−22		7

$$\begin{array}{l} \text{Perceived Efficacy } (+7) \\ - \quad \text{Perceived Threat } (-22) \\ \hline \text{Discriminating Value } (-15) \end{array}$$

In this example, the threat scores are very high and the efficacy scores are very low. In line with the threat-by-efficacy interactions found in the literature, we would expect fear control processes to dominate, resulting in defensive avoidance or denial. Likewise, the discriminating value equation predicts fear control responses because perceived threat exceeds perceived efficacy, yielding a negative value (i.e., −15) that predicts greater defensive avoidance and/or reactance.

Alternatively, following is an example of a positive discriminating value where perceived efficacy exceeds perceived threat, indicating danger control dominance.

Item Scores for Perceived Threat		*Item Scores for Perceived Efficacy*	
susceptibility item 1:	6	response efficacy item 1:	6
susceptibility item 2:	5	response efficacy item 2:	5
severity item 1:	7	self-efficacy item 1:	7
severity item 2:	4	self-efficacy item 2:	5
(assign negative value)	−22		23

$$\begin{array}{l} \text{Perceived Efficacy } (+23) \\ - \quad \text{Perceived Threat } (-22) \\ \hline \text{Discriminating Value } (+1) \end{array}$$

Notice that the threat scores are identical to those in the first example, but the efficacy scores are much higher. Thus both the threat and efficacy scores are high in this example. The literature shows that under conditions of high threat and high efficacy, people adopt recommended responses and protect themselves against a threat (e.g., Kleinot & Rogers, 1982; Maddux & Rogers, 1983; Witte, 1992c). Similarly, the discriminating value equation in this example yields a positive value, indicating that danger control responses, such as attitude, intention, or behavior change, are likely.

It is important to observe that fear control outcomes and danger control outcomes are qualitatively different. Danger control responses include attitude, intention, or behavior changes; fear control responses include defensive avoidance, message minimization, and/or perceived manipulation (reactance). In other words, positive (danger control) discriminating values predict phenomena that are qualitatively different from those predicted by negative (fear control) discriminating values. With these analyses in mind, the following hypotheses are advanced:

H1. *Danger control responses:* Those individuals with positive discriminating values (indicating danger control dominance) will have higher levels of attitude, intention, and behavior change than will those individuals with negative discriminating values (indicating fear control dominance).

H2. *Fear control responses:* Those individuals with negative discriminating values (indicating fear control dominance) will have higher levels of defensive avoidance, message minimization, and perceived manipulation than will those individuals with positive discriminating values (indicating danger control dominance).

Summary

Risk managers and public health practitioners need diagnostic tools to help determine which types of risk messages will be most effective for targeted audiences. In an extension of the EPPM, I have developed a "discriminating value" formula. This formula should determine whether audiences are engaging in fear control or danger control processes with regard to a given threat or hazard. In the following section, I describe two studies that tested the validity of this formula.

TWO PILOT STUDIES

Two studies were conducted to evaluate the role of perceived threat and perceived efficacy on AIDS-preventive behaviors following the evaluation of an AIDS prevention message. Study 1 assessed perceptions and outcomes at a single time point; Study 2 assessed perceptions and outcomes at two time periods separated by six weeks. Similar questionnaire items were used in both studies.

Methods

Study 1

Procedures. Participants were students who received extra credit or course credit for reading an AIDS prevention message and completing a questionnaire (described below) assessing HIV-related perceptions of threat, efficacy, and outcome variables (e.g., attitudes, defensive avoidance).

Subjects. Participants in the study were 40 primarily heterosexual (97.5%) subjects with an average of 1.5 sexual partners in the previous three months. Most of the subjects were Anglo (60%); 17.5% were African American, 17.5%

were Hispanic, and 5% were Filipino. There were approximately equal numbers of men (52.5%) and women (47.5%), and nearly all of the participants were between the ages of 17 and 24 (97.5%).

Study 2

Procedures. This study was part of a larger project on the role of threat and efficacy in AIDS prevention. After reading an AIDS prevention message, subjects completed an initial questionnaire soliciting perceptions of threat, efficacy, fear arousal, danger control outcomes, and fear control outcomes. Six weeks later, subjects returned to report behavioral changes. To increase the likelihood of honest and accurate behavioral self-reports, the anonymous nature of the questionnaires was stressed repeatedly. Anonymity was ensured by having subjects develop their own secret codes, so the initial questionnaires and six-week follow-up questionnaires could be matched (e.g., "You may use your personal ID code for your ATM, your middle name, or anything else that you'll remember ").

Subjects. Participants were 146 prescreened students who were (a) not in long-term monogamous relationships, (b) had had sexual intercourse, and (c) had not taken a course on AIDS or human sexuality. Nearly all of the participants were between the ages of 17 and 24 (93%) and had had an average of 1.4 sexual partners in the previous six months (range 0 to 22). Most participants were heterosexual (97%), and 66.4% were white, 17.8% were Asian, 11% were Hispanic, and 0.7% were African American. Approximately equal numbers of males (45.2%) and females (54.8%) participated. Six weeks later, 115 subjects completed follow-up questionnaires (approximately 21% attrition). Attrition appeared to be random across all demographic variables.

The Questionnaire

Efficacy. The components of efficacy, response efficacy (e.g., "I think that condoms prevent AIDS") and self-efficacy (e.g., "A sex partner[s] and I are able to use condoms to prevent AIDS"), were measured with two items each on scales ranging from *strongly disagree* to *strongly agree*. The efficacy items were averaged to create an overall index (Study 1, $\alpha = .75$; Study 2, $\alpha = .71$).

Threat. The components of threat, susceptibility and severity, were also measured separately. Perceived susceptibility to AIDS was assessed with four items (e.g., "How possible is it for you to get AIDS?"—*not at all possible* to *extremely possible*).[2] In terms of perceived severity, pilot studies indicated a strong ceiling effect for Likert-type responses (e.g., "How serious is AIDS?"—*not at all serious* to *extremely serious*) in that, regardless of the threat condition, most subjects thought AIDS to be extremely serious. Therefore, a two-question "gruesomeness" scale was developed. Participants were asked to rank (a) the *least* to *worst* "way to die," and (b) the *least* to *most* "painful way to die" with the following items: drowning in the ocean, burning to death in a fire, suffocating to death, dying from AIDS, dying from throat cancer, dying from torture, dying from being buried alive in sand. In computing the results to the gruesomeness scale, whatever the subjects ranked as the worst way to die was assigned a value of 7, the next worst way to die was assigned a value of 6, and so on. Therefore, the scale was a 7-point scale ranging from 1 = *least* worst way to die to 7 = *worst* way to die. Wherever "dying from AIDS" appeared in the rank order of ways to die was the "perceived severity" value it was given. For example, if it was ranked the third worst way to die, it was given a value of 5 for perceived severity. This way, the ceiling effect for perceived severity was successfully resolved (there was variance on the scale), and then this scale was used to validate the low-, moderate-, and high-threat messages. Although this perceived severity measure solved the ceiling effect problem, it contributed to a slightly unstable alpha for the overall threat index (Study 1, $\alpha = .66$; Study 2, $\alpha = .57$).

Danger control outcomes. The danger control (message acceptance) dependent variables were attitudes toward "my using condoms," intentions to use condoms, and self-reported behaviors (Study 2 only). In Study 2, attitudes and intentions were assessed at time 1, and behaviors were measured at time 2.

Attitudes. Attitudes toward condoms were assessed with five semantic differential scales (e.g., bad/good, desirable/undesirable, favorable/unfavorable, not pleasurable/pleasurable, romantic/not romantic) in Study 1 ($\alpha = .90$), and two additional items were added for Study 2 (safe/not safe, effective/not effective; $\alpha = .82$).

Intentions. Intentions to use condoms were measured with five questions (e.g., "Do you intend to use condoms at all during the next 4-6 weeks?"—*definitely no* to *definitely yes*; "I plan to use condoms during the next 4-6 weeks"—*not at all* to *every time I have sex*) (Study 1, $\alpha = .84$; Study 2, $\alpha = .83$).

Behaviors. Behaviors were assessed in Study 2 only at a six-week follow-up with four questions (e.g., "Did you and a partner[s] use condoms?"—*no, never* to *yes, frequently*; "Did you plan to use condoms since you first participated in this study?"—*no, never* to *yes, planned and used them*; "Did you practice any safe sex skills since you first participated in this study?"—*definitely no* to *definitely yes*) ($\alpha = .80$). Only those participants who had had sexual intercourse since time 1 were included in any of the behavioral analyses.

Fear control outcomes. The fear control (message rejection) dependent variables were defensive avoidance, message minimization (only in Study 2), and perceived manipulation, and were solicited with reference to the specific threat (i.e., AIDS) and the AIDS prevention message. Readers will notice that for Study 2, the defensive avoidance and message minimization measures are a bit unstable. It is my belief that these low reliabilities stem from the fact that these variables are "hidden" processes that we cannot directly measure. For example, we can only infer from participant responses that defensive avoidance is occurring (i.e., it is difficult to ask people if they are defensively avoiding a threat, because if they are, they won't know it). Therefore, these measures were validated with thought-listing tasks and a memory test (described in Witte, 1991).

Defensive avoidance. Defensive avoidance was determined through an examination of the degree to which subjects wanted to avoid thinking further about AIDS and AIDS prevention in response to a written message. In Study 1, participants were asked to complete the following with two different responses: "When I was first reading the message and looking at the pictures, my first instinct was to . . . " The two sets of responses were as follows: (a) *"want* to do something to keep myself from getting AIDS"—*"not* want to do something to keep myself from getting AIDS"; and (b) *"want* to protect myself from AIDS"—*"not* want to protect myself from AIDS" ($\alpha = .92$). One additional response item was added to Study 2: *"want* to think about AIDS"—*"not* want to think about AIDS" ($\alpha = .61$)

Message minimization. Message minimization, or denial of the importance of an AIDS prevention message, was determined through the measurement of the degree to which subjects derogated or minimized the message (i.e., feelings and impressions of the message). For example, the message minimization questions assessed whether subjects thought the message was "distorted," "overblown," "exaggerated," "boring," or "overstated" (Study 2, $\alpha = .78$).

Perceived manipulation. The perceived manipulation questions were designed to determine the degree of reactance subjects had against the AIDS prevention message. For example, participants were asked whether they felt "manipulated" or whether the message "deliberately tried to manipulate my feelings" (Study 1, 4 items, $\alpha = .76$; Study 2, 3 items, $\alpha = .66$).

The AIDS Prevention Messages

The messages consisted of (a) a core message based on a public health service brochure, (b) a case study of a fictitious AIDS patient, and (c) a message about the effectiveness of condoms. Four photos were embedded in the core message and the case study. The threat message discussed the severity of AIDS and individuals' susceptibility to AIDS. The efficacy message discussed the effectiveness of condoms in preventing AIDS and the ease with which condoms can be used. To prevent confounding of other variables, each message was equated for length, order of arguments, and number of pictures. Messages and measures were subjected to extensive pilot testing and validation in three phases (for detailed information on the messages, see Witte, 1992c).

Results

Analysis Procedures

The analysis procedures were identical for both studies. First, the threat measure and the efficacy measure were standardized. Then, the discriminating value was calculated in each study as Z-Score Efficacy – Z-Score Threat. Next, those individuals with positive discriminating values were separated from those with negative discriminating values to create a danger control group (Study 1, $N = 20$;

Study 2, $N = 78$) and a fear control group (Study 1, $N = 19$; Study 2, $N = 67$). The hypotheses were tested with MANCOVA procedures because of the multiple dependent variables and the existence of several covariates with the discriminating value as the factor with two levels (positive values = danger control group; negative values = fear control group).

Caveats

I must make one important caveat concerning the results reported here. Because the present work is a first attempt to quantify the critical point in the EPPM, these results should be viewed as preliminary only. These data act as pilot illustrations of what the discriminating value can do, rather than as vigorous hypothesis tests. Because of the exploratory nature of the studies, the *pattern* of results is of more interest than the statistical significance of the results. Future research should examine the discriminating value with diverse topics and populations to test its validity.

Study 1

Danger control responses. As predicted, those people with positive discriminating values (indicating dominance of danger control processes) had higher mean scores for danger control responses than did those with negative discriminating values (indicating dominance of fear control processes). Table 10.1 shows that those people with positive discriminating values had stronger AIDS-preventive attitudes and intentions than did those with negative discriminating values. MANCOVA analysis revealed a marginally significant multivariate effect on attitudes and intentions by discriminating value group (Wilks's lambda = .85, $F[2, 34] = 2.91$, $p = .07$) with number of different sex partners and familiarity of previous sexual partners acting as covariates. Univariate F tests indicated significant differences between the positive and negative discriminating value groups for attitudes ($F[1, 35] = 5.49$, $p < .05$), but not for intentions ($F[1, 35] = 1.66$, $p = .21$).

Fear control responses. As predicted, those people with negative discriminating values (indicating dominance of fear control processes) had higher mean scores for the fear control responses than did those with positive discriminating values (indicating dominance of danger control processes). Table 10.1 shows that those people with negative discriminating values were more likely to defensively avoid the threat of AIDS and to perceive manipulation from AIDS prevention messages than were those with positive discriminating values. MANCOVA analysis revealed a marginally significant multivariate effect on perceived manipulation and defensive avoidance by discriminating value group (Wilks's lambda = .85, $F[2, 29] = 2.55$, $p = .096$) while controlling for the effects of gender, number of different sex partners, and familiarity of previous sexual partners. Univariate F tests indicated significant differences between the positive and negative discriminating value groups for defensive avoidance ($F[1, 30]$

$= 4.35$, $p < .05$) and marginally significant differences between groups for perceived manipulation ($F[1, 30] = 2.96$, $p = .096$).

Study 2

Danger control responses. As predicted, those people with positive discriminating values (indicating dominance of danger control processes) had higher mean scores for danger control responses than did those with negative discriminating values (indicating dominance of fear control processes). Table 10.1 shows that those people with positive discriminating values had stronger AIDS-preventive attitudes, intentions, and behaviors than did those with negative discriminating values. Attitudes and intentions (measured at time 1) were analyzed separate from behavior (measured at time 2) because of the discrepancy between sample sizes from time 1 to time 2. MANCOVA analysis revealed a significant multivariate effect on attitudes and intentions by discriminating value group (Wilks's lambda = .92, $F[2, 133] = 5.90$, $p < .01$) while controlling for the effects of age, prior condom use, number of different sex partners, and familiarity of sexual partners. Univariate F tests indicated significant differences between the positive and negative discriminating value groups for attitudes ($F[1, 134] = 4.98$, $p < .05$), but not for intentions ($F[1, 134] = .69$, $p = .41$). When behavior was added as a dependent variable to the MANCOVA, the number of subjects dropped significantly (down to 59) and the univariate F test indicated no significant difference between positive and negative discriminating value groups for behavior ($F[1, 51] = 1.27$, $p = .26$).

Fear control responses. Those people with negative discriminating values (indicating dominance of fear control processes) had higher mean scores for two of the three fear control responses than did those with positive discriminating values (indicating dominance of danger control processes). Table 10.1 shows that those people with negative discriminating values were more likely to defensively avoid the threat of AIDS and to perceive manipulation from AIDS prevention messages than were those with positive discriminating values. Contrary to predictions, those with positive discriminating values had higher message minimization scores than did those with negative discriminating values. Perceived manipulation and message minimization (measured at time 1) were analyzed separate from defensive avoidance (measured at time 2) because of the discrepancy between sample sizes from time 1 to time 2. MANCOVA analysis failed to reveal a significant multivariate effect on perceived manipulation and message minimization by discriminating value group (Wilks's lambda = .97, $F[2, 116] = 1.86$, $p = .16$) while controlling for the effects of age, gender, sexual orientation, prior condom use, number of different sex partners, and familiarity of sexual partners. Univariate F tests indicated no significant differences between the positive and negative discriminating value groups for message minimization ($F[1, 117] = 2.18$, $p = .14$) or perceived manipulation ($F[1, 117] = .54$, $p = .47$). Similarly, the univariate F test indicated no significant

TABLE 10.1
Mean Responses by Positive Discriminating Value (Indicating Dominance of Danger Control Processes) and Negative Discriminating Value (Indicating Dominance of Fear Control Processes)

| | Danger Control Responses | | | Fear Control Responses | | |
	Attitudes	Intentions	Behavior	Defensive Avoidance	Message Minimization	Perceived Manipulation
Study 1						
danger control group (positive discriminating value)	5.06	5.15	NM	1.77	NM	2.99
fear control group (negative discriminating value)	4.24	4.70	NM	2.36	NM	3.53
Study 2						
danger control group (positive discriminating value)	5.59	5.68	3.96	2.02	2.39	2.40
fear control group (negative discriminating value)	5.08	5.64	3.63	2.26	2.14	2.53

NOTE: NM = not measured.

differences between positive and negative discriminating value groups for defensive avoidance ($F[1, 87] = .91, p = .34$).

Discussion

The results of these two pilot studies indicate that the discriminating value formula has some predictive utility in determining whether individuals are engaging in danger control or fear control processes with respect to a given threat, in this case AIDS. Thus, in general, the patterns predicted for Hypotheses 1 and 2 were supported although statistical support was weak. As expected, the means of those individuals with positive discriminating values—indicating the dominance of danger control processes—had more positive attitudes toward condoms, intended to use condoms, and reported greater condom use than did those with negative discriminating values. Conversely, the means of those people with negative discriminating values—signifying the dominance of fear control processes—were more likely to avoid defensively and react against AIDS prevention messages (i.e., perceive manipulation) than were those with positive discriminating values. One unpredicted finding was that of message minimization, where the danger control group minimized the message more than the fear control group. It may be that if individuals are controlling the danger of AIDS, then they may minimize any messages coming their way because they believe they are adequately protecting themselves. Future work should examine closely the relations among message minimization, attitude, intention, and behavior change to evaluate whether message minimization tends to be a danger control or fear control response.

Overall, the discriminating value formula yielded patterns that distinguished between those engaged in fear control processes and those engaged in danger control processes. The formula appeared to discriminate between the danger control and fear control groups (with the exception of message minimization in Study 2) across the two separate studies.

Limitations

These results should be viewed cautiously, given that this is a first attempt to provide risk managers and practitioners with an easy-to-use diagnostic formula. As noted above, the *pattern* of the means is of more interest in this chapter than is the statistical significance. Though the discriminating value differentiated between those engaging in fear control and those engaging in danger control, as indicated by the means in Table 10.1, they often failed to reach conventional levels of statistical significance. The discriminating value formula should be tested in large-scale correlational studies to determine more fully its predictive validity. Readers also should note that the discriminating value formula simply offers a rough cut between those currently engaged in danger control processes and those currently engaged in fear control processes. Unfortunately, the current formula does not offer any further precision than this. However, the formula offers important information to risk message designers in that it can be useful for them in diagnosing, a priori, the likelihood of their fear appeals' pattern backfiring. Overall, the results for the formula are encouraging, given the consistency of the findings across two studies and two samples. Future studies should utilize randomly sampled populations to test the ideas presented here.

Practical Applications

The discriminating value formula appears to distinguish between those engaging in danger control processes and those engaging in fear control processes. This user-friendly discriminating value formula has great practical utility and offers practitioners an easy method for determining what type of fear appeal to use. For example, the results of the two studies reported here suggest that when danger control processes dominate, fear appeals targeted toward these populations should focus on both the threat of HIV for college students and the efficacy of recommended responses to avert HIV transmission. Focusing on the threat of HIV while also depicting effective and easy methods to prevent transmission should elicit protection motivation and result in safer sex behaviors among these sexually active, nonmonogamous, heterosexual individuals. Of course, for those currently engaging in fear control processes, the fear appeals would need to focus on ways to deter HIV transmission and omit any references to the threat. When fear control processes dominate, perceived threat is already too high. Thus risk messages targeted toward those engaging in fear control processes should especially emphasize response and self-efficacy issues. Future research should explore which groups of people tend to engage in danger control processes and which groups tend to engage in fear control processes with a variety of health threats (e.g., lung cancer, automobile accidents, heart disease).

USING THE EPPM
TO GENERATE RISK MESSAGES

The EPPM has the capacity to be expanded and applied to the area of risk communication, given its focus on how risks induced by perceptions of threat interact with how perceptions of efficacy or control over a hazard produce either danger control or fear control outcomes. Previously, many in the risk field have considered fear appeals to be inappropriate strategies for gaining adherence to risk communication recommendations. For example, Covello, von Winterfeldt, and Slovic (1986) assert that "people seldom respond appropriately to high-threat or fear communications, such as photographs or films graphically depicting the physical symptoms of disease or the results of a disfiguring or fatal accident. Such communications may induce excessive fear and anxiety, which, in turn, may reduce people's attention, induce defensive responses, and evoke hostility toward the source of the communication" (p. 175). The operative word in this quotation is "may." Risk communications *may* initiate adverse outcomes such as those outlined here, but only under certain conditions, according to the EPPM. When people feel out of control or helpless in the face of a grave threat, they are more likely to react against the risk message and control their fear by defensively avoiding the risk or by becoming angry at the communicator for using blatant manipulation techniques. However, high-threat messages can be extremely effective in motivating self-protective behaviors *if* people believe they can easily and effectively avert the threat (e.g., see Kleinot & Rogers, 1982; Rogers & Mewborn, 1976; Witte, 1992c).

Experts on emergency management for natural and technological disasters have long pointed out that an effort "must be made by emergency managers to establish a clear relationship between taking the suggested protective measures and the minimization of negative consequences of the hazard. Any imminent-threat message should explain *how* public safety will be enhanced if citizens comply with these instructions" (Perry & Nigg, 1985, p. 76). Thus, common wisdom matches empirical and theoretical conclusions. That is, risk messages must not only depict the threat as severe and probable; to promote danger control responses, they *must* offer specific solutions that the public can easily carry out with a minimum of complexity and labor. For example, in the case of a natural hazard, public response to risk messages is more likely if the information about averting harm "is specific regarding the hazard. . . . Specific information is more likely to be believed, as is information that is consistent, certain, frequently delivered, from official sources, and then confirmed" (Mileti & Fitzpatrick, 1992, p. 394).

Too often, it appears that risk messages contain information about the threat only, with no information (or information given too late) about how to avert harm from or minimize exposure to the threat. Unfortunately, when no information is given about how to avert and/or minimize the threat (i.e., no efficacy information is given), people are more likely to engage in fear control responses. One way to increase perceived efficacy in order to promote danger control responses in the face of a serious threat is to increase the public's perception of individual control. For example, the consistent release of information (as it comes in) about particularly threatening or alarming risks can act as a safety valve, in that people feel informed and in control; their efficacy is increased because they believe they know what to do if the threat should become actual, and perceived threat is adequately balanced by perceived efficacy. In such a case, people are able to remain cognizant and rational as they believe in their ability to control the danger. If information about a threat is withheld, people's perceived efficacy in averting any harm from the threat is low. They feel uninformed and unsure of what to do if the threat becomes real; perceived threat exceeds perceived efficacy, resulting in fear control responses, where people react against risk managers and lash out at them. "Withholding information angers people, in part because they lose their power to take action. By withholding information, even in cases where exposure is minimal, agencies pre-empt people's right to make decisions and control their exposure to risk" (Chess & Hance, 1989, p. 14). Similarly, Devgun (1991) notes, "To avoid the perception of involuntary risk thrust upon them, the local public needs to be involved throughout the remediation process and should be a partner in the decision-making process" (p. 7).

When individuals' levels of perceived efficacy remain high—that is, when they believe they know what to do and believe they are able to do something to avert a threat—they will engage in danger control processes, even in situations of high threat. For example, in one potentially threatening situation involving private wells that needed to be tested for contamination, "people were alerted to each step of the process before it happened. As a result, discussion centered on the risk itself and not on the way people were treated by the health department" (Chess & Hance, 1989, p. 14). Because perceived threat was balanced by perceived efficacy, the public engaged in danger control responses.

When threatening information about a risk is released all at once, people are overwhelmed emotionally because they feel a lack of control (i.e., low perceived efficacy) in the face of a grave threat (high perceived threat) and engage in fear control responses, lashing out in anger at risk managers and/or reacting emotionally (as one grassroots activist stated, "I got into it because of my kids. I *stayed* in it because I got so angry"; Chess & Hance, 1989, p. 14).

In sum, to prevent fear control responses and to maintain danger control responses, risk managers should (a) work *with* communities and listen to and address their concerns, (b) keep people informed of risks and hazards as they emerge, and (c) involve the public in decisions and the development of regulations (Chess & Hance, 1989). By doing these things, risk managers can balance perceptions of threat—however high they may be—with perceptions of control over the threat (i.e., high perceived efficacy), and danger control processes should dominate. The EPA's recent protocol for developing risk communications includes getting community input on the management of risks (Thomas, 1986). By doing this, risk managers can ascertain levels of perceived threat and fear as well as levels of perceived efficacy in averting any risks. They can then develop messages, based on the assessment of community perceptions, that yield the maximum level of understanding and effectiveness.

ETHICAL ISSUES IN RISK COMMUNICATION

The development of risk-related messages often presents ethical dilemmas concerning choices between simply informing the public and persuading the public to act or react. Risk messages can inform, educate, and promote and/or direct behavior (Covello et al., 1986). However, *any* risk message, by virtue of presenting certain facts to the exclusion of others (because of time or other constraints), will influence its audience in some manner. There is no such thing as a neutral risk message. As Cannell and Otway (1988) note: "The only satisfactory solution to this dilemma is for those engaged in risk communications consciously to serve the information needs perceived by their audience, whoever that audience happens to be and in whatever context it finds itself. This implies a commitment to people, rather than technology" (p. 524).

Risk influence messages appear to be most acceptable when they promote better health and/or the prevention of disease (National Research Council, 1989). For example, risk messages that persuade persons to quit smoking cigarettes, to wear seat belts, to use condoms to prevent transmission of HIV, or to seek mammograms to detect cancer are traditionally seen by the government and the public as appropriate. It appears that "when a class of personal action (such as drunk driving) affects a large portion of the populace or threatens individuals who do not engage in that action, people are more willing to accept, and even to demand, that government agencies be proactive and try to influence beliefs and actions. Under such conditions, people are more willing to compromise the autonomy, privacy, or freedom of some individuals for the good of others" (National Research Council, 1989, p. 89). Also, "the more clearly it has been established that an activity is dangerous or that it may harm persons generally considered to deserve societal protection (e.g., children), the more acceptable influence attempts seem to become" (National Research Council, 1989, p. 88).

The EPPM provides a theoretical rationale and specific procedures for manipulating risk perceptions of audience members in order to motivate them to act or react in the manner desired by message designers. However, policy makers and risk managers must behave ethically, with the common good in mind, when designing risk messages. Clearly, the "good of the masses" must come before the "good of the agency." Obviously, target audiences should not be persuaded that a risk is safe and acceptable when in fact it is not (or we do not know whether it is safe or not). Even if the "true" risk of a hazard is unknown, risk managers can prevent panic in audiences by (a) acknowledging this uncertainty (which is likely to increase perceptions of threat) and (b) offering specific steps that people can take to reduce effectively the chances of the threat occurring and/or to minimize harm from the threat should it occur. For example, there is great uncertainty in exactly how many ways HIV can be transmitted, which results in strong perceptions of threat about HIV transmission. However, the known strategies for reducing the chances of contraction of HIV can be spelled out in a step-by-step manner to reduce public fears. In short, risk message designers must be ethical, responsible, and committed to the general welfare of the audience. The tremendous responsibility attached to deciding the "right" answers or the "correct" behaviors cannot be ignored.

CONCLUSION

Although risk messages, and especially fear appeals, have great potential for promoting self-protective behaviors, until now there has been no way to determine *prior* to message development *which* kinds of messages will be most effective for targeted audiences. The formula I have described in this chapter represents one relatively simple method for determining appropriate messages for specific audiences. The results of the pilot tests reported here reveal that the formula may be useful as a diagnostic tool for public health practitioners and risk managers interested in devising effective targeted risk communications that yield the greatest public good.

NOTES

1. Originally, Fischhoff et al. (1978) labeled the two factors "technological risk" and "severity." In later work, these researchers reexplored the factor structure, which resulted in a shifting of some of the qualitative dimensions and the renaming of the two factors to "dreaded" and "unknown risk" (e.g., Slovic, 1987; Slovic et al., 1982).

2. Susceptibility did not receive disproportionate weight in the perceived threat index even though it was measured with four items and severity was measured with only two. First, separate composites were developed for perceived susceptibility and perceived severity, then these composites were averaged to create the perceived threat variable.

REFERENCES

Cannell, W., & Otway, H. (1988, October). Audience perspectives in the communication of technological risks. *Futures,* pp. 519-531.

Chess, C., & Hance, B. J. (1989). Opening doors: Making risk communication agency reality. *Environment, 31,* 11-39.

Covello, V. T., von Winterfeldt, D., & Slovic, P. (1986). Risk communication: A review of the literature. *Risk Abstracts, 3,* 171-182.

Devgun, J. S. (1991, June). *Role of risk assessment in remediation of contaminated sites.* Paper presented at the 11th Annual Meeting of the International Association for Impact Assessment, Urbana-Champaign, IL.

Douglas, M. (1985). *Risk acceptability according to the social sciences.* New York: Russell Sage Foundation.

Fischhoff, B., Slovic, P., Lichtenstein, S., Read, S., & Combs, B. (1978). How safe is safe enough? A psychometric study of attitudes towards technological risks and benefits. *Policy Sciences, 9,* 127-152.

Hovland, C., Janis, I., & Kelly, H. (1953). *Communication and persuasion.* New Haven, CT: Yale University Press.

Janis, I. L. (1967). Effects of fear arousal on attitude change: Recent developments in theory and experimental research. In L. Berkowitz (Ed.), *Advances in experimental social psychology* (Vol. 3, pp. 166-225). New York: Academic Press.

Johnson, F. R., Fisher, A., Smith, V. K., & Desvousges, W. H. (1988). Informed choice or regulated risk? *Environment, 30,* 12-15, 30-35.

Kishchuk, N. A. (1987). Causes and correlates of risk perceptions: A comment. *Risk Abstracts, 4,* 1-4.

Kleinot, M. C., & Rogers, R. W. (1982). Identifying effective components of alcohol misuse prevention programs. *Journal of Studies on Alcohol, 43,* 802-811.

Leventhal, H. (1970). Findings and theory in the study of fear communications. In L. Berkowitz (Ed.), *Advances in experimental social psychology* (Vol. 5, pp. 119-186). New York: Academic Press.

Maddux, J. E., & Rogers, R. W. (1983). Protection motivation and self-efficacy: A revised theory of fear appeals and attitude change. *Journal of Experimental Social Psychology, 19,* 469-479.

Mileti, D. S., & Fitzpatrick, C. (1992). The causal sequence of risk communication in the Parkfield earthquake prediction experiment. *Risk Analysis, 12,* 393-400.

National Research Council. (1989). *Improving risk communication.* Washington, DC: National Academy Press.

Perry, R. W., & Nigg, J. M. (1985). Emerging management strategies for communicating hazard information. *Public Administration Review, 45,* 72-76.

Rogers, R. W. (1975). A protection motivation theory of fear appeals and attitude change. *Journal of Psychology, 91,* 93-114.

Rogers, R. W. (1983). Cognitive and physiological processes in fear appeals and attitude change: A revised theory of protection motivation. In J. Cacioppo & R. E. Petty (Eds.), *Social psychophysiology* (pp. 153-176). New York: Guilford.

Rogers, R. W., & Mewborn, C. R. (1976). Fear appeals and attitude change: Effects of a threat's noxiousness, probability of occurrence, and the efficacy of the coping responses. *Journal of Personality and Social Psychology, 34,* 54-61

Sandman, P. M. (1988, December). *Hazard versus outrage: The case of radon.* Paper presented at the Symposium on Science Communication, Annenberg School for Communication, Los Angeles, CA.

Slovic, P. (1987). Perception of risk. *Science, 236,* 280-285.

Slovic, P., Fischhoff, B., & Lichtenstein, S. (1982). Why study risk perceptions? *Risk Analysis, 2,* 83-93.

Thomas, L. M. (1986). Risk communication: Why we must talk about risk. *Environment, 28,* 4-5, 40.

Witte, K. (1991). *Preventing AIDS through persuasive communications: Fear appeals and preventive action efficacy.* Unpublished doctoral dissertation, University of California, Irvine.

Witte, K. (1992a). Message and conceptual confounds in fear appeals: The role of threat, fear, and efficacy. *Southern Communication Journal, 58,* 147-155.

Witte, K. (1992b). Putting the fear back into fear appeals: Reconciling the literature. *Communication Monographs, 59,* 329-349.

Witte, K. (1992c). The role of threat and efficacy in AIDS prevention. *International Quarterly of Community Health Education, 12,* 225-249.

Witte, K. (1994). Fear control and danger control: A test of the extended parallel process model (EPPM). *Communication Monographs, 61,* 113-134.

11 Corporate Environmental Risk Communication: Cases and Practices Along the Texas Gulf Coast

ROBERT L. HEATH
University of Houston

Industries that manufacture and discharge toxic and hazardous materials into the environ-ment, especially chemical companies, are increasingly seeing it in their interest to improve communication with community members. Framed by what has been termed a *risk democracy* perspective, this chapter examines risk communication cases and practices of the Texas coast chemical industry. These cases demonstrate the value of communi-cation outreach efforts that accommodate key publics' cognitive involvement, desire for control, uncertainty, efforts to balance harms and benefits, knowledge of risks and their solutions, trust, and problem definition. By contrasting five cases featuring successful and unsuccessful communication efforts, the author attempts to create greater aware-ness of risk communication processes and strategies and seeks to enhance under-standing and agreement between those entities that create risk and persons who are risk intolerant.

E VEN when they do not work for chemical plants or enjoy their contribution to local tax bases, millions of people benefit from such plants because their products enhance the quality of life. On the other hand, environ-mental quality and health risks posed by exposure to toxic materials or hazard-ous processes are everyone's problems. Toxic materials released into the air, water, and soil may affect health. Each year, tons of emissions enter the air and harm the aesthetics of the environment. Recent charges have been voiced that the siting and policing of chemical facilities and waste storage or disposal opera-tions are more likely to affect low-income neighborhoods, whose populations use the terms *environmental racism* and *environmental equity* in their indict-ments of regulatory practices.

Correspondence and requests for reprints: Robert L. Heath, School of Communication, University of Houston, Houston, TX 77204-3786.

Communication Yearbook 18, pp. 255-277

The cost of reducing emissions and lessening risks of exposure to toxic materials will affect the U.S. economy. The National Petroleum Council, an industry advisory committee to the federal Department of Energy, predicts the bill for meeting new environmental regulations will be $166 billion over the next two decades. That is the cost of standing still rather than expanding plant operations, a sum that is twice the annual expenditure during the second half of the 1980s (Sullivan, 1993). That sum will factor into the price of products made from chemicals, along with the cost of gasoline and other petroleum products. Parts of some plants will be closed rather than remodeled. Some plants will be put out of business.

All is not bleak, however, even on the economic front for chemical facilities. They have learned that by cleaning up their manufacturing processes they may be able to enhance their productivity. For example, Du Pont realized that by redesigning its plant in Beaumont, Texas, it could utilize more of the materials processed and reduce its discharge by 110 million pounds of waste each year (McMurray, 1991).

These changes and challenges are the result of three decades of activism as well as improved plant operations on the part of responsible companies. Communication is a vital part of this change. Plant operations cannot be allowed to harm public health and damage the environment. Wise regulation avoids extreme measures that do not accomplish the goals intended and unnecessarily harm the companies and industry to be constrained. Opinions, particularly those of people in communities near chemical plants, play a vital role in the way this regulation is shaped and imposed.

With the above as context, in this chapter I report on five examples of risk communication along the Texas gulf coast that feature practices by members of the chemical manufacturing industry that have failed or succeeded. Based on these examples, I draw conclusions to clarify the directions that risk communication practice and research should take.

The Texas gulf coast is an ideal location to examine risk communication practices. Along the "Chemical Coast," the environment is subject to trade-offs whereby air and water quality and health are balanced against the need for products, profits, food, clothing, and shelter. For instance, after the 1980s oil bust devastated the Texas economy, the industry helped diversify the area's economic base, and in 1987 pumped $2 billion in wages and salaries into the economy. The region has the largest concentration of petrochemical plants in the world, which employ 120,000 workers and operate close to neighborhoods. One industry group located in the shadows of Houston, Texas, is the East Harris County Manufacturers Association (EHCMA), the heart and soul of the chemical industry. Representing most of the large chemical companies of the world, its 80 members account for a major part of the employment and revenue generated by the Texas chemical industry. In conjunction with the Chemical Manufacturers Association (CMA), EHCMA provides research and counsel for the improvement of plant operations and the enhancement of communication with relevant stakeholders.

By working to maximize industrywide uniformity, it lessens the perils of change. The association recommends industry standards to members so that their executive managements can be less apprehensive that when they improve plant designs and enhance operations other members in the industry may not make similar costly improvements, thereby creating unfair market advantages. Uniform change is a reasonable part of maintaining marketplace competition while making wise progress toward an improved environment.

Frequently, the analysis of risk communication features an information exchange and shared knowledge model. That model assumes a knowledgeable sender speaking to allay fears felt by targeted audiences who are concerned about the level of risk from hazardous processes and toxic substances that exist in living and working environments (Covello, Sandman, & Slovic, 1988; Covello, von Winterfeldt, & Slovic, 1987; Davies, Covello, & Allen, 1987). In that vein, Covello (1992) defines risk communication as "the exchange of information among interested parties about the nature, magnitude, significance, or control of a risk" (p. 359).

In contrast to what may be called a shared understanding model, the examples in this chapter stress the importance of the communication *infrastructure* that exists in communities where residents and private sector and government organizations are confronted with adapting to complex and often conflicting interests and evaluations of what level of risk is tolerable. This multiple-player, dynamic process view assumes that each community consists of a multitude of interests that are not always compatible and that constitute different levels of understanding and risk tolerance. Rather than merely featuring understanding, in this analysis I highlight the importance of different evaluative heuristics. I assume that some of the issues that result in misunderstanding and conflict are matters of unsubstantial opinion and reflect a struggle for control in which knowledge of chemicals and operating processes may be unpersuasive and even thought to be irrelevant.

In the discussion that follows, I nominate key variables as central to risk communication: cognitive involvement, struggle for control, knowledge of risks and their solutions, uncertainty, problem recognition or definition, trust, and benefit/harm ratios. Acknowledging that the mass media play a role in this infrastructure, I stress that all communication levels must be scrutinized if we are to understand risk communication processes. The outcome of these processes does not depend so much on what one party says, as on the quality of dialogue in a community that originates once key publics experience uncertainty about whether chemical plant operations result in health or environmental problems. Risk communication deals with risk estimates, whether they are appropriately tolerable, and risk consequences, whether ingesting or breathing chemicals emitted by plants harms people and other organisms. Persons engaged in operating plants and living close to them ask questions; the answers may depend on the side of the fence where they originate. Does risk exit? Is it tolerable? What are its consequences? How can undesirable consequences be eliminated or reduced to tolerable levels? Can persons who create the risk be trusted, because of their ethics or knowledge, to contain it?

The sections of this chapter illustrate ineffective or effective risk communication practices. Companies may underestimate or dismiss community concerns about environmental hazards; those that make this mistake stand a good chance of becoming distrusted and having projects defeated or indefinitely delayed. Recognizing the perils of ignoring their neighbors' fears and uncertainty, savvy organizations are (a) developing communication infrastructures and adopting practices, such as citizens' advisory councils, for soliciting and responding to community sentiments; (b) training technical experts in place of public relations practitioners as spokespersons on technical issues; and (c) encouraging open-door practices whereby the public can scrutinize plant permits and operating standards, which are enhanced through programs that reward employees who improve plant operations. Despite the responsible efforts of other members of their industry, some chemical plant managements have not learned that if they do not have a track record of responsible performance the community has reason to doubt their ability and willingness to protect the environment and the health of their neighbors.

UNDERESTIMATING OPPOSITION, OR
HOW CITIZENS DEFEAT THE GOOD OL' BOY SYSTEM

The case described in this section concerns a failed attempt by one of the world's largest companies to locate a copper smelter on the shore of the vibrant but environmentally strained Galveston Bay. This example demonstrates how a plant management can be defeated during the permitting process when it fails to listen to and heed the concerns of a public who believes that its interests are likely to be harmed by proposed plant operations. The management team assumed that the good ol' boy permitting process would once again work to the advantage of any company no matter how questionable its analysis regarding its environmental impact on the community. This example also supports the assumption that base appeals to the financial benefits in a community constitute a monologue if the company does not respond to the dialogue of concern where key publics seek control of their environment.

As part of its economic and manufacturing expansion, Mitsubishi Corporation, through a subsidiary named Texas Copper Corporation (TCC), sought state and federal air and water quality commissions' approval to build and operate a $200 million copper smelter near Texas City, Texas. Approximately 26 state and federal construction and operating permits were required to operate the plant, a process that required extensive public hearings. If approved, the smelter, the first major plant to be constructed in Texas City since 1967, would have employed 1,000 workers during construction and 200 when operations began. An area suffering 9% unemployment, Texas City has a long history with the chemical industry. Many of its residents have worked for or are employed in the industry or have family members so employed. Local businesses and school districts draw revenues from chemical plants and their employees.

The company had options to purchase a tract of land large enough for the plant as well as a wildlife reserve. The bay supports sport and commercial seafood harvest and allows for many water recreation activities. It is encircled with upscale residential resort neighborhoods. Across the bay from the plant site, Galveston, Texas, has enjoyed a decade of economic recovery because of tourists drawn by its efforts to reestablish itself as an attractive vacation spot.

Several area municipal governments were likely to be affected by the siting of the plant. Texas City would gain a substantial increase in its tax and wage base. Its businesses and residential neighborhoods would partially recover from a deep recession. Thus its municipal leaders and others in the region supported the plant's efforts to obtain permits. In contrast, other area municipal leaders and many part-time, leisure residents opposed the granting of those permits.

The facility was designed to discharge into Galveston Bay 2,000 pounds of copper, zinc, arsenic, lead, and other trace metals annually. Opponents argued that the 23 million gallons of warm water and toxic heavy metal discharges would harm marine life and damage the seafood and tourism industries. The smelter's owners and their hired experts said that the metals were insignificant compared with the amount of metals already in the bay as well as those discharged by petrochemical plants, and that the temperature of the water to be discharged would meet state requirements. Opponents challenged TCC executives to agree to implement superior wastewater treatment processes that would lower the toxic discharge. Similar appeals were made privately by technical experts from the local chemical industry who feared that the bad-apple syndrome would lead to demands for more stringent restrictions on the industry. The company responded that the facility was state-of-the-art and environmentally sensitive.

The U.S. representatives of the project were well known in the region. One of them, Thomas Mackey, had a long list of industry achievements, but he was also associated with a plant in the region that had manufactured tin during World War II; in the past decade the site of that plant had been found to be laden with toxic substances, including lead. It eventually was listed as a Superfund site, one of the most damaged by industrial wastes in the United States. In the initial stages of the permitting effort, no representatives from the parent company were directly involved. Responsibility for buying land, obtaining permits, and initiating construction rested with the U.S. representatives.

Texas's regulatory system has a history of favoring petitioners for operating permits of facilities. The permitting process has been a good ol' boy system that listens patiently to the proponents of projects and their opponents (if any) and then grants permits. A theme has prevailed that "you can't make an omelet without breaking an egg." Jobs and economy have often been given priority over long-term planning for the consequences of toxic buildup. This process began to change in the mid-1980s as a consequence of heightened concern for public health and safety. The federal government has led in spirit if not in practice by failing to promulgate a firmly enforced and well-defined environmental policy. Managements who had a long history with chemical manufacturing were prone to believe that the permitting system would sustain them forever, or at least one more time. That spirit permeated the thinking of TCC's U.S. representatives.

The issue of environmental responsibility is apparent not only during permitting processes, but also during plant operation. A state representative commented during the TCC permitting process that environmentalists typically press for the establishment of high performance standards. If pressed hard enough, companies eventually agree to those standards, knowing that state regulatory staffs are inadequate to monitor all sites to assure that performance standards are met.

TCC representatives employed traditional communication tactics to gain public support and allay fears about the proposed plant's operations. They prepared and circulated position papers and used other publications to extol the economic virtues of the plant's construction and operation. They described its technology and marshaled experts in its defense. They purchased newspaper ads to promote the project. They sought endorsements by editorialists. They lined up local business and government leaders to voice approval for the project as a safe and vital remedy for the local economy. They spoke on these issues at public hearings, where they emphasized their long-time association with the community and asserted that they wanted everyone to know that they were doing the right thing.

At each milestone victory in the permitting process, a company spokesperson proudly proclaimed how fair the review process was and how the proposed plant design was being vindicated against critics. Local newspapers published that kind of statement, sometimes expressing relief at the progress and sometimes exhibiting a note of apprehension that the executives might be portraying a rosier picture than would come true during operations. Local newspapers published letters to the editors by plant spokespersons who wrote to clarify previous statements that had been printed or to refute critics by claiming that they were misinformed regarding technical aspects of the smelting or wastewater discharge process. A central theme was that the review process was adequate to safeguard public health and safety as well as environmental quality. If the regulatory agencies said the plant was safe to construct and operate, then that was fact, not controversial opinion and speculation. Throughout this effort, TCC provided a lot of data on the assumption that increased knowledge would allay public fear. On August 12, 1990, the *Galveston Daily News* saluted the new facility for its environmental responsibility and contribution to the local economy in its feature titled "Hats Off to Success!" (p. 5A).

TCC spokespersons claimed that, along with one in Timmins, Canada, a similar facility was operating responsibly in Naoshima, Japan. Videotaped presentations about the Naoshima site included scenes of plant operations, along with testimonials from local residents and fishermen about the lack of environmental harm from the plant. TCC spokespersons took their show on the road. Ready to speak at local civic associations, they stressed three themes: safe, state-of-the-art operations; strong need for domestic production of copper; and a shot in the arm for the local economy.

This project would have progressed through construction to operation if its representatives had not blundered in their approach to the project's critics. Municipal leaders in communities adjacent to Texas City feared that property values would be hurt by the plant. Opponents from other sectors of the economy, particularly tourism and fishing, worried that the plant would harm the environment and damage their industries. Local toxicologists insisted that too much is known about these toxic metals to feel safe and that too little is known about their accumulative effect on life forms in the bay and on its shores. Lead is well known to be a harmful substance. Its effects were made salient by locally publicized discussions of the need for lead removal as old homes in the region were being restored. Stories abounded about the discovery of sites in the region where toxic substances, including lead, had been found. Some sites, including the World War II tin plant, had remained virtually unchanged, not degrading, and could be placing toxic materials into public water systems. Lead is particularly scary to parents of young children, whose nervous systems are susceptible to permanent damage from lead poisoning. People were uncertain about the design specifications of the wastewater treatment system, the long-term build up in the bay, and current movements in the bay that could distribute metals to areas not foreseen by planners and regulators.

Several groups protested the plant's petition for operating permits. Many of them were small and had little financial or human resources to sustain them, but they did attract attention. Such groups concocted names for themselves that were shortened to clever acronyms proclaiming dire consequences. For instance, a group known as TOCSICK (Texans Opposed to Copper Smelters in Communities with Kids) fanned the apprehension parents have regarding exposing children to lead. The media seemed to like the groups and perhaps gave them more attention than they deserved. On their own, they lacked political savvy and popular support and therefore posed little threat to TCC's efforts, but they helped keep the issue visible and made better organized groups more effective. In this discussion climate, persons concerned about health were likely to have been alarmed by the discovery that two flounders, a popular sports fish, caught in the bay contained a level of 2.5 parts per million of lead, a level high enough to harm children and pregnant women.

Other protest groups opposing TCC had earned records that should have been read with caution by any company that intended to do business in ways thought to be environmentally unsound. These groups were worthy opponents for huge international companies and the Texas good ol' boy regulatory system. The Galveston Bay Foundation and the Galveston Bay Conservation and Preservation Association had long, distinguished track records of protecting and promoting Galveston Bay. They had battle scars from encounters with chemical companies, municipalities, and the international shipping industry that navigates the channel in the bay.

TCC made a grave mistake when it did not distinguish the powerful from the fringe groups and try to work with the former to ascertain and meet community expectations. Activists were able to fill small auditoriums with persons who opposed TCC during permit hearings. They gave the impression of representing a larger segment of the public than was probably the case.

As protesters gained momentum and passed out more flyers, the project representatives increased their campaign. More ads were placed in local newspapers. Three billboards associated Texas Copper Corporation with positive attributes: good neighbor, strong local tax base, jobs, and environmental responsibility. If the issue were left to a vote by local citizens, a majority of them would have supported the plant. Many of them exhibited high risk tolerance. An independent survey of Texas City residents found that 52% supported and 36% opposed construction of the smelter; 12% would not commit to a position (Nathan, Heath, & Douglas, 1992).

By this time, however, TCC representatives had made a fatal mistake. They had begun to think of their critics in denigrating terms, a sentiment that filtered into their public statements. These comments were intended to marginalize critics by calling them "outsiders," "Yankees" (a damning term in Texas), "bird lovers," "jerks," "pipsqueak politicians of the leisure set," "crackpots," and "meddlers." TCC voiced confidence that state officials would see the critics as whiners. Instead of seeking out leaders of opponent groups and discussing issues with them in private, TCC representatives alleged that their opponents lacked expertise, operated from base motives, and failed to see the big picture of economic growth for a troubled region. These newsworthy statements showed an uncaring spirit for concerned citizens.

To the recommendation that they hire ethical public relations counsel, TCC representatives responded that no one trusts PR people and anyone with half a brain can do PR. To the suggestion that they invite responsible activists to serve as advisers, the response was that they could no longer talk to those folks because they would not listen to reason. To the advice that they needed to lessen criticism by giving the public more say over the design of the plant and evaluation of its impact, TCC representatives said the critics could have that influence when they had investment money on the line. A smug reliance on the good ol' boy system underpinned every reaction to advice.

Then TCC ran up against a local environmental attorney, Jim Blackburn, who used two tactics decisively. He put together a loose coalition of critics and had them endorse him as their sole representative. That kept activists from looking like a tattered, ragtag array of marginalized whiners. He filed an injunction against a recently awarded permit, one of many, and asked for new hearings based on the charges that TCC had engaged in distortion and less than full disclosure. He vowed to fight the issue in court, as well as in the regulatory arena.

By May 1991, the CEO of Texas Copper and general manager of TCC's parent company, Mitsubishi Materials Corporation, Izumi Sukekawa, had arrived. He had to confront the issue of trust, which had been severely damaged by the discovery that TCC had withheld or distorted crucial data. A major report submitted by TCC was honored by the review panel despite the fact that it contained substantial flaws in the models used to analyze the potential impact of wastewater discharge. In contrast to lenient treatment of TCC data, the commission ignored independent reports from three prominent local scientists, including a nationally famous toxicologist.

The activists were ready to play tough. One condition for ongoing negotiation was that prominent U.S. representatives of TCC could no longer be on the negotiating team. One member of that group, the president of TCC, had been found to have misrepresented Galveston Bay Foundation's position to Mr. Sukekawa. At this point in the proceedings, TCC still had to receive permits from Texas Air Control, the U.S. Army Corps of Engineers, and the Environmental Protection Agency. Many critics wondered in the press whether this process would be eased by the presence of a prominent TCC employee who had worked for the U.S. Corps of Engineers.

In August 1991, participants in the permitting process publicly claimed that they had never been betrayed and lied to so often as they had been by the representatives of TCC. These persons believed that hostility would persist for years. Sukekawa took over the negotiations and invited Blackburn to his home for dinner and conversation. Promising to use a superior process for removing toxic materials from the wastewater discharge, Sukekawa agreed to allow an environmental engineer selected by the activists to be the watchdog for the process.

Nevertheless, distrust was high. Even though Sukekawa promised to distance himself from Thomas Mackey, president of TCC, many doubted that would be the case. Mackey was a personal friend of Takeshi Nagano, chairman of Mitsubishi Materials Corporation. One of Mackey's companies held options on the land where the plant would be built. His 34 years of residence in the area had earned him an insider's place in the game. Critics of TCC were split over their opposition. Some believed that the new deal lessened the effect of the plant on Galveston Bay and wanted to allow the start of construction. Others doubted that Sukekawa was any different from Mackey, and thought he was merely pretending to favor conciliation. Close analysis of the other two plants owned and operated by Mitsubishi revealed that both operated at higher levels of environmental responsibility than would the Texas City plant. Critics used the Timmins and Naoshima plants as analogies to improve the Texas City plant design. One reporter asked, "Texas Copper promises to minimize its proposed smelter's pollution of Galveston Bay. Why doesn't everybody believe it?" (Barth, 1991).

Events had reached a point where trust, technical explanation and evaluation, conciliation, and compromise were becoming ineffective. Concern over the situation was expressed in the outdoor and recreation column of the *Houston Post,* written by Ken Grissom. On January 19, 1992, he voiced the worries of sports fishermen, commercial fishermen, local residents, and environmentalists: "Did the Galveston Bay Foundation cop out on Texas Copper? Will the Japanese-owned copper smelter become a millstone around the neck of the conservation organization? Or will it be the good neighbor its billboards promised, bringing needed jobs to the area without sacrificing the already overstressed ecology?" Concern centered on the agreement by the Galveston Bay Foundation and the Galveston Bay Conservation and Preservation Association to cease opposition to the Texas Water Commission (TWC) permit allowing discharge of wastewater into Galveston Bay. In exchange, Sukekawa agreed to a treatment process that was 5 to 10 times cleaner than TWC required. The parties indicated that they were having fruitful negotiations on other permits.

On March 12, 1992, TCC management proclaimed the death of its project, naming "red tape" as the culprit. Long delays in the permitting process had destroyed the resolve of the company, which had better use for its capital than holding it in reserve while a handful of critics filed for rehearings on the permits it had received. The irony of this front-page news was the reported comment by "two environmental groups [that] scoffed at the company's explanation, claiming that Texas Copper's biggest problem was that it just couldn't get the hang of the application procedure" (Loddeke, 1992, p. A20). Expressing disbelief and outrage over loss of the project were the mayors of Texas City and Galveston, the two largest cities in the area, and Senator Phil Gramm.

The case described above features ingredients important to risk communication: knowledge, uncertainty regarding the extent of a problem, cognitive involvement based on self-interest, control, conflicting interests, risk intolerance, and trust based on personal reputations and relationships among key players. Lacking faith in TCC and the regulatory system, activists wanted to control the operation and reduce risks to a tolerable level. This case demonstrates the importance of the infrastructure in each community and reminds plant management of the importance of not lying, of not assuming that base appeals to community financial rewards can override uncertainty about public health and environmental impact, and of not underestimating the power of cognitively involved activists.

CREATING CITIZENS' ADVISORY COUNCILS

In marked contrast to the strained and unproductive relationships among the players in the TCC case, the following example emphasizes how all of the variables in a community communication infrastructure can work for a company and the members of the community at risk. A theme of activism in the 1960s was "Power to the People!" The challenge to corporate and government authority voiced in that slogan caught many people off guard. Industry, perhaps, was the most startled. The environmental movement included the petrochemical industry in its lineup of bad guys, despite the fact that the industry had reason to believe that it had made society better through its products. But friction existed and tensions mounted. What savvy chemical company managements have learned is the value of bringing the people to the chemical plant and the plant to the people. This example demonstrates the importance of sharing control with and listening to members of the community as means for increasing trust through dialogue. Rather than forcing cognitively involved members of the community to a confrontational stance, citizens' advisory boards allow long-term opportunities for active members of a community to voice concerns and technically expert personnel from a plant to explain technical concepts and processes. This dialogic approach exemplifies the importance of developing positive relationships slowly and patiently.

One of the first major responses to the dissent and difference of opinion regarding plant operations was initiated by the Chemical Manufacturers Association (CMA) through a series of ads placed in newsmagazines to proclaim that chemical plants are safe. Plant safety is associated with commitment to community. Spokespersons featured in the ads said that they had raised their families in neighborhoods near chemical plants, and that their children would eventually do the same. The plot of this narrative was "All is well." The tactic did not work. It was too general, it was self-serving, and it failed to address key publics whose interpretations of the data were different from those of company or industry spokespersons. Concerned citizens had their own data and drew their own conclusions.

A new option promoted by CMA to enhance the quality of risk communication seems to be making progress. It entails creation of citizens' advisory councils (CACs), two of which have been implemented by one of the most responsive chemical companies in the Houston area. These councils were initiated in 1990 as part of CMA's Responsible Care program. (Sometimes *care* is used as the acronym CAER, community awareness and emergency response.) The project began with a proposal by the public affairs group to executive management. The proposal preached the theme of community outreach and included a design of the CACs and a statement of project outcomes. The proposal acknowledged that if the CACs were going to work, the company had to be prepared to relinquish some control over information and acknowledge that legitimate grievances by CAC members would have to be addressed, perhaps through improved plant performance. Making that commitment was a serious undertaking, because it assumed capital expenditure and recognized that, once initiated, the CACs could not be abandoned without embarrassment. Creation of the CACs could, probably would, result in increased costs, which might hurt the profit margin and demand other changes on the part of the company if it were to remain competitive. This kind of proposal is not easy for managements to approve in times when profit margins are paper thin.

After careful deliberation, executives approved the creation of two CACs, one each for two plant locations. The goal for the creation of the CACs was to improve the dialogue between industry and community. No specific performance standards were set as measures of the success of the dialogue; it was intended to be organic and take on its life through the membership rather than being used by the company merely to pass information to the community.

A third-party facilitator was hired and assigned the responsibilities of constituting a steering committee and drafting a charter. This activity took six months. The steering committee of each council consisted of seven members who were invited to participate because of their records of community service. Once the charter was in place, the next task was to enlarge the councils, which began meeting once a month in 1991 and continue to meet. CAC members are well known for their participation in local business, civic groups, churches, and schools. Also selected have been members of activist groups. Some of these persons are interested in public health and environmental problems, such as members of CCAP (Concerned Citizens Against Pollution). A prominent member of the Sierra Club who does not live in the neighborhood was nevertheless willing to participate. He could contribute valuable insights and raise issues derived from years of activism in a major national environmental group.

The size of each council varies, but averages 15 members from the community and 4 from the sponsoring company. Some members remain on a council for a long time, and others drop out for a variety of reasons. For a while, a member of one CAC represented an aggressive and vocal environmental group in Southeast Texas; other members of that group attended meetings. For the most part, the most vocal and demanding activists lose interest in the CAC, which seems to move more slowly and quietly than they prefer. Radical activists thrive on claims that companies are inaccessible and unconcerned about public sentiments. The CACs refute that claim by their presence and by their slow, methodical discussion and resolution of issues.

Each CAC meeting centers on an agenda that is prepared by the facilitator, who continuously polls CAC members to determine which topics are most important to them. The facilitator then sets priorities for the order in which topics are discussed. If a topic comes up in the community as an expression of public concern, it can be placed on the agenda at any meeting. The CAC meetings are public, but only members can participate for most of the meeting. The agenda includes the opportunity for other persons, including industry representatives, to present and discuss hot topics. Often the company reports on its activities and shares reports that it believes might be useful to the CAC. For instance, if the company has engaged in some operation that has caused community concern, an explanation of the activity may be provided and people may have an opportunity to ask questions and voice concerns. At each meeting, resource people are available to handle special issues, especially those requiring technical details about operations, chemical processes, or policies. The public is welcome to sit as an audience, but may voice opinions and raise issues only at the end of the meeting. Some issues that are raised by the public serve as topics for agendas at subsequent meetings, but most concerns are addressed at the time they are raised. The CACs are designed to avoid or at least lessen the appearance that tough issues are postponed and eventually forgotten. The presence and operation of the CACs are intended to be rhetorical statements of the company's responsive concern for the public interest.

Measures of success that one could use to assess the effects of the CACs are as much a matter of what does not happen as of what does. No formal measures, such as attitude toward the company, have been used; none have been proposed. Some indicators consist of positive and negative comments that are volunteered by CAC members about the company and the CAC process. These comments have become increasingly positive and are interpreted by the company's manager of public affairs to indicate that the company is building a constructive relationship with its key publics. These comments are believed to be widely held throughout the community, based on the assumption that if influence leaders in the community are more favorable toward the chemical company they are likely to voice positive or neutral comments to their friends and neighbors rather than negative ones.

Members of the CACs see the company as honest, open, and willing to engage in candid dialogue, not merely as using the CACs as a public relations tool for hyping company accomplishments, putting the best spin on problems, or glossing and ignoring issues that demand significant change. A strong measure of the CACs' success is the fact that community leaders use them as means for raising issues, seeking information about plant operations, and voicing concerns. This forum is preferred over voicing concerns to reporters and raising issues in the media to force the company to respond. Company personnel believe that the CACs are an excellent listening post for finding out about the sentiments of the community. Company members think that the CACs help them to obtain a sense of how key publics view their company, to understand which aspects of their operations are troubling, and to grasp how accurately key publics understand plant operations.

The CACs serve as focus groups that company personnel employ to understand how to communicate better with members of the community. For example, the plant used comments from CAC members as it began to implement its community alert system. Typical of those used by many other chemical plants, the alert system includes a siren that is sounded in the event that a toxic or hazardous emission occurs and moves airborne beyond the plant boundary. As soon as possible after the release occurs and the siren is sounded, the company broadcasts on a dedicated special AM radio channel that the substance was released and announces measures the public should take. These can range from continuing normal activities, to staying indoors until the material has dissipated, to evacuation in the event of a massive release of some highly dangerous material.

CAC members aided the company in the design of messages that are put out on the "Careline." These are recorded messages that people can obtain by dialing a designated telephone number. Such messages are made available to explain occurrences or plant processes that may disturb members of the community. For instance, some chemicals stink, even in extremely low parts-per-million volumes. Persons who smell them may be legitimately concerned about the safety of breathing them. In such an event, a message is made available for residents who dial the Careline. Members of the community complained that some messages insulted their intelligence, pandered to them, or glossed over or dismissed concerns they had for their safety and welfare. They felt that some messages conveyed an inappropriate or offensive tone (e.g., suggesting little concern about the event) or were uninformative (e.g., using technical jargon unfamiliar to callers). Because the messages are stored and used for any recurrences of events, the company had reason to develop standardized messages that convey the information the public wanted, and in the proper tone. The company played the Careline messages for the CACs and received suggestions on how to frame them more effectively. Now, to the extent possible, all new messages are screened through the CAC prior to being placed on the Careline. One measure of the success of this process is a decreased number of complaints about the tone and/or content of these messages.

Of similar importance was the complaint that plant personnel used an interrogating tone when people called to talk to them about some event. The standardized form used by plant personnel included, for instance, a place to record the caller's name, address, and phone number. The plant representatives had not been instructed to indicate to callers that giving this information was optional, and members of the public feared that it could be used to mete out retribution (high constraint recognition; Grunig, 1992). The form was changed to emphasize that personal details were optional but important to the company so that its representatives could get back to the person with an explanation of the event. Complaints regarding giving personal data ceased.

A current undertaking of the CACs is the work of a subcommittee to discuss action plans for reducing emissions of chemicals that are listed as hazardous by the Superfund Amendment Reauthorization Act of 1986. Dialogue in the subcommittee and that will transpire in the entire CAC will focus on the problems, solutions, and risks associated with reducing the emission of those materials. That dialogue can assist the company in its planning efforts and help CAC members (and eventually the community at large) to understand the problems and corrective measures associated with changing plant design and operations. The discussion demonstrates the care and attention the company is willing to invest in doing business in a way that asserts its stewardship role in the community. Although ever likely to be impatient at the speed at which plants change, the members of the CAC get a much better sense of how difficult such changes are and how carefully planned change needs to be to avoid unnecessary expenditures or unwise safety measures.

The CAC is not only a communication vehicle that seems to work because it gives members of the community a sense of sharing power with the company; it is also a planning device that can help the company sense and avoid problems through the way they are approached. It gives the plant personnel a barometer of the priorities among issues as viewed by influential members of the community. It helps plant management communicate with the community. The dialogue seems to be genuine, acknowledging the interests and needs of both parties. Even more important, it appears to meet the standard of helping the company to be an honest and effective member of the community (Kruckeberg & Starck, 1988).

The citizens' advisory council operationalizes the spirit of risk democracy advocated by the National Research Council (1989). The council notes that risk communication is *"an interactive process of exchange of information and opinion among individuals, groups, and institutions. It involves multiple messages about the nature of risk and other messages, not strictly about risk, that express concerns, opinions, or reactions to risk messages or to legal and institutional arrangements for risk management."* It is "successful only to the extent that it raises the level of understanding of relevant issues or actions and satisfies those involved that they are adequately informed within the limits of available knowledge" (p. xi).

Many risk communication lessons can be learned from these CACs. Communities want to feel that they have sufficient control over harmful processes that transpire in them. Attempts to inform publics about technical issues, concepts, and processes must be accompanied by patience, tolerance for disagreement, openness, trust, and the development of opinion leaders who convey and translate technical information to key publics. Communication styles matter. The company must demonstrate its stewardship through an honest desire to be understood and to understand not only through words but through actions.

TRAINING TECHNICAL EXPERTS
AS RISK COMMUNICATORS

Some companies that manufacture chemicals have discovered that plant operating personnel and employees in charge of environmental compliance are excellent candidates to be public communicators. Often overlooked in the past because they are not polished speakers and may be hesitant as they show genuine concern for expressing technical issues properly, these personnel present themselves and their ideas with depth of knowledge and a strong commitment to exploring issues with scientific certainty. Their cautious attention to detail and firm resolve that they understand technical issues offer such personnel public speaking qualities that are rarely found in persons who are polished communicators but lack the knowledge of technical issues and operations required to answer the tough questions that concern the public. These technically educated personnel are often frustrated by the slow progress they make in informing audiences who lack technical education. These communicators would prefer a linear, hypodermic communication process, whereby technical information could be injected into nontechnical audiences. Once they realize that this model does not work, they become resolved to explain patiently the processes and controls exerted to achieve safety and environmental responsibility. During such discussions, they become increasingly sensitive to what key publics do not know and how difficult it is for them to grasp technical issues.

Because of these positive attributes, such personnel have begun to emerge from behind plant boundaries to take their places on panels and as company spokespersons. They often are the best participants in dialogue programs with environmental activists, regulators, technicians, and scientists. Two of these people in the Houston area, for instance, have taken on a role they had not imagined as they studied chemical engineering and achieved the status of professional engineers. Instead of being in front of the audience, public relations personnel in these companies are behind the scenes helping these experts to prepare themselves and their materials to make effective presentations. These experts speak with authority that comes from commitment to use scientific research to solve problems. They are not glib, but they can be assertive when presenting facts or in the discussion of technical concepts.

These individuals are the new breed of risk communicator. They attend conferences on technical risk topics and regulatory processes. They give testimony at hearings. They get involved with trade associations and help to create in those associations a spirit of friendly cooperation with environmentalists and concerned citizens. Not only can they challenge statements made by outrageously misinformed critics, they are also prepared because of their scientific education to appreciate the concerns people have about things they do not understand. This kind of spokesperson has become increasingly valuable as environmentalists and concerned citizen groups have begun to commission studies of their own and to hire their own experts. They understand technical reports and the scientific methodologies used in conducting those studies. They can critique the methodologies or applaud findings that add new, important insights into technical problems they are trying to solve for their companies. Rather than exhibiting the bold, assertive persona that is easy for public relations persons to adopt, these spokespersons convey a sense of inquiry and learning. Open to comments and criticism from external audiences and groups of apprehensive employees, they realize that displays of scientific expertise can sometimes count for a lot when people are uncertain about the health hazards of living or working in proximity to toxic materials.

A case in point: Following a release of cyanide in a plant, some workers voiced grave concern about their safety. Known to be used for capital punishment and predator control, cyanide is a chemical that most people believe is dangerous. An environmental engineer used a device that tests the amount of cyanide in the air to determine whether it exceeded safe limits. The engineer announced that the levels were okay, quite safe. The workers were not satisfied —they feared a company cover-up. The engineer then asked one of the workers to light a cigarette. The smoke from the cigarette was drawn into the measuring device, which indicated that the amount of cyanide in tobacco smoke was five times higher than that in the ambient air of the plant, despite the release. The workers were amazed and no longer fearful.

Spokespersons with technical expertise work hard to get their messages across. They oversee the content of training tapes used to instill in technical and operations plant personnel the corporate culture that their managements do not tolerate pollution. They stress to operations workers that they are responsible for assuring compliance rather than being expected to cover up environmental problems or covertly contribute to them by sloppy operations or by committing illegal actions, such as dumping or discharging toxic materials in violation of regulations. The lesson to be learned is this: Technical topics require expertise that most public relations personnel do not have. Trust comes through the process of technical communication as much as from the content.

IMPLEMENTING AN OPEN-DOOR POLICY

One chemical plant in the Texas gulf coast region has undertaken an aggressive employee empowerment effort to stress to its personnel, as well as report to the public, how well empowered engineering and operating personnel do in abating environmental discharges. The employees benefit from improving the performance of their plant. For instance, when new engineering techniques are proven and patented, the relevant personnel receive monetary rewards when proprietary processes are used by other plants. The result: Although this is the largest plant in the region, its environmental emission levels are among the lowest. This favorable outcome results from a culture that empowers employees to improve plant operations. It results in openness to those members of the public who have sufficiently high levels of cognitive involvement that they are motivated to monitor plant operations.

Another part of the company's risk communication effort entails the construction of a small building near the main gate to the plant. In the building are located, for public scrutiny, all of the performance reports the company files with regulatory agencies. All of the permits, whether pending or approved, are available for public review. A clerk is available to take requests for additional information that visitors might desire and to assist them in their efforts to locate particular documents. When the building was first opened, it attracted a steady stream of concerned citizens. Now it rarely has a visitor but remains fully available to anyone seeking information. The dwindling stream of visitors may indicate that surrounding community members believes the company is operating in their interest and does not pose an intolerable risk. Uncertainty about risks is lowered by the demonstration of openness as well as by the documented progress toward achieving zero emissions.

LOSING THE BATTLE FOR TRUST

The first example in this chapter pointed to failures on the part of chemical plant management to satisfy the uncertainty experienced by neighbors who worried that plant operations would harm public health or the environment. The following, and final, example also focuses on failed efforts to respond to public needs. It demonstrates how a dominant sender can mistakenly assume that it can design and convey a message to allay fears of a public on the assumption that the concern will be allayed if the public understands issues as the company and its expert do. A company that has superior technical insights into chemical processes and plant operations, according to this view, can build community understanding and support merely by reporting its operations and plant design decisions. Such a company tends to exhibit a high degree of paranoia when its technical and operating expertise is challenged. Its culture hinders its ability to listen to critics and to design messages and conduct communication campaigns that address issues from audiences' points of view and give them answers they find useful.

The major problem with the plant in this example is its miserable history of violating state and federal regulations, a history of performing in ways that destroy key publics' trust. For instance, Delaware revoked one of the company's facilities' 37 operating permits in 1985 because it had violated state air quality standards. The Texas facility had, by January 1992, been assessed nearly $350,000 in penalties for 32 violations since 1984. In addition, the EPA had imposed a $3.37 million fine for contamination of soil and water. The attorney for Calhoun County Resource Watch asked during a permit hearing that the state close the plant and pursue criminal charges for willful pollution violations. Critics charged plant management with engaging in deception while ostensibly providing accurate and full information about its operating standards and its parent company's environmental record.

Despite all of the news of environmental violations by the company, a survey conducted by an independent research team found that 66% of the local residents in this small community supported the company because of its economic benefits, whereas 26% opposed it (Heath, Liao, & Douglas, 1993). The plant had created 4,000 jobs during the construction period and 1,000 permanent positions when operations started. When the plant started construction in 1990, local unemployment fell from 5.4% to 5.0% in one month. Sales tax collections for September 1990 were up 540% compared with the same month a year earlier.

The Texas Building and Construction Trades Council joined ranks with local environmental groups to protest operations at the plant that it characterized as "one of the most sloppily built chemical facilities in the history of the state." In response to claims by the union and inquiries by state permitting agencies, plant officials reported that they had made appropriate progress with the changes required by law (Thomas, 1992).

As part of a petition to receive permits for a $1.3 billion plant expansion, a controversy arose over the location of the wastewater discharge outflow. Environmentalists and state officials opposed the location of discharge proposed by the plant because of fear of damage to a shallow estuary. The discharge volume was estimated to be 10 million gallons each day. Alternative discharge points were available, but each option presented by the plant to the permitting agency would cost the company more money. Company spokespersons assured its critics that additional costs were unnecessary because of the results of a study regarding the volume of water carried in the estuary. Opposing that conclusion was the Gulf Coast Conservation Association, a group that has environmental concerns in part because of its interest in sports fishing, which countered that the study had been conducted under abnormally rainy conditions and did not take account of drought conditions.

Is this company making progress toward erasing its bad reputation and moving to earn community trust? Perhaps. In 1992, it signed an agreement that allowed outside auditors to monitor its compliance with safety and environmental regulations. Rather than relying exclusively on the company as the source of information, the public now had a watchdog. This commission was authorized to force the company to take needed corrective actions.

Two aggressive environmental groups opposed this move, complaining that the accord created the false impression that the company had changed its organizational culture and was now willing to be a model citizen. Raw edges existed among the company critics. One local activist had demonstrated her opposition by staging a hunger strike that drew a lot of media attention, especially when she was hospitalized after one month of protest. This agreement between one faction and plant management frustrated efforts by two unions that had wanted guarantees to allow unionization as a means of assuring worker safety. Praising the accord, the attorney representing it called it an environmental protection plan that would achieve higher standards of plant performance than existed for any other facility in the United States.

In turbulent times, uncertainty and distrust soar. Highly involved people struggle to control sources of risk that affect their self-interests. Information and knowledge become less relevant to the need to exert control because they are only loosely related to risk tolerance. Overregulation and long-term distrust are likely to result when companies operate from the premise that they have solutions to abate risks despite the absence of track records of community stewardship. Whereas the first example presented in this chapter featured the failure of the communication style of plant management to convince the public to buy a pig in a poke, the failure in this last example is of a different kind. Instead of having no track record to use to judge the plant management's sense of social responsibility, key members of the public have had ample opportunity to see the fruits of an unconstructive dialogue with plant management. The management tends to opt for a communication style that assumes that key activists would agree, "If you knew what I knew, you'd make the same decision" (Gaudino, Fritsch, & Haynes, 1989, p. 299).

CONCLUSION

Risk communication constitutes an array of options. They include a technical expert's attempt to explain chemical processes and meteorological modeling of wind currents to a group of concerned citizens who live near a plant, periodically smell odors, and worry that emissions harm them, their property, their families, and the community. Communication tactics include chemical plants sponsoring Audubon Society bird counts on their premises to determine the impact plant operations have on bird populations. Plant tours conducted by technical experts who explain processes and operating policies to concerned members of the community can replace stonewalling as a communication tactic. However, no strategy is universally effective; no magic buttons can be pushed to explain technical concepts or processes and thereby allay fears.

Nevertheless, an information-based approach to risk communication seems to dominate. Hadden (1989), Kalikow (1984), and Otway and Wynne (1989) all argue that if information and knowledge are fundamental to the regulation of industrial risks, then policy makers and risk experts must consider carefully the kinds of information laypersons need and can use. The informational model features experts as sources, messages as information about risk levels, media reporters and editors as channels, and receivers—an amorphous public. A typical weakness of this model is that risk messages suffer from "deficiencies in scientific understanding, data, models, and methods, which result in large uncertainties in risk estimates; and highly technical analyses that are often unintelligible to lay persons" (Covello et al., 1987, p. 110). Other source problems include "lack of trust and credibility; disagreements among scientific experts; limited authority and resources for addressing risk problems; lack of data addressing the specific fears and concerns of individuals and communities; failure to disclose limitations of risk assessments and resulting uncertainties; limited understanding of the interests, concerns, fears, values, priorities, and preferences of individual citizens and public groups; and use of bureaucratic, legalistic, and technical language" (pp. 110-111). Channels are affected by "selective and biased media reporting that emphasizes drama, wrongdoing, disagreements, and conflict; premature disclosures of scientific information; and oversimplification and distortions of, as well as inaccuracies in, interpreting technical risk information" (p. 111). Receivers suffer "inaccurate perceptions of levels of risk; lack of interest in risk problems and technical complexities; overconfidence in the ability to avoid harm; strong beliefs and opinions that are resistant to change; exaggerated expectations about the effectiveness of regulatory actions; desire and demand for scientific certainty; reluctance to make trade-offs among different types of risk or among risks, costs, and benefits; and difficulties in understanding probabilistic information related to unfamiliar technology" (pp. 111-112).

Although information and knowledge are vital to risk estimation and control, an approach to risk communication that too singularly features those variables can underemphasize other relevant concepts. Such an approach can fail to recognize that no matter how strong the informative effort of risk experts, different levels of risk tolerance exist in a community. These levels change over time, for each person and throughout a community. Too many variables exist in each risk case for one to be able to argue reasonably that enough time can be spent informing people of risks, the estimates of the harms, and the corrective measures that bring them to tolerable levels. To be viable, a risk communication model needs to acknowledge community dynamics, especially a demonstrated earnestness by responsive players to understand all of the issues, solve problems, and improve conditions. Analysis should center on the processes of risk decision making and shared control by concerned members of a community at risk.

Views on risk communication are inadequate to the extent that they slight the political dynamics that emerge in communities when a motivated segment of the population experiences a sufficiently high level of risk intolerance to express concern about health and safety. Vital to understanding the dynamics of this process are variables such as cognitive involvement, perceived balance of benefits and harms associated with the sources of risk, knowledge of risk and its abatement, control of the source of risk as well as personal destiny, and uncertainty (Nathan et al., 1992). Research has discovered that cognitive involvement is motivated by the degree to which persons believe their self-interests are positively or negatively affected (Petty & Cacioppo, 1981, 1986), in this case by losses and gains associated with chemical plant operations.

As postulated by Grunig's (1983, 1992) situational theory, persons experiencing higher levels of cognitive involvement are prone to use more informative and analytic communication sources and to take strategic actions to impose public policies that protect their interests. Of importance to risk communication research is the realization that a majority of residents in a community support a local chemical plant because of financial benefits, despite controversy over the plant's environmental record. In contrast to studies that feature people who oppose the sources of risk, researchers should capture the dynamic exchange and power struggle between supporters and opponents, a community contesting its standards (Heath & Douglas, 1990, 1991; Heath et al., 1993).

Community communication infrastructures have only begun to receive research attention (Conn, Owens, Rich, & Manheim, 1988; Hadden, 1989; Rest, Krimsky, & Plough, 1991). Such analysis centers on organizations such as local emergency planning committees that can, but often do not, serve as points of influence for the community to exert self-control. Such studies often treat these groups as sources of information rather than as forums for dialogue.

Heath and Nathan (1991) have argued that when environmental health risk is created by a source over which the cognitively involved individual has minimal control, the risk model must emphasize community politics and conflicting levels of risk tolerance. Key elements of that model are the idiosyncratic personal and community standards of what constitutes a tolerable level of risk. Whereas policy makers typically base risk estimates on morbidity rates, community members use personal bases for estimating levels of risk. One key to understanding the community decision heuristic is the analysis of the idiosyncratic ways in which individuals, technical professionals, and policy makers evaluate risks (Tversky & Kahneman, 1986). Different levels of tolerance exist. Evaluations of what levels are appropriate are subjected to public debate (often involving community and environmental activism).

Future research needs to place more emphasis on community dynamics: collective efforts to assess and control risks, at multiple levels of analysis, reflecting different amounts of risk tolerance and assuming conflicting interests. Researchers and commentators tend to stress aspects of technical sources of information and opinion as central to the discussion of risk communication as though their standards of risk estimation and abatement can prevail in a community if they design messages properly. In contrast, the model of risk communication that is most likely to be productive is one that compares the expectations of self-performance, expectations of regulatory interests, and expectations of vested interests in the community. Gaps between what is known and what needs to be known, and between what is known and what is tolerated, are the heart of environmental risk communication. Research and practice of risk communication are likely to be most productive when they emphasize the centrality of a community of self-interests and a desire to exert control in behalf of those interests.

REFERENCES

Barth, L. (1991, August). Troubled waters. *Houston Metropolitan*, pp. 56-63.

Conn, W. D., Owens, W. L., Rich, R. C., & Manheim, J. B. (1988). *Processing hazardous materials risk information* (EPA Report). Washington, DC: Government Printing Office.

Covello, V. T. (1992). Risk communication: An emerging area of health communication research. In S. A. Deetz (Ed.), *Communication yearbook 15* (pp. 359-373). Newbury Park, CA: Sage.

Covello, V. T., Sandman, P. M., & Slovic, P. (1988). *Risk communication, risk statistics, and risk comparisons: A manual for plant managers.* Washington, DC: Chemical Manufacturers Association.

Covello, V. T., von Winterfeldt, D., & Slovic, P. (1987). Communicating scientific information about health and environmental risks: Problems and opportunities from a social and behavioral perspective. In J. C. Davies, V. T. Covello, & F. W. Allen (Eds.), *Risk communication* (pp. 109-128). Washington, DC: Conservation Foundation.

Davies, J. C., Covello, V. T., & Allen, F. W. (Eds.). (1987). *Risk communication.* Washington, DC: Conservation Foundation.

Gaudino, J. L., Fritsch, J., & Haynes, B. (1989). "If you knew what I knew, you'd make the same decision": A common misperception underlying public relations campaigns? In C. H. Botan & V. Hazleton, Jr. (Eds.), *Public relations theory* (pp. 299-308). Hillsdale, NJ: Lawrence Erlbaum.

Grissom, K. (1992, January 19). Agreement creates smelter watchdog. *Houston Post*, p. B20.

Grunig, J. E. (1983). Communication behaviors and attitudes of environmental publics: Two studies. *Journalism Monographs, 81,* 1-54.

Grunig, J. E. (Ed.). (1992). *Excellence in public relations and communication management.* Hillsdale, NJ: Lawrence Erlbaum.

Hadden, S. G. (1989). *A citizen's right to know: Risk communication and public policy.* Boulder, CO: Westview.

Heath, R. L., & Douglas, W. (1990). Involvement: A key variable in people's reaction to public policy issues. In J. E. Grunig & L. A. Grunig (Eds.), *Public relations research annual* (Vol. 2, pp. 93-204). Hillsdale, NJ: Lawrence Erlbaum.

Heath, R. L., & Douglas, W. (1991). Effects of involvement on reactions to sources of messages and to message clusters. In L. A. Grunig & J. E. Grunig (Eds.), *Public relations research annual* (Vol. 3, pp. 179-193). Hillsdale, NJ: Lawrence Erlbaum.

Heath, R. L., Liao, S., & Douglas, W. (1993). *Effects of perceived economic harms and benefits on issue involvement, information seeking, and action: A study in risk communication.* Paper presented at the annual meeting of the International Communication Association, Washington, DC.

Heath, R. L., & Nathan, K. (1991). Public relations' role in risk communication: Information, rhetoric and power. *Public Relations Quarterly, 35*(4), 15-22.

Kalikow, B. N. (1984). Environmental risk: Power to the people. *Technology Review, 87*(7), 55-61.

Kruckeberg, D., & Starck, K. (1988). *Public relations and community: A reconstructed theory.* New York: Praeger.

Loddeke, L. (1992, March 12). Mitsubishi drops plan for plant. *Houston Post,* pp. A1, A20.

McMurray, S. (1991, June 11). Chemical firms find that it pays to reduce pollution at source. *Wall Street Journal,* p. A1.

Nathan, K., Heath, R. L., & Douglas, W. (1992). Tolerance for potential environmental health risks: The influence of knowledge, benefits, control, involvement and uncertainty. *Journal of Public Relations Research, 4,* 235-258.

National Research Council. (1989). *Improving risk communication.* Washington, DC: National Academy Press.

Otway, H., & Wynne, B. (1989). Risk communication: Paradigm and paradox. *Risk Analysis, 9,* 141-145.

Petty, R. E., & Cacioppo, J. T. (1981). *Attitudes and persuasion: Classic and contemporary approaches.* Dubuque, IA: William C Brown.

Petty, R. E., & Cacioppo, J. T. (1986). *Communication and persuasion: Central and peripheral routes to attitude change.* New York: Springer-Verlag.

Rest, K., Krimsky, S., & Plough, A. (1991). *Risk communication and community right-to-know: A four community study of SARA Title III* (U.S. EPA assistance agreement no. CR813481). Medford, MA: Tufts University, Center for Environmental Management.

Sullivan, A. (1993, August 31). Oil industry projects a surge in outlays to meet U.S. environmental standards. *Wall Street Journal,* p. A2.

Thomas, K. (1992, March 4). Labor adds its muscle to state's quarrel with Formosa Plastics. *Houston Post,* p. C1.

Tversky, A., & Kahneman, D. (1986). Judgment under uncertainty: Heuristics and biases. In H. R. Arkes & K. R. Hammond (Eds.), *Judgment and decision making* (pp. 38-55). Cambridge: Cambridge University Press.

12 Attaining a State of Informed Judgments: Toward a Dialectical Discourse on Risk

NAPOLEON K. JUANILLO, Jr.
CLIFFORD W. SCHERER
Cornell University

The inadequacy of direct regulatory control of health, environmental, and technological hazards has triggered an accelerating interest in risk communication as an alternative form of risk management. This chapter discusses the assumptions and issues inherent in two paradigms of risk communication. The first paradigm, classical risk communication, follows a linear model that structures communication into senders, media, messages, and receivers. It aims to persuade the public in accepting scientific and bureaucratic judgments of risk acceptability as well as decisions on risk management. The second paradigm, dialectical risk communication, goes beyond ensuring that one's message is transmitted and listened to. Rather, it is a process of empowering stakeholders to appreciate different perspectives on risk, scrutinize opinions and perceptions about risk, and sharpen the skills necessary to make informed judgments that consequently have impacts on individual and community lifestyles and policies. The authors argue that the dialectical model of risk communication is best suited for providing the public a better understanding of issues that affect their decisions on health and safety.

R ISK communication, as currently practiced, evolved out of an imperative to offset the limitations of regulatory control over health, environmental, and technological hazards. As evidenced by the surge of large-scale awareness, safety information, and emergency response programs, risk communication became another form, if not a pragmatic alternative to, risk management. Designed to convey to the public the rational-technical knowledge grounded in risk assessment and risk management technologies, classical risk communication essentially translates as advocacy for determining which risks are acceptable.

Recently, however, questions have been raised over the assumptions of classical risk communication. Can this framework sufficiently address different communication needs and accommodate conflicting perspectives from various sources?

Correspondence and requests for reprints: Napoleon K. Juanillo, Jr., School of Communication Studies, Nanyang Technological University, Singapore 2263.

Communication Yearbook 18, pp. 278-299

Is it enough to see risk communication as a set of mechanical procedures that merely deal with the appropriate mix of persuasive and public relations techniques? Is it plainly a propagandistic communication that downplays the risks and pushes for their acceptance?

In this chapter we argue that, given the increasing public concern over what constitutes safety and risk, there is a need to reflect further on the meaning, context, structures, and assumptions of risk communication. We argue that a dialectical model of risk communication, which is essentially what "communication" is all about, is best suited for providing the public a better understanding of issues that affect their decisions on health and safety.

Dialectical risk communication is a democratic exchange of information, opinions, and issues concerning the assessment of risk and its acceptability among different stakeholders (that is, experts, policy makers, interest groups, and the general public). Reflecting a more Jeffersonian approach, this paradigm recognizes the complex scientific as well as sociopolitical values that the different actors bring into the process of transaction. Given the quality and quantity of information that can be derived from these interactive exchanges, dialectical risk communication can potentially foster critical thinking and provide stakeholders a better chance of attaining informed judgments or decisions about risk.

In this chapter, we discuss the assumptions and dilemmas inherent in both the classical risk communication model and the emerging dialectical paradigm of risk communication. In order to introduce the context in which risk controversies generally occur, we present a detailed background of the food safety debate. We examine the major issues that cast serious questions about the presumed societal benefits of conventional risk communication, and highlight some of the important principles that serve as the bases for shaping risk communication as a dialogue.

We conclude that, in principle, dialectical risk communication provides an effective framework through which policy decisions affecting public health and safety can be arrived at meaningfully. Such policy decisions acquire relevance as stakeholders engage in open dialogue about the different perspectives of an issue and suggest alternative solutions. However, dialectical risk communication is not a panacea to current public debates on acceptable levels of risk and safety. Any dialectical transaction, by nature, can potentially open up other avenues for debate and questioning. Perhaps it will not even provide an answer to the oft-repeated question, Is it safe or not safe? Rather, it will enable those involved to consider reasonable perspectives and form their judgments accordingly.

THE POLITICS OF RISKS:
THE CASE OF FOOD SAFETY

Questions about the safety of the food supply have challenged public trust and generated heated debates over the past two decades. The issues most familiar to consumers include the use of pesticides on food crops, possible carcinogenicity of color additives, dioxin leaching into milk from paperboard containers, and outbreaks of illness caused by salmonella bacteria in eggs and poultry. Recently, concerns over the potential risks of growth hormones such as bovine somatotropin (bST) and other products of agricultural biotechnology have exacerbated the public's confusion and sensitivity to matters of food safety (Archibald et al., 1988; Scherer, 1991; Segal, 1990).

Public outcry over food safety was particularly evident in 1989, which saw 250 organized boycotts of food products, compared with 100 to 150 in a usual year. A survey conducted among consumers that year showed that 62% changed their buying habits because of fear of food-related risks. Consumer confidence about the safety of the food supply dropped from 81% in January 1989 to 65% by June 1989 (Mueller, 1990). Likewise, trust in the ability of government to safeguard human health and safety plummeted. In another survey, 90% of the respondents said that they believed the government should do more to protect citizens from environmental and health risks. However, 90% of the respondents also said they did not trust the Environmental Protection Agency (EPA), the federal agency in which that function is vested (Kennedy, 1989).

Extensive mass media coverage of food safety controversies in 1989 added drama and intensity to the public's perceptions of food safety. On February 26, 1989, the popular television newsmagazine *60 Minutes* aired a segment titled "A Is for Apple," indelibly linking the all-American symbol of health, the apple, with questions of cancer risks in children. The program was shown one day before the release of a report by the Natural Resources Defense Council (NRDC) titled *Intolerable Risk: Pesticides in Our Children's Food*. The broadcast was introduced with an illustration showing a big red apple emblazoned with a skull and crossbones. It highlighted two major points found in the NRDC report: First, the Environmental Protection Agency has not paid adequate attention to children and infants in estimating dietary risks from pesticides; and second, when the EPA finds a pesticide used on food hazardous, it takes an unreasonable amount of time to limit further exposure (Arnold, 1990; Russell, 1990; Zeise, Painter, Berteau, Fan, & Jackson, 1991).

With an estimated 50 million television viewers, the *60 Minutes* segment on Alar had some telling consequences. According to reports, schools nationwide removed apples and apple products from cafeteria menus. Mothers dumped apple juice down the drain. Organic food stores were overrun with sudden demand for Alar-free apples as well as for organic and certified pesticide-free produce. The apple industry incurred irretrievable losses up to $200 million owing to lower sales, and beleaguered mom-and-pop apple growers brought a lawsuit for damages of more than $700 million (Arnold, 1990; Beck et al., 1989; Derr, 1989; Zind, 1990). A survey by the Wirthlin Group after the *60 Minutes* broadcast found that 6 out of 10 people had heard or read something that made them think apples were unsafe; 4 out of 10 specifically mentioned reports linking apples to pesticides that cause cancer (Arnold, 1990).

In March 1989, even as the controversy over Alar in apples smoldered, the discovery of Chilean grapes laced with negligible amounts of cyanide became the next staple of news headlines. All Chilean fruit already in the United States at that time was then withdrawn from the market. The cyanide incident was later found to be an apparent case of tampering. On September 2, 1989, United Press International reported highly toxic dioxins found in milk cartons, the result of chemicals used in the papermaking process. At various times during the year, there were news reports about salmonella bacteria showing up in a third of supermarket chickens; lethal *Listeria monocytogenes* bacteria being detected in cabbage, cucumbers, potatoes, and radishes; and fish contamination resulting from the *Exxon Valdez* oil spill in Alaska (Arnold, 1990; Beall, Bruhn, Craigmill, & Winter, 1991).

Public disapprobation and cynicism toward the safety of the food supply have remained unabated. Consumers persist in seeking categorical answers to questions about risks and safety. A survey conducted by the Food Marketing Institute (FMI) in 1991 showed that although 82% of the respondents expressed confidence that the food in supermarkets is safe, 75% indicated wariness of potential food hazards (Wolf, 1992).

Deaths in the Northwest in February 1993 caused by tainted hamburger also brought under public suspicion the efficiency of the government's meat inspection procedures and technology. Suggestions have been made concerning the use of irradiation for killing pathogens in meat. However, irradiation, although declared safe by many scientists, has met resistance from consumer groups that believe irradiation is unfit for use in preserving or disinfecting food because it causes harmful chemical changes and loss of vitamins.[1]

In March 1993, *Frontline,* a PBS television series, reexamined the potential risks of pesticide residues on children's health in a program titled "In Our Children's Food." Hosted by prominent journalist Bill Moyers, the show focused on how the government has failed to certify the safety of agricultural chemicals heavily used for decades and why the only source of data on pesticide safety is the industry that profits from pesticide use. While condemning no particular fruit or vegetable, the program castigated everyone from the chemical industry to the EPA and Congress for a clogged regulatory system that fails to ban harmful chemicals and does not address the special risks to children, who eat a lot more produce in relation to their body weight than do adults. The maximum levels of pesticide residues that are allowed to remain on produce are based on estimates of what adults, not children, eat. Like most media coverage of food-related risks, the show used melodramatic footage to prove its points. In one segment on a school playground, Bill Moyers asked a scientist from an environmental group if we know how much exposure to pesticides children are getting. The scientist said no, and the segment ended with a slow pan to an empty swing (Sugarman, 1993).

Later reinforcing this unsettling television documentary were the results of "Pesticides in the Diets of Infants and Children," a five-year study of the National

Academy of Sciences (NAS) on agricultural chemicals and how they affect children. In a report released June 30, 1993, the NAS acknowledged that infants and children may be uniquely sensitive to pesticides on food. The report noted that children consume more than 60 times what adults consume for their body weight and so tend to get higher doses of the pesticides used on fruits early in life. It faulted the government's method of calculating the safe level of pesticides on food and claimed that the three federal agencies that control the amount of pesticides permitted on food—the Agriculture Department, the Environmental Protection Agency, and the Food and Drug Administration—have outmoded policies that make it possible for children to get the same pesticide from several sources, and end up eating amounts of it that are unsafe (Hilts, 1993).

FOCUSING THE DEBATE:
SCIENCE AND PUBLIC VALUES

The intensification of debate over health and environmental risks manifests a decline of public confidence in scientific risk analysis, risk management decisions, and government regulations. The popular dispute over the safety of the food supply reflects other acrimonious conflicts that are being waged over such issues as landfill siting, groundwater quality, toxic wastes, and nuclear power. Until the 1970s, health or environmental risks identified with new technologies were generally accepted by the public as an unfortunate but inevitable price for the many material benefits that such technologies bring. Confidence remained high that more science would successfully resolve the problems created by science (Dickson, 1984).

Ironically, scientific progress has increased not only our ability to detect potential risks, but our ability to uncover previously unknown risks. As our understanding of the world grows, we are constantly confronted with uncertainties that leave considerable space for conflicting interpretations. This almost daily barrage of uncertainties and the widespread publicity they generate have led the public to view themselves as the victims, rather than as partakers and beneficiaries, of science and technology (Slovic, Fischhoff, & Lichtenstein, 1982). The questions are no longer so much, How safe is safe enough? or How fair is safe enough? Perhaps even more important, the question is now, Who shall decide? (Bazelon, 1979).

As von Schomberg (1993) argues, the relationship between science and public policy is built on precarious ground in the first place. Traditionally, the relationship between science and policy has always been functional. Decision making based on the data of scientific research manifests a belief in a scientific system that produced that information. The belief in science is functional because it is not founded on veracity, but rather on the competence and legitimacy of the scientific system. The complexity of certain questions and problems is so enormous that an intermediate party is needed for the production of information.

Because science information is considered reliable and practical, the scientific system is seen as fulfilling a social function.

However, controversy can shake the functional authority of science. The belief that the production of truth or facts is a function of the scientific institution cannot be built on conflicting versions of truths by experts. These conflicting interpretations cast doubt on the certainty and inclusiveness of previously accepted knowledge. They generate disputes about the methods used and what scientific discipline should lay claim to the best solution to the problem in question. Consequently, no consensus can be formed because the experts are not able to explicate the truth conditions of statements. Whatever consensus may exist among scientists can always be proven wrong at any moment by the discovery of some new phenomenon or simply by a change in scientific fashion (Collingridge & Reeve, 1986).

In discussions of scientific controversy, the plausibility of knowledge claims is laid out for judgment. The conflicting knowledge claims of the experts constitute epistemic uncertainty that eventually induces public debate. What constitutes significant and meaningful evidence? Whose judgment is to be considered in the evaluation of the severity and acceptability of risk? What rules of evidence should guide decision making and policy formation? What are the appropriate roles of government and of citizens in risk management? Who should be involved in decisions about risk? Who should control crucial policy choices related to the protection of human health and safety (Nelkin, 1985; von Schomberg, 1993)?

Growing disillusionment with the power of scientific knowledge to transform and rationalize the decisions and actions of government has led to a sober reassessment of the role of science in public life (Ezrahi, 1980).[2] Science has become both a source of progress and a harbinger of apprehension as the public has begun to fear not only the depersonalized knowledge represented by science, but also the uncertainties associated with technical advances such as those in biotechnology. Thus recombinant DNA research is, to some, a way of improving the human condition; to others it presents a threat to health (Nelkin, 1985).

Public ambivalence is not only a response to the obscurity and complexity of science. Controversies over science and technology also reflect broader social and political tensions in U.S. society—disagreement over the appropriate role of government, the struggle between individual autonomy and community goals, and the threat to the power of the citizen (Nelkin, 1985). It has been widely perceived that the growing importance of scientific expertise in policy decisions appears to limit the democratic process.

Although people's resentment toward health and environmental risks in the absence of compensating benefits is not a novelty,[3] what is new in the public's response to risks is its increased assertiveness as a part of the decision-making process on how those risks should be managed (Fischhoff, 1985). Litigation has increased as individuals seek redress and compensation for health problems resulting from exposure to toxic substances. Calls for legislative reform and regulatory action have escalated as advocacy groups have sought to change the standards regulating the use of agricultural chemicals on food crops and to assure the strict implementation of these standards (Nelkin, 1985). In 1984, for example, after research had suggested that ethylene dibromide (EDB) poses a risk of inducing cancer, an explosion of public fears pushed the EPA to restrict drastically the use of this fumigant to control pests in grain and cereal products. In 1985, public opinion kept the Oregon Department of Agriculture from using its preferred pesticides in a battle against gypsy moths (Fischhoff, 1985). Much of the criticism, focused through public interest groups such as the Natural Resources Defense Council, was aimed at the failure of traditional political institutions to inject social values into decision making on scientific and technological regulations that affect human health and safety. People now want to be informed about the risks they face, to have a role in setting regulatory limits, and to vote on the legitimacy of emerging agricultural and food-processing technologies (Fischhoff, 1985). Increasingly, the public has become reluctant to commit the resolution of such issues to the exclusive jurisdiction of experts and the state (Jasanoff, 1986).

Even among scientists, there have been efforts to develop the concept of "public interest science." Public interest science seeks greater community participation in decisions previously left to professional groups. It argues for the creation of decision-making mechanisms, with the government subsidizing public interest groups that lack the competence or technical expertise to mount complex technical arguments or challenge such arguments when made by others. Scientists Joel Primack and Frank von Hippel (1974), the prime movers behind this concept, note, "If scientists make available to citizens the information and analysis they need for the defense of their health and welfare, they can help bring more open and democratic controls on the uses of science and technology."

Because scientific assessments of risk have implications for public health and safety as well as political power, they are often contentious and emotional. Disputes over risk are not just about numbers; they are also about values. Agreements on the validity of the numbers do not resolve the differences. Although a dispute may seem to center on dose-response data, a closer examination will reveal that it also includes the issue of fairness, fear, and anger. For example, to some people, the mere possibility of an increase in cancer risk, no matter how small or speculative, is sufficient to justify stringent regulations on the use of a suspect chemical. Others argue that in the light of the many economic benefits many chemicals provide, people should not worry about such risks until they are convincingly proven to be substantial. Still others argue for various intermediary positions (Graham, Green, & Roberts, 1988). As Brunk, Haworth, and Lee (1991) note in their study of value judgments in the debate over the registration of alachlor, a chemical herbicide:

> The debate over the risk of alachlor is not primarily a debate between those who accept the verdict of scientific risk assessment and those who do not. It is not a conflict

between those who understand the "objective" risks of alachlor and those who are guided by an irrational "subjective" perception of risks. Neither is it primarily a debate within science itself. Rather, it is primarily a political debate—a debate among different value frameworks, different ways of thinking about moral values, different conceptions of society, and different attitudes toward technology and toward risk-taking itself. (pp. 6-7)

Hence, because conflicts about risk assessment and risk management decisions pit values against each other, such values need to be debated and weighed in a political process (National Research Council, 1989). The probabilistic data generated by scientific and technical experts must be viewed together with the interpretation and meaning that people give to such data (Covello, Menkes, & Nehnevajsa, 1982). The involvement of the public in the risk assessment and risk management debates helps to represent societal values to the scientists and experts and to clarify the necessary choices that the political process must make.

However, the ensuing political contest has always been frustrating for both experts and the public. Experts are frequently puzzled by the "irrationality" of the public's attitude toward scientific risk assessment. On the other hand, the public is frustrated by the inaccessibility of the knowledge they need to develop informed opinions (Fiorino, 1989; National Research Council, 1989).

Advocates of industry and government agencies defending their regulatory agendas argue that the public has a bad sense of perspective. They often distinguish between *objective* and *subjective* risk. The former refers to the product of scientific research, primarily public health statistics, experimental studies, epidemiological surveys, and probabilistic risk analyses. The latter refers to nonexpert perceptions of that research, embellished by whatever other considerations seize the public mind (Fischhoff, Watson, & Hope, 1984). The public, they claim, demands that enormous efforts be directed at small but scary-sounding risks while virtually ignoring larger, more commonplace ones (Morgan, 1993). Given the "transscientific" nature of the factual premises, and the rapid changes in the definition of problems and their solutions, the lay public lacks the time, information, and inclination to take part in technically based problem solving (Fiorino, 1990).

Other evidence, however, suggests that disagreements between the public and the experts cannot be attributed simply to ignorance and irrationality (Fischhoff et al., 1984). Citizens are often sensible about the risks they face. Debates on risks and safety have witnessed precipitous drops in the rate and social acceptability of smoking, widespread shifts toward low-fat, high-fiber diets and other healthful foods, dramatic improvements in automobile safety and the passage of laws making use of seat belts mandatory. As Brown (1987) also observes in his essay on popular epidemiology, a public that relied solely on the diagnostic and preventive methods of experts would have missed such risks as those connected to diethylstilbestrol (DES) and Agent Orange. In another study, Fessenden-Raden, Fitchen, and Heath (1987) found that residents of small towns facing water quality problems can quickly educate themselves about complicated chemical risk issues. These examples indicate that the public can be very sensible about risk when companies, regulators, and other institutions provide the opportunity. Laypeople have different, broader definitions of risk that, in important respects, can be more rational than the parameters set by experts. They may have a better capacity than experts alone for accommodating uncertainty and correcting errors over time through deliberation and debate (Barber, 1984).

It has been argued that in our system of participatory democracy, members of the public have the right to provide input into policy decisions that will affect them directly. Democracy presumes that the political system embodies greater wisdom than any specialized community (Stern, 1991). Public participation confers political legitimacy on the policy choices that are made and secures public acceptance and cooperation in the actual implementation of these choices. A technocratic orientation ignores the value dimension of policy analysis and disenfranchises the public, who, in a democracy, ought to control that policy (Schrader-Frechette, 1985). The alternative of entrusting policy to panels of experts working behind closed doors has been proven a failure, both because the resulting policy may ignore important social considerations and because it may prove impossible to implement in the face of grassroots resistance (Morgan, 1993). William Ruckelshaus (1983, 1985), twice administrator of the Environmental Protection Agency, has noted that to manage risk effectively and formulate workable policies on risk assessment and risk management, the public must be involved in the decision-making process. As Thomas Jefferson long ago articulated, public decisions that require specialized knowledge raise questions about political power:

> I know no safe depository of the ultimate powers of society but the people themselves; and if we think them not enlightened enough to exercise their control with a wholesome discretion, the remedy is not to take it from them, but to inform their discretion. (letter to William Charles Jarvis, September 20, 1820; in Ford, 1899)

Communicating about risk is crucial to the process of arriving at societal decisions on risk analysis and management. The understanding of science in general and the likely consequences of particular technological choices call for a continuing exchange of concerns and viewpoints among individuals, groups, and institutions. In this context, communication works toward the confluence of scientific learning, value choices, and democratic participation. A successful dialogue on risk does not guarantee that risk management decisions will maximize general welfare or vouch for the certainty of knowledge claims. It ensures, however, that those involved in the decision-making process will understand the consequences of available options (National Research Council, 1989).

CLASSICAL RISK COMMUNICATION:
THE DILEMMAS OF LIMITED DISCOURSE

The inadequacy of direct regulatory control of health, environmental, and technological hazards and the need to gain public acceptance for policies grounded in scientific risk assessment methodologies have triggered an accelerating interest in risk communication as an alternative form of risk management (Plough & Krimsky, 1987). Classical risk communication focuses on the goals of the communicator, following a linear model that structures communication into senders, media, messages, and receivers. In practice, it is a process whereby government regulators and industry persuade the public to accept scientific and bureaucratic judgments of risk acceptability as well as decisions on risk management. Seeking a "rational" or "technocratic" approach, classical risk communication stresses the vital role of the expert as the source of accurate and unbiased assessment of risk (Kraft, 1991). Although it purports to encourage some form of public participation in the process of consensus formation, the fact remains that the basic political structures and communication channels, through which the solutions and decisions are expressed and carried through, are essentially top-down in orientation (Dickson, 1984).

In itself, classical risk communication is directed at easing the tension between what Plough and Krimsky (1987) call the "demosphere," or popular culture, and the "technosphere" (culture of experts). It seeks to bring the public perception of risk into conformity with scientific rationality. Hence the success of classical risk communication hinges on the degree to which popular knowledge reflects the technical rationality of risk and the extent to which popular behavior and attitudes harmonize with scientific-technocratic values and principles (Plough & Krimsky, 1987). In this context, the social and cultural facets of risk are of marginal concern.

There are several problematic assumptions inherent in the classical approach to risk communication. First, scientists or experts are seen as the only (or certainly major) legitimate providers of "accurate," "objective," and "value-free" information on risk. As initiators of risk communication, they presumably know what kind of information is beneficial for the target audience. The prevailing view is that experts should be left alone to calculate or determine the acceptability of risks associated with a product or technology. Because of society's tradition of relying on experts and scientists for solutions to complex scientific and technical problems, expert information has always been regarded as more rational and valid than the experiential, subjective, and perceptual judgments of the lay public.

Plough and Krimsky (1987) have attributed society's long dependence on scientists and experts in risk assessment on three major preconditions: (a) direct government intervention, (b) the rapid developments in public health and medicine, and (c) the emergence of decision analysis. Since the beginning of the twentieth century, the government of the United States has taken it upon itself to protect citizens against threats to public health and safety. In particular, it has recognized as its goal the protection of citizens from adverse health risks in the marketplace, the workplace, and the environment. Supported by general consensus is the idea that everything should be made safer through direct government intervention. Government efforts to ensure public health and safety perhaps reached their height in the 1970s, when new federal regulatory agencies were established or expanded to deal with risks attached to food and drugs (Food and Drug Administration), the environment (Environmental Protection Agency), the workplace (Occupational Safety and Health Administration), and consumer products (Consumer Product Safety Commission) (Plough & Krimsky, 1987).

Rapid developments in medicine and the establishment of public health institutions, which substantially redefined health risks and redirected intervention strategies, have likewise abetted the professionalization of risk assessment and analysis. Under new government mandates, public health departments began the first large-scale environmental risk monitoring in such areas as sanitation and food safety. Risk messages were formulated to communicate the danger of hazards such as unsafe water and unpasteurized milk. At the helm of these developments in public health and medicine were experts who commanded the public's trust as they applied new technologies to reduce the risks of infectious diseases, for example (Plough & Krimsky, 1987).

Decision analysis constitutes the third tributary to the expert-driven field of risk assessment as the government heavily supported research in new fields such as operations research and systems analysis. Quantitative methodologies used in understanding chance processes and in economic and strategic military decisions have been applied to the practical problems of predicting and altering the course of risk factors in public health, medicine, and the environment (Grier, 1980, 1981; Plough & Krimsky, 1987).

Quantitative decision methodologies have thus provided a rational basis for complex policy decisions concerning technological risks. Advances in laboratory tests, environmental modeling, computer simulations, and epidemiological methods have enabled scientists routinely to detect faults in extremely complex engineering systems—even weak causal links between hazards and deleterious outcomes—and infinitesimally small amounts of potentially harmful carcinogenic or mutagenic substances (Grier, 1981; Plough & Krimsky, 1987).

The second assumption of classical risk communication pertains to the superiority of technical rationality. It assumes that science, by itself, can provide "objective truths," as expressed through hypothetico-deductive methods, measurements, and quantitative comparison across risk events. Logical consistency has become a necessity. Technical rationality dictates that science exists in order to predict with precision, scope, and accuracy, including prediction of the consequences of risk management decisions and policies (Brunner & Ascher, 1992; Plough & Krimsky, 1987). Hence scientific analyses and results are primordial to defining the problem, shaping proposed solutions, and justifying the legitimacy of political policies (Burns & Ueberhorst, 1988).

Unfortunately, the elevation of technical rationality as an imperative to policy decisions affecting risk assessment and risk acceptability has resulted in disdain for lay opinion and values. For instance, the U.S. Department of Energy reportedly funded a study to demonstrate that opponents of nuclear power are mentally ill. In other cases, public perceptions of risk have been labeled as "primitive," "inconsistent," colored by the superstition, and driven by some fundamentalist notion of "purity" (Schrader-Frechette, 1990).

Third, classical risk communication views the public as a passive receiver of scientific risk information; that is, the expert speaks and the citizen listens. Because issues of risk are presumably too complex for the lay public to understand, the assumption is that once citizens are exposed to risk information, they will unconditionally form an opinion consistent with the views or arguments of the communicator. From this perspective, a key problem is scientific illiteracy on the part of members of the public, who tend to let their values and "unscientific" beliefs color their interpretations of the evidence and are often swayed by unscientific analysis (Robinson, 1992).

Viewing the public as passive recipients of risk information is consistent with two overlapping theoretical frameworks that appear to guide this typical process of risk communication: the direct-effects model and the persuasion model.

Risk Communication and the Direct Effects Model

The classical approach to risk communication sharply distinguishes between sources of information and the receivers of that information. Local officials and government regulatory experts constitute the source and the lay public is the receiver. Notwithstanding the benevolent intentions of the sources, the fact remains that they dictate the process by which issues can be discussed. The initiative is exclusively that of the communicators, the effects being exclusively on the audience. The agenda for discussion has been set by the experts, and communication is judged to have an effect to the extent that it is followed by an observable response on the part of the receiver.

Risk Communication and the Persuasion Model

Public hearings and the involvement of citizens' advisory groups, however, do not necessarily create an interactive process. They often appear to have served as instruments of persuasion. They are means of engineering support for prestructured information, risk assessment findings, and risk management decisions made by local officials and experts. Using Heberlein's (1976) categories of strategic types of public involvement mechanisms, it can likewise be said that classical risk communication performs the following functions.

Informational function. Information about risks has been predetermined by planners acting on behalf of the citizens and in the name of public welfare. The public's involvement in advisory groups, public hearings, focus groups, and other types of "semi-interactive" communication mechanisms serves only to legitimate and sanitize the process of top-down information dissemination. Local citizens are informed about the nature of the project. Although the public is given an opportunity to ask questions, responses to public opinion and concern are not the most important considerations in the planning process. Citizens or citizens' groups are convened and later directed toward preset goals. They actually do not take the initiative and do not have control over the discussion of the issues.

Co-optation function. Classical risk communication involves citizens in order to avoid obstructions to risk assessment findings and risk management decisions. Citizens are not seen as partners in assessing risks and making relevant decisions concerning the management of risk. However, because they may pose possible obstructions, their cooperation and sanction are necessary. Public hearings where citizens are encouraged to vent their complaints serve to provide only a semblance of interaction—of being listened to and of being a part of the decision-making process.

Ritualistic function. Public hearings or other types of mechanisms are provided usually to fulfill a legal requirement. From the outset, there have been no explicit intentions on the part of the planners to solicit the public's input in the risk assessment process or in the shaping of policies related to risk management.

Indeed, public participation in risk communication can be a token—an instrument to gain credibility and trust and not really to engage people in a communication process, but to build support for the plans of regulatory agencies or officials. As Kasperson (1986) puts it, agency-initiated risk communication characteristically has as its goal "correcting misperception," "educating the public," "reducing conflict," "easing implementation," or "increasing legitimacy." Participation in risk communication from the perspective of the bureaucrat is one of co-optation—a means for maximizing rationality, a catalyst for implementing decisions, a means for changing public attitudes and behavior.

TOWARD A DIALECTICAL VIEW
OF RISK COMMUNICATION:
EXPANDING THE DISCOURSE ON RISK

The validity of the assumptions and theoretical underpinnings that guide classical risk communication have been put to question. Indeed, what has been subjected to criticism is the process of classical risk communication itself. What is now called for is an elemental reassessment concerning the nature of risk information and the roles of the different actors involved in the risk communication process.

First, as can be noted in the case studies on classical risk communication as well as in everyday discourse on risk, science is not "neutral, objective, and free of social interests" (Nowotny, 1987). Objectivity is an aspiration, but it can never be an achievement of science (Brunner & Ascher, 1992). Because scientific knowledge is socially constructed and negotiated, the definition of a scientific problem cannot be dissociated from the political decisions it helped shape. Although science-based information is vital to risk communication, it should not be seen as the only input into the decision process. As Krimsky and Plough (1988) point out, even the scientific aspects of risks are embedded in complex layers of social, political, and cultural orientations that influence the perceptions of the problem. Science-based risk information may help minimize ambiguities and organize complex data, but it cannot be taken as incontrovertible factual evidence. Risk assessments are constructed from theoretical models that are based on assumptions and subjective judgments. Limitations in the quality and comprehensiveness of the models, methods, and analysis as well as improper rules for combining estimates can seriously compromise the reliability, validity, and robustness of scientific risk assessments (Ahearne, 1990; Covello, 1989; Rip, 1985).

Second, the objectivity of scientists or experts in decision processes is partially misconstrued. The fact that most scientists strive to be objective in their research on risks does not mean that they can be entirely objective. When scientists and experts, like everyone else, make choices among perceived alternatives, they do so in the context of their own expectations and values. Their choices cannot be objectively rational with respect to the real situation, nor can their choices be independent of their own points of view (Brunner & Ascher, 1992). They tend to oscillate between a usually informal context of contingency, in which they admit the uncertainty and provisional nature of the knowledge in question, and an empirical, formal context in which they justify the conclusions reached by emphasizing solely the certainty and absoluteness of the results they obtained (Mulkay & Gilbert, 1983; Nowotny, 1987). Moreover, even within the scientific community, value-laden disputes exist concerning the accuracy and method of ascertaining health and environmental risks. As Douglas and Wildavsky (1982) point out:

> Scientists disagree on whether there are problems, what solutions to propose, and if intervention will make things better or worse. One scientist thinks of Mother Nature as merely secreting a healthy amount of dirt and another thinks of her being forced to inject lethal pollutants. No wonder the ordinary lay person has difficulty in following the argument, and no wonder the scientists have difficulty presenting themselves to the public. (pp. 63-64)

Hence scientific and technical experts are principal extenders of science-based risk information, but they are not the only sources of risk information. As key participants in the risk communication process, scientists and experts help generate important information and bring in perspectives on risks that are accurate and rational, but no more valid than the interpretations and perspectives brought in by the public. Scientists and experts bring in tools for assessing risks, whereas the public brings in tools (i.e., social, cultural, and political values) to evaluate scientific risk assessments. However, scientists and experts can help the public understand the scientific process and the bases for risk assessment.

Third, with the precipitous decline of public confidence in the ability of government and industry to generate objectivity in risk assessment and plurality in risk management decisions,[4] the public has ceased to be a mere receiver of risk information. Large segments of the public now demand more involvement in debates over risk issues and challenge conclusions and recommendations from scientists and experts regarding risk assessment and risk management measures. What to scientific and technical experts are rational and objective criteria of scientific assessment and formal analysis are to others (i.e., the lay public) a more intuitive, experiential process of cultural assessment and sociopolitical analysis, such as the perceived fairness of the risk, long-term effects, degree of personal control, voluntariness, and intrusion into the cultural environment (Fiorino, 1989). When public and experts disagree, it is a clash between sets of differently informed opinions (Fischhoff et al., 1984).

Indeed, in light of changing societal relations and a growing realization that the issues of risk are to a large extent constructed by social, cultural, and political norms and values, the typical practice of packaging and marketing a set of risk messages to an unquestioning public is no longer the normative risk communication scenario. The content and process of risk communication cannot be removed from the risk generation process, assessment activities, social interactions, and the broader array of actors composing risk management as a whole (Kasperson & Stallen, 1991). As common misconceptions and assumptions about the nature of risk and the actors involved in risk communication have been dispelled, efforts have been geared toward shaping risk communication into an interactive process by which concerned parties can participate in formulating more effective risk assessment guidelines and risk management decisions. Focus has shifted toward examining the underlying principles and goals of an interactive risk communication and what it should constitute operationally in order to be a more responsive, meaningful, and dialogical process.

Features of Dialogical Risk Communication

Multiple stakeholders/multiple perspectives. In contrast to conventional risk communication, which normally emanates from a monolithic source that diffuses its information to target receivers, dialectical risk communication involves several stakeholders who bring into the communication process their own perspectives about an issue. It is built on the premise that each stakeholder has much to learn from the others and vice versa. Because the exchange is interactive, the theoretical delineation between "sources" and "receivers" becomes irrelevant. Stakeholders are accorded an equal chance to propose opinions and ideas for consideration by others. Although, in reality, the communication process is initiated by a particular stakeholder (e.g., FDA, NRDC, local environmental group), it becomes "interactive" only when efforts are made to pull in participants who are directly or indirectly affected by the issue.

Free flow of information. The typical model used to involve the public in policy decisions is a strategy often described as the decide-announce-defend approach. In this approach, a group or agency (e.g., EPA) typically commissions a study, uses the results to determine what it considers the best alternative, and then announces a decision. This is followed commonly by a public hearing in which the group involved defends the decision.

On the other hand, dialectical risk communication presumes a free flow of information among stakeholders about the problem, policies, evidence, and potential solutions. Dialectical risk communication provides all affected individuals or groups with the same opportunity to share information, to become informed, to understand the dimensions of an issue, and to weigh the viability of proposed solutions. One major reason some solutions proposed by groups or individuals have appeared unrealistic or simplistic may be the lack of recognition of the complexity of the issue. Dialectical risk communication potentially opens up the process for appreciating the different facets of an issue and enables the different stakeholders to look at proposed solutions in their appropriate context.

Access to communication channels and resources. Implicit in dialectical risk communication is accessibility of communication channels and resources for different stakeholders. Several interpersonal communication mechanisms hold potential for stimulating public involvement, such as workshops, citizen panels, quasi-experiments, and advisory committees. Forums such as these are likely to facilitate group interaction and allow for immediate feedback. Regardless of the format, however, the most important consideration is the extent to which these public forums are designed and organized to meet the following objectives (Renn, Webler, & Johnson, 1991):

1. *Identify the problem:* What is the problem? What are the possible options and decision procedures?
2. *Elicit values:* What personal, social, and political values are affected by the possible options?
3. *Validate values:* How do individual values relate to those of other stakeholders?
4. *Present or generate options:* What are the possible options and what are their advantages and disadvantages? What are their costs to individuals and society?
5. *Evaluate options:* How do these different options relate to the different values just expressed by the stakeholders?
6. *Holistic judgment:* What are the priorities of individuals and groups? What is now the judgment on prioritizing options?
7. *Discuss potential differences:* What are the explanations for these differences in priorities and judgments regarding options?
8. *Final holistic judgment:* What are the individual and group decisions? What are the major justifications for these decisions?

Implicit in these operational characteristics of dialectical risk communication are the goals of democratic participation, critical thinking, and autonomy in decision making. It is democratic because it accommodates various groups or individuals who believe that their involvement can have an impact on policies that will affect society as a whole. It fosters critical thinking as it engages stakeholders in the process of reasoning, abstracting, and processing myriad information about risks. It nurtures autonomy in decision making as it allows participants to understand different viewpoints, unfettered by one-sided enthusiasms or affiliations.

Achieving genuine dialogue and public participation may at first appear to be a nearly impossible task. But the notion of public involvement in decision making itself has been driven by the contemporary needs of society for a more holistic assessment and resolution of issues. Given the right impetus, a genuine dialogue among the different parties involved is attainable.

Dialectical risk communication does not aim to make the lay public the "judges" in scientific battles. Rather, it seeks to create a process whereby all the parties involved are informed of the ambiguities, uncertainties, and potential of scientific as well as other types of risk assessments to contribute to political decisions. From this point of view, for example, the meaning of "scientific mediation" and "popularization of science" is to point out those kinds of uncertainties. It is not to find a "unified front" or a unanimous scientific standpoint, but to enable the parties involved to recognize legitimate ways of searching for the truth amid competing claims and evidence (Nowotny, 1987, p. 74).

Hence, consistent with the ideal of democratic discourse, an interactive discussion of competing ideas about risk leads to a critical evaluation of varying perspectives, and eventually to an informed judgment. As the participants in the discourse present their views and interests, they also improve their understanding of the issues. They may even come to a point of decision grounded in reason.

CONCLUSION

In this chapter we have examined two paradigms of risk communication. The first paradigm, classical risk communication, is a process whereby government regulators, scientists, experts, policy makers, industry, and others steer the public toward accepting technical-scientific judgments of risk acceptability as well as decisions on risk management. Inherent in the classical risk communication model are the following assumptions: (a) Scientists or experts are the only legitimate providers or sources of "accurate," "objective," and "value-free" information on risk; (b) technical rationality is superior to lay rationality; and (c) the public is a passive receiver of scientific risk information. The dependence on the experts and scientific risk assessments was presumably engendered by (a) government interventions to ensure public health and safety, (b) rapid developments in science and medicine, and (c) advances in quantitative decision methodologies.

The second paradigm, dialectical risk communication, is conceived of as an alternative framework to classical risk communication. Dialectical risk communication goes beyond ensuring that one's message is transmitted and listened to. Rather, it is a process of empowering stakeholders as they begin to appreciate different perspectives on risk, scrutinize opinions and perceptions about risk, and sharpen the skills necessary to make informed judgments that consequently have impacts on individual and community lifestyles and policies. The movement from a linear to a more interactive orientation in risk communication has been spurred by several factors, such as (a) increasing disenchantment with the power of scientific knowledge to justify regulatory actions; (b) a growing realization that issues of risk acceptability are to a large extent constructed by social, cultural, and political factors; and (c) public demand for participation in policy making. Moreover, the need to examine risk information critically and to arrive at informed judgments regarding risk issues has summoned a communication framework that allows for an interactive sharing of ideas and opinions that reflect the complexity and multidimensionality of risk. The controversy over food safety, discussed at length in this chapter, clearly depicts this phenomenon.

Dialectical risk communication is characterized by at least three important elements: (a) It has multiple stakeholders carrying multiple perspectives, (b) it establishes a free flow of information between and among all stakeholders, and (c) it provides easy access to communication channels and resources. At least some elements of an open, interactive, and democratic risk communication process are attainable. Implicit in dialectical risk communication are the principles of democratic participation, critical thinking, and autonomy in decision making.

Dialectical risk communication continues to be an evolving framework, albeit with very few documented success stories that can clearly provide guidance on how best to initiate and sustain the process. There is a need to recapture and adapt workable structures and procedural techniques carefully, as well as a need to generate important observable indicators of success.

Apart from searching for answers concerning its practical application, the challenge of dialectical risk communication lies in exploring further its theoretical and philosophical underpinnings. A more profound examination of the overarching theoretical and philosophical principles of dialectical communication can also help set directions for its practical application. Dialectical risk communication and its relationship with scientific and public discourse, critical thinking and reasoning, ethics, and political participation are just a few of the possible arenas that await further reflection and research.

Moreover, there are theoretical issues that dialectical risk communication must grapple with. First, the idea of public involvement in resolving disputes concerning risk acceptability must take into account the preparedness and capacity of the public to sift discriminately through facts and evidence. Dialectical risk communication assumes that stakeholders are all equipped with adequate information that will allow them to participate effectively in the process. However, even where adequate process skills for decision making are assumed, stakeholders who are poorly informed about the scientific process and technical risk assessment, for instance, can cripple effective and sound decision making. The success of the anti-Alar campaign, for example, was partly a result of the public's unfamiliarity with science in general and with toxicology in particular (Arnold, 1990). Russell (1990) has likewise noted that "image has become as important as law and science"—a phenomenon made evident by the use of movie personalities as spokespersons for food safety causes. Thus dialectical risk communication, if misconstrued as a free-for-all clash of ideas and symbols, can bring the issues away from the arena of reasonable and responsible debate and move the locus of decision to uninformed, emotion-based opinion.

Second, dialectical risk communication must find a way to resolve the issue of micro and macro rationality. The layperson sees risk in relation to how it will affect him or her personally. Policy makers, in contrast, view risk in terms of its overall impact on society. Thus, for example, it is rational for a person to reject a landfill to be located in his or her community, but it is irrational for society as a whole not to be able to locate a landfill.

Third, dialectical risk communication has to deal with the emotional-psychological baggage that individuals bring to the process. The phenomenon of exaggeration of even minor risks, for example, may clog the transaction at the expense of other stakeholders. In short, there is no guarantee that dialectical risk communication will be successful most of the time.

Fourth, dialectical risk communication has to explicate that stakeholders should be prepared to take responsibility for their actions. Even democratic processes do not guarantee error-free outcomes (Formaini, 1990). Dialectical risk communication views the individual as the ultimate judge of what is safe or what constitutes an acceptable risk. Although interaction and participation in risk communication are consistent with principles of democracy and individual autonomy, the process can facilitate certain outcomes and suppress others. In other words, judgments and decisions can be seriously flawed but still determine public policy. For instance, if some interest groups demand zero risk as a goal, notwithstanding its impossibility, have they considered the expense and trade-offs that accompany such a demand?

The goals implicitly set forth in dialectical risk communication are, without doubt, ambitious. But the concept of recapturing the essence of communication as interaction has long been overdue. The time has come, and the issues confronting today's society demand it.

NOTES

1. Of those surveyed, 80% rated the use of pesticides and herbicides as "a serious hazard"; 17% said that it is "something of a hazard." Some 56% said that antibiotics and hormones in poultry and

meat are "a serious hazard," and 35% said that they are "something of a hazard"; 42% said that irradiation of foods is "a serious hazard," and 31% said that it is "something of a hazard" (Puzo, 1992).

2. The change in attitude toward science may have been in part the result of the impact created by the publication in 1962 of Rachel Carson's *Silent Spring,* which equated science with destruction. Although many of Carson's data about the potential carcinogenicity of DDT were somewhat speculative, they later proved crucial in debates about the threats of chemicals to human health. Carson's main contribution, however, was to bring together in a popular form the evidence against DDT from a number of scientific disciplines, building these into a generalized critique of the narrow focus of contemporary science and technology, of their apparent blindness to broad social and environmental effects, and ultimately of the gulf between the values of laboratory life and those of surrounding society (Dickson, 1984, p. 223).

3. Discussions on the social impact of scientific knowledge or regulatory controls by the government have always been accompanied by political controversy. Some of these disputes concerned the effect on consumers' health of food additives such as caffeine and sodium benzoate, and the occupational hazards of new production techniques in the chemical and food-processing industries. In the early 1950s, even at the height of the public's confidence in science and technology, fears of the carcinogenic properties of artificial food additives led Senator James J. Delaney to introduce one of the strictest controls on the application of science ever passed by the Congress, an amendment to the Food and Drug Act requiring that the government set a zero tolerance for any chemical found to cause cancer in laboratory animals (Dickson, 1984, p. 222).

4. Many people still have faith and confidence in scientific experts and science in general, but a growing number of citizens have become skeptical. Between 1966 and 1976, the percentage of the public expressing a great deal of confidence in the scientific community declined from 56% to 43% (Nelkin, 1981; cited in DeSario & Langton, 1987), and a 1979 survey indicated that 42% of the public believed that "you can't trust what experts like scientists and technical people say because often what they say isn't right" (National Science Board, 1981; see also DeSario & Langton, 1987).

REFERENCES

Ahearne, J. F. (1990, Fall). Risk communication: Some common myths and unpleasant realities. *E.N.D.*

Archibald, S. O., Bruhn, C., Dowling, N., Fan, A., Hazlett, T. W., Hurel, B., Lane, S., Marsh, R., & Wallace, L. T. (1988). *Regulating chemicals: A public policy quandary.* Report of the 1987-1988 Study Group on Chemicals in the Human Food Chain: Sources, Options, and Public Policy; sponsored by the University of California Agricultural Issues Center, Davis.

Arnold, A. (1990). *Fear of food.* Bellevue, WA: Free Enterprise.

Barber, B. R. (1984). *Strong democracy: Participatory politics for a new age.* Berkeley: University of California Press.

Bazelon, D. (1979). Risk and responsibility. *Science, 205,* 272-280.

Beall, G. A., Bruhn, C. M., Craigmill, A. L., & Winter, C. K. (1991). Pesticides in your food: How safe is "safe"? *California Agriculture, 45*(4), 4-11.

Beck, M., Hager, M., Miller, M., Hutchison, S., Hackett, G., & Joseph, N. (1989, March 27). Warning! Your food, nutritious and delicious, may be hazardous to your health. *Newsweek,* pp. 16-26.

Brown, P. (1987). Popular epidemiology: Community response to waste-induced disease in Woburn, Massachusetts. *Science, Technology and Human Values, 12*(3/4), 78-85.

Brunk, C., Haworth, L., & Lee, B. (1991). *Value assumptions in risk assessment: A case study of the Alachlor controversy.* Waterloo, ON: Wilfred Laurier University Press.

Brunner, R. D., & Ascher, W. (1992). Science and social responsibility. *Policy Sciences, 25,* 295-331.

Burns, T. R., & Ueberhorst, R. (1988). *Creative democracy.* New York: Praeger.

Collingridge, D., & Reeve, C. (1986). *Science speaks to power.* New York: St. Martin's.

Covello, V. T. (1989). Informing people about risks from chemicals, radiation, and other toxic substances: A review of obstacles to public understanding and effective risk communication. In W. Leiss (Ed.), *Prospects and problems in risk communication* (pp. 1-50). Waterloo, ON: University of Waterloo Press.

Covello, V. T., Menkes, J., & Nehnevajsa, J. (1982). Risk analysis, philosophy, and the social and behavioral sciences: Reflections on the scope of risk analysis research. *Risk Analysis, 2*(2), 53-68.

Derr, D. (1989, May 15). [Statement by the International Apple Institute, McLean, VA].

DeSario, J., & Langton, S. (1987). *Citizen participation in public decision making.* Westport, CT: Greenwood.

Dickson, D. (1984). *The new politics of science.* New York: Pantheon.

Douglas, M., & Wildavsky, A. (1982). *Risk and culture: An essay on the selection of technical and environmental dangers.* Berkeley: University of California Press.

Ezrahi, Y. (1980). Utopian and pragmatic rationalism: The political context of scientific advice. *Minerva, 18,* 111-131.

Fessenden-Raden, J., Fitchen, J. M., & Heath, J. S. (1987). Providing risk information in communities: Factors influencing what is heard and accepted. *Science, Technology and Human Values, 12*(3/4), 94-101.

Fiorino, D. J. (1989). Technical and democratic values in risk analysis. *Risk Analysis, 9,* 293-298.

Fiorino, D. J. (1990). Citizen participation and environmental risk: A survey of institutional mechanisms. *Science, Technology and Human Values, 15,* 226-243.

Fischhoff, B. (1985). Managing risk perceptions. *Issues in Science and Technology, 2,* 83-96.

Fischhoff, B., Watson, S. R., & Hope, C. (1984). Defining risk. *Policy Sciences, 17,* 123-139.

Ford, P. L. (1899). *Writings of Thomas Jefferson* (Vol. 10). New York: G. P. Putnam.

Formaini, R. (1990). *The myth of scientific public policy.* New Brunswick, NJ: Transaction.

Graham, J. D., Green, L. C., & Roberts, M. J. (1988). *In search of safety: Chemicals and cancer risk.* Cambridge, MA: Harvard University Press.

Grier, B. (1980). *One thousand years of mathematical psychology.* Paper presented at the annual meeting of the Society for Mathematical Psychology, Madison, WI.

Grier, B. (1981). *The early history of the theory and management of risk.* Paper presented at the meeting of the Judgment and Decision Making Group, Philadelphia.

Heberlein, T. A. (1976). Some observations on alternative mechanisms for public involvement: The hearing, public opinion poll, the workshop, and the quasi-experiment. *Natural Resources Journal, 16,* 197-212.

Hilts, P. J. (1993, July 5). Results of study on pesticide encourage effort to cut use. *New York Times,* p. A8.

Jasanoff, S. (1986). *Risk management and political culture.* New York: Russell Sage Foundation.

Kasperson, R. E. (1986). Six propositions on public participation and their relevance for risk communication. *Risk Analysis, 6,* 275-281.

Kasperson, R. E., & Stallen, P. J. M. (1991). Risk communication: The evolution of attempts. In R. E. Kasperson & P. J. M. Stallen (Eds.), *Communicating risks to the public: International perspectives.* Dordrecht, Netherlands: Kluwer Academic.

Kennedy, D. (1989). Humans in the chemical decision chain. *Choices, 4*(3), 4-7.

Kraft, M. E. (1991). Risk perception and the politics of citizen participation: The case of radioactive waste management. In B. J. Garrick & W. C. Gekler (Eds.), *The analysis, communication, and perception of risk* (pp. 105-118). New York: Plenum.

Krimsky, S., & Plough, A. (1988). *Environmental hazards: Communicating risks as a social process.* Dover, MA: Auburn House.

Morgan, M. G. (1993). Risk analysis and management. *Scientific American, 269*(1), 32-41.

Mueller, W. (1990). Who's afraid of food? *American Demographics, 12*(9), 40-43.

Mulkay, M., & Gilbert, G. N. (1983). Scientists theory talk. *Canadian Journal of Sociology, 8*(2), 179-198.

National Research Council. (1989). *Improving risk communication.* Washington, DC: National Academy Press.

National Science Board. (1981). *Science indicators.* Washington, DC: Government Printing Office.

Nelkin, D. (1981). Science and technology policy and the democratic process. In A. Teich (Ed.), *Technology and man's future* (3rd ed.). New York: St. Martin's.

Nelkin, D. (1985). *The language of risk.* Beverly Hills, CA: Sage.

Nowotny, H. (1987). A new branch of Science, Inc. In H. Brooks & C. L. Cooper (Eds.), *Science for public policy* (pp. 61-76). Oxford: Pergamon.

Plough, A., & Krimsky, S. (1987). The emergence of risk communication studies: Social and political context. *Science, Technology and Human Values, 12*(3/4), 4-10.

Primack, J., & von Hippel, F. (1974). *Advice and dissent: Scientists in the political arena.* New York: Basic Books.

Puzo, D. (1992, December 31). Irradiation: The waiting game. *Los Angeles Times,* p. H2.

Renn, O., Webler, T., & Johnson, B. B. (1991). Public participation in hazard management: The use of citizen panels in the U.S. *Risk-Issues in Health and Safety, 2,* 197-226.

Rip, R. (1985). Experts in public arenas. In H. Otway & M. Peltu (Eds.), *Regulating industrial risks: Science, hazards, and public protection* (pp. 94-110). London: Butterworth.

Robinson, J. B. (1992). Risks, predictions, and other optical illusions: Rethinking the use of science in social decision-making. *Policy Sciences, 25,* 237-254.

Ruckelshaus, W. (1983). Science, risk, and public policy. *Science, 221,* 1026-1028.

Ruckelshaus, W. (1985). Risk, science, and democracy. *Issues in Science and Technology, 1*(3), 19-38.

Russell, C. (1990). A crisis in public confidence. *EPA Journal, 16*(3), 2-5.

Scherer, C. W. (1991). Strategies for communicating risks to the public. *Food Technology, 45*(10), 110-116.

Schrader-Frechette, K. S. (1985). *Risk analysis and scientific method: Methodological and ethical problems with evaluating societal risks.* Boston: D. Reidel.

Schrader-Frechette, K. S. (1990). Scientific method, anti-foundationalism, and public decisionmaking. *Risk-Issues in Health and Safety, 1,* 23-41.

Segal, M. (1990). Is it worth the worry? Determining risk [Special report]. *FDA Consumer,* pp. 7-11.

Slovic, P., Fischhoff, B., & Lichtenstein, S. (1982). Why study risk perception? *Risk Analysis, 2*(2), 83-93.

Stern, P. C. (1991). Learning through conflict: A realistic strategy for risk communication. *Policy Sciences, 24,* 99-119.

Sugarman, C. (1993, March 30). Frontline: Pesticides revisited. *Washington Post,* p. E2.

von Schomberg, R. (1993). Controversies and political decision making. In R. von Schomberg (Ed.), *Science, politics, and morality* (pp. 1-6). Dordrecht, Netherlands: Kluwer Academic.

Wolf, I. D. (1992). Critical issues in food safety, 1991-2000. *Food Technology, 46*(1), 64-70.

Zeise, L., Painter, P., Berteau, P. E., Fan, A. M., & Jackson, R. J. (1991). Alar in fruit: Limited regulatory action in the face of uncertain risks. In B. J. Garrick & W. C. Gekler (Eds.), *The analysis, communication, and perception of risk* (pp. 275-284). New York: Plenum.

Zind, T. (1990). Fresh trends: A profile of fresh produce consumers. In *The Packer Focus 1989-1990* (pp. 37-68). Overland Park, KS: Vance.

13 What Risk Communicators Need to Know: An Agenda for Research

KATHERINE E. ROWAN
Purdue University

AT a 1993 conference on risk assessment, a military general, whom I won't name, gave a presentation on risk communication. During the course of his presentation he explained to the audience of risk assessors that public meetings about hazardous sites can become hostile; therefore, government risk communicators speaking at such meetings need to have their wits about them. For instance, he noted, it's a good idea to tie the auditorium chairs together in advance of your presentation. That way, you will be protected from hostile, chair-throwing citizens.

The general's approach to audience adaptation is obviously extreme (although there have been public meetings where chair throwing would not have been unexpected), but his remarks suggest one reason risk communication itself is viewed as a hazardous activity, particularly by government and industry representatives. It is easy to believe *all* difficulties in communicating with the public result from the irrationality of uninformed citizens or ardent environmentalists. Occasionally, this analysis has merit. But it is also the case that communicating about physical hazards, particularly those that are humanly produced, is an inherently difficult task, one that requires good "mental models" of the risk communication process and a sophisticated sense of effective listening and speaking options.

In this commentary, I argue for lines of work in risk communication research that would ultimately provide practitioners like the general with these and other conceptual tools. In addition, I argue that because risk communication is ultimately a pragmatic endeavor, its research agenda should be charted on a practical course. The study of risk communication is also an excellent arena for testing basic theory; because of their difficulties, risk situations create interesting

Correspondence and requests for reprints: Katherine E. Rowan, Department of Communication, Purdue University, West Lafayette, IN 47907-1366.

Communication Yearbook 18, pp. 300-319

contexts for exploring purely theoretical questions. However, the field of risk communication must have as a central mission genuine aid for risk communication practitioners. Consequently, the question, What do risk communicators need to know? is used here as (a) a framework for organizing extant work, (b) a basis for commenting on the four risk communication studies presented in this volume of *Yearbook,* and (c) a heuristic generating an agenda for risk communication research.

From reviewing the literature and working with practitioners in risk communication seminars, I have formed the belief that these individuals would benefit from a wide array of research and "traditional wisdom" in communication. However, they most need four types of communication knowledge. First, and most important, they need to know how to think well and philosophize about risk situations and risk management. Second, they need to know what kinds of policies, regulations, and procedures should govern conduct, both communicative and otherwise, in risk situations. Third, they need to know how people of all sorts interpret risk situations and the factors influencing those perceptions. Fourth, they need to know how to communicate effectively about risks. They need knowledge of multiple communication skills, including credibility management, informing-explaining, persuading, and motivating action. Risk communicators may need other bodies of information as well, but they all need at least these four.

NOTIONS OF IDEAL RISK
COMMUNICATION UNCOVERED AND REFINED

Communicating about danger creates fear, anger, apathy, and needs for comforting, information, listening, negotiation, patience, and respect. Because of the emotional and intellectual challenges of their enterprise, risk communication practitioners need ethical and philosophical frameworks with which to consider their activities. In addition, they need a sense of the common, intuitive notions everyday people have about how "danger information" is best shared. Frequently, these intuitions are deeply held. Frequently, too, intuitions held by one group clash with those of another.

Because practitioners have these needs, risk communication scholars can perform an important service by providing philosophical frameworks that illuminate people's everyday notions and provide bases for refining and extending them. That is, scholars can contribute to the risk communication literature by providing both phenomenological analyses of common, intuitive notions of "how risk communication ought to work" and formal analyses establishing philosophical frameworks for understanding and guiding risk communication activities.

Extant Work Uncovering
Intuitive Risk Communication Frameworks

Currently, the risk communication literature contains three kinds of work that may undergird a philosophical framework for risk communication. First, there are numerous depictions of the two most common orientations to risk communication, the "technical" and the "democratic" (Fiorino, 1989) or, as Juanillo and Scherer term them in their chapter in this volume, the classical and the dialectical. Second, there are phenomenological analyses of people's everyday notions of environmental risk, such as those offered by the German theorist Niklas Luhmann (e.g., 1989, 1993; see also Wandersman, Hallman, & Berman, 1993). Third, there are works sketching broad philosophical principles for what constitutes good risk communication (e.g., Bradbury, 1989; Douglas & Wildavsky, 1982; Hadden, 1989; National Research Council, 1989; Schrader-Frechette, 1985). All of this work provides important first steps toward a systematic philosophy of risk communication.

Depictions of the two most common orientations to risk communication. Numerous scholars have identified two common and contrasting ways that people intuitively orient to risk communication situations (e.g., Davies, Covello, & Allen, 1987; Hadden, 1989; Heath & Nathan, 1991; National Research Council, 1989; Plough & Krimsky, 1987; Sandman, 1987, 1993). "Technicals" orient to news of a bovine growth hormone in milk or the discovery of abandoned toxic waste by focusing attention on the nature and severity of the hazard. Because of this focus, they tend to privilege scientific and technical information in discussions about its management and view risk communication as a hierarchical, one-way communication process where they as experts inform the decision making of less-expert publics.

In contrast, "democratics" are concerned more with matters of justice and fairness than they are with information about the precise nature and severity of the hazard. Democratics may be those who feel a certain risk or a wide array of health and environmental threats have been unfairly imposed upon them or others. Given this focus, they view risk communication as a context where all stakeholders—those who are exposed to danger as much as those who generate it—should have some control over its management.

The depiction of these two contrasting stances toward risk communication has been an important tool for understanding why risk communication contexts are frequently confrontational. A key problem is that the technical and democratic approaches to risk communication delegitimate each other. When technicals feel a physical hazard (e.g., the discovery of traces of carcinogens in city drinking wells) is negligible in its health effects, they find discussions of injustice in connection with such nearly nonexistent risk absurd. In contrast, if democratics feel that little or no concern has been displayed by a company for the health and welfare of innocent community members (when, for example, the company allows carcinogens in drinking water), they tend to dismiss discussions about the actual severity of the hazard as irrelevant.

The strength of the technical response to risk situations is its emphasis on the importance of gathering and conveying accurate information. The weakness is that it is ultimately elitist. The technical model narrowly focuses on the importance of one kind of expertise, technical expertise, and one kind of information, that about risk severity and likelihood. The strength of the democratic model is its emphasis on listening and open dialogue as fundamental communicative processes. Democratics usefully assume that all parties affected by a risk have some expertise to bring to a discussion of its management. The weaknesses of the democratic model may not be as immediately obvious as those of the technical, but they exist. First, the democratic model assumes a fair process equals a fair product. Democratics believe that as long as there are rules preventing industry or government officials from taking over discussion, eventually truth will emerge. But although continual efforts to assure fair process are vital to effective risk communication, by themselves they do not assure careful problem analysis and skilled communication. A second weakness in the democratic model is that it tries to outlaw an important communication skill: persuasion. Toxic substances, hazardous wastes, and ozone-harming emissions are difficult to understand and manage. Even people with similar backgrounds and access to identical information often disagree about how best to cope with them. There is nothing inherently wrong with attempts to gain agreement. The problem with persuasion is that it often occurs *prematurely,* when people should be listening or gathering information rather than attempting to persuade.

Transcending the
Technical/Democratic Dichotomy

Delineation of these two models provides an important beginning to a phenomenology of risk communication. However, as yet we really do not have a rigorous phenomenology of conceptions of risk, beliefs about risk management, or related concepts such as fairness and hazard. Specifically, what we need is a much more systematic analysis of these notions as they are grounded in people's everyday understandings of risk and consideration of how these dialectical poles can be meaningfully transcended. Like Juanillo and Scherer, most commentators currently tend to opt for the democratic side of this debate, applauding its focus on encouraging participation from all parties affected by an environmental or health risk. Krimsky and Plough (1988) take a somewhat more balanced approach in their presentation of a "cultural" perspective on risk communication, maintaining that the technical and democratic perspectives are equally legitimate, but different, perspectives on risk situations. Although this recognition is useful, it stops short of providing principles that would guide practitioners through especially rough communication terrain. For example, should all stakeholders be apprised of a potential risk prior to an analysis of whether it exists? To what extent can citizens shape the activities of private industry? Under what conditions would we want such oversight?

Ultimately, I would argue that we can transcend the technical and democratic orientations by embracing the strengths and jettisoning the weaknesses of each. Good risk management requires *both* scientific knowledge and social justice. A transcendent approach to risk communication would be one that describes the *social conditions* most likely to secure the best possible technical knowledge about hazards and the best possible methods of addressing stakeholders' concerns. In focusing on the social conditions necessary for the production of knowledge and justice, I am looking for a Habermasian way of resolving the clash between technical and practical interests (e.g., Habermas, 1971). The work of Habermas and other political theorists may be helpful in meeting the need for a comprehensive philosophical analysis of risk communication. This grand conceptual engine would ultimately inform all other lines of risk communication work, such as those on policy and regulation, risk perception, and communication skills for risk situations.

RISK COMMUNICATION POLICIES: THOSE THAT WORK AND THOSE THAT DON'T

Practitioners need improved policies and procedures for communicating with multiple stakeholders (citizens, industry, government) in risk assessment and locally unwanted land use (LULU) controversies (e.g., Freudenberg, 1984; Popper, 1985; Unger, Wandersman, & Hallman, 1992). Current federal and state legislation often mandates only a token role for public participation in decisions such as how a hazardous waste site will be cleaned up or whether an industry will be allowed to build in a given area. Regulations need to address better the nature of the public input required in risk situations and the timing of requests for input. For example, a complex set of federal and state regulations governs cleanup of hazardous waste sites (see, e.g., Ohio Environmental Protection Agency, 1993). First, a site is studied to determine whether the materials it contains are, in fact, hazardous. Second, various cleanup options are considered and the option considered the safest, most economical, and most feasible is ultimately recommended to citizens in the area. Unfortunately, studies of cleanup options frequently take several years (Ohio Environmental Protection Agency, 1993). Affected citizens know about the hazard and the risk assessors' presence in their area, but are not asked for input. When they are asked to comment, it is after a cleanup or remediation option has been selected. After waiting years for some kind of control over processes that seem to affect their lives, health, and property values, they essentially are asked if the proposed option is acceptable. Frequently, affected citizens are not especially knowledgeable about the science and engineering involved in site remediation and are vulnerable to suggestions or feelings that the recommended option is dangerous or inadequate in some way.

For example, in Ohio there have been several disputes when Ohio Environmental Protection Agency risk assessors have recommended building incinerators to clean up hazardous waste sites, and citizens have become convinced that incinerator emissions are unhealthful (see, e.g., Ohio Environmental Protection Agency, 1992). So public meetings aimed at creating contexts for citizen comment frequently devolve into a series of stoic, technical presentations by agency officials, punctuated by angry shouts from local citizens upset about having the option forced on them. At one meeting, a citizen shouted, "We have seen all your charts before. Why don't you listen to *us* for a change?" The citizen was told that there would be an hour and a half of presentations by state and federal officials and time for public comment at the end. Angry audience members showed their disgust by interrupting the presentations with pointed questions and occasional outbursts. Across the nation, extremely difficult meetings like this one are not atypical.

After being shouted down at public meetings or yelled at over the phone, government risk communicators decide that risk communication with the public is itself risky. However, their solutions to risk communication difficulties are often poorly informed. Frequently, they come to believe that if only they could learn "magic words" or be better public speakers, they would somehow win over angry citizens who shout at them during public meetings (Sandman, 1993). Similarly, citizens' groups often try to oppose some new industrial facility or the siting of a toxic waste cleanup facility. When their opposition fails, they feel that the system has let them down and that they have no power over fundamental decisions affecting their health, the health of their children, and their property values.

What citizens, industrialists, and government officials need are better policies, regulations, and procedures governing risk management and public communication about risks. Better procedures would involve making risk information (e.g., about a facility's stored hazardous materials or emissions) more accessible and easily retrievable by local emergency personnel or through on-line services (Hadden, 1989). Better policies would involve stakeholders meeting with one another early and often. Better regulations would allot citizens roles larger than that of "comment givers" at points in the decision-making process when decisions have already been made. Thus detailed policy studies and comparative studies of what works and what does not, such as that presented by Heath in his chapter in this volume, are potentially quite helpful to practitioners.

Existing and Needed Research on
Risk Communication Policies and Procedures

Scholars have been working to develop the area of risk communication policy studies. Several methodologies have been used, including case studies, historical analyses, and comparative assessments. For example, Krimsky and Plough

(1988) offer an excellent array of detailed cases in a text that implicitly compares contexts where citizens were highly opposed to some humanly created risk (e.g., the "ice minus" case, in which a new genetically engineered substance was sprayed near strawberry crops) to cases where citizens saw no reason for concern in connection with some physical risk (e.g., an arsenic-emitting copper smelter in Tacoma that had been in operation for nearly a century). Other researchers have offered cases contrasting successful and unsuccessful citizen efforts directed at thwarting the building of an incinerator and other unwanted projects (e.g., Bacow & Milkey, 1982; Bauer, 1988; Buchanan, 1988). In addition, there are historical analyses of risk management efforts such as Lowrance's (1976) excellent history of DDT and Covello and Mumpower's (1985) historical view of risk management (see also Lowi, 1990).

A growing body of work explores risk management policies internationally. Scholars have studied nuclear power regulation in Europe, Japan, the United States, and other countries (e.g., Dauvergne, 1993; Inaba, 1993; Jinzaburo, 1988). For example, in Japan nuclear power facilities make themselves more acceptable by rewarding their local communities with financial incentives and other amenities (Inaba, 1993). Other work has examined LULU siting in Europe, Canada, and the United States (e.g., Fiorino, 1990; McDaniels & Gregory, 1991; Meyer & Solomon, 1984; Wiegman, Boer, Gutteling, Komilis, & Gadet, 1992). In Canada, one highly successful case involved a somewhat different approach: The government of a Canadian province asked communities to bid on acceptance of a hazardous waste site. Communities were allowed to participate only if they held referenda to determine citizen support for the site's acceptance. Further, the province funded efforts to educate local citizens in hazardous waste site management and oversight (even flying citizens to "model dumps" in Europe). And the company was required to meet citizen-generated policies for safe operation (Tomsho, 1991; also see McLellan, 1989). A similar approach to siting LULUs is called a "reverse Dutch auction" (Inhaber, 1991), which is a procedure in which communities bid to take hazardous waste facilities and the lowest bid wins. The bidding communities can specify accountability procedures the waste management company must abide by if it is allowed to use the community as a site.

Some of the most useful policy studies are those that compare effective and ineffective risk communication and management practices. Heath's work in this volume fits in this category and is interesting because of the specifics he provides about what has and has not worked in risk communication efforts on the Texas gulf coast. Scholars and practitioners should find especially interesting Heath's comparison of effective and ineffective methods of having industry and community members work together in risk decision making. The Texas Copper Corporation (TCC) case he presents illustrates *ineffective* methods of involving a community in efforts to build a copper smelter in Galveston Bay. The international company involved failed because its representatives made several risk communication errors. For example, they did not distinguish the powerful from the fringe groups and work with the former to ascertain and meet community expectations for keeping the bay area clean. Eventually, TCC's efforts to build the copper smelter in Galveston Bay were defeated by well-organized opposition from fishing, tourist, and sporting groups as well as citizens with homes near the smelter's proposed site. These opposing groups defeated the company by questioning the results of permit hearings, delaying construction of the facility until the company grew tired of having capital tied up in a nonexistent plant.

A contrasting case reviewed by Heath involves the Chemical Manufacturers Association's "citizens' advisory councils" as vehicles for both identifying and meeting community objections to chemical emissions. Heath explains that the CACs are run by a hired third-party facilitator charged with constituting the steering committee and drafting its charter. Steering committee members are individuals active in local business, civic, religious, and other community activities. Environmental activists are asked to join, as are four individuals from the sponsoring company. The CACs' mission is to identify topics of concern to the community regarding a chemical plant's activities or emissions. These concerns become the agenda items for CAC meetings.

According to Heath, the CACs have become forums for raising issues and concerns. Company officials listen to CAC members to learn what aspects of their operations are troubling. Additionally, the CACs serve as focus groups for refining public relations messages. Clearly, CACs may be used as serious contexts for problem solving or as token appeasement of irate community members. Although there is always the possibility that a CAC might be exploited as a rubber stamp for company plans, Heath's discussion of the Galveston Bay CACs is intriguing because it offers a specific set of procedures that seem to instantiate the dialogic ideals advocated by Juanillo and Scherer, among many others (e.g., Bradbury, 1989; Krimsky & Plough, 1988).

A second contribution Heath makes is his novel support for the use of technically trained personnel as risk communicators. The idea that informed answers by technically trained individuals are more credible, in the long run, than those of less-informed public relations officers makes sense. Heath's example of a technical person demonstrating that the amount of cyanide in a plant falls within acceptable levels nicely illustrates his point. In sum, Heath's chapter presents a rich set of detailed examples concerning effective and ineffective risk communication procedures. Any procedure can be used for good or ill, so the motives of any particular company or agency in communicating should always be carefully considered. But by describing very specific communication methods, such as CACs, using the technically trained as spokespersons, and the "open-door" policy one company adopted, Heath makes an effective and pragmatically useful contribution to the policy and regulation literature.

Scholarly efforts to identify effective and ineffective features of risk management and communication procedures have real benefits for practitioners. Just knowing about the possible use of reverse Dutch auctions, CACs, and other well-specified forums for risk communication can help practitioners avoid becoming cynical about the possibility of improved risk communication among stakeholders with conflicting interests. Well-specified procedures make concrete the beautiful, but remote-seeming, ideals advanced by Juanillo and Scherer.

INFORMED MODELS OF RISK PERCEPTION

Risk communication practitioners frequently work as environmental protection agents or health department officials. As a consequence of their positions, they need to call public attention to health or environmental hazards, or they need to reduce disproportionate fear. Frequently, these individuals have sophisticated "mental models" of health and environmental hazards—their jobs require that they do. However, they are much less likely to have sophisticated mental models of their publics, how their publics perceive risk, and how to communicate about risk with these individuals.

Some indicators of practitioners' notions about their publics can be gleaned from interview data. Recently, in preparation for a seminar on risk communication given to 130 state environmental risk assessors, I surveyed participants to elicit their perceptions about risk communication. Among other questions, I asked why their publics did not understand the degree of hazard posed by local hazardous waste sites. Here are some of their responses:

Paranoia of hazardous wastes.

Fear that government is pulling a "fast one" on [the] public.

Ignorance of risk assessment and that "voodoo" science.

When I talk to people at a site, the first thing I hear is all the cancer in the neighborhood. The site is not the cause—lifestyle is.

People have been conditioned to react to names (e.g., dioxin, PCBs, radiation) rather than on the degree of risk from an exposure to a site.

They are only concerned about short-term risks to themselves and diverting the issues to an "us" versus "them" scenario.

Some of these responses are insightful; some are not. But note the emphasis they all place on such ideas as paranoia, ignorance, fear, and conditioning. What this sampling suggests is that these individuals do not feel especially optimistic about risk communication. They see their publics as irrational, and they see communication with irrational people as futile. In my experience, these responses are not atypical. Consequently, I believe practitioners need alternative ways of construing people's reactions to risks, ones that suggest people are not as irrational as they may seem, and that when people do act irrationally, there are ways of combating that. In brief, practitioners need mental models of risk perception that are accurate and that point toward productive modes of risk communication.

Scholars can, and have, assisted risk communication practitioners by identifying psychological and social factors associated with risk perception. Currently, work on psychological factors predictive of risk perception among lay audiences is quite extensive. Less work is available on social factors.

Psychological Factors Associated With Risk Perception

The largest body of research relevant to risk communication is that on psychological factors affecting risk perception. Numerous studies have identified dimensions along which "experts" or technicals' evaluations of a risk will vary from those of "lay audiences" or democratics (e.g., Covello, 1992; Fischhoff, Slovic, & Lichtenstein, 1982; Goleman, 1994; Lichtenstein, Slovic, Fischhoff, Layman, & Combs, 1978; Slovic, 1987; Tversky, Sattath, & Slovic, 1988; Wandersman & Hallman, 1993). In brief, physical risks are perceived to be *more hazardous* by lay audiences if these risks are viewed as not observable, unknown to those exposed, delayed in their effects, unfamiliar, uncontrollable, globally catastrophic, fatal, not fair, risky to future generations, and involuntary. In contrast, physical risks are perceived as *less hazardous* if they are observable, known to those exposed, immediate in their effects, familiar, controllable, not globally catastrophic, not fatal, equitable, individual, of minimal danger to future generations, and voluntary. The result of all this is that risks such as traces of chemical carcinogens in drinking water will generally be more upsetting to individuals than the discovery of, for example, a naturally occurring, illness-causing parasite in their drinking water.

Recent work has explored mass media coverage as a factor in risk perception, and several findings are noteworthy. First, people assume that news coverage of a risk suggests that the risk is more important and more severe than other not-reported or less-reported risks (Fischhoff, 1989). For example, news reports about the dangers of asbestos in schools may have exacerbated concern about this risk. In some communities recently, more money was spent on asbestos removal per student than on education for students (Fisher, Chestnut, Chapman, & Rowe, 1993). Additionally, negative events are usually more psychologically vivid than are positive ones. Thus, as Slovic says, news about an accident at a chemical plant will be more memorable than stories depicting numerous competent and positive activities in which the same plant engaged (cited by Goleman, 1994; see also Griffin & Dunwoody, 1992; Plous, 1991).

In their chapter in this volume, Griffin, Neuwirth, and Dunwoody shed light on the role particular mass media message features may play in people's judgments of health and environmental risks after reading news stories. These researchers were interested in the extent to which the severity and likelihood of a hazard, along with journalistic message design factors such as headlining and personalizing leads, might be associated with readers' perceptions of mass media-reported risk.

To explore this question, they drew from Fishbein and Ajzen's (1975; Ajzen & Fishbein, 1980) theory of reasoned action, which is based on the assumption that people generally behave in rational ways. In addition, they also drew upon Kasperson's (1992) theory of mass media coverage of risk, which says that mass media coverage essentially "amplifies" or makes phenomena seem more dramatic, compelling, important, dangerous, or serious than they would have without such coverage.

Griffin et al. report a number of findings, at least two of which should be of interest to practitioners. First, as one would predict if one assumes people are essentially rational, students who read stories where the likelihood or level of risk was high (i.e., that it was highly likely one would become ill from drinking the infested tap water) were more likely to believe that drinking tap water would lead to illness than were those who read stories where this risk was said to be much lower. This finding supports the notion that risk information reported in the mass media is associated with people's appraisals of that risk.

Second, Griffin et al.'s findings in connection with the stylistic factors assessed were more complex than expected. When the risk of illness was reported as *low* in the body of the story but mentioned in the headline, students tended to *overestimate* the perceived risk of getting ill. However, when the likelihood of illness was reported as *high* in the story and also mentioned in the headline, the "amplification" effect disappeared. In fact, when the risk in the story was high, reading a risk-mentioning headline reduced aversion to the risk, a puzzling finding. Griffin et al. suspect it may be accounted for by discounting. That is, the headline may have seemed to exaggerate the risk reported in the relatively brief story. Thus there was some support for Kasperson's amplification theory of mass media effects, though that support was qualified. The amplification phenomenon occurred only in conditions where a story reported a risk to be low but the risk was graphically "blared" in the story's headline.

The strength of Griffin et al.'s work in their chapter here and in other sources (e.g., Dunwoody & Russow, 1989; Russow & Dunwoody, 1991) is its systematicity and use of powerful theory to study risk communication. In fact, the theory they employ in their chapter in this volume is so fully detailed and explored that the phenomenon they study—risk communication—may receive a somewhat less thorough conceptualization than ideal. However, this study is one of several in a systematic research program exploring psychological, social, and mass media factors associated with risk perception. (Social factors include such concerns as the size and economic diversity of a perceiver's community.) The real force of the work Griffin, Neuwirth, Dunwoody, and their associates have undertaken will come from the broad picture their research program will paint of the relationships among psychological, social, and mass media factors' associations with risk perception.

Self-Efficacy and Risk

Some of the most interesting research in risk perception and risk communication has been that conducted by Kim Witte, who has explored the psychological factor of self-efficacy and risk. Self-efficacy concerns the extent to which one feels able to defend oneself against a physical danger. In her chapter in this volume, Witte is interested in helping practitioners determine people's states of mind about some risk so that they can take this information into account in designing risk messages, particularly messages urging people to take some voluntary precautionary action. Witte's prior studies have identified ways of determining whether individuals are orienting more toward control of a danger or toward mitigating their fear of it through psychological processes such as denial (Witte, 1992). As her extended parallel process model (EPPM) predicts, when individuals evaluate a risk message, one of three responses is possible. If they view the threat as minimal, they will ignore the message. If they view the threat as severe and feel they know how to combat it, they will take steps to do so. But if they view the threat as severe and feel unable to control it, fear sets in and they resort to psychological processes, such as recasting the threat as less severe or even denying its existence.

Knowing how an audience is perceiving a risk allows risk communicators to adjust their messages appropriately. If audience members see the danger as trivial and it is not, information about the danger (or need for fear) can be presented. But if the danger is high, communicators need to know whether audience members' orientation is toward danger control or fear control. If it is fear control, then Witte recommends giving the audience information about ways they can control exposure to the risk, that is, self-efficacy information.

Risk communication practitioners I have talked with are enthusiastic about Witte's work because it increases their perceived self-efficacy *as communicators.* Her work illustrates the power of refining practitioners' mental models of risk communication. Witte's explorations of the EPPM's utility provide risk communicators with an understanding of why people are responding as they do to risk as well as guidance in how to either heighten people's sense of some danger or increase awareness of steps available for controlling exposure to the danger. In sum, Witte's work suggests concrete, practical steps practitioners can take to improve the effectiveness of their communication efforts. Because it does, it is being eagerly received by numerous practitioners and scholars in public health and safety fields.

Social Factors Associated With Risk Perception

Unlike the psychological factors associated with risk perception, less is known about social factors and risk perception. There has been some work conducted to examine social factors such as age, gender, and race correlates of risk perception (e.g., Benthin, Slovic, & Severson, 1993; Drotiz-Sjoberg & Sjoberg, 1991; Otani, Leonard, & Ashford, 1992; Spigner, Hawkins, & Loren, 1993; Wood, Hillman, & Sawilowsky, 1992), and cross-cultural studies of risk perception have been undertaken (e.g., Ayish, 1991; Dake, 1991; Kasperson & Stallen, 1991). However, there has been less work on, for example, relationships among social factors such as occupation, socioeconomic status, race, community size, and region as predictors of risk perception. A notable exception is a line of work by Dunwoody, Griffin, and their associates on community pluralism and newspaper coverage of risk (e.g., Dunwoody & Russow, 1989; Griffin & Dunwoody, 1992). In brief, these researchers have found associations between the "pluralism" of a community (frequently a correlate of community size) and coverage of environmental risk. Griffin and Dunwoody (1992) found, for example, that if a community is labeled by a federal agency as a "top polluter," the way this news is presented will vary as a function of community pluralism. Smaller communities dependent upon the branded company for jobs may focus on solutions to the problem in their reporting or may downplay the report. Newspapers in larger communities, which are less dependent upon single employers, are more apt to focus their coverage on the problem and on spotlighting culpable parties. Clearly, factors such as community size and type of news coverage are associated with judgment about risk just as psychological factors are. There is a need for more research of the kind Griffin, Dunwoody, and their colleagues have undertaken on social factors and risk perceptions.

In sum, research on risk perception has examined the differences between technical and lay perceptions of physical risks in great detail. For the most part, researchers have focused on risk features and psychological factors that account for these differences. Less work is available on the mass media's association with risk perception and on social factors such as community size and their connections to patterns in risk judgment. Much of the work on characteristic patterns of risk perception is useful to practitioners who need to consider how a given audience may view some hazard. Perception research by itself, however, does not provide practitioners with the conceptual tools they need for effective communication. Practitioners also need heuristics for audience analysis and message generation.

A SYSTEMATIC AND RHETORICAL
UNDERSTANDING OF RISK COMMUNICATION

Currently in the risk communication literature there is a tendency to view findings about risk perception as equivalent to information about risk communication. For example, Covello (1992) presents a discussion of risk comparisons as a way of indicating what is known about risk communication. Risk comparisons are analogies or other comparisons practitioners use to help those without technical training understand statistical estimates of a risk's severity or likelihood. For example, a message noting that you have a greater chance of being killed walking down the street than you do of being harmed by a nuclear power plant accident would count as a risk comparison. As a number of scholars have noted, this example suggests precisely what is irritating about some risk comparisons (Covello, 1992; Slovic, 1987): Although they frequently reflect accurate information about a risk's likelihood, risk comparisons annoy lay audiences when familiar, mundane risks (those of walking down the street) are compared with risks perceived as exotic and potentially catastrophic (nuclear power plant accidents).

Practitioners Need
a Rhetoric of Risk Communication

Information supplied in risk comparisons is specific and useful in a narrow sense, but ultimately it misleads. It wrongly suggests to practitioners that risk communication with the public is a matter of knowing "what answers people get wrong on the risk quizzes life offers" and teaching them the correct answers. This, of course, is a dimension of the "technical" perspective on risk situations that publics find upsetting.

Instead of simply learning how to generate good risk comparisons, practitioners need information about why people act and feel as they do and how practitioners can build working relationships with them. Practitioners need to be able to create contexts for supportive, informative, persuasive, and action-engendering communication—whatever the risk or situation at hand calls for.

Risk communicators would be more benefited if researchers, rather than focusing on specific message *forms,* such as comparisons, focused instead on helping practitioners analyze risk situations and achieve certain *goals.* Too often, current research provides practitioners bits and pieces of information about communication but fails to offer an integrated, comprehensive theory. What practitioners need is a theory detailing the difficulties risk communication generally involves and the best methods for addressing those difficulties through communication. This is what I mean by a *rhetoric.*

Without a rhetorical approach to risk communication, practitioners and scholars tend to present "rules" for risk communication. Covello and Allen (1988) present such rules in a pamphlet for the U.S. Environmental Protection Agency. Their seven rules include "Speak clearly and with compassion" and "Accept the public as a legitimate partner" in risk decision making. These rules are useful as guidelines instantiating the best features of the technical ("Speak clearly") and democratic ("Accept the public") orientations to risk communication, but ultimately, rules must be complemented with analytic tools. When practitioners speak clearly and with compassion but are still shouted down or misunderstood, they have no bases for diagnosing why communication failed in their encounters. In contrast, a rhetoric provides analytic tools for situation analysis and response. For example, a rhetoric of risk communication would offer practitioners a heuristic delineating the most likely tensions in risk communication situations.

Assume, for example, the following difficult risk communication situation: A set of environmental protection officials is facing an angry crowd at a public meeting. The meeting is the first opportunity a community has had to learn about cleanup options at a local hazardous waste site. Citizens attending the meeting are angry because they have had no role to this point in the decision-making process, despite the cleanup's clear effect on their lives. The most obvious tensions in this situation would come from profound distrust on the parts of both citizens and the state officials toward one another. However, practitioners who have the situation-analysis tools a rhetoric provides would be better equipped to operate in such a situation than would practitioners who lack this information. Rhetorically reflective practitioners would first consider classic obstacles to trust in any situation (doubts about competence, trustworthiness) and think quickly about what rhetoric-suggested actions would be most appropriate in this particularly distrustful context. Such an analysis might suggest steps, such as offering a 5-minute rather than a 50-minute presentation, offering to listen and take notes on audience members' concerns, offering to share their concerns with one's superiors, and providing the group with one's office phone number so they have some way of holding speakers accountable for their promises. There are no magic words or easy responses in difficult risk situations such as public meetings over landfills. Indeed, the unpleasantness of such meetings may be precisely what is needed to encourage adoption of better methods for waste site decision making. In the meantime, practitioners equipped with the conceptual tools a rhetoric provides would at least be able to diagnose their situations more carefully and speak more clearly to audience concerns than would those having access only to broad guidelines and rules.

Scholars Need a Rhetoric of Risk Communication

Research in risk communication would benefit as well from a rhetoric of risk communication. With such a theoretical tool, both Griffin et al. and Witte could make their already systematic work in risk communication even more so. When deciding which message features were relevant to a given effect or goal, they could draw from a comprehensive theory of message effects. These researchers present sophisticated analyses of persuasion and the attitude-behavior relationship. However, their theoretical apparatuses for selecting message features are less than comprehensive. Witte equates fear appeals with risk messages, implying that all risk messages are solely a matter of balancing two message features—danger depiction and efficacy information. This narrow definition is fine for an analysis of fear control, but it is limited if one also wants to explore a broader range of risk communication goals.

For example, suppose one wanted to test the effect of supplying accountability information (that is, information on how one could monitor another's activities) on perceptions of trustworthiness in hazardous waste site controversies (see Sandman, 1993, on the utility of accountability in building trust). Such a question is clearly relevant to risk communication. Currently, however, the theoretical frameworks Griffin et al. and Witte draw upon to identify testable message features are not capable of pointing to message features associated with credibility. A comprehensive theory of message features would delineate major communication goals pursued in risk communication and identify message features likely to facilitate or hinder those goals.

Building a Comprehensive
Rhetoric of Risk Communication

To locate the fundamental goals of risk communication, one must first identify the communication tensions inherent in risk communication situations. I have argued elsewhere that there are five such tensions (Rowan, 1991). Because communicating about unfamiliar physical risks makes people uneasy and skeptical, risk communication is plagued by *distrust*. Because it often involves information about newly discovered risks or newly discovered technologies and substances, risk communication is harmed by a *lack of awareness* about, for example, what bovine growth hormone is. Because risk communication involves complex scientific, legal, and philosophical issues, it is harmed by *ignorance* about how bovine growth hormone works or about the legal rights of consumers. Because risk communication frequently deals with phenomena about which even well-informed individuals disagree, it is affected by *dissatisfaction and disagreement*. And last, because risk communication also involves topics about which nearly all of us agree but that we find difficult to act upon (e.g., the importance of reducing dietary fat and increasing exercise), risk messages sometimes need to move people from states of psychological *inertia to action*.

In sum, these five fundamental tensions suggest five fundamental communicative goals. I list them with the mnemonic, CAUSE, referring to the goals of

credibility establishment,
awareness creation,
understanding enhancement,
satisfaction (i.e., agreement), and
enactment, or moving from agreement to action (Rowan, 1994).

Extensive social scientific research is available on message features associated with accomplishment or hindrance of each of these communication goals (for sketches of this work, see Rowan, 1991, 1994). Unfortunately, message research goes by numerous names and is scattered throughout a variety of social scientific fields. An important task for risk communication research is to offer detailed and integrated reviews of these literatures. Such reviews would high-light a wide array of message features that researchers studying risk communication effectiveness could tap.

With a systematic theory of message features, coupled with well-established theories of attitude and behavior change, we could provide practitioners with a highly refined sense of the ways in which risk communication is likely to go awry and the communication options available for addressing or avoiding these difficulties. Information about risk perception is necessary but not sufficient to help practitioners improve their understanding of and skill at risk communication. In addition, risk communicators need analytic tools for analyzing risk situations and generating responses consistent with their analyses. A rhetoric of risk communication would provide these conceptual tools.

SUMMARY

I have argued in this commentary that risk communicators could benefit from a wide array of communication research. But if we focus on what they need most, scholars should be assisting them in, first, generating a systematic philosophy of risk communication, one that transcends the unnecessary dichotomy posed by the technical and democratic orientations to risk situations. Second, scholars can benefit practitioners substantially by offering them detailed policy studies about what does and does not work in resolving complex siting disputes and information access questions. Third, scholars can assist practitioners by extending understanding not only of the psychological factors associated with risk perception but also of key social factors such as occupation, race, schooling, socioeconomic status, and broader community characteristics. And finally, scholars can assist practitioners by integrating and extending the information available about communication skills relevant in risk communication, skills such as listening, credibility management, informing-explaining, persuading, and motivating action.

The pursuit of this kind of an agenda in risk communication research is likely to have a real impact on practitioners and, one hopes, on the quality of human health and the environment. There is one more turn in the story of the general who viewed tying chairs together as an effective risk communication option. After the general gave his talk, a second speaker rose. She gave her presentation on the limitations of the linear model of risk communication and the importance of engaging the public in dialogue with risk assessors from the earliest stages of the assessment process. After listening to this presentation, the general leaned over to a copanelist and whispered, "My approach to risk communication was too linear, wasn't it?" With conversions like this, risk communication scholars should feel motivated to continue their work. Research in risk communication can and does make a difference in the world.

REFERENCES

Ajzen, I., & Fishbein, M. (1980). *Understanding attitudes and predicting social behavior.* Englewood Cliffs, NJ: Prentice Hall.

Ayish, M. (1991). Risk communication: A cross-cultural study. *European Journal of Communication, 6,* 213-222.

Bacow, L., & Milkey, J. (1982). Overcoming local opposition to hazardous waste facilities: The Massachusetts approach. *Harvard Environmental Law Review, 6,* 265-305.

Bauer, U. (1988). The river that wouldn't die. In B. Hall (Ed.), *Environmental politics: Lessons from the grassroots* (pp. 70-79). Durham, NC: Institute for Southern Studies.

Benthin, A., Slovic, P., & Severson, H. (1993). A psychometric study of adolescent risk perception. *Journal of Adolescence, 16,* 153-168.

Bradbury, J. A. (1989). The policy implications of differing concepts of risk. *Science, Technology and Human Values, 14,* 380-399.

Buchanan, M. (1988). No safe haven for Mr. Foushee's incinerator. In B. Hall (Ed.), *Environmental politics: Lessons from the grassroots* (pp. 85-91). Durham, NC: Institute for Southern Studies.

Covello, V. T. (1992). Risk communication: An emerging area of health communication research. In S. A. Deetz (Ed.), *Communication yearbook 15* (pp. 359-373). Newbury Park, CA: Sage.

Covello, V. T., & Allen, F. W. (1988). *Seven cardinal rules of risk communication.* Washington, DC: Environmental Protection Agency, Office of Policy Analysis.

Covello, V. T., & Mumpower, J. (1985). Risk analysis and risk management: An historical perspective. *Risk Analysis, 5,* 103-120.

Dake, K. (1991). Orienting dispositions in the perception of risk: An analysis of contemporary worldviews and cultural biases. *Journal of Cross-Cultural Psychology, 22,* 61-82.

Dauvergne, P. (1993). Nuclear power development in Japan. *Asian Survey, 33,* 576-591.

Davies, J. C., Covello, V. T., & Allen, F. W. (Eds.). (1987). *Risk communication.* Washington, DC: Conservation Foundation.

Douglas, M., & Wildavsky, A. (1982). *Risk and culture: An essay on the selection of technical and environmental dangers.* Berkeley: University of California Press.

Drotiz-Sjoberg, B., & Sjoberg, L. S. (1991). Adolescents' attitudes to nuclear power and radioactive waste. *Journal of Applied Social Psychology, 21,* 2007-2036.

Dunwoody, S., & Russow, M. (1989). Community pluralism and newspaper coverage of a high-level nuclear waste siting issue. In L. A. Grunig (Ed.), *Environmental activism revisited: The changing nature of communication through organizational public relations, special interest groups and the mass media* (pp. 5-19). Troy, OH: North American Association for Environmental Education.

Fiorino, D. J. (1989). Technical and democratic values in risk analysis. *Risk Analysis, 9,* 293-298.

Fiorino, D. J. (1990). Citizen participation and environmental risk: A survey of institutional mechanisms. *Science, Technology and Human Values, 15,* 226-243.

Fischhoff, B. (1989). Risk: A guide to controversy. In National Research Council, *Improving risk communication* (pp. 211-319). Washington, DC: National Academy Press.

Fischhoff, B., Slovic, P., & Lichtenstein, S. (1982). Lay foibles and expert foibles in judgments about risk. *American Statistician, 36,* 240-255.

Fishbein, M., & Ajzen, I. (1975). *Belief, attitude, intention, and behavior: An introduction to theory and research.* Reading, MA: Addison-Wesley.

Fisher, A., Chestnut, L. G., Chapman, R. H., & Rowe, R. D. (1993). Schools respond to risk management programs for asbestos, lead in drinking water and radon. *Risk: Issues in Health and Safety, 4,* 309-328.

Freudenberg, N. (1984). *NOT in our backyards! Community action for health and the environment.* New York: Monthly Review Press.

Goleman, D. (1994, February 1). Hidden rules often distort ideas of risk. *New York Times,* pp. B1-B9.

Griffin, R. J., & Dunwoody, S. (1992). *Press coverage of risk from environmental contaminants* (Report to the U.S. Environmental Protection Agency, Office of Policy, Planning, and Evaluation). Washington, DC: Government Printing Office.

Habermas, J. (1971). *Knowledge and human interests* (J. J. Shapiro, Trans.). Boston: Beacon.

Hadden, S. G. (1989). *A citizen's right to know: Risk communication and public policy.* Boulder, CO: Westview.

Heath, R. L., & Nathan, K. (1991). Public relations' role in risk communication: Information, rhetoric, and power. *Public Relations Quarterly, 35,* 15-22.

Inaba, H. (1993, February). Information: The key to acceptance of expanded nuclear power generation. *Japan 21st,* pp. 43-44.

Inhaber, H. (1991). A market-based solution to the problem of nuclear and toxic waste disposal. *Journal of the Air and Waste Management Association, 41,* 808-816.

Jinzaburo, T. (1988, October-December). Nuclear power's credibility crunch. *Japan Quarterly,* pp. 403-408.

Kasperson, R. E. (1992). The social amplification of risk: Progress in developing an integrative framework. In S. Krimsky & D. Golding (Eds.), *Social theories of risk* (pp. 153-178). New York: Praeger.

Kasperson, R. E., & Stallen, P. J. M. (Eds.). (1991). *Communicating risks to the public: International perspectives.* Dordrecht, Netherlands: Kluwer Academic.

Krimsky, S., & Plough, A. (1988). *Environmental hazards: Communicating risks as a social process.* Dover, MA: Auburn House.

Lichtenstein, S., Slovic, P., Fischhoff, B., Layman, M., & Combs, B. (1978). Judged frequency of lethal events. *Journal of Experimental Psychology: Human Learning and Memory, 4,* 557-578.

Lowi, T. J. (1990). Risks and rights in the history of American governments. *Daedalus, 119,* 17-40.

Lowrance, W. W. (1976). *Of acceptable risk: Science and the determination of safety.* Los Altos, CA: William Kaufmann.

Luhmann, N. (1989). *Ecological communication* (J. Bednarz, Jr., Trans.). Chicago: University of Chicago Press.

Luhmann, N. (1993). *Risk: A sociological theory* (R. Barrett, Trans.). New York: Aldine de Gruyter.

McDaniels, T. L., & Gregory, R. S. (1991). A framework for structuring cross-cultural research in risk and decision making. *Journal of Cross-Cultural Psychology, 22,* 103-127.

McLellan, J. A. (1989). Hazardous substances and the right to know in Canada. *International Labour Review, 14,* 639-650.

Meyer, M. W., & Solomon, K. (1984). Risk management in local communities. *Policy Sciences, 16,* 245-265.

National Research Council. (1989). *Improving risk communication.* Washington, DC: National Academy Press.

Ohio Environmental Protection Agency, Division of Emergency Response and Remediation. (1992). [Skinner Landfill (Butler County) public meeting tape]. Dayton: Author.

Ohio Environmental Protection Agency, Division of Emergency Response Remediation. (1993, February). *Superfund sites in Ohio.* Columbus: Author.

Otani, H., Leonard, S. D., & Ashford, V. L. (1992). Age differences in perceptions of risk. *Perceptual and Motor Skills, 74,* 587-594.

Plough, A., & Krimsky, S. (1987). The emergence of risk communication studies: Social and political context. *Science, Technology and Human Values, 12,* 4-10.

Plous, S. (1991). Biases in the assimilation of technological breakdowns: Do accidents make us safer? *Journal of Applied Social Psychology, 21,* 1058-1082.

Popper, F. J. (1985, March). The environmentalist and the LULU. *Environment, 27,* 7-11, 37-40.

Rowan, K. E. (1991). Goals, obstacles, and strategies in risk communication. *Journal of Applied Communication Research, 19,* 300-329.

Rowan, K. E. (1994). Why rules for risk communication fail: A problem-solving approach to risk communication. *Risk Analysis, 14,* 365-374.

Russow, M. D., & Dunwoody, S. (1991). Inclusion of "useful" detail in newspaper coverage of a high-level nuclear waste siting controversy. *Journalism Quarterly, 68,* 87-100.

Sandman, P. M. (1987, November). Risk communication: Facing public outrage. *EPA Journal,* pp. 21-22.

Sandman, P. M. (1993). *Responding to community outrage: Strategies for effective risk communication.* Fairfax, VA: American Industrial Hygiene Association.

Schrader-Frechette, K. S. (1985). *Risk analysis and scientific method: Methodological and ethical problems with evaluating societal risks.* Boston: D. Reidel.

Slovic, P. (1987). Perception of risk. *Science, 236,* 280-285.

Spigner, C., Hawkins, W., & Loren, W. (1993). Gender differences in perception of risk associated with alcohol and drug use among college students. *Women and Health, 20,* 87-97.

Tomsho, R. (1991, December 27). Small town in Alberta embraces what most reject: Toxic waste. *Wall Street Journal,* pp. A1, A4.

Tversky, A., Sattath, S., & Slovic, P. (1988). Contingent weighting in judgment and choice. *Psychological Review, 95,* 371-384.

Unger, D. G., Wandersman, A., & Hallman, W. (1992). Living near a hazardous waste facility: Coping with individual and family distress. *American Journal of Orthopsychiatry, 62,* 55-70.

Wandersman, A. H., & Hallman, W. K. (1993). Are people acting irrationally? Understanding public concerns about environmental threats. *American Psychologist, 48,* 681-686.

Wandersman, A. H., Hallman, W. K., & Berman, S. (1993). How residents cope with living near a hazardous waste landfill: An example of substantive theorizing. *American Journal of Community Psychology, 17,* 575-583.

Wiegman, O., Boer, H., Gutteling, J. M., Komilis, E., & Gadet, B. (1992). The development of reactions of the public to warning and emergency situations in France, Greece, and the Netherlands. *Journal of Social Psychology, 132,* 101-116.

Witte, K. (1992). The role of threat and efficacy in AIDS prevention. *International Quarterly of Community Health Education, 12,* 225-249.

Wood, P. C., Hillman, S. B., & Sawilowsky, S. S. (1992). Self-concept among African-American at-risk adolescents. *Perceptual and Motor Skills, 74,* 465-466.

14 Moving Toward a Framework for the Study of Risk Communication: Theoretical and Ethical Considerations

RAJIV NATH RIMAL
BJ FOGG
JUNE A. FLORA
Stanford University

T HE National Research Council (1989) defines risk communication as "an interactive process of exchange of information and opinion among individuals, groups, and institutions" (p. 2). Inherent in this definition are two elements risk communicators have generally overlooked. One is the idea that risk communication involves a two-way flow of information. The second is the necessity of including cross-level linkages in studying risk.

The field of risk communication, as young as it is, has grown tremendously in the past two decades. It has attracted researchers from a wide variety of disciplines—from sociologists interested in the social implications of risk to psychologists interested in cognitive biases in risk perception. In this chapter we demonstrate how communication, as a discipline, can make a set of unique contributions to the systematic study of risk.

Four aspects of risk are pertinent to communication as a field of study. First, questions about the cultural meaning ascribed to risk and the determination of a collective course of action involve issues of communication. They require consensus and negotiation of meaning. Second, the processes associated with risk-related decisions—that is, decisions made under conditions of uncertainty —are determined by communication. Heuristics that people employ in making judgments, for example, are heavily influenced by the manner in which issues are framed (Tversky & Kahneman, 1973, 1974). Framing, in turn, is a function

Correspondence and requests for reprints: Rajiv Nath Rimal, Department of Communication, McClatchy Hall, Stanford University, Stanford, CA 93405-2050.

Communication Yearbook 18, pp. 320-342

of communication. Third, communication of risk information is intrinsically linked to behavior. In few other areas does communication itself have such a great likelihood (and mandate) to change behavior. Communication scholars increasingly need to embrace theories and methods that enhance our understanding of behavior change.

Finally, we are not the first researchers to argue that any comprehensive study of risk has to adopt a multilevel approach that includes individuals, institutions, and whole societies (National Research Council, 1989; Renn, Burns, Kasperson, Kasperson, & Slovic, 1992). Because interactions among individuals, institutions, and societies are linked through communication (Paisley, 1984; Pan & McLeod, 1991), the field of communication is in a unique position to accommodate this multilevel approach. Next, we consider some of the reasons a multilevel approach is germane and theoretically heuristic.

LEVELS OF ANALYSIS
IN RISK COMMUNICATION

Risk communication is inherently a process that occurs at multiple levels of society, among institutions and political systems as well as among individual citizens. Further, there is a great deal of "cross-level" communication. The communication of risk typically involves senders at the institutional or societal level and receivers at the individual level. Government institutions, social organizations, interest groups, and the scientific community are just a few examples of higher-order entities that have an interest in disseminating risk-related information to the public. However, individuals also send messages to institutions (Rakow, 1989). Individuals and groups demand more and/or different information about risk. They also advocate change in institutional and political systems. A multilevel approach, though often neglected, is especially germane to enhancing our understanding of effective risk communication.

Individual-Level
Risk Communication

The central questions of concern to risk-related research—Why do people take precautions? How can we encourage people to act?—have generally been asked at the individual level (Weinstein, 1987). Crawford (1987) notes, for example, that the popular understanding of wellness in the 1970s and 1980s emphasized individual responsibility. The theme of individual responsibility was also manifest in the growth of self-help and self-care movements during that period. Research on risk perception focused on cognitive biases associated with individuals' ability to make judgments under conditions of uncertainty (Tversky & Kahneman, 1974) and demonstrated how such judgments diverge from normative standards (Kahneman & Tversky, 1972; Tversky & Kahneman,

1971, 1973). Individual behavior change was also the central concern of many large-scale public health campaigns in the 1980s, such as the Stanford Five-City Project (Farquhar et al., 1985) and the Minnesota Heart Health Program (Blackburn, Leupker, Kline, Bracht, & Carlaw, 1984).

Macro-Level
Risk Communication

The intuitive understanding of how risk affects us as individuals and the proliferation of research at the individual level neglect the consideration that individuals *as members of groups* are affected by risks. There are several shortcomings associated with analysis that is restricted to the individual level.

An exclusive concentration on individuals implies that, because the problem affects individuals, the source of the problem must also lie with individuals. When individuals are held accountable, solutions come to be framed entirely at the individual end. Those who are not capable of or do not possess the means to counter the threat are left to their own devices and are effectively blamed for not taking the requisite steps.

Although individuals may be held responsible for some risks they take voluntarily, many risks originate in institutions and so solutions are more efficiently obtained by attacking the problem at the source. As Weinstein (1987) points out, "A worker should not be expected to wear burdensome protective clothing when a better factory ventilation system would achieve the same result" (p. 7). For these reasons, a growing number of researchers have begun to suggest alternate paradigms (Crawford, 1987; Crouch & Wilson, 1982; Douglas, 1985; Hilgartner, 1992; Waterstone, 1992; Weinstein, 1987).

Framing groups, as opposed to individuals, as populations at risk is both practically and politically expedient. The sense of urgency is heightened when social groups are perceived to be vulnerable. Not only are social and legislative actions more easily secured when large numbers of people are affected, but social mobilization and collective effort strategies are also more likely to be effective when there is shared concern about risk factors.

Framing risk issues at the institutional level shifts our consideration of risk in several ways. First, an exclusive focus on the assessment, perception, and communication of risk constitutes an implicit acceptance of the status quo. Given such a restrictive orientation, communication has to focus on the management of risks, not on their reduction. Encouraging people to take protective measures against skin cancer is a case in point. Providing coping mechanisms in the face of growing threats is certainly a worthwhile strategy. However, locating the problem only at the protection end is an implicit acknowledgment of society's inability to contain the increased concentration of ultraviolet rays. A more effective strategy may be to focus on controlling the risk object itself by demanding a stringent policy on industrial emission levels.

Cross-Level
Risk Communication

Although individual well-being is at the center of many efforts designed to assess, manage, and study risk-related concerns, an effective approach has to be more comprehensive in scope, incorporating higher-order entities (Renn et al., 1992). How individuals process risk is shaped by their perceptions of how others in their surroundings construe and react to the same information (Fessenden-Raden, Fitchen, & Heath, 1987).

The impact of higher-order entities on individuals' risk perception and management strategies has been documented in a variety of settings, for example, in studies of the role of social networks and occupational environments (Hallman & Wandersman, 1992; Nordenstam & Vaughan, 1991), in studies concerned with cultural and ethnic identity (Dake, 1992; Dake & Wildavsky, 1991; Vaughan & Nordenstam, 1991), and in studies involving community and government agencies (Crawford, 1987; Ferguson & Valenti, 1991; Hance, Chess, & Sandman, 1989; Hansson, 1989). Collectively, these studies underscore the importance of embracing the larger social context in which risks are framed, construed, processed, and acted upon. The analysis we have offered so far also supports the need for an orientation that accommodates a multilevel approach. However, from a theoretical perspective, the adoption of a multilevel approach to the study of risk communication has more often been the exception than the rule. We have few theories that cut across levels, thus our explication is restricted mostly to the individual level.

The absence of a coherent organizing framework for analyzing theoretical, methodological, and practical implications of risk communication has also led to the creation of a body of literature that is more idiosyncratic than systematic. There is little agreement about theoretical issues as fundamental as the appropriate unit of analysis. Is the unit of analysis the individual, as the use of dispositional terms such as *risk averse* and *risk seeking* would indicate (Kahneman, Knetsch, & Thaler, 1991; Kahneman & Lovallo, 1993)? Or is the appropriate unit of analysis the situation, as another risk-related term, *conditions of uncertainty* (Tversky & Kahneman, 1974), would imply? In addition, what is the appropriate level of concept explication? After all, we talk about risk-seeking tendencies of individuals, groups (Bazerman, 1990; Douglas, 1985), and societies (Waterstone, 1992). Finally, as a practical matter, what are the important ethical considerations that risk communicators have to address?

In this chapter we argue for a framework that serves as a heuristic device for organizing theory and research, as well as for examining ethical concerns. The framework we suggest is not meant to be comprehensive in scope; we offer it only as a set of guidelines for conceptually arranging three critical issues: theory, ethics, and levels of analysis.

INTERPRETIVE CONTINUUM
OF RISK COMMUNICATION

In the literature, risk issues are broadly classified into two categories: risk assessment and risk management (Bogen, 1990; Rowe, 1992).[1] These categories represent two domains on a continuum that can be defined by the extent to which meaning is infused into risk messages. At one end of this interpretive continuum is the *descriptive* domain, within which risks are presented as pure data, with minimal subjective interpretation. At the other extreme of the interpretive continuum is the *injunctive* domain, within which risk messages are presented as harmful elements whose effects are to be avoided and overcome through behavior modification. Messages in the injunctive domain are unambiguous in how they interpret risks and advocate behavior change. Between these extreme points on the continuum, we locate the *evaluative* domain, which includes risk messages that contain intermediate levels of interpretation and injunction.

Consider, as an example of a message from the descriptive domain, the publication of crime statistics or vehicle accident rates, in which the associated risks are expressed as numerical probabilities of chance encounters. Little interpretation of the data is provided and no behavior change is advocated. A message from the evaluative domain, in contrast, is illustrated by the use of warning labels on cigarette packages, where risks to health are made explicit. An example of a message from the injunctive domain would be the Centers for Disease Control's "America Responds to AIDS" campaign, urging the use of condoms to fight AIDS, in which an explicit call is made for behavior modification.

In the practice of risk communication, there is a considerable amount of overlap among these concepts, which is why we classify the various communication strategies into domains and place domains on a continuum. Within the descriptive domain itself, for example, we can locate data at one end and information at the other.[2] Similarly, within the injunctive domain, we can differentiate between advocacy for behavior change and the less injunctive call for change in behavioral intention. In Figure 14.1 we have arranged the four studies included in this volume according to the theoretical and ethical issues they raise along the interpretive continuum.

The placement of risk messages along the interpretive continuum has a number of benefits. First, it allows for the explication of communication goals in each domain. A risk message in the descriptive domain has different sets of goals (conveying information, for example) from one in the evaluative domain (changing attitudes) or in the injunctive domain (changing behavior).

Second, once the communication goal has been defined, placement of the message on the interpretive continuum will set the boundary conditions for the pertinent theory, appropriate research questions, and expected outcomes. Only then can the effectiveness of various messages be evaluated. As McGuire (1989) points out, without an appropriate correspondence between goals and outcomes, communication efforts are doomed to fail, and evaluation efforts are likely to

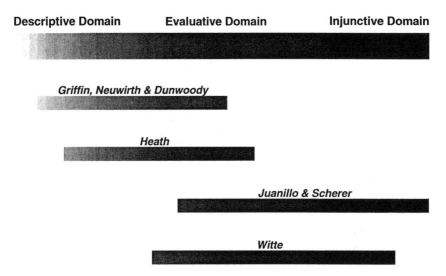

Figure 14.1. Interpretive Continuum

suffer from the "distant-measure fallacy," which represents a mismatch between the level at which messages are executed and the level at which they are evaluated.

The third benefit of locating messages on the interpretive continuum has to do with the various ethical issues that are invoked along the continuum. Messages in the descriptive domain, for example, raise substantially different ethical questions from those in the evaluative and injunctive domains. We discuss the theoretical and ethical issues in the following sections.

THEORETICAL ISSUES

Different sets of theoretical issues are raised within the different domains along the interpretive continuum. Theories can be distinguished along a number of dimensions, but we adopt a message design perspective and use an outcome expectancy criterion. In other words, our placement of theory into various domains is determined by the nature of the expected outcome. Further, out of the review of domain-specific theories and concepts arise implicit research questions about the relations among concepts within a level, relations among levels of analysis within risk communication, and the efficacy of the risk communication process.

Concepts in the Descriptive Domain

Knowledge Enhancement

An important goal of communication in this domain is the enhancement of knowledge about risk factors. Communicators have an obligation to provide access to accurate information, the prerequisite for knowledge enhancement—notwithstanding evidence of a tenuous link between knowledge gain and higher-order effects. Of particular interest are channel factors and message formats within channels (Flora, Maibach, & Maccoby, 1989) that determine optimum levels of information density, message complexity, and frequency.

Equally important for consideration are differential levels of audience abilities that facilitate information acquisition. The knowledge gap hypothesis (Donohue, Tichenor, & Olien, 1975; Tichenor, Donohue, & Olien, 1970) is a particularly important conceptual framework that should guide message design. It demonstrates how individuals and societies with higher competence levels (correlates of socioeconomic status) gain disproportionately more knowledge than those with lesser prior abilities. A failure to account for differential abilities among audience members can lead to self-defeating outcomes, where messages intended to reduce societal differences in knowledge result in increasing the "gap."

Communication

Many government agencies and industries are mandated to publish risk-related information periodically. The purpose of such communications quite often is the communication act itself. The "open-door policy" implemented by one chemical plant in the Texas gulf coast region (Heath, Chapter 11, this volume) illustrates this example. Although the effect of the disclosure may be the alleviation of public fears about the plant's environmental record, the purpose ostensibly is to promote an image of openness. Strategies of openness reflect genuine concerns to disseminate information only to the extent that the communication is presented in a simple manner that is readily digested by concerned individuals. Shrouding even authentic gestures of openness in a veil of complex jargon, however, can seriously undermine the communication effort.

Agenda-Setting and Media Advocacy

From a research evaluation perspective, dissemination of information is another important criterion in the descriptive domain. The extent of coverage of risk information in the media, audience exposure to the message, and issue salience may be of particular interest to the source. Agenda-setting research (McCombs & Shaw, 1972) provides the conceptual link between the media's agenda and the public's agenda (see also Manheim, 1987, for the interaction among various agendas in the public realm). A particularly illustrative example is provided by Rogers, Dearing, and Chang (1991), who demonstrate the convergence of the media agenda, the public agenda, and the policy agenda in the AIDS epidemic. Of special interest here is the cross-level linkage that agenda-setting research provides between individuals at the micro end and communities and institutions at the macro end.

Whereas agenda-setting research is concerned with the effects *of* the media, media advocacy is concerned with effects *on* the media. Media advocacy is the strategic use of public relations techniques to stimulate coverage and influence the framing of public health issues in the media (Wallack, 1990; Wallack, Dorfman, Jernigan, & Themba, 1993). The ultimate goal of media advocacy is to shape the public policy agenda. Media advocates pursue this goal by increasing the frequency of coverage and by influencing the manner in which public health issues are framed in the media. We discuss additional framing issues below.

Concepts in the Evaluative Domain

Whereas descriptive risk messages are concerned with presenting the data, evaluative messages are concerned with the manner in which the presentation occurs. In the evaluative domain, risk messages are provided with sufficient interpretation to highlight the potential threats of hazards. The goals of communication in this domain include influencing judgment, enhancing perceptions of risk, and changing attitudes and beliefs.

Influencing Judgment

Literature on risk perception leaves little doubt that judgment is influenced heavily by the manner in which risks are framed (Kahneman & Tversky, 1984; Tversky & Kahneman, 1974). Under conditions of uncertainty, individuals employ cognitive shortcuts, or heuristics, to make judgments. The extent to which these judgments are biased is determined by the kinds of heuristics that are brought to bear on the decision process. Representativeness, availability, and insufficient adjustment (Tversky & Kahneman, 1974) are three heuristics that lead individuals to make biased judgments. Their influential role in the decision-making process highlights the importance of paying attention to the manner in which risks are framed and presented to the public.

Perceived Risk

We assume that risk communicators are interested in motivating their audiences to attend to and understand the evaluated risks. In other words, the "risk" component of risk communication in this domain is used as an independent variable ("perceived risk"); the dependent variable is the extent to which the audience is motivated to attend to or seek information about the evaluated message. Indeed, perceived risk has been found to be directly related to information seeking (Atkin, 1973). The implication of this finding, however—that increasing levels of perceived risk will promote information seeking—has to be taken with caution. As Witte points out in her chapter in this volume, such strategies taken beyond the "critical point" are likely to backfire, as they induce fear control responses over danger control responses, effectively stifling the onset of coping mechanisms.

Grunig's (1983) situational theory provides supporting evidence: Information-seeking behavior is typical of those whose awareness of prevailing problems is high and perception of constraints is low. Although increasing problem recognition increases the first dimension, it also influences constraint recognition and inhibits information seeking. Witte's extended parallel processing model provides a convenient, albeit tentative, guide for determining the threshold of heightened risk awareness.

Attitude Change and Involvement

Literature on persuasion suggests that involvement is an important variable that determines how information is processed. Ray's (1973) model lists three hierarchies that are invoked under different conditions. Under conditions of high involvement with clear alternative choices (learning hierarchy), cognitions lead to affective changes that in turn lead to behavior. When there is no clear choice among alternatives but involvement is high (dissonance attribution hierarchy), behaviors influence affect and, subsequently, through attributional processes, cognitions (Festinger, 1957). Under conditions of low involvement (low involvement hierarchy), cognitions influence behavior, which, in turn, influences affect.

Petty and Cacioppo's (1981) elaboration likelihood model predicts similar outcomes. Under conditions of high involvement, individuals tend to focus on information central to the message—strength of the argument, for example—and information processing follows the "central route." Under conditions of low involvement, the "peripheral route" is invoked and the focus is on components not crucial to the message, such as source attractiveness and message appeal. Messages that have been processed through the central route are likely to be elaborated upon extensively and thus are enduring. Messages processed through the peripheral route are likely to endure only as long as the peripheral cues are present (Cialdini et al., 1975). Because involvement determines which route will be invoked, it will also determine the extent of message elaboration and hence retention.

Working on Petty and Cacioppo's (1981) model, Flora and Maibach (1990) have demonstrated that at low levels of cognitive involvement, emotional messages are particularly important for recall. The implication for risk communicators is obvious: When it is difficult to motivate individuals, use emotion-eliciting messages; when involvement in a topic is already high, use thought-eliciting messages that facilitate long-term changes.

Concepts in the Injunctive Domain

When risks are presented with an explicit call for action, the message is said to lie within the injunctive domain. On the interpretive continuum, the injunctive domain constitutes risk messages infused with the maximum amount of interpretation, leaving little ambiguity about the harm posed by various hazards. "Just say no" is an example of a message in the injunctive domain. The interpretation provided by the communicator leaves little doubt that drugs are "bad," or even that the morality issue is open to debate. It advocates behavior modification consistent with the preinterpreted message.

Although the practical goal of the communication in this domain is behavior modification, the theoretical tools employed toward that end are somewhat ambiguous. The source of ambiguity, by far, has been the failure to make adequate theoretical distinctions between behavioral intentions and actual behaviors. Notwithstanding Ajzen and Fishbein's (1980) admonition—that behavioral intentions can act as proxy for actual behaviors only to the extent that intentions "correspond to the behavioral criterion in action, target, context, and time" (p. 51) and that they are within individuals' volitional control—researchers have generally used the two concepts interchangeably. We distinguish between theories based on behavioral intentions and those that deal directly with behavior change. The following list of theories is not meant to be comprehensive; it represents only a handful of the most commonly invoked application-oriented approaches.

Theories on Behavioral Intention

The theory of reasoned action. Fishbein and Ajzen's (1975, 1981; Ajzen and Fishbein, 1980; Fishbein, 1980) theory posits that individuals' behavioral intention is a function of attitudes toward the behavior and perceptions of normative pressures to perform the behavior (see, for example, Griffin, Neuwirth, & Dunwoody, Chapter 9, this volume). Despite several limitations of the theory (for example, its application only to those behaviors under a person's volitional control and its failure to distinguish between expectations and intentions), its predictive power has generally withstood strong theoretical scrutiny in a variety of domains. Two meta-analyses done by Sheppard, Hartwick, and Warshaw (1988) of 87 separate studies that employed the theory of reasoned action revealed, for example, not only that the theory is robust across several conditions, but also that the application of the theory to situations beyond the model's original boundary conditions (measures of behavioral intention involving single behavior without choice among alternatives) has resulted in consistent findings.

Of particular interest here to risk communicators is the higher correlation observed between intention and performance for activities involving choice than that for activities without choice among alternatives. Postdecisional evaluation of performance, from a cognitive dissonance (Festinger, 1957) perspective, also predicts more positive evaluation of choice-related outcomes than non-choice-related, though identical, outcomes. Taken together, these findings suggest that, in order to change behavioral intentions, presenting individuals with choice among options in combating a threat against a potential risk is a more effective strategy than presenting an "ideal" solution. This strategy will result not only in a higher likelihood of change from the status quo, but, once such changes have been adopted, they will be evaluated more positively. This will likely result in higher maintenance rates.

The health belief model. The health belief model (Becker, 1974; Janz & Becker, 1984; Rosenstock, 1960, 1966, 1974) was developed in the context of the study of people's propensity to seek preventive action against tuberculosis (Rosenstock, 1990) in the 1950s; since then, it has been used in a variety of health domains. The model predicts that people will be ready to adopt a preventive measure if a sequence of cognitive components is invoked. These components are (a) perceived threat, which includes perceptions of susceptibility to and severity of the disease; (b) high levels of perceived benefits in taking the preventive action; and (c) low perceived costs in taking the preventive action. In general, people are expected to adopt a preventive action if the perceived levels of threat and benefit are high and the perceived costs associated with the preventive action are low. In addition to these components, people are more likely to adopt a behavior in the presence of internal or external cues (or "prompts") to action.

As with the theory of reasoned action, the health belief model is grounded in assumptions about the powerful role of rational decision-making processes that induce individuals to take action. Janz and Becker's (1984) review of 29 studies that employed the health belief model between 1974 and 1984, and 17 others conducted prior to 1974, demonstrated that factors related to the model were significantly related to prevention behavior. Because of a heavy reliance on retrospective measures, however, the causal link of the various components of the model has been difficult to establish. Thus the health belief model falls short of prospectively inducing behavior change, which is why it is included here under behavioral *intention.*

Protection motivation theory. Closely related to the health belief model is protection motivation theory (Maddux & Rogers, 1983; Rogers, 1975, 1983), which relates reactions to threats to attitude change. In the original formulation of protection motivation theory (Rogers, 1975), intent to adopt the recommended response was conceptualized as an outcome of responses to fear. The relationship between intent and fear was mediated by cognitive processes, such as appraisal of severity, expectancy of exposure, belief in the efficacy of coping response, and protection motivation.

Subsequent improvements in protection motivation theory have incorporated the notion of self-efficacy and the interplay of adaptive and maladaptive responses. Experiments done by Maddux and Rogers (1983) and Kirscht and Joseph (1989) have indicated powerful main effects of self-efficacy on intention to adopt the recommended coping behavior and a three-way interaction among self-efficacy, outcome expectancy, and behavioral intention (Maddux & Rogers, 1983; Maddux, Sherer, & Rogers, 1982). The interaction was such that when any two of the three components were high, additional information had little effect; however, when fear of exposure to danger was high, intentions to adopt the recommended behavior were also high if either the self-efficacy was high or perceptions about the coping strategy's ability to avert the danger were high.

From a risk communication perspective, protection motivation theory is an improvement over the health belief model because of its shift in focus from entirely on the negative aspects associated with threats to positive aspects associated with coping mechanisms.

Theory of Behavior Change

Social-cognitive theory (Bandura, 1977, 1986) is based on the principle that reciprocal interactions among behavioral, personal, and environmental factors determine psychological functioning. Although the models we have considered so far (the theory of reasoned action, the health belief model, and protection motivation theory) treat behavior as an outcome of a series of antecedents, social-cognitive theory's strength lies in its conceptualization of behavior as an ongoing process that determines and is determined by environmental and personal factors. The three components of the theory—personal, environmental, and behavioral factors—continuously interact with one another such that a change in one has implications for the others. For example, an individual's behavior is shaped by his or her environment; however, a change in behavior can alter both the environment and the individual's perception of self-efficacy to bring about the change.

From the perspective of injunctive risk messages designed to change individuals' behavior, social-cognitive theory underscores the importance of taking into account the totality of the situation in which individuals exist. It is not enough simply to advocate behavior change. In the absence of cognitive skills *and* environmental modifications, change will be difficult to achieve, and, when achieved, difficult to maintain. Instead, requisite cognitive skills, such as perceptions of self-efficacy, must be modified, and cognitive barriers must be removed. In addition, substantial changes in environmental conditions must be brought about if behavioral modifications are to be sustained.

As we pointed out earlier, behavior change is a process that includes both theoretical and ethical concerns. Such concerns also guide communication efforts along the entire range of the interpretive continuum. Having pointed out some of the theoretical concerns, we next turn to the ethical side of risk communication.

ETHICAL ISSUES

The Growing Need for Ethical Awareness

Our premise in this section is that risk communication is a value-laden activity (Salmon, 1989; Warwick & Kelman, 1973). In other words, the values and motives of message senders—in this case, risk communicators—are expressed through the process of risk communication. Even though risk communication scholars sometimes disagree on the specifics of what constitutes ethical behavior (Greenberg, 1991; National Research Council, 1989), we cannot afford to neglect ethics as part of our ongoing research and discussion (Greenberg, 1991; Morgan & Lave, 1990). Indeed, risk communication efforts will fail to serve society if risk communicators neglect careful consideration of ethical issues.

To date, the primary focus of ethical discussions of risk communication has been to identify the values of scientists and technical sources as the senders of risk communication messages. For example, scientists may express their values through choosing numbers to summarize knowledge about the magnitude of risk and through weighting different attributes of hazards (National Research Council, 1989). In contrast, the roles of channel values (such as journalistic norms) and of message receivers' values have been less well examined. To be sure, ethical communication concerns not just the sender; messages can be modified substantially in both the dissemination process and the receiving process. For example, Morgan and Lave (1990) have argued that ethical problems in risk communication arise when there is a mismatch between the objectives of the sender and those of the receiver.

In this chapter, we do not deal comprehensively with all issues of ethical risk communication. Instead, our intent is to highlight the importance of ethical issues by presenting five illustrative examples of values for ethical communication and by showing how the framework of the three domains can inform our understanding of potential ethical problems. The five illustrative values germane to risk communication that we consider here are as follows: *voice,* the extent to which receivers have a voice in the risk communication process; *self-determination,* the extent to which receivers can determine their own actions; *honesty,* the extent to which messages conform to standards of honesty; *pluralism,* the extent to which alternative views are allowed to exist in the risk communication process; and *equality,* the extent to which risk messages are available to and efficacious for all individuals in the focal audience. These values have been discussed in various places in the communication literature (Andersen, 1991; Arnett, 1991; Cronen, 1991; Doxiadis, 1987a, 1987b; Eisenberg, 1987; Greenberg, 1991; Jaksa & Pritchard, 1988; Makau, 1991; Morgan & Lave, 1990; National Research Council, 1989; Warwick & Kelman, 1973).

Issues in the Descriptive Domain

A host of ethical issues arise in the descriptive domain. We discuss below three of the most salient: equality, honesty, and self-determination.

Threats to Equality

Ethical problems within the descriptive domain are likely to arise because of the nature of data and people: Data require interpretation, and people have differing interpretation abilities (Morgan & Lave, 1990; National Research Council, 1989). In other words, descriptive messages may be understood by one person (who can bring his or her own interpretive skills to the data), whereas the same message may not be understood (or understood in the same way) by another person. This presents an ethical concern about equality of information delivery.

In his chapter in this volume, Heath unintentionally presents an example of the inequality data can create. In one scenario, he explains how a chemical company opened its records to public view to allow the public "to scrutinize plant permits and operating standards." We suspect that the citizens who read the plant records probably had insufficient training to make sense of the data. Heath cites this communication strategy as a good example of openness, but this strategy may have had a stronger effect—one that brings up ethical questions. Even though the plant's data were ostensibly available to everyone, the information that could be extracted from the data was not. After what we might guess were frustrating attempts to understand the plant and its impact, most citizens likely gave up their investigation, figuring they should simply listen to "expert" opinion.

Threats to Honesty

The next ethical problem that arises from descriptive risk messages is lack of honesty regarding presentation of information—sometimes intentional, sometimes not. Of course, doctoring data is a breach of honesty; however, dishonesty can be more subtle than that (National Research Council, 1989). Honesty—or the lack thereof—can be understood through the examination of senders' intentions regarding messages (Morgan & Lave, 1990) as well as through an understanding of the larger scientific and technical communities that collect and interpret data. Intentional deceit occurs when an agency selectively chooses which data to release. Other threats to honesty may be unintentional. As Salmon (1989) writes, "While numbers themselves may be neutral, the means through which numbers are procured and interpreted certainly are not" (p. 39). Indeed, all observations include some sort of bias, because instruments are biased and because the humans who use the tools or methods are inevitably imprecise (National Research Council, 1989).

Potential for Self-Determination

Despite the inevitable bias of "pure" data, descriptive campaign messages are the least biased of all risk communication messages. They also allow for the greatest degree of self-determination. If data can be easily and appropriately interpreted by all focal audiences, individuals can reach their own conclusions about personal meaning and appropriate behavior. For example, in their chapter in this volume, Juanillo and Scherer cite a hopeful case in which "residents of small towns facing water quality problems can quickly educate themselves about complicated chemical risk issues." In this instance, people learned to interpret data, and this process allowed them to choose their own behaviors relative to the risks. Certainly, laypeople can—and should—become more conversant with the interpretation of data (National Research Council, 1989).

Issues in the Evaluative Domain

As we stated at the beginning of this chapter, evaluative risk messages impose an interpretive framework on data that makes possible some conclusion about risk level or risk behavior. In their chapter, Juanillo and Scherer capture the distinction between descriptive and evaluative messages well: "Disputes over risk are not just about numbers; they are also about values. Agreements on the validity of the numbers do not resolve the differences." Because interpretive frameworks are by nature biased, messages in the evaluative domain present some of the most complex ethical issues in risk communication. Many ethical concerns arise in the evaluative domain, but we focus here on threats to voice, pluralism, and equality.

Threats to Voice

Interpretive risk messages may raise ethical questions because they often do not allow people to voice their opinions in ways that bring about change (National Research Council 1989). Indeed, too few risk campaigns have designed systems for making the interpretation of data an interactive, negotiated process. In their chapter, Juanillo and Scherer focus on the issue of voice, a concept they call "dialectical risk communication." Under this model, people would negotiate the interpretation of data—an ethical ideal that other scholars endorse (National Research Council, 1989). Rakow (1989) extends the voice value much further, suggesting not merely "a reciprocity of interaction between institutions and individuals or publics" (p. 180), but a subordination of institutions to individuals.

In his chapter in this volume, Heath presents an example of citizens participating with industry and civil leaders in the process of interpreting risk. Although the plan appears to promote voice, the details of the plan raise suspicion: During certain advisory council meetings, only council members (who are chosen by the company) can participate for most of the meetings. Juanillo and Scherer condemn this kind of faux voice, explaining that instead of allowing negotiation of risk, "public hearings and the involvement of citizens' advisory groups . . . appear to have served as instruments of persuasion" (p. 32).

Threats to Pluralism

Perhaps the most serious ethical problem in evaluative messages is the lack of pluralism. In other words, creators of evaluative messages usually do not allow other viewpoints to be generated or supported from the same data. In contrast, a highly ethical message would allow for—or at least acknowledge—a variety of interpretations, depending on the framework or set of values used (National Research Council, 1989).

Many other values exist, including what is most efficient, what yields highest benefit/cost ratio, what is simplest, what is practical, what improves the quality of life, what reduces risk, what eliminates risk, and what is not in my backyard. These values affect how data are interpreted. Therefore, if we accept the validity of competing value systems, it seems we must also accept the competing interpretations that people make based on those values. Unfortunately, in most risk situations, those who define the problem inevitably bring their interpretive framework to the data (National Research Council, 1989). As Salmon (1989) notes, "This power [to define problems] resides disproportionately with government, corporations and other institutions . . . [with] access to the mass media" (p. 25). Other scholars also are alarmed over the prevalence of narrow interpretive messages. Morgan and Lave (1990) contend that "telling a story in any *one* way may mean telling it in a biased way" (p. 356). Risk communicators will raise the ethical standard of their campaigns by allowing for various interpretations and opinions on a given issue.

Threats to Equality

Although people usually understand evaluative messages better than descriptive ones (National Research Council, 1989), messages in the evaluative domain present a distinct aspect of inequality. Appropriate behavior inferred from evaluative messages may be clearer to educated people than to uneducated people (Eisenberg, 1987), thus resulting in inequality (see also our earlier discussion on the knowledge gap hypothesis). For example, the evaluative message "The exchange of body fluids can transmit HIV" may not inform all people equally about what behavior they need to take to minimize HIV risk. Some may wonder, "Does this mean sweat can transmit HIV? Teardrops? These are body fluids, after all."

In her chapter in this volume, Witte addresses the issue of interpretation and behavior: "Too often, it appears that risk messages contain information about the threat only, without information . . . about how to avert harm from or minimize exposure to the threat." Witte then advocates a kind of message that provides both interpretation and behavior: "Risk messages must not only depict the threat as severe and probable; to promote danger control responses, they *must* offer specific solutions that the public can easily carry out with a minimum of complexity and labor." Although the purpose behind Witte's advice is not to make messages more ethical, the effect of following her advice increases the likelihood of equality.

Issues in the Injunctive Domain

Many ethical issues arise when risk communicators design messages in the injunctive domain. Here we focus on issues of honesty, self-determination, and equality.

Threats to Honesty

Although injunctive messages clearly outline what experts feel is appropriate behavior to reduce or avoid a risk, injunctive messages can pose threats to honesty on a variety of levels. First, because many injunctive interventions are simple and memorable, they may compromise accuracy. For example, the "Just Say No" campaign is a simplistic answer to a complex problem. Because the "drug problem" can be defined in many ways (Salmon, 1989), no single solution will work for every situation.

Second, injunctive messages can raise ethical questions because they often must fit a time constraint or an attention limitation, as is typically the case with short television spots (National Research Council, 1989). This often requires that a risk message "focus on only one or two points or viewers may miss the message entirely" (Calvert, Cocking, & Smrcek, 1991, p. 257). However expedient this focusing strategy may be, injunctive messages then become more likely to distort both the perception of risk and the range of responses available for avoiding or reducing that risk (National Research Council, 1989).

Third, some injunctive messages compromise honesty by not explaining how much a risk can be reduced if a person follows the advocated behavior. Morgan and Lave (1990) show that reducing a risk factor by 50% might seem quite significant until the probability is shown: from .0000001 to .0000002. In such cases, injunctive messages can mislead people into overestimating the efficacy of the advocated action.

Finally, injunctive messages sometimes compromise honesty because they fail to reveal the values involved in the adoption of the advocated behavior. This means that if the audience does not have the same values as the message designer, the behavior advocated will likely be inappropriate or irrelevant for that audience (National Research Council, 1989). For example, some public schools teach safer-sex practices to students, advocating the use of condoms. Certain people object to the values in which safer-sex messages are based, as they view abstinence as the ideal intervention for teens. Making clear the interpretive framework of the message (in this case, the belief that teens will engage in sexual conduct despite pleas for abstinence) can make the communication more ethical.

Threats to Self-Determination

Perhaps the most common ethical issue associated with injunctive messages is the threat to self-determination. In presenting injunctive messages, risk communication planners may attempt to take too much control over people's lives. Because self-determination is an important value in American life (National Research Council, 1989), attempting to dictate the behavior of others presents an ethical problem.

As is shown by the contrast between two of the four chapters under review here—Witte's and Juanillo and Scherer's—self-determination in injunctive risk messages is one of the most hotly debated issues in the literature. On the one hand, some scholars believe that risk communicators have a responsibility to "persuade people either to reduce or to engage in certain behaviors in order to decrease health risks" (Witte, Chapter 10, this volume; see also Beauchamp, 1987). This is the "expert knows best" approach to communication. Witte, for example, concludes her chapter with the assertion that experts should provide the answers: "The tremendous responsibility attached to deciding the 'right' answers or the 'correct' behaviors cannot be ignored." On the other hand, Juanillo and Scherer would condemn this approach as paternalistic (see also Rakow, 1989).

Instead of advocating a single behavior, risk communicators would do well to present the data, outline the various interpretive frameworks, and suggest a variety of sample behaviors. However, we concede that certain forms of paternalism have a place in exceptional cases. As the National Research Council (1989) has noted, "The more clearly it has been established that an activity is dangerous or that it may harm persons generally considered to deserve societal protection (e.g., children), the more acceptable influence attempts seem to become" (p. 88; see also Salmon, 1989). All in all, maintaining an effective balance of expert assistance and expert paternalism in injunctive messages and campaigns is not a trivial task.

Threats to Equality

Although most audience members readily understand injunctive messages, a great amount of variation exists in people's abilities to carry out advocated behaviors (National Research Council, 1989). In accordance with many theories of communication and persuasion, Calvert et al. (1991) discuss how difficult changing actual behavior is. Catchy phrases are not enough to motivate people to change addictive, habitual, or rewarding behaviors. Calvert et al. point out that for many behaviors that incur risk, messages must do more than present information: "Addictive behaviors like smoking tobacco or using drugs, then, require both information about the problem and follow-up support in order to change those behaviors" (p. 259). Programs that provide follow-up and support make injunctive messages less exclusive and thereby more ethical, because they give audience members more equal chances to perform the advocated behaviors successfully.

SUMMARY

We began this chapter by arguing that communication, as a field, has a set of unique contributions to make to the study of risk. Many of the processes involved in the communication of risk are intrinsically linked to the field of communication. Communication scholars have made numerous contributions to the study of risk in a relatively short amount of time. However, despite the abundance of studies generated in the field on this topic, the absence of a set of organizing principles has limited the conceptual contribution of research. We have presented one such framework for integrating theoretical as well as ethical issues.

We have also raised arguments for the need to frame risk communication in individual-level, societal-level, and cross-level terms. We can accomplish this only if we can explicate the various risk-related concepts along cross-level linkages. Our review of the literature—in the field of communication in general and that of risk communication in particular—makes it clear that an absence of cross-level linkages has limited the scope of our theories and restricted our thinking. This is an appropriate setting to call for further research in the area, and we believe such efforts should concentrate on questions of cross-level relationships in communication. Among the four studies included in this volume, two ask questions at the individual level and two at the institutional level. Although this distribution is encouraging with respect to informing our understanding of individual- and institutional-level risk communication, we believe that further work also needs to consider cross-level influences.

NOTES

1. *Risk assessment* is the "characterization of potential adverse effects of exposures to hazards; includes estimates of risk and of uncertainties in measurements, analytical techniques, and interpretive models; quantitative risk assessment characterizes the risk in numerical representations" (National Research Council, 1989, p. 321). *Risk management* is the "evaluation of alternative risk control actions, selection among them (including doing nothing), and their implementation" (National Research Council, 1989, p. 322).

2. In differentiating between descriptive and interpretive risk messages, we must point out the difference between two words: *data* and *information*. Although they are often used interchangeably, we believe these words have different meanings. We agree with Davis and McCormack (1979), who maintain that data by themselves are only facts, and that facts become information only after the infusion of meaning. In other words, data have a much lower level of bias and personal interpretation than does information.

REFERENCES

Ajzen, I., & Fishbein, M. (1980). *Understanding attitudes and predicting social behavior.* Englewood Cliffs, NJ: Prentice Hall.
Andersen, K. E. (1991). A history of communication ethics. In K. J. Greenberg (Ed.), *Conversations on communication ethics.* Norwood, NJ: Ablex.
Arnett, R. C. (1991). The status of communication ethics scholarship in speech communication journals in 1915 to 1985. In K. J. Greenberg (Ed.), *Conversations on communication ethics* (pp. 55-74). Norwood, NJ: Ablex.
Atkin, C. (1973). Instrumental utilities and information seeking. In P. Clarke (Ed.), *New models for communication research* (pp. 205-242). Beverly Hills, CA: Sage.

Bandura, A. (1977). *Social learning theory.* Englewood Cliffs, NJ; Prentice Hall.

Bandura, A. (1986). *Social foundations of thought and action.* Englewood Cliffs, NJ: Prentice Hall.

Bazerman, M. H. (1990). Decision making with more than two parties. In M. H. Bazerman (Ed.), *Judgment in managerial decision making* (2nd ed., pp. 142-152). New York: John Wiley.

Beauchamp, D. (1987). Life-style, public health and paternalism. In S. Doxiadis (Ed.), *Ethical dilemmas in health promotion* (pp. 69-81). New York: John Wiley.

Becker, M. H. (Ed.). (1974). The health belief model and personal health behavior [Special issue]. *Health Education Monographs, 2,* 324-473.

Blackburn, H., Leupker, R. V., Kline, F. G., Bracht, N., & Carlaw, R. (1984). The Minnesota Heart Health Program: A research and demonstration project in cardiovascular disease prevention. In J. D. Matarazzo, S. H. Weiss, J. A. Herd, N. E. Miller, & S. W. Weiss (Eds.), *Behavioral health: A handbook of health enhancement and disease prevention* (pp. 1171-1178). New York: John Wiley.

Bogen, K. T. (1990). *Uncertainty in environmental health risk assessment.* New York: Garland.

Calvert, S. L., Cocking, R. R., & Smrcek, M. (1991). AIDS public service announcements: A paradigm for behavioral science. *Journal of Applied Developmental Psychology, 12,* 255-267.

Cialdini, R. B., Vincent, J. E., Lewis, S. K., Catalan, J., Wheeler, D., & Darby, B. L. (1975). Reciprocal concessions procedure for inducing compliance: The door-in-the-face technique. *Journal of Personality and Social Psychology, 31,* 206-215.

Crawford, R. (1987). Cultural influences on prevention and the emergence of a new health consciousness. In N. D. Weinstein (Ed.), *Taking care: Understanding and encouraging self-protective behavior* (pp. 95-113). New York: Cambridge University Press.

Cronen, V. E. (1991). Coordinated management of meaning theory and postenlightenment ethics. In K. J. Greenberg (Ed.), *Conversations on communication ethics* (pp. 21-54). Norwood, NJ: Ablex.

Crouch, E. A. C., & Wilson, R. (1982). *Risk/benefit analysis.* Cambridge, MA: Ballinger.

Dake, K. (1992). Myths of nature: Culture and the social construction of risk. *Journal of Social Issues, 48,* 21-37.

Dake, K., & Wildavsky, A. (1991). Individual differences in risk perception and risk-taking preferences. In B. J. Garrick & W. C. Gekler (Eds.), *The analysis, communication, and perception of risk* (pp. 15-24). New York: Plenum.

Davis, W., & McCormack, A. (1979). *The information age.* Reading, MA: Addison-Wesley.

Donohue, G. A., Tichenor, P., & Olien, C. N. (1975). Mass media and the knowledge gap: Hypothesis reconsidered. *Communication Research, 2,* 3-23.

Douglas, M. T. (1985). *Risk acceptability according to the social sciences.* New York: Russell Sage Foundation.

Doxiadis, S. (1987a). Conclusions. In S. Doxiadis (Ed.), *Ethical dilemmas in health promotion* (pp. 225-229). New York: John Wiley.

Doxiadis, S. (Ed.). (1987b). *Ethical dilemmas in health promotion.* New York: John Wiley.

Eisenberg, L. (1987). Value conflict in social policies for promoting health. In S. Doxiadis (Ed.), *Ethical dilemmas in health promotion* (pp. 99-116). New York: John Wiley.

Farquhar, J. W., Fortmann, S. P., Maccoby, N., Haskell, W. L., Williams, P. T., Flora, J. A., Taylor, C. B., Brown, B. W., Solomon, D. S., & Hulley, S. B. (1985). The Stanford Five-City Project: Design and methods. *American Journal of Epidemiology, 122,* 323-334.

Ferguson, M. A., & Valenti, J. M. (1991). Communicating with environmental and health risk takers: An individual differences perspective. *Health Education Quarterly, 18,* 303-318.

Fessenden-Raden, J., Fitchen, J. M., & Heath, J. S. (1987). Providing risk information in communities: Factors influencing what is heard and accepted. *Science, Technology and Human Values, 12*(3/4), 94-101.

Festinger, L. (1957). *A theory of cognitive dissonance.* Evanston, IL: Row, Peterson.

Fishbein, M. (1980). A theory of reasoned action: Some applications and implications. In H. Howe & M. Page (Eds.), *Nebraska Symposium on Motivation* (pp. 65-116). Lincoln: University of Nebraska Press.

Fishbein, M., & Ajzen, I. (1981). Acceptance, yielding, and impact: Cognitive processes in persuasion. In R. E. Petty, T. M. Ostrom, & T. C. Brock (Eds.), *Cognitive responses in persuasion* (pp. 339-359). Hillsdale, NJ: Lawrence Erlbaum.

Fishbein, M., & Ajzen, I. (1975). *Belief, attitude, intention, and behavior: An introduction to theory and research.* Reading, MA: Addison-Wesley.

Flora, J. A., & Maibach, E. W. (1990). Cognitive responses to AIDS information: The effects of issue involvement and message appeal. *Communication Research, 17,* 759-774.

Flora, J. A., Maibach, E. W., & Maccoby, N. (1989). The role of media across four levels of health promotion intervention. *Annual Review of Public Health, 10,* 181-201.

Greenberg, K. J. (Ed.). (1991). *Conversations on communication ethics.* Norwood, NJ: Ablex.

Grunig, J. E. (1983). Communication behaviors and attitudes of environmental publics: Two studies. *Journalism Monographs, 81,* 1-54.

Hallman, W. K., & Wandersman, A. (1992). Attribution of responsibility and individual and collective coping with environmental threats. *Journal of Social Issues, 48,* 101-118.

Hance, B. J., Chess, C., & Sandman, P. M. (1989). Setting a context for explaining risk. *Risk Analysis, 9,* 113-117.

Hansson, S. O. (1989). Dimensions of risk. *Risk Analysis, 9,* 107-112.

Hilgartner, S. (1992). The social construction of risk objects: Or, how to pry open networks of risk. In J. F. Short, Jr., & L. Clarke (Eds.), *Organizations, uncertainties, and risk* (pp. 39-53). Boulder, CO: Westview.

Jaksa, J. A., & Pritchard, M. S. (1988). *Communication ethics: Methods of analysis.* Belmont, CA: Wadsworth.

Janz, N. K., & Becker, M. H. (1984). The health belief model: A decade later. *Health Education Quarterly, 11,* 1-47.

Kahneman, D., Knetsch, J. L., & Thaler, R. H. (1991). Anomalies: The endowment effect, loss aversion, and status quo bias. *Journal of Economic Perspectives, 5,* 193-206.

Kahneman, D., & Lovallo, D. (1993). Timid choices and bold forecasts: A cognitive perspective on risk taking. *Management Science, 39,* 17-31.

Kahneman, D., & Tversky, A. (1972). Subjective probability: A judgment of representativeness. *Cognitive Psychology, 3,* 430-454.

Kahneman, D., & Tversky, A. (1984). Choices, values, and frames. *American Psychologist, 39,* 341-350.

Kirscht, J. P., & Joseph, J. G. (1989). The health belief model: Some implications for behavior change, with reference to homosexual males. In V. M. Mays, G. W. Albee, & S. F. Schneider (Eds.), *Primary prevention of AIDS: Psychological approaches* (pp. 111-127). Newbury Park, CA: Sage.

Maddux, J. E., & Rogers, R. W. (1983). Protection motivation and self-efficacy: A revised theory of fear appeals and attitude change. *Journal of Experimental Social Psychology, 19,* 469-479.

Maddux, J. E., Sherer, M., & Rogers, R. W. (1982). Self-efficacy expectancy and outcome expectancy: Their relationship and their effects on behavioral intentions. *Cognitive Therapy and Research, 6,* 207-211.

Makau, J. M. (1991). The principles of fidelity and veracity: Guidelines for ethical communication. In K. J. Greenberg (Ed.), *Conversations on communication ethics* (pp. 111-122). Norwood, NJ: Ablex

Manheim, J. B. (1987). A model of agenda dynamics. In M. L. McLaughlin (Ed.), *Communication yearbook 10* (pp. 499-516). Newbury Park, CA: Sage.

McCombs, M. E., & Shaw, D. L. (1972). The agenda-setting function of the mass media. *Public Opinion Quarterly, 36,* 176-187.

McGuire, W. J. (1989). Theoretical foundations of campaigns. In R. E. Rice & C. K. Atkin (Eds.), *Public communication campaigns* (2nd ed., pp. 43-65). Newbury Park, CA: Sage.

Morgan, G. M., & Lave, L. (1990). Ethical considerations in risk communication practice and research. *Risk Analysis, 10,* 355-358.

National Research Council. (1989). *Improving risk communication.* Washington, DC: National Academy Press.

Nordenstam, B., & Vaughan, E. (1991). Farmworkers and pesticide exposure: Perceived risk and self-protective behavior. In B. J. Garrick & W. C. Gekler (Eds.), *The analysis, communication, and perception of risk* (pp. 163-173). New York: Plenum.

Paisley, W. (1984). Communication in the communication sciences. In B. Dervin & M. J. Voigt (Eds.), *Progress in the communication sciences* (pp. 1-43). Norwood, NJ: Ablex.

Pan, Z., & McLeod, J. M. (1991). Multilevel analysis in mass communication research. *Communication Research, 18,* 140-173.

Petty, R., & Cacioppo, J. T. (1981). *Attitudes and persuasion: Classic and contemporary approaches.* Dubuque, IA: William C Brown.

Rakow, L. F. (1989). Information and power: Toward a critical theory of information campaigns. In C. T. Salmon (Ed.), *Information campaigns: Balancing social values and social change* (pp. 164-196). Newbury Park, CA: Sage.

Ray, M. L. (1973). Marketing communication and the hierarchy-of-effects. In P. Clarke (Ed.), *New models for communication research* (pp. 147-176). Beverly Hills, CA: Sage.

Renn, O., Burns, W. J., Kasperson, J. X., Kasperson, R. E., & Slovic, P. (1992). The social amplification of risk: Theoretical foundations and empirical applications. *Journal of Social Issues, 48,* 137-160.

Rogers, E. M., Dearing, J. W., & Chang, S. (1991). AIDS in the 1980s: The agenda-setting process for a public issue. *Journalism Monographs, 126,* 1-47.

Rogers, R. W. (1975). A protection motivation theory of fear appeals and attitude change. *Journal of Psychology, 91,* 93-114.

Rogers, R. W. (1983). Cognitive and physiological processes in fear appeals and attitude change: A revised theory of protection motivation. In J. Cacioppo & R. Petty (Eds.), *Social psychophysiology: A sourcebook* (pp. 153-176). New York: Guilford.

Rosenstock, I. M. (1960). What research in motivation suggests for public health. *American Journal of Public Health, 50,* 295-301.

Rosenstock, I. M. (1966). Why people use health services. *Milbank Memorial Fund Quarterly, 44,* 94-124.

Rosenstock, I. M. (1974). Historical origins of the health belief model. In M. H. Becker (Ed.), *The health belief model and personal health behavior* [Special issue]. *Health Education Monographs, 2,* 328-335.

Rosenstock, I. M. (1990). The health belief model: Explaining health behavior through expectancies. In K. Glanz, F. M. Lewis, & B. K. Rimer (Eds.), *Health behavior and health education: Theory, research and practice* (pp. 39-62). San Francisco: Jossey-Bass.

Rowe, W. D. (1992). Risk analysis: A tool for policy decisions. In M. Waterston (Ed.), *Risk and society: The interaction of science, technology, and public policy* (pp. 17-31). Dordrecht, Netherlands: Kluwer Academic.

Salmon, C. T. (1989). Campaigns for social "improvement": An overview of values, rationales, and impacts. In C. T. Salmon (Ed.), *Information campaigns: Balancing social values and social change* (pp. 19-53). Newbury Park, CA: Sage.

Sheppard, B. H., Hartwick, J., & Warshaw, P. R. (1988). The theory of reasoned action: A meta-analysis of past research with recommendations for modifications and future research. *Journal of Consumer Research, 15,* 325-343.

Tichenor, P. J., Donohue, G. A., & Olien, C. N. (1970). Mass media and the differential growth in knowledge. *Public Opinion Quarterly, 34,* 158-170.

Tversky, A., & Kahneman, D. (1971). The belief in the "law of small numbers." *Psychological Bulletin, 76,* 105-110.

Tversky, A., & Kahneman, D. (1973). Availability: A heuristic for judging frequency and probability. *Cognitive Psychology, 5,* 207-232.

Tversky, A., & Kahneman, D. (1974). Judgment under uncertainty: Heuristics and biases. *Science, 185*, 1124-1131.

Vaughan, E., & Nordenstam, B. (1991). The perception of environmental risks among ethnically diverse groups. *Journal of Cross-Cultural Psychology, 22*, 29-60.

Wallack, L. (1990). Improving health promotion: Media advocacy and social marketing approaches. In C. Atkin & L. Wallack (Eds.), *Mass communication and public health: Complexities and conflicts* (pp. 147-164). Newbury Park, CA: Sage.

Wallack, L., Dorfman, L., Jernigan, D., & Themba, M. (1993). *Media advocacy and public health: Power for prevention.* Newbury Park, CA: Sage.

Warwick, D. P., & Kelman, H. C. (1973). Ethical issues in social intervention. In G. Zaltman (Ed.), *Processes and phenomena of social change* (pp. 377-418). New York: John Wiley.

Waterstone, M. (1992). Introduction: The social genesis of risks and hazards. In M. Waterstone (Ed.), *Risk and society: The interaction of science, technology, and public policy* (pp. 1-12). Dordrecht, Netherlands: Kluwer Academic.

Weinstein, N. D. (1987). Introduction: Studying self-protective behavior. In N. D. Weinstein (Ed.), *Taking care: Understanding and encouraging self-protective behavior* (pp. 1-13). New York: Cambridge University Press.

SECTION 3

Modes of Connecting Through Communication: Discourse, Relationships, Technology, and Ideology

15 Micromanaging Expert Talk: Hosts' Contributions to Televised Computer Product Demonstrations

ROBERT E. NOFSINGER
Washington State University

Conversation analysis of interactive talk on the television program *Computer Chronicles* indicates that both the host and the guests shape the product demonstration. The host overtly contributes ideas to the ongoing interaction, fine-tuning the demonstration through the use of prompts and clarifications. Guests respond to these in topically informative ways. Although the host performs much the same opening, closing, and direction management functions as do interviewers in broadcast news interviews, these computer product demonstrations are cooperatively informational rather than challenging or combative in tone.

R ECENT conversation-analytic studies of talk in the broadcast media have emphasized the interactive character of mass-mediated messages in news interviews and other "talk show" programs (Clayman, 1989, 1991, 1993; Greatbatch, 1986a, 1986b, 1988; Heritage, 1985; Heritage, Clayman, & Zimmerman, 1988; Heritage & Greatbatch, 1991; Nofsinger, 1994). In these and other studies, real-time person-to-person talk—communicative interaction—is shown to be a primary system through which the broadcast message gets produced. This approach narrows the distinctions conceptualizing communication as an interpersonal phenomenon on the one hand and a mass-mediated phenomenon on the other. It contrasts with the perspective that treats broadcast messages more as texts or products than as sets of communicative behaviors (Pingree, Wiemann, & Hawkins, 1988). It is clear, however, that the participants on such broadcast talk programs jointly produce the structure of the mediated message through their social interaction. These analyses of the organizing practices that participants employ make an important contribution to our understanding both of interpersonal communication processes and of the broadcast media (Heritage et al., 1988).

Correspondence and requests for reprints: Robert E. Nofsinger, School of Communication, Washington State University, Pullman, WA 99164-2520.

Communication Yearbook 18, pp. 345-370

Over the past decade, the most extensively studied type of broadcast "talk" program (in this conversation-analytic research tradition) has been the news interview. In describing the underlying structure of news interview programs, analysts have focused on turn taking in news interviews, compared with that in ordinary conversation. Another major focus has been on how participants establish themselves as representing certain institutions: how the interviewer produces a display of journalistic neutrality, for example, and how he or she, as the representative of the news organization, controls the time and other parameters of the program. A third area of focus in this research is how speaking turns are designed for an "overhearing" audience—the viewers—rather than exclusively for the copresent participants. A brief review of these three areas provides a base from which to discuss the televised product demonstrations that are the focus of this chapter.

Everyday conversation is organized to provide for local, turn-by-turn management by the participants of how long a speaking turn lasts, who speaks next, what types of communicative or social actions they produce through their turns, and when the conversation is brought to an end (Heritage, 1984; Hopper, 1992; Nofsinger, 1991; Sacks, Schegloff, & Jefferson, 1978; Schegloff & Sacks, 1973). Any participant is potentially free to produce questions, answers, offers, requests, and a wide range of other communicative actions. These aspects of ordinary conversation are not normatively determined ahead of time, but vary according to the practices of the participants.

News interview talk, however, is markedly different from everyday conversation. One set of differences is related to role expectations in broadcast programs. The types of communicative action that a participant may properly perform in his or her turn are allocated in advance to each type of participant, to each role (Greatbatch, 1988; Heritage et al., 1988; Heritage & Greatbatch, 1991). Specifically, one type of participant (the interviewer, or IR) predominantly asks questions and the other (the interviewee, or IE) predominantly gives answers. This constraint, *turn-type preallocation,* is one major respect in which the turn-taking system for news interviews differs from that of everyday conversation (Atkinson & Drew, 1979; Greatbatch, 1988). IEs orient to this constraint by withholding talk until the IR has produced a recognizable question. This allows IRs to construct complex turns that include a preface or "lead-in" to the question as well as the question itself (Greatbatch, 1988; Heritage & Greatbatch, 1991). For example, in the confrontational 1988 *CBS Evening News* interview between Dan Rather and (then) Vice President George Bush, Rather's first "live" turn (after broadcast of a taped report) comprised several components that led up to the actual question. Data Segment 1 displays this opening.[1]

Data Segment 1 [Rather-Bush Tape 2, 0501, simplified]
01 DR: ((end of taped report)) •hh Mister Vice President,
02   thank you for being with us tonight, •hh

03	Donald Gregg still serves as your trusted advisor,
04	he was deeply involved in running arms to the
05	contras, an' he didn't inform you. •hhh
06	Now when President Reagan's (.) trusted advisor
07	Admiral Poindexter (0.5) failed to inform <u>him.</u>
08	(0.8) the President (.) <u>fi</u>red him.
09	(0.5) Why is Mister Gregg still inside the White
10	House an' still a trusted advisor.
11 GB:	Because I have confidence in him, (.)
12	an' because this matter, Dan, as you well
13	know, an' your editors know, has been looked
14	at by the <u>ten million dol</u>lar st<u>u</u>dy by the Senate
15	an' the House, •hh it's been <u>look</u>ed at by the
16	<u>Tow</u>er Commission . . . ((Bush's answer runs a total of 1 minute, 26 seconds))

Rather's turn includes a welcome (lines 1-2), two statements about Donald Gregg (lines 3 and 4-5), a statement about what President Reagan did under presumably similar circumstances (lines 6-8), and the actual question for Bush (lines 9-10). In everyday conversation, any one of these components might have been treated by other participants as a complete turn, as the occasion for producing a response. But Bush waits for the question component before beginning his answer in line 11. IRs orient to these same constraints by withholding acknowledging talk while the IE produces an extended answer (Heritage, 1985; Heritage & Greatbatch, 1991). In this instance, Rather remains silent while Bush takes a turn of almost one and a half minutes. Although both Rather and Bush can be seen to employ the turn-taking system of the news interview at the outset, it should be noted that their later departure from those constraints is one of the things that made this particular encounter so controversial (Clayman & Whalen, 1988-1989; Nofsinger, 1988-1989; Schegloff, 1988-1989). This turn-taking system gives rise to other important differences between news interviews and conversations. For example, because IEs are under a constraint to respond to the IR's questions, the IR has effective control over the topics that can be talked about, although IEs do employ several practices that allow them to comment on issues not mentioned by the IR (Greatbatch, 1986a).

A second set of differences between news interviews and everyday conversation involves the performance of certain "official" duties. In broadcast news interviews, participants orient to (usually) one of their number as being a representative of the institution producing the program. This person is treated as being responsible for opening and closing the program, and for certain other functions necessary for its smooth progression. This differs from ordinary conversation among peers, where talk may be initiated by anyone, using a wide variety of "start-up" practices, and where conversations are jointly brought to an end through a kind of negotiation process among participants (Hopper, 1992; Schegloff & Sacks, 1973). In addition, potential participants may be introduced into the conversation, and their relationship to the matters potentially being discussed may be made clear in a variety of ways, including self-introduction and introduction by mutual acquaintances. In news interviews, however, the IR announces the news item or issue that will be discussed in the interview (using a turn formatted as a *headline* or an *agenda projection*), initiates the presentation of relevant background information, and produces an *introduction* of the IE(s)— to the audience, not primarily to the participants themselves (Clayman, 1991). It is also the IR who brings the interview to a close, initiating a preclosing (typically a "warning" to IEs that very little time is left), followed by a terminal closing turn (e.g., "thank you"), neither of which must be overtly responded to by IEs (Clayman, 1989). As the closing develops, IEs withhold talk while IRs produce the closing actions. In general, the adaptation of conversational sequences to the needs of managing broadcast news interviews involves a reduction and specialization of the devices used in ordinary everyday talk (Clayman, 1989; Heritage & Greatbatch, 1991). The range of turn-taking practices is more limited and some aspects of the talk are managed more unilaterally by one participant (the IR) than is the case in ordinary conversation (Clayman, 1989).

A third set of issues researched in the conversation-analytic literature concerns the ways in which talk in news interviews is designed for the broadcast audience. In everyday conversation, messages are routinely designed for their intended recipients (Sacks & Schegloff, 1979). Ordinarily, these recipients are present either face-to-face or via two-way audio connection, as in telephone conversation. So participants' turns are designed for those who are copresent and (potentially, at least) participating in the interactive talk. In news interviews this is also the case—turns are designed in certain respects for potential recipients who are copresent in the studio or interacting via two-way remote link. But participants also orient to the nonpresent, "overhearing" audience. In a variety of ways, turns in news interviews and other broadcast "talk" shows are designed for the viewing/listening audience (Heritage, 1985; Nofsinger, 1994). For example, moderators or hosts of question-answer talk shows initiate repairs when a guest says something that would likely not be understood by the viewing audience—and guests typically respond by repeating or otherwise confirming these clarifying versions of their turns (Nofsinger, 1994).

We know how the practices used in ordinary conversation are modified to accomplish news interviews. It makes sense that language-in-use is adapted to the situated requirements of particular activities (see Levinson, 1992). Indeed, understanding those practices is an important step toward understanding the nature of the activity and the context of which it is a part. It is important, therefore, to extend our understanding of how interaction is accomplished and how practices of talk are adapted to other mediated contexts and other types of broadcast activities. One such activity is the product demonstration.

Televised demonstrations of processes and products are common, especially on PBS and the cable channels. When product demonstrations are produced in an interactive format, some practices of talk are likely to resemble those in the news interview.[2] For example, in the data examined for this study, product demonstrations are characterized by turn-type preallocation similar to that in news interviews. Also in these demonstrations, the host manages the opening, closing, and transitions from one guest to another. And participants orient to designing messages for a nonpresent, "overhearing" audience. The activity of demonstrating a product may also be different in important respects from that of interviewing a newsworthy figure. The situated identities of host and guest are not the same as those of IR and IE. IRs often challenge or counter IEs' answers in interviews with public figures, especially political ones (Clayman, 1988, 1993; Greatbatch, 1986b; Heritage & Greatbatch, 1991). In the product demonstrations studied here, however, the hosts did not challenge guests, nor did the guests respond evasively or defensively as IEs sometimes do in news interviews (Clayman, 1993; Greatbatch, 1986b). In addition, guests may be product experts in a different way from IEs who are experts on particular news stories. Guests who demonstrate products are usually official representatives of the companies that manufacture or market the products. They often have product demonstration as part of their official duties and, in that sense, are experts on the particular products. IEs, on the other hand, are frequently involved in the newsworthy events that are discussed in news interviews, but may or may not be official spokespersons for the institutions involved. Finally, product demonstrations involve a more complex mix of actions than do news interviews. Demonstrations rely more on *showing* (visibly operating or displaying something while talking about it) than interviews do.

The television program *Computer Chronicles* typifies the sorts of social interactional issues raised by this kind of televised product demonstration. Analysis of interactive talk in the studio sessions of these programs (described below) indicates that product demonstrations on *Computer Chronicles* are distinguished by these characteristics: (a) Both the host and guest shape the product demonstration. Hosts overtly contribute ideas to the ongoing interaction (which might naively be thought of as "the guest's" demonstration). (b) The host fine-tunes, adjusts, or guides the product demonstration in a "cooperative" way. That is, the host prompts for actions that the guest can be expected to be willing and able to perform. The host seeks clarification by proposing items that guests might have said themselves (but did not) or with which guests can be expected to agree. (c) Guests respond in informationally or topically informative ways. They do not evade answering questions or reformulate questions before answering. In other words, these computer product demonstrations are jointly produced, thoroughly interactive, and cooperatively informational, rather than controversial, in tone.

Computer Chronicles is a weekly TV program that presents information about currently available computer equipment and software, with an emphasis on PC-compatible or DOS products and, to a lesser extent, products related to Apple's Macintosh. Its objective is to deliver up-to-date technical information about various computer products. The usual format includes a combination of remote reports by the program's staff and two or three face-to-face discussions in the studio. These discussions normally take the form of "conversations" between the host (and sometimes a cohost) and one of several guests, each representing a product or point of view.[3] The study reported below focused on face-to-face talk in the studio and was based on 27 studio sessions from 12 different programs.

In several respects, the participants in these exchanges can be seen to orient to the same concerns that shape broadcast news interviews. First, there is a division of labor in the communicative work the participants do. The host and cohost ask questions and prompt the guest to give certain information or to demonstrate the featured product in certain ways. The guest provides the answers and the indicated demonstrations. In other words, turn-type preallocation operates in these studio sessions. Second, the host announces the topical focus of the program, introduces the guests (and cohost, if there is one), and uses questions and other prompts to "get the demonstration started." Third, participants (the host especially) orient to time limits presumably imposed by the half-hour format of the show (and the even shorter time available for each of two or three studio segments during the half hour). The host routinely brings each segment of the program to a close, employing practices similar to those used by broadcast news interviewers to achieve what Clayman (1989) calls "the production of punctuality." The host also takes steps to ensure that there is time within a segment for the several guests to present their products or points of view. We shall see, however, that the host is deeply involved in the product demonstration itself.

THE PROMPT

As indicated above, the host employs standard techniques to orient the audience (and the copresent participants) to the topical focus of the studio segment, to introduce the guests and characterize their expertise, to get a demonstration started, and to close each demonstration and each studio segment. But the host on *Computer Chronicles* participates in the development of the product demonstration to an extent that goes far beyond these direction-setting and boundary-management functions. The host and guest collaborate to produce and shape the product demonstration itself. One contribution by the host to the overall shape of the demonstration is to *prompt* the guest to perform specified demonstration duties, discuss specified items or issues, or move on to other (unspecified) matters. A prompt is displayed in Data Segment 2, line 3.

Data Segment 2 [MM92-1, 1897]

01 SC:	. . . A'ri- this is one of the games
02	you worked on called Operation Neptune.
03	And tell us what you do here.
04 ML:	•h Well right now- I'm a submari:ne
05	(.) a:n' my station: (.) •h is signaling
06	me that there's a problem . . .

The host (SC) has just been discussing the process of testing new computer games for children with ML, the guest, who is a sixth grader. In lines 1-2, SC draws attention to the computer program showing on the monitor. He then prompts the guest to explain the game: "And tell us what you do here." ML then begins describing how the game works and is soon operating the game for the television camera (data not shown). This movement from a discussion of testing "beta" versions of computer games to the actual demonstration of a game is instigated by the host and performed by the guest. The *prompt* comprises three host practices: (a) requesting that the guest perform a certain communicative action; (b) inquiring of the guest about a component, process, or issue related to the product; and (c) eliciting from the guest a new topic or focus of discussion.

The Action Request

The host of a product demonstration program faces not only the interactional problem of how to get a demonstration started, but also, potentially, the problem of how to alter the guest's approach to the demonstration when such a change is deemed advisable. One solution to both problems is for the host to design a turn that names the action or set of behaviors the guest should perform and that requests him or her to do so. This is the *action request*. Such a turn also typically mentions the topical focus that the guest should take. In the first instance to be examined, the product demonstration per se has not yet begun. In Data Segment 3, an action request is used to prompt the guest to begin the demonstration. The host, SC, has just introduced two guests (including DG) and characterized the focus of this session as questions that new (beginner) computer owners face.[4]

Data Segment 3 [93-1, 4186]

01 SC:	(.) •h Dave let's start out with this issue
02	of memory.= >Y'know y'go home you bought
03	your computer you think it has everything
04	you needed you put in the first game an'
05	it says (.) can't run not enough memory.<
06	•h Give us a quick tutorial (.) on ram the
07	different kinds of memory and how you

```
08        solve those pro ⌈ blems.
09 DG:                   ⌊•hh >Okay< memory is
10        where work (.) gets done (0.2) in the
11        computer. (0.2) The more memory y'have
12        (0.2) the more work y'can get done.
13        •h It's that simple.
```

Using an action request in lines 6-8, SC requests that the guest, DG, give a tutorial on computer memory. DG immediately begins a description of memory, overlapping the end of the host's turn at lines 8-9, and continues on to display memory hardware and software (data not shown). SC's action request is prefaced by his own talk orienting the broadcast audience, as well as the copresent participants, to a specific focus, the "issue of memory." Action requests in *Computer Chronicles* are commonly, though not universally, prefaced by the host's talk. The action request itself characterizes the action or actions the guest is to perform ("give us a quick tutorial"), mentions memory as the suggested focus, and is recognizable as a request. SC's turn prompts the requested tutorial by DG.

In this instance, the host has solved the problem of getting the demonstration started. Once the demonstration has begun, however, there may be need for a change in the guest's approach. The host can use the same practice, the action request, to alter the way in which the demonstration progresses. In Data Segment 4, the program is about portable computers. The guest, RM, has been describing the capabilities of a fax modem card in his notebook computer, the Safari, so the product demonstration is under way. SC (the host) uses an action request to prompt RM to actually operate the fax modem.

Data Segment 4 [MM93-4, 2680]

```
01 RM:    . . . and also it's a fax modem.
02        ⌈ So this is a very powerful=
03 SC:    ⌊ okay
04 RM:    =little card
05 SC:    A'ri- Robert I have a fax
06        machine over he::re a::nd
07        can you show me how you could use the
08        Safari (0.5) and a cellular phone
09        (0.4) t' send out a fax to somebody
10        even though you're not hard
11        wired anywhere.
12 RM:    Absolutely. uh we've got'p- we got
13        t' program already loaded (.) we've
14        got t' PCMCI modem card in . . .
((RM sends a fax to SC's machine))
```

Here, SC's turn includes an orienting preface (lines 5-6), which ties back to RM's mention of "fax modem" in line 1, and the action request itself (lines 7-9). The expected action is specified ("show me how") and the focus of that action is described. Notice that even though the action request is phrased as a question about the recipient's ability ("can you . . . "), this format is a standard way of packaging a request. The host's turn prompts the requested "showing" by RM. Presumably, this request to operate the equipment (specifically, to send a fax to the fax machine sitting on the table in the studio) was anticipated before the studio session began. Both host and guest knew of the plan to demonstrate the product in this way,[5] so SC's action request was a method of triggering this preplanned demonstration.

Sometimes a guest fails to employ an obvious behavior to further the demonstration. In such a case, the action request may be utilized to bring about a modification in the ongoing demonstration. In Data Segment 5, JB (a guest) is describing the special features of a notebook computer that is open in front of him on the table. His hands are at either side of the computer (the computer is between his hands). The new focus of his talk is a red "button" in the middle of the keyboard. SC is the host.

Data Segment 5 [MM93-4, 2832]

```
01 JB:     . . . •hh Another feature that
02         makes it easy to use for those
03         kinds of things is 'n integrated=
((JB gestures toward the keyboard))
04         =pointing device. •hh
((JB returns hands to sides of case))
05         right here in the c ⌈ enter of the key-
06 SC:                        ⌊ (wha-) that little
07         red dot explain that t' ⌈ me.
08 JB:                             ⌊ pt •h That's
09         called Trackpoint Two,=
10 SC:     =uh huh
11 JB:     •h and it's uh insa- in the middle
12         of the keyboard, (0.4) so you don't
13         have to move your hands from the home
14         row typing position to use it (.) •h
15         and 's better than a ty- than either
16         ay (0.5) uh mouse or ay ⌈ trackball.
17 SC:                             ⌊ So could
18         you show us you would put your index=
((JB moves finger toward red button))
```

19   =fing ⌈ er say on there,   ⌉
20 JB: ⌊ Put your finger on it ⌋ =
((camera has moved to show close-up of JB's finger on the red button))
21   =and you are able would be able
22   t'move the . . .

JB begins to describe this feature of the product (lines 1-5) and, as he says "integrated pointing device," he gestures toward the keyboard with both hands. But he does not actually point at the red dot specifically or touch it with his finger. As he takes a breath in line 4, his hands return to the sides of the computer. SC immediately produces an action request ("explain that t' me") with a brief orienting preface ("that little red dot"), overlapping JB's turn (line 5). This prompt occasions further explanation from JB focusing on "Trackpoint Two." As he continues his explanation (lines 11-16), the guest still does not point to or manipulate the "little red dot." The host then produces another action request (lines 17-19), this one specifying actions different from the prior one (i.e., "show us" and "put your index finger . . . on there," instead of "explain that t' me"). Note that this second action request does not follow an orienting preface by the host, but rather is built off of JB's adjacent turn (lines 11-16), in which the guest described what he is now being prompted to show. JB complies with the request and the camera shows his finger manipulating the red button. Thus the host's action requests alter the trajectory of the demonstration from mention of and explanations about the feature to the actual operation of it.[6]

It is routine in *Computer Chronicles* for the host to use this practice not only to prompt the guest to begin a product demonstration, but also to manage the ongoing demonstration and prompt the guest to shift to other communicative actions. Guests are routinely cooperative and forthcoming in the subsequent turns. Through the host's action requests and the guests' responses to them, the particular mix of demonstration actions and their topical focus are interactively and recurrently achieved. But the host prompts guests in other ways as well, including the use of specific, itemized inquiries.

The Itemized Inquiry

Hosts of product demonstration programs and interviewers alike face an interactional problem that is closely related to the one considered above. Either at the beginning of a guest's talk or during the ongoing presentation, the problem may arise of how to induce a guest to talk about a specific issue or event—or, in the case of *Computer Chronicles,* a component, process, or other item related to the product. One solution is for the host to use another version of the prompt: a question-formatted turn that inquires about some specific item. This is the *itemized inquiry* (see Button & Casey, 1985).[7] In Data Segment 6, SC (the host) has been demonstrating a peripheral device for connecting a computer to a television set. He then focuses on notebook computers and the number of different models available (lines 1-3).

Data Segment 6 [MM93-4, 2562]
```
01 SC:    ... Let's talk about the machines
02        themself though, there are zillions
03        of notebook computers out there
04        how in the world does a guy decide
05        which one t'buy (.) how to figure
06        out the right machine.
07 PO:    W'I think there are a lot of different
08        considerations: but first of all I
09        think that the- that person needs to
10        assess their own needs ...
```

Following this preface, SC asks a question about a specific, related issue: how to decide which computer to buy. This itemized inquiry (lines 4-6) prompts an answer about that item, and PO's part of the studio session begins. Itemized inquiries are similar to action requests in that they are commonly prefaced with orienting talk by the same speaker who produces the prompt itself—the host. They also mention a specific item as their topical focus. They differ from action requests in that itemized inquiries do not explicitly name the communicative action the guest is being prompted to produce. Because itemized inquiries are formatted as questions (note the interrogative "how" and the subject-verb reversal of "does" and "a guy" in Data Segment 6), the type of action expected in reply is clear: Questions are first actions that make relevant answers as second actions (Nofsinger, 1991; Schegloff & Sacks, 1973). So itemized inquiries occasion answers by the guest. It is also the case, however, that guests' answers are often accompanied or followed by demonstrations of the product in operation.

Although itemized inquiries are normally deployed in the environment of prefacing talk by the host, the preface may be fairly short. In Data Segment 7, which is from a different (later) studio session than the previous segment, PO has been explaining the usefulness of his notebook computer's having two slots for PCMCIA cards. The computer is open on the table in front of him.

Data Segment 7 [MM93-4, 2659]
```
01 PO:    ... so that you don't have
02        to remove it. So it's just
03        a a (.) convenience really
04 SC:    A'ri- one quick thing I see y' got
05        all these button controls ⌈ over here
06 PO:                                ⌊ yes.
```

```
07 SC:   what uz that do.
08 PO:   Okay. (0.4) These button controls
09       •h uh affect the contrast right
10       here? a:nd the brightness . . .
```

At a possible ending point of PO's turn, the host produces a brief preface that sequentially disassociates his turn from PO's ("A'ri- one quick thing") and mentions some buttons on PO's computer (lines 4-5). Continuing his turn, SC then produces an itemized inquiry (line 7). This prompts PO to talk about the buttons. So the prefacing talk may only be long enough to provide whatever orientation to this impending new focus is needed, given the immediate context.

In rare cases, an itemized inquiry may occur without any prefacing statement. In Data Segment 8, a guest (TR) has been describing the potential advantages of the optical mouse. DN is the host.

Data Segment 8 [CC13, 4388]
```
01 TR:   . . . So it's not really better,
02       it's just a little different.
03 DN:   pt What's thee uh what's the
04       price on the optical mouse.
05 TR:   Uh the PC Mouse Three by Mouse
06       Systems is a hundred an' sixty
07       nine dollars.
```

Here, DN's itemized inquiry (lines 3-4) prompts from the guest a statement of the product's price. But note that there is no prefacing talk by DN that might orient the viewing audience and the guest that this question is forthcoming. And yet, the host's turn does not seem to be directly occasioned by anything the guest has just said. The price of the optical mouse had not previously been talked about on this program (although the price of another input device, a trackball, had been given earlier by another guest). It seems that some topical items are "standard" for this sort of product demonstration. In the few instances where itemized inquiries are not prefaced by the host, the items specified in the question tend to be ones that are nearly always raised about a product—the price, in this case. If this speculation is correct, the preface to itemized inquiries may be dispensed with when the item is one that is generally relevant for this type of product and for this kind of demonstration.

Through the use of the itemized inquiry, the host of a product demonstration program can influence the item or set of items that a guest will talk about next. This practice is employed throughout an ongoing demonstration and results in an interactively achieved, recurrently managed topical focus for the demonstration. Guests' responses are immediately and cooperatively forthcoming. Itemized inquiries and action requests are not the only means by which the host can prompt a guest to focus on a new aspect of the product being demonstrated, however. The host can elicit a changed, but unspecified, topical focus in the guest's next turn.

The Topic Elicitor

Button and Casey (1984) discuss the everyday practice of eliciting what could become the first or initial topic in an ordinary conversation. They examine *topic initial elicitors,* turns such as "what's up" and "how's it going," for their potential to prompt the recipient to talk about something of his or her choosing. First topics in a product demonstration are usually specified by either of the two prompts discussed previously. But hosts of broadcast talk shows do face an interactive problem for which a similar turn, an eliciting turn of some kind, can be a solution. The problem is how to get the guest to move on to talk about *another* item, without choosing or specifying for the guest what that item should be. The host in *Computer Chronicles* can prompt a guest to choose a new or changed item to talk about in an ongoing demonstration by employing a *topic elicitor.* In an action request prior to Data Segment 9, the host (SC) has prompted RK to describe the components of a computer: "•h I wanna begin by asking you to give us a guided tour (0.3) inside (0.4) this little box over here. . . . " As the segment begins, RK talks about the case (the "box") itself.

Data Segment 9 [93-1, 4132]
```
01 RK:   Yes thee uh th'computer cas:e is
02       the housing, it's the main box that comes
03       (.) with a ┌ computer system ┐
04 SC:            └ (     )  'kay  ┘
05 RK:   ┌ •hhh
06 SC:   └ Use that a pointer if you'd like,
         ((SC hands a screwdriver to RK))
07 RK:   Uh ┌ (whe-)
08 SC:      └ (So) what's in here.
09 RK:   When y'take the top off pro'ly the
10       first thing you'll see: is this
11       large (.) plastic laminated board.=
12       =that's called the mother board
```

RK removes the case from the computer, revealing the components inside. In line 6, SC offers the guest a screwdriver to use as a pointer. As the inbreath (line 5) and the "uh" (line 7) indicate, RK's demonstration is momentarily suspended. At this point, the host produces a topic elicitor (line 8), a short "what" question. This prompts RK to continue the "guided tour" by discussing another component (the "motherboard"). Note that the guest does not treat SC's "so what's in here" as the occasion for a listing of components, but rather as the occasion to point out and describe a next item. Of course, the overall frame of reference here is presumably based on the way the program has been introduced and on the host's action request for a guided tour. But within the set of relevant items available for demonstration, the guest is prompted to make a selection and resume talking. Later, in that same demonstration, the guest is describing the computer's expansion slots, as displayed in Data Segment 10.

Data Segment 10 [93-1, 4140]

```
01 RK:    •h um you'll also find on every
02        computer you'll find some expansion
03        slots: uh which allow you: to expand
04        the capabilities of your computer
05        ⌈ system
06 SC:    ⌊ And add car:ds or boar:ds,
07 RK:    That's correct.
08 SC:    A'right what else do we have.
09 RK:    U:m we'll find an on every computer
10        there will be some sort of storage
11        capacity, on this particular system
12        there are three drives: . . .
```

After RK mentions the expansion slots (pointing them out in the computer at the same time), SC offers an interpretation or clarification (line 6) of RK's turn. The guest confirms this (line 7), but does not immediately continue his discussion. At this point, SC prompts the guest with a topic elicitor (line 8). Again the format is a short "what" question that does not specify which of the available relevant items the guest should talk about. RK begins to talk about the computer's disk drives. Shortly thereafter, as RK displays and describes the third disk drive, the interaction continues as indicated in Data Segment 11.

Data Segment 11 [93-1, 4145]

```
01 RK:    . . . and then underneath thee:
02        CD rom drive on this unit is where
03        they have stored thee t'hard di ⌈ sk
04 SC:                                    ⌊ Right
05        (0.2)
06 RK:    the main storage area on the computer.=
07 SC:    =What else is in there.
08 RK:    •hh Uh every computer will have (0.2) ram
09        memory (0.2) on the system, in this
```

10   particular system (.) we have slots
11   where . . .

Following RK's mention of the hard disk and SC's overlapping acknowledgment ("right"), there is a silence of two-tenths of a second. Then RK adds
another description of the same component, the hard disk (line 6). SC immediately produces a topic elicitor (line 7). This prompts RK to talk about yet another
component of the computer, random access memory ("ram memory"). In effect,
the host has prompted the guest to move on to another item. Topic elicitors are
used in other environments as well (for example, in demonstrations of software),
but the host's use of three elicitors in this one demonstration illustrates the
extent to which the progression of a product demonstration can be driven by
such practices. Again, guests routinely cooperate in providing the prompted
demonstrations.

The three host practices of action request, itemized inquiry, and topic elicitor
are the first pair parts of adjacency pairs (Schegloff & Sacks, 1973). That is,
they are each members of a pair of communicative actions such that the first action
makes specifically relevant just a few possible second actions by the recipient.
For example, the host's action request makes relevant either a performance of
the requested action by the guest or an account for why that action will not be
forthcoming. This adjacency-pair status makes these three practices powerful
tools for managing the ongoing demonstration and results in a much more
interactively achieved product demonstration than the expertise of the guests
and the technical complexity of the products might suggest. The host prompts
not only a reply by the guest, but (in the case of action requests and itemized
inquiries) a specific type of action or topic focus by the guest.

The prompt, consisting of the three practices reported on here, does not involve
the host in making substantive comments or contributions. Except for remarks
that serve as preface to a prompt, the host's turn avoids describing or commenting on the items it focuses on. Rather, the host prompts the *guest* to make additional
comments or contributions in specified ways or regarding specified items
(except in the case of topic elicitors, where guests are prompted simply to move
on to something else). And guests uniformly provide the prompted information
or demonstrations and often go on to demonstrate other aspects of the products.
But hosts *do* make substantive contributions and manage the microdetails of
guests' demonstrations to a surprising extent. They do this through clarification
practices.

THE CLARIFICATION

It might be thought that with the communicative practices available for
beginning and ending a product demonstration program (and segments thereof),
introducing the guests, managing a guest's approach to the demonstration, and

managing the ongoing topical focus, the interactional demands on the host would largely be met. It is important to recall, however, that programs such as *Computer Chronicles* are produced primarily for an "overhearing" audience: people watching the broadcast. This means that the demonstration, although designed in part for the immediate local interaction, must also be designed for that viewing audience (Heritage, 1985). This raises a number of additional interactional problems for the host, who, although not producing much of the substance of the demonstration, might nevertheless be presumed responsible for ensuring that the program is intelligible to the audience. These interactional problems include how to make technical terms and operations clear, how to make explicit something the guest has left unsaid, how to insert important information the guest has omitted, and so on. Thus a recurrent concern of product demonstration program hosts is to provide for clarifying exchanges of talk. These may begin with the host producing a *clarification,* a turn that either (a) states a version of what the guest has said, what the product or guest is doing, what a guest's prior turn might mean, and so on, or (b) inquires about such matters.

The Clarifying Formulation

Heritage and Watson (1979, 1980) discuss what happens when a participant describes or attempts to say in so many words the meaning or gist of the conversation so far (or some part of it). They call such an utterance a *formulation.* Formulations routinely occasion confirmations, disconfirmations, or similar "decisions" from their recipients (Heritage & Watson, 1979, 1980). When a participant formulates a part of the conversation, he or she may not only propose its sense or gist, but may emphasize certain elements over others, say explicitly what had been left implicit, or even propose an inference or elaboration of that prior talk (Heritage, 1985). Formulations are routinely used in broadcast news interviews to prompt the interviewee to confirm, to expand upon, or to defend his or her remarks (Heritage, 1985). In this analysis, I use the concept more broadly to indicate that the host formulates not only a guest's prior talk, but what the guest has just *done* or *is doing.* For example, when the guest has used the computer keyboard or the mouse, the host may say, "Okay, Robert, you just sent Russ a message." Even saying what the *computer* is doing (what is showing in the display on the monitor screen, for example) is termed a formulation: The light bar on the screen highlights an item named "D:" and the host says, "So that will look like your D drive." The host uses such *clarifying formulations* to propose additional descriptions and inferences based on a guest's prior turn, make more explicit certain of the guest's points, and otherwise fine-tune the demonstration.

The names of featured products are routinely voiced, even though they may be displayed visually as well. This is in keeping with the fact that the audience must obtain the names of products from the demonstrations themselves. They cannot examine the materials in the studio or ask questions of the participants.

In Data Segment 12, JL has been describing a computer program as a potential Christmas gift. She has not said the name of the product, but she has held it up to the camera so the audience can see the front of the package. The host (SC) can be seen to orient toward the presumed interests and understanding of the audience.

Data Segment 12 [CC05, 2282]

```
01 JL:     . . . •h and it's fun software. What=
           ((JL holds the package up with its name toward the camera.))
02         =it does is allows you to play with
03         fractals. ⌈ •hh
04 SC:              ⌊ uh hu ⌈ h
05 JL:                      ⌊ uh (.) right now fractals=
           ((J puts the package back down.))
06         =are things that people are hearing
07         about an awful lo ⌈ t.
08 SC:                       ⌊ this is Frac ⌈ tools,
09 JL:                                      ⌊ Fractools
10         is the u:m (0.7) name of the package . . .
```

It appears by line 6 that JL may not explicitly mention the product's name in her introductory remarks; she has put the package back down on the table (so the audience can no longer see the name) and is talking about fractals, the changing color patterns that this product produces. The host deftly inserts a formulation of the name in line 8. JL quickly confirms the product's name (line 9). Her presentation is thus reshaped somewhat. The host's formulation explicitly supplies something that had been omitted from the talk while preserving the guest's basic focus on the product.

The host also uses clarifying formulations to supply relevant information other than a product's name. In Data Segment 13, the guest (PS) is demonstrating how data stored on disk by a DOS (or PC) computer can be transferred to a Macintosh. She begins with a DOS floppy disk, but fails to identify it specifically as belonging to the DOS system.

Data Segment 13 [CC03, 2962]

```
01 PS:     . . . and for demonstration purposes
02         what I'm gonna do here is •hh take a
03         standard three sixty K (.) disk
04         (1.2)
05         five and a quarter (0.3) pop it in
06         •h ⌈ h and
07 SC:        ⌊ Okay so that's a dos formatted disk,=
```

```
08 PS:    =this is a dos format diskette, right?
09        (0.6)
10        •hh (.) a:nd what you're gonna see
11        here is . . .
```

As the disk slides into the disk drive unit, SC formulates the character of the disk (line 7) and gets immediate confirmation from PS (line 8). This formulation produces an adjustment to—a refinement of—the demonstration presented to the viewing audience. In this case, the information explicitly conveyed by the formulation was already implicitly available in the guest's prior behavior. PS had characterized the disk as "three sixty K" (360 kilobytes of storage capacity) and as "five and a quarter" (the 5.25-inch diameter of the disk). These characterizations are sufficient to identify the disk as a DOS (rather than a Macintosh) disk, though perhaps only for computer aficionados. It is in this sense that the host shows an orientation to fine-tuning the demonstration for the audience.[8]

In other cases, the host's clarifying formulation proposes an inference based on the guest's prior turn and other actions. In Data Segment 14, DH is demonstrating a touch pad that sits on the desk and controls the mouse pointer on the screen (and other functions). The large number of silences in his turn is accounted for by his pausing while he touches the pad and waits for the display to change. TB is the cohost.

Data Segment 14 [CC13, 4514]
```
01 DH:    . . . An' you can see (0.5) in
02        this hypercard (0.4) um: (0.9)
03        application: th't (.) by just
04        pressing dow:n a little bit harder
05        on (1.1) on the unit (0.4) um we're
06        able to (1.2) um applica- a- um
07        (0.5) do the uh: the mouse button.
08 TB:    •h So in essence (.) my finger now
09        is the pointing device.
10 DH:    Yes: exactly. an' it operates in
11        (.) •h absolute mode . . .
```

The guest conveys, albeit in a somewhat fragmented fashion, that extra pressure on the touch pad is the functional equivalent of clicking a mouse button. The cohost then formulates an inference (lines 8-9) from this demonstration: that the user's finger becomes the pointing device. That is, by touching certain locations on the pad the user directs the pointer symbol to corresponding locations on the monitor screen. The guest had been *doing* that as part of the demonstration, but had not *expressed* it that way. DH confirms this (line 10) and continues talking about the product. Thus the cohost has introduced a substantive contribution into the demonstration: a clarification of how the product works. With this confirmed by the guest, the demonstration has become more collaboratively produced, the cohost making a more substantive contribution than would otherwise have been the case.

The inferences expressed in clarifying formulations can be designed to make explicit a connection between information produced in the demonstration and related information that the viewing audience might be expected to have. In Data Segment 15, SS is showing how cell formulas work in his spreadsheet program and the advantages over the older generation of spreadsheets. The host is SC.

Data Segment 15 [MM93-4, 3354]
01 SS: . . . a::n- an' if you wanted to
02   cut 'n' copy this formula across all
03   pages you would just click on the
04   global icon an' then •h define
05   the scope of this formula select
06   okay an' it gets copied across.
07 SC: So you're not stuck with cells
08   which just happen to be adjacent
09   to each other in the old fashioned
10   ⌈ (model. yeh) ⌉
11 SS: ⌊ That's corre ⌋ct. Exactly.
12   •h Now, six months down the road
13   you wanna go in an' analyze this
14   model again . . .

The guest has selected a formula to be copied into certain cells in a set of business financial worksheets. In lines 1-6 he describes the copying operation while actually carrying it out. SC formulates a characteristic of this operation —that the target cells can be distributed throughout the worksheets and do not have to be adjacent to each other—and contrasts that with the "old fashioned" spreadsheets (lines 7-10). In so doing, the host produces a reminder to viewers of their experiences with the older generation of spreadsheet programs, which could copy only to a rectangular block of adjacent cells. This is a substantive contribution by the host—one that the guest might have made, but did not. The guest quickly confirms the clarification (actually overlapping SC's turn in line 10) and continues with the demonstration. Again, the demonstration is a collaborative and cooperative affair.

Clarifying formulations are directly linked to a guest's prior turn and offer a version of what the guest said or may have meant. These contributions by the host may be regarded as cooperative in the sense that they express descriptions, minor inferences, and the like, that the guest can be expected to agree with, or even information that the guest *might* have said, but did not. Another clarifying practice is to *ask* what the guest meant, what the product is doing, what is going on. This involves building a question-formatted turn from a guest's prior turn.

The Clarifying Inquiry

As described above, one type of clarification involves the host's formulating (summarizing, re-presenting) talk or inferences from a guest's prior turn and thereby occasioning a confirmation by the guest. In contrast, the host may design the clarifying turn as a question about a guest's immediately prior—or possibly more distant—turn. This *clarifying inquiry* occasions an answer by the guest. Note that this practice is not the same as the itemized inquiry previously reported on. Although the clarifying inquiry does ask about a specific item or issue (a characteristic of the itemized inquiry), this item is to be found in the prior talk of the guest, rather than in a preface or preliminary talk by the host. That is, the clarifying inquiry focuses on something the guest has recently said, as can be seen in Data Segment 16. The host (SC) has asked JO to compare two of his company's spreadsheet programs: Lotus 123 and Improv (the focus of this demonstration). JO characterizes the new software in rather general terms.

Data Segment 16 [MM93-4, 3385]

```
01 JO:   Okay, •h well Improv is the
02       first dynamic spreadsheet for
03       Windows. It's it's a reinvention
04       of the spreadsheet. •hh um You'll
05       find that it's a dramatic- (0.4)
06       dramatically different approach
07       (.) t' spreadsheets um as compared
08       to traditional (.) cell based
09       spreadsheets like 123.
10 SC:   Okay what d'ya mean by dynamic
11       and different approach to a
12       spreadsheet.
13 JO:   Well um the interaction is
14       very different an- and why
15       don't I show (this) . . .
```

In lines 10-12, the host asks a question designed to bring about a further elaboration or clarification of JO's description. The "what d'ya mean" question itself is supplemented by a direct topical tie to JO's turn through the repetition of the expressions "dynamic," "different approach," and "spreadsheet." This occasions an answer in which the guest shows SC what he means by those terms. The resulting elaborated demonstration has been interactively achieved.

The clarifying inquiry is used not only to bring about explanations of expressions in prior talk, but also to engender further discussion about product components and operations. In Data Segment 17, PO (a guest) has been pointing out features of his favorite notebook computer in response to an earlier action request by SC.

Data Segment 17 [MM93-4, 2647]

```
01 PO:   . . . •hh On this side
02       (1.0) pt there are two
03       (0.6) PCMCIA (0.5) slots
04 SC:   uh huh
05 PO:   A:nd (0.6) it's just a- a
06       terrific machine overall
07 SC:   >Wha' wou- wha' would< you
08       use two slots for then.
09 PO:   •h well (0.3) for example I
10       think- (0.3) if you had a
11       modem (0.4) and a lan card (.)
12       ⌜you c'n plug 'em both ⌜ and have
13 SC:   ⌞uh huh              ⌞ okay
14 PO:   'em both in at the same ti:me . . .
```

PO has explained earlier what a PCMCIA card is and now mentions that his computer has two slots for such cards (lines 1-3). After PO's "overall" evaluative statement about the computer, SC produces a clarifying inquiry focused on the possible uses of two slots (lines 7-8). This occasions an answer by PO and the usefulness of the slots is explained.[9] Again, the host's turn includes not only the actual question, but a topical tie to PO's prior talk (the words "two slots").

This clarification practice can also be used to "reach back" into earlier portions of the guest's demonstration. The key to this is referencing the earlier talk in such a way that its relevance to the current turn can be recognized. Data Segment 18 begins 45 seconds after the guest (SS) last demonstrated changing to the third and fourth dimensions of a multidimensional spreadsheet. SS is now talking about how spreadsheet formulas are expressed in ordinary language terms rather than in codes.

Data Segment 18 [MM93-4, 3367]

```
01 SS:   •h An' it shows you in English
02       language terms •h how this formula
03       was described.
```

```
04 SC:   H- how do I shift those dimensions
05       you were showing me before if I
06       wan'to- you know represent two (0.9)
07       two ⌐ other dimensions (   )
08 SS:     └ Okay basically let- let me show
09       y'an example if I wanted to sh- uh
10       see the sales of my nineteen
11       ninety two year . . .
```

At a possible ending of SS's turn, the host (SC) produces a clarifying inquiry (lines 4-7). The question is not about the focus of the guest's most recent turn, but about something that SS had talked about and demonstrated earlier. The reference to these earlier matters is conveyed in the expressions "those dimensions you were showing me before," and "represent two . . . other dimensions." SS is able to locate those earlier matters and immediately (in overlap with SC at line 7) answers the "how" question by showing another example. Thus an earlier discussion is renewed and the current trajectory of the demonstration is altered along lines initiated by the host and followed by the guest.

The clarification, comprising the two host practices discussed above, can be seen as a host's way of providing for clarifying talk about specific matters presented by the guest. Using a clarifying formulation, the host proposes a summary, characterization, fine-tuning, or interpretation of a guest's talk and occasions the guest's confirmation (or disconfirmation) of it. Employing a clarifying inquiry, the host raises specific questions about specific matters presented by a guest and thus occasions an answer—often an elaboration or demonstration— by the guest. These responses are immediate and are overwhelmingly confirming or informative. Through these practices, the ongoing demonstration is adjusted, clarified, refocused, and extended through an interactive and collaborative process.

CONCLUSION

The task of *Computer Chronicles* is the communication of technical information to a viewing audience. Each guest is specifically expert in his or her product (and possibly in the demonstration of it), and the hosts (and cohosts) seem broadly competent in computer matters. But even though the guests are the subject-matter experts, the hosts orient to the presumed informational needs of the audience in employing two sets of practices to alter the progress of the product demonstration. Clayman (1989) says of broadcast news interviews that certain techniques *micromanage* the length of an interviewee's final turn. In analogous ways, the host of *Computer Chronicles* micromanages the trajectory, topical focus, clarity, and potential implications of the ongoing series of a guest's turns. Through the use of prompts—action requests, itemized inquiries, and topic elicitors—the host occasions a specified type of action, treatment of a specified topic item, or movement on to other unspecified matters. Guests routinely perform the prompted actions. By using clarifications—clarifying formulations and clarifying inquiries—the host introduces statements as well as questions about what is going on or what is meant. These occasion immediate confirmations or other answers (including further demonstrations) by the guest. The resulting product demonstration is collaboratively achieved, not unilaterally constructed by the guest within boundaries provided by the host. This achievement is a cooperative one as well, in the sense that the host does not (except rarely) challenge the guest, as may occur in broadcast news interviews (Greatbatch, 1986b; Heritage, 1985). Guests respond to prompts and clarifications cooperatively as well; that is, they do not respond defensively. For example, guests do not evade answering questions or reformulate questions before answering, as news interviewees may do (Clayman, 1993; Greatbatch, 1986b). And guests overwhelmingly respond to clarifications by confirming the host's formulations, often by repeating them (Nofsinger, 1994).

In light of these findings, it can be seen that the interactive format is a strategy for adapting an ongoing product demonstration to the presumed needs of an overhearing, nonpresent audience. It makes available "conversational" (i.e., social-interactional) resources for the micromanagement of guests' turns. Hosts who do not need the current moment of a demonstration to be modified or clarified for their own benefit can engineer changes on behalf of the intended audience. The classic issues of what to talk about next and how to express it are thus collaboratively resolved in this mass-mediated context through practices of interpersonal communication.

APPENDIX: TRANSCRIBING CONVENTIONS

The primary transcription symbols used in the data segments are explained below. This system for transcribing talk to written form was devised by Gail Jefferson and is explained more extensively in Atkinson and Heritage (1984, pp. ix-xvi) and in Beach (1989, pp. 89-90). The symbols are used to represent characteristics of talk besides the words themselves, such as silences, overlapping talk, unusual volume, pronunciation, and audible breaths.

Symbol	Meaning
. . .	Ellipses indicate talk omitted from speaker's turn.
[ ]	Square brackets between lines of talk indicate the beginning ([) and end (]) of overlapping talk.
(0.4)	Numbers in parentheses represent silence measured to the nearest tenth of a second.

(.)	A dot enclosed in parentheses indicates a short, untimed silence, generally less than two- or three-tenths of a second.
end of line=/=start of line	Equal signs are latching symbols. When attached to the end of one line and the beginning of another, they indicate that the later talk was "latched on to" the earlier talk with no hesitation, perhaps without even waiting the normal conversational rhythm or "beat."
>no no no<	Angles pointing toward each other enclose talk that is noticeably faster; outward-pointing angles enclose slower talk: <I just don't know>.
<u>Wait</u> a minute	Underlining shows vocal stress or emphasis.
FBI, 911	All-upper-case initials indicate separate pronunciation of each letter; numerals indicate separate pronunciation of each digit. Otherwise, the item is spelled out.
Oh: no:::	Colons indicate an elongated syllable; the more colons, the more the syllable or sound is stretched.
Wait a mi-	A hyphen shows a sudden cutoff of sound.
(safari)	Parentheses around words indicate transcriber doubt about what those words are, as in the case of overlapped or off-camera talk.
( )	Empty parentheses indicate that some talk was not audible or interpretable at all.
((looks up))	Double parentheses enclose transcriber comments.
When? 'ats right.	Punctuation marks are generally used to indicate pitch level rather than sentence type. The apostrophe (') indicates missing speech sounds and normal contractions. The period indicates a drop in pitch; the question mark shows rising pitch (not necessarily a question); and the comma represents a flat pitch or a slight rising-then-falling pitch. When used, the exclamation point (!) shows "lively" or animated talk.
•h	The h preceded by a raised dot represents an audible inbreath. Longer sounds are transcribed using a longer string: •hhh
•hh, heh	The h without a leading dot represents audible exhaling, sometimes associated with laughter; laughter itself is transcribed using "heh" or "hah" or something similar. When laugh tokens are embedded in a word, they are often represented by an h in parentheses: Ye(hh)s.
pt	The letters pt by themselves represent a lip smack, which may occur just as a speaker begins to talk.
Didjuh ever	Modified spelling is used to suggest something of the pronunciation. For example, "A'ri-" is a quick version of "all right."

NOTES

1. Refer to the appendix to this chapter, to Atkinson and Heritage (1984, pp. ix-xvi), or to the spring 1989 issue of *Western Journal of Speech Communication* (Beach, 1989, pp. 89-90), for a more complete explanation of the special symbols used by conversation analysts.

2. Product demonstrations can also be noninteractive, involving one person on camera. Examples may be found in various woodworking, painting, and cooking programs; in automobile review programs such as *MotorWeek* on PBS; and in consumer product programs on the "shopping" channels (e.g., QVC).

3. Two different hosts and three cohosts appear in the studio sessions reported on here, but SC is by far the most frequent host. Nevertheless, persons other than SC can and do use the practices that he uses.

4. Personal names in the talk are represented by pseudonyms (as when SC calls the guest by his first name in line 1).

5. RM's preparedness as stated in lines 12-14 is evidence of this.

6. The "show us" action request is not prefaced by the host—a departure from the usual shape of such a turn. It may be that the prior action request preface ("that little red dot") and the intervening turn by the guest serve the needed orienting functions.

7. Button and Casey (1985, pp. 4-20) describe a practice common in everyday conversation and call it the "itemized news enquiry." The present term is intended to finesse the issues of whether and for whom the item may be "news."

8. In Data Segment 10, line 6 is another example of this.

9. This data segment leads into the beginning of Data Segment 7 above.

REFERENCES

Atkinson, J. M., & Drew, P. (1979). *Order in court: The organisation of verbal interaction in judicial settings.* Atlantic Highlands, NJ: Humanities Press.

Atkinson, J. M., & Heritage, J. C. (Eds.). (1984). *Structures of social action: Studies in conversation analysis.* Cambridge: Cambridge University Press.

Beach, W. A. (Ed.). (1989). Sequential organization of conversational activities [Special issue]. *Western Journal of Speech Communication, 53*(2).

Button, G., & Casey, N. (1984). Generating topic: The use of topic initial elicitors. In J. M. Atkinson & J. C. Heritage (Eds.), *Structures of social action: Studies in conversation analysis* (pp. 167-190). Cambridge: Cambridge University Press.

Button, G., & Casey, N. (1985). Topic nomination and topic pursuit. *Human Studies, 8,* 3-55.

Clayman, S. E. (1988). Displaying neutrality in television news interviews. *Social Problems, 35,* 474-492.

Clayman, S. E. (1989). The production of punctuality: Social interaction, temporal organization, and social structure. *American Journal of Sociology, 95,* 659-691.

Clayman, S. E. (1991). News interview openings: Aspects of sequential organization. In P. Scannell (Ed.), *Broadcast talk* (pp. 48-75). London: Sage.

Clayman, S. E. (1993). Reformulating the question: A device for answering/not answering questions in news interviews and press conferences. *Text, 13,* 159-188.

Clayman, S. E., & Whalen, J. (1988/89). When the medium becomes the message: The case of the Rather-Bush encounter. *Research on Language and Social Interaction, 22,* 241-272.

Greatbatch, D. (1986a). Aspects of topical organization in news interviews: The use of agenda shifting procedures by interviewees. *Media, Culture & Society, 8,* 441-455.

Greatbatch, D. (1986b). Some standard uses of supplementary questions in news interviews. In J. Wilson & B. K. Crow (Eds.), *Belfast working papers in language and linguistics* (Vol. 8, pp. 86-123). Jordanstown: University of Ulster.

Greatbatch, D. (1988). A turn-taking system for British news interviews. *Language in Society, 17,* 401-430.

Heritage, J. C. (1984). *Garfinkel and ethnomethodology.* Cambridge: Polity.

Heritage, J. C. (1985). Analyzing news interviews: Aspects of the production of talk for an overhearing audience. In T. A. van Dijk (Ed.), *Handbook of discourse analysis: Vol. 3. Discourse and dialogue* (pp. 95-117). London: Academic Press.

Heritage, J. C., Clayman, S., & Zimmerman, D. H. (1988). Discourse and message analysis: The micro-structure of mass media messages. In R. P. Hawkins, J. M. Wiemann, & S. Pingree (Eds.), *Advancing communication science: Merging mass and interpersonal processes* (pp. 77-109). Newbury Park, CA: Sage.

Heritage, J. C., & Greatbatch, D. (1991). On the institutional character of institutional talk: The case of news interviews. In D. Boden & D. H. Zimmerman (Eds.), *Talk and social structure* (pp. 93-137). Berkeley: University of California Press.

Heritage, J. C., & Watson, D. R. (1979). Formulations as conversational objects. In G. Psathas (Ed.), *Everyday language: Studies in ethnomethodology* (pp. 123-162). New York: Irvington.

Heritage, J. C., & Watson, D. R. (1980). Aspects of the properties of formulations in natural conversations: Some instances analyzed. *Semiotica, 30,* 245-262.

Hopper, R. (1992). *Telephone conversation.* Bloomington: Indiana University Press.

Levinson, S. C. (1992). Activity types and language. In P. Drew & J. C. Heritage (Eds.), *Talk at work* (pp. 66-100). Cambridge: Cambridge University Press.

Nofsinger, R. E. (1988-1989). "Let's talk about the record": Contending over topic redirection in the Rather/Bush interview. *Research on Language and Social Interaction, 22,* 273-291.

Nofsinger, R. E. (1991). *Everyday conversation.* Newbury Park, CA: Sage.

Nofsinger, R. E. (1994). Repeating the host: An interactional use of repetition by guests on televised episodes of "Computer Chronicles." In B. Johnstone (Ed.), *Repetition in discourse: Interdisciplinary perspectives* (Vol. 2, pp. 84-95). Norwood, NJ: Ablex.

Pingree, S., Wiemann, J. M., & Hawkins, R. P. (1988). Editor's introduction: Toward conceptual synthesis. In R. P. Hawkins, J. M. Wiemann, & S. Pingree (Eds.), *Advancing communication science: Merging mass and interpersonal processes* (pp. 7-17). Newbury Park, CA: Sage.

Sacks, H., & Schegloff, E. A. (1979). Two preferences in the organization of reference to persons in conversation and their interaction. In G. Psathas (Ed.), *Everyday language: Studies in ethnomethodology* (pp. 15-21). New York: Irvington.

Sacks, H., Schegloff, E. A., & Jefferson, G. (1978). A simplest systematics for the organization of turn-taking for conversation. In J. Schenkein (Ed.), *Studies in the organization of conversational interaction* (pp. 7-55). New York: Academic Press.

Schegloff, E. A. (1988-1989). From interview to confrontation: Observations of the Bush/Rather encounter. *Research on Language and Social Interaction, 22,* 215-240.

Schegloff, E. A., & Sacks, H. (1973). Opening up closings. *Semiotica, 7,* 289-327.

16 Studying Conversational Interaction in Institutions

ROBERT W. HOPPER
University of Texas at Austin

I N the past decade, conversation analysts have embraced the study of talk in institutional settings. This focus is celebrated in the title of a recent volume, *Talk at Work* (Drew & Heritage, 1992b), that suggests common ground between conversation analysis and organizational communication. These institutional studies include descriptions of discourse in the media (see Clayman, 1992; Greatbatch, 1992; see also Nofsinger, Chapter 15, this volume). These studies pose prospects relevant to any scholars who describe message details using evidence made available by electronic recordings. Connections between conversation analysis and traditional areas of communication study may promote theory, but this moment also entails examining our ongoing dis-ease about how to conceptualize settings and other features of communicative context.

We have grown used to organizing our disciplinary subfields by communicative setting: public address, group communication, organizational communication, and so on. This classification by setting is more a historical than an analytic artifact, and our best scholars denounce the practice (e.g., Miller, 1978). Yet we continue to train novice teacher-scholars to focus on what is specific to such setting domains as "political speeches," "interaction in business organizations," and "speaking practices in X culture."

When we pursue area concentrations in organizational, mass-mediated, or interpersonal communication, we pretend to hold a theory of context that supports the division of our phenomena into these setting-specified specialties. Our tradition, rich with appreciation of setting but including no viable theory of context, has brought us to the kinds of problems chemists would experience if there were no periodic chart to relate diverse elements in terms of common properties.

Conversation analysts have developed an approach to context that communication scholars may use in addressing this problem. It is argued that a theory of

Correspondence and requests for reprints: Robert W. Hopper, Department of Speech Communication, University of Texas, Austin, TX 78712.

Communication Yearbook 18, pp. 371-380

conversation (and, by extension, any communication theory) must describe both context-sensitive and context-free phenomena:

> Conversation can accommodate a wide range of situations, interactions in which persons in varieties of identities . . . are operating; it can be . . . capable of dealing with a change of situation within a situation. Hence there must be some formal apparatus that is itself context-free. (Sacks, Schegloff, & Jefferson, 1974, p. 699)

Because speakers must adapt each moment to changing contextual relevancies, we must explain these moment-to-moment adaptations. Each context may have unique properties, but context-specifying practices must extend across contextual variation. As Sacks et al. note, "It is the context-free structure that defines how and where context-sensitivity can be displayed" (p. 699, n. 8).

Any communication theorists could seek to specify context-free features of communicative practices and to test these specifications against empirical details of communicative performances in the world. Let us consider how conversation analysts use this stance to study talk in institutional settings.

CONVERSATION ANALYSES
OF TALK IN INSTITUTIONS

Numerous conversation analyses of institutional talk follow the premise that practices of mundane conversation provide certain context-free components underpinning the interactive uses of talk in any setting:[1]

> The basic forms of mundane talk constitute a kind of benchmark against which other more formal or "institutional" types of interaction are recognized and experienced. . . . "institutional" forms of interaction will show systematic variations and restrictions on activities in their design relative to ordinary conversation. (Drew & Heritage, 1992a, p. 19)

Analyses of talk in institutional settings frequently proceed by posing comparisons between practices used in that setting and those in mundane conversation—practices that seem relatively context-free.

How does one judge the validity of such arguments? Schegloff (1992) proposes a criterion of "relevance." Given that we refer to persons and to settings by various contextualizing category terms, any moment in any interaction might truthfully be described by many such terms.[2] But are all true characterizations equally salient to the course of interaction at any moment? Of course not—the problem is to specify the relevance of a category term *to interacting speakers* at a particular moment.

If we describe talk that occurs in a setting (e.g., a medical interview), we should rely on empirical evidence that the participants orient to that setting. For example, two persons meet in a physician's examining room and perform this encounter opening:

UTCL Street:14

D: Hello Mister Steen=
P: =Good morning
          (2.0)
D: I'm Doctor Krone

In this exchange of greetings and name identifications, D calls both himself and P by title plus last name. This asymmetrical pair of reference terms, mister/doctor (and who speaks them both), shows at least one participant characterizing this encounter as one between a physician and a patient. This can be taken as a modest display-in-message of the relevance of the institutional setting "doctor-patient" to that speaker.

Of course, this occasion provides markings of setting before these parties speak to one another. The patient has walked into a clinic building, spoken to a receptionist, been shown to a small white room, had his blood pressure measured by a nurse, and waited alone. Actions at each of these moments invest the occasion with institutional qualities—even before the opening of the speech event we label as a "doctor-patient" encounter. Still, the person references supplied in this encounter opening align with institutional qualities and perform work within institutional roles.

Most essays about talk within institutions have treated just one setting, which foregrounds setting-based explanations for things happening as they do. We can follow Schegloff's tests for the "relevance" of messages to setting, and infer that the use of the person-reference term "doctor" (spoken in the instance above) is relevant to the characterization of this event as a doctor-patient encounter. However, this cannot resolve the root problem of the seductiveness of setting as *the* explanation for action. This is not just an analyst's problem, but a member's problem to which analysts are also vulnerable. As such, this problem can become a topic for study.

SETTING APPEARS ON CUE

In the doctor-patient example just above, there may be features preserved by a video record of this event that are not related to the contextual frame, doctor-patient encounter. But would we discover such structurating practices while studying the topic "doctor-patient interaction"? Does specifying the setting help us find connection to the setting? May the current turn to the study of "institutional settings" thereby blunt the cutting edge of conversation analysis?

Sacks (1992) recommends that analysts adopt "unmotivated listening" practices rather than limit the work to issues specifiable in advance:

> A first rule of procedure in doing analysis, a rule that you absolutely must use or you can't do the work, is this: In setting up what it is that seems to have happened, preparatory to solving the problem, do not let your notion of what could conceivably happen decide for you what must have happened. (p. 115)

Conversation analysts have frequently eschewed hypothesis testing to rely upon the surprising insight. However, recent "institution" essays take a mainstream procedural tack, delineating a problem area, reviewing literature, and specifying comparisons among kinds of settings. Is this a consequence of the anchoring of analysis in institutional materials? Recall that the early Sacks lectures are based almost exclusively in institutional materials![3] What distinguishes Sacks's lectures from current conversation analyses of institutional discourse? A partial answer is that Sacks used "institutionally situated" materials to mount many observations about mundane practices; he was not primarily studying an "institutional context."

A problem with analyses of institutional talk is embedded in describing *it* as "institutional talk." This terminology carries the traditional setting divisions of communication study. Given a characterization of a strip of talk as "the opening of a medical interview," or given a title of an essay as "Host Talk on X TV Show" it becomes difficult to resist offering an institutional setting explanation as *the* explanation for whatever we find in these materials.

Conversation analysts maintain within research activities some methodical practices that can position the investigator inside (but not only swept along by) versions of what I provisionally call "setting appears on cue"—alluding to Sacks's discussion titled "character appears on cue." This concept traces how it is that when an institutional explanation for a marked event gets advanced, it routinely becomes *the* explanation.

"Character appears on cue" turns on examples such as the following, about which Sacks (1992) notes that a telephone counselor who has been speaking with a caller for only a few seconds detects a probable lie:

B:	When she stepped between me and the child, I went to move her out of the way. And then about that time her sister had called the police. I don't know how she . . . what she . . .
→ A:	Didn't you smack her one?
B:	No
→ A:	You're not telling me the story, Mr B. (p. 113)

Mr. B subsequently admits that he "shoved her." Sacks ponders how A detects such a distortion in the story of a stranger (pp. 114, 183-185). A apparently expects that police would be called pursuant to some sort of act. Hearing no such act in

B's story, A guesses that such an act has occurred—and that that act cued the call to the cops.

Sacks (1992) further illustrates "character appears on cue" with another police-appearance story (from a group therapy session) in which the officer appears after a hypothetical drag race. Yet neither the race nor the police officer is mentioned:

> Joe: . . . in the same car, same color, same year the whole bit, roll up his pipes and he's in a dirty grubby tee
>
> →   shirt, and the guy'll pick the guy up in the dirty grubby tee shirt . . . (p. 182)

Sacks notes how unproblematic it seems for the participants in this event to figure out that "the guy" proposed by the teller (as doing the picking up) is in fact a police officer. There is another "guy" in the story ("in the dirty grubby tee shirt"). This guy has been carefully introduced, and might get lexically confused with the guy doing the picking up. The police officer's character is not introduced. Instead:

> What occurs is good grounds for the cop to do what he ought to do; he's on the scene and he does it. So he's introduced via the action he does, where the grounds for that action are laid out, though how he happens to be there need not be indicated. (p. 183)

The cop is introduced by his action within a scene, making his appearance institutionally appropriate: The "character appears on cue" (p. 182). Because that institutional explanation is available, it gets treated as *the* explanation for this point in the narrative. The details of that setting making get somewhat effaced from the telling.

The institutional character of Sacks's examples is readily apparent. Each takes for granted the entrance of a police officer performing role-incumbent occupational activity. It is partly by their "institutionality" that these instances demonstrate Sacks's points about how we make context and action. When an institutional explanation pops up, that explanation can quickly get advanced as *the* explanation for a variety of things. That accomplishment, the appearance and advancing of setting/institution-as-explanation, is something we must study.

Are we all, participants in interaction and observational analysts, doomed to be dupes of life's institutionalizing presumptions? Yes, to a degree, we are; and that is part of what we should describe.

DIALECTICS OF INSTITUTIONAL AND CONTEXT-FREE PRACTICES

In this discussion I have taken the institutional/mundane contrast as one starting point. I have noted some pitfalls in specifying an "institutional" setting as a focus for analysis. Another complication, however, is that certain mundane practices of conversation, those I have labeled relatively "context-free," operate somewhat similarly to the practices labeled "institutional." We interact with each other and within dialectic interplay of these social forces.

For example, when a speaker utters the first part of an adjacency pair, context-free systematics evoke difficult to isolate and still harder to resist constraints to perform a matching category of rejoinder. The turn-taking system apparently includes procedures by which participants in interaction scrutinize any current turn for its status as a possible first pair part. This constraint is institutional in the sense that languages and cultures are institutions—in which we are inmates. In any speech community, a first pair part proffers to a next speaker certain overwhelmingly obvious analyses, which the next speaker is invited to treat as *the* analysis at this moment.

Adjacency-pair first parts, such as questions, are enormously commonplace in what we label "institutional" talk. But do we best specify the institution as just the setting within a professional organization? Is not the question-answer pair another source of institutional organization interacting with the buildings, organizational chart, and human factors? And what about the turn-taking practices of which adjacency pairs are only an example?

For empirical reasons, Sacks et al. (1974) select turn taking as their primary example of context-free practices of conversation:

> Major aspects of the organization of turn taking are insensitive to such parameters of context, and are, in that sense, "context free"; but it remains the case that examination of any particular materials will display the context-free resources of the turn-taking system to be employed, disposed in ways that are fitted to particulars of context. (p. 699, n. 8)

Sacks et al. propose certain features of turn-taking organization as relatively context-free, including the following: One party talks at a time; any first speaker gains rights to a turn-constructional unit the end point of which can be approximately projected during its unfolding course; turn transitions are finely coordinated to keep speech overlaps brief; and a current speaker gets the first opportunity to select a next speaker.

These specifications describe mundane conversation in a large number of speech communities; there is something primordial about them. Speakers may mark any utterance with reference to these practices. Speakers may, for instance, constrain the course of a next speaker's turn by speaking a question. However, no member has special role-defined privileges to ask questions.

In some "institutional" settings participants do modify turn-taking practices, thereby orienting to the "procedural consequentiality" of the setting (Schegloff, 1992). To exemplify procedural consequentiality in "institutional" talk, Schegloff argues that question-answer sequencing in "news interview" settings modifies mundane practices by assigning inflexible roles of interviewer (question asker) and interviewee (question answerer) (pp. 121ff.; see also Nofsinger, Chapter 15, this volume). One procedural consequence of this institutional role division is that a news interviewer may set up a question with numerous preliminaries, keeping an interviewee from speaking until a recognizable question occurs. This point is made vivid in the opening of a 1988 interview between then Vice President George Bush and news anchor Dan Rather. In this encounter Rather structures his turn by stating a series of unflattering preliminaries:

Rather/Bush [simplified transcript]
Rather: Donald Gregg still serves as your trusted advisor
           He was deeply involved in running arms to the
           Contras and he didn't inform you
→   (0.5)
           Now when President Reagan's trusted advisor
           Admiral Poindexter (0.6) failed to inform him,
           (0.8) the President- fired him.
→   (0.5)
           Why is Mister Gregg still (.) inside the White
           House and still a trusted advisor.
Bush: Because I have confidence in him ((continues))

This simplified transcription shows two transition-relevant pauses following unpleasant allegations by Rather. Yet Bush waits until Rather completes a recognizable question before beginning to speak. Schegloff argues that this news interview respondent is constrained within this institutional context to wait for a question to be asked.[4]

Procedural consequentiality (for these instances at least) is consequentiality to context-free conversation practices. Specification of such practices, and their uses, deserves a central place in communication research. But if "institutional" constraints may modify the "context-free" practices of turn taking, then those practices must be taken to be in some sense context-sensitive. Sacks et al. appear to endorse this proposal when they note that context-free practices guide context-sensitive activity. If we try to make the categories "institutional" and "context-free/mundane" stand aside from each other, in separate test tubes, we may stunt our understanding of conversational practices. It is not mainly these categories we should describe, but the moment-to-moment unfolding of conversational interaction.

CONCLUSIONS

The current moment in scholarship, in which conversation analysts describe talk in institutional settings, is rich with opportunity for all of communication studies. Analysts have fashioned some beginnings of a theory of context, constructed some exemplars of rigorous method, and addressed description in specific institutional contexts. This makes conversation analysis accessible to new clients and audiences. These same developments provide a theory of context to which scholars, throughout communication studies, may respond.

But the theoretical backdrop of such work takes on risks of prematurely assessing a communicative pattern as consequential to any "institution" so addressed. For example, do we want to argue that physicians are "being unresponsive" after question-answer pairs (Jones, 1993; Treichler, Frankel, Kramarae, Zoppi, & Beckman, 1984) and that news interviewers who act quite similarly are "achieving neutrality before an overhearing audience" (Clayman, 1992; Greatbatch, 1992; Heritage & Greatbatch, 1991)? These are each attractive hypotheses, but specific support for them remains provisional. Could further evidence show that interactive responsiveness is curtailed for the interviewer-questioner role in a variety of "interview" formats?

As we tackle these issues, we may use Schegloff's criterion of "relevance" as a caution against Type I error. Scholars describing talk in an institutional setting should not only compare features, but also show participants' orientations to the relevance of the setting.

Schegloff's second criterion, "procedural consequentiality," is formulated as somewhat specific to context-free procedures for turn taking, repair, and so on. In some other domain it may take a different shape. We should not turn Schegloff's criteria of "relevance" and "procedural consequentiality" into cookie cutters, nor should we ask any theorist to fulfill both sets of criteria up to some standard level.

> Establishing relevance and establishing procedural consequentiality cannot be "threshold issues," that is, once you have "enough" to show it you are finished. Rather they are questions for continuing analysis. . . . Invoking social structure or the setting of the talk at the outset can systematically distract from, even blind us to, details of those domains of events in the world. (Schegloff, 1992, p. 127)

The detailed conversation-analytic study of events in the world has provisionally isolated a problem that I hereby dub the "institution" problem. It seems to be a feature of communicative events in the world that (a) an explanation can easily come to be treated as *the* explanation, and (b) this is particularly the case with names for settings. These are not just analysts' problems but participants' problems as well, for which most schools of analysis have no descriptive remedy. This participants' problem itself is an important domain of study within the study of interaction. All interaction, whatever its setting, illuminates dialectics between the context-sensitive and the context-free, between the institutional and the mundane.

This essay has provided one conversation analyst's method-centered rejoinder to current studies of talk in institutions. Coherence has not been possible here, only a series of reflections. But perhaps these pages may be taken as one turn at talk within a specifically institutionalized moment. Other responses are still to come from scholars in organizational communication, mass communication, and other traditional setting areas in our discipline. Such responses might reshape our discipline's subcultural landscape.[5] So will the responses to these works from everyday communicators in all walks of life, to the betterment of whose experience all communication scholarship is dedicated.

NOTES

1. *Mundane conversation* can be roughly described as interaction between previously acquainted peers at moments in which no institutional purpose strongly constrains what is occurring (see Zimmerman, 1988).

2. This problem is discussed for characterizations of individuals by Schegloff (1992), Hopper and Drummond (1992), and Mandelbaum (1990-1991). In the current essay I use examples of "setting" terms, but the problem of reference to persons persists in any complex interaction—along with the problem of reference to setting and other features of context.

3. The 1964 lectures are based on phone calls to a suicide prevention hot line, and the overwhelming majority of lectures during 1965-1967 are based on group therapy sessions for troubled teens.

4. Schegloff contrasts this instance with one in which a speaker tries a similar tack to that used by Rather, but (without the added restriction of news interview procedure) his cointerlocutor mishears his purpose and responds prematurely. Schegloff details a subtle methodical point about procedural consequentiality: "'Leading up' to something . . . can pose problems of sequential organization for the participants in ordinary conversation. And . . . there are specific practices of talking in interaction which are addressed to it" (p. 120). Schegloff argues that in mundane talk there is a constraint limiting a speaker to a single turn unit at the end of which a coparticipant may decode this utterance as a speech act (e.g., a request or apology). This entails a vulnerability for a speaker who undertakes a request prefaced by some storytelling. The (context-free) systemics of ordinary talk include resources for dealing with this problem (e.g., the pre-pre). However, in the news interview instance between Rather and Bush, we see the interviewer achieving a compound turn (against the will of the other) because of an apparent constraint that the interviewee forestall responding until a hearable question has been enacted. There are grounds, therefore, for claiming that the setting characterization "news interview" is procedurally consequential to the turn-taking practices in this instance.

5. I would like to acknowledge responses to this essay-in-progress by Curtis LeBaron, Leslie Jarmon, Dan Modaff, and Judy Shetler. These responses have helped me see how far this vein of scholarship must yet travel before it effectively addresses its most important audiences.

REFERENCES

Clayman, S. E. (1992). Footing in the achievement of neutrality: The case of news-interview discourse. In P. Drew & J. Heritage (Eds.), *Talk at work: Interaction in institutional settings.* (pp. 163-198). Cambridge: Cambridge University Press.

Drew, P., & Heritage, J. (1992a). Analyzing talk at work. In P. Drew & J. Heritage (Eds.), *Talk at work: Interaction in institutional settings* (pp. 3-65). Cambridge: Cambridge University Press.

Drew, P., & Heritage, J. (Eds.). (1992b). *Talk at work: Interaction in institutional settings.* Cambridge: Cambridge University Press.

Greatbatch, D. (1992). On the management of disagreement between news interviewees. In P. Drew & J. Heritage (Eds.), *Talk at work: Interaction in institutional settings* (pp. 268-301). Cambridge: Cambridge University Press.

Heritage, J., & Greatbatch, D. (1991). On the institutional character of institutional talk: The case of news interviews. In D. Boden & D. H. Zimmerman (Eds.), *Talk and social structure* (pp. 93-137). Berkeley: University of California Press.

Hopper, R., & Drummond, K. (1992). Accomplishing interpersonal relationship: Telephone openings of strangers and intimates. *Western Journal of Speech Communication, 3,* 185-195.

Jones, C. (1993). *Supportive communication in physician-patient interviews: The case of the missing assessments.* Unpublished doctoral dissertation, University of Texas.

Mandelbaum, J. (1990/91). Beyond mundane reasoning: Conversation analysis and context. *Research in Language and Social Interaction, 24,* 333-350.

Miller, G. R. (1978). The current status of theory and research in interpersonal communication. *Human Communication Research, 4,* 164-178.

Sacks, H. (1992). *Lectures on conversation* (Vol. 1) (G. Jefferson, Ed.). Oxford: Basil Blackwell.

Sacks, H., Schegloff, E. A., & Jefferson, G. (1974). A simplest systematics for the organization of turn taking for conversation. *Language, 50,* 696-735.

Schegloff, E. A. (1992). On studying talk in institutions. In P. Drew & J. Heritage (Eds.), *Talk at work: Interaction in institutional settings* (pp. 101-134). Cambridge: Cambridge University Press.

Treichler, P. A., Frankel, R. M., Kramarae, C., Zoppi, K., & Beckman, H. B. (1984). Problems and problems: Power relationships in a medical encounter. In C. Kramarae, M. Schulz, & W. O'Barr (Eds.), *Language and power* (pp. 55-62). Beverly Hills, CA: Sage.

Zimmerman, D. H. (1988). On conversation: The conversation analytic perspective. In J. A. Anderson (Ed.), *Communication yearbook 11* (pp. 406-432). Newbury Park, CA: Sage.

17 An Experimental Approach to Social Support Communications: Interactive Coping in Close Relationships

ANITA P. BARBEE
MICHAEL R. CUNNINGHAM
University of Louisville

This review covers four major topics. First, the authors discuss previous studies on social support that document the content of supportive communications. Next, the discussion turns to the development and validation of the Interactive Coping Behavior Coding System and its converse, the Support Activation Behavior Coding System. A third focus is research stemming from sensitive interaction systems theory, which makes predictions, based on numerous variables, concerning whether an interaction will be ameliorative or harmful. The final section presents findings on the effects of interactive coping variables on relationship maintenance.

A common complaint among people who are in distressed marriages, rocky romantic partnerships, or estranged friendships is that they feel misunderstood and unsupported (Baxter, 1986). People in these kinds of relationships often have arguments over how one partner fails to help the other with problems or bad moods during times of stress. Emotional support has been found to be one of the best predictors of satisfaction in relationships (Buhrmester, Furman, Wittenberg, & Reis, 1988). As a consequence, understanding the communication behaviors that lead to the solving of problems or the amelioration of a partner's distress has become a focus of a number of investigators (Burleson, 1994). Cataloging the individual, relationship, and contextual variables that influence the likelihood that supportive or problem-solving communications will be offered for various types of issues also has become an important goal for a number of disciplines, including communication and clinical and social psychology.

Correspondence and requests for reprints: Anita P. Barbee, Kent School of Social Work, University of Louisville, Louisville, KY 40292.

Communication Yearbook 18, pp. 381-413

In this review we cover four major topics. First, we discuss the history of research on social support, with a particular focus on previous efforts to document the content of supportive communications. Next, we discuss the development of the Interactive Coping Behavior Coding System (ICBCS; Barbee, 1988, 1990), which is used to categorize problem- and emotion-focused supportive behaviors provided by the erstwhile helper, and its converse, the Support Activation Behavior Coding System (SABCS; Barbee, Cunningham, et al., 1993), which is used to categorize the verbal and nonverbal behaviors from the person in need of such support. A primary focus of our research has been on documenting the *content* of communications in the social support situation. Our category systems have allowed us to examine the tit-for-tat sequential interplay of help-seeking support activation communications and help-giving interactive coping behaviors. We believe that understanding which support-seeking communications and support-giving messages lead to the successful amelioration of a friend's distress, and which lead to failure, can help us to understand the support process in particular and the nature of close relationships in general.

A third focus in this chapter is sensitive interaction systems theory (SIST), which suggests that the social support situation often stimulates multiple internal conflicts *within* the partners and covert conflict *between* the partners. These conflicts create opportunities for mixed messages and misunderstandings in the communication process. A central postulate of SIST is that people often experience ambivalence when faced with the need to ask for, or provide, social support. There is tension within the help seeker between the need for assistance and the individual's face-saving concerns (Goldsmith, 1994), and that tension can influence the person's choice of social support activation behaviors. There are also tensions within the help giver among such concerns as loyalty to the partner, attributions that blame the partner for the partner's difficulties, and the help giver's desired and actual competence to handle the help seeker's problems (Spitzberg & Cupach, 1984). All of these concerns can influence the helper's use of interactive coping behaviors.

Previously, little attention has been paid to the subtle emotional and cognitive states of partners that affect the dynamics of their communications in supportive interactions. There has been limited focus on how a potential helper rises, or fails to rise, to a partner's signals of distress as a result of his or her own pressures and emotions. SIST makes predictions, based on variables pertaining to the help giver, the help seeker, their relationship, and the context in which support seeking occurs, concerning whether the interaction will be ameliorative or harmful. By experimentally manipulating variables influencing one or both players in a support interaction, we have been able to test SIST's predictions concerning how conflicting concerns may influence the sensitive dynamics of seeking and giving support.

Because most of the problems for which people need help are part of the ebb and flow of daily life, we have focused our research on how support messages are transmitted for coping with daily hassles between people in ongoing relationships. Our interest in daily hassles meshes with the increasing tendency for researchers to monitor day-to-day performance in relationships (Duck, 1990). In the final section of our review, we present findings from a variety of methodologies, including contemporaneous thought-listing methods, short-term diary self-reports, and longitudinal follow-up investigations that are concerned with the effects of social support on relationship satisfaction, maintenance, and stability.

PREVIOUS RESEARCH
ON SUPPORTIVE COMMUNICATIONS

Many commentators have pointed to the need for more research on supportive transactions and the variables that affect the support process (Hobfoll & Stokes, 1988). There are several systemic and historical reasons why researchers in the area of social support have neglected study of the helper and the process of support. The social support literature initially grew out of the fields of clinical and community psychology (Gottlieb, 1978) and behavioral medicine (Matthews, Davis, Stoney, Owens, & Caggiula, 1991). As a result, interest began with examination of people's *perceptions* of support from members of their networks as the people experienced major life events or endured chronic stressors. The studies have been primarily correlational in nature, and the typical dependent measures have focused on mental and physical health outcomes.

The strengths of the perspective offered by the social support tradition are threefold. First, social support is a form of helping that occurs primarily in the context of close relationships (Leatham & Duck, 1990). Second, support giving is not simple, but entails multiple helping behaviors that must be tailored for the person and problem at hand. Finally, outcomes have been investigated that are significant beyond the immediate context, such as the recipient's health and longevity. Although the social support literature has made great contributions to our understanding of the effects of perceived social support and social networks on a recipient's well-being, an extension of the work is needed.

This orientation deterred investigation of the roles of contextual variables and microcommunication dynamics in social support. Only a few studies have examined the variables that affect a *helper*'s willingness and ability to support a close associate (e.g., Simpson, Rholes, & Nelligan, 1992), the influence of environmental variables on the support process (Lepore, Evans, & Schneider, 1991), or specifically *how* individuals provide social support to help regulate the moods and solve the problems of their associates (Cutrona & Suhr, 1992; Winstead & Derlega, 1991).

The social psychological literature on helping provides additional clues for the study of social support in close relationships (Dunkel-Schetter & Skokan, 1990). There are several strengths of this perspective. First, the use of experimental designs to manipulate variables affecting both the helper and the recipient enables the examination of cause-and-effect relationships between important

components in the helping process. Second, exploration of variables that enhance or discourage a helper's ability or willingness to assist another person has
yielded insight regarding the intrapersonal and situational deficits that must be
overcome before help is offered (Darley & Latané, 1968). Finally, analysis of
short-term solutions to daily problems is useful in light of the research that
shows daily hassles to have a cumulative impact on health that can equal that
of major life events (DeLongis, Folkman, & Lazarus, 1988).

Yet there also are gaps in the social psychological literature. The helping
behaviors studied have typically been *simple* ones that are easily observed in
the field or in the laboratory. Thus much of the helping literature that has focused
on help between *strangers* may differ substantially from the literature that has
focused on close associates (Williamson & Clark, 1992).

The communication literature emphasizes that problems may be solved and
emotions soothed through conversational messages between friends (Burleson,
1990; Leatham & Duck, 1990; Miller & Ray, 1994). Although a number of communication researchers have used methods similar to those noted above (Albrecht
& Halsey, 1992; Tardy, 1994), other communication researchers have reminded
us that we have to *listen* to people as well as watch them (Albrecht & Adelman,
1987). Burleson, Albrecht, Goldsmith, and Sarason (1994) note that it is important
to study "the *messages* through which people seek and express support, the
interactions in which supportive messages are produced and interpreted, and
the *relationships* that are created by and contextualize the supportive interactions in which people engage." The examination of what prohibits or enhances
a helper's willingness and ability to give helpful or unhelpful *messages* to
another person provides insight regarding the intrapersonal and situational
deficits that must be overcome in order for a person to help those in need. Our
program of research strives to incorporate the strengths of the clinical, helping,
and communication literatures in hopes of enhancing the study of social support
in each discipline.

Previous Efforts to
Document Social Support Behaviors

Gottlieb (1978) was one of the first contemporary researchers who attempted
to develop a classification scheme of social support behaviors. In his investigation, coders empirically derived 26 categories of helping behaviors from a
subset of 40 transcribed protocols. Gottlieb subsequently grouped these categories into four general types of influence: emotionally sustaining behaviors,
problem-solving behaviors, indirect personal influence, and environmental
action. More recently, Gottlieb and Wagner (1991) have extended their list of
support behaviors to include criticizing/undermining behaviors.

Barrera, Sandler, and Ramsay (1981) expanded on Gottlieb's earlier work by
developing the Inventory of Socially Supportive Behaviors. The 40 items used
in the scale were based on a broad conceptualization of social support that

included aid in the form of supplying goods and services as well as more abstract forms of support, such as positive regard.

Cutrona (1986) used a diary approach to extend the work done by these researchers. She had participants register in a diary when stressful events occurred and when each of six behaviors occurred each day. The behaviors included "listened to confidences," "offered advice," "expressed point of view," "tangible assistance," "expressed caring or concern," and "positive feedback," reflecting the four most commonly cited social support functions: emotional sustenance, self-esteem bolstering, information/feedback, and tangible assistance. Cutrona and Suhr (1992) went on to develop a behavioral coding system based on the categories of the Social Provision Scale (Russell & Cutrona, 1984).[1]

Although the studies noted above are commendable for attempting to delineate the actual behaviors that constitute social support, there were some limitations in most of the investigations. First, the work tended to use retrospective self-report methods that relied on the memories of the subjects to recall accurately what kind of social support was given or received in various situations. Some of these events may have occurred years prior to the study, and the recollections may have been influenced by biases in memory or in self-presentational dynamics. Second, the researchers seldom described specific, concrete social support communication behaviors. Instead, they tended to reference broad behavior categories (e.g., Cutrona, 1986; Gottlieb & Wagner, 1991) and ambiguous actions such as "he was there for me." As a consequence, many putative lists of social support behaviors may refer more to perceived social support than to overt communication behaviors. Furthermore, excluding the work of Gottlieb's group, the studies tended to employ lists of social support behaviors generated through informal expert opinion rather than either explicit theory or exhaustive empirical sampling of the domain. Finally, except for Gottlieb and Wagner (1991), the researchers focused exclusively on the positive aspects of social support, ignoring the negative behaviors often used with someone in need of support.

Burleson (1983) examined the content of supportive communications using a functional-hierarchical approach. His coding system includes nine categories with three major levels of comforting messages. The levels of comforting messages vary in the extent to which others' feelings and perspectives are explicitly acknowledged, elaborated, and granted legitimacy. The lowest level of comforting messages deny the feelings and perspectives of the distressed other, whereas the middle levels implicitly recognize the perspectives and feelings of the partner. The highest levels of comforting messages provide more explicit acknowledgment and elaboration of the other's feelings and perspective. Burleson provides an excellent system—similar to the scoring codes for stages of cognitive development, such as moral maturity and role taking—for analyzing the level of interpersonal and communication competence displayed in different comforting messages. Burleson's developmental scoring system may also be a valuable supplement to other scoring systems that focus on more descriptive and molecular aspects of social support.

Goldsmith (1994) suggests that politeness theory (Brown & Levinson, 1987) provides a useful framework for evaluating supportive messages. She notes that provisions of advice, offers of help, and expressions of concern may be framed in ways that vary from abrupt and direct to polite and indirect. Goldsmith found that messages that she terms "bald-on-record" (e.g., "You should study harder next time") tended to be seen as less helpful than communications with similar content that were phrased to convey "positive face" (e.g., "I know you work hard, and if you study even harder, I know that you can do even better next time"). Thus politeness is a second qualitative dimension that may underlie the concrete categories of behavior that people use to convey support.

VALIDATION OF THE
INTERACTIVE COPING TYPOLOGY

We have developed a typology of the specific communication behaviors that may be expected during an episode of interactive coping (see Barbee, 1990, 1991). We define *interactive coping* as a dynamic behavioral process in which one individual responds verbally and nonverbally, in either helpful or unhelpful ways, to another individual's problem or emotion (Barbee, Cunningham, et al., 1993). We prefer the term *interactive coping* to the more traditional *social support.* As Pearlin and Schooler (1978) and Thoits (1986) have observed, it is likely that the behaviors people use in personal coping would also be used in interaction to assist a friend with coping. Yet the coping literature has made clear that many of the behaviors that people use when engaged in individual coping, such as denial or escape behaviors, could be considered *negative* or detrimental to effective adaptation (Carver, Scheier, & Weintraub, 1989; Folkman & Lazarus, 1985). In the same way, people do not *always* use positive behaviors or messages when interacting with friends or loved ones who are trying to handle distress (Burleson & Samter, 1985; Dakof & Taylor, 1990; Gottlieb & Wagner, 1991; Lehman, Ellard, & Wortman, 1986). The terms *social support* and *comforting messages* primarily convey the use of positive and helpful behaviors, rather than the full spectrum of behaviors that may occur with a friend in need. Thus we believed it was important to include these potentially negative messages in our typology.

The reliance on the term *social support,* and the lack of theory for guiding the development of previous typologies of support behaviors, may account for why negative support behaviors have been ignored. In developing our behavioral list, we continued to draw on the theoretical framework of the coping literature. Pearlin and Schooler's (1978) personal coping typology delineated three major styles of coping: changing the situation, changing the meaning of the stressor, and controlling distressed feelings. Billings and Moos (1984) have extended Pearlin and Schooler's typology by including an avoidance dimension. Folkman and Lazarus (1985) argue that the primary difference in coping behaviors is that some are problem focused (dealing with the issue itself) whereas others are emotion focused (dealing with the emotional repercussions of life stresses). Carver et al. (1989) factor analyzed most of the extant personal coping scales and found problem-focused, emotion-focused, and negative factors.

Other investigators have emphasized other dimensions of coping. Roth and Cohen (1986) argue that an important dimension of dealing with any stressor is the tendency either to approach the stressor or to avoid it. Endler and Parker (1990) and Amirkhan (1990) have found partial support for both the Folkman and Lazarus and Roth and Cohen dimensions. These investigators report a three-factor solution for their scales: problem-focused behaviors, emotion-focused behaviors, and avoidant behaviors. Caution must be exercised, however, in drawing conclusions from factor-analytic investigations. The number of factors extracted is partially a function of the nature and number of items in the original matrix. None of the factor-analytic studies that we have reviewed has balanced the number of approach and avoidance coping behavior items provided to subjects; avoidance options have always been fewer in number. The use of a limited number of avoidance items may have caused all avoidant behaviors to cluster together, rather than to sort into separate problem-focused and emotion-focused avoidant factors. The number of factors extracted also is a function of the correlation of the behaviors in the self-report of the subjects. If undersocialized subjects report high frequencies of use of both problem-focused and emotion-focused avoidance behaviors, whereas oversocialized subjects report low frequencies of use of both categories of behavior, the two categories will emerge as a single factor, regardless of conceptual and empirical distinctions in other domains. As a consequence, factor-analytic results provide ambiguous evidence concerning the underlying dimensions of social support.

The interactive coping typology (Barbee, 1988) is concerned with the behaviors individuals use in supporting lovers and friends. The typology integrates two of the major theoretical dimensions used in the investigation of personal coping. The interactive coping typology includes Roth and Cohen's (1986) dimension of either *approaching* or *avoiding* the problem or emotion, which is crossed with Folkman and Lazarus's (1985) dimension of *focusing on the problem* versus *focusing on the emotion.* The resulting interactive coping typology includes *solve* behaviors, which are problem-focused/approach behaviors that attempt to find an answer to the problem, such as the provision of informational and tangible support, asking clarifying questions, and making suggestions; *solace* behaviors, which are emotion-focused/approach behaviors that strive to elicit positive emotion and express closeness, such as saying the friend is a good person;[2] *dismiss* behaviors, which are problem-focused/avoidance behaviors that tend to minimize the significance of the issue, such as saying the problem is not serious; and *escape* behaviors, which are emotion-focused/avoidance behaviors that distract the help seeker or discourage the expression of negative emotion by the seeker of support, such as encouraging the help seeker to watch television or to drink, making fun of the help seeker, or showing irritability toward the help seeker. The current inventory of interactive coping behaviors is presented in Table 17.1. Several studies have been devoted to validating the Interactive Coping Behavior Coding System (Barbee, 1988, 1990) and to expanding the behaviors included in the four categories (Berry, Barbee, Cunningham, & Yankeelov, 1993; Gulley, 1993).

It should be noted that whereas we tend to emphasize the interactive coping dimensions of approach versus avoidance, problem versus emotion focus, and the resulting categories of solve, solace, dismiss, and escape behaviors, we do not wish to lose sight of the complexity of the individual communications within each category. The two dimensions and four categories offer theoretical unity and parsimony, but each interactive coping behavior has unique meaning as a communication act within the context of the social relationship, and can be studied independent of our summary categories.

Validation of the
Interactive Coping Typology

Our initial goal in developing the Interactive Coping Behavior Coding System was to develop a scoring approach based on meaningful theoretical dimensions that was diverse enough to capture the variety of human behaviors during a support interchange yet brief enough to be used during observation of live or videotaped conversations. Eighteen behaviors were initially gleaned from polling subjects about what they did to cheer up their friends (Barbee, 1988), and these behaviors were rationally allocated to the four interactive coping categories. A codebook that defined each interactive coping behavior and provided examples of each one was created through pilot testing and then employed in several studies that combined experimental and observational methods (Barbee, 1990, 1991). In the first study, pairs of friends came to the laboratory, and one friend had an emotion-arousing experience that involved either failing a test or watching a sad film. The experience was discussed with the partner while the pair was unobtrusively videotaped.

The communications are evaluated by coders who have been trained in several steps. Coders first learn the underlying logic of the typology and become familiar with the entire coding system and instances of each behavior. For example, they learn that for an event to be coded as "solve/question" (see Table 17.1), the helper must ask a question about the details of the problem itself, such as "What is on your mind?" "What do you think the test results mean?" "What happened next?" A comment such as "Why do you let that get to you?" would not be coded as a "solve/question" but as a "dismiss/minimization."

Coders are given substantial training, from sample tapes, in distinguishing between seemingly similar codes. For instance, the difference between "solace/ giving reassurance" and "dismiss/minimizing the importance of the problem" often hinges on the structure of the language and the tone of voice in which the communication is delivered. Giving reassurance involves saying something

TABLE 17.1
Interactive Coping Behavior Coding System, Revised

Solve Behaviors: Problem-Focused/Approach

QUES: Asks questions about the details of the problem; asks questions about how the seeker will continue to handle; asks what's on the seeker's mind, "What's bothering you?" in positive tone; asks "Are you okay?"*

CAUSE: Figures out the *cause* of the problem; gathers extra information about the problem.

PERSP: Gives the seeker perspective; reframes the situation for the seeker; takes the perspective of the third party; provides insight into the event; clarifies the event.*

SUGGSO: Gives suggestions on how to solve the problem; suggests resources to help; recommends professional or nonprofessional help; suggests that the person confront the problem; suggests that the person take some time to relax; suggests that the person stand up for him- or herself; suggests that the person compromise; suggests that the person do what makes him or her happy; suggests how to handle the problem.*

SOLUTION: Gives information to help solve the seeker's problem; tells seeker how the situation can be changed; comes to a conclusion about what seeker could do to solve the problem; tells about a book that could help; looks for solutions with the seeker; lists options of how to solve the problem; describes how he or she would handle the problem if it were his or hers.

TANGIBLE: Does something active or physical to help the seeker; gives money or a loan; offers to help now; offers to follow up in the future.

Solace Behaviors: Emotion-Focused/Approach

AFFECTION: Gives seeker a hug; touches seeker on the shoulder; puts arm around seeker's shoulder; gives a kiss; verbal affection; conveys attachment to seeker.*

EMPATHY: Shows understanding; makes empathic remarks such as uh-huh, oooh; cries with seeker; gets angry along with seeker about the problem's cause.

COMPLIMENT: Compliments the looks of seeker; compliments ability of seeker.*

AVAILABLE: Assures seeker of future availability to help with the problem; leans forward and displays quiet attentiveness; stifles impulse to interrupt seeker.

REASSURE: Tells the seeker that he or she is a good person; tries to boost the seeker's self-esteem; shows shock/sorrow at hearing the problem; give reassurance that everything will be okay; agrees with seeker; assures the seeker that it was not his or her fault; criticizes the behavior of the third party.*

LIFT MOOD: Offers to buy the seeker a gift or take him or her out to lunch in order to cheer the seeker up; exercises with the seeker to lift spirits; encourages seeker to engage in a creative task to lift spirits.

CONFIDENTIALITY: Assures seeker of confidentiality; promises to mislead others about problem.

FEELINGS: Asks how the seeker feels about the problem; asks why the seeker feels that way; encourages disclosure of feelings and emotional displays.

Dismiss Behaviors: Problem-Focused/Avoidance

AVOIDPROB: Tells the seeker about his or her own problem rather than dealing with the seeker's problem; avoids dealing with the problem; changes the topic of conversation; talks, but doesn't address the real problem; talks about own interest.*

SHOWDIS: Shows disinterest in problem; says, "I don't care about problem"; says, "There's nothing you can do."

(continued)

TABLE 17.1
Continued

Dismiss Behaviors: Problem-Focused/Avoidance

CRITICIZE: Criticism about how the seeker handled the problem; blames the seeker for the problem; says, "Don't get upset until it is really a problem"; suggests problem could have been handled with easily available information.*

MINIMIZE: Says that the seeker's problem is not serious; says, "That's life"; says, "It's not a problem"; says, "Forget about it"; suggests that others have similar problems and that the seeker is not unique.*

SARCASM: Uses sarcastic tone of voice; ridicules the seeker; says, "Good luck"; patronizing.

POLLYANNA: Feigns sympathy; says, "Don't worry"; says, "Look on the bright side"; suggests the problem is a "blessing in disguise"; tells seeker that problem could be worse; tells seeker to think of other people's suffering.

Escape Behaviors: Emotion-Focused/Avoidance

AVOID VERBALLY: Tells the seeker to leave; uses excuses not to talk to seeker; reminds seeker of things helper has to do; passes off the seeker to another.

DISTRACT: Turns on TV or radio; begins to read a book or magazine while the seeker is talking or instead of answering the seeker; acts distracted; ignores the seeker's emotional displays or mood state.*

NONVERBAL ESCAPE: Withdraws physically in room—moves chair away from seeker, turns away from seeker, pulls back; leaves room; avoids eye contact.*

ENCOURAGE ESCAPE: Encourages seeker to get drunk or take drugs; encourages seeker to have sex or to engage in fantasy; changes activity.

AGGRESSIVE JOKE: Makes fun of the seeker or the seeker's feelings, not with the intention to cheer up the seeker; laughs at the seeker and his or her situation, tells a joke that is out of context for the seeker's problem.*

SHOW IRRITATION: Shows irritation at the seeker or the seeker's problem; reports annoyance that the seeker is depressing.

MEAN: Says, "I don't care about you"; says, "Shut up," "Be quiet," or "Quit talking about it"; says, "Grow up."

SUPPRESSEM: Encourages the seeker to suppress emotions; encourages seeker not to cry; helper takes seeker to a public place to discourage open display of emotions.

*Indicates behaviors used in first coding system.

positive, in a pleasant tone, such as "You usually do really well on tests; this probably is not an indication of your true ability." Minimizing the problem, by contrast, involves saying something like "Forget about it; the test is probably bogus," often in a hurried or irritated tone of voice. The solace message validates the partner's concern while building up his or her self-esteem, whereas the dismiss message denies the importance of the event.

The tapes are coded using a tally system (Bales, 1970) for the words and actions of the helper as he or she responded to the partner's description of the experience. The unit of analysis for tallying is the complete thought. A simple sentence generally receives a single code, whereas a complex sentence, with several conjunctions or other extensions, usually merits several codes. Thus the message "I know you are very talented and I'm sure you won't quit" would be tallied as a solace/compliment and a solace/reassure. Expressive sequences and overt behaviors, such as hugs, are also coded as single units. A tally is given for the occurrence of each behavioral action. There has been minimal difficulty in assigning all behaviors to one of the categories on the coding sheet.

Once the coders begin to view the tapes of experimental sessions, they are always blind to the experimental design and hypotheses of the study on which they are working. Each coder works alone and codes the same number of randomly assigned interactions from each experimental condition. Two coders rate each videotape segment, with a third coder resolving the small number of discrepancies in categorization. The first coding system was reliably used as an observational coding system in two laboratory studies with interrater reliabilities ranging from .91 to .95 (Barbee, 1990; Yankeelov, Barbee, Cunningham, & Druen, 1991).

Berry et al. (1993) conducted a series of studies to examine social support behaviors using the memorable message approach (Knapp, Stohl, & Reardon, 1981; Miller & Ray, 1994). In one study using this method, Berry et al. asked 58 undergraduates to record the details of four problems, two of which they had discussed with close associates and two of which close associates had discussed with them. They were then instructed to record the five specific things they or their close associates said or did in response to hearing about the problem, including both helpful and unhelpful behaviors. From these questionnaires, we ultimately generated a full list of 100 interactive coping behaviors, with 25 behaviors in each of the four categories of solve, solace, dismiss, and escape. Not all of these 100 behaviors are observable in the lab; we have found that 28 types of behaviors are sufficient for observational purposes.

We found, in a third laboratory study (Gulley, 1993), that the 28-behavior-type coding system was also highly reliable, with an interrater reliability of .95 (see Table 17.1). This study used same-sex friends, opposite-sex friends, and romantic partners. It also differed slightly from the previous laboratory studies in that the sources of the problems for the recipients were not manipulated, but were recalled from their everyday lives. Furthermore, instead of having the raters code from videotapes, each videotaped interaction was transcribed, so as to minimize knowledge of the gender and relationship configuration of each dyad. Despite a wider range of problems being discussed, interactive coping behaviors were observed that were similar to those found in the first two observational studies. The most frequent forms of solve behaviors were asking questions about the event, giving a perspective about the event through clarification, and giving advice through suggestions. Solace was evident in the form of empathic remarks, complimenting and reassuring the person, and doing things to lift the person's mood. Dismiss behaviors primarily came in the form of changing the topic, including talking about one's own problems, criticizing the partner, and minimizing the importance of the problem. The most frequent escape behaviors were making fun of the person's feelings, showing irritation through sarcastic teasing, and ignoring the person through physical withdrawal.

Recipients report that the approach behaviors of solve and solace are more desirable and more effective in helping them than are the avoidance behaviors of dismiss and escape (Barbee, 1990, 1991; Gulley, 1993; Yankeelov et al., 1991; Yankeelov, Barbee, Cunningham, Druen, & Berry, 1993). Other researchers examining support for current chronic stressors have found results that corroborate these findings (Gottlieb, 1978). Most recently, Dakof and Taylor (1990) interviewed cancer patients about the helpful and unhelpful behaviors their network members engaged in when the patients were first diagnosed with the disease. They found that the most helpful behaviors from family and friends took the form of informational (i.e., solve) and emotional support (i.e., solace), whereas the most unhelpful behaviors were minimization of the problem; criticism of how the patient handled the situation; lack of concern, empathy, and affection; and withdrawal by close others—all behaviors that fit into our dismiss and escape categories.

Solve and solace behaviors tend to be viewed positively and dismiss and escape behaviors tend to be viewed negatively, and these two pairs tend to correlate in our research. Our results provide some support for Burleson's (1983) hierarchical typology of comforting messages. Burleson's less sophisticated or less competent messages involve a blend of what we would term *dismiss* and *escape* statements. His sophisticated comforting messages include a mixture of behaviors that we would classify as solves and solaces. Burleson's coding system may be preferred when the research focuses on the development of communication competence. When the goal of the research is to document the specific behaviors that people use to cheer up their partners, or the help giver's tendency to approach or avoid focusing on the partner's problem or emotion, the ICBCS may be preferred.

Studies of the effectiveness of various forms of support indicate that different behaviors may be effective for different types of problems. We have tended to examine the effects of negative events that have already occurred, rather than events that are expected. Winstead and Derlega (1991) found that if just *one* member of a dyad is *anticipating* an anxiety-provoking situation, then encouraging the distressed person to disclose feelings is a good social support strategy and unrelated talk is a poor social support strategy. The effectiveness of these two behaviors reverses when *both* people are depressed or anxious about the same upcoming event. Thus there may be times when dismissing or escaping is a helpful method of interactive coping. Consistent with the contention that each interactive coping behavior may have its place, Lehman et al. (1986) found that solve behavior, in the form of advice, is unwanted by those who are grieving. Metts, Geist, and Gray (1994) found that informational and emotional support were not uniformly effective in reducing stress in nurses. A focus on the problem, in the form of a solve, may work best if it is preceded by a focus on the person, in the form of solace, or if it is requested. An unsolicited solve for an event that appears to the help seeker to have no solution may seem like an impolite dismiss.

Recipient's Support Activation Behaviors

We have also examined the dynamics of the recipient friend in need, including the behaviors that help or hinder a person in obtaining support. Our a priori model of social support activation behaviors involves the dimensions of *verbal* versus *nonverbal,* which is crossed with the dimension of whether the help seeker is *direct* about the desire for help versus *indirect* and ambiguous about whether help is being sought (Cutrona, Suhr, & MacFarlane, 1990). Direct support-seeking behaviors may be verbal, with a person asking for help, which includes talking about the problem in a factual manner, telling the helper about the problem, giving details of the problem, and telling what he or she has done so far about the problem. Direct support seeking may also be nonverbal, with a person showing obvious distress about the problem through crying or other direct behaviors, such as eye contact with furrowed brow, dramatic pouting, or putting his or her head on the partner's shoulder. Seekers using these behaviors convey their emotional state and convey that they want some form of help to solve the problem or make them feel better.

Indirect support-seeking behaviors, by contrast, are more subtle and less informative. Indirect strategies for activating social support can be verbal, as when a person globally complains about a situation or hints that a problem exists without requesting aid. Hints may let the helper know there is a problem, or how the seeker feels, without the seeker's directly stating his or her problem or feelings. Hints and complaints may protect the help seeker's self-esteem, but they may not convey the nature of the problem in such a way that the help giver can provide effective solves. If the helper is confused or put off by the hints or complaints, he or she may respond with a dismiss behavior. Indirect support activation behaviors may also be nonverbal, as when a person subtly shows negative affect in the form of sighing, sulking, or fidgeting. Different negative emotions may lead to different indirect nonverbal support activation displays. Sadness may lead to sighing, annoyance may lead to sulking, and anxiety may lead to fidgeting. Seekers using these behaviors may wish to maintain face by avoiding open admission of distress, to test the interest and compassion of the potential helper, or to avoid obligating the potential help giver through a direct approach. Individuals may be unaware, or may deny, that such nonverbal behaviors are intended to elicit social support. There is a risk, however, that sighing, sulking, or fidgeting may not elicit solace, but instead may cause irritation in the partner and produce escapes. The current inventory of support activation behaviors is presented in Table 17.2.

The Support Activation Behavior Coding System (Gulley, 1993) was developed using the same approach employed by Berry et al. (1993) and described in the previous section. We asked 40 undergraduates to record the details of four problems, two of which they had discussed with close associates and two of which close associates had discussed with them. They were then instructed to record the five specific things that they or their close associates said or did when

TABLE 17.2
Support Activation Behavior Coding System

Ask Behaviors: Direct/Verbal

TELLP: Tells *what* the problem is; sits down and speaks one-on-one with partner; says, "I have this problem."

TELLD: Tells *details* of the problem; describes entire situation; explains the reasons for the problem; talks openly and states factual evidence; sticks to the facts; becomes more serious and shares more details; gives both sides of the problem.

ASKH: Ask directly for help: "I have a problem that I need your help with"; asks if the other has time to talk.

ASKQ: Asks questions of the helper; asks if the helper knows why the other person acted that way; asks if the helper has also had this problem.

ASKS: Asks for suggestions on how to solve the problem; asks what he or she should do about the problem; asks for advice or opinion on what the helper would do; compares viewpoints.

ASKR: Ask for reassurance: asks for physical support, a hug or kiss; requests understanding.

ASKD: Asks to be distracted or get the problem off his or her mind; asks to hear funny joke to take mind off the problem; asks the helper to talk about happy things; asks to go out.

RETURN: Returns to the subject; repeatedly brings up subject when partner finishes talking about the problem; keeps talking about the problem when partner changes the subject.

TALKF: Talks about and shares feelings: makes partner understand how he or she hurts; openly expresses fear about the problem; tells partner he or she is going crazy with the problem.

EXACT: Exact labeling of emotion; says, "I feel sad" or "angry" or "depressed" or "lonely" or "afraid."

Cry/Pout Behaviors: Direct/Nonverbal

CRY: Actually cries or holds back tears while talking about the problem.

SAD: Appears sad, with raised eyebrows and frown; rubs at eyes; covers eyes; drops head and looks as though about to cry.

POUT: Feigns being really upset just to get attention; holds head down; looks away from partner; exaggerates emotions to get more attention.

STOUCH: Seeker physically touches helper: hugs; touches partner's arm and holds hand; touches partner to get his or her attention.

NLAUGH: Nervous laughter about the problem or in response to partner's suggestion; laughs while still showing negative affect; laughs to try to cheer self up; laughs in disbelief to keep from crying.

ANGER: Shows anger or frustration; throws things; throws hands up in exasperation and frustration; raises voice; starts breathing hard; hits leg out of anger.

LEANT: Leans toward the partner; puts elbows on knees and leans toward partner.

CLOSET: Gets close to partner; moves toward partner; sits next to partner without saying anything; moves closer to partner.

EYEC: Has or maintains eye contact; looks partner in the eye while talking; focuses all attention on partner, with direct eye contact.

FACEP: Looks in the face of the helper to show how serious the problem is; sits close to partner; tries to maintain eye contact.

Hint/Complain Behaviors: Indirect/Verbal

HYPO: Speaks hypothetically about the problem; speaks rhetorically about the problem; makes up "I know a friend who needs some help" scenario.

COMPLAIN: Complains about the problem or source of the problem without making it clear that help is desired; criticizes the person causing the problem; asks, "Why me?"; complains about the details of the problem.

WHINE: Uses high-pitched voice while talking about the problem; says, "It's not my fault" in childish tone.

SEJOKE: Downplays the severity of the problem; masks true feelings by laughing about own problem; makes a joke of the situation so it seems like it doesn't bother him or her; says, "Well, at least my problem is not as bad as yours"; pretends to be happy.

DENY: Denies that the problem is serious when it obviously is; leaves out important information; pretends there is no problem; says, "It's no big deal" or "It doesn't really bother me"; says, "I'm fine" or "It's okay."

AVOID: Avoids talking about real issues in the problem; talks about only a few aspects of the problem without expressing that he or she actually has a problem; avoids discussing the problem in detail so as to downplay the problem; talks around the problem without talking about the core of the problem; rambles about other things unrelated to the problem; lies about having a problem; avoids any questions; changes the subject; talks about the helper's problem.

VAGUE: Labels emotions in vague terms; says, "I feel out of sorts" or "out of it" or "weird" or "unusual."

Sigh/Sulk/Fidget Behaviors: Indirect/Nonverbal

SIGH: Repeatedly releases breaths; shows hurt feelings by being very quiet and providing very brief answers to questions.

SULK: Makes sounds of sullen irritation; refuses to answer questions; folds arms in defiance while listening to advice.

FIDGET: Nervous habits to try to calm self; bites fingernails; cracks knuckles; smokes a lot; rocks in chair; nervously taps pencil, taps feet, or scratches face and neck (any self-grooming behaviors); paces; moves in chair out of embarrassment and tries to get comfortable; wrings hands.

STAREO: Stares out in space and seems like not paying attention to the helper; seems to be thinking about something else; seems distracted and looks at the floor; looks at hands and fingernails as if in deep concentration.

LOOKAP: Deliberately looks away from partner; avoids eye contact; avoids looking at the helper; looks at book or TV to avoid looking at partner.

MOVEAP: Moves away from partner; moves chair away or walks away; takes hand from partner's and moves back in chair; walks to another room; moves chair away from partner to show irritation with partner.

they brought up the problem or concern. They were also asked to recall both straightforward and vague attempts to seek help. From these questionnaires, we ultimately generated a list of 68 support activation behaviors, 17 behaviors for each of the four categories of ask, cry, hint, and sigh.

In a second study, we attempted to see if laypeople conceptualized support activation in the same way we did. We asked 95 subjects to sort each of the 68 behaviors into one of the four categories. The naive subjects sorted 82% of the ask behaviors, 88% of the cry behaviors, 100% of the hint behaviors, and 76%

of the sigh behaviors consistent with our expectations. We subsequently used this information to develop a coding scheme for observational research (see Table 17.2), which was employed by Gulley (1993). The system was highly reliable, with an interrater reliability of .95. The most frequently used seeking behaviors within each category were as follows. *Ask* included telling details of the problem, asking questions about how to handle the problem, and telling the helper exactly how the seeker feels. Three specific forms of *hint/complain* behaviors were employed: complaining about the problem, being vague about how the problem made the seeker feel, and denying the seriousness of the problem. *Cry* behaviors tended to appear as tears and touching the partner. *Sigh* behaviors came in the form of moving or looking away from the partner and fidgeting.

Relations Between Support-Seeking and Support-Giving Behaviors

In order to integrate the role of talk over time (Duck, 1990) into the study of social support, we considered the microdynamics of the interactive coping process. *Microdynamics* refers to the tit-for-tat process in which the support activation behavior of one member of a dyad affects the interactive coping behavior of the partner, which, in turn, produces another support activation behavior.

If interactive coping dynamics were simple and symmetrical, *ask* support activation behaviors from the help seeker might consistently elicit *solve* efforts from the help giver. A *cry* might always produce a *solace* message. A *complain* or *hint* behavior might result in a *dismiss*. Finally, a *sigh, sulk,* or *fidget* might induce an *escape*. But we never expected human communication to be that neat and predictable. A help seeker could *ask* for a *solace*. A sensitive partner could respond to either a *hint* or a *sigh* with the *solve* question: "What's on your mind?" An estranged partner, by contrast, could respond to a *cry* with an *escape*.

Statistical, as well as conceptual, complexities emerge when the probabilities of one set of four categories is crossed with the probabilities of a second set of four categories. As a consequence, the decision was made to investigate the microdynamic relation of support activation behaviors to interactive coping behaviors using only one dimension from each of the two communication typologies. Sequential analyses were used to examine the communication behavior of 120 pairs of close associates who were discussing a number of different types of problems (Gulley, 1993). The microdynamic analyses focused on how the direct support activation behaviors of ask and cry, versus the indirect categories of hint and sigh, influenced the interactive coping approach categories of solve and solace, versus the avoidance categories of dismiss and escape.

Gulley (1993) found that direct requests for support were more likely to produce approach than avoidance behaviors. Indirect support activation behaviors also were more likely to produce approach than avoidance behaviors, but direct behaviors more reliably led to approach behaviors than did indirect behaviors. Further microdynamic analysis also showed that a support seeker more often employed a direct behavior following a helper's use of an approach behavior and employed an indirect behavior most often in response to an avoidant behavior.

These results demonstrate that partners were communicating in synchrony, such that each individual's behavior tended to elicit a complementary behavior from the interaction partner. Similar results were reported in a diary study examining partners' perceptions of supportive behaviors (Sullivan, 1989).

The interdependent nature of partners' communication behaviors in Gulley's study was further illustrated by analyses showing that the best predictors of the behaviors employed by either support seekers or givers were their partners' previous behaviors. Other variables, such as the subject's gender, whether the relationship was romantic or a friendship, and the type of problem discussed did not effectively predict the patterns of behaviors employed during the conversations.

These findings bolster the notion that support seekers share some of the responsibility for the type of support they receive. Helpers may not be solely responsible if they provide poor support, because it is the support seeker who must convey the form of support that is needed. Support seekers may differ in the competence with which they communicate their needs, similar to the differences between support givers documented by Burleson (1983).

Although Gulley (1993) found that both direct and indirect support activation behaviors could lead to approach interactive coping behaviors, her subjects and methods may have been optimal for obtaining that outcome. Her research participants were in close, nondistressed relationships; they were allowed to choose the problem to be discussed; and they were not operating under external stressors. Clearly, matters are not always so ideal; many variables can upset the delicate equilibrium of the give and take of support between friends and romantic partners.

SENSITIVE INTERACTION SYSTEMS THEORY

Relationships are often robust and resilient, but specific interactions can be delicate and easily thrown off track by variables internal or external to the system. For some years now, we have been working on what we call *sensitive interaction systems theory* to reflect the dialectics of flexibility and delicacy, and the essential complexity that is inherent in communication between members of close relationships. SIST, which is illustrated in Figure 17.1, is predicated on the notion that internal conflict and ambivalence may be reflected in the communications of both the help seeker and the help giver.

An interactive coping episode begins with a problem and a help seeker who communicates the need for assistance. The use of a direct support activation behavior, such as an ask or a cry, seems like a straightforward way to obtain assistance from a friend. Yet a problem that suggests an embarrassing personal weakness, or a solution that is elusive because of a lack of personal social

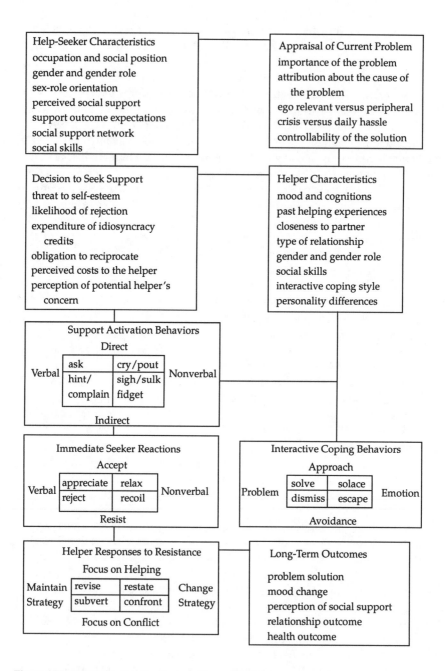

Figure 17.1. Sensitive Interaction Systems Theory Variables

competence, may reduce a distressed person's willingness to disclose openly the need for support. Because of self-presentational concerns (Goldsmith, 1994), the individual in need of assistance may be more willing to seek help if he or she is of lower status than the help giver, whereas the converse may be the case if the person in need is of higher status. Males may be more averse to seeking help than females, although we have found that males are willing to take both task and relationship problems to male friends (Barbee, Gulley, & Cunningham, 1990). Those who have perceptions of a poor social support network, those who have low self-esteem and thereby fear using up their limited welcome and idiosyncrasy credits, and those who anticipate rejection or who are reluctant to burden their partners also may be hesitant to seek support. When a person in need of support is ambivalent about seeking it directly, the result may be the use of indirect social support activation behaviors, with all of the opportunities for misunderstanding previously noted.

The SIST perspective notes that contextual variables in the situation that produce negative thoughts, or internal dynamics of the helper that produce ambivalent feelings, may upset the delicate balance of interactive coping communications. If the relationship is close, if the problem is viewed as a crisis that is highly important, if the problem is attributable to external causes, if the problem does not make the helper feel personally threatened and seems like it has a controllable solution, the help giver may feel strongly motivated to provide all the assistance that is required. Yet, just as the help seeker's self-esteem is at risk when he or she presents a problem, the help giver's self-esteem is challenged when he or she attempts to provide an effective solution or to relieve distress. If the help seeker's problem seems insoluble, the help giver may feel threatened by the fact that he or she can provide only limited assistance. If the help seeker's problems seem trivial, if the issues or emotions seem to be the help seeker's own fault, or if the help seeker has not followed advice that the help giver offered earlier, then the help giver may feel annoyance toward the help seeker. If the helper is in a negative mood because of his or her own problems, he or she may feel little empathy for the help seeker. Under those circumstances, the interaction may produce more disappointment, distress, or anger than it alleviates.

Sensitive interaction systems theory suggests that social support interchanges between friends or romantic partners are emotionally charged, but are also resistant to disruptions and are often self-correcting when one occurs. If the help seeker does not receive the desired response, he or she may try another support activation behavior. Conversely, if one interactive coping behavior does not cheer up the partner, the help giver may try another one. If there are too many negative variables in the equation because of either the help seeker or the help giver, however, the conversation may spiral into ineffectiveness. SIST proposes that there may be no one variable that is critical to the outcome of the interaction, but a combination of several may add up to the straw that breaks the camel's back. A combination of negative variables over a limited time interval may overwhelm the support communication system within a relationship in a manner

similar to the complex pattern of interactions that chaos theory uses to characterize the occurrence of an avalanche, or a wave breaking on the beach (McCauley,
1988).

Experimental Investigations
of the Interactive Coping Process

Based on the SIST perspective, we have conducted 20 empirical studies to
test systematically the effects of affective, cognitive, relationship, and personal
variables on the process of giving and receiving interactive coping behaviors.
We have primarily employed an experimental approach to understand the support process among people in ongoing relationships. In our basic paradigm for
examining the effects of emotion and cognition on the behaviors that people choose
to engage in when interacting with distressed friends, people in close relationships (i.e., friends, romantic partners) volunteered to participate in a study of
"communication." Once in the laboratory, each partner filled out questionnaires,
including demographic, personality, and mood measures. Then each person was
randomly, but covertly, assigned to be either a recipient in need of comfort or a
helper. The recipients then were exposed to a saddening event, such as a tragic
movie, or a failure experience on a cognitive or physiological test. In several
studies, the helpers were simultaneously induced to be in a positive, negative,
or neutral mood. Once the pair was reunited, their conversation about the first
person's experience with the movie or test was covertly videotaped for five
minutes. After the interaction, participants gave self-report accounts of their
feelings, such as empathy and annoyance; their thoughts, such as attributions
concerning the importance, cause, and controllability of the problem; and the
behaviors they engaged in during the interaction. Participants also indicated
how they believed their partners felt and acted during the interaction. The
videotapes were later coded by trained coders using both the ICBCS and SABCS
(Barbee, 1990, 1991; Yankeelov et al., 1991, 1993). Below, we review the effects
of specific variables from the model on the use of various interactive coping
behaviors.

Mood

Cunningham has provided support for the view that positive and negative
moods operate as separate processes (see, e.g., Cunningham, Shaffer, Barbee,
Wolff, & Kelly, 1990; Cunningham, Steinberg, & Grev, 1980). A positive mood
generally increases helping behavior (Carlson, Charlin, & Miller, 1988). Positive-
mood helpers may be more helpful because they are more outwardly and socially
focused (Cunningham et al., 1980, 1990) and because they are cued to concomitants of positive affect (Manucia, Baumann, & Cialdini, 1984), such as liking for
others (Mayer & Gaschke, 1988), optimism (Cunningham, 1988b), and recall
of positive experiences (Isen, 1984). Finally, people are helpful in positive

moods in order to enhance their good feelings (Mayer, DiPaolo, & Salovey, 1990) or to maintain their positive moods (Isen, Shalker, Clark, & Karp, 1978).

Negative mood may decrease or increase helping behavior, depending on the helper's focus of attention and feelings of personal responsibility to help (Carlson & Miller, 1987). People in negative moods tend to be self-focused (Cunningham, 1988a), because focusing inward enables distressed people to process why they are distressed and then mobilize the energy to alleviate the negative state (Pratto & Johns, 1992). They also have negative thoughts and other concomitants of negative affect such as pessimism (Cunningham, 1988b), risk avoidance (Isen, 1984), and low energy levels (Cunningham, 1988a). All of these factors can inhibit those in negative moods from helping.

In our research on the interactive coping process, we found that people in experimentally induced positive moods were much more likely to notice a friend's distress and to address it with effective supportive and problem-solving strategies than were people who were in either neutral or negative moods (Barbee, 1991; Yankeelov et al., 1991). In fact, people who were sad and depressed often were so self-focused and passive that they rarely realized their friends were in need of support. And even when they did notice, saddened helpers lacked the energy to act effectively.

We replicated and extended the lab work using role-playing scenario experimental designs (Barbee, 1991) and structural equation modeling. These studies showed that induced positive affect, as well as feelings of subjective closeness, caused help givers to regard the problem as more important, which increased empathy. Feelings of empathy, in turn, increased the likelihood that solve and solace behaviors would be used. Future studies will explore the effects of different types of problems and emotions on helper-seekers' use of activation behaviors.

Attributions

The helper's attributions about the legitimacy of the depressed person's mood also have an impact on the helper's feelings and on the interactive coping strategy employed (Barden, Garber, Lieman, Ford, & Masters, 1985). Weiner (1980) reports that subjects expected to feel sympathy and pity for strangers in need, and would offer assistance, provided they attributed the problem to circumstances beyond the stranger's control. When subjects believed the stranger could control the problem, they anticipated feeling anger and lower inclination to help. Our studies used people in close relationships, but obtained similar outcomes. In three studies, we found that the more the helper attributed the help seeker's problems to internal, controllable causes, the more the helper blamed the help seeker; further, the more the helper blamed the help seeker, the more the helper displayed the avoidance behaviors of dismiss and escape (Barbee, 1991).

Thought Listing

In order to understand more fully the effects of specific cognitions, gender, and relationship variables on the process of social support, we have extended our experimental work to include a variety of methods. In our fourth observational laboratory study (Yankeelov et al., 1993), we included a thought-listing procedure (Ickes, Bissonnette, Garcia, & Stinson, 1990) to capture participants' cognitions and feelings more closely. After subjects completed their interactive coping conversation, they were asked individually to view the videotapes of their communications. Each subject was asked to stop the videotape at each point where he or she recalled having had a specific thought or feeling, and to report the affective tone of that thought or feeling.

This approach has added to our growing knowledge of the effects of gender on interactive coping (Barbee, Cunningham, et al., 1993; Barbee et al., 1990; Derlega, Barbee, & Winstead, 1994). Path analyses revealed that females' provision of support was influenced by their positive appraisal of their partners' use of verbal seeking behaviors. The more open the male seekers were in their description of the problem issues, the more the females generated positive thoughts and feelings about their partners, and those reactions, in turn, led to more approach behaviors. There was no direct effect of male behavior on female reactions. This may be because many male seekers are deterred from engaging in direct support seeking because of gender role expectations (Costrich, Feinstein, Kidder, Marecek, & Pascale, 1975). The indirect and ambiguous nature of males' support-seeking behavior may lead their female partners to depend on their *own* internal emotional appraisals to guide their support giving.

Males' provision of support to their partners, by contrast, was most influenced by the females' nonverbal support activation behaviors, including the amount of tears, sad expressions, and sighs the females expressed. The males' thoughts and feelings about these behaviors had much less influence than the support activation behaviors themselves. Because female seekers utilized unambiguous tactics to gain support, their male partners could react to their apparent need without additional cognitive or affective elaboration.

Interaction Record Diary

To increase our understanding of the effects of gender on the daily give and take of social support, we conducted a diary study in which 156 subjects reported every conversation they had that lasted 10 minutes or more over a two-week period (Barbee, Felice, Cunningham, & Berry, 1993). We defined social support as "any interaction in which either you or any of the people you are with directly or indirectly talks about a problem, concern, irritation, conflict, bad mood, or sadness about someone or something." Using that definition, males and females did *not* differ in the frequency of such interactions, which occurred at least once a day. In addition, there were no gender differences in the provision of problem-focused behaviors, but differences were found for emotion-focused behaviors. Male helpers reported giving more solace behaviors to females than to other males. Female seekers, however, reported receiving more escape behaviors from both male and female partners than did male seekers. Despite receiving a mixed set of behaviors from males, and contrary to sex role stereotypes, females rated males as better than females in cheering them up. Consistent with our lab results, we also found that more negative psychological states, including less positive mood and greater conflict, accompanied the provision or receipt of support, compared with other types of conversations.

These four findings add a qualification to previous research that has found women to be more supportive than men and supportive interactions to be more socioemotionally positive than other communications. It is possible that the need for solve behaviors may produce disagreements about the adequacy of different solutions to a problem. The need for solace may bring with it the risk of disappointment over halfhearted nurturance or incomplete care. Such difficulties may have produced the higher conflict scores and less positive moods that we found to be associated with supportive interactions. Prior research that has focused on positive emotional support behaviors may have neglected those help-seeking interactions that did not go well.

Effects of Interactive Coping on Participant and Relationship Outcomes

We have examined the effects of successful and unsuccessful interactive coping patterns on the long-term consequences for the relationships in which they took place (Barbee & Yankeelov, 1992). One of our studies examined the extent to which one member of each of 120 couples provided effective or ineffective interactive coping behaviors to the other in a laboratory situation. Both partners of each couple were called 10 months after their participation in the study, to see which couples were still together and which had separated. We found that the lack of an attempt to cheer up a partner and the use of dismiss behaviors during the experimental session were significant predictors of later romantic relationship dissolutions. It is likely that the inattentiveness and poor interactive coping displayed in the experimental context was a representative sample of the communication problems that led to the deterioration of the relationship.

Responses to Interactive Coping Behaviors

The recipient of *effective* social support may experience such outcomes as solutions to problems, improved mood, perception of an effective social support network, and enhanced prospects for good health. Based on Cheuck and Rosen's (1992) intriguing findings concerning the spurned helper and our diary findings of negative mood and conflict accompanying supportive interactions, we are currently developing a typology of the help seeker's immediate response to the help giver's interactive coping efforts. In our current conceptualization, such reactions may have the content of acceptance versus resistance, and they may have the form of being verbal or nonverbal. A help seeker who conveys verbal *appreciation* of the help giver's efforts, or who conveys the same acceptance nonverbally by *relaxing* or smiling, may encourage the help giver to persist with the current problem and to help the next time a problem comes up. By contrast, a help seeker who verbally *rejects* a proposed solve or solace, or who conveys the same resistance with a *recoil* or a sneer, may reduce the help giver's willingness to remain engaged in the interactive coping process. We know that depressed roommates exhaust the willingness of their partners to be supportive (Coyne, 1976), but it is not yet clear how many rejects and recoils it takes to reach that point.

A help seeker may follow the expression of resistance to the helper's interactive coping behavior with another support activation behavior. In that case, the cycle of support activation and interactive coping behaviors may continue through several more turns. If the help seeker does not convey a support activation behavior, then the helper has the choice of letting the conversation die or responding to the resistance with another initiative. Helpers who attempt approach behaviors but receive resistance from the help seeker are in a position similar to that of therapists who work with difficult clients.

Our final communication typology, on helper responses to resistance, does not involve a new coding scheme, but instead is based on analysis of strings of three turns of communication involving interactive coping and resistance. Because the typology of immediate seeker reactions is still in development, however, these suggestions are necessarily speculative. We propose that helpers who encounter resistance from the seeker when presenting approach interactive coping behavior must implicitly address the initial issue of whether they wish to focus on providing continued help or on the conflict inherent in resistance. Then helpers must consider whether to maintain or change their interactive coping strategy.

A helper who wishes to persist in helping may choose to retain the same strategy, by restating or reframing the original approach behavior. A behavioral string of solve-resist-solve or solace-resist-solace would be tallied as a *restate*. By contrast, a run of solve-resist-solace or solace-resist-solve would be coded as a *revise*. A revise may occur when the helper interprets the seeker's resistance as an indication that the current focus of interactive coping on the seeker's problem, or on the seeker's emotion, is not appropriate. A wise helper recognizes that a rebuff may occur when the seeker needs emotional nurturance and is given advice for which he or she is not ready. By contrast, some seekers know that their emotions will lift the moment their problems are solved; they may resist pleasantries and warmth when they want bottom-line suggestions. Attentive helpers adaptively desist from an initial empathic, nondirective approach with such seekers. Based on our earlier findings, we speculate that positive-mood helpers, those in healthy relationships, and those facing help seekers whose problems are both serious and externally caused may be more likely than others to display restate and revise responses to seekers' resistance.

Yet, as Cheuck and Rosen (1992) have artfully demonstrated, having a sincere helping effort rebuffed is an unpleasant experience, and may cause the helper to react to the conflict. A conflict-focused pattern of responding to resistance is to *confront* it, by shifting from a problem- or emotion-focused approach interactive coping behavior to a behavior in the same category that is avoidant, especially one delivered with a pointed tone of voice. In the confront sequence of solve-reject-dismiss, a helper may blurt out, "You obviously don't want my advice, so maybe the problem isn't that serious!" Similarly, in the confront string of support-recoil-escape, the helper might say sarcastically, "Well, you don't like reassurance, do you just want to get drunk?" At best, confront sequences such as these provide the help seeker with a metacommunication perspective on the dynamics of the supportive interaction. At worst, these sequences may alert the help seeker to the limits of the helper's patience with resistance. Either insight may stimulate additional support activation behaviors from the help seeker, which may repair the conversation and facilitate approach interactive coping behaviors from the helper.

The final response to resistance involves switching across categories of behavior, and is termed *subvert*. In the subvert pattern of solve-reject-escape, the helper offers suggestions about the help seeker's problem, has the first advice rejected, and then recommends an escape that conveys termination of the conversation, such as turning on the television set. The subvert pattern of support-recoil-dismiss is similar, but in this case the helper provides warmth and encouragement, the help seeker continues to be glum and unresponsive, and the helper reacts by saying that the seeker's problem is silly. The double jump, from approach to avoidance and from emotion to problem focus, is likely to leave the help seeker bewildered and unlikely to express additional support activation behaviors. In the final pattern of subvert, the helper who meets resistance switches from providing interactive coping approach behaviors to expressing support activation behaviors. A help giver who pouts, complains, or sulks when facing resistance implicitly suggests the need for a role reversal. The subtext is that the help seeker should forget the initial issue and cheer up the help giver. This, of course, undermines the interaction goal of the help seeker, who may be in no position to provide cheer. Both people could end up having grounds to resent each other.

The responses to resistance typology is predicated on the helper's providing an approach behavior prior to the seeker's resistance. Additional conflict may occur when the helper provides an avoidance behavior and the help seeker rejects or recoils from that. Although we have not yet examined any of these conjectures using empirical data, a string of avoidance-resist-avoidance communications, such as dismiss-resist-escape, may indicate a downward spiral in the support conversation and, possibly, the relationship.

CONCLUSIONS

Our integrative approach to the study of social support has made progress in achieving a number of goals since we began this work seven years ago. We have extended the study of social support beyond the focus on the perceptions of the recipient by including observations of actual supportive episodes, manipulating variables affecting the potential helper, and examining the effect of these variables on the provision of support for everyday types of problems. In conducting observational research, we have been able to capture a large measure of what is actually said and done during supportive conversations.

Our observational research has provided further documentation of a phenomenon suggested by self-report research (e.g., Dakof & Taylor, 1990), that potential helpers do not always approach the problems or the emotions of their friends in distress with compassion and helpful suggestions. Sometimes, helpers avoid the problems and emotions of their friends and thereby cause the friends to feel bitter and unsupported. The clinical literature on coping gave us some clues about the motivation and form of unhelpful responses to a friend in need. The experimental approach, borrowed from the social psychological tradition, allowed us to isolate some of the variables, such as mood and causal attributions, that lead to such avoidant responses. The communication research tradition was essential for focusing our attention on the dynamic, interactive nature of social support conversations.

Our interest in the determinants of the helper's provision of interactive coping behaviors, combined with our interest in support as a communication process, led us to examine the messages from the seeker that instigated the support episode. As we observed support activation behaviors, we noted that help seekers were not always clear in expressing the nature of their problems, nor were they direct in conveying the types of responses they wanted from their partners. Such behaviors had consequences: Direct support activation behaviors more reliably led to approach interactive coping behaviors than did indirect activation behaviors (Gulley, 1993).

Our research also reinforced the view that social support communications are reciprocally causal, and that neither the seeker nor the helper is solely responsible for supportive conversations going downhill and for failing to be effective. Our microdynamic analyses of two turns of conversation revealed that seekers often used an indirect support activation behavior *following* a helper's avoidant interactive coping behavior (Gulley, 1993). When our typology of resistance to support is perfected, and we have analyzed sequences of three turns of communication behaviors, we may be able to pinpoint further some of the seeker's resistance behaviors that contribute to poor outcomes. Analyses of four-turn communication chains, in the form of support activation behavior→interactive coping behavior→seeker reactions to support→helper responses to resistance, will provide even more insight into this complex process.

Sensitive interaction systems theory has provided a useful conceptual base for integrating predictions about when supportive approach behaviors will be forthcoming, when avoidance will prevail, and the consequence of both tendencies for the relationship. Our findings are compatible with Gottman's (1993) demonstration of the predictive significance of criticism, defensiveness, contempt, and withdrawal behaviors during marital communications. We found that low levels of effort to cheer up a partner (compare Gottman's withdrawal) and the use of dismiss behaviors (compare Gottman's criticism and contempt) predicted dissolution in dating relationships (Barbee & Yankeelov, 1992). More research is needed, however, to determine how many negative variables and avoidance messages it takes to topple an interaction, to lead to overt friction and recriminations rather than to closeness and feelings of support.

Although we have found some evidence to support the notion that the use of dismissive behaviors may undermine a relationship so much that it is ultimately terminated, we need to examine this process of deterioration more closely. We need to conduct more frequent assessments of supportive episodes, using a longitudinal design. Another issue that remains to be explored is how some couples come to be more effective over time in the give and take of support activation and interactive coping messages, whereas other couples become more alienated from each other.

Those who feel that two-dimensional typologies oversimplify the complex reality of human communication will find much to abhor in our research. Yet, although we have achieved high levels of interrater reliability, and others have obtained some success using our coding system for both interactive coping (Jones, 1993) and support activation (Barnes, 1992), we try to remain flexible in our methodological applications and mindful of their conceptual limitations. We are willing to collapse four categories into two, as circumstances dictate.

We also recognize that help-seeking and help-giving messages can be infinitely complex, and that the ability to understand them may depend on the history of communication within the couple. Discerning accurately, for example, whether a given facial movement is a pout that is asking for support or a frown warning the partner to stay away may require experience within the relationship. Similarly, whether a message is supportively humorous or dismissively sarcastic may depend on both the actual tone and a guess about the partner's intentions. When the help giver is partially responsible for *causing* the problem that is distressing to the help seeker, then blaming, face-saving, and apology communications may be interwoven into the fabric of the interactive coping conversation.

Our two-dimensional typologies may seem unnaturally tidy, but they have been useful for documenting some of the complexities of human communication. We have found that males are not incompetent in providing emotional support, as some popular accounts have suggested (Barbee, Cunningham, et al., 1993), and that romantic relationships are not always the best context for seeking solace or solutions to life's problems (Gulley, 1993). Our multimethod observational approach has also been able to contribute support and clarification to other lines of research.

For example, Cutrona (1990) suggested the optimal matching hypothesis, which proposed that controllable problems should elicit problem-focused helping and uncontrollable problems should elicit emotion-focused helping. Although the idea made intuitive sense, and Cutrona's self-report data seemed to support it, the hypothesis was not confirmed in observational or scenario studies, either in her lab or in ours (Barbee, 1991; Cutrona & Suhr, 1992; Gulley, 1993). It may be that people alternate between solace and support behaviors, depending on the flow of the conversation and what they guess will work at any given point in the dialogue.

The chaos theory component of sensitive interaction systems theory reminds us that human communication behavior may involve components of lawfulness as well as random oscillations. Barrera et al. (1981) found that the total frequency of helping behaviors received did not correlate significantly with psychological well-being among pregnant adolescents. If the help seeker does not provide clear guidance in his or her social support activation behavior, an effective help giver may alternate between problem-focused and emotion-focused behavior, in hopes that one or the other will be on target. Burleson (1983) found that the most competent communicator employs comforting messages that blend problem- and emotion-focused support, which may thereby double the chances of success in cheering up the friend.

Thus, consistent with Cutrona, the number of helpful behaviors that a person receives after a stressful event may not matter as much as specific fit of the helpful behavior to the problem or emotion at hand. That is why tracking what is said and done, through both observational and self-report techniques, is important for understanding which behaviors lead to the amelioration of negative feelings following a distressing event.

It is our hope that if individuals become more aware of how their own emotions and thoughts affect their willingness and ability to cheer up their friends and loved ones, they will monitor those variables, counteract them, and give better support. Instructors and applied researchers could examine the benefits, for both short-term support and long-term relationship maintenance, of teaching people the insights gleaned from research on effective interactive coping.

A curriculum on the communication of social support could counteract less-informed sources of information about how to cheer up others. It has been our informal observation that television programs, especially situation comedies, often model indirect requests and dismissive responses to the disclosure of personal problems. A curriculum component on social support activation might concentrate on teaching clear, polite, and face-saving strategies for *how* to ask for a little help from one's friends. A curriculum component on the provision of interactive coping would not turn amateurs into therapists, but it could provide members of relationships with the skills to provide better first aid to their lovers and friends for the problems and emotional travails of everyday life. A curriculum focused on social support could enhance communication competence in an area that seems crucial for relationship maintenance.

Our investigation of the dynamics of social support communications has provided a series of conceptual typologies and empirical scoring systems; replicable results concerning the effects of mood, cognitions, and relationship variables on the process; distinctions concerning the effects of gender and type of relationship on communication dynamics; evidence of the reciprocally causal nature of communications for seeking and giving support; and some tantalizing leads concerning the long-term outcomes of effective and ineffective interactive coping. Many issues remain to be addressed, however. We hope that this review will stimulate others to join us in the multidisciplinary and multimethod investigation and application of the communication dynamics of help seeking and help giving in close relationships.

NOTES

1. We developed our coding system before Cutrona and her associates reported theirs, so we did not have the benefit of their research when we began our investigations. Our system overlaps with theirs in the positive domains, but we include an array of negative behaviors that are not in their system.

2. In previous work, we referred to the emotion-focused/approach category as *support*. We are now calling that category *solace* so as to reduce confusion between overall supportiveness and the specific category of behavior that is emotion focused and approach oriented.

REFERENCES

Albrecht, T. L., & Adelman, M. A. (1987). *Communicating social support.* Newbury Park, CA: Sage.

Albrecht, T., & Halsey, J. (1992). Mutual support in mixed-status relationships. *Journal of Social and Personal Relationships, 9,* 237-252.

Amirkhan, J. H. (1990). A factor analytically derived measure of coping: The coping strategy indicator. *Journal of Personality and Social Psychology, 59,* 1066-1074.

Bales, R. F. (1970). *Personality and interpersonal behavior.* New York: Holt, Rinehart & Winston.

Barbee, A. P. (1988). *The effects of positive and negative moods on the cheering up process in close relationships.* Unpublished doctoral dissertation, University of Georgia.

Barbee A. P. (1990). Interactive coping: The cheering-up process in close relationships. In S. W. Duck (Ed.), *Personal relationships and social support* (pp. 46-65). London: Sage.

Barbee, A. P. (1991, October). The role of emotions and cognitions in the interactive coping process. In R. Baumeister (Chair), *Interpersonal causes of emotions.* Symposium conducted at the meeting of the Society of Experimental Social Psychologists, Columbus, OH.

Barbee, A. P., Cunningham, M. R., Winstead, B., Derlega, V., Gulley, M. R., Yankeelov, P. A., & Druen, P. B. (1993). The effects of gender role expectations on the social support process. *Journal of Social Issues, 49,* 175-190.

Barbee, A. P., Felice, T., Cunningham, M. R., & Berry, M. (1993, June). Studying socially supportive and nonsupportive interactions in daily life. In *Unique features of the RIR diary method.* Symposium conducted at the International Conference on Personal Relationships, Milwaukee, WI.

Barbee, A. P., Gulley, M. R., & Cunningham, M. R. (1990). Support seeking in close relationships. *Journal of Social and Personal Relationships, 7,* 531-540.

Barbee, A. P., & Yankeelov, P. A. (1992, July). *Social support as a mechanism for relationship maintenance.* Paper presented at the annual meeting of the International Society for the Study of Personal Relationships.

Barden, R. C., Garber, J., Lieman, B., Ford, M. E., & Masters, J. C. (1985). Factors governing the effective remediation of negative affect and its cognitive and behavioral consequences. *Journal of Personality and Social Psychology, 49,* 1040-1053.

Barnes, M. K. (1992, November). *"How do I tell you what I need?" A typology of support eliciting strategies.* Paper presented at the annual meeting of the Speech Communication Association, Chicago.

Barrera, M., Sandler, I. N., & Ramsay, T. B. (1981). Preliminary development of a scale of social support: Studies on college students. *Journal of Community Psychology, 9,* 435-447.

Baxter, L. A. (1986). Gender differences in the heterosexual relationship rules embedded in break-up accounts. *Journal of Social and Personal Relationships, 3,* 289-306.

Berry, M. M., Barbee, A. P., Cunningham, M. R., & Yankeelov, P. A. (1993). *Using the act frequency approach to delineate support behaviors.* Unpublished manuscript, University of Louisville.

Billings, A. P., & Moos, R. (1984). Coping, stress and social resources among adults with unipolar depression. *Journal of Personality and Social Psychology, 46,* 877-891.

Brown, P., & Levinson, S. C. (1987). *Politeness: Some universals in language usage.* London: Cambridge University Press.

Buhrmester, D., Furman, W., Wittenberg, M. T., & Reis, H. T. (1988). Five domains of interpersonal competence in peer relationships. *Journal of Personality and Social Psychology, 55,* 991-1008.

Burleson, B. R. (1983). Social cognition, empathic motivation, and adults' comforting strategies. *Human Communication Research, 10,* 295-304.

Burleson, B. R. (1990). Comforting as social support: Relational consequences of supportive behaviors. In S. W. Duck (Ed.), *Personal relationships and social support* (pp. 66-82). London: Sage.

Burleson, B. R. (1994). Comforting messages: Significance, approaches, and effects. In B. R. Burleson, T. L. Albrecht, & I. G. Sarason (Eds.), *Communication of social support: Messages, interactions, relationships, and community* (pp. 3-28). Thousand Oaks, CA: Sage.

Burleson, B. R., Albrecht, T. L., Goldsmith, D. J., & Sarason, I. G. (1994). Introduction: The communication of social support. In B. R. Burleson, T. L. Albrecht, & I. G. Sarason (Eds.), *Communication of social support: Messages, interactions, relationships, and community* (pp. xi-xxx). Thousand Oaks, CA: Sage.

Burleson, B. R., & Samter, W. E. (1985). Consistencies in theoretical and naive evaluations of comforting messages. *Communication Monographs, 52,* 103-123.

Carlson, M., Charlin, V., & Miller, N. (1988). Positive mood and helping behavior: A test of six hypotheses. *Journal of Personality and Social Psychology, 55,* 211-229.

Carlson, M., & Miller, N. (1987). Explanation of the relation between negative mood and helping. *Psychological Bulletin, 102,* 91-108.

Carver, C. S., Scheier, M. F., & Weintraub, J. K. (1989). Assessing coping strategies: A theoretically based approach. *Journal of Personality and Social Psychology, 56,* 267-283.

Cheuck, W. H., & Rosen, S. (1992). Helper reactions: When help is rejected by friends or strangers. *Journal of Social Behavior and Personality, 7,* 445-458.

Costrich, N., Feinstein, J., Kidder, L., Marecek, J., & Pascale, L. (1975). When stereotypes hurt: Three studies of penalties for sex-role reversals. *Journal of Experimental Social Psychology, 11,* 520-530.

Coyne, J.C. (1976). Depression and the response of others. *Journal of Abnormal Psychology, 85,* 186-193.

Cunningham, M.,R. (1988a). Does happiness mean friendliness? The effects of mood and self-esteem on social interaction and self-disclosure. *Personality and Social Psychology Bulletin, 14,* 283-297.

Cunningham, M. R. (1988b). What do you do when you're happy or blue? Mood, expectancies and behavioral interest. *Motivation and Emotion, 12,* 309-331.

Cunningham, M. R., Shaffer, D. R., Barbee, A. P., Wolff, P. L., & Kelly, D. J. (1990). Separate processes in the relation of elation and depression to helping: Social versus personal concerns. *Journal of Experimental Social Psychology, 26,* 13-33.

Cunningham, M. R., Steinberg, J., & Grev, R. (1980). Wanting to and having to help: Separate motivations for positive mood and guilt-induced helping. *Journal of Personality and Social Psychology, 38,* 181-192.

Cutrona, C. E. (1986). Behavioral manifestations of social support: A microanalytic investigation. *Journal of Personality and Social Psychology, 51,* 201-208.

Cutrona, C. E. (1990). Stress and social support: In search of optimal matching. *Journal of Social and Clinical Psychology, 9,* 3-14.

Cutrona, C. E., & Suhr, J. A. (1992). Controllability of stressful events and satisfaction with spouse support behaviors. *Communication Research, 19,* 154-174.

Cutrona, C. E., Suhr, J. A., & MacFarlane, R. (1990). Interpersonal transactions and the psychological sense of support. In S. W. Duck (Ed.), *Personal relationships and social support* (pp. 30-45). London: Sage.

Dakof, G. A., & Taylor, S. E. (1990). Victims' perception of social support: What is helpful from whom? *Journal of Personality and Social Psychology, 58,* 80-89.

Darley, J. M., & Latané, B. (1968). Bystander intervention in emergencies: Diffusion of responsibility. *Journal of Personality and Social Psychology, 10,* 202-214.

DeLongis, A., Folkman, S., & Lazarus, R. S. (1988). Hassles, health, and mood: Psychological and social resources as mediators. *Journal of Personality and Social Psychology, 54,* 486-495.

Derlega, V. J., Barbee, A. P., & Winstead, B. A. (1994). Friendship, gender, and social support: Laboratory studies of supportive interactions. In B. R. Burleson, T. L. Albrecht, & I. G. Sarason (Eds.), *Communication of social support: Messages, interactions, relationships, and community* (pp. 136-151). Thousand Oaks, CA: Sage.

Duck, S. W. (1990). Relationships as unfinished business: Out of the frying pan and into the 1990s. *Journal of Social and Personal Relationships, 7,* 5-28.

Dunkel-Schetter, C., & Skokan, L. A. (1990). Determinants of social support provision in personal relationships. *Journal of Social and Personal Relationships, 7,* 437-450.

Endler, N. S., & Parker, J. D. A. (1990). Multidimensional assessment of coping: A critical evaluation. *Journal of Personality and Social Psychology, 58,* 844-854.

Folkman, S., & Lazarus, R. S. (1985). If it changes it must be a process: A study of emotion and coping during three stages of a college examination. *Journal of Personality and Social Psychology, 48,* 150-170.

Goldsmith, D. J. (1994). The role of facework in supportive communication. In B. R. Burleson, T. L. Albrecht, & I. G. Sarason (Eds.), *Communication of social support: Messages, interactions, relationships, and community* (pp. 29-49). Thousand Oaks, CA: Sage.

Gottlieb, B. H. (1978). The development and application of a classification scheme of informal helping behaviours. *Canadian Journal of Behavioural Science, 10,* 105-115.

Gottlieb, B. H., & Wagner, F. (1991). Stress and support processes in close relationships. In J. Eckenrode (Ed.), *The social context of coping* (pp. 165-188). New York: Plenum.

Gottman, J. M. (1993). *What predicts divorce? The relationship between marital processes and marital outcomes.* Hillsdale, NJ: Lawrence Erlbaum.

Gulley, M. R. (1993). *Sequential analyses of social support elicitation and provision behaviors.* Unpublished doctoral dissertation, University of Louisville.

Hobfoll, S. E., & & Stokes, J. P. (1988). The process and mechanics of social support. In S. W. Duck (Ed.), *Handbook of personal relationships* (pp. 497-519). New York: John Wiley.

Ickes, W., Bissonnette, V., Garcia, S., & Stinson, L. (1990). Using and implementing the dyadic interaction paradigm. In C. Hendrick & M. Clark (Eds.), *Review of personality and social psychology.* London: Sage.

Isen, A. M. (1984). Towards understanding the role of affect in cognition. In R. S. Wyer & T. K. Srull (Eds.), *Handbook of social cognition* (Vol. 3, pp. 179-236). Hillsdale, NJ: Lawrence Erlbaum.

Isen, A. M., Shalker, T. E., Clark, M., & Karp, L. (1978). Affect, accessibility of material in memory, and behavior: A cognitive loop? *Journal of Personality and Social Psychology, 36,* 1-12.

Jones, D. C. (1993, June). *The development of hypothetical helping strategies among adolescents: Sex role and friendship expectations.* Paper presented at the International Conference on Personal Relationships, Milwaukee, WI.

Knapp, M., Stohl, C., & Reardon, K. (1981). "Memorable" messages. *Journal of Communication, 31,* 27-41.

Leatham, G., & Duck, S. W. (1990). Conversations with friends and the dynamics of social support. In S. W. Duck (Ed.), *Personal relationships and social support* (pp. 1-29). London: Sage.

Lehman, D. R., Ellard, J. H., & Wortman, C. B. (1986). Social support for the bereaved: Recipients' and providers' perspectives on what is helpful. *Journal of Consulting and Clinical Psychology, 4,* 438-446.

Lepore, S. J., Evans, G. W., & Schneider, M. L. (1991). Dynamic role of social support in the link between chronic stress and psychological distress. *Journal of Personality and Social Psychology, 61,* 899-909.

Manucia, G. K., Baumann, D. J., & Cialdini, R. B. (1984). Mood influences on helping: Direct effects or side effects? *Journal of Personality and Social Psychology, 46,* 357-364.

Matthews, K. A., Davis, M. C., Stoney, C. M., Owens, J. F., & Caggiula, A. R. (1991). Does the gender relevance of the stressor influence sex differences in psychophysiological responses? *Health Psychology, 10,* 112-120.

Mayer, J. D., DiPaolo, M., & Salovey, P. (1990). Perceiving affective content in ambiguous visual stimuli: A component of emotional intelligence. *Journal of Personality Assessment, 54,* 772-781.

Mayer, J. D., & Gaschke, Y. N. (1988). The experience and meta experience of mood. *Journal of Personality and Social Psychology, 55,* 102-111.

McCauley, J. L. (1988). *An introduction to nonlinear dynamics and chaos theory.* Stockholm: Royal Swedish Academy of Sciences.

Metts, S., Geist, P., & Gray, J. L. (1994). The role of relationship characteristics in the provision and effectiveness of supportive messages among nursing professionals. In B. R. Burleson, T. L. Albrecht, & I. G. Sarason (Eds.), *Communication of social support: Messages, interactions, relationships, and community* (pp. 229-246). Thousand Oaks, CA: Sage.

Miller, K., & Ray, E. B. (1994). Beyond the ties that bind: Exploring the "meaning" of supportive messages and relationships. In B. R. Burleson, T. L. Albrecht, & I. G. Sarason (Eds.), *Communication of social support: Messages, interactions, relationships, and community* (pp. 215-228). Thousand Oaks, CA: Sage.

Pearlin, L. I., & Schooler, C. (1978). The structure of coping. *Journal of Health and Social Behavior, 19,* 2-21.

Pratto, F., & Johns, O. P. (1992). Automatic vigilance: The attention-grabbing power of negative information. *Journal of Personality and Social Psychology, 61,* 380-391.

Roth, S., & Cohen, L. J. (1986). Approach, avoidance, and coping with stress. *American Psychologist, 41,* 813-819.

Russell, D., & Cutrona, C. E. (1984, August). *The provisions of social relationships and adaptation to stress.* Paper presented at the annual meeting of the American Psychological Association, Toronto.

Simpson, J. A., Rholes, J. A., & Nelligan, J. S. (1992). Support seeking and support giving within couples in an anxiety-provoking situation: The role of attachment styles. *Journal of Personality and Social Psychology, 62,* 434-446.

Spitzberg, B. H., & Cupach, W. R. (1984). *Interpersonal communication competence.* Beverly Hills, CA: Sage.

Sullivan, L. A. (1989). *Social support: Sex differences in the exchange of emotional support.* Unpublished doctoral dissertation, Michigan State University.

Tardy, C. H. (1994). Counteracting task-induced stress: Studies of instrumental and emotional support in problem-solving contexts. In B. R. Burleson, T. L. Albrecht, & I. G. Sarason (Eds.), *The communication of social support: Messages, interactions, relationships, and community* (pp. 71-87). Thousand Oaks, CA: Sage.

Thoits, P. A. (1986). Social support as coping assistance. *Journal of Consulting and Clinical Psychology, 54,* 416-423.

Weiner, B. (1980). A cognitive (attribution)-emotion-action model of motivated behavior: An analysis of judgments of help giving. *Journal of Personality and Social Psychology, 39,* 186-200.

Williamson, G. M., & Clark, M. S. (1992). Impact of desired relationship type on affective reactions to choosing and being required to help. *Personality and Social Psychology Bulletin, 18,* 10-18.

Winstead, B. A., & Derlega, V. J. (1991). An experimental approach to studying social interaction and coping with stress among friends. In W. H. Jones & D. Perlman (Eds.), *Advances in personal relationships* (Vol. 2, pp. 107-131). Greenwich, CT: JAI.

Yankeelov, P. A., Barbee, A. P., Cunningham, M. R., & Druen, P. (1991, May). *Interactive coping in romantic relationships.* Paper presented at the International Conference on Personal Relationships, Normal, IL.

Yankeelov, P. A., Barbee, A. P., Cunningham, M. R., Druen, P., & Berry, M. (1993, June). *Cognitive and emotional influences on the interactive coping process in romantic couples.* Paper presented at the International Conference on Personal Relationships, Milwaukee, WI.

18 The Communicative Microdynamics of Support

DAENA J. GOLDSMITH
University of Illinois, Urbana-Champaign

THERE is much to commend in sensitive interaction systems theory (SIST) and in the program of research on which it is based. As their report in the preceding chapter shows, Barbee and Cunningham have recognized the need to study the conversations in which persons seek and receive support for their problems. They have developed innovative ways to study actual conversations between friends and romantic partners in experimental settings, and they have gone on to replicate their findings with other methods. They have begun to catalog and examine the multiple cognitive, emotional, relational, and social influences that impinge upon supportive interactions. Readers familiar with research in social support and in helping behavior will recognize the significance of these innovations.

However, this move to examine new phenomena and new types of data has not been accompanied by changes in theoretical frames. Barbee and Cunningham succeed in providing a catalog of features that could affect or result from supportive interaction; however, their conceptualization of the features and their explanations for the linkages are diverse and loosely coupled. Implicit in this approach to theorizing is the assumption that the "microdynamics" of supportive communication can be adequately conceptualized and explained as a product of various and disparate psychological and sociological processes.

I interpret the study of "microdynamics" of supportive interactions to include consideration of the factors that influence production, interpretation, coordination, and effects of supportive messages and conversations (see Burleson, Albrecht, & Goldsmith, 1993). The concepts and models Barbee and Cunningham propose are most responsive to two questions: What conditions influence a potential helper's motivation to provide support? Under what conditions do

Correspondence and requests for reprints: Daena J. Goldsmith, Department of Speech Communication, University of Illinois, Urbana-Champaign, 244 Lincoln Hall, 702 South Wright Street, Urbana, IL 61801.

Communication Yearbook 18, pp. 414-433

partners synchronize their motivations to approach or avoid supportive interaction? Without denying the significance of these questions, I wish to propose an alternative set of questions about the microdynamics of support and to indicate why a different set of theories and approaches is required to answer these questions. To achieve Barbee and Cunningham's broader goals of understanding which support-seeking and support-giving messages ameliorate distress and how these sequences unfold, we need not only theories of motivation but also theories of communication; I hope to illustrate what the latter might look like.

CONCEPTUALIZING
"SOCIAL SUPPORT COMMUNICATIONS"

Typologies of support-seeking and -providing behaviors and a model of how these behaviors may be chained together in interaction are at the heart of the research that Barbee and Cunningham report. Their results suggest that coders can reliably use the typologies.[1] Their results also indicate that provision behaviors can be predicted by helper mood, attribution of problem cause, gender, and seeker's behavior, and, in turn, different provision behaviors are associated with a recipient's perception of helpfulness and with relational breakup. Granting the reliability and predictive utility of the typologies, I wish to examine what kinds of distinctions are captured by the typologies and the model and for what sorts of questions these distinctions are useful.

Interactive Coping

Barbee and Cunningham explain that they developed the typology of interactive coping behaviors in order to provide an observational coding system that includes "negative" behaviors as well as positive ones. In redressing this limitation in the social support literature, they turn to research on individual coping. The problem-/emotion-focused distinction is common to both the coping and social support literatures; although previous typologies of social support behaviors (Barrera & Ainlay, 1983; Cutrona, 1986; Gottlieb, 1978) draw distinctions among types of problem solving and emotional support, the use of this dimension does not introduce new types of behaviors or concepts. In contrast, the avoid/approach dimension does entail a range of behaviors not included in the previous taxonomies. It is also this dimension that has most often produced significant results in Barbee and Cunningham's research.

Conceptualizing supportive interactions as "interactive coping" and utilizing dimensions from the literature on individual coping suggests that the process of seeking and providing support is akin to individual coping. Yet interactive coping differs from individual coping in requiring the negotiation of meaning and coordination of action. An individual coping with his or her own stress does not have the additional challenge of producing messages that indicate to others his or her current state and desired response. Similarly, individual coping does not require interpretation and coordination with the states and responses of another. Finally, the effects of individual coping strategies are dependent on the interface between one person and his or her situation, whereas the effects of interactive coping are also dependent on communication between people.

These differences are evident when we consider that in conversation about a problem there is more than one problem and more than one set of emotions with which to cope. In addition to the problem and associated emotions experienced by one of the parties, a conversation introduces the "problems" of interacting (conveying one's intention, interpreting one another's utterances, coordinating one another's utterances, attending to face wants) and the emotional responses to these interactive demands. The 2 × 2 interactive coping typology fails to capture this additional complexity and conflates avoiding problem/emotion with avoiding interaction. Approach behaviors approach both interaction with the other person and the other person's problem or emotional distress. We might expect the avoid behaviors would similarly approach interaction with the other person but would avoid talking about the other person's problem or emotion. Instead, avoid behaviors such as "tells the seeker to leave," "begins to read a book or magazine while the speaker is talking," "says, 'shut up,'" "ridicules the speaker," and "says, 'I don't care about the problem'" (see Table 17.1, in Chapter 17) avoid the other person's problem or emotion by avoiding or rejecting interaction with the other person. The conflation is also evident if we consider the focus of "coping" in the two categories: Approach behaviors attempt to help the *other* person cope with his or her problem, although most of the avoid behaviors appear to be attempts by the speaker to cope with his or her *own* anxiety, discomfort, or frustration in interacting (see Barbee, 1990, p. 50).

There are two consequences of this conflation. First, the typology overlooks forms of interaction that ambiguously approach the problem or emotion and forms that approach interaction but avoid problem/emotion. The potential utility of "ambiguous approach" and "assisted avoidance" will be discussed later. Second, the approach/avoid dimension does not differentiate types of suppor-tive behavior; it differentiates supportive behaviors from rejecting behaviors.[2] Viewed in this light, Barbee and Cunningham's findings that approach behav-iors are preferred to avoidance behaviors are less informative: Most people don't like it when other people ignore them, ridicule them, or try to escape interaction with them. Instead, their findings are most interesting for what they tell us about the circumstances under which individuals in close relationships would engage in such counternormative behavior: Why would people in close relationships reject their partners in their hour of need?

Another way of demonstrating this interpretation of the interactive coping typology is to consider a range of ways in which behaviors could have detri-mental effects. When they explain the class of behaviors they are adding to their typology, Barbee and Cunningham define "negative behaviors" by their effect: "negative or detrimental to effective adaptation." Interactions could have detrimental effects in at least three qualitatively different ways: (a) Messages intended to help the other person could have both helpful effects and negative side effects, (b) messages intended to help the other person could have negative effects, and (c) messages that are *not* intended to help the other person could have negative effects. Differentiating these possibilities suggests different questions about microdynamics of support.

The first class of messages (help intended, both helpful and unhelpful effects) might be illustrated by a friend who receives advice about a problem at work. The support is well intentioned and helpful with the problem at work but simultaneously has negative effects on other outcomes, such as the receiver's self-esteem and equality in the relationship with the advice giver. Considering this class of supportive interactions alerts us to consider multiple outcomes in drawing conclusions about whether or not a message is "effective" or "helpful." The second class of messages (help intended but unhelpful) might occur if a helper gives bad or inept advice or offers advice when empathy is desired or offers advice in a way that implies criticism. Distinguishing this type of "negative" behavior focuses attention on questions of message form and adaptation: For that class of messages we recognize as intended to be helpful, what additional requirements must be met if the message is actually to be helpful? What abilities must a speaker possess to produce such a message? The third kind of "negative" behavior involves a would-be helper who does not actually wish to help and instead tries to terminate the interaction or even to harm the other person. This possibility leads us to look at motivation. What factors influence whether someone intends to help or not help or harm?

Cast in these terms, the approach-avoid dimension contrasts well-intended and (presumably) helpful behaviors with ill-intended (or at least not-help-intended) and (presumably) harmful behaviors and is most useful in examining questions of whether a speaker wishes to help or not. It tells us less about how messages might be adapted to achieve effects or about how messages might be differentially effective at different outcomes. In other words, the interactive coping typology can help us learn about the microdynamics of *intention* to support but does not tell us about how messages are constructed from intentions, how intentions are interpreted from messages, or about the communicative processes that go on between intentions and outcomes.

Support Activation

In their support activation typology, Barbee and Cunningham redress several blind spots in previous research on supportive interactions. They attend to the role of the support seeker, examine nonverbal as well as verbal communication, and recognize the potential importance of indirect message forms. Attention to these phenomena is overdue, but this does not preclude the need for conceptual elaboration and justification of these dimensions.[3] A shortage of previous research makes it even more critical that "support activation," "direct/indirect," and "verbal/nonverbal" be clearly defined and linked to other components of the model. Several difficulties result from the lack of theoretical grounding for these concepts.

There are unexplained inconsistencies in the treatment of communication processes in the interactive coping typology and the support activation typology. The interactive coping typology is based on content of utterances, but the support activation typology focuses on form (direct/indirect, verbal/nonverbal). The two typologies also differ in how nonverbal behaviors are assumed to function. In support-seeking messages, nonverbal behaviors are treated as separate from verbal behaviors. For support-giving messages, coders are instructed to code nonverbal behaviors into the same categories as verbal behaviors (e.g., the "affection" category of solace behaviors) or to use nonverbal behaviors as cues to the meaning of verbal behaviors (e.g., tone of voice is used to differentiate between the categories "giving reassurance" and "minimizing the problem").

There are a number of problems with the way in which verbal/nonverbal and direct/indirect are conceptualized in the support activation typology. Four of nine verbal/direct behaviors do not directly ask for help ("telling about the problem," "telling details of the problem," "returns to the subject," and "talks about feelings"). It may be that in any close relationship "telling" about a problem is normally interpreted as a request for help. If so, "telling" utterances are conventionally indirect message forms ("phrases and sentences that have contextually unambiguous meanings which are different from their literal meanings"; Brown & Levinson, 1987, p. 132). "Communicating the facts of their dilemma and/or their emotional distress" is treated as indirect help seeking by Cutrona, Suhr, and MacFarlane (1990, p. 38), the source Barbee and Cunningham cite in support of the direct/indirect distinction. It is also inconsistent to code various forms of "telling" about a problem as direct but to classify "complains about the problem" or "whining" as indirect. Complaining and whining may be less pleasant than telling, but they are no more or less direct.

Another problem with the direct/indirect dimension is that many behaviors classified as indirect are not necessarily help seeking at all: The verbal/indirect categories of "deny" and "avoid" and the nonverbal/indirect categories "sulk," "stare out in space," "look away from partner," and "move away from partner" appear to convey a desire *not* to engage in discussion of the problem. The authors acknowledge this possibility, saying "individuals may be unaware, or may deny, that such nonverbal behaviors are intended to elicit social support." We can interpret all of these behaviors as indirect seeking only if we assume all persons with problems *must* want to receive help, no matter what they say or do.

It would be more useful to reconceptualize the behaviors labeled "direct" and "indirect" as "approach" and "avoid," only this time, by the person with the problem. The behaviors classified as direct have in common the expression of emotion and affiliation with the partner: they openly discuss the problem and/or feelings, they explicitly ask for help, they do not attempt to hide negative affect, they express nonverbal affiliation and conversational involvement (see Burgoon

& Newton, 1991). In contrast, with the exception of "hypo," "complaining," and "whining," the indirect behaviors involve minimization and/or denial of the problem, minimal responses or attempts to change the topic, and nonverbal distancing behaviors.

The verbal/nonverbal dimension also needs revision. The nonverbal categories include verbal behaviors: The direct/nonverbal category includes "verbal labeling of emotion" and the indirect/nonverbal category includes "labels emotions in vague terms." In the nonverbal/direct category, "cry" is defined as "actually cries or holds back tears *while talking about the problem*" and "eye contact" includes in the definition "looks partner in the eye *while talking*" (emphasis added). In the indirect/nonverbal category, behaviors coded "sigh" include "shows feelings by being very quiet and *providing very brief answers to questions*" (emphasis added).

This blurring of verbal and nonverbal in the actual use of the typology underscores the absence of a conceptual justification for treating these as separate means of support elicitation. Traditional treatments of nonverbal communication recognize that although some types of nonverbal behaviors can stand alone in conveying meaning (e.g., "iconic" gestures), many nonverbal behaviors function to complement, reinforce, or modify the meaning of verbal behavior. Recently, a number of researchers have taken the stronger stance that some nonverbal actions are integral parts of the verbal messages they accompany (e.g., Bavelas, 1990; McNeil, 1985; Streeck, 1993). What may be most distinctive about some attempts at seeking support is the relationship *between* verbal and nonverbal parts of the message (e.g., verbally acknowledging a problem while nonverbally playing down its seriousness; verbally denying a problem while nonverbally indicating its seriousness; see Goldsmith & Parks, 1990).

The nonverbal category also fails to distinguish between nonverbal *behavior* and nonverbal *communication.* Barbee and Cunningham use *support activation* as synonymous with *support seeking,* yet behaviors such as "scratches face and neck," "hits leg out of anger," "nervous laughter," and "nervously taps pencil" might be involuntary behaviors rather than communicative attempts to solicit support. Researchers in nonverbal communication have recently advocated recognizing degrees of intent, control, or purpose in nonverbal behavior (for a brief summary, see Manusov & Rodriguez, 1989); some even go so far as to say that the relatively intentional forms of nonverbal behavior and the relatively unintentional forms "are sufficiently different from one another to warrant their being identified and treated as distinctly different phenomena, or at least to preclude generalizing certain research results from one to the other" (Motley & Camden, 1988, p. 2). Even researchers who define a broad range of nonverbal behaviors as communicative have taken pains to provide experimental evidence for their position (e.g., Bavelas, Black, Chovil, Lemery, & Mullett, 1988; Bavelas, Chovil, Lawrie, & Wade, 1992; Chovil, 1991).

Barbee and Cunningham provide evidence that the nonverbal behaviors in the typology *could* be used to communicate a desire for help: The typology was originally based on behaviors individuals reported having used in real-life attempts to get help. However, that a behavior could, under particular circumstances, be used to seek help does not mean the behavior conventionally and normally functions this way in conversation. Partners in a close relationship might come to agree that "when I fidget, it really means I want you to ask me what's wrong" or, alternatively, "when I hit my leg it means I want to be left alone." However, a behavioral coding scheme that is to be used in a wide array of situations and in more than one close relationship should reflect typical meanings and functions of behavior rather than possible but idiosyncratic uses. Asking laypeople to sort behaviors into four categories of support seeking does not provide the needed justification either, because the procedure appears to assume that the behaviors *are* forms of seeking support and only asks respondents to sort them into four types.

A final problem with the support activation typology concerns the combination of the verbal/nonverbal dimension with the direct/indirect dimension. It is debatable whether nonverbal behavior can ever be "direct" in the same way that verbal behavior is "direct," and nonverbal communication researchers go to considerable effort to document consensually recognizable interpretations for particular nonverbal behaviors (for a summary, see Burgoon, Buller, & Woodall, 1989). Even if we accept that some of the nonverbal behaviors in the support activation typology have relatively unambiguous and consensually shared meanings, it is necessary to consider *what* they directly convey. Behaviors such as crying, "appearing sad," "throwing things," "covering eyes," and "breathing hard" may have relatively unambiguous interpretations as *expressions of distress,* but even direct expressions of distress are at best indirect requests for assistance. The would-be provider confronted with crying by another must make an inference about what the crying means in the situational and relational context; that crying indicates distress probably requires little inference, but that crying indicates a desire for help is not so clear. Several of the other nonverbal/direct cues are probably relatively unambiguous *expressions of conversational involvement* (see Coker & Burgoon, 1987). However, even if we were to assume that an expression of one's own involvement is a relatively unambiguous request for the other's involvement, "help" is not the only type of other-involvement one might seek. In contrast, verbal/direct requests for help (e.g., "asks for help," "asks for suggestions," "asks for reassurance") leave little doubt that another person means to seek help.

There are at least two implications of these difficulties with the support activation typology. First, these problems are a reminder that reliability does not ensure validity, and they indicate that the typology needs conceptual clarification and justification. Second, these problems point to an alternative research agenda that explicitly considers rather than assumes the interpretive processes through which behaviors of a distressed individual come to count as help seeking (Gergen & Gergen, 1983). Explorations of help seeking in close relationships and particularly in forced laboratory interactions make it tempting to assume that all behavior is problem relevant and potentially support activating. But this takes for granted the interpretive dynamics of supportive communication rather than making them the object of our theorizing. How do the relationships between verbal and nonverbal behaviors influence a would-be helper's interpretation of a would-be seeker's intent? Which verbal and nonverbal ways of seeking support have ambiguous meanings, and what are the processes (both over the history of a relationship and in the moment of interaction) through which close relational partners interpret a desire for help out of potentially ambiguous verbal and nonverbal behaviors? How might behaviors that are not help seeking come to be interpreted as help seeking through the interaction between would-be provider and would-be seeker?

It is revealing that Barbee and Cunningham choose to label this taxonomy "support activation." The verbal/nonverbal and direct/indirect dimensions do not differentiate coherently between involuntary behavior and other-oriented communication, between communicating a desire not to discuss a problem and indirectly communicating a desire for help, or between the communication of distress and the communication of a desire for help. In effect, any behavior emitted by a person with a problem is treated as a means of activating support. As is the case with the interactive coping typology, this focus is more relevant to motivation to communicate than it is to questions of communication process. The typology focuses our attention on the degree to which persons with problems attempt to control their expressions of distress and the degree to which they seek help rather than avoid it.

INTERPRETING RESULTS

These questions about the typologies amount to more than just taxonomic aesthetics. Considering how categories are operationalized clarifies what the typologies tell us about "which support-seeking communications and support-giving messages lead to the successful amelioration of a friend's distress" and about the "sequential interplay of help-seeking support activation communications and help-giving interactive coping behaviors" (Barbee & Cunningham, Chapter 17, this volume).

Ameliorating Distress and Other Message Effects

Barbee and Cunningham report that recipients find approach behaviors more helpful than avoidance behaviors. They note that the approach behaviors resemble those reported as helpful by Gottlieb (1978) and the avoidance behaviors resemble those reported as unhelpful by Dakof and Taylor (1990). They acknowledge research indicating that approach behaviors are not always desired and that talk unrelated to a problem (an "avoid" behavior) was found to be helpful in a study by Winstead and Derlega (1991). Given this variability in the utility of approach and avoidance behaviors, we should consider how useful the interactive coping typology would be in future research into the conditions under which approach behaviors are preferred to avoidance behaviors.

To the extent that the avoidance category is skewed toward behaviors that reject the other person, this stacks the deck in favor of approach strategies. To illustrate: Contrast the interactive coping typology with the approach taken in the Winstead and Derlega (1991) study to which Barbee and Cunningham refer. One of the support strategies considered by Winstead and Derlega involved "talking about other topics unrelated to the problem." If we were to use the interactive coping typology to study this support strategy, it would be coded as "avoid problem" and considered together with other dismiss behaviors such as "says, 'I don't care about problem,' " "blames them for problem," and "uses sarcastic tone of voice." Coded in this category, it seems unlikely that we would detect the perceived helpfulness of "talking about other topics unrelated to the problem."

Talking about other topics is one example of "assisted avoidance": acts that avoid the problem/emotion but *do not* avoid interaction with the other person. For some types of problems and in some types of situations, it may be functional for an individual to forget a problem or pretend it does not exist. Roth and Cohen (1986) suggest that avoidance is a useful individual coping strategy for reducing short-term stress and preventing crippling anxiety in the face of uncontrollable stress. Thoits (1984) suggests a variety of helpful ways to assist others in managing disruptive emotions, including such "avoidant" behaviors as escaping an upsetting situation; changing physiological responses with drugs, alcohol, or relaxation; "playacting" positive emotions; and reinterpreting negative emotions as positive. Changing the topic, engaging in diversionary activities, and putting on a happy face can be functional ways of dealing with stress, and others may assist us in these forms of avoidance.

Assisted avoidance behaviors appear in the interactive coping typology but are not consistently treated as approach or avoidance, and either coding would group assisted avoidance with dissimilar behaviors that might mute its effects. "Lift mood" behaviors (emotion-focused/approach) avoid both problem and emotional distress by engaging in other activities (buying a gift, going to lunch, exercising, engaging in a creative task). Yet the effects of this behavior would be indistinguishable from effects of other behaviors that explicitly deal with emotional distress. It is also difficult to see how "lift mood" behaviors are distinct from "encourage escape" behaviors (emotion-focused/avoidance) that encourage getting drunk, doing drugs, having sex, or changing activity. We might make value judgments about the relative healthfulness of the activities, but both "lift mood" and "encourage escape" essentially involve assisted avoidance of both problem and emotion. As a result, assisted avoidance behaviors are codable but not very researchable in this taxonomy.

Another form of behavior that is neglected in the interactive coping typology might be labeled "ambiguous approach." Several theories of the relationship between message features and their functions suggest that equivocal, off-record messages may be adaptive in situations in which a speaker faces conflicting goals or demands (e.g., Bavelas, Black, Chovil, & Mullett, 1990; Brown & Levinson, 1987). Barbee and Cunningham note that "a central postulate of SIST is that people often experience ambivalence when faced with the need to ask for, or provide, social support"; however, messages that are ambiguous in the provision of support (and thus potentially responsive to these difficulties) are not well represented in the interactive coping typology. All of the solve behaviors clearly and directly address the problem experienced by the other and five of eight solace behaviors clearly and directly address the emotions experienced by the other ("empathy," "compliment," "available," "reassure," "feelings").

The utility of ambiguous approach and its neglect in the interactive coping typology may be illustrated by considering "experience swapping" (Glidewell, Tucker, Todt, & Cox, 1983), in which a support provider does not explicitly talk about the other person's problem but instead shares a story of a similar experience. Glidewell et al. (1983) found that experience swapping was an adaptive way for teachers to get support with work-related problems: Teachers who valued equality and professional autonomy felt explicit and direct support (i.e., solves or solaces) would imply an asymmetric relationship and would be inappropriate in suggesting how a fellow teacher should act. Experience swapping might be coded as "solution" in the problem-focused/approach category ("describes how he or she would handle the problem if it were his or hers"), but doing so would group experience swapping with predominantly direct and unambiguous helping strategies. Alternatively, experience swapping might be coded as "avoid problem" in the problem-focused/avoidance category ("tells the seeker about his or her own problem rather than dealing with the seeker's problem"), but this would group these instances with behaviors such as talking about irrelevant topics, showing disinterest, and criticizing the other.

Like assisted avoidance, ambiguous support responds to dual concerns intrinsic to *interactive* coping: Ambiguity enables a speaker to address both the problem/ emotion experienced by the other and the problems/emotions associated with interaction (e.g., autonomy, power, face). Utterances in which support is ambiguous appear to be problematic for the interactive coping coding scheme, and presumably this is handled by coder instruction and training; alternatively, utterances in which support is ambiguous could be a theoretically interesting and distinguishable category.

Similar problems emerge in the interpretation of results based on the support activation typology. Just as ambiguity may be functional for managing interactive dilemmas in support provision, equivocal and off-record forms of support seeking may also be adaptive for avoiding risks of asking for help (Goldsmith & Parks, 1990). Inclusion of the "indirect" category in the support activation typology seems to recognize the utility of indirect seeking. However, there is a subtle but substantial shift in the treatment of indirect strategies: Barbee and Cunningham focus on the conditions that might *motivate* the use of indirect strategies and discount the potentially adaptive *message effects* of indirect strategies. Their findings might appear to support this shift: Direct seeking behaviors are more reliably associated with approach behaviors than are indirect seeking behaviors. However, we should not necessarily conclude that indirect seeking behaviors are less effective in soliciting support, because the support activation typology treats as indirect a number of involuntary behaviors and behaviors that convey a desire *not* to receive support. In addition, a number of behaviors that are probably indirect means of seeking support (conventionally indirect verbal behaviors, nonverbal expressions of distress and involvement) are categorized as direct. The direct and indirect categories of support activation more accurately tap a distinction between expression and affiliation with the other versus suppression and distance from the other. Consequently, the operationalization of "indirect" in this research is unlikely to reveal the utility of truly indirect seeking.

Barbee and Cunningham's broad categories and their particular way of selecting, grouping, and contrasting the range of social support behaviors are ill suited to examining ambiguous approach, assisted avoidance, or indirect seeking. Yet the labels given to dimensions in the typologies and conclusions drawn from their use may suggest to readers unfamiliar with the details of the coding system that these forms of behavior have been evaluated and found wanting. For example, Barbee and Cunningham offer the following interpretation of the finding that indirect seeking was less reliably linked to approach behaviors: "Helpers may not be solely responsible if they provide poor support, because it is the support seeker who must convey the form of support that is needed. Support seekers may differ in the competence with which they communicate their needs." This interpretation represents avoidance behavior as a poor type of *supportive* behavior even though many of the behaviors categorized as avoidance are rejecting behaviors rather than supportive attempts at assisted avoidance. This conclusion also seems to suggest that indirect behaviors are less competent means of seeking support, when many of the indirect behaviors do not appear to be seeking support at all and some of the direct behaviors are indirect. It seems likely but problematic that readers will interpret findings and conclusions such as these as suggesting that open and direct communication is optimal in some or most circumstances, and yet this conclusion is based on an overly simplified contrast between open, direct communication and rejecting and distancing behavior. There are a range of strategies in between that are competent and well suited to addressing multiple goals.

Sequential Models

Barbee and Cunningham are pioneers in the laudable goal of modeling how support seeking and support provision are chained in a conversation. In interpreting their findings on two-behavior sequences and in evaluating the utility of the proposed longer sequences, it is useful to clarify what is being linked and what kind of "microdynamics" are being modeled.

The sequential models focus on one dimension each from the provision and seeking typologies: approach/avoid and direct/indirect. I have suggested that the direct category might more accurately be interpreted as "seeker approach" behaviors that openly discuss the problem and/or feelings, explicitly ask for help, do not attempt to hide negative affect, and express nonverbal conversational involvement. In contrast, the indirect category (with the exceptions of "hypo," "complaining," and "whining") is more like "seeker avoidance," including minimization and/or denial of the problem, minimal responses or attempts to change the topic, and nonverbal distancing behaviors. Similarly, the approach/avoid dimension of support provision most clearly contrasts help-intended behaviors and not-help-intended behaviors. In other words, we can view these dimensions as reflecting whether or not the seeker and provider want to have an interaction about the problem or emotional distress and the sequential models indicate whether interlocutors match their desires to engage or not engage in an assistance-oriented conversation. Viewed in this way, it is perhaps less surprising that direct seeking strategies are more consistently linked to approach provision strategies. Instead, we might consider why some of the indirect strategies that appear to convey a desire *not* to receive help elicit help nonetheless.[4]

Clearly it is important to study circumstances under which relational partners agree about whether or not to have a supportive interaction. An inability to agree on whether or not a supportive interaction will occur seems likely to affect the perceived helpfulness of a partner's responses and satisfaction in the relationship. If a seeker conveys a request for help or expresses distress or conversational involvement ("direct" behaviors) and is met with rejection ("avoid" behaviors), this would probably lead to low perceived helpfulness of the partner's behavior and to relational dissatisfaction. It could also be perceived as unhelpful and relationally dissatisfying if a "seeker" conveys a desire to minimize the problem, change the topic, and distance him- or herself from the other ("indirect" behaviors) and is met with problem and emotion-focused talk ("approach" behaviors) instead. Sequences of direct/indirect and approach/avoid behaviors inform our understanding of the sequential matching of desires for supportive interaction. However, these models are limited in illuminating the processes through which support is communicated (or through which refusal to seek or provide support is communicated).

Matching behaviors based on statistical likelihood does not reveal the processes through which respondents attribute meaning to utterances and coordinate their contributions. That is, we may observe the likelihood *that* approach and avoid tendencies are matched, but we do not see the interpretive and discursive processes through which this coordination (or lack of coordination) occurs. Jefferson's (1984a, 1984b) research on laughter in troubles talk serves to illustrate the difference in approaches. She shows how features such as who initiates laughter, when laughter occurs, and even how hard each person laughs are part of the process through which interlocutors coordinate responsiveness to problems and shifts from problem talk to other topics. This is not to say that Jefferson's conversation-analytic approach is "better" than Barbee and Cunningham's sequential approach, but it points to the difference between demonstrating *that* matching between general types of behavior occurs and demonstrating *how* synchronization and coordination come about.

Similarly, coding a variety of behaviors into one of two categories obscures how respondents may modulate form and type of responses within categories. For example, a repetition of a direct-approach-direct-approach sequence tells us that both seeker and provider are interested in having a supportive interaction rather than avoiding one. And we could discriminate whether the support offered was, generally speaking, problem-solving or emotion-focused. However, to conclude from these matches that partners' behaviors are complementary and synchronized, as Barbee and Cunningham do, may obscure significant variation within those global categories. A sequence in which "ask to be distracted" ("direct" behavior) is met with "asks questions about the details of the problem" ("approach" behavior) would be treated as "synchronized" despite the obvious mismatch between what is requested and what is provided. Similarly, the expanded sequences of responses and repeated attempts at support would treat a support provider's progression from "asking questions" to "gathers extra information about the problem" to "gives suggestions on how to solve the problem" to "comes to a conclusion about what seeker could do to solve the problem" as a repetitive sequence of "restated" solves rather than a careful progression from information seeking to possible solution to recommendation. The sequential model may be able to identify gross mismatches in partners' *desires* to engage in supportive interaction, but it is less useful in tracking highly competent negotiation and coordination of support provision or in capturing subtly mismatched or misunderstood attempts.

Finally, the proposed sequential models require that each turn at talk be coded into a single category. This precludes us from examining how a single utterance could include multiple means of seeking or providing support. The way in which a provider might "double the chances of success" by offering multiple kinds of support could be captured by the sequential model only if the dual provisions occurred in separate turns. For example, the sample message "I know you work hard, and if you study even harder, I know that you can do even better next time" was rated by a group of students as a highly helpful response to a friend who has failed an exam (Goldsmith, 1994). Coding this as "solve" could not account for why this message was rated as significantly more helpful than "You should study harder next time" (also a "solve" behavior) and would not help us understand why a receiver might respond with "appreciation" to the former message and with "rejection" or "recoil" to the latter.

In sum, the sequential models are not sufficiently sensitive to the dynamics of interpretation, coordination, and evaluation of messages in a conversation. They suggest when partners are in agreement that they wish to have a supportive interaction and when they are not, but the sequential models cannot explain what goes "wrong" (or "right") communicatively in the achievement of these states of match or mismatch.

TOWARD THEORIES OF
COMMUNICATION PROCESSES

Sensitive interaction systems theory suggests a compelling research agenda, and results thus far are particularly valuable for understanding what thoughts and emotions motivate individuals to provide support and for representing whether partners coordinate their potentially conflicting motives to approach or avoid one another in emotionally difficult circumstances. However, before communication researchers embrace this particular model, it is worthwhile to consider the questions to which it is *not* addressed: It tells us relatively little about message production, interpretation, coordination, and effects. And it may well be that Barbee and Cunningham never intended for it to answer these sorts of questions! One problem with SIST is ambiguity about the questions to which the theory is addressed. Phrases such as "dynamics of communications in a supportive interaction," "sequential interplay" of seeking and providing, and "sensitive dynamics of giving and seeking support" serve a valuable rhetorical function in reminding researchers that "social support" has too often been treated as a static property of an individual or a network. However, once researchers are persuaded to study supportive conversations, a more precise set of concepts and research questions is needed to guide research.

A theory of motivation to give support does not necessarily explain ability to give support, just as a theory of how people provide support would not necessarily explain the conditions under which they would do it. When our questions concern how people produce, interpret, coordinate, and evaluate conversations, we need questions and concepts grounded in a recognition of the distinctive processes that characterize communication between persons. Investigation of the *communicative* microdynamics of supportive communication should begin with dimensions and features of messages (or conversations) based on a conceptualization and explanation of communication processes. Attempts to explain differences in individual ability to produce helpful messages should embody a theory of message production: What capabilities of individuals enable them to accomplish (or prevent them from accomplishing) particular message forms? Models of the processes through which utterances are interpreted as seeking or providing support and through which these lines of action are coordinated should grow out of a theoretical framework concerned with situated meaning and action. Explanations for the effects of messages or conversations (e.g., which messages ameliorate distress) would benefit from a theory of how and why particular features accomplish outcome-relevant functions.

Two of the taxonomies of supportive behaviors to which Barbee and Cunningham refer serve to illustrate this grounding of typologies in theory.

Barbee and Cunningham present these as alternative schemes for coding supportive behavior, but these taxonomies also represent an alternative approach to developing theory. Burleson's (1982) scheme for examining comforting messages originated in questions about differences in the kinds of messages produced by speakers. The selection of "person-centeredness" as the basis for a taxonomy of comforting messages was based on a theory of how personal constructs are related to a speaker's production of messages. In subsequent work, Burleson and Samter have turned their attention to the outcomes of person-centered messages, and this has been accompanied by a move to develop theoretical explanations of message effects (i.e., how and why person-centeredness would be linked to amelioration of distress and relationship development; see Burleson, 1994, in press).

My own research on facework and support (Goldsmith, 1992, 1994) is less well-developed and researched than either Burleson's or Barbee and Cunningham's work, but it can provide another example of how the features of messages selected for examination might be grounded in a theory of communication processes (in this case, message effects). My interest in the use of facework strategies in supportive messages came about because I noticed that many of the negative effects of supportive interactions appeared to involve threats to an individual's sense of acceptance and/or autonomy (Goldsmith, 1992). Brown and Levinson's (1987) theory of politeness identifies and explains what features of messages convey ritual respect for positive face (the want to be accepted) and negative face (the want not to be unduly imposed upon). This theory of how message features are adaptive for particular functions provided a basis for suggesting how some facets of a supportive message might make it more or less effective at mitigating risks of receiving support. Admittedly, this account needs further refinement and testing (Goldsmith, 1994), but it illustrates how theories of message effects can provide a principled basis for the selection of features and dimensions to examine in supportive interactions.

Burleson's person-centered message typology and my politeness message typology utilize existing theories of communication processes. Supportive interactions might have positive and negative effects through a variety of mechanisms (Albrecht, Burleson, & Goldsmith, 1994), and identification of these mechanisms could serve as an impetus for the creation of original taxonomies of message or conversation features. For example, Thoits (1984) suggests that distress can be ameliorated through the management of the experience of emotion. She suggests four components of emotion and six ways in which these components may be behaviorally or mentally manipulated. Using Thoits's theoretical explanation, we might create a typology of message features (or our unit of analysis might involve larger "chunks" of communicative activity) through which various types of manipulation of emotion are achieved. A variety of alternative outcomes, explanations, and message features might be examined from different theoretical perspectives. For instance, a focus on the ways in which supportive interactions influence identity, esteem, and mastery (e.g., Thoits,

1985) or uncertainty reduction (e.g., Albrecht & Adelman, 1987) might produce different taxonomies of different features.

As these examples demonstrate, I am not advocating a parochial attitude that only theories developed by communication researchers should be used to study supportive communication: The person-centered hierarchy draws from developmental psychology and sociolinguistics, politeness theory has origins in sociology and sociolinguistics, and Thoits's work is based in the social psychological study of emotion. What is distinctive in these examples is that the particular features of messages or conversations selected for observation are justified by theoretical explanations for communication processes and for the links between communication processes and other variables of interest. This reflects a different approach to theory building than that taken by Barbee and Cunningham. Based on the description in their chapter, it appears that their selection of dimensions for each typology occurred independent of the selection of other dimensions and variables in their Figure 17.1. Approach/avoid, problem/emotion, verbal/nonverbal, direct/indirect, and the like can be and have been used by others to categorize supportive or coping behaviors; but the selection of these dimensions does not appear to have been based on theoretical linkages to the other kinds of variables that are hypothesized to precipitate support or to occur as a consequence. Barbee and Cunningham later propose possible linkages between the dimensions of the typologies and a variety of other conditions, but this results in a catalog of variables that *might* affect communication rather than explanations for *how* and *why* these linkages occur.

Similarly, the decision to use two dimensions in each typology is not theoretically based. The authors acknowledge that 2 × 2 typologies gloss some differences within categories, and they anticipate objections to this simplification. However, reasoned decisions about trade-offs between parsimony and complexity cannot be made in a theoretical vacuum. For example, Thoits (1984) proposes that supportive behaviors have positive effects through helping individuals to manage their emotional distress; on this basis, she speculates that messages attempting to build the self-esteem of the other person will be less effective than messages focusing on eliminating the disruptive emotional states that threaten self-esteem. Consequently, for Thoits's purposes, Barbee and Cunningham's solace category would be too broad; it combines messages that have different effects and different explanations in her theoretical account. Similarly, the 2 × 2 typologies would not be sufficiently sensitive to variations in the politeness of behaviors such as "gives suggestions," "offers help," and "criticizes seeker" or variation in the person-centeredness of "gives reassurance" and "shows understanding." My point is not that the interactive coping typology is flawed because it would not work for Thoits or Goldsmith or Burleson; rather, I mean to demonstrate that these other programs of research provide a theoretical basis for evaluating the substance and number of dimensions. Any typology of supportive communication will focus on some features and overlook others; the question is whether there is a coherent, internally consistent basis for believing that one's focus is useful for the questions one wishes to ask. Barbee and Cunningham defend the 2 × 2 typologies by pointing to empirical results, and if our concern is primarily with prediction, this may be sufficient. But this does not necessarily provide satisfactory explanation or direction for future research. That the typology has successfully predicted perceived helpfulness or relational breakup does not explain *why* these associations among variables are observed. Nor does it readily direct our attention to other associations that might occur. Likewise, the 2 × 2 circumplexes may produce easily operationalized and reliably coded categories, but it is more theoretically satisfying to base our conceptualization on discursive structures and practices rather than on statistical structures and practices.

The alternative approach I am advocating is unlikely to produce a model of the scope in Figure 17.1 and is unlikely to result in a single set of message typologies being linked to all possible antecedents and consequences. Different features of messages may be useful for examining different antecedents, different contexts, different mechanisms or processes, and different outcomes. Similarly, the unit of analysis may not always be the message. This approach would probably not produce a single megamodel of supportive interactions, but would instead settle for a variety of theoretically driven explanations of particular communicative processes—"micromodels" of the "microdynamics" of the communication of support.

Grounding research in theories of communicative processes is not only essential to our understanding of the communicative dynamics of social support; it also enables research on supportive interactions to speak to more general concerns in the study of communication. Barbee and Cunningham provide convincing evidence that conversations about problems can be emotionally charged, relationally significant, and motivationally complex. Their research suggests some of the circumstances under which individuals will be motivated to engage in or attempt to escape these interactions. These same sorts of conversations are also an excellent site for examining variation in communicative competence, the workings of interpretation, challenges to coordination, and multiple types of communication effects. Applying or developing theories of communication in these particular kinds of conversation could make a distinctive contribution to interdisciplinary research on social support and also has great potential for facilitating our understanding of communication processes more generally.

NOTES

1. However, it is unclear what measure of reliability is being reported and whether the reported reliabilities are for each of the subcategories in the typology or for the broad 2 × 2 categories.

2. It is somewhat unclear how Barbee and Cunningham mean for this dimension to be interpreted. They would appear to share my interpretation when discussing their research on mood and attribution

(e.g., "All of these factors can *inhibit* those in negative moods from *helping*"; emphasis added). However, in explaining the broader applications of the typology, they appear to imply that they are contrasting different forms of helping behaviors (e.g., "may account for why *negative support behaviors* have been ignored"; emphasis added).

3. Barbee and Cunningham cite Cutrona, Suhr, and MacFarlane (1990) as a source; however, these dimensions were simply a part of Cutrona and colleagues' discussion of their findings and not a systematically derived or defended basis for a taxonomy. For example, Cutrona et al. suggest that one way of interpreting differences in strategy use between married couples and friends is to contrast the directness of requests for support; however, that friends and spouses differ in the directness of their requests does not necessarily indicate directness would be related to the kind of support provided, the variable Barbee and Cunningham seek to predict. Similarly, Cutrona et al. mention that women more frequently displayed emotions nonverbally but do not indicate that this difference affects the kinds of support received.

4. Barbee and Cunningham suggest that the tendency to provide help regardless of what the seeker does may reflect optimal relational circumstances. An alternative reading might question why, in well-functioning relationships, the would-be seeker would attempt to avoid asking for help, or why a would-be helper would ignore indications that discussion is not desired and persist in discussing the problem or emotion anyway. It might be that forced laboratory conversations also contribute to the frequency with which partners talk about problems or emotions; to do otherwise would appear to violate their explicit instructions.

REFERENCES

Albrecht, T. L., & Adelman, M. A. (1987). *Communicating social support.* Newbury Park, CA: Sage.

Albrecht, T. A., Burleson, B. R., & Goldsmith, D. J. (1994). Supportive communication. In M. L. Knapp & G. R. Miller (Eds.), *Handbook of interpersonal communication* (2nd ed., pp. 419-449). Thousand Oaks, CA: Sage.

Barbee A. P. (1990). Interactive coping: The cheering-up process in close relationships. In S. W. Duck (Ed.), *Personal relationships and social support* (pp. 46-65). London: Sage.

Barrera, M., Jr., & Ainlay, S. L. (1983). The structure of social support: A conceptual and empirical analysis. *Journal of Community Psychology, 11,* 133-143.

Bavelas, J. B. (1990). Nonverbal and social aspects of discourse in face-to-face interaction. *Text, 10,* 5-8.

Bavelas, J. B., Black, A., Chovil, N., Lemery, C. R., & Mullett, J. (1988). Form and function in motor mimicry: Topographic evidence that the primary function is communicative. *Human Communication Research, 14,* 275-299.

Bavelas, J. B., Black, A., Chovil, N., & Mullett, J. (1990). *Equivocal communication.* Newbury Park, CA: Sage.

Bavelas, J. B., Chovil, N., Lawrie, D. A., & Wade, A. (1992). Interactive gestures. *Discourse Processes, 15,* 469-489.

Brown, P., & Levinson, S. C. (1987). *Politeness: Some universals in language usage.* London: Cambridge University Press.

Burgoon, J. K., Buller, D. B., & Woodall, W. G. (1989). *Nonverbal communication: The unspoken dialogue.* New York: Harper & Row.

Burgoon, J. K., & Newton, D. A. (1991). Applying a social meaning model to relational message interpretations of conversational involvement: Comparing observer and participant perspectives. *Southern Communication Journal, 56,* 96-113.

Burleson, B. R. (1982). The development of comforting communication skills in childhood and adolescence. *Child Development, 53,* 1578-1588.

Burleson, B. R. (1994). Comforting messages: Significance, approaches, and effects. In B. R. Burleson, T. L. Albrecht, & I. G. Sarason (Eds.), *Communication of social support: Messages, interactions, relationships, and community* (pp. 3-28). Thousand Oaks, CA: Sage.

Burleson, B. R. (in press). Comforting messages: Features, functions, and outcomes. In J. A. Daly & J. M. Wiemann (Eds.), *Communicating strategically: Strategies in interpersonal communication*. Hillsdale, NJ: Lawrence Erlbaum.

Burleson, B. R., Albrecht, T. L., & Goldsmith, D. J. (1993). Social support and communication: New directions for theory, research, and practice. *ISSPR Bulletin, 9,* 5-9.

Chovil, N. (1991). Social determinants of facial displays. *Journal of Nonverbal Behavior, 15,* 141-154.

Coker, D. A., & Burgoon, J. K. (1987). The nature of conversational involvement and nonverbal encoding patterns. *Human Communication Research, 13,* 463-494.

Cutrona, C. E. (1986). Behavioral manifestations of social support: A microanalytic investigation. *Journal of Personality and Social Psychology, 51,* 201-208.

Cutrona, C. E., Suhr, J. A., & MacFarlane, R. (1990). Interpersonal transactions and the psychological sense of support. In S. W. Duck (Ed.), *Personal relationships and social support* (pp. 30-45). London: Sage.

Dakof, G. A., & Taylor, S. E. (1990). Victims' perception of social support: What is helpful from whom? *Journal of Personality and Social Psychology, 58,* 80-89.

Gergen, K. J., & Gergen, M. M. (1983). The social construction of helping relationships. In J. D. Fisher, A. Nadler, & B. M. DePaulo (Eds.), *New directions in helping: Vol. 1. Recipient reactions to aid* (pp. 143-163). New York: Academic Press.

Glidewell, J. C., Tucker, S., Todt, M., & Cox, S. (1983). Professional support systems: The teaching profession. In A. Nadler, J. D. Fisher, & B. M. DePaulo (Eds.), *New direction in helping: Vol. 3. Applied perspectives on help-seeking and receiving* (pp. 189-212). New York: Academic Press.

Goldsmith, D. J. (1992). Managing conflicting goals in supportive interaction: An integrative theoretical framework. *Communication Research, 19,* 264-286.

Goldsmith, D. J. (1994). The role of facework in supportive communication. In B. R. Burleson, T. L. Albrecht, & I. G. Sarason (Eds.), *Communication of social support: Messages, interactions, relationships, and community* (pp. 29-49). Thousand Oaks, CA: Sage.

Goldsmith, D. J., & Parks, M. R. (1990). Communicative strategies for managing the risks of seeking social support. In S. W. Duck (Ed.), *Personal relationships and social support* (pp. 104-121). London: Sage.

Gottlieb, B. H. (1978). The development and application of a classification scheme of informal helping behaviours. *Canadian Journal of Behavioural Science, 10,* 105-115.

Jefferson, G. (1984a). On stepwise transition from talk about trouble to inappropriately next-positioned matters. In J. M. Atkinson & J. C. Heritage (Eds.), *Structures of social action: Studies in conversation analysis* (pp. 191-222). Cambridge: Cambridge University Press.

Jefferson, G. (1984b). On the organization of laughter in talk about troubles. In J. M. Atkinson & J. C. Heritage (Eds.), *Structures of social action: Studies in conversation analysis* (pp. 346-369). Cambridge: Cambridge University Press.

Manusov, V., & Rodriguez, J. S. (1989). Intentionality behind nonverbal messages: A perceiver's perspective. *Journal of Nonverbal Behavior, 13,* 15-24.

McNeil, D. (1985). So you think gestures are nonverbal? *Psychological Review, 92,* 350-371.

Motley, M. T., & Camden, C. T. (1988). Facial expressions of emotion: A comparison of posed versus spontaneous expressions in an interpersonal communication setting. *Western Journal of Speech Communication, 52,* 1-22.

Roth, S., & Cohen, L. J. (1986). Approach, avoidance, and coping with stress. *American Psychologist, 41,* 813-819.

Streeck, J. (1993). Gesture as communication: I. Its coordination with gaze and speech. *Communication Monographs, 60,* 275-299.

Thoits, P. A. (1984). Coping, social support, and psychological outcomes: The central role of emotion. In P. Shaver (Ed.), *Review of personality and social psychology: Vol. 5. Emotions, relationships, and health* (pp. 219-238). Beverly Hills, CA: Sage.

Thoits, P. A. (1985). Social support and psychological well-being: Theoretical possibilities. In I. G. Sarason & B. R. Sarason (Eds.), *Social support: Theory, research, and applications* (pp. 51-72). Boston: Kluwer Academic.

Winstead, B. A., & Derlega, V. J. (1991). An experimental approach to studying social interaction and coping with stress among friends. In W. H. Jones & D. Perlman (Eds.), *Advances in personal relationships* (Vol. 2, pp. 107-131). Greenwich, CT: JAI.

19 Social Impacts of Electronic Mail in Organizations: A Review of the Research Literature

LAURA GARTON
BARRY WELLMAN
University of Toronto

E-mail is a communication network operating on a computer network that supports social networks. It combines locational flexibility, rapid transmission to multiple others across time and space, and the ability to store and process information. This chapter reviews research into how e-mail shapes—and is shaped by—organizational structures and processes. Although social phenomena strongly affect the use of e-mail, many discussions of media use have treated it as a voluntary, individual act of matching task to media. They have paid less attention to the influence of organizational power, group perceptions, and social network relations. E-mail provides fewer cues than face-to-face communication about interactions, physical context, or social roles. As this fosters status equalization, there is less awareness of group members' expertise, organizational niche and power, and ascribed characteristics. Under certain conditions, people are more uninhibited, nonconformist, and conflictual when using e-mail; groups are more polarized and take longer to reach consensus. However, groups using e-mail tend to produce more diverse opinions and better contributions to the decision-making process. E-mail increases access to new people; weakens spatial, temporal, and status barriers; and provides access to information that would otherwise be unavailable. When people communicate electronically, work groups become more fluid. People can participate actively in more groups, and those on the periphery get more involved.

DISENTANGLING RESEARCH FROM HOPE AND HYPE

Electronic mail (e-mail) has grabbed the attention of policy and propaganda machines. Major newspapers run at least one story per week about e-mail, the Internet, videomail, and other forms of computer-mediated communication

Correspondence and requests for reprints: Barry Wellman, Centre for Urban and Community Studies, University of Toronto, 455 Spadina Avenue, Toronto, Ontario, Canada M5S 2G8.

Communication Yearbook 18, pp. 434-453

(CMC). The U.S. government is promising to do for communications in the 1990s what the interstate highway system did for transportation in the 1960s: provide convenient, high-speed, high-capacity text/data highways with reduced accident rates. Corporate use is widespread and increasing at an estimated rate of 32% per year: in 1991 there were 8.9 million corporate e-mail users in *Fortune* 2000 companies, estimated to grow to 15.6 million corporate users in 1993 and 25 million in 1995 (Electronic Mail Association, 1992). Moreover, these figures exclude noncorporate use.[1]

All of this activity and visibility has generated much speculation about the social implications of e-mail. The inherently social nature of CMC means that this technology is likely to have both intended and unintended outcomes. The hoped-for advantages of CMC include productivity and efficiency gains; greater organizational communication, commitment, and solidarity; more participatory and egalitarian decision making; better decisions; and administrative and geographic decentralization (e.g., Hiltz & Turoff, 1978; Johnson-Lenz & Johnson-Lenz, 1994; Sproull & Kiesler, 1991b). Yet Jeremiahs have warned that CMC can also lead to increased management surveillance and control, more standardized work, centralized power and loss of branch autonomy, disrupted group processes and decision making, and increased worker alienation (e.g., Clement, 1992; Sproull & Kiesler, 1991a; Zuboff, 1988).

In this chapter we review social scientific research into how e-mail, the most prevalent type of CMC, shapes and is shaped by the social environment. Our goal is to disentangle empirical evidence from speculation. What do we know, as opposed to what do we hope, fear, or want to sell? More than most research reviews, this represents a Sisyphean task. It is impossible to keep up with the proliferation of research, especially because relevant studies are published in many disciplines, and often only in poorly circulated reports and conference proceedings. To keep this discussion under control, we focus on the *social* implications of *electronic mail within organizations*. We want to know about how people communicate with each other electronically within relatively bounded work groups. We look only at the predominant modes of communication: text-based services providing electronic mail among individuals, distribution lists from one individual to many, and computer conferencing among many organization members. We do not pay much attention to other forms of CMC, such as videoconferencing, public bulletin boards, and the sprawling interorganizational connectivity provided by the Internet. Ours is not an arbitrary focus on organizational e-mail; it coincides with the preponderance of CMC research on "computer-supported cooperative work" in North American organizational milieus.[2]

AUTHORS' NOTE: Our research has been supported by the Social Science and Humanities Research Council of Canada and by the Ontario Ministry of Science and Technology (through the Information Technology Research Centre and the Ontario Telepresence Project). We thank the *Communication Yearbook* reviewers and Baljeet Bhachu, Dimitrina Dimitrova, Caroline Haythornthwaite, Emmanuel Hergott, Marilyn Mantei, Gale Moore, and Janet Salaff for their advice and assistance.

SOCIALLY RELEVANT
CHARACTERISTICS OF ELECTRONIC MAIL

E-mail is "the entry, storage, processing, distribution and reception, from one account to one or more other accounts, of digitized text by means of a central computer [now becoming unnecessary] and remote terminals connected by a telecommunications network" (Rice, Grant, Schmitz, & Torobin, 1990, p. 28), with the following characteristics (based on Culnan & Markus, 1987; Rice & Associates, 1984; Sproull, 1991):

Asynchrony. E-mail users do not need to be in the same place at the same time. Like telephone communication and regular mail, e-mail transcends space, but unlike face-to-face (FTF) or telephone communication (without voice mail), e-mail also transcends time.[3] Although this aids communication across time zones and eliminates telephone tag, it increases uncertainty about if and when a message has been received. Distance is more of a spur to use than time, as many e-mail systems support synchronous conversation.

Rapid transmission and reply. E-mail's rapid transmission of messages, even across continents, supports collaborative work.[4] Indeed, e-mail devotees often refer to regular postal mail as "snail mail."

Textual nature. The text-based nature of e-mail makes it less able than FTF communication to convey conventional nonverbal social cues. This increases uncertainty about how to interpret messages, more so when they are from strangers.

Dyadic and multiple connections. E-mail may be sent one to one, one to many, or many to many (computer conferencing). Little effort is needed to send or forward messages to multiple sites. Individuals may belong to many groups, and groups can easily expand and contract. Work groups may form for specific tasks and then dissolve, or they may break into smaller groups with all members aware of subgroup proceedings. In many systems, it is as easy to communicate outside of one's own work group as within it, although many organizations keep all e-mail within their boundaries for security reasons.

Storage and manipulation. E-mail can be stored in external memory for future retrieval, searching, editing, and forwarding to others. People can edit their own and others' messages to change their meaning. The historical record of interaction may be used for surveillance of individual and group interactions, to review past decisions (as Oliver North belatedly learned), and to bring new members up to date.

WHEN IS E-MAIL USED?

Task, Perception, and Interaction

Although investigations of the circumstances under which people use e-mail fall under the rubric of "media choice," defining issues only in terms of choice commits a voluntaristic fallacy by not considering organizational and normative constraints on individual behavior (Fulk & Boyd, 1991). It is impossible to avoid using e-mail when the organization sends all of its important messages on it or when using e-mail is a condition of employment. It is fruitless to send e-mail to coworkers who do not have access to the system or who never use it. In most organizations, e-mail is neither mandated nor rejected, but is one of several ways to communicate, along with telephoning (including voice mail), paper memos, faxing, scheduled FTF meetings, and unscheduled FTF encounters.

Many studies of media choice have looked at matches among the communication needs of a task, the capabilities of a communication medium, and the organization and individuals' perceptions about a medium's appropriateness for that task. Although analysts disagree about the details of task-media matches, some argue that a medium is chosen to reduce *uncertainty* in the absence of information (Rice et al., 1990; Rice & Shook, 1990; Steinfield, 1986). Others argue that *equivocality* is the key to task-media matches (Daft & Lengel, 1986; Daft, Lengel, & Trevino, 1987; Valacich, Paranka, George, & Nunamaker, 1993). Whereas *uncertainty* refers to the need to acquire information to accomplish a task, *equivocality* refers to participants' interpretation of the task itself. Other proposed keys to media choice are *routineness* (the extent of task variation) and *analyzability* (the extent to which persons can describe and complete a task by following known procedures) (Perrow, 1967; Rice et al., 1990).

We fear that this analytic approach has *a*socially concentrated on a single individual choosing among media, without taking into account the social relationships involved in communication. The "social presence" concept expands horizons a bit by including such elements as the ability of a medium to convey awareness of the other person and to support interpersonal relations (Short, Williams, & Christie, 1986). A somewhat similar concept, "media richness," involves the capacity of different media to provide immediate feedback and to support multiple verbal and nonverbal cues (Daft & Lengel, 1984, 1986; Daft et al., 1987). Rich media help participants to understand each other through feedback, multiple cues (similar to social presence), language variety, and personal focus (infusion of emotion and feelings; Daft et al., 1987). By contrast, lean media rely on rules, forms, and procedures. Working before the widespread proliferation of CMC, Daft and Lengel (1986) ranked media in order of richness: FTF, telephone, personal written documents such as letters or memos, impersonal unaddressed documents (e.g., bulletins, standard reports), and numeric documents. More recent research has placed e-mail between personal and formal written text (Schmitz & Fulk, 1991) or in some instances closer to the telephone (Lea, 1991). However, Schmitz and Fulk (1991) argue that the real difference is between FTF and simple alphanumeric text; formal/informal documents, e-mail, and the telephone all tend to cluster in the middle realm of media richness. Although the social presence and media richness approaches consider the capacity of media to support interaction, the rankings attached to these approaches still assume that individuals operate as isolated rational choosers: assessing a task, appraising media, and making the best match.

Consistent with the task-oriented nature of these approaches, several studies have related the nature of the task to the media chosen to deal with it. One study found that 84% of the managers of a large company preferred to use FTF communication to deal with an equivocal task rather than the telephone, letters, fliers, and the public address system. Of these managers, 62% preferred to use written, addressed communication to deal with unequivocal tasks. Higher-performing managers were more sensitive to the interplay between the nature of the task and the choice of media (Daft et al., 1987). This study did not include e-mail, however. More recently, Rice et al. (1990) found that people use e-mail to deal with complex tasks, often in conjunction with other media. Their findings suggest that much communication is about multiple, complex tasks that are not suitable for simple task-media matching (see also Lea, 1991). Thus Lea (1991) found that the members of a large firm considered e-mail to be similar to FTF and the telephone in terms of spontaneity, and to be an appropriate choice for inconsequential as well as important communication (see also Rice et al., 1990; Rice & Shook, 1990).

As the medium is also a message, analysts must consider the social meanings attributed to a communication medium and the context within which it is used. One study found that managers often communicated face-to-face "to signal a desire for teamwork, to build trust, goodwill, or to convey informality," but they communicated on paper to signify authority and legitimacy (Trevino, Daft, & Lengel, 1990, p. 86). Perin (1991) has noted, "Although top-down policies may first appear on electronic mail . . . , their legitimation depends on being printed out as hard copy that arrives in paper mail" (p. 77).

Such findings raise the matter of how different communication media come to be perceived as appropriate for various tasks. Schmitz and Fulk (1991) propose that media evaluations are formed by social influence as well as by a person's experience and expertise (see also Fulk, Schmitz, & Steinfield, 1990). Under their social influence model, rational choice is only one possible reason people use different communication media. It is through interaction with others that people come to perceive the attributes of specific media as useful for specific tasks. Thus social networks are not only the fruits of interaction; they are also reference groups that define the appropriate use of media (Rogers & Kincaid, 1981).

Social Networks

The presence of a critical mass of users affects the extent to which people use e-mail. For instance, Steinfield (1986) found that people with more e-mail access to others in a large decentralized corporation used e-mail more than did people who had less such access. Those who had e-mail access to people *outside* their own work group were especially likely to use it; access to immediate coworkers was less important because FTF communication with them was accomplished easily. Another study of a small office showed that those who were more involved in existing communication networks were more likely to follow group norms about whether or not to use e-mail (Rice et al., 1990). Schmitz and Fulk (1991) similarly found that people in the same communication network usually agreed about what medium to use for what purpose.

Substitute, Addition, or Booster?

Does the use of e-mail reduce the use of other forms of communication (a substitution effect), is it an addition to the total amount of communication, or does it also boost the use of other means of communication? One study showed a booster effect: Work groups that used e-mail had a higher level of overall communication than those that did not. This suggests that "the electronic super-structure is not a simple substitute for in-person contact, telephone calls, print correspondence, or any other conventional medium" (Bikson & Eveland, 1990, p. 286). The evidence is not clear, however; another study showed that e-mail use reduced the use of other media: Those groups that used e-mail heavily spent less time in FTF meetings, on the telephone, and exchanging paper memos (Finholt, Sproull, & Kiesler, 1990). Still another study found that frequent e-mail use was associated more with frequent informal FTF contact than with frequent formal FTF meetings, and that e-mail was often used to deal with emotional stress (Haythornthwaite, Wellman, & Mantei, 1994). These findings suggest that it is the way in which e-mail is used, and not the frequency of e-mail use, that affects the use of other communication media.

GROUP PROCESSES

Research into differences between FTF and e-mail groups has looked mainly at computer conferencing, a type of e-mail in which all of a group's messages are available to all members. Most of the work undertaken so far has consisted of experimental laboratory studies of two to five persons, comparing how FTF and computer conferencing groups solve specified problems within fixed time limits. Although some consistent findings have emerged, generalizations have been limited by the diversity of research designs: synchronous/asynchronous, experienced/inexperienced users, specially formed/ongoing groups (see also Culnan & Markus, 1987).

Just as task groups are a primary market for e-mail vendors, research into e-mail's impact on group processes has concentrated on decision making in focused, bounded task groups. Researchers have paid less attention to the use of e-mail to maintain socioemotional relationships (but see Johnson-Lenz & Johnson-Lenz, 1994) or to maintain the routine, nonfocused intercourse necessary to sustain organizational life, and they have paid less attention to diffuse, unbounded relationships that cut across organizations.

Organizational analysts describe task groups as having regular interactions, stable identities, interdependent members, collective orientations toward common goals, motivation to work together, structured interactions based on common roles and norms, and group members who are open to one another's influences. As these criteria were developed for task groups that interact face-to-face, often in a common space where all are accessible to all, analysts have wondered if they apply also to groups using e-mail, whose members are rarely in the same place at the same time. It may be more difficult to maintain group focus and identity when people cannot tell what other e-mail users are doing when they are not signed on or what else they are doing when they are signed on.

Much of this problem-solving-oriented research has focused on the consequences of e-mail filtering out nonverbal cues in communication (Culnan & Markus, 1987). E-mail does not supply nonverbal *interactional cues* to group members, such as eye contact, gestures, nodding approval, frowning, or hesitating before replying. There are no *contextual cues,* either: Participants cannot use seating arrangements to identify coalitions and cleavages, or choose meeting sites to identify the importance or sponsorship of meetings. Because e-mail users typically are identified by name only, people are not constantly reminded of the *social roles* others have beyond the narrow confines of the task group. Users may not be aware of another group member's gender, race, expertise, or organizational position.

The relative absence of such cues can foster extreme language, difficulties in coordination and feedback, problems in reaching group consensus, and group polarization (Goode & Johnson, 1991; Harasim & Winkelmans, 1990; Hiltz, Johnson, & Turoff, 1986; Kiesler, Siegal, & McGuire, 1984; Kiesler & Sproull, 1992). However, e-mail users may use nonverbal cues, either explicitly, by adding status information to their signatures, or implicitly, by their writing style or by forwarding communications to important persons (Walther, 1992).

E-mail's filtering of cues can have positive effects as well. Because of the need for coordinated focus, effective FTF groups can typically accommodate fewer than a dozen members. If more members are needed, FTF groups subdivide or some members become passive. Turn taking is regulated, so that only one person speaks at a time. By contrast, e-mail is less restrictive and can accommodate more ideas from more people. People may offer comments simultaneously and make proposals without a formal sequence. Subgroups can form to deal with particular problems without disturbing overall group focus. Larger group sizes are possible because passive voyeurs are less noticeable.

Status Equalization

In FTF groups, higher-status people talk more than lower-status people, men talk more than women, and managers talk more than subordinates. Those who participate have more opportunities to influence decisions. Because e-mail reduces status cues, status-induced imbalances also are weaker. E-mail can encourage more open and equal discussion, leading to decisions based on knowledge rather than on the influence of high-status members (e.g., Kiesler & Sproull, 1992). However, we have not found any research addressing the possibility that high-status people may be reluctant to use e-mail because it can diminish their influence.

Members of e-mail groups tend to participate more equally than do members of FTF groups (Kiesler et al., 1984; Rice, 1987; Sproull & Kiesler, 1991a). For example, Kiesler and Sproull (1992) found that when a three-person group held e-mail discussions there was half the inequality in participation than when they talked FTF; for one thing, e-mail users could communicate simultaneously. But more equal participation and reduced status differences do not necessarily help an e-mail group to reach consensus. E-mail hinders the emergence of leaders, and this lack of leadership may inhibit group coordination (Hiltz et al., 1986). We caution that much of the evidence on equal participation and absence of leadership is the product of laboratory experiments conducted with university students, and may not be generalizable to paid-work situations. For example, one study that used respondents who were older than most university students did not find that the type of media used affected the equality of participation. Furthermore, those respondents who were experienced e-mail users tended to be more active participants in FTF as well as in e-mail groups (Adrianson & Hjelmquist, 1991).

E-mail's suppression of differences may extend to achieved expertise as well as to ascribed social status—a caution to those who believe that the lower salience of status on e-mail may lead to more-focused discussions and better decisions. One study found that e-mail significantly equalized both the actual and perceived performance of people with differing expertise as well as those with high and low social status. It was an undiscriminating "muffler" of all differences (Dubrovsky, Kiesler, & Sethna, 1988).

Nonconforming Behavior

In FTF groups, participation and influence are correlated with social status (Berger & Conner, 1973; Ridgeway, 1983; Webster & Driskell, 1978). The process of developing group norms and roles involves both verbal and nonverbal communication. In most cases, it results in movement toward consensus. E-mail's reduction of nonverbal cues and suppression of status information can hinder a group's movement to consensus by fostering nonconforming behavior and disagreement. Even in experimental task groups e-mail is often blunt, with uninhibited "flaming" language such as swearing and insults (Hiltz, Johnson, & Agle, 1978; Siegal, Dubrovsky, Kiesler, & McGuire, 1986). In one study of 54 student e-mail users, Siegal et al. (1986) recorded 34 instances of swearing, insults, and name-calling; by contrast, no such behavior took place in FTF discussions. Another study comparing task performance in FTF and e-mail conditions found that students were less efficient and more uninhibited while using e-mail (Dubrovsky et al., 1988). This use of uninhibited, often-conflictual language may be related to a lack of visible social control and fewer nonverbal cues to help convey meaning (Sproull & Kiesler, 1991a). Attempts to introduce typographic cues become thin substitutes for nonverbal cues: There is no way to distinguish mild amusement from hilarity with a "smiley," :-). There are few reminders in e-mail of others or of the social context. When cues and controls are weak, people may pay less attention to the presence and opinions of others (Rice et al., 1990).

Some analysts argue that e-mail's speed and ephemerality encourage nonconforming behavior (Kiesler, Zubrow, Moses, & Geller, 1985). Others contend that e-mail encourages deindividuation through reduced self-awareness and increased feelings of anonymity (Siegal et al., 1986). Still others argue that it is inexperience with e-mail, and not the medium itself, that fosters uninhibited language. As groups establish a communication style that includes e-mail, uninhibited language may either decline or become normative (Adrianson & Hjelmquist, 1991). However, some researchers have found a lack of inhibition among experienced e-mail users as well as novices, adults as well as students, and strangers as well as friends (Kiesler et al., 1984).

Group Polarization

Do e-mail's weaker interactional cues and fostering of nonconformist behavior promote the polarizing movement of groups toward more caution or risk (McGrath, 1984)? E-mail groups shift to extreme positions more than do FTF groups (Kiesler et al., 1985; Kiesler & Sproull, 1992; Sproull & Kiesler, 1991a). Less social control and fewer normative constraints in e-mail promote more polarized groups. This may be because e-mail submerges individual identity. However, Lea and Spears (1991) argue that because people have social as well as individual identities, if e-mail submerges individual identities, then group membership should become more important and encourage group polarization. This suggests that it is social network pressure, and not deindividuating alienation, that is important for group polarization in e-mail.

Consensus

With few nonverbal mechanisms to guide e-mail groups, reaching agreement in them is lengthier and more complex than in FTF groups (Adrianson & Hjelmquist, 1991; Hiltz et al., 1986; Kiesler et al., 1984; Sproull & Kiesler, 1991a). It took 4 times as long for a three-person group to reach consensus in a real-time computer conference than in FTF meetings, and nearly 10 times as long for a four-person group that had unlimited time. It took more time to type and to read e-mail than to talk and to listen in FTF meetings. Feedback lags and weak interactional cues made it harder to know how others were interpreting messages and how confident others were in their positions. People also had difficulty interpreting when the group was ready to come to a decision (Kiesler & Sproull, 1992).

Although both FTF and e-mail groups will initially propose a variety of alternatives and solutions, the process of reaching consensus in FTF groups is usually more gradual and sequential than that in e-mail groups. In e-mail groups, initial and subsequent proposals are less related to each other, and members spend more time and effort reconciling diverse ideas to reach consensus. E-mail groups tend to hold more votes, probably because they converge on decisions more slowly (Kiesler & Sproull, 1992).

Decision Quality

The difficulties that e-mail groups have in reaching consensus do not weaken the quality of their decisions. Indeed, e-mail discussion may increase decision quality by increasing the diversity of opinions presented and considered. In one experiment, participants dealt with a technical problem in which the facts were known, as well as a human relations problem with more ambiguous information. Both the FTF and e-mail groups improved the quality of their decisions after discussing the technical problem. By contrast, although the FTF groups reached agreement about the human relations problem, only one of eight e-mail groups did so. Yet external judges thought that the minority opinions in the e-mail groups tended to be better than those in the consensus FTF groups. These higher-quality suggestions were the result of the greater variety of opinions offered in the e-mail groups (Hiltz et al., 1986).

Another study showed that when e-mail users were isolated from each other, they produced higher-quality and more original ideas than did FTF groups (Valacich et al., 1993). The greater ability of the isolated e-mail users to communicate simultaneously meant that they could focus on the task without the distraction of other verbal and nonverbal communication. Small group research has shown that although the number of opinions given in a group is negatively correlated with reaching agreement in the group, it is positively correlated with the quality of decisions. This suggests that e-mail may produce more communication that aids high-quality decisions, but less communication that leads to consensus (Hiltz et al., 1986).

CONNECTIVITY

Access to New People and New Information

Research into the use of e-mail in actual organizational settings has employed a variety of methods and designs: experiments, ethnographic observation, closed-ended surveys, open-ended interviews, and electronic data collection. Actual e-mail users interact in organizational contexts, and not in laboratories. Unlike the experimental groups discussed above, their interactions are not focused on one single task concentrated into two- or three-hour time limits. Group membership often fluctuates, people may have prior relationships, and they may be aware of one another's social characteristics and organizational positions.

E-mail extends the number and range of contacts and information in organizations. Many organizations use voluntary and required distribution lists (DLs) that send e-mail messages to many employees. They are a means of seeking and receiving information from a wide range of contacts and groups. In one study, employees in a large corporation received messages from 700 DLs that accounted for 80% of their daily e-mail (Finholt & Sproull, 1990). Respondents reported that these DLs extended their communication reach, supplying information that they would not receive in any other way. Some 58% of DL messages came from strangers, and 68% came from locations outside of the recipients' buildings; 63% of their e-mail came from people external to their department or chain of command. These messages were sent across as well as within DLs, and they helped integrate the firm (Finholt & Sproull, 1990; Kiesler & Sproull, 1988).

Similar evidence comes from a study of an office systems company where most messages were sent to DLs. Almost half of these messages were from people the recipients did not know, and 60% of the messages would not have been received if there had been no e-mail. Messages that respondents felt they were unlikely to have received without e-mail were also more apt to have been sent by people who were spatially or organizationally distant (Feldman, 1987). Similarly, a study of collaboration between scholars located in three countries and two continents found that e-mail aided networking among those who were already acquainted and connected previous strangers who had common interests (Carley & Wendt, 1989; Harasim & Winkelmans, 1990; Schwartz & Wood, 1993).

E-mail links people and work groups over space, time, and group boundaries. The frequently large memberships of DLs help maintain weaker ties. Indeed, the absence of constraining nonverbal cues and social controls may make it easier to communicate with weak ties by e-mail than FTF. Such wide-ranging ties are especially useful for linking heterogeneous people, getting new information, and integrating organizations (Granovetter, 1973; Feldman, 1987; Wellman, 1988). Thus e-mail users in one large multinational corporation reported an improved sense of connectedness with the company and greater access to high-quality information (Rice & Steinfield, 1994). Indeed, some people join many DLs precisely because they don't want to miss anything (Finholt & Sproull, 1990; Rice & Steinfield, 1994). Overload can be a problem: One study of a lab found that those who were responsible for delegating tasks felt in control of their e-mail, whereas those who received orders and could not delegate tasks felt overwhelmed (Mackay, 1988).

Informal Interaction

Informal interactions using e-mail sustain organizational processes and integrate peripheral members (Eveland & Bikson, 1988). In one decentralized corporation, more than half of those surveyed used e-mail at least occasionally to "keep in touch with others, take breaks from work, and participate in entertaining events such as games" (Steinfield, 1985, p. 241). Although task-related use was more frequent, people also used e-mail for play and pleasure. Similarly, Haythornthwaite et al. (1994) found that most members of a research group used e-mail to socialize, and many used it for emotional support.

In one study, Finholt and Sproull (1990) found that the messages in extracurricular, voluntary DLs placed a greater emphasis on fun and symbolic communication, whereas the messages in required, task-related DLs were designed to direct attention, coordinate activities, solve problems, and demonstrate competence. The extracurricular DLs were five times larger and more geographically dispersed than were required DLs. People were more likely to reply to messages in extracurricular DLs, although there was no difference from the required DLs in other measures of activity.

Informal e-mail helps to relieve workplace stress (Steinfield, 1985), to integrate new and peripheral employees into a group (Eveland & Bikson, 1988; Rice & Steinfield, 1994; Steinfield, 1985), and to encourage organizational involvement, cohesiveness, and commitment (Huff, Sproull, & Kiesler, 1989; Kaye, 1992; Sproull & Kiesler, 1991a). Although organizational research has shown that socializing with colleagues on and off the job promotes positive organizational attitudes, research has not yet clearly shown the benefits of socializing on e-mail for performance (Sproull & Kiesler, 1991a). However, Finholt and Sproull (1990) suggest that increased e-mail participation may improve performance in the long term because increased links among employees are useful in times of crisis and participation helps employees build skills and absorb ideas.

Cross-Cutting Group Boundaries

Geography has strongly affected the social structure of organizations, with the plant or the office being a key building block. Even when employees report to superiors located elsewhere, they usually spend most of their time communicating with people working nearby. Yet e-mail can support large, complex, and fluid groups that cut across existing organizational and territorial structures (Castells, 1989; Finholt & Sproull, 1990; Kaye, 1992). Thus Bikson and Eveland (1990) found that department-based communication clusters in the RAND Corporation became more open after e-mail was introduced.

On the basis of these preliminary findings, Bikson and Eveland (1990; Eveland & Bikson, 1988) designed a field experiment to investigate changes in the structure of relationships among 79 high-status men from a large corporation who were split into two groups: one with access to e-mail and the other without. In the standard media group, people tended to belong to only one subcommittee, and relatively well defined clusters emerged that reflected these subcommittee boundaries. By contrast, the members of the e-mail group belonged to at least two subcommittees, and their interactions were less confined to subcommittees. The e-mail group also had broader leadership and formed a coordinating committee to link various subcommittees. "The technology supplied to the electronic group enabled a much richer and more dense interaction structure than could be supported by the technology available to the standard group" (Bikson & Eveland, 1990, p. 269). Kiesler and Sproull (1992) have noticed similar phenomena occurring with software development teams; they suggest that e-mail has the ability to create in-groups without creating out-groups.

Linking Core and Periphery

As it helps overcome the constraints of geography, e-mail can increase contact between head office and peripheral employees. "Core" and "periphery" can also have a metaphorical connotation, because e-mail has the potential to give low-status people more access to information and organizational power (e.g., Sproull & Kiesler, 1991a). One group has studied retirees who were more organizationally peripheral than continuing employees. Formed into two groups, one using e-mail and one not, those retirees in the e-mail group increased their involvement with other group members more than those in the other group, as measured by name/face recognition, making acquaintances, and frequency of contact. The e-mail retirees went from recognizing less than 10% of their group to recognizing more than 90%. Their contact with group members during two weeks increased from less than 20% to more than 50%, whereas contact between retirees in the non-e-mail group remained at less than 10%. The e-mail group held scheduled meetings, and retirees participated in 75% of scheduled meetings. By contrast, retirees in the non-e-mail group participated in only 19% of their group's meetings, principally because the non-e-mail group held many unscheduled meetings in offices that less than 12% of the retiree members were able to attend (Eveland & Bikson, 1988).

E-mail enables peripheral persons to increase their group involvement, fostering, in turn, a more positive orientation to the group. Thus the originally peripheral retirees had more time than employees to learn e-mail techniques, and they used their e-mail skills as well as their organizational experience and expertise to become central contributors to the group. Although members of the e-mail group initially rated their own performance lower than the members of the non-e-mail group rated their own performance, e-mail group members ranked themselves higher by the end of the project. By contrast, non-e-mail group members lowered their rating of their group's performance over time, with the peripherally connected retirees reporting the lowest evaluations (Eveland & Bikson, 1988).

Similarly, a study of a mid-sized city government found that e-mail use fostered increased participation by peripheral shift workers (Huff et al., 1989). The number of e-mail messages was correlated more strongly with increased participation (a measure of behavior) than with increased feelings of being informed (a measure of attitudes). Correlations with participation and attitudes were stronger for the number of messages sent than for the number received. Because the retirees in the Bikson and Eveland (1990) study were proportionately higher senders of messages than were the current employees, the frequency of sending e-mail messages may be an important predictor of overall organizational participation. By contrast, merely receiving information passively on DLs may not increase participation in organizational activities.

Social Control

Issues of control have been important themes in predicting e-mail's effects on organizations. Sproull and Kiesler (1991a) note the potential conflict between management's desire to maintain control over the organization and the attributes of e-mail that extend traditional communication patterns. They observe that open communication leads to unsupervised information sharing, through which employees might discover more about the company than management wants them to know. Management may fear that employees will use e-mail to organize collective action (Sproull & Kiesler, 1991a, p. 110). Increased connectivity through e-mail can also accelerate the flow of (mis)information, rumors, complaints, subversive communications, and practical jokes. Finholt and Sproull (1990) provide an example of a message circulated in a DL designed to report company news. The message explained how a division would be reorganized, who would have management responsibilities, and how the transition would proceed. Twelve days later, the sender issued another message, apologizing for the April Fool's Day joke. At IBM, an e-mail "gripenet" became the locale of so many organized complaints against corporate practices that management quickly shut it down (Emmett, 1982). Concern over what information is being communicated, and to whom, continues to rattle management's sense of propriety and control. Even when organizations encourage informal e-mail, managers often view it with distrust (Perin, 1991). For example, one corporation's managers monitored messages between professional women who were discussing career options because management feared their discussion would lead to demands for unionization and affirmative action (Zuboff, 1988).

In addition to e-mail's subversive potential, it can also extend managerial control, especially over outlying branches. Sproull and Kiesler (1991a) suggest that attempts to use CMC to strengthen centralized control may lead to organizational conflict. They expect that management practices will change "when people work in multiple groups, when groups are composed of members who collaborate only electronically, and when soft structures emerge without management directive" (p. 160).

CONCLUSIONS

Summary

E-mail is a communication network operating on a computer network that supports social networks. E-mail combines locational flexibility, rapid transmission to multiple others across time and space, and the ability to store and process information. These features make it an attractive tool for organizations that are geographically dispersed, work collaboratively, and are information-intensive. E-mail's technical characteristics condition but do not determine CMC. Changes associated with e-mail are determined by social as well as technical factors: organizational policies on the use of various media, the extent to which organizations support an open communication system, the nature of the task environment, influential users' perception of what media are appropriate for which tasks, and a critical mass of users.

Discussions of media choice within organizations have largely treated it as an individual, voluntary act of matching tasks to media; they have paid less attention to the influence of organizational power, group perceptions, and social network relations. Although e-mail is text based, like writing, in practice it is flexibly used, like FTF and telephonic communication, for complex tasks and spontaneous communication. The medium is also the message: FTF communication may be used to promote goodwill and build trust, e-mail may be used to gather opinions and discuss alternatives, and paper may be used to formalize decisions. It is not clear if e-mail substitutes for, adds to, or boosts the use of other communication media. The nature of interpersonal relationships, social networks, social influence, and organizational power structures all affect how groups and individuals use e-mail.

E-mail provides fewer cues than does FTF communication about interactions, physical context, and social roles. This fosters status equalization, as there is less awareness of group members' expertise, organizational niche and power, and ascribed characteristics, such as age and gender. Under certain conditions, people are more uninhibited, nonconformist, and conflictual when using e-mail to accomplish certain types of tasks. As it is more difficult to interpret the intentions of the sender in e-mail than in FTF communication, misunderstandings are more likely to emerge and more difficult to resolve. Although e-mail groups are slower to develop leaders and reach consensus, their greater range of ideas may produce more innovative and better decisions. To date, the narrow focus of e-mail-related research on decision making has led to the neglect of studies that (a) take into account previous relationships among group members and (b) analyze interactions over longer periods (c) that occur in real organizations where people must (d) simultaneously attend to a variety of (e) tasks and (f) social networks (see Walther, 1992).

It is such social networks that structure flows of resources (including information) in organizations. E-mail increases access to new people; weakens spatial, temporal, and status barriers; and provides access to information that would otherwise be unavailable. When people communicate electronically, work groups become less fixed entities; they provide individuals with opportunities to participate actively in more groups. It is this participation in e-mail that is the key—not the mere passive receipt of information. The fluidity of communication structures can allow people with expertise to share their knowledge more broadly. Leadership and participation are broader, and those on the periphery get more involved. Information can spread more rapidly and widely than management would like, but the same technology enables those in the core to become more aware of what the periphery is doing. Branch workers may lose their autonomy, and middle managers may become less necessary and even unemployed.

Implications

We suspect that the differences we have discussed here between research focusing on task groups and that focusing on organizational connectivity reflect two ways to organize work (Wellman, 1993). Experimental research on task group performance is more relevant to an *open office* fishbowl, where a small number of densely knit persons work only with each other and are focused on a common goal. They are in a bounded space and have visual, physical, and verbal access to each other. There is little privacy, and it is easy for supervisors and peers to exercise social control. To support virtual open offices, CMC systems must make it easy for people to know coworkers' availability at a glance and to communicate instantly. It would be enough to click on each coworker's icon.

By contrast, research on organizational connectivity is more relevant to the *networking office,* in which workers move between interactions with many others. Such a situation often occurs among professionals who make multiple, often unexpected, contacts with colleagues in their own and other organizations. The Internet is an e-mail example familiar to many scholars. As people move between projects, they move between relationships. CMC must allow them to interact selectively with many of their potential correspondents and to maintain privacy and autonomy. Many design aspects of a CMC system to support this virtual networking office will be different from those needed to support a virtual open office.

E-mail is the precursor to more powerful, multimedia CMC systems with even broader social implications. If CMC brings increased connectivity with individuals and groups across space and time, will this alter the structure of organizational relations and of the social systems in which they are embedded? Will it result in the formation of new groups and communities of interest independent of organizational structures?

The effects of CMC may spread well beyond today's narrow focus on organizational tasks, productivity, and structure. CMC may increase the dispersal of work, not only the current movement from the central business district to suburban offices, but from offices to homes. Informants tell us that a large Toronto corporation saves $7,500 (Canadian) per year in real estate costs when one central office employee becomes a teleworker. CMC may lead to a new kind of piecework, with families huddled in their former "rec rooms," spinning words on their computers. We wonder if a follow-up article to this one will be titled "The Social Implications of CMC for Domestic Relationships."

NOTES

1. We caution that counts and forecasts are quite unreliable in the field because of rapid proliferation, numerous small buyers and sellers, and excessive optimism by hopeful vendors.

2. The best way to keep track of the field is to read the proceedings of the semiannual CSCW conferences (held in North America) and the ECSCW conferences (held in alternate years in Europe). See also the aforementioned CHI proceedings and Baecker (1993). Both the CSCW and CHI groups are affiliated with the Association for Computing Machinery.

3. Answering machines and, more recently, voice mail are two recent attempts to solve the need for temporal synchronicity when using the telephone. The digital nature of some voice mail means that it can offer some of the same features as e-mail, such as the ability to be forwarded. However, voice mail consumes many more bytes per message than e-mail and cannot be manipulated as easily.

4. Such long-distance speed is truer for communications that are within organizations than it is for the Internet, which often uses a complex set of computer transfers at intervening sites between the sender and the receiver.

REFERENCES

Adrianson, L., & Hjelmquist, E. (1991). Group processes in face-to-face and computer mediated communication. *Behaviour and Information Technology, 10,* 281-296.

Baecker, R. M. (Ed.). (1993). *Readings in groupware and computer-supported cooperative work: Assisting human-human collaboration.* San Mateo, CA: Morgan Kaufmann.

Berger, J., & Conner, T. L. (1973). Performance expectations and behavior in small groups. In R. J. Ofshe (Ed.), *Interpersonal behavior in small groups* (pp. 131-140). Englewood Cliffs, NJ: Prentice Hall.

Bikson, T. K., & Eveland, J. D. (1990). The interplay of work group structures and computer support. In J. Galegher, R. E. Kraut, & C. Egido (Eds.), *Intellectual teamwork: Social and technological foundations of cooperative work* (pp. 245-290). Hillsdale, NJ: Lawrence Erlbaum.

Carley, K., & Wendt, K. (1989). *Electronic mail and scientific communication: The study of soar and its dominant users* (Working paper of the Department of Social and Decision Sciences). Pittsburgh: Carnegie Mellon University.

Castells, M. (1989). *The informational city: Information technology, economic restructuring and the urban-regional process.* Oxford: Basil Blackwell.

Clement, A. (1992). Electronic workplace surveillance: Sweatshops and fishbowls. *Canadian Journal of Information Science, 17*(4), 18-45.

Culnan, M. J., & Markus, M. L. (1987). Information technologies. In F. Jablin, L. L. Putnam, K. Roberts, & L. Porter (Eds.), *Handbook of organizational communication* (pp. 420-443). Newbury Park, CA: Sage.

Daft, R. L., & Lengel, R. H. (1984). Information richness: A new approach to managerial information processing and organization design. In B. Staw & L. Cummings (Eds.), *Research in organizational behavior* (pp. 191-233). Greenwich, CT: JAI.

Daft, R. L., & Lengel, R. H. (1986). Organizational information requirements, media richness and structural design. *Management Science, 32,* 554-571.

Daft, R. L., Lengel, R. H., & Trevino, L. K. (1987). Message equivocality, media selection, and manager performance: Implications for information systems. *MIS Quarterly, 11,* 355-366.

Dubrovsky, V., Kiesler, S., & Sethna, B. N. (1988). *Expected and unexpected effects of computer media on group decision making.* Unpublished manuscript, Carnegie Mellon University, Committee on Social Science Research in Computing.

Electronic Mail Association. (1992). *Electronic mail market research results.* Arlington, VA: Author.

Emmett, R. (1982). VNET or GRIPENET. *Datamation, 4,* 48-58.

Eveland, J. D., & Bikson, T. K. (1988). Work group structures and computer support: A field experiment. *ACM Transactions on Office Information Systems, 6,* 354-379.

Feldman, M. S. (1987). Electronic mail and weak ties in organizations. *Office Technology and People, 3,* 83-101.

Finholt, T., & Sproull, L. (1990). Electronic groups at work. *Organization Science, 1,* 41-64.

Finholt, T., Sproull, L., & Kiesler, S. (1990). Communication and performance in ad hoc task groups. In J. Galegher, R. E. Kraut, & C. Egido (Eds.), *Intellectual teamwork: Social and technological foundations of cooperative work* (pp. 291-325). Hillsdale, NJ: Lawrence Erlbaum.

Fulk, J., & Boyd, B. (1991). Emerging theories of communication in organizations. *Journal of Management, 17,* 407-446.

Fulk, J., Schmitz, J., & Steinfield, C. W. (1990). A social influence model of technology use. In J. Fulk & C. W. Steinfield (Eds.), *Organizations and communication technology* (pp. 117-140). Newbury Park, CA: Sage.

Goode, J., & Johnson, M. (1991, November). Putting out the flames: The etiquette and law of e-mail. *Online,* pp. 61-65.

Granovetter, M. (1973). The strength of weak ties. *American Journal of Sociology, 78,* 1360-1380.

Harasim, L. M., & Winkelmans, T. (1990). Computer-mediated scholarly collaboration. *Knowledge: Creation, Diffusion, Utilization, 11,* 382-409.

Haythornthwaite, C., Wellman, B., & Mantei, M. (1994). Media use and work relationships in a research group. In J. Nunamaker, Jr., & R. Sprague, Jr. (Eds.), *Proceedings of the 27th Hawaii International Conference on Systems Science* (pp. 94-103). Washington, DC: IEEE Press.

Hiltz, R. S., Johnson, K., & Agle, G. (1978). *Replicating Bales problem solving experiments on a computerized conference* (Research Report No. 8). Newark: New Jersey Institute of Technology.

Hiltz, R. S., Johnson, K., & Turoff, M. (1986). Experiments in group decision making: Communication process and outcome in face-to-face versus computerized conferences. *Human Communication Research, 13,* 225-252.

Hiltz, R. S., & Turoff, M. (1978). *The network nation.* Reading, MA: Addison-Wesley.

Huff, C., Sproull, L., & Kiesler, S. (1989). Computer communication and organizational commitment: Tracing the relationship in a city government. *Journal of Applied Social Psychology, 19,* 1371-1391.

Johnson-Lenz, P., & Johnson-Lenz, T. (1994). Groupware for a small planet. In P. Lloyd (Ed.), *Groupware in the 21st century: Computer supported cooperative working toward the millennium* (pp. 269-285). London: Adamantine.

Kaye, A. R. (1992). Computer conferencing and mass distance education. In M. Waggoner (Ed.), *Empowering networks: Using computer conferencing in education.* Englewood Cliffs, NJ: Educational Technology.

Kiesler, S., Siegal, J., & McGuire, T. W. (1984). Social psychological aspects of computer-mediated communication. *American Psychologist, 39,* 1123-1134.

Kiesler, S., & Sproull, L. (1988). *Technological and social change in organizational communication environments* (Working paper). Pittsburgh: Carnegie Mellon University, Department of Social and Decision Sciences.

Kiesler, S., & Sproull, L. (1992). Group decision making and communication technology. *Organization Behavior and Human Decision Processes, 52,* 96-123.

Kiesler, S., Zubrow, D., Moses, A. M., & Geller, V. (1985). Affect in computer-mediated communication: An experiment in synchronous terminal-to-terminal discussion. *Human-Computer Interaction, 1,* 77-104.

Lea, M. (1991). Rationalist assumptions in cross-media comparisons of computer mediated communication. *Behaviour and Information Technology, 10,* 153-172.

Lea, M., & Spears, R. (1991). Computer mediated communication, de-individuation and group decision-making. *International Journal of Man-Machine Studies, 34,* 283-301.

Mackay, W. E. (1988). Diversity in the use of electronic mail: A preliminary inquiry. *ACM Transactions on Office Information Systems, 6,* 380-397.

McGrath, J. D. (1984). *Groups: Interaction and performance.* Englewood Cliffs, NJ: Prentice Hall.

Perin, C. (1991). Electronic social fields in bureaucracies. *Communications of the ACM, 34*(12), 75-82.

Perrow, C. (1967). A framework for the comparative analysis of organizations. *American Sociological Review, 32,* 194-208.

Ridgeway, C. L. (1983). *The dynamics of small groups.* New York: St. Martin's.

Rice, R. E. (1987). Computer-mediated communication and organizational innovation. *Journal of Communication, 37*(4), 65-94.

Rice, R. E., & Associates. (1984). *The new media: Communication, research, and technology.* Beverly Hills, CA: Sage.

Rice, R. E., Grant, A. E., Schmitz, J., & Torobin, J. (1990). Individual and network influences on the adoption and perceived outcomes of electronic messaging. *Social Networks, 12,* 27-55.

Rice, R. E., & Shook, D. E. (1990). Relationships of job categories and organizational levels to use of communication channels, including electronic mail: A meta-analysis and extension. *Journal of Management Studies, 27,* 195-229.

Rice, R. E., & Steinfield, C. W. (1994). New forms of organizational communication via electronic mail and voice messaging. In J. H. Adrianson & R. Roe (Eds.), *Telematics and work,* (pp. 109-137). Hillsdale, NJ: Lawrence Erlbaum.

Rogers, E. M., & Kincaid, D. L. (1981). *Communication networks: Toward a new paradigm for research.* New York: Free Press.

Schmitz, J., & Fulk, J. (1991). Organizational colleagues, media richness, and electronic mail. *Communication Research, 18,* 487-523.

Schwartz, M., & Wood, D. C. (1993). Discovering shared interests using graph analysis. *Communications of the ACM, 36*(8), 78-88.

Short, J., Williams, E., & Christie, B. (1986). *The social psychology of telecommunications.* London: John Wiley.

Siegal, J., Dubrovsky, V., Kiesler, S., & McGuire, T. (1986). Group processes in computer-mediated communication. *Organizational Behavior and Human Decision Processes, 37,* 157-187.

Sproull, L., & Kiesler, S. (1991a). *Connections: New ways of working in the networked organization.* Cambridge: MIT Press.

Sproull, L., & Kiesler, S. (1991b). A two-level perspective on electronic mail in organizations. *Journal of Organizational Computing, 2*(1), 125-134.

Sproull, R. (1991). A lesson in electronic mail. In L. Sproull & S. Kiesler, *Connections: New ways of working in the networked organization* (pp. 177-194). Cambridge: MIT Press.

Steinfield, C. W. (1985). Dimensions of electronic mail use in an organizational setting. In J. Pearce & R. Robinson (Eds.), *Proceedings of the annual meeting of the Academy of Management* (pp. 239-243). Mississippi State: Academy of Management.

Steinfield, C. W. (1986). Computer-mediated communication in an organizational setting: Explaining task-related and socioemotional uses. In M. L. McLaughlin (Ed.), *Communication yearbook 9* (pp. 777-804). Beverly Hills, CA: Sage.

Trevino, L. K., Daft, R. L., & Lengel, R. H. (1990). Understanding managers' media choices: A symbolic interactionist perspective. In J. Fulk & C. W. Steinfield (Eds.), *Organizations and communication technology* (pp. 71-94). Newbury Park, CA: Sage.

Valacich, J. S., Paranka, D., George, J. F., & Nunamaker, J. F., Jr. (1993). Communication concurrency and the new media. *Communication Research, 20,* 249-276.

Walther, J. B. (1992). Interpersonal effects in computer-mediated interaction: A relational perspective. *Communication Research, 19,* 52-90.

Webster, M., Jr., & Driskell, J. E., Jr. (1978). Status generalization: A review and some new data. *American Sociological Review, 43,* 220-236.

Wellman, B. (1988). Structural analysis: From method and metaphor to theory and substance. In B. Wellman & S. D. Berkowitz (Eds.), *Social structures: A network approach* (pp. 19-61). Cambridge: Cambridge University Press.

Wellman, B. (1993). Models of community, models of communication. In C. Belisle (Ed.), *Communications et nouvelle technologies,* (pp. 373-389). Lyon: PPSH.

Zuboff, S. (1988). *In the age of the smart machine.* New York: Basic Books.

20 Don't Blink or You'll Miss It: Issues in Electronic Mail Research

MICHAEL E. HOLMES
University of Utah

IN the preceding chapter, Garton and Wellman observe that reviewing electronic mail research is a Sisyphean task. The metaphor is only partly apt;
Sisyphus was condemned to roll a boulder up a mountain only to have it roll
down again, so he had to repeat the effort. He enjoyed a temporary completion
of his onerous task. In contrast, no survey of e-mail research is likely to be
complete, or even temporarily so. The rapid diffusion of organizational e-mail
has earned it vigorous popular and scholarly attention, but has also accelerated
its technical and social development. E-mail remains a moving target. The title
of this commentary on Garton and Wellman's effort underscores the rapidly
changing nature of the state of the art in e-mail and e-mail research.

Garton and Wellman seek to disentangle the hope and hype about e-mail by
surveying the results of empirical research. They focus on research efforts
concerned with the dynamics of media choice and the impacts of computer-
mediated communication on group processes and organizational connectivity.
Although this approach can be faulted for failing to discuss the theoretical
foundations of the research, it is similar to prior outcome-driven reviews such
as the one offered by Culnan and Markus (1987). The review is not exhaustive,
but it is adequately representative of current research threads. What it reveals
is a loosely interwoven body of findings that fails to coalesce into a coherent
representation of e-mail and its relationship with organizational communication
processes.

E-mail research is difficult to survey because it is burgeoning and interdisciplinary. Review and synthesis are further complicated by the literature's relative
immaturity. Garton and Wellman frequently note inconsistent results between
studies, and some findings must be treated as tentative because they are based
on only one or two studies. However, a more fundamental barrier to making

Correspondence and requests for reprints: Michael E. Holmes, Department of Communication,
University of Utah, Salt Lake City, UT 84112.

Communication Yearbook 18, pp. 454-463

sense of the research arises from diverse conceptions of e-mail itself. It is important to take stock of these concepts in order to interpret past efforts and fashion new research directions. Garton and Wellman emphasize prior research; in this commentary, I suggest an alternative grouping of that research based on its underlying concepts of e-mail. I also stress future research directions.

Garton and Wellman offer Rice, Grant, Schmitz, and Torobin's (1990) technical definition of e-mail: "the entry, storage, processing, distribution and reception, from one [computer] account to one or more other accounts, of digitized text" (p. 28). This definition distinguishes e-mail from other electronic media that organizations use in a similar fashion, such as fax, voice mail, and videoconferencing. However, a technical definition can capture only part of what researchers envision when they consider e-mail. At least four root metaphors drive e-mail research: e-mail as a tool, e-mail as a message delivery system, e-mail as an object of social meaning, and e-mail as a genre of written communication.[1] Each vision of e-mail subtly emphasizes or obscures different facets of the technology and influences selection of theoretical frameworks and empirical research questions.

VISIONS OF ELECTRONIC MAIL

E-Mail Is a Tool for Accomplishing Tasks

Situating e-mail as a component of computer-supported cooperative work emphasizes its use in organizational task accomplishment. Unsurprisingly, much of the task-oriented research proceeds from a managerial orientation and a concern with efficiency and effectiveness. Media choice research applies theories of social presence (Short, Williams, & Christie, 1986) and media richness (Daft & Lengel, 1986) to the question of task-to-technology fit. Media choice models are implicitly deterministic: they assume media have relatively fixed characteristics, rooted in channel constraints, of information capacity and ability to reduce equivocality and uncertainty. Effective media use therefore is a matter of rational choice that individuals may accomplish by analyzing task information requirements and matching them to media capacity. Studies in this tradition seek to compare and rank media by their social presence or media richness (Short et al., 1986) and to identify relationships between media selection and managerial performance (Daft, Lengel, & Trevino, 1987).

Task-centered e-mail research suffers from two weaknesses. First, it focuses on media choice at the expense of media content and use. Tool choice (the appropriate matching of media to task requirements) is elevated as the dominant concern; issues of tool use become secondary. This narrow focus is a deficiency because patterns of tool choice and use are interdependent. Second, it is an overly narrow view of organizational tasks that treats them as unitary actions of isolated individuals. Two alternative perspectives on "e-mail as a tool" can address these weaknesses: task-artifact analysis and media homology.

Kuutti and Arvonen (1992) argue that tools are artifacts that mediate between subjects (human agents of action) and objects (targets of action). Tools have consequences; they are artifacts "into which the historical development of the relationship between subject and object thus far is condensed" (p. 235). Tools both enable and constrain practices. This is inherent in the task-artifact cycle: "A task implicitly sets requirements for the development of artifacts to support it; an artifact suggests possibilities and introduces constraints that often radically redefine the task" (Carroll, Kellogg, & Rosson, 1991, p. 79). Traditional media choice models presume stable, objective task characteristics. Task-artifact analysis can explore how tools redefine tasks. The iterative relationships between organizational tasks and e-mail system designs could be explored through (a) examination of the task assumptions that are embedded in e-mail systems, (b) exploration of the evolution of e-mail system designs over time, and (c) analysis of task-related claims made by e-mail system providers (Bødker, 1991; Carroll et al., 1991; Norman, 1991).

A broader view of media fitness for organizational tasks can be found in management philosophies that advocate business process reengineering to support rapid adaptation to market forces. For example, high-speed management (King & Cushman, 1994) and enterprise agility (Ligus, 1993) prescribe organizational market maneuverability and speed of response to market-niche opportunities. Both philosophies identify electronic communication and e-mail as suitable tools for achieving these ends. Such unquestioning insistence on the fit between e-mail and contemporary organizational needs is surprising, given the possibility that the deluge of e-mail may actually lower productivity and efficiency (Pearl, 1993). The media homology hypothesis (Brummett, 1988) may prove a useful framework for understanding the zeal of e-mail adherents.

According to Brummett (1988), a homology consists of "formal parallels among seemingly disparate things or experiences" (p. 203). He argues that a homology among media content, media form, and experience is "powerfully motivating" (p. 207). Such a homologous relationship may exist among e-mail content, e-mail form, and contemporary organizational experiences. Each emphasizes speed, reach, and impermanence. E-mail messages tend to be direct, short, and ephemeral. The formal structure of e-mail allows communication to transcend barriers of time and space. Managers seek salvation in various forms of high-speed management, defined in part by rapid response to changing global conditions and brief tactical alliances rather than enduring strategic partnerships with other organizations. The choice of e-mail as an organizational tool may be influenced as much by this homology as it is by the task at hand. The experience of e-mail use may resonate with, and validate, a managerial worldview and philosophy of organizational action. Systematic inquiry into homology of content, form, and experience in e-mail use would require careful rhetorical analysis; as Brummett (1988) notes, such study requires "the exercise of sensibilities trained to recognize forms and their rhetorical appeals" (p. 214).

E-Mail Is an Object
With Social Meaning

Communication media are socially defined as well as materially constructed (de Sola Pool, 1983; Finlay, 1987). Perceptions of a medium, including evaluation of its fitness for various tasks, arise from its technical features and from attitudes toward the medium shared within a work group (Fulk, Schmitz, & Steinfield, 1990). Media choice is shaped by these social influence processes as well as by channel constraints and task characteristics. Research on the role of social influence in media choice (Fulk et al., 1990; Schmitz & Fulk, 1991) therefore offers a valuable correction to rationalistic and deterministic models driven by "objective" media and task characteristics.

Social influence research could be expanded beyond the level of social groups. Current research labors at the level of communication networks and examines the role of group membership in media perceptions. At a more micro level of analysis, social influence theory could be pursued by probing the construction of media meaning in ongoing talk, with attention to the interaction routines and critical episodes in which the meaning of e-mail and its usage norms are negotiated.

At a macro level of analysis, social influence theorists could investigate the influence on organizational meanings of cultural discourse about new technologies. Fulk et al. (1990) address influence processes operating through communication networks within the organization. This treats the organization as an impermeable container of meaning; however, discourse about new communication technologies and their potential effects pervades American popular culture and constitutes part of organization members' social knowledge (Finlay, 1987). Finlay's (1987) analysis of new technology discourse in the mass media reveals that its features and operations (such as use of the imperative voice—"You will"—and exploitation of fictive scenarios) tend to narrow, rather than broaden, visions of possible futures. The discourse also obscures opportunities for audience participation in defining the future. It may be profitable to study the degree to which popular discourse about new communication technology is reflected in organizational discourse, and to determine if its restrictive features are also present and operating on media perceptions in that context.

E-Mail Is a Message Delivery System

The technical definition of e-mail noted earlier accents its function as a message delivery system. Electronic message delivery systems transcend constraints imposed by face-to-face interaction. Communication media are time and space shifters (Danowski, 1991). They separate the location and/or time of message production from that of reception and thus extend our communicative reach.

Communication networks in organizations historically have been shaped by physical and social propinquity (Danowski, 1991). E-mail can alter organizational networks by allowing new links to emerge and new coalitions to be formed irrespective of physical and hierarchical barriers (Korzenny, 1978, calls this "electronic propinquity"). The connectivity impact of e-mail is one of the most developed areas of e-mail study. Historical analyses and empirical research on the introduction of new media demonstrate that communication media can alter the very shape of organizations (de Sola Pool, 1983; Yates, 1989). They transform communication networks and are in turn shaped by those networks (Contractor & Eisenberg, 1990; Rice et al., 1990).

A fundamental question has failed to garner attention from researchers in the message delivery system framework: Is all e-mail created equal? That is, is the fundamental dynamic of computer-based messaging so robust that differences among delivery systems are immaterial? If technical differences among systems are unimportant, the connectivity findings from e-mail may be relevant to emerging forms of electronic messaging, such as desktop videoconferencing (Fitzgerald, 1994). If technical differences are important, relationships between system features and impacts should be systematically incorporated in research designs, and caution should be exercised in the generalization of findings based on a specific e-mail system.

Technical features of e-mail that may be relevant to this concern include hardware adequacy, software ease of use, and message structuring. For example, I have three ways to send e-mail: a locally developed menu-based e-mail system on the department LAN (local area network), DEC's VaxMail on a university mainframe account, and the Pine e-mail program on a Unix workstation account. The LAN mail system is convenient for departmental communication, but it is time-consuming to search for addresses on other LANs in the campus WAN (wide area network). The addressing convention to reach Internet addresses is clumsy, and the LAN does not provide off-campus "dial-up" access. The VaxMail system provides easy Internet access, but is housed in an overburdened and unbearably slow machine. Its command-line interface can be intimidating, and the built-in editor is primitive at best. In contrast, the Unix e-mail system is the fastest and friendliest of the three. The clear differences in these e-mail systems suggest that not all e-mail is created equal in features or performance.

The systems described above vary in speed and ease of use, but all structure e-mail messages as electronic memoranda (Yates & Orlikowski, 1992). The formal heritage of the e-mail message is evident in the familiar "To," "From," and "Subject" header. No additional content structuring is provided; however, this is not the case with all systems. For example, the Coordinator e-mail system structures messages as speech acts in "conversations for action" (Winograd, 1987-1988, p. 7). It encourages users to subscribe to a particular model of conversational moves in the accomplishment of shared tasks. Design differences are not limited to message composition features. E-mail systems differ in their capacities for filtering incoming messages (Churbuck, 1991) and for organizing and retrieving stored messages (Pearl, 1993).

Marked differences can also be found among e-mail systems for computer conferencing. Rapaport (1991) identifies three conceptual structures for organizing messages in computer conferencing: the linear, comb, and branching models. Systems based on the linear model organize comments chronologically within a topical conference, though some selection and filtering by keywords or other mechanisms may be available. The comb model provides subtopic organization within conferences. The subtopics constitute the spine of the comb, and chronologically organized message threads are the comb's teeth. The branching model imposes a tree structure on message threads. A response to a message can be designated as the start of a new thread; its responses are consequently attached to it rather than identified as part of the original thread. Each message structure encourages a different cognitive map of a computer conference, and mastery of the underlying model may be crucial to effective participation. As Rapaport (1991) asserts, "A user needs to understand the particulars of this logical structure as it pertains to his or her environment" (p. 116).

Given these differences, it may be unwise to treat all e-mail or conferencing systems as functionally equivalent. Message delivery systems can vary in ease of use and design assumptions about message functions and structures. These variations could condition connectivity impacts and other outcomes of e-mail. It is an overreaction to assume that no results generalize across systems; on the other hand, it is overly optimistic to assume that system differences are always unimportant.

Poole, Holmes, Watson, and DeSanctis (1993) identify the same dilemma in another context of new technology research, that of group decision support systems (GDSS): "If two GDSSs differ in some aspects of design, philosophy, and configuration of features, can results from studies on the two be generalized to the 'GDSS' genre, or must they be considered independent because of technological differences?" (p. 178). E-mail researchers should take note of the solution advocated by these authors and by Poole, Holmes, and Watson (1991). They suggest decomposing the feature-to-impact relationships of the technology in question. This requires that researchers (a) produce a general model consisting of a list of hypotheses about possible impacts of the technology and the features responsible for these impacts, (b) identify the features present in the specific system under study in order to identify the impacts that should result, and (c) determine whether the predicted impacts occurred and modify the general model in accordance with the results. This approach is intended to aid in the cumulation of results across systems and to help in the determination of which features of a technology produce various outcomes. It may also help clarify inconsistent results across studies.

E-Mail Is a Genre
of Written Communication

One important social impact neglected by Garton and Wellman is the role of e-mail in new genres of organizational discourse. Communicative genres are "recognized types of communication characterized by structural, linguistic, and substantive conventions" (Yates & Orlikowski, 1992). Garton and Wellman's review comprises research essentially unconcerned with linguistic features of e-mail content. They mention language only in reference to uninhibited or nonconforming behavior in e-mail. The language-oriented studies of e-mail omitted from their review tend to concentrate on linguistic features that define the genre (Black, Levin, Mehan, & Quinn, 1983; Ferrara, Brunner, & Whittemore, 1991; Murray, 1985, 1991). One weakness of these studies is their tendency to equate medium with genre; that is, to identify e-mail as a singular and consistent form of discourse and to concentrate on discourse features determined by channel constraints.

Many researchers caution against a deterministic view of media. They argue that other communicative resources may be as important as channel characteristics in shaping interaction within a medium (Poole & DeSanctis, 1990; Yates & Orlikowski, 1992). For example, Reder and Schwab's (1989) organizational media ethnography reveals the place of e-mail in a complex communicative environment characterized by multiple channels, multiple genres of task-related communication, and multichannel genres. They found that at times e-mail was a substitute for telephone and face-to-face communication, at other times it substituted for written communication, and it gave rise to "new genres . . . uniquely associated with electronic mail" (p. 183). Such attention to genre variations is one way to avoid a monolithic view of the medium.

Neither communication technologies nor discourse genres are ahistorical. Both are shaped by prior technologies and genres. One promising direction for the study of e-mail genres is the examination of the interplay of organizational environment, technology, and discourse genres over time. In her study of now-familiar technologies, Yates (1989) examined the development of the organizational memorandum at the turn of the century. She traced how industrial productivity, geographically expanding mass markets, the typewriter, carbon paper, flat file technology, and new management philosophies converged to shape the emergence of the modern organizational memorandum. Her impressive combination of social, technical, and communication history does much to reveal, by contrast, the simplistic nature of our experimental and contemporary field studies of organizational e-mail. Although her study has the advantage of the perspective provided by intervening decades, the same theoretical and methodological energies can be turned to current changes in organizational media. Yates and Orlikowski (1992) argue that studies of genre evolution can illuminate relationships between genre and medium and provide a means for examining "reciprocal and recursive relationships between media and communication in organizations over time" (p. 310).

CONCLUSION

I have examined various visions of e-mail here in order to reveal their influences on research efforts and to suggest alternative directions for future research. Of course, e-mail is all of these things: tool, message delivery system, social object, and discourse genre. These visions are separated in research only for clarity and convenience. The lack of cohesion among the perspectives is troubling to some, and the need for further theoretical development and integration has been noted before (Fulk & Boyd, 1991). Yet it is neither possible nor necessary to integrate the four conceptions of e-mail into an encompassing theory of e-mail and its impacts. Simple recognition of the diverse interpretive frameworks can enhance future research.

I have noted a number of possible research directions in this commentary. Those who conceive of e-mail as a tool might examine the task-artifact cycle and the homology of e-mail and popular management philosophies. Researchers concerned with the social meaning of e-mail could push down to the micro level of negotiation of that meaning in everyday talk and push up to the level of futurist discourses that permeate popular culture. Scholars who frame e-mail as a message delivery system could refine models of feature-to-impact relationships. Investigators of e-mail as a genre of discourse could identify important differences of form and content between subgenres of e-mail and explore the reciprocal interdependence of medium and genre.

The alternative directions I have suggested here share a common purpose: to move us beyond the linear causal models of media choice and media effects evident in Garton and Wellman's review. The suggestions are intended to encourage complexity in e-mail research. E-mail scholarship should be founded on reciprocal, recursive, and refined models. E-mail is becoming more pervasive and complex; if we are to keep pace with its rapid diffusion and evolution, our theories and methods must evolve as well.

NOTE

1. The metaphors "e-mail is a community infrastructure" and "e-mail is a surveillance tool" are omitted from this discussion. The first is beyond the scope of this essay because its focus on social uses of e-mail de-emphasizes questions of organizational impacts; it is reflected, however, in the research on e-mail and communication networks in organizations. The second metaphor is omitted because it appears most often in contexts of constitutional law and policy analysis.

REFERENCES

Black, S. D., Levin, J. A., Mehan, H., & Quinn, C. N. (1983). Real and non-real time interaction: Unraveling multiple threads of discourse. *Discourse Processes, 6,* 59-75.

Brummett, B. (1988). The homology hypothesis: Pornography on the VCR. *Critical Studies in Mass Communication, 5,* 202-216.

Bødker, S. (1991). *Through the interface: A human activity approach to user interface design.* Hillsdale, NJ: Lawrence Erlbaum.

Carroll, J. M., Kellogg, W. A., & Rosson, M. B. (1991). The task-artifact cycle. In J. M. Carroll (Ed.), *Designing interaction: Psychology at the human-computer interface* (pp. 74-102). Cambridge: Cambridge University Press.

Churbuck, D. (1991, January 7). Bozo filters: Screening software for electronic mail. *Forbes,* p. 286.

Contractor, N. S., & Eisenberg, E. M. (1990). Communication networks and new media in organizations. In J. Fulk & C. W. Steinfield (Eds.), *Organizations and communication technology* (pp. 143-172). Newbury Park, CA: Sage.

Culnan, M. J., & Markus, M. L. (1987). Information technologies. In F. Jablin, L. L. Putnam, K. Roberts, & L. Porter (Eds.), *Handbook of organizational communication* (pp. 420-443). Newbury Park, CA: Sage.

Daft, R. L., & Lengel, R. H. (1986). Organizational information requirements, media richness and structural design. *Management Science, 32,* 554-571.

Daft, R. L., Lengel, R. H., & Trevino, L. K. (1987). Message equivocality, media selection, and manager performance: Implications for information systems. *MIS Quarterly, 11,* 355-366.

Danowski, J. A. (1991). Organizational media theory. In J. A. Anderson (Ed.), *Communication yearbook 14* (pp. 187-207). Newbury Park, CA: Sage.

de Sola Pool, I. (1983). *Forecasting the telephone: A retrospective technology assessment.* Norwood, NJ: Ablex.

Ferrara, K., Brunner, H., & Whittemore, G. (1991). Interactive written discourse as an emergent register. *Written Communication, 8,* 8-34.

Finlay, M. (1987). *Powermatics: A discursive critique of new communications technology.* New York: Routledge & Kegan Paul.

Fitzgerald, M. (1994, February 7). Videoconferencing catches on. *Computerworld,* p. 41.

Fulk, J., & Boyd, B. (1991). Emerging theories of communication in organizations. *Journal of Management, 17,* 407-446.

Fulk, J., Schmitz, J., & Steinfield, C. W. (1990). A social influence model of technology use. In J. Fulk & C. W. Steinfield (Eds.), *Organizations and communication technology* (pp. 117-140). Newbury Park, CA: Sage.

King, S. S., & Cushman, D. P. (Eds.). (1994). *High speed management and organizational communication in the 1990's.* Albany: State University of New York Press.

Korzenny, F. (1978). A theory of electronic propinquity: Mediated communication in organizations. *Communication Research, 5,* 3-23.

Kuutti, K., & Arvonen, T. (1992). Identifying potential CSCW applications by means of activity theory concepts: A case example. In J. Turner & R. Kraut (Eds.), *CSCW 92 proceedings: Sharing perspectives* (pp. 233-240). New York: Association for Computing Machinery.

Ligus, R. G. (1993, November-December). Enterprise agility: Maneuverability and turbo power. *Industrial Management,* p. 27.

Murray, D. E. (1985). Composition as conversation: The computer terminal as medium of communication. In L. Odell & D. Goswami (Eds.), *Writing in nonacademic settings* (pp. 203-227). New York: Guilford.

Murray, D. E. (1991). The composing process for computer conversation. *Written Communication, 8,* 35-55.

Norman, D. A. (1991). Cognitive artifacts. In J. M. Carroll (Ed.), *Designing interaction: Psychology at the human-computer interface* (pp. 17-38). Cambridge: Cambridge University Press.

Pearl, J. A. (1993). The E-mail quandary. *Management Review, 82*(7), 48-51.

Poole, M. S., & DeSanctis, G. (1990). Understanding the use of group decision support systems: The theory of adaptive structuration. In J. Fulk & C. W. Steinfield (Eds.), *Organizations and communication technology* (pp. 173-193). Newbury Park, CA: Sage.

Poole, M. S., Holmes, M. E., & Watson, R. (1991). Conflict management in a computer-supported meeting environment. *Management Science, 8,* 926-953.

Poole, M. S., Holmes, M. E., Watson, R., & DeSanctis, G. (1993). Group decision support systems and group communication: A comparison of decision making in computer-supported and non-supported groups. *Communication Research, 20,* 176-213.

Rapaport, M. (1991). *Computer mediated communications.* New York: John Wiley.

Reder, S., & Schwab, R. G. (1989). The communicative economy of the workgroup: Multi-channel genres of communication. *Office: Technology and People, 4,* 177-195.

Rice, R. E., Grant, A. E., Schmitz, J., & Torobin, J. (1990). Individual and network influences on the adoption and perceived outcomes of electronic messaging. *Social Networks, 12,* 27-55.

Schmitz, J., & Fulk, J. (1991). Organizational colleagues, media richness, and electronic mail. *Communication Research, 18,* 487-523.

Short, J., Williams, E., & Christie, B. (1986). *The social psychology of telecommunications.* London: John Wiley.

Yates, J. (1989). The emergence of the memo as a managerial genre. *Management Communication Quarterly, 2,* 454-484.

Yates, J., & Orlikowski, W. J. (1992). Genres of organizational communication: A structurational approach to studying communication and media. *Academy of Management Review, 17,* 299-326.

Winograd, T. (1987-1988). A language/action perspective on the design of cooperative work. *Human-Computer Interaction, 3,* 3-30.

21 A Kinder, Gentler Discipline: Feeling Good About Being Mediocre

MICHAEL BURGOON
University of Arizona

This essay offers challenges to currently popular schools of thought in the discipline of communication. The argument is made that research and teaching, whether allied with groups claiming to be anywhere on the political spectrum from critical theory to the communication sciences, has become imbued with a political ideology that wrongheadedly defines communication competence as behaviors that value the collective over the individual. Such definitions also value congeniality above all else. It is further suggested that now accepted definitions of communication competence proscribe what is acceptable or unacceptable scholarship. Such political hegemony has led to the premature abandonment of lines of research that provide insights on how communication can be used as a tool of social policy, allowing ideas and people to be judged on the basis of intellectual merit rather than the political correctness of positions advocated.

L ET me begin by saying that I am *not* by nature a quiet man. But I too believe in a kinder, gentler world, where one can feel good about being mediocre. Some believe that if such a philosophy is acceptable for the largest democracy in the world, then perhaps it ought to be good enough for the discipline of communication. I shall argue that our theoretical predilections, ideological predispositions, and most of all our discipline's dominant social scientific research prescriptions form the Holy Trinity that allows us to live in

AUTHOR'S NOTE: I am deeply indebted to two of my friends and colleagues whose constant interest in and conversation about my work enrich my intellectual life. Dr. Calvin Morrill, a sociologist educated at Harvard but now on the faculty of the Department of Sociology at the University of Arizona, frequently guides me to the words and works of people smarter than me, who have already said better than I can what I really want to say. Dr. William Bailey, my sometimes coauthor and coconspirator, came to the desert from Northwestern University sometime around the Pleistocene epoch. He is a man of immense knowledge and uncommon common sense who comforts me, because most of what is happening in this field makes no more sense to him than it does to me. Although both have greatly influenced me, they should remain blameless for the thoughts contained in this chapter; what is said here is what I wanted to say.

Correspondence and requests for reprints: Michael Burgoon, Department of Communication, University of Arizona, Tucson, AZ 85721.

Communication Yearbook 18, pp. 464-479

that kinder, gentler disciplinary world. But I will certainly not embrace that world with any kind of enthusiasm.[1]

Those of us who have haunted the corridors and meeting rooms of convention hotels and perused our journals for the past quarter century or so know that the questions of "whither" or "whether" communication theory have been asked in some form for a very long time. Thus this essay is only one of many that have attempted to take stock of questions about the state of theoretical development and/or dominant scholarly directions in the discipline. However, I am not going to repeat the shibboleths frequently offered up about the dearth of theories of human communication, even though that is probably what some might expect. In fact, I am going to depart from that particular "party line" for a moment and offer a digression about the question of "whether" theory before mounting my offensive on the "whither" issue.

I found myself agreeing with almost everything Charles Berger (1991) had to say in the *Communication Monographs* Chautauqua titled "Why Are There So Few Communication Theories?" However, I would add a disclaimer to the general discussion about our lack of identifiable theories in this field. We may be relatively unsuccessful in developing "grand theories" of human communication, or for that matter ineffective at even developing names, labels, or acronyms for our theoretical positions that garner attention widely in this discipline or even marginally creep into the lexicon of other social sciences. However, the bulk of the research in this discipline is driven more by theory now than in the recent past. Clearly variable-analytic efforts earlier disparaged by others as "dustbowl empiricism," or maybe in this field we should now say "Country Roads/Mountain Mama data crunching," no longer entitle one to admittance as a Brahmin in our own normative-status-driven professional caste system. So we are making theoretical progress much in the same way normal sciences progress. Albeit slow by any measure or yardstick, the values and standards are "a changin'." Thus I am less concerned about this question of "whether" than are some others.

Rather, the concerns that are of paramount interest to me have their genesis in two recent articles, "Strangers in a Strange Land" (Burgoon, 1992) and "PC at Last! PC at Last!" (Burgoon & Bailey, 1992). The position advanced in these essays is rather simple to articulate: the discipline of communication has taken a far left-of-center turn in terms of the guiding political philosophy that imbues our present scholarly attempts. We have embraced a mutant, and continually mutating, Marxist-like philosophical stance toward what communication behavior *ought* be that limits the domain of scholarly discourse and proscribes what are acceptable and unacceptable lines of inquiry. I will advance more of that argument later in the chapter, but this is the argument, in a nutshell, that I will advance.

In those two articles, critical theorists in general, and the postmodernists specifically, were exempted from my attack because I thought they were just the obvious target. The leftist political leanings of much of that kind of discourse is apparent to all. I wanted then, and still do, to focus my frontal assault on the politicalization of the social scientific study of what we now call interpersonal communication. However, I do have some comments to make about the "isms" and "ists" now present in this discipline and many others that can be arrayed on some sort of recognizable political continuum for the purposes of this discussion.

THE POLITICAL LEANINGS
AND MEANINGS OF VARIOUS "ISMs" AND "ISTs"

People interested in the political sociology of this particular discipline have erred in lumping several disparate groups with very different social goals and rhetorics into the category of politically correct groups with a supposed leftist liberal social-political agenda. I do not think all of the groups representing "isms" and populated with "ists" even approach constituting a truly intellectual liberal hegemony. Rather, I would array these groups along a somewhat traditional right-to-left political continuum in a tripartite category scheme: fascism, opportunism, and Marxism.

It appears to me that the recent rhetoric, scholarship, and social agenda of many, but not all, associated with *specific* genres of radical feminism and Afrocentrism have little to do with the "deprivileging" of *any* voice. Rather, it appears that what is being called for is the mere substitution of one set of privileged voices with another. Such blatant attempts to shift power to specific groups are not unlike those used by other mostly right-of-center elements in any political arena. It was suggested to me that I would make my arguments much more palatable, perhaps even persuasive, to many in the discipline if I would avoid categorizing such groups as "right-wing," but rather temper my prose or couch my comments in terms of dogmatism (of the left), as social psychologists have done. Although I am sincerely grateful to those who offered such prepublication advice, I opted *not* to take that course, for I am not talking about closed-mindedness, but appropriate political ideology and strategic intent that guides the rhetoric and behavior of these groups. As such, I am uninterested in separating these kinds of self-interest from the self-interest that militant youth groups are currently using in Germany to privilege German citizens over foreign nationals. Substantive differences in rhetorical strategy are not apparent to me, but I do know that certain self-interest groups are more politically correct than others in this discipline, as well as in this country. As such, one raises howls of protest when these groups are criticized and/or compared to rhetorical movements that appear to be very similar in goals, actions, and behaviors. However, I am not overly concerned about whether my comments are well received. I also do not believe that this currently faddish concern with privilege substitution will have much real impact on the creation of knowledge within our discipline. This too shall pass.

A second group of academics are pure and simple opportunists. Indeed, if no voices are to be privileged in postmodern communication scholarship, then the mediocre, or even the sincerely stupid, have as much to say about the text (or the action) as the most able, more brilliant research scholars who have spent decades attempting to make contributions to knowledge. Cumulative knowledge is neither possible nor desirable if the text (or communication behavior) is to be totally divorced from any objective assessment. So each day is a new day for postmodern opportunists. This so-called postmodern leveling is not even very modern. The French social historian Alexis de Tocqueville wrote in 1834 in *Democracy in America* that "there is indeed a manly and legitimate passion for equality which rouses in all men a desire to be strong and respected. This passion tends to elevate the little man to the rank of the great. But the human heart also nourishes a debased taste for equality which leads the weak to want to drag the strong down to their level" (Mayer, 1969, p. 57). As one can see, in 1834 we had not yet desexed the language of the intelligentsia.

Critiques can appear in outlets like *Communication Education* telling us that we should not "privilege our voices as teachers by telling others what we have learned," but rather we can all exist in this age of mediocrity and teach other folks to feel good about themselves and this new community of equals we will create. I note with some (no, make that much) amusement that some of the folks who were around in the late sixties and early seventies to lead us down the "garden path" of experiential learning now call themselves critical theorists or postmodernists. I did not think they had much to say then and believe that they have merely found a new forum for not saying much now. Again, all of this is not exactly modern or postmodern, as Tocqueville spoke of our educational system more than 150 years ago when he claimed that a "middling standard has been established in America for all human knowledge. All minds come near to it, some by raising and some by lowering their standards" (Mayer, 1969, pp. 55-56). Perhaps we in communication are only now catching up with the analysis of the insightful Frenchman of the first part of the nineteenth century. It would not be the first time we have lagged a bit behind in "things."

However, I take none of these disciplinary voices very seriously either. The vested self-interest of opportunism is apparent to all so as to make these folks pretty unthreatening to the continuation of knowledge creation (and probably privilege) in this and most other disciplines. So I guess the opportunists land somewhere in the middle of my political continuum, flipping here and flopping there.

But there are groups to the left of center intellectually and politically that *are* having an impact on the discipline. Clearly, postmodern deconstructivists who free the text from any meaning, save that of the *in situ* interpretivist, are not unlike the proponents of Marxism, now mostly institutionalized in academia, or of Karl Marx, himself. If one exempts Marx's economic theory, his writings, like those of most critical theorists of the deconstruction type, have no plan, are devoid of much contact with any sort of present reality, and offer little more than negative critiques of what currently exists. The conundrum yet unfaced by communication practitioners with postmodern leanings is that they do not yet recognize, as did Marx, that certain voices will continue to be privileged. Marx allowed as how the intellectual elite would have to remain in privileged positions when the proletariat gained power. Lenin, Stalin, and Mao understood this position on privileged voices well as they justified their means by always pointing to the supposed end result of equality to come. Perhaps we will have to come to grips with that same sort of privilege question if present-day critical theorists and/or postmodernists prevail in this discipline.

The other group that I have been willing to label as guided by a political philosophy far to the left of center is one that came as a surprise to most who read my previous essays: that is the group of empirically trained social scientists whose primary interest is interpersonal communication.

POLITICAL IDEOLOGY AND SCIENTIFIC
RESEARCH IN INTERPERSONAL COMMUNICATION

Perhaps the most efficacious manner in which to proceed is to articulate carefully the previously published (Burgoon & Bailey, 1992) self-examination questions that must be answered satisfactorily before one can proclaim that our research in interpersonal communication, as a whole, is guided by a dominant left-of-center political ideology. In the original essays, our discussion focused on three questions about our scholarly efforts in an attempt to illuminate the political biases present in our social scientific research efforts. I shall repeat those questions and examples for the purposes of discussion in this essay.

The First General Question

Are our scholarly efforts sufficiently guided, even proscribed, by some ideological doctrine that clearly establishes what is acceptable for admission in the domain of scholarly discourse? That general question prompts several follow-up interrogatories: (a) Are there clear and agreed-upon conceptual boundaries delimiting what is acceptable for scrutiny and what is not? (b) Have we progressed to the state where extant data have very little impact on what we choose to conclude or even consider? (c) Are our assumptions about appropriateness sufficiently rigid so as to preclude lines of inquiry that might, in fact, challenge those said ideological assumptions? And (d) Are appropriate and dependable surveillance mechanisms in place to prevent the incursion on our scholarly discourse by patently disagreeable notions?

I believe that most active communication researchers with a social science orientation would eschew the notion that their research is guided, let alone controlled, by political ideology. However, at the risk of being redundant both within this chapter and with previously published essays, it can be argued that most, if not all, of the allied social sciences are currently anchored in an ideology that is politically left of center. Thus I would argue with the so-called critical theorists' claims that science is an oppressive enterprise with a rightist orientation that seeks to maintain the privilege of some amorphous ruling class of intellectuals. Rather, social sciences in general, and communication in particular, have embraced a Marxist orientation that glorifies the collective while diminishing the importance of the individual. I dismiss as false consciousness the claim that empirical research in communication is, at present, ideologically pure or value neutral. These self-same researchers are not aware of the hegemony that dominates their own investigations.

Although, as I said, I could make the point solely by my focus above on the so-called critical theorists or postmodern deconstructionists as living proof of our claim that the discipline has drifted markedly left of center, that would be too easy. Instead, I wish to deal with, if not challenge, the dominant paradigm of research in communication. Few would argue with the claim that interpersonal communication has emerged as a preeminent, even glamorous, area of research in this discipline. However, it might not be apparent to all that this supposedly scientific, empirical, objective content domain in fact operates with all of the restrictions, inhibitions, and failures accruing to what I contend is a rather ubiquitous conceptual mooring closely resembling the tenets of Marxist thinking.

The entire human relations approach, which I believe that most in the interpersonal communication camp have embraced, makes certain assumptions about how things *ought* be, and then uses and abuses the epistemologies of science to promulgate what are statements only slightly removed from the status of myth. As has been argued elsewhere, the kind of thinking that brought us participative management spawned a school of organizational communication that is, in fact, prescriptively injunctive about how prosocial managers ought be (Burgoon, 1992; Burgoon & Bailey, 1992). The good of the group or organization is presumed to override the concerns of the individual, and we have in fact come dangerously close to accepting the premise that individual needs can be met only through the establishment of healthy, functioning work groups and organizations.

The fact that little, if any, data have ever been offered in support of such a human relations approach is of little concern. The kind of thinking that democratized the classroom, probably concomitantly decreased actual learning, and made student satisfaction the prime dependent variable in the world of higher education was born of this human relations movement. This human relations approach, with the same ideological assumptions about the desirability of prosocial behaviors, forms the basic paradigm of interpersonal communication. The prototypical competent communicator is described as open, warm, caring, and so on. He or she is presumed capable of successfully fostering group communication and satisfies everyone touched by his or her communication conduct.

Although such definitions of communication competence may be aesthetically pleasing to many, the assumptions brought forth by people who cling to such a restrictive view of what it means to communicate effectively are so ubiquitous as to be basically unchallengeable in a political sense in this field at the moment. At present, a kind of "McCarthyism of the Left" sets the intellectual boundaries and proscribes the research domain of communication and a number of other social sciences. This intellectually socialistic dogma emphasizes the good of the collective being met by politically correct communication behaviors that are inherently prosocial in orientation and outcome. Social scientists who believe that such a view of interpersonal communication is sheer nonsense have been generally unwilling to challenge such "do-gooder" programs of research in any meaningful way lest their comments be termed impolite, uncivil, or, in some cases, rhetorical excess.

Intellectual and scientific challenges have been advanced against what I have called a kind of "secular humanism" in the social sciences (Burgoon, 1992). Parks (1982) and Bochner (1982) (although I am not sure, given Art Bochner's recent written revelations that he would stick to his position of a decade ago) offered to the folks studying interpersonal communication the kinds of challenges that are warranted, with little impact on the research that followed in the next decade. In fact, such challenges are often treated as little more than literary curios that cannot be allowed to stem the tide of empirical research and data collection, tautologically reaffirming our notions of good while simply ignoring the bad.

I have already provided a detailed examination of the impact of such ideological pressures on the currently quite faddish concern with the health communication context that bears repeating here (Burgoon, 1992). I argued that although such political ideologies may not have done any real harm in many interpersonal communication contexts, the same cannot be said of the medical context, "where the only models [statistical] that make any sense are probit models with 'Dead/Not Dead' as the prime dependent measures." Concerns for increased patient satisfaction, patient empowerment, and patient self-efficacy are labeled as mostly misguided efforts to fit the dominant human relations/ interpersonal communication paradigm on a context that is clearly noninterpersonal in all ways, shapes, and forms. I also claimed that commonly held assumptions by interpersonal communication researchers concerning communicator style, warmth, prosocial communication strategies, and peerlike relationships may not only be uncharacteristic of the clinical practice of medicine, but any attempt to *change* the situation to fit the conceptual preferences and political ideology of our interpersonal communication brethren is foolish.

If one examines the relevant health communication research literature, it is clear that the bulk of behavioral scientists' efforts is based upon some version of the following set of ideological assumptions: (a) The clinical medicine context is best conceptualized as some sort of communication transaction in which a caregiver is advised to make the care receiver feel good about the situation, the provider, and the patient, if we can still use such a stigmatizing term; (b) the care receivers are always presumed to be motivated to gain all the information they can, or if they are not currently so motivated, then it is the task of the competent physician to provide that motivation, usually through some increased amount of sensitive interpersonal communication; (c) it follows then that noncompliance, which is obviously a major concern, is a communication problem inextricably linked to failures of the physician to accomplish a and b above, that is, to satisfy the interpersonal needs of the patient while providing sufficient information *and* motivation to ensure action. It is not much of a stretch to suggest that the above are not much different from a Marxist interpretation of managers' rights and obligations vis-à-vis the proletariat.

An equally careful examination of the *data* would reveal that these guiding assumptions are based on a model of the world that has little isomorphism with objective reality. The voluminous body of research relating to patient satisfaction consistently finds that (a) most people are relatively satisfied with their physicians, and (b) the correlation between satisfaction with any element in the health care context and compliance is not significantly different from zero. Moreover, there is absolutely no evidence to suggest that so-called open communication styles of the physician, the interpersonal nature of the physician-patient interaction, or any conveniently collected measures of satisfaction are at all correlated with objective measures of health status. It would not be unreasonable, then, to conclude that noncompliance is likely not a problem that will be solved by any of the behaviors mandated by what has been called the interpersonal communication school of thought. Thus the extant empirical evidence is strikingly disappointing to devotees of this communication-centered approach to the medical care context, yet it seems to be uninfluential in changing ideology or practice.

However, I recognized that it was a far argumentative leap from suggesting that the research evidence shows *no* effects to claiming that present communication behaviors in the clinical practice of medicine are harmful. Such an argumentative leap is based upon some simple premises. The first premise advanced was that the primary concerns of medical communication researchers should focus on compliance, objective health status, and, ultimately, morbidity-mortality rates. Any direct link between communication and those criterion variables is of obvious import. Any secondary lags from communication to patient satisfaction, and a host of other variables commonly studied, must obviously be causally linked to one of more of these outcome variables (and back to communication), or be deemed perhaps interesting, but technically trivial and scientifically unimportant. That does not mean that I do not recognize that there are multiple communication goals and potential outcomes present in the clinical practice of medicine. Rather, I do argue that some goals and outcomes require more primary research attention than others.

One line of reasoning that I have advanced strongly suggests that the human relations approach to medical care may be correlated with, if not deterministically responsible for, declines in patient compliance. To elaborate, few would deny that this social marketing/human relations approach, replete with ideological constraints, has been thrust upon the medical profession with some force from a number of disciplines and a variety of funding agencies for the past two decades. However, concomitant with such efforts, we have witnessed an increasing, not decreasing, rate of noncompliance with suggested medical regimens and proposed disease prevention protocols. Moreover, even with dramatic cultural-level changes in the amount of available health information and concern for wellness, there have been unremarkable changes in objective health status of the population.

Most in this discipline would consider it absurd to suggest any causal link between the human relations approach to medicine and such dire outcomes— sort of a "killing them with kindness" argument. However, those same people are more than willing to argue for untenable stochastic links between their prescriptive views of how physicians ought to behave and some sort of social *good.* Again, this is a case of ideological rigidity overriding empirical evidence, or just plain good sense.

Another form of argument would point to extant evidence, not easily ignored, but just the same roundly dismissed. This suggests that noncompliers are most responsive to verbally aggressive physicians. In that same vein, different kinds of research would be completed if this discipline conceptualized the context of medical treatment as a noninterpersonal situation in which status differentials are maximized, perceptions of control and sanction are preeminent, social distance is established, and doctor-patient communication is examined from the perspective of how compliance-gaining strategies are used by powerful physicians plying their trade, all in the name of increased benefit to patients.

Although I drew heavily on an ideological analysis of but one subfield, doctor-patient communication, I could have selected any of a number of research areas to illuminate the central thesis that (a) our research is guided, even controlled, by unarticulated but ever-present ideology; (b) we are relatively immune from the influence of data, especially when it does not fit our preconceptions; (c) political preference for what ought to be can prevail even in the face of evidence of potentially severe harm; and (d) we have adequate mechanisms in place to protect us from unpopular ideas. Thus we can indeed rest assured that all of this will combine to create the kinder, gentler world I spoke of at the beginning of this essay. Perhaps we will learn to feel good not only about mediocrity but also about illness, death, and disease as the price to pay for maintaining "civil" communication behaviors.

The Second General Question

Does political ideology determine what is reality? The new leftist scholarly agenda often rejects the traditional, commonsense notion of an objective reality, and therefore rejects also the notion of external value-free criteria by which the truth or falsity of discourse can be judged. Instead, reality is socially constructed through language, and the dominant culture's ideology is imbued in that reality.

Such an analytic perspective is distinctly European, taking its program from hermeneutics (Burgoon & Bailey, 1992). In the previously published political correctness article ("PC at Last!"), Bill Bailey and I attempted to analyze the politics of the sixties and seventies that brought us to our present state of affairs in the study of interpersonal communication. Some of those arguments are worth repeating here.

As social reality is constituted in and through language, a major PC program is the control of language. That control takes two forms: control in the form of language deconstruction necessary to lay bare ideological bias and oppression (e.g., Lakoff, 1975), and control in the form of the language construction necessary to the emancipation of the oppressed. In this view, desexing the language is a program to reconstruct "reality" in ways more favorable to females. Efforts to regulate hate speech are a program to reconstruct "reality" to benefit a broader minority base. We bought from whole cloth the notion that we can rename a problem out of existence.

Albeit not always knowingly, interpersonal communication research and theory have from their beginnings been guided by collectivist concerns, whatever the question. In any historical account, the initial academic interests in interpersonal communication must be ascribed, in some large measure, to the influence of the Palo Alto group. The relationship between that group's interest in communication and insanity and the present political leanings of the communication discipline is by no means a chance occurrence.

The clinical/therapeutic orientation of early interpersonal communication studies did much to dissipate the then extant standards of objectivity in social science. Gregory Bateson (1960) postulated two universes: the Newtonian universe of object and the communication universe, in which there were no objects, only messages. Consequently, sanity was no longer a matter of being in contact with objective reality, and insanity was the consequence of being in contact with crazy and crazy-making messages (Bateson, Jackson, Haley, & Weakland, 1956). With such formulations, Bateson and his colleagues flew into the very teeth of medical science and physiological models of insanity.

Watzlawick, Beavin, and Jackson (1967) further pushed back the frontiers of objectivity with their conception of individual communication behavior as an expression of a communication system, typically a family. Because individual behavior was an excrescence of the system, individual intentionality and meaning could have no role in communication study. Consequently, the field did not see that Watzlawick et al. had anticipated later hermeneutic scholars who were to cut the text free from all historical accidents of authorship, situation, and purpose, thus making *any* form of meaning obsolete (e.g., Branham & Pearce, 1985; Ricoeur, 1973).

Watzlawick et al. may be forgiven if, at this early time, they did not yet see the political advantage of dissolving individual consciousness into the universal solvent, linguistic intersubjectivity (Niklas, 1984). The mantra these authors gave to communication students of the sixties and seventies—Thou canst not

not communicate!—should not be underestimated in effect. It, perhaps more than anything else, demonstrated to communication scholars that individual epistemic processes and psychological projection (although excluded from meaning!) were nevertheless to be studied as equivalent to overt social behavior. (Although fortunately too late to reverse social progress, recent disclaimers have been made; see Bavelas, 1990; Motley, 1990.) This equivalency represents a major deconstruction of objectivist reality, the closest equating of fantasy and reality yet achieved by social constructivism. It appears that the study of schizophrenia begat a kind of schizophrenic analysis. On the one hand, the collective is presumed to be etiology of meaning; on the other hand, no voice is privileged above any other in decoding and interpreting all behavior. Subjectivity reigned in a way that would make Marx proud. I would argue that Michael Motley (1990), while making an important attempt to set the record straight in regard to the Palo Alto group, missed the mark in that ideologues were setting the boundaries for communication study that would be harmful for two decades or more. Those who have chimed in with some esoteric debate on the role of intent in communication seem equally oblivious to the political ideology promulgated by this influential research group. Far more important questions than intent were raised in this early work by Watzlawick et al.

It remained for R. D. Laing, himself steeped in Marxist theory and the philosophy of Watzlawick et al., to deconstruct the politics of experience (Laing, 1967) and of the family (Laing, 1969). Such deconstruction revealed that the oppressive forces behind madness were the broader sociopolitical and economic forces of the system. Madness was madness only when viewed outside of its generating system; put back into the context of the schizophrenogenic family, a microcosm of the insane society, the communication made good sense (Laing & Esterson, 1964). In brief, Laing and his colleagues taught communication that the madness of the system was its politics.

Simultaneously, the rhetoric of the sixties and the seventies—"Let it all hang out," and "If it feels good, do it!"—directly fueled interpersonal communication's deconstruction of social praxis. Rational discourse was deconstructed to be the bane of the campus and the main weapon of the oppressive establishment.

Ever relevant and current, communication met the challenge. In communication classrooms and journals, Openness and its reciprocal, Receptivity, became god-terms. If the politics of activism required that the substance of the private individual was to be traded for the transparency of public self-disclosure (Jourard, 1964), interpersonal communication was equal to the task. Even occasional feelings of self-consciousness on the part of reactionaries or revisionists quickly dissipated in the redundant, interrogative echoes of Rogerian summaries (Rogers, 1951) (e.g., "You're feeling confused because you killed your mother and raped her dog? in that order?").

In the complementarity of boundless psychological striptease and indifferent psychological voyeurism, interpersonal communication reached its political zenith. Not much had not been hung out; little that had felt good had not been done. And so, receptive and positive toward all things plural and different, antagonistic toward singularity and hegemony, communication arrived in the eighties politically correct, and wholly unaware of it. Family bliss, secular cities, corporate solvency, national mental and physical health, and world peace—it was but a matter of time before the Mary Poppinses of the communication world achieved it all, and with a mere spoonful of sensitivity to make the compromise go down. I give all of the credit for the colorful and delightful language in the above to my friend and colleague Bill Bailey, but his politics and mine lead us to the same conclusions.

We were prepared for the eighties and hardly blinked when Carol Gilligan (1982) told us of different voices. Moral development, nurturance, responsibility, and relationship were already a part of our conversational and professional topoi. Perhaps the feminization of communication even preceded the feminization of Gilligan herself. Communication had already accepted the mother figure of a kinder, gentler discipline, although some thought it more analogous to submitting to the discipline of Nurse Ratched.

As alert to social trends and political ideology as communication was, the discipline soon found that all of the questions that could be asked of a politically guided discipline had not yet been posed.

The Third General Question

Have old concerns and commitments been jettisoned to live in the New Order? About the time our leftist political orientation solidified its hold on the discipline, and communication discovered its true self, holding such sociopolitically liberal tenets became more difficult. The let-it-all-hang-out variety of freedom of speech, which had worked so well in dismantling the bourgeois morality, paved the way to letting more hang out than was politically desirable in mass media. Explicitly violent and sexually degrading treatment of women, deconstructed as a mode of masculine social control, was obviously not politically "sensitive." Such material was deemed obscene and censorship became more attractive to many.

Another censorship issue, the banning of "hate speech," especially on campuses, found favor with some very liberal thinkers. Even some old liberals who cheered the *New York Times v. Sullivan* (1964) decision opined that it was a good law for its day, but times had changed. The argument advanced is that the college campus has always been a haven for rational discourse, at least for the last four or five years. Why should not irrational hate speech be banned? Such speech is a mere assault, according to one argument (Sunstein, 1991), and not different from an obscene phone call. Many traditional conservatives, always happy to embrace reason and discipline, and those groups I earlier arrayed on the right edge of my modified political continuum may also find a new attraction in such censorship of communication. Indeed, our politics have created strange bedfellows and forced us all to endure the ancient Chinese curse: We do live in interesting times.

WHITHER THOU (WE) GOEST, I KNOW NOT

It has always appeared to me that Robert Altman and Francis Ford Coppola are magnificent directors whose major flaw is that they just cannot figure out how to end their films. I am perplexed by that same problem in attempting to bring this essay to its close.

On the one hand, my friend and mentor the late Gerald Miller and I argued that thinking and research in this discipline follows a pendulumlike motion, with periods of certain kinds of research being preeminent for a time, only to be followed by a return to what was temporarily not in vogue (Burgoon & Miller, 1990). My own personal read on the situation is that postmodernism, critical theory, or whatever label one wishes to apply to the intellectual barbarism and nihilism that has so affected disciplines traditionally associated with the humanities (e.g., the study of literature), is having less real impact on disciplines like communication and sociology. To use a metaphor of contemporary import, given the not-so-distant in the recent past natural disasters in Florida and Hawaii, the eye of the storm missed us and we have just been bruised and brushed a bit by the trailing edge of the destructive winds.

Although not in any way politically correct, I believe that there *are* canonical texts in literature. I also believe that such canons will survive the contemporary call for the elimination of such thought. The strident insistence on replacement of same with "diversity and multiculturalism" is probably little more than a swing of the same kind of pendulum that Miller and I discussed. It is my position that this field also contains canonical texts, derived from classical rhetorical studies and contemporary social science research, that will survive and prosper long after the present cast of characters answers their final professional curtain call. So I am not overly exercised about what I have called the currently faddish postmodern movement. That is, undoubtedly, because I do not take it very seriously.

On the other hand, I am not so sanguine about the ultimate outcome of our present fascination with social science research in interpersonal communication. It is probably abundantly clear that I am convinced that focusing on a large range of criterion measures assuming cooperation and caring are "good" and competition or using various forms of strategic communication are things we can learn not to do (e.g., relational satisfaction, self-esteem enhancement, patient empowerment, participative decision making, interpersonal solidarity, and much conflict resolution research) is evidence of our political, collectivist orientations and horribly misguided.

Because it may be less clear, let me state directly that I also believe we have prematurely jettisoned important lines of inquiry simply because we have been in a rush to divorce ourselves from an established discipline like experimental social psychology. When persuasion became a political "devil-word" in the sixties, associated with control, maintenance of the establishment, and often unethical communication behavior, we were quick to abandon several lines of fruitful research in social influence. Another premature death in this discipline has been proclaimed by many, but none quite so forcefully as the eminent textbook writer Daniel O'Keefe (1990), when he told us that learning theories are no longer of much interest or use to communication people. I should note that this is the same O'Keefe who, a decade or so earlier, gave last rites to all of logical positivism.

These are but examples of premature abandonment of as yet unmined veins of scholarly inquiry that still should be front and center stage in this discipline. Our insecurities about the accuracy of purely political assaults on our concern with applied social influence research, coupled with our understandable desire to "stake out" our own disciplinary boundaries, did separate us from social psychology, and I fear interpersonal communication studies became little more than the pop psychology of "feeling good" in the process.

My problem is, simply stated, making people understand that I think much social science research in communication is guided and constrained by a ubiquitous political ideology that is invisible to the participants (researchers) engaged in the process. The people I most want to reach think they are already members of the choir, and that science has been their salvation. It has not!

It is not acceptable for social scientists to behave as if everyone can continually operate in win-win situations, decide that we ought to have happiness and/ or satisfaction (by whatever label we name our criterion measures), operate as the sole or even primary outcomes of most or all communication transactions, or proceed as if prosocial behaviors are usually superior to other kinds of communication. Yet many ongoing programmatic social science efforts in interpersonal communication, implicitly or explicitly, proffer such operating assumptions. Instantiating such research as the dominant scientific paradigm in this discipline is our own particular, and peculiar, way of deprivileging voices who wish to quarrel with what I have argued is this now pervasive definition of the competent communicator.

To continue to do so is to participate in the systematic elimination of excellence in this society, as Alexis de Tocqueville argued would be the hallmark of American democracy. Perhaps excellence is obtainable only through privileged voices who become very, very good at contingent reinforcement, analysis, control, and influence. Although our democratic values proclaim people to be equal under the law, there is little reason to believe that people either are born or develop to be intellectual or social equals; people have and will continue to have disparate amounts and kinds of power that will influence all kinds of human behavior, including communication. Thus I find no great comfort in our disciplinary efforts to make communication (and the world) into a "level playing field" for all. If we deceive people into believing that equal they are, and equal they must remain, then we commit the ultimate cruelty in the name of kindness: namely, allowing people to feel good about being at the Golden Mean, which may be no more than being mediocre.

NOTE

1. I wish to make it clear that I have liberally used passages, some edited and some not, of my own previously published work in this chapter (Burgoon, 1992; Burgoon & Bailey, 1992). I do this with my own permission as well as that of Bill Bailey. This is easier to do with present word processing technology than when I had only a correcting IBM Selectric typewriter. My apologies for some redundancy to the few who might have read the two prior pieces expressing my concerns about misguided political ideology in this discipline. I would also again like to express my gratitude to Mary Anne Fitzpatrick, University of Wisconsin, and Lawrence Grossberg, University of North Carolina, for making it possible for the two earlier pieces even to appear in print. I also wish to acknowledge the willingness of the current editor of the *Communication Yearbook*, Brant Burleson, to allow me to articulate these arguments, which are not likely to be well received by many in this discipline.

REFERENCES

Bateson, G. (1960). Toward minimum requirements for a theory of schizophrenia. *Archives of Psychiatry, 2,* 477-491.

Bateson, G., Jackson, D., Haley, J., & Weakland, J. (1956). Toward a theory of schizophrenia. *Behavioral Science, 1,* 251-264.

Bavelas, J. (1990). Behaving and communicating: A reply to Motley. *Western Journal of Speech Communication, 54,* 593-602.

Berger, C. R. (1991). Communication theories and other curios. *Communication Monographs, 58,* 101-113.

Bochner, A. (1982). On the efficacy of openness in close relationships. In M. Burgoon (Ed.), *Communication yearbook 5* (pp. 109-144). New Brunswick, NJ: Transaction.

Branham, R., & Pearce, W. (1985). Between text and context: Toward a rhetoric of textual reconstruction. *Quarterly Journal of Speech, 71,* 19-36.

Burgoon, M. (1992). Strangers in a strange land: The Ph.D. in the land of the medical doctor. *Journal of Language and Social Psychology, 11,* 101-106.

Burgoon, M., & Bailey, W. (1992). PC at last! PC at last! Thank God almighty, we are PC at last! *Journal of Communication, 42,* 95-104.

Burgoon, M., & Miller, G. R. (1990). Paths. *Communication Monographs, 57,* 152-160.

Gilligan, C. (1982). *In a different voice: Psychological theory and women's development.* Cambridge, MA: Harvard University Press.

Jourard, S. (1964). *The transparent self.* New York: Van Nostrand.

Laing, R. (1967). *The politics of experience.* New York: Ballantine.

Laing, R. (1969). *The politics of the family.* New York: Random House.

Laing, R., & Esterson, A. (1964). *Sanity, madness and the family.* New York: Basic Books.

Lakoff, R. (1975). *Language and woman's place.* New York: Harper & Row.

Mayer, J. P. (Ed.). (1969). *Alexis de Tocqueville: Democracy in America* (G. Lawrence, Trans.). Garden City, NY: Anchor.

Motley, M. (1990). On whether one can(not) communicate: An examination via traditional communication postulates. *Western Journal of Speech Communication, 54,* 1-20.

New York Times v. Sullivan, 386 U.S. 254 (1964).

Niklas, U. (1984). An empiricist approach to the problem of intersubjectivity of language and C. S. Pierce's concept of the sign. In J. Pelc et al. (Eds.), *Sign, system, and function* (pp. 241-246). Berlin: Mouton.

O'Keefe, D. J. (1990). *Persuasion: Theory and research.* Newbury Park, CA: Sage.

Parks, M. (1982). Ideology in interpersonal communication: Off the couch and into the world. In M. Burgoon (Ed.), *Communication yearbook 5* (pp. 79-107). New Brunswick, NJ: Transaction.

Ricoeur, P. (1973). The model of the text: Meaningful action considered as text. *New Literary History, 5,* 91-117.

Rogers, C. (1951). *Client centered therapy.* Cambridge, MA: Riverside.

Sunstein, C. (1991). Ideas, yes; assaults, no. *American Prospect, 6,* 36-39.

Watzlawick, P., Beavin, J., & Jackson, D. (1967). *Pragmatics of human communication: A study of interaction patterns, pathologies, and paradoxes.* New York: W. W. Norton.

22 Ideology in Interpersonal Communication: Beyond the Couches, Talk Shows, and Bunkers

MALCOLM R. PARKS
University of Washington

S OCIAL ideology and social science meet across a long, tense border. Traffic across this border may either contribute to an enlarged sense of public argument or dissolve into a cacophony of complaint and countercomplaint. Learning to speak thoughtfully across this border is, I believe, one of the most critical challenges facing the field of interpersonal communication. In this essay I explore several ideological components in current discourse about interpersonal communication. My essay is occasioned by Professor Burgoon's essay in the present volume. Being asked to write a commentary on Burgoon's essay leaves me in the enviable rhetorical position of being able to say nearly anything I please and still be viewed as a comparative moderate. I do not plan to waste such an opportunity, though my essay is intended more as parallel piece than as a direct response. This is not my first foray into the ideology of interpersonal communication. I will be revisiting several of the themes I originally raised in an essay on "ideology of intimacy" in *Communication Yearbook* more than a decade ago (Parks, 1982). I will certainly travel many of the paths hacked out by my colleague, even substantially agree with his criticisms, but ultimately I find that the question of ideology in interpersonal communication leads me in a different direction.

My primary purposes are to enrich our sense of ideological influences on methods and topics and to consider ways that ideological and empirical voices can engage in meaningful discussion rather than merely cancel each other out. To frame the discussion, I begin by contrasting Professor Burgoon's essays on the topic (Chapter 21 in this volume, as well as Burgoon, 1992; Burgoon & Bailey, 1992) with another recent essay on the same topic by Lannamann (1991). I will

Correspondence and requests for reprints: Malcolm R. Parks, Department of Speech Communication, DL-15, University of Washington, Seattle, WA 98195.

Communication Yearbook 18, pp. 480-497

then turn to an exploration of the more specific ideological influences in current popular and scholarly discussions of interpersonal communication. This will involve revisiting the "ideology of intimacy" as well as sampling three new ideological influences that are finding their way into discourse about interpersonal communication. Finally, I will note a few of the understandings I think we must reach if we are to have a truly useful conversation about scientific and ideological concerns.

FRAMING IDEOLOGICAL CONCERNS

According to Burgoon, the study of interpersonal communication is held hostage by the members of an ideological conspiracy (see the preceding chapter, as well as Burgoon, 1992; Burgoon & Bailey, 1992). That conspiracy has penetrated our choice of research questions, our theoretical approaches, and our willingness to accept the findings of social scientific studies as truth. Burgoon describes the conspirators as a loose, perhaps unwitting, alliance of opportunists and leftists. For Burgoon, these conspirators have faces. Some are radical feminists and Afrocentrists who are more interested in privileging their own voices than in creating a level rhetorical playing field. Others are mere opportunists who embrace the "postmodern leveling" because it allows them to publish mediocre work. Still others are traditional social scientists who have adopted what Burgoon labels as a leftist ideological bias. In the preceding chapter, Burgoon contends that communication scholars in this latter group have "embraced a Marxist orientation that glorifies the collective while diminishing the importance of the individual."

The examples Burgoon uses to support his indictments are, if not convincing, at least intriguing and deserve to be taken seriously. First on the culprits' list is the human relations school of organizational communication, which is never quite specified, but which is accused of placing group needs over individual needs while at the same time making individual satisfaction the primary variable in medical and educational settings. One might wish for a more thorough review of the literature on these points, but nonetheless Burgoon is on solid empirical ground when he observes that student satisfaction is not very strongly related to learning. The argument can easily be extended even further. We should, for example, question whether the recent emphasis on "teacher immediacy" runs the risk of creating a generation of teachers who are overly concerned with their popularity and a generation of students who believe that they can learn only from people they like. Burgoon is also on solid empirical ground when he observes that patient satisfaction is not very strongly related to either health status or compliance with treatment regimens. Thus ideologies that prioritize social harmony and individual satisfaction in these settings may make us happier, but not necessarily more intelligent or healthy.

Having scored direct hits on these targets, Burgoon reloads and unleashes a barrage that probably hits as many innocent parties as ideologues. There is a striking irony in these attacks. Although Burgoon criticizes Carl Rogers, Sidney Jourard, and other humanistic psychologists for placing undue importance on expressiveness and disclosiveness, his essay gathers most of its own rhetorical force from Burgoon's personal expressiveness and disclosiveness.

Be that as it may, Burgoon's essay does confront us with two vital questions in its remaining sections. First, Burgoon raises the question of whether the anti-objectivist, deconstructivist agenda so levels the rhetorical field that it becomes impossible to appeal to systematic observation as a way of adjudicating competing knowledge claims. This is a legitimate concern, one that should be shared by social scientists and postmodernists alike. Second, Burgoon challenges us to consider whether new scholarly fashions have caused us to renounce traditional commitments to persuasion and freedom of speech. This, too, is a legitimate concern. It is, for example, difficult to find an introductory text in interpersonal communication that addresses the issue of persuasion (save for Burgoon, Hunsaker, & Dawson, 1994). And it is difficult not to have sympathy for Burgoon's position when one considers the eagerness with which many embrace the concept of censorship in the media and the classroom. In today's campus climate, freedom of speech is too often limited to the freedom to say only those things that no one will find offensive. Perhaps Burgoon's essay is hotly contentious only because academic debate has become so pallid.

One way to frame the discussion of ideology in interpersonal communication is to compare Burgoon's essay with another recent essay on the same topic by J. W. Lannamann (1991). Like Burgoon, Lannamann views interpersonal communication research as a hostage of unexamined ideological assumptions. Based on his review of the studies published in a two-year period in *Human Communication Research* and *Communication Monographs,* Lannamann concludes that mainstream interpersonal communication research is guided by four ideological tendencies. The first of these is the emphasis on individualism and cognitivism. In spite of paying lip service to the reciprocal nature of communicative influence, to the social origins of the self, and to larger social structural considerations, most research is conducted at a purely individual level. This tendency has a number of deleterious effects, according to Lannamann, not the least of which is the implicit acceptance of existing power relationships in society. Second, our understanding of interpersonal communication is distorted by the ideological tendency to engage in "subjectivist reduction." This sin is exemplified by the fact that so many studies are restricted to self-report measures. Such a practice, Lannamann claims, not only ignores the actual content of messages, but also encourages us to ignore "the powerful influences of material conditions beyond the interpretive and rational control of the subject" (p. 190). Third, the focus on the desires and intentions of individual communicators as primary explanatory mechanism for interpersonal behavior reflects an ideological commitment that further blocks our search for broader understandings.

It does so by reducing collective action to individual subjective perceptions, by conceptualizing action in terms of individual goal directedness rather than as a product of larger material and social conditions, and by making it impossible to see the unintended macro-level consequences of individual behavior. Finally, Lannamann indicts social scientific research as being ahistorical. Others have made similar points, but Lannamann goes further with his claim that the ahistoricism of interpersonal communication actually represents an ideological position because it has the effect of placing the field in a conservative political position.

The juxtaposition of these two approaches to ideology in interpersonal communication is more revealing than either of them taken individually. For Burgoon, the prevailing ideological bias is one of collectivism over individualism, whereas for Lannamann, the prevailing ideological bias is one of individualism over collectivism and historicism. Burgoon and Lannamann also differ strongly in their assessment of the political implications of interpersonal communication research. For Burgoon, the prevailing ideology is subversive. It upsets legitimate authority structures and undermines the value placed on the results of empirical research. For Lannamann, on the other hand, the prevailing ideology of interpersonal communication is politically conservative. Researchers ignore the larger historical and social antecedents of individual behavior and therefore tacitly affirm existing power arrangements. That such contrasting assessments could be about the same literature may mean that we are in better shape than we thought. Certainly it implies that the field of interpersonal communication is not quite the ideological hostage that either writer imagines.

The most important contrast between these essays, however, is a more subtle one. Burgoon and Lannamann proffer markedly different visions of the proper role of ideology in interpersonal communication research. Burgoon's position, though not explicitly stated, appears quite straightforward: Ideological interests have no place in interpersonal communication research and should be eliminated whenever they are discovered. In Lannamann's (1991) view, such a strategy is impossible, if not delusional. "It is impossible," he says, "to have no ideology" (p. 186). If everything in interpersonal communication is ideological, then we are left only the choice of which ideology to embrace. And even though Lannamann retreats to the safety of the critic's perch, we can decipher (dare I say, deconstruct?) his ideological prescription for the field of interpersonal communication by reversing his critical lenses. Thus what Lannamann is really doing is asking us to reject one ideology and embrace another. His ideology views individual behavior as reactive rather than proactive, presumes that contemporary behavior is fully determined by historical forces, discounts individual differences, and disconnects personal intention and social action.

These essays exemplify the two dominant choices available for relating issues of value to interpersonal communication research. One choice is deny the possibility of ideological influences, to be vigilant, and to purge them. Empirical data are allowable only to the degree that they can be shown to be free of

ideological contaminants. The other choice is to deny the impossibility of ideological influences and to embrace a particular ideological position as the right
and proper one. Here, empirical data are allowable only to the degree that they
can be shown to be consistent with prior ideological commitments.

Neither of these choices is a good one. Or, to be more precise, neither of these
choices is sufficient if we are to bring the full scope of human intelligence and
spirit to the interpersonal issues of the day. Ideological influences cannot and
should not be banished from the study of interpersonal communication. It is
inconceivable to me that any question of genuine human import should be
resolved without reference to human values, that is, to ideology. It is equally
inconceivable to me, however, that we would try to resolve such questions
without reference to our strongest powers of systematic observation, that is, to
empiricism and science. The first option leaves complex individual and social
questions in the hands of specialists. The second option leaves important issues
to be settled by highly combustible mixtures of moral vision and force. Neither
option is acceptable. Instead of purging the ideological or censoring the empirical, we should be constructing an arena of discourse, an "intellectual commons,"
in which questions of value and questions of fact can each contribute in disciplined ways to discussions of larger personal and societal issues.

In thinking about the shape such discussions might take it is vital to appreciate
just how varied and how extensive the ideological influences on interpersonal
communication have become. Burgoon and Lannamann identify only a few of
these influences. To gain a more complete picture, I will first revisit "the
ideology of intimacy" (Parks, 1982) and then note three new ideologies that are
having or soon will have profound effects on research and pedagogy in interpersonal communication.

THE IDEOLOGY OF INTIMACY REVISITED

Ideological components have long been prominent in the study of interpersonal communication. In the early 1980s, I surveyed the ideological scene and
found evidence that interpersonal communication research and pedagogy were
being influenced by what Sennett (1977) had called "the ideology of intimacy."
This ideology had several components, including (a) the conceptualization of
interpersonal communication as something independent of cultural roles or group
identities; (b) the valorization of openness and honesty and the corresponding
devaluation of privacy, tact, and deception as positive forces in interpersonal
relationships; and (c) the tendency to equate the overall quality and level of
development of relationships with their level of disclosure and intimacy (Parks,
1982). Surveying the present scene, I find that with some notable exceptions
these ideological components have not only survived, they have prospered in
the intervening decade.

Definitions of Interpersonal Communication

The prevailing definition of interpersonal communication has changed little in the past decade. Whether accomplished by reference to Martin Buber's (1970) "I-thou" distinction or Miller and Steinberg's (1975) distinction between the interpersonal and the noninterpersonal, most texts continue to define interpersonal communication as communication based on the unique personal qualities of the participants (see Adler & Towne, 1990; DeVito, 1989; Stewart & Logan, 1993). Most researchers and nearly all texts view interpersonal communication as developmental. It is something people work up to as they shed impersonal social roles.

The continuing ideological commitments of this definition are revealed in two of its features. First, equating interpersonal communication with the unique personal features of the individual implies that our shared qualities and shared roles are not very informative about us as individuals—they are merely part of the "herd experience" (Stewart & Logan, 1993, p. 5). Second, it is clear in most texts that interpersonal communication is the only good or true communication. It is where we are most likely to learn, to relate, to influence, to play, and to give and receive help (DeVito, 1989). It is through interpersonal communication that we find the bulk of our "humanness" and do the most to enrich our lives and protect our health (Stewart & Logan, 1993). Although I find myself agreeing in part with these views, I cannot help wondering if impersonal relationships do not also make a significant contribution. As I noted in my earlier essay, our impersonal relationships, our "weak links," serve vital personal and social functions that cannot be served by our more personal relationships (Parks, 1982). In some settings the emphasis on developing personal relations may even be damaging. I think this is what Burgoon is pointing out in his example of how emphasizing personal satisfaction in one's relationship with a physician may in fact get in the way of objectively more important factors, such as compliance with a medical regimen.

The Quest for Openness and Honesty

Jourard's (1971) "transparent self" is alive and well in the 1990s. Most introductory texts in interpersonal communication continue to assert that true interpersonal communication can best or perhaps only be accomplished when participants honestly and mutually open their private selves for inspection and comment. Of course, no one endorses indiscriminate openness, and most discussions have always identified some conditions under which openness is inappropriate or unwise. Indeed, as I survey recent editions of several of the texts I critiqued a decade ago, it seems that writers have become more sensitive to the risks associated with the humanistic model of openness and unguarded honesty. It is heartening to see texts presenting more detailed recommendations for distinguishing appropriate and inappropriate openness, recognizing that openness and honesty may be used manipulatively, and even treating the decision to be open as a strategic choice as opposed to a moral imperative (see, for example, Adler & Towne, 1990; DeVito, 1989; Stewart & Logan, 1993). In spite of these laudable cautionary notes, however, the benefits claimed for openness still overshadow discussions of risk.

Contemporary texts also continue to display a lack when it comes to incorporating theory and research regarding openness and honesty. In addition to my discussion of the topic (Parks, 1982, 1994), several other lines of research in the 1980s and early 1990s converged to underscore the practical limits on the humanistic model of openness, unguarded honesty, and expressiveness. I will note just three examples. One is Bavelas's reconceptualization of equivocation as a strategic message choice rather than a simple lack of clarity (see Bavelas, Black, Chovil, & Mullett, 1990). Another is the work that imports politeness theory into research on interpersonal communication (e.g., Lim, 1990; Lim & Bowers, 1991). Still another is the research on message design logics by O'Keefe (1988, 1992). Each of these projects leads us to recognize that the humanistic model's ideological endorsements are fraught with pragmatic difficulties. Each portrays the structure of communication and the choices available to communicators in more complex ways than does the humanistic model. It is disappointing that so few introductory texts even mention this material. When it is mentioned, it remains at the theoretical periphery, or the discussion is just plain simplistic. One text, for example, labels lying and equivocation as unethical interpersonal acts except in cases where the speaker is saying something the listener will like (see DeVito, 1989, pp. 82-85).

The Valorization of Intimacy and Disclosure

At the heart of the ideology of intimacy as I first viewed it was the belief that interpersonal relationships are real and valuable only to the extent that they develop toward intimacy through high levels of self-disclosure (Parks, 1982). Today the scene is considerably more complex. On the one hand, the research literature on interpersonal communication is no longer so uniform in its treatment of self-disclosure and intimacy. The list of developmental dimensions has broadened to include factors such as interdependence and code specialization. Ideological components still remain, but new perspectives have given credence to a more balanced view. Chief among these is the dialectical perspective. Researchers such as Altman and Baxter have created the theoretical space that I only loosely envisioned in my 1982 essay (see Altman, Vinsel, & Brown, 1981; Baxter, 1988). In the dialectical perspective, relational development occurs within the ongoing tensions between disclosure and privacy and between intimacy and autonomy. The dialectical perspective can now be found in specific studies of relationship development, relationship maintenance, and social support (e.g., Baxter & Simon, 1993; Baxter & Widenmann, 1993; Goldsmith, 1988; Goldsmith & Parks, 1990).

There remains, however, a considerable gap between theory and pedagogy. Although introductory texts today are less breathless in their endorsements of intimacy and disclosure than they were a decade ago, no text pauses to consider the virtues of less intimate, "weak" relationships before celebrating the joys of intimacy. Little of the dialectical perspective has worked its way down to this level. The most popular introductory texts, and many of popular advanced texts, rarely mention the risks of intimacy. When they are mentioned, they are usually described in ways that ultimately reinforce the virtues of intimacy. One popular reader (Stewart, 1990), for example, contains an excerpt from a piece on "the dangers of intimacy" by Hatfield. All the dangers, however, turn out to be personal fears that prevent people from disclosing in healthy ways that build intimacy. Popular texts on interpersonal communication almost never ask their readers to consider that intimacy itself has risks, or that intimacy could actually be enhanced by privacy, or that self-disclosure might not be the primary tool for relational development.

The ideology of intimacy thus survives, albeit more in pedagogy than in research. But in the past decade it has been joined by new ideological streams emptying into academic and popular discourse about interpersonal communication. I will not attempt to catalog all of these factors, but will instead focus on three that I think are particularly influential: the feminization of intimacy, the cult of the universal victim, and the diversity celebration.

THE FEMINIZATION OF INTIMACY

As the ideology of intimacy mingled with feminist agenda and gender research the concept of intimacy itself was feminized. Actually, the trend toward equating intimacy with stereotypically feminine communication styles dates at least as far back as Parsons and Bales (1955). Since then, researchers have generally taken the position that men's behavior emphasizes shared instrumental activities, whereas women's behavior prioritizes disclosure and talk about feelings. Because of its supposedly lower levels of verbal self-disclosure and emotional support, men's interpersonal behavior has routinely been judged to be less intimate than women's (e.g., Caldwell & Peplau, 1982; Davidson & Duberman, 1982; Griffin & Sparks, 1990; Hays, 1984; Komarovsky, 1964; Rubin, 1983).

Discourse about sex differences took a decidedly ideological path in the 1980s with the rise of cultural feminism and the inexplicable popularity of works like Gilligan's (1982) *In a Different Voice*. Not only were sex differences exaggerated, but stereotypically feminine ways of relating came to be valorized (Swain, 1989; Tavris, 1992; Wood & Inman, 1993). As the impact of Gilligan's work and related works spread, so did the breadth of the claim. By the mid-1980s, numerous popular and academic writers argued either implicitly or explicitly that only women are capable of genuine intimacy (e.g., Belenky, Clinchy, Goldberger,

& Tarule, 1986; Schaef, 1985). Cancian (1986) labeled this trend the "feminization of love."

If feminine ways of relating have been glorified, the more stereotypically male ways of expressing closeness have been devalued. In their recent review, Wood and Inman (1993) observe, "Not only were women dubbed intimacy experts, but men were alternately pitied and chided for their alleged shortcomings" (p. 281). Men were judged to be inexpressive, threatened by, unskilled at, or just plain incapable of "real intimacy" and thus doomed to poor-quality relationships (e.g., Basow, 1992; Brehm, 1992; Mazur & Olver, 1987; Williams, 1985). When men's behavior was measured with a feminine yardstick, it was bound to be found wanting (Cancian, 1987).

The feminization of intimacy is problematic for at least three reasons. First, the actual research does not support the sharp gender differences claimed by the feminist version of the ideology of intimacy. In their meta-analysis of more than 200 studies on sex differences in self-disclosure, for example, Dindia and Allen (1992) found that female disclosure was typically only "slightly" greater than that of males, averaging less than a fifth of a standard deviation. And Gilligan's (1982) claim of sharp gender differences in the orientation toward moral issues and interpersonal attachments does not stand in the light of either a careful inspection of her own data or the results of other research, as Tavris (1992) points out in her thoughtful review of Gilligan's work. That this statement will strike many as heresy only underscores my point. The intuitive appeal of Gilligan's claim is so strong for many women that the fact that it is empirically dubious becomes irrelevant (Greeno & Maccoby, 1986). Second, the feminist version of the ideology of intimacy distorts our conceptualization of interpersonal communication by encouraging us to ignore or discount the ways in which males express intimacy. Although the data are far from complete, recent research does indeed point to previously ignored masculine ways of expressing intimacy, such as the complex use of humor as a bonding device (Swain, 1989). Finally, the easy adoption of ideological assumptions about gender differences and different voices not only obscures our path toward a common language, but also ironically contains the potential for locking women into a limited conception of their own communicative abilities.

RECOVERY AND THE UNIVERSAL VICTIM

If you browse in the self-help aisles of the bookstore, electronically jog through the talk-show circuit, or, increasingly, study introductory texts on interpersonal communication, you will soon discover that you are a victim of a disease, either yours or somebody else's. You are an alcoholic, a drug abuser, a food abuser, a workaholic, a sexaholic, a gambler, addicted to anger, a fitness addict, a sports addict, a compulsive shopper, a religion addict. Perhaps you are just unhappy. If so, then you may be "addicted to misery" (Becker, 1989). If not, you must certainly have been affected by someone who is addicted to something. That means you have a universal disease: codependency. According to Beattie (1987), a codependent is someone who "has let another person's behavior affect him or her, and who is obsessed with controlling that person's behavior" (p. 31). Such a vague definition, of course, implies that we are nearly all codependents, nearly all victims of dysfunctional interpersonal relationships. Indeed, the sages of self-help estimate that as many as 96% of us are victims of addiction and dysfunction (Bradshaw, 1988a).

The only way to relieve universal victimhood is to be in recovery. One is never recovered, only in recovery. The prime model for recovery is the 12-step program developed by the founders of Alcoholics Anonymous a half century ago. Today, however, the recovery movement has become flypaper for a bewildering cast of pop therapists, spiritual gurus, celebrity victims, and, of course, writers who seek profit from their own and others' dysfunctions.

Images of universal victimization and generalized recovery imply a particular model of interpersonal communication. Once one has admitted powerlessness over one's disease and submitted to a higher spiritual power, one is instructed to embark on an interpersonal quest to "heal the child within" (Whitfield, 1987) and "heal the shame that binds" (Bradshaw, 1988b). The primary tools for doing so are self-analysis of how one has been previously abused in relationships and disclosure to others in recovery. We must share our "toxic secrets" because, in the parlance of the recovery movement, "you are only as sick as your secrets." Testimony is reality. This model repackages much of the ideology of intimacy. It equates relational quality with disclosure, judges interpersonal effectiveness in terms of openness and honesty, and renders the larger social world meaningful only in terms of the individual's personal problems and relationships.

I do not take issue with the fact that millions of people suffer with addictive disorders or that they have been helped by groups like Alcoholics Anonymous. Issue can be taken, however, with the expansion of this model to the point where it becomes a generalized metaphor for all problems and all relationships. If nothing else, the cult of the universal victim does not square very well with the data. Spouses of substance abusers, for example, do not appear to manifest any predictable personality disorders as a group (Edwards, Harvey, & Whitehead, 1973; Gomberg, 1989). They simply do not conform to the codependency model.

Universal victimhood undermines the individual's sense of competence. It encourages spiritual passivity and helplessness. At the same time, the recovery movement imposes unrealistic expectations for what healthy interpersonal relationships should be. Bradshaw (1988a), for example, defines a healthy relationship as one "based on equality, the quality of two self-actualizing spiritual beings who connect at the level of their beingness" (p. 47). At the individual level, then, the recovery movement simultaneously demands more than most people can give and questions their ability to give anything at all. But the greatest dangers of this ideology, it seems to me, lie at the political level. It reduces the political to the personal (Kaminer, 1992; Katz & Liu, 1991; Tavris,

1992). It does so by denying any reality that cannot be linked to one's own personal journey from victimhood to recovery and by dissipating the will to act collectively. Personal testimony replaces conversation and argument directed toward larger social goals (Kaminer, 1992). Because suffering is reduced to personal experience, the concepts of abuse and disease are ultimately trivialized. Children of alcoholics are the same as Holocaust survivors (Bradshaw, 1988a). As Kaminer (1992) observes:

> At its worst, the recovery movement's cult of victimization mocks the notion of social justice by denying that there are degrees of injustice. It equalizes all claims of abuse, actual and metaphoric. The personal subsumes the political, with dire consequences for both politics and personality development. (pp. 155-156)

THE DIVERSITY CELEBRATION

Multiculturalism is the next wave to wash over interpersonal communication research and pedagogy. At least in the United States, we are in the midst of a celebration of a cultural diversity so very broadly defined that it includes matters of gender, age, race, ethnicity, sexual orientation, and a dozen more. Professional scholars are under great pressure to incorporate multicultural perspectives in their work. Studies of cultures and cultural differences abound, new units are added to courses, and relatively standard interpersonal texts are given fashion makeovers so that they may be marketed as "culturally sensitive" (e.g., Berko, Rosenfeld, & Samovar, 1994).

The diversity celebration would generate very little heat if it were simply the recognition that we live in a varied interpersonal world and that both our theories and our students would be better served if this fact were more fully acknowledged. But, of course, it is much, much more than that. It is often a celebration, as Burgoon rightly points out, with the explicit political goal of "deprivileging" the dominant group (usually white males) and elevating everybody else. Only certain people are invited to the party. It is a celebration policed by ideologues whose ears are so sharp that a speaker's fate can be determined by something as simple as a preposition. Call someone a "person of color" and you have shown cultural sensitivity, but call someone a "colored person" and you are off to the reeducation camps. I thus abandon any hope that my general support for the diversity celebration will save me when I note some of its excesses and contradictions.

Much of the multiculturalist agenda in academia rests, its seems to me, on two dubious empirical assumptions. The first of these is that multicultural training, whether in interpersonal contexts or in the larger curriculum, has the effect of boosting the self-esteem of disadvantaged cultural groups. I certainly endorse the goal; indeed, I think that self-esteem and communicative competence go hand in hand (Parks, 1994). What I question is the assumption that giving people intense training in their cultural background actually raises their self-esteem in any socially meaningful way. Does a crash course in how cultural groups differ actually cause people to treat others with greater tolerance, thus allowing them to experience the kind of success that bolsters their self-esteem? I confess to not knowing the answer to these questions. What is disturbing is that no one in the diversity celebration is even pausing to ask them.

The second dubious empirical assumption ungirding the multiculturalist agenda is that all cultural differences make a difference. One problem with evaluating this assumption, of course, is that it is impossible to know where to begin. Nearly every difference has been reified into a cultural difference: separate cultures not just for ethnic groups but also for the sexes, for sexual orientations, for occupational groups, age groups, weight groups, and so on. When every difference is elevated to the cultural level, the concept of cultural difference becomes meaningless. Another problem with the assumption that all differences make a difference is that there is considerable evidence against it. Not every study of cultural difference finds statistically significant, let alone socially meaningful, differences. To give just one example, Gudykunst, Yang, and Nishida (1985) found that uncertainty reduction theory models fit equally well across cultures in the United States, Korea, and Japan. By presuming on a priori ideological grounds that every difference must make a difference, we are prevented from exploring the generality of our theories and sorting out which cultural differences are truly important in which circumstances.

Beyond its empirical difficulties, the diversity celebration has limited itself to a celebration of the subjective, which ultimately, I think, makes for both bad scholarship and bad politics. Multiculturalists, including feminist methodologists, have appropriated attacks on the search for the objective and have instead championed the personal and subjective. Traditional social science, we are told, falsely separates the knower from the known (Harding, 1986; Keller, 1985). Quantitative methods "break living connections" (Mies, 1991, p. 67). They are just part of the machinery of cultural and sexual oppression. Concepts like culture and gender, it is said, are so fundamental that they cannot be treated as mere variables in an analytic framework (Wood, 1993). The problem with such views is that they radically personalize and localize communicative phenomena to such a degree that it is difficult to make any empirical statement that goes beyond the individual. As one critic put it:

> The diversification of student populations and concern for multiculturalism have made respect for subjective experiences and points of view political imperatives. Fashions in literary and legal theory and historical research focus on knowledge as a matter of perspective, disdaining the "pretense" of objectivity. Scholars get to talk about themselves. Theory is nothing but testimony. (Kaminer, 1992, p. 41)

Surely this is too harsh. Or is it? Foss and Foss (1994) recently identified personal testimony as the proper, presumably the only proper, material for feminist scholarship on communication. What about the problem of sorting out which testimonies to trust, which to include? "Irrelevant," say Foss and Foss (p. 39). The researcher is only a "presentational expert" who acts as a "midwife, coaching and assisting others to give voice to their experiences" (p. 40).

The balkanizing influence of radical multiculturalist thought is even more dangerous in the political realm. I take no issue with the moderate multiculturalist position that truly celebrates diversity within a common whole. But the notion that cultural and ethnic identifications are primary, immutable political realities runs counter to the American experiment (Schlesinger, 1992). First, it devalues the individual. The American myth is built around the aspirations of the individual, not the aspirations of the group. True, the group is an important source of identity, but so too is individual achievement. Recognizing diversity is one thing, but limiting people's conceptions of themselves to cultural factors is not likely to help them. Second, radical multiculturalist positions shrink the sphere of common discourse and understanding. Their "offshoot is the rhetoric of cultural separatism" (Hughes, 1993, p. 83). Armed with its fascination with subjectivism, the radical multiculturalist project corrodes us into smaller and smaller factions. The "melting pot" fractures into gender cultures, which break into ethnic cultures, which crumble still further into the many cultures of the "differently abled." The process continues until the possibility of common discourse and understanding is turned to dust. The melting pot may be an outmoded metaphor, failing as it does to value our diversity, but there are alternatives that allow us to envision both diversity and unity. Robert Hughes (1993) gives us one example: "Reading America is like scanning a mosaic. If you look at the big picture, you do not see its parts—the distinct glass tiles, each a different color. If you concentrate only on the tiles, you cannot see the picture" (p. 14). I celebrate diversity, but I also worry that the diversity celebration too often leaves us down on our hands and knees looking for our little tiles, afraid that we'll be stepped on, unable and unwilling to see the larger picture.

TOWARD AN INTELLECTUAL COMMONS

When I wrote about ideology in interpersonal communication just over a decade ago, one of my main concerns was that "the ideology of intimacy" created too large a gap between the world of the interpersonal and the world of the public and political. I still have that concern because the ideology of intimacy is still very much with us. Burgoon and Lannamann, though Lannamann more than Burgoon, also seem to share this concern in their own ways. Each of the three new ideological influences raises this concern as well. Feminized intimacy defines men out of the intimate realm and may lock women into it. The cult of the universal victim reduces the political to the personal and replaces collective action with spiritual acceptance. The diversity celebration poses the specter of retribalization.

As a working social scientist, I am also committed to the increasingly quaint notion that systematic observation both is possible and ought to count for something. Thus part of my original essay was to debunk some of the false empirical claims made by the ideology of intimacy. Burgoon's essays point to other cases in which ideological imperatives have led to the acceptance of false claims. In this essay I have noted additional examples of this same phenomenon. Feminized intimacy perpetrates false or insufficiently supported claims regarding the sex differences in disclosure and relational orientations. The cult of the victim asks us to accept unsubstantiated stereotypes about the amount and nature of interpersonal dysfunction. The diversity celebration rests on unexplored empirical claims regarding the relationships among culture, self-esteem, and communication.

The discussion of the relationship between the interpersonal and the political, between observation and ideology, ultimately leads me to a more general concern with the nature of our discourse about communication processes. It seems to me that communication scholars, like those in many other disciplines, have often lost interest in the connection between empirical and ideological issues and have fractured into warring camps. Our value to each other and to society is thus dissipated in mixtures of posturing and complaint. We may not be able to argue our way to the sort of universal consensus Habermas (1979) envisioned, but neither do we need to think that we are incapable of constructing arguments that transcend anything but the most local setting (e.g., Lyotard, 1984). I don't know if it is possible to achieve consensus, but I think it is possible to have a good conversation, and that the results of this conversation may contribute to practical argument in both public and private spheres.

To have a good conversation, we must first get beyond the posturing. I am not going to resolve the subjectivist-objectivist debate, nor do I think we need to. In fact, I think it is generally a good thing. What we need, however, is some plain talk that helps us appreciate the limits of our positions. So, to the postmodernist-subjectivist critics of social science, I have this to say: We don't need you. Contrary to what you may think, social science is a tremendously successful enterprise. No other epistemological perspective is as capable of summarizing commonalities across individuals and groups and of identifying patterns of covariation. So believe, if you wish, that you have shown social science to be philosophically flawed. It probably is, but we don't care. We will quietly continue to design the messages of the political candidates you vote for, program your media, design your children's schools, structure your workplaces, influence social policies that affect you, help manufacturers tailor their products to your whims and desires (and vice versa), and predict your marriages and divorces. Oh yes, when you are sitting at home congratulating yourselves on proving the futility of a science of human behavior and a woman calls to sell you this or that, you might remember that we told her what to say. We may do these things well or poorly, morally or immorally, but we are doing them nonetheless.

To my fellow social scientists, I say: We are not as special as we think we are. Our claims to knowledge are part of, not separate from, the larger questions of value and policy that swirl about. Our objectivity, although crucial, is slight, and we are far more easily co-opted by language, ideology, and fashion than we like to think. If nothing else, we are too often fodder for the relentless maw of the consumer economy. We spend too much time with methods and analysis and not enough time with the introduction and discussion sections, and as a result we end up with statistically complex but trivial work. If we were not so certain of our special status, we might find that our critics are asking some very helpful questions. A modest starting point might be the questions Hawes (1994) recently posed in an article on reflexivity in communication research: "What is your stake in the work you're doing? What's the point? What are your political inclinations and objectives? To what uses is your research put? Whose interests are being served? Whose are being overlooked?" (pp. 9-10).

We should neither embrace nor purge ideological concerns in social science. Instead, I believe we should pull apart the border separating ideological and scientific interests to create space for an intellectual commons, a communicative equivalent to the common areas where people once grazed their animals. I admit that my image of a commons is romantic, but then I'm a social scientist and therefore given to romantic enterprises. Still, I like the image of the commons because its rules provide a commonsense metaphor to guide the discussion of ideological and empirical issues. The first rule of the commons to remember is that you don't own the place. Much of the "ferment in the field"—most of the philosophical debates and nearly all of the methodological debates—has been, it seems to me, about ownership. Surely we all own our little pieces of the action, of the mosaic, but the commons is a place we go to talk. If we are to contribute in meaningful ways to the important issues of the day, we must drop our claims to ownership of the commons.

The second rule of the commons is to remember who owns each animal. I translate this to mean that we should avoid trying to synthesize all points of view into one critical stance. Questions of value and questions of fact are intimately related, but they are not the same thing. Everything may be ideologically influenced, but there are degrees of influence, and it is vital to respect them. Aside from the fact that synthesis is usually an ownership move, efforts to achieve higher-order synthesis have a dismal history. They spin off into higher and higher levels of metatheory that rise up like glass walls without a single handhold.

A third rule is related: Don't overgraze your animals. Each camp has things it does better than others. Just as no scientific study can decide a question of value, no ideological perspective can decide an empirical question. Yet nearly all questions of value contain assumptions about what the facts are and nearly all social scientific findings contain implications for value positions. Wise use of the commons requires us to recognize explicitly what questions we can and cannot answer and to acknowledge when we switch from talking about one type of question to the other. Failure to do so promotes squabbling, but, more important, it drains the conversation of its vitality.

The final rule of the commons is to look for ways to be useful to your neighbor. By devising systematic tests of the empirical components in ideological positions, social scientists may help refine discussions of value. By critiquing the unexamined ideological assumptions in social science, our critics may help us do better science. Ultimately, we should hope that the important questions of the day will be decided not by any one voice, but by the practical arguments that can be constructed from the many voices. If my image of the intellectual commons is too simplistic, I invite alternatives. Unless we find better ways to engage in disciplined conversation and debate about questions of fact and value, our voices will cancel each other out. We will have abandoned the field of discourse. The only sound that will remain will be the announcer telling us that *Oprah* is on next.

REFERENCES

Adler, R. B., & Towne, N. (1990). *Looking out, looking in* (6th ed.). Fort Worth, TX: Holt, Rinehart & Winston.

Altman, I., Vinsel, A., & Brown, B. B. (1981). Dialectic conceptions in social psychology: An application to social penetration and privacy regulation. In L. Berkowitz (Ed.), *Advances in experimental social psychology* (pp. 107-160). New York: Academic Press.

Basow, S. A. (1992). *Gender: Stereotypes and roles* (3rd ed.). Pacific Grove, CA: Wadsworth.

Bavelas, J. B., Black, A., Chovil, N., & Mullett, J. (1990). *Equivocal communication.* Newbury Park, CA: Sage.

Baxter, L. A. (1988). A dialectical perspective on communication strategies in relationship development. In S. W. Duck (Ed.), *Handbook of personal relationships* (pp. 257-273). Chichester: John Wiley.

Baxter, L. A., & Simon, E. P. (1993). Relationship maintenance strategies and dialectical contradictions in personal relationships. *Journal of Social and Personal Relationships, 10,* 225-242.

Baxter, L. A., & Widenmann, S. (1993). Revealing and not revealing the status of romantic relationships to social networks. *Journal of Social and Personal Relationships, 10,* 321-337.

Beattie, M. (1987). *Codependent no more.* New York: Harper/Hazeldon.

Becker, R. A. (1989). *Addicted to misery.* Deerfield Beach, FL: Health Communications.

Belenky, M. F., Clinchy, B. M., Goldberger, N. R., & Tarule, J. M. (1986). *Women's ways of knowing: The development of self, voice, and mind.* New York: Basic Books.

Berko, R. M., Rosenfeld, L. B., & Samovar, L. A. (1994). *Connecting: A culture-sensitive approach to interpersonal communication competency.* Fort Worth, TX: Harcourt Brace Jovanovich.

Bradshaw, J. (1988a). *Bradshaw on: The family.* Deerfield Beach, FL: Health Communications.

Bradshaw, J. (1988b). *Healing the shame that binds you.* Deerfield Beach, FL: Health Communications.

Brehm, S. S. (1992). *Intimate relationships* (2nd ed.). New York: McGraw-Hill.

Buber, M. (1970). *I and thou.* Magnolia, MA: Peter Smith.

Burgoon, M. (1992). Strangers in a strange land: The Ph.D. in the land of the medical doctor. *Journal of Language and Social Psychology, 11,* 101-106.

Burgoon, M., & Bailey, W. (1992). PC at last! PC at last! Thank God almighty, we are PC at last! *Journal of Communication, 42,* 95-104.

Burgoon, M., Hunsaker, F. G., & Dawson, E. J. (1994). *Human communication* (3rd ed.). Thousand Oaks, CA: Sage.

Caldwell, R., & Peplau, L. (1982). Sex differences in same-sex friendship. *Sex Roles, 8,* 721-732.

Cancian, F. (1986). The feminization of love. *Signs, 11,* 692-709.

Cancian, F. (1987). *Love in America: Gender and self-development.* Cambridge: Cambridge University Press.

Davidson, J., & Duberman, L. (1982). Same-sex friendships: A gender comparison of dyads. *Sex Roles, 8,* 809-822.

DeVito, J. A. (1989). *The interpersonal communication book.* New York: Harper & Row.

Dindia, K., & Allen, M. (1992). Sex differences in self-disclosure: A meta-analysis. *Psychological Bulletin, 112,* 106-124.

Edwards, P., Harvey, C., & Whitehead, P. (1973). Wives of alcoholics: A critical review and analysis. *Quarterly Journal of Studies on Alcohol, 34,* 112-132.

Foss, K. A., & Foss, S. K. (1994). Personal experience as evidence in feminist scholarship. *Western Journal of Communication, 58,* 39-43.

Gilligan, C. (1982). *In a different voice: Psychological theory and women's development.* Cambridge, MA: Harvard University Press.

Goldsmith, D. J. (1988, November). *To talk or not to talk: The flow of information between romantic dyads and networks.* Paper presented at the annual meeting of the Speech Communication Association, New Orleans.

Goldsmith, D. J., & Parks, M. R. (1990). Communicative strategies for managing the risks of seeking social support. In S. W. Duck (Ed.), *Personal relationships and social support* (pp. 104-121). London: Sage.

Gomberg, E. S. L. (1989). On terms used and abused: The concept of "codependency." *Drugs and Society: Current Issues in Alcohol/Drug Studies, 3,* 113-132.

Greeno, C. G., & Maccoby, E. E. (1986). How different is the "different voice"? *Signs, 11,* 310-316.

Griffin, E., & Sparks, G. (1990). Friends forever: A longitudinal exploration of intimacy in same-sex friends and platonic pairs. *Journal of Social and Personal Relationships, 7,* 29-46.

Gudykunst, W. B., Yang, S., & Nishida, T. (1985). A cross-cultural test of uncertainty reduction theory: Comparisons of acquaintances, friends, and dating relationships in Japan, Korea, and the United States. *Human Communication Research, 11,* 407-454.

Habermas, J. (1979). *Communication and the evolution of society* (T. McCarthy, Trans.). Boston: Beacon.

Harding, S. (1986). *The science question in feminism.* Ithaca, NY: Cornell University Press.

Hawes, L. C. (1994). Revisiting reflexivity. *Western Journal of Communication, 58,* 5-10.

Hays, R. B. (1984). The development and maintenance of friendship. *Journal of Social and Personal Relationships, 1,* 75-98.

Hughes, R. (1993). *Culture of complaint.* New York: Oxford University Press.

Jourard, S. M. (1971). *The transparent self.* New York: Van Nostrand Reinhold.

Kaminer, W. (1992). *I'm dysfunctional, you're dysfunctional: The recovery movement and other self-help fashions.* Reading, MA: Addison-Wesley.

Katz, S. J., & Liu, A. (1991). *The codependency conspiracy.* New York: Warner.

Keller, E. (1985). *Reflections on gender and science.* New Haven, CT: Yale University Press.

Komarovsky, M. (1964). *Blue-collar marriage.* New York: Vintage.

Lannamann, J. W. (1991). Interpersonal communication research as ideological practice. *Communication Theory, 3,* 179-203.

Lim, T. (1990). Politeness behavior in social influence situations. In J. P. Dillard (Ed.), *Seeking compliance: The production of interpersonal influence messages* (pp. 75-86). Scottsdale, AZ: Gorsuch Scarisbrick.

Lim, T., & Bowers, J. W. (1991). Facework: Solidarity, approbation, and tact. *Human Communication Research, 17,* 415-450.

Lyotard, J. F. (1984). *The postmodern condition: A report on knowledge* (G. Bennington & B. Massumi, Trans.). Minneapolis: University of Minnesota Press.

Mazur, E., & Olver, R. R. (1987). Intimacy and structure: Sex differences in imagery of same-sex relationships. *Sex Roles, 16,* 539-558.

Mies, M. (1991). Women's research or feminist research? The debate surrounding feminist science and methodology. In M. M. Fonow & J. A. Cook (Eds.), *Beyond methodology: Feminist scholarship as lived research* (pp. 60-84). Bloomington: Indiana University Press.

Miller, G. R., & Steinberg, M. (1975). *Between people: A new analysis of interpersonal communication.* Chicago: Science Research Associates.

O'Keefe, B. J. (1988). The logic of message design: Individual differences in reasoning about communication. *Communication Monographs, 55,* 80-103.

O'Keefe, B. J. (1992). Developing and testing rational models of message design. *Human Communication Research, 18,* 637-649.

Parks, M. (1982). Ideology in interpersonal communication: Off the couch and into the world. In M. Burgoon (Ed.), *Communication yearbook 5* (pp. 79-107). New Brunswick, NJ: Transaction.

Parks, M. (1994). Communicative competence and interpersonal control. In M. L. Knapp & G. R. Miller (Eds.), *Handbook of interpersonal communication* (2nd ed., pp. 591-620). Thousand Oaks, CA: Sage.

Parsons, T., & Bales, R. (1955). *Family, socialization, and interaction process.* New York: Free Press.

Rubin, L. (1983). *Intimate strangers.* San Francisco: Harper & Row.

Schaef, A. W. (1985). *Women's reality: An emerging female system in a white male society.* New York: Harper.

Schlesinger, A. M., Jr. (1992). *The disuniting of America.* New York: W. W. Norton.

Sennett, R. (1977). *The fall of public man.* New York: Vintage.

Stewart, J. (Ed.). (1990). *Bridges not walls: A book about interpersonal communication.* New York: McGraw-Hill.

Stewart, J., & Logan, C. (1993). *Together: Communicating interpersonally.* New York: McGraw-Hill.

Swain, S. (1989). Covert intimacy: Closeness in men's friendships. In B. Risman & P. Schwartz (Eds.), *Gender in intimate relationships: A microstructural approach* (pp. 71-86). Belmont, CA: Wadsworth.

Tavris, C. (1992). *The mismeasure of woman.* New York: Simon & Schuster.

Whitfield, C. L. (1987). *Healing the child within.* Deerfield Beach, FL: Health Communications.

Williams, D. G. (1985). Gender, masculinity-femininity, and emotional intimacy in same-sex friendship. *Sex Roles, 12,* 587-600.

Wood, J. T. (1993). Enlarging conceptual boundaries: A critique of research in interpersonal communication. In S. P. Bowen & N. Wyatt (Eds.), *Transforming visions: Feminist critiques in communication studies* (pp. 19-49). Cresskill, NJ: Hampton.

Wood, J. T., & Inman, C. C. (1993). In a different mode: Masculine styles of communicating closeness. *Journal of Applied Communication Research, 21,* 279-295.

INDEX

Abelson, R., 108, 119

Abstracting, and mindlessness-mindfulness, 114–116

Acquired immunodeficiency syndrome, fear, use of, in risk message, 229–254

Action assembly theory, message production:
cognitive encoding, 26–53
conceptual attributes, 27–28
empirical attributes, 28–29
methodological attributes, 28–29
multiple goal, 26–53, 31–35
speech-onset latency, 34, 40, 47
theoretical attributes, 27–28

Adaptation model, message design, 74–79

Agenda-setting, risk communication, 326–327

Agre, P. E., 58, 67

Ajzen, I., xiv, 202, 203, 204, 207, 329

Albrecht, T. L., 384, 397

Anderson, D. R., 138, 152, 153

Antecedents, of mindlessness-mindfulness, in social interaction, 108–110

Appelt, D. E., 58

Applegate, J. L., 96

Appraisal, constructivist research program, 86–92

Aristotelian logic, language and, 112–114

Armstrong, G. B., 143

Arvonen, T., 456

Ashby, W. R., 172, 173

Attention:
as communication variable, 134–135
misconceptions regarding, 137–141
research on, significance of, 135–137
to television, measurement of, 133–161, 141–151
capacity model, 143–144
covert process measurement, 142–151
overt behavior, 151–154
preload task methodology, 147–149
psychophysiological measure, 149–151
reaction time, 145–146

Attitude:
change, risk communication, 328
and reasoned action theory, 202–203

Baddeley, A. D., 147

Bailey, W., 115

Bales, R., 487

Barbee, A., xvi

Bargh, J. A., 108

Barrera, M., 384, 408

Bateson, G., 473

Baxter, L., 182

Beattie, M., 489

Beatty, M. J., 19, 88

Becker, M. H., 330

Behavior:
and reasoned action theory, 202–203
overt, as measure of attention, 151–154

Behavioral change, risk communication, 331

Behavioral intention, risk communication, 329–331

Berger, C. R., 180, 191, 195, 465

Berry, M. M., 391, 393

Bikson, T. K., 445

Bochner, A., 470

Bransford, J. D., 45

Brown, P., 30, 428

Brummett, B., 456

Brunk, C., 284

Buber, M., 485

Bull, V., 19

Burgoon, J. K., xiii, 119

Burgoon, M., xvii

Burke, J. A., 75

Burleson, B. R., 96, 384, 385, 392, 397, 408, 428

Button, G., 357

Cacioppo, J. T., 328

Capacity model, in measurement of attention, 143–144

Cappella, J. N., 172

Carter, R. F., 134

Carver, C. S., 387

Casey, N., 357

Cegala, D. J., 187, 191

Chafe, W. L., 59, 61

Chaffee, S. H., 134, 195

Chaiken, S., 17–19

Chang, S., 326

Chanowitz, B., 111

Chapman, D., 58, 67

Cheuck, W. H., 403, 405

Cialdini, R. B., 121
Citizens' advisory councils, creation of,
    264–269
Clayman, S. E., 366
Cognition:
    during communication, 189–191
    requirement-centered perspective, 180–197,
        186–189
    compartmentalization of research, 183–184
    emotion and, 183
Cognitive encoding, action assembly theory,
    26–53
    message production
        cognitive encoding, 26–53
        conceptual attributes, 27–28
        empirical attributes, 28–29
        methodological attributes, 28–29
        multiple goal, 26–53, 31–35
        speech-onset latency, 34, 40, 47
        theoretical attributes, 27–28
Cognitive interdependence, requirement-
    centered perspective, 191–192
Cognitive interpersonal communication
    research, 162–179
    assumptions, 163–164
    modern theories, 162–179
Cognitively based pause, social pause,
    contrasted, 35–38
Cognitive rules:
    construct differentiation, 14–20
    heuristic processing, 16–20
    interaction goals, 3–21
    schema development, 14–16
Cognitive structure, and reasoned action
    theory, 203–204
Cohen, L. J., 422
Cohen, P. R., 56
Communicative microdynamics of, of
    emotional support, 414–433
Compatibility, v. incompatibility, in message
    features, in message assembly, in
    multiple-goal message production, 38–42
Complexity account, in multiple-goal message
    production, 42–47
Compliance-gaining message, theme identifi-
    cation, 65–66
Computer product demonstration, micro-
    management of expert talk, by
    television host, 345–370
Conceptual attributes, message production,
    27–28

Condom use, fear, use of, in risk message,
    229–254
Congitively-based pause, social pause,
    contrasted, 35–38
Connectivity, and electronic mail, 443–445
Consequences, of mindlessness-mindfulness,
    in social interaction, 110–111
Construct differentiation:
    alternative conception of, 6–99–13
    cognitive rules model, 14–20
    goal formation, 6–13
    traditional conception of, 6–9
Constructivist research program:
    appraisal of, 86–92
    corroboration, 89–91
    degeneration, 91–92
    explanation, 89–91
    methodology, 84–86
    negative heuristic, engagement of, 96–98
    parsimony, 91
    positive heuristic, 92–96
    prediction, 89–91
    progression, 91–92
    protective belt, 87–89
    revision, 92–99
    scope, 91
Content, conversational, requirement-centered
    perspective, 191
Conversation:
    content, requirement-centered perspective,
        191
    interaction, in institutions, 371–380
Cook, R., 207
Coping, interactive, in close relationships,
    381–413
Corporations, environmental risk
    communication, 255–277
    citizens' advisory councils, 264–269
    open-door policy, 271
    training technical experts, 269–271
    trust, 271–273
Corroboration, constructivist research
    program, 89–91
Corty, E., 17
Covello, V. T., 249, 257, 312
Covert process measurement, 142–151
Cross-level, of risk communication, 323
Culnan, M. J., 454
Cunningham, M., xvi
Cutrona, C. E., 385, 408

Daft, R. L., 437
Dakof, G. A., 421
Daley, J. A., 92
Davis, K. E., 23
Dearing, J. W., 326
Decision quality, and electronic mail, 443
Degeneration, constructivist research program, 91–92
Delia, J. G., 86–88, 90, 95
Derlega, V. J., 392, 421, 422
Design of message, 54–79, 59–67
  adaptation model, 74–79
  complex interpersonal tasks, 61–64
  compliance-gaining message, theme identification, 65–66
  description, structure of, 59–61
  knowledge organization, 68–70
  local management, 67–70
  message generation model, 70–74
    antecedents, 70–72
    relevance, 72–73
  planning, 67–68
  problem-solving model, 55–59
  speech, flow of thought, 59–67
Devgun, J. S., 251
Dialectical discourse, on risk, 278–299
Diary, interaction record, sensitive interaction systems theory, 402–403
Dileo, D., 115
Diversity, in interpersonal communication, 490–494
Doise, W., 174
Douglas, M., 298
Dozier, D., 208
Drechsel, B., 140
Drew, D. G., 139
Dunwoody, S., xiv, 207, 208, 312

Eagly, A., 17–19
Edwards, D., 182
Electronic mail, 434–463
  access to new information, 443–444
  and connectivity, 443–445
  consensus, 442–443
  decision quality, 443
  group polarization, 442
  group processes and, 439–443
  nonconforming behavior, 441–442
  social control, 447
  social impact of, 434–453
  social network, 438–439
  socially relevant characteristics of, 436
  status equalization, 440–441
E-mail. *See* Electronic mail
Emotion, rise of, as communication variable, 183
Emotional support:
  behavior seeking, relationship to support-giving behavior, 396–397
  communicative microdynamics of, 414–433
  interactive coping, 381–413
Empirical attributes, message production, 28–29
Endler, N. S., 387
Environmental risk communication, corporate, 255–277
  citizens' advisory councils, 264–269
  open-door policy, 271
  training technical experts, 269–271
  trust, 271–273
Equality, threats to, risk communication, 332–333, 335, 337
Erev, I., 126
Ethical issues, in risk communication, 331–337
Eveland, J. D., 445
Expert talk, micromanagement of, 345–370
Explanation, constructivist research program, 89–91
Extended parallel process model, risk message, 230–253

Fallacious reasoning, and mindlessness, 120–122
Fear:
  acquired immunodeficiency syndrome, risk message, 229–254
  risk message, 229–254
    extended parallel process model, 230–253
Feminization, of intimacy, 487–488
Fessenden-Raden, J., 285
Finholt, T., 445, 447
Finlay, M., 457
Fishbein, M., xiv, 203, 205, 206, 222, 329
Fiske, S. T., 14
Fitchen, J. M., 285
Fletcher, G. J., 19
Flora, J. A., xv, 328
Flow of thought, and speech, 59–67
Fogg, B., xv
Folger, J. P., 170
Folkman, S., 386
Food safety, risk

politics of, 279–282
public values and, 282–286
Foss, K. A., 496
Foss, S. K., 491
Fulk, J., 437, 438, 439, 457

Garton, L., xvi
Geist, P., 392
Gilligan, C., 475, 487
Gilovitch, T., 121
Glidewell, J. C., 423
Glucksberg, S., 118
Goal formation:
    construct differentiation, 6–13
    individual differences, 3–21
"Golden age of cognition," 180–197
Goldsmith, D. J., xvi, 384, 386, 397
Gottlieb, B. H., 384, 421
Gottman, J. M., 407
Gray, J. L., 392
Greenberg, B. S., 143
Greene, J. O., xii, 34–35, 41, 45, 47
Griffin, R. J., xiv, 312
Grimes, T., xiii, 139, 140, 146
Grosz, B. J., 60, 75
Group polarization, electronic mail, 442
Group processes, and electronic mail, 439–443
Grunig, J. E., 275, 328
Gulley, M. P., 396, 397

Habermas, J., 493
Hackett, R., 207
Hadden, S. G., 274
Hartwick, J., 329
Hawes, L. C., 494
Hawkins, R. P., 153
Haworth, L., 284
Hazard characteristics, health risk messages,
    reasoned action theory, 206–207
Health behavior, reasoned action theory, 204
Health risk messages, reasoned action theory,
    201–228
    attitude, 202–203, 218–220
    behavior, 202–203, 202–204
    cognitive structure, 202–203, 218–220
    control variables, 213
    dependent measures, 212–213
    dependent variables, 209

design, 210–211
hazard characteristics, 206–207
health behavior, 204
hypotheses, 209–210
illness belief, 214–218
manipulated variables, 206
model component relationships, 220–221
norms, 202–203
procedure, 212
research questions, 209–210
risk communication, 204–209
statistical analysis, 213–214
stimulus materials, 212
stylistic structure, 207–209
subjects, 210–211
Heath, J. S., 285
Heath, R. L., xiv, 275
Heffner, M. B., 134
Heider, F., 10
Hermann, T., 70–72
Heuristic processing:
    cognitive rules, 16–20
    negative, in constructivist research
        program, 96–98
    positive, in constructivist research
        program, 92–96
Hewes, D. E., xiii, 168, 170, 173, 174
Higginbotham, J., 122
Hitch, G., 147
Holmes, M. E., xvii, 459
Honesty, threats to, risk communication, 333,
    336
Hopper, R., xvi
Hovy, E., 57, 58
Howe, G. W., 11
Hughes, R., 492

Ideology:
    interpersonal communication, 480–497
        diversity and, 490–494
        of intimacy, 484–487
        victim, 488–490
Incompatible message features, v. compatible,
    in message assembly, in multiple-goal
    message production, 38–42
Individual differences, in goal formation, 3–21
Individual level, risk communication, 321–322
In goal formation, individual differences in,
    3–21

Injunctions, in risk communication, 328–331
Institutions, conversational interaction in, 371–380
Integrative conflict tactics, cognitive bases of, 192–195
Interaction:
    coping:
        interaction record diary, sensitive interaction systems theory, 402–403
        mood, 400–401
        responses to, 403–405
        sensitive interaction systems theory, 397–405
        social support communication, 381–413
        thought listening, 402
    goals, cognitive rules model, 3–21
Interdependence, cognitive, requirement-centered perspective, 191–192
Interpersonal tasks, and message design management, 61–64
Interpretive continuum, risk communication, 324–325
Intimacy:
    feminization of, 487–488
    and ideology, 484–487
Iyengar, S., 208

Jackson, K. M., 134
Janz, N. K., 330
Jefferson G., 425
Johnson, M. K., 45
Jones, E. E., 9, 10, 18
Joseph, J. G., 330
Jourard, S. M., 485
Juanillo, N., xv
Judgment, influencing, with risk communication, 327

Kahneman, D., 143
Kalikow, B. N., 274
Kaminer, W., 490
Kasperson, R. E., 207, 310
Kellermann, K., 108
Kennamer, J. D., 208, 217
Kiesler, S., 441, 446, 447
Kinder, D. R., 208
Kirscht, J. P., 330
Knowledge:
    enhancement, risk communication, 325–326
    organization, 68–70

Korzybski, A., 112
Kosicki, G. M., 139
Krimsky, S., 291, 303, 305
Kuutti, K., 456

Labov, W., 60
Laing, R. D., 474
Lakota, I., 84–85
Lambert, B. L., xii–xiii, 61, 63, 64, 70, 73, 75–76
Lang, A., 149, 150, 156
Langer, E., xiii, 110, 111, 117, 119, 120, 125
Language:
    achieving mindfulness through, 122–126
    role of, in mindlessness-mindfulness, 111–120
Lannamann, J. W., 480, 482, 483
Lave, L., 332, 336
Lazarus, R. S., 386
Lea, M., 442
Lee, B., 284
Lee, J. Y., 63–64
Lehman, D. R., 392
Lemert, J. L., 207
Lengel, R. H., 451
Le Poire, B. A., 119
Levelt, D. M., 70
Leventhal, H., 231
Levin, S. R., 152, 153
Levinson, S., 30, 428
Levy, D. M., 59
Liberman, A., 17–19
Linde, C., 60
Lindsey, A. E., 35
Lorch, E. P., 152, 153–154
Lutz, R. J., 205

Macro-level, of risk communication, 322
Maddux, JE, 330
Maibach, EW, 328
Management of message design, 54–79
    adaptation model, 74–79
    complex interpersonal tasks, 61–64
    description, structure of, 59–61
    knowledge organization, 68–70
    local management, 67–70
    message generation model, 70–74
        antecedents, 70–72
        relevance, 72–73
    planning, 67–68

problem-solving model, 55–59
speech, flow of thought, 59–67
Markus, M. L., 454
McGuire, W. J., 217, 324
McLeod, J. M., 139
Meadowcroft, J. M., xiii, 145–146, 155
Mediocrity, acceptance of, 464–479
Message production, 70–74
  antecedents, 70–72
  conceptual attributes, 27–28
  empirical attributes, 28–29
  generation model, 70–74
    antecedents, 70–72
    relevance, 72–73
  methodological attributes, 28–29
  multiple-goal, 31–35
  for multiple social goals, 26–53
  relevance, 72–73
  speech-onset latency, 34, 40, 47
  theoretical attributes, 27–28
Methodological attributes, message production,
  28–29
Metts, S., 392
Micromanagement, of expert talk, 345–370
Middlestadt, S. E., 205, 222
Middleton, D., 182
Miller, G. R., 476, 485
Mindlessness-mindfulness, in social interaction,
  105–132
  abstracting, 114–116
  achieving through language, 122–126
  antecedents of, 108–110
  Aristotelian logic, 112–114
  characteristics of, 107–108
  consequences of, 110–111
  fallacious reasoning and, 120–122
  links to, 116–120
  nature of, 107–111
  role of language, 111–120
Misconceptions, about attention, 137–141
Mitzman, B., 207
Monsour, M., 168
Mood, sensitive interaction systems theory,
  400–401
Morgan, G. M., 332, 336
Motley, M., 474
Multiple-goal message production, 31–35
  compatible, v. incompatible message features, in message assembly, 38–42
  complexity account, 42–47
  pause, phonation, ratio, 45

Nathan, K., 275
National Research Council, 320, 337
Neal, M., 126
Negative heuristic, engagement of, in
  constructivist research program, 96–98
Neuwirth, K., xiv
New York Times v. Sullivan (1964), 475
Newell, A., 68
Newman, H., 119
Nisbett, R. E., 9, 18
Nofsinger, R., xv–xvi
Nolt, J., 122
Nonconforming behavior, electronic mail,
  441–442
Norms, and reasoned action theory, 202–203

O'Keefe, B. J., xii–xiii, 63–64, 90, 92, 98
O'Keefe, D. J., 16, 477
Organization, of knowledge, and message
  management, 68–70
Orlikowski, W. J., 460
Otway, H., 274
Overt behavior, as measure of attention,
  151–154

Pan, Z., 139
Parker, J. D. A., 387
Parks, M. R., xvii, 470
Parsimony, in constructivist research program,
  91
Parsons, T., 487
Pause:
  phonation, ratio, 45
  social v. congitively based, 35–38
Payne, S. K., 19, 88
Pearlin, L. I., 386
Perception, of risk, 308–312
  risk communication, 327–328
Perin, C., 438
Perrault, C. R., 56
Persuasion model, risk communication,
  289–290
Petty, R., 328
Phonation, pause, ratio, 45
Piper, P., 117
Planalp, S., 170
Planning, as message design management,
  67–68
Plough, A., 291, 303, 305

Pluralism, threats to, risk communication, 334–335
Political ideology, and interpersonal communication research, 468–476
Poole, M. S., 170, 459
Positive heuristic, in constructivist research program, 92–96
Prediction, constructivist research program, 89–91
Preload task methodology, in attention measurement, 147–149
Primack, J., 284
Progression, in constructivist research program, 91–92
Protective belt, constructivist research program, 87–89
Psychological factors, and risk perception, 309–311
Psychologization of communication, disenchantment with, 182–183
Psychophysiological measure, of attention, 149–151
Public values, and food safety risk, 282–286

Rakow, L. F., 324
Ramsay, T. B., 384
Rapaport, M., 459
Ray, M. L., 328
Reaction time, attention measurement, 145–146
Reasoned action theory, health risk messages, 201–228
    attitude, 202–203
    behavior, 202–203
    cognitive structure, 202–203, 218–220
    control variables, 213
    dependent measures, 212–213
    dependent variables, 209
    design, 210–211
    hazard characteristics, 206–207
    hypotheses, 209–210
    illness belief, 214–218
    manipulated variables, 206
    model component relationships, 220–221
    norms, 202–203
    procedure, 212
    research questions, 209–210
    risk communication, 204–209
    statistical analysis, 213–214
    stimulus materials, 212
    stylistic structure, 207–209

    subjects, 210–211
Reder, S., 460
Reeder, G. D., 19
Reeves, B., 145–146, 149
Relationship to support-giving behavior, support seeking behavior, 396–397
Relevance, and message generation, 72–73
Requirement-centered perspective
    cognition, 180–197, 186–189
    during communication, 189–191
    compartmentalization of research, 183–184
    emotion and, 183
    cognitive interdependence, 191–192
    conversational content, 191
    interdependence, cognitive, 191–192
Research:
    compartmentalization of, 183–184
    on risk communication:
        agenda, 300–319
        policies, 304–305
        risk perception, 308–312
Revision, constructivist research program, 92–99
Rhetoric, of risk communication, 312–316
Rice, R. E., 438
Rimal, R. N., xv
Risk:
    communication:
        agenda-setting, 326–327
        attitude change, 328
        behavioral change, 331
        behavioral intention, 329–331
        cross-level, 323
        citizens' advisory councils, 264–269
        direct effects model, 289
        environmental, corporate, 255–277
        equality, threats to, 332–333, 335, 337
        ethical issues, 331–337
        expanding discourse, 290–294
        framework for, 320–342
        health risk messages, reasoned action theory, 204–209
        honesty, threats to, 333, 336
        individual level of, 321–322
        injunctions, 328–331
        interpretive continuum, 324–325
        judgment, influencing, 327
        knowledge enhancement, 325–326
        levels of analysis, 321–323
        macro-level, 322
        perceived risk, 327–328

persuasion model, 289–290
pluralism, threats to, 334–335
policies, 304–305
risk perception, 308–312
rhetoric of, 312–316
self-determination, 333–334
threats to, 336–337
training technical experts, 269–271
voice, threats to, 334
dialectical discourse on, 278–299
food safety, politics of, 279–282
limited discourse, dilemmas of, 287–290
message, fear, 229–254
extended parallel process model, 230–253
perception, 308–312
psychological factors, 309–311
self-efficacy, and risk, 311
social factors, 311–312
research agenda, 300–319
self-efficacy, 311
Rogers, E. M., 326
Rogers, R. W., 330
Rohatyn, D., 122
Roloff, M. R., 170
Rosen, S., 403, 405
Roth, S., 422
Rowan, K., xv
Rucinski, D. M., 139
Ruesch, J., 116
Ruggles, W. L., 134
Russell, C., 296
Rutherford, D. K., 168
Ryan, M. J., 205

Sacks, H., 375–376
Saeki, M., 63–64
Salmon, C. T., 333
Sandler, I. N., 384
Sandman, P. M., 236
Schema development, cognitive rules, 14–16
Scherer, C., xv
Schleuder, J., 144, 146, 158
Schmitz, J., 438, 439
Schooler, C., 386
Schwab, R. G., 460
Seibold, D. R., 170
Seither, M., 207
Self-determination:
risk communication, 333–334
threats to, risk communication, 336–337
Self-efficacy, and risk, 311

Sennett, R., 484
Sensitive interaction systems theory, 397–405
interaction record diary, 402–403
mood, 400–401
thought listening, 402
Shegloff, E. A., 372
Shepherd, G. J., 15–16
Sheppard, B. H., 203, 329
Sherman, S. J., 17
Sibun, P., 59, 67
Siegal, J., 441
Simon, H., 68
Smolensky, P., 69
Social control, and electronic mail, 447
Social factors, and risk perception, 311–312
Social goals, multiple, production of messages in, 26–53
Social interaction, mindlessness-mindfulness in, 105–132
abstracting, 114–116
achieving through language, 122–126
antecedents of, 108–110
Aristotelian logic, 112–114
characteristics of, 107–108
consequences of, 110–111
fallacious reasoning and, 120–122
links to, 116–120
nature of, 107–111
role of language, 111–120
Social network, electronic mail, 438–439
Social pause, congitively based pause, contrasted, 35–38
Social support communication, interactive coping, 381–413
Sokolov, E. N., 150
Spears, R., 442
Speech-onset latency, 34, 40, 47
Spencer, J. W., 208
Sperber, D., 72
Sproull, L., 441, 445, 446, 447
Stasson, M., 206
Status equalization, electronic mail, 440–441
Steinberg, M., 485
Steinfield, C. W., 438
Stylistic structure, reasoned action theory, health risk messages, 207–209
Suhr, J. A., 385
Support, emotional:
communicative microdynamics of, 414–433
seeking behavior, relationship to support-giving behavior, 396–397
Swanson, D. L., 91

Taylor, S. E., 14, 421
Technical experts, training of, corporate environmental risk communication, 269–271
Television:
    attention, measurement of, 133–161, 141–151
    capacity model, 143–144
    covert process measurement, 142–151
    overt behavior, 151–154
    preload task methodology, 147–149
    psychophysiological measure, 149–151
    reaction time, 145–146
    host, micromanagement of expert talk by, 345–370
Texas gulf coast, environmental risk communication, corporate, 255–277
Theme identification, compliance-gaining message, 65–66
Theoretical attributes, message production, 27–28
Thoits, P. A., 413, 422, 429
Thorson, E., 144, 150
Thought listening, sensitive interaction systems theory, 402
Training, of technical experts, corporate, environmental risk communication, 269–271
Trank, D. M., 15–16
Trungpa, C., 113
Trust, and corporate environmental risk communication, 271–273

Ullmer-Ehrich, V., 60

Variables, manipulated, in reasoned action theory, 206
Victim, ideology of, 488–490
Voice, threats to, risk communication, 334
von Hippel, F., 284
von Hippel, W., 119
von Schomberg, R., 299
von Winterfeldt, D., 249

Wagner, F., 384
Waldron, V. R., xiii, 187, 190
Walsten, T., 126
Warshaw, P. R., 329
Watson, R., 459
Watt, J. H., 145
Weinstein, N. D., 322
Weisberg, R. W., 118
Wellman, B., xvi
Wildavsky, A., 298
Wilson, D., 72
Wilson, S. R., xii
Winstead, B. A., 392, 421, 422
Witte, K., xiv
Woods, E., 96
Wynne, B., 274

Yagade, A., 208
Yates J., 460

Zajonc, R. F., 179
Zhao, X., 153
Zorn, T. E., 90

ABOUT THE EDITOR

BRANT R. BURLESON (Ph.D., University of Illinois, Urbana-Champaign, 1982) is a Professor in the Department of Communication at Purdue University, where he teaches courses in communication theory, interpersonal communication, and the philosophy of the social sciences. His research interests center on communication skill acquisition and development, social-cognitive foundations of strategic communication, effects of communication skills on relationship formation and development, and prosocial supportive forms of communication. His research has appeared in several edited volumes and journals, including the *American Journal of Family Therapy, Child Development, Communication Monographs, Communication Research, Family Relations, Human Communication Research, Journal of Language and Social Psychology,* and *Quarterly Journal of Speech.* He has held several offices in both the International Communication Association and the Speech Communication Association, and has served on the editorial boards of more than a dozen major journals. Recently, he coedited (with Terrance Albrecht and Irwin Sarason) *Communication of Social Support: Messages, Interactions, Relationships, and Community* (Sage, 1994).

ABOUT THE AUTHORS

ANITA P. BARBEE (Ph.D., University of Georgia, 1988) is a social psychologist who is currently serving as a Research Scientist for the Child Welfare Training Assessment Project at the Kent School of Social Work, University of Louisville. She was the recipient of the International Network on Personal Relationships Dissertation Award in 1989. She is on the editorial boards of the *Journal of Social and Personal Relationships, Motivation and Emotion,* and *Journal of Social Behavior and Personality.* Her research focuses on social support, which is fueled by interests in the development and maintenance of personal relationships, gender issues, and health. She is currently working on a book on social support in close relationships.

JUDEE K. BURGOON is Professor of Communication at the University of Arizona, where she also serves on the faculty of the Business and Public Administration Arizona Executive Program. She is former editor of *Communication Monographs,* a Fellow of the International Communication Association, and a member of the Society for Experimental Social Psychology. Her current research interests and publications relate primarily to aspects of interpersonal communication and nonverbal communication, including expectancy violations theory, relational communication, dyadic interaction patterns, deception, impression management, and information management. Her writing credits include seven books and more than 130 articles, chapters, and reviews in communication, psychology, mass communication, and argumentation journals. Among her most recent books are *Nonverbal Communication: The Unspoken Dialogue* (Harper Collins, 1989; revised edition forthcoming from McGraw-Hill), with David Buller and Gill Woodall, and *Interpersonal Adaptation: Dyadic Interaction Patterns* (Cambridge University Press, in press), with Lesa Stern and Leesa Dillman.

MICHAEL BURGOON (Ph.D., Michigan State University) is Professor of Communication and Professor of Family and Community Medicine at the University of Arizona. He is a Fellow of the International Communication Association and a member by election of the Society for Experimental Social Psychology. He has published widely in communication, psychology, medicine, education, and management.

MICHAEL R. CUNNINGHAM (Ph.D., University of Minnesota, 1977) is a Professor in the Department of Psychology at the University of Louisville. He is on the editorial boards of *Journal of Personality and Social Psychology, Journal of Personality,* and *Motivation and Emotion.* Besides social support, his research interests include evolutionary variables in interpersonal attraction, social allergies, and individual differences in prosocial behavior in the workplace, such as honesty and service orientation. He and Anita Barbee are currently writing a book on attraction and love.

SHARON DUNWOODY (Ph.D., Indiana University) is Evjue-Bascom Professor of Journalism and Mass Communication and is on the instructional staff of the Institute of Environmental Studies at the University of Wisconsin—Madison. She is also Head of the Center for Environmental Communications and Education Studies, which conducts research on various aspects of communicating science to the public. Her research interests include understanding how mass media select and construct science accounts and the ways in which individuals use that information. Her most recent studies have focused on individuals' use of messages about environmental risks. Her recent publications have examined impacts of information subsidies and community structure on local press coverage of environmental contamination (*Journalism Quarterly,* 1994), the mass media and risk perception (in *Risk Is a Construct,* edited by B. Ruck, 1993), and journalistic strategies for reporting long-term environmental issues (in *The Mass Media and Environmental Issues,* edited by A. Hansen, 1993). She also recently authored a book, *Reconstructing Science for Public Consumption: Journalism as Science Education* (Deakin University).

JUNE A. FLORA (Ph.D., Arizona State University) is an Assistant Professor in the Department of Communication at Stanford University and Associate Director of the Center for Research in Disease Prevention at Stanford University. She has published research concerning theoretical and applied issues regarding health communication campaigns and message effectiveness. She is Chairperson of the Health Communication Division of the International Communication Association, and her research interests include communication campaigns designed for social change.

BJ FOGG (M.A., Brigham Young University) is a Ph.D. student in the Institute for Communication Research at Stanford University.

LAURA GARTON is a doctoral student in the Department of Sociology, University of Toronto, and a researcher for the university's Telepresence Project and the Centre for Urban and Community Studies. Her dissertation research uses a social network-analytic perspective to examine the impact of computer-mediated communication systems on the structure of organizational control. As a member of a multidisciplinary longitudinal research project at the University of Toronto, she is collecting data on the effects of introducing computerized desktop audio/video/screen-sharing communication technology on organizational structure, work practices, and interpersonal relations. She has also worked as a survey researcher and a community organizer in Canada and the United States.

JOHN GASTIL (Ph.D., University of Wisconsin—Madison, 1994) is a researcher at the University of New Mexico Institute for Public Policy. His primary research interests include democracy, small group behavior, political psychology, and critical theories of politics and society. His most recent publication is *Democracy in Small Groups: Participation, Communication, and Decision Making* (New Society, 1993). Some of his previous writings have appeared in *Discourse & Society, Human Relations, Journal of Applied Social Psychology, Political Psychology, Sex Roles,* and *Small Group Research.*

DAENA J. GOLDSMITH is Assistant Professor of Speech Communication at the University of Illinois, Urbana-Champaign. Her research examines the influence of culture in interpersonal communication. She is currently studying how the evaluation of advice giving varies depending on the use of facework strategies, the sequential placement of advice, attempts to define situations and relationships, and cultural expectations. She has published in *Communication Research, Communication Education,* and *Research on Language and Social Interaction.*

JOHN O. GREENE (Ph.D., University of Wisconsin—Madison, 1983) is Professor of Communication, Purdue University. His research interests center on human information-processing approaches to verbal and nonverbal message production. This focus is reflected in his work on developing action assembly theory and the application of that theory in a variety of domains, including social skill and social performance deficits, the nature of the self and its role in social interaction, and the nonverbal concomitants of deception. His work has appeared in a variety of books and scholarly journals, including *Communication Monographs, Communication Theory, Human Communication Research,* and *Quarterly Journal of Speech.*

ROBERT J. GRIFFIN (Ph.D., University of Wisconsin—Madison) is Associate Professor in the College of Communication at Marquette University in Milwaukee, Wisconsin. He is director of the Center for Mass Media Research and is former director of the college graduate program. Most of his research involves mass communication and environmental concerns, but he also conducts research into a variety of other communication topics. With Sharon Dunwoody, he has been conducting research into risk communication, funded by grants from the U.S. Environmental Protection Agency and the National Science Foundation. His recent publications include articles addressing the impacts of information subsidies and community structure on local press coverage of environmental contamination (*Journalism Quarterly,* 1994), journalistic strategies for reporting long-term environmental issues (in *The Mass Media and Environmental Issues,* edited by A. Hansen, 1992), and the impact of risk message content (*Journal of Language and Social Psychology,* 1992).

TOM GRIMES (Ph.D., Indiana University, 1986) is Ross Beach Professor of Journalism and Mass Communications at Kansas State University. He previously spent 10 years in television news, primarily in Dallas, Texas, as a general assignment reporter, news anchor, and news director. After earning a Ph.D., he took a faculty position at the School of Journalism and Mass Communication at the University of Wisconsin—Madison, where he remained until his move to Kansas State University. His research areas cover human information processing, with an emphasis on memory and attention. His recent publications, with coauthors, include an examination of the way human faces enhance memory for abstract messages when faces are paired with those messages (*Personality and Social Psychology Bulletin*, 1994) and a study that examines how certain TV production techniques can distort a viewer's memory for the content of televised news stories (*Communication Reports*, 1994).

ROBERT L. HEATH is Professor of Communication at the University of Houston. He is engaged in a series of research projects as well as community service projects involving chemical companies, health organizations, environmental and community activists, regulatory bodies, and members of the scientific community. The results of these efforts have been published in *Public Relations Quarterly* and *Journal of Public Relations Research*, as well as in the books *Enacting Organizational Communication: From Interpersonal Contacts to External Affairs* (Lawrence Erlbaum, 1994) and *Strategic Issues Management* (in preparation).

DEAN E. HEWES is Professor of Speech Communication at the University of Minnesota, Minneapolis. His work has appeared in *Communication Monographs, Quarterly Journal of Speech, Human Communication Research*, and *Communication Research*, as well as in *Communication Yearbook* and numerous other edited books. His most recent effort is the edited book *The Cognitive Bases of Interpersonal Communication* (Lawrence Erlbaum, in press). He is currently completing *Cognition in Communication* (Guilford Press). His research interests include social cognition, personal relationships, small group communication, research methodology, and the concept of "emergence" in communication theory. He is also a better-than-average fisherman.

MICHAEL E. HOLMES (Ph.D., University of Minnesota, 1991) is Assistant Professor in the Department of Communication, University of Utah. His research focuses on group decision support systems, crisis conflict, and sequential analysis of communication episodes. His work has been published in *Belfast Working Papers in Language and Linguistics, Journal of Organizational Computing, Management Science, Communication Yearbook*, and *Communication Research*.

ROBERT W. HOPPER (Ph.D., University of Wisconsin) is Charles Sapp Professor of Communication at the University of Texas at Austin. His most recent book, *Telephone Conversation* (Indiana University Press, 1992), applies conversation analysis to our most important electronic communications medium—the electronic medium for interpersonal communication. He is the founder of the International Communication Association's Special Interest Group in Language and Social Interaction.

NAPOLEON K. JUANILLO, Jr., (Ph.D., Cornell University, 1994) is a member of the faculty at the School of Communications Studies, Nanyang Technological University, Singapore. His research interests focus on information and communication issues relating to environmental management, biotechnology, food safety and nutrition, risk assessment, and risk management. His current research examines the impact of dialectical discourse of scientific uncertainty on the public's information-processing and decision-making strategies. His other research interests focus on media and public discourses of scientific and technical controversies in the United States and developing countries. He has published in *Communication Yearbook, Agriculture and Human Values,* and the *Asian Journal of Communication.*

BRUCE L. LAMBERT (Ph.D., University of Illinois, Urbana-Champaign, 1992) teaches health communication as an Assistant Professor in the Department of Pharmacy Administration and the Department of Pharmacy Practice at the University of Illinois, Chicago. His current research focuses on situated cognitive models of message production and on the antecedents and consequences of individual differences in communication skill among practicing pharmacists. Of particular interest to him are the effects of improved communication on patients' satisfaction, understanding, and compliance with health recommendations. He has investigated patients' perceptions of pharmacists' hypertension compliance-gaining messages as well as the impact of power and social distance on pharmacists' messages to physicians. His work has appeared in the *Quarterly Journal of Speech, International Journal of Psychology,* and *Proceedings of the Cognitive Science Society.*

ELLEN J. LANGER is Professor of Psychology at Harvard University, where she is Chair of the Social Psychology Program and a member of the Division on Aging of the Faculty of Medicine. She has been the recipient of a Guggenheim Fellowship and the American Psychological Association's Award for Distinguished Contributions to Psychology in the Public Interest. She is the author of many articles and three books, *Personal Politics* (with Carol Dweck), *The Psychology of Control,* and *Mindfulness.* Her current research interests include memory, the illusion of calculated decisions, and the phenomenon of horizontal hostility among social groups.

JEANNE MEADOWCROFT (Ph.D., University of Wisconsin—Madison) is a member of the faculty in the Department of Agricultural Journalism at the

University of Wisconsin—Madison. She previously taught in the Department of Telecommunications at Indiana University. Her research areas include memory and attentional processes. Two of her publications on attention include articles examining the influence of story schema development on children's attention to television (with Byron Reeves, in *Communication Research,* 1989) and attention span cycles (in *Patterns in Communication Processes,* edited by Watt and Van Lear, in press).

KURT NEUWIRTH is a doctoral candidate in the School of Journalism and Mass Communication at the University of Wisconsin—Madison. His research interests include public opinion processes, with particular interest in the spiral of silence and the role of risk communication in opinion formation and change. His recent publications include studies of the impact of risk message content (*Journal of Language and Social Psychology,* 1992), coming to terms with the impact of communication on scientific and technological risk judgments (in *Risky Business,* edited by L. Wilkins and P. Patterson, 1991), and perceptions of opinion climates and the willingness to discuss the issue of abortion (*Journalism Quarterly,* 1990).

ROBERT E. NOFSINGER (Ph.D., University of Iowa) is Associate Professor in the School of Communication, Washington State University. His research interests focus on the organization of conversation and other systems of interactive talk, such as broadcast news discussion programs, education and product demonstration programs, and call-in talk shows. He teaches courses in language and social interaction, conversation analysis, and interpersonal and small group communication. He is the author of *Everyday Conversation* (Sage, 1991) and has published articles in *Communication Monographs, Communication Reports, Research on Language and Social Interaction,* and the *Western Journal of Communication.*

BARBARA J. O'KEEFE (Ph.D., University of Illinois, Urbana-Champaign, 1976) is Associate Professor in the Department of Speech Communication, University of Illinois, Urbana-Champaign. Her research has addressed a wide range of questions related to the development of a theory of message design, including the development of skill at designing appropriately adapted messages; the structure and effects of persuasive messages, regulative messages, request refusals, and compliment responses; the management of multiple communicative goals, particularly instrumental and identity goals; and the nature of the cognitive processes underlying message adaptation and generation. In addition, she has addressed broader issues involved in the construction of theories of communication and has been a leading contributor to constructivist theory. Her recent publications, which focus on the role of implicit models of means-ends relations in guiding message design, have appeared in *Human Communication*

Research, Communication Monographs, and *Communication Research,* as well as in a number of edited books.

MALCOLM R. PARKS (Ph.D., Michigan State University, 1976) is Associate Professor of Speech Communication at the University of Washington. His primary research interests include the development of personal relationships and personal networks, communicative competence, and deceptive communication. He has served as Vice President of the International Communication Association and Chair of its Interpersonal Communication Division. His recent work includes chapters in the *Handbook of Interpersonal Communication* and *Communication and Social Influence Processes.*

RAJIV NATH RIMAL (M.A., Southern Illinois University at Carbondale) is a Ph.D. candidate in the Institute for Communication Research at Stanford University. His research interests include social and health influences of mass media messages. His recent work has concentrated on the role of communication in influencing children's health practices. He is also working on the analysis of public service announcements on AIDS from around the world.

KATHERINE E. ROWAN (Ph.D., Purdue University, 1985) is an Associate Professor in the Department of Communication at Purdue University. She teaches courses in journalism, public relations, and mass communication. Her scholarship draws from principles of classical rhetoric and contemporary social scientific research. The focus of her research is on features of effective written and oral discourse, particularly discourse designed to explain difficult ideas, and on risk communication, or discourse about physical hazards. Her publications have appeared in *Written Communication, Journal of Technical Writing and Communication, Journal of Applied Communication Research,* and *Risk Analysis,* as well as other outlets. She also presents seminars and public lectures on effective risk communication for citizens, scientists, and government officials.

CLIFFORD W. SCHERER (Ph.D., University of Wisconsin—Madison, 1976) is Associate Professor of Communication at Cornell University. His research focuses on the communication of scientific and technical information and the role of communication in public policy formation. He is particularly interested in issues concerning policy formation involving scientific uncertainty. He has published in a variety of journals and books, including *Communication Yearbook, Journal of Soil and Water Conservation, Agriculture and Human Values,* and *Journal of Communication.*

VINCENT R. WALDRON (Ph.D., Ohio State University, 1989) is currently Associate Professor in the Department of Communication Studies at Arizona State University West. His research addresses the role of emotion and cognition in the production of strategic messages in both interpersonal and organizational contexts. He has published his work in such journals as *Communication Monographs, Human Communication Research, Management Communication Quarterly,* and *Language and Social Psychology.*

BARRY WELLMAN (Ph.D., Harvard University) is Professor of Sociology at the Centre for Urban and Community Studies, University of Toronto, and a researcher in the university's Telepresence Project. He has developed the study of communities *as* social networks. His recent research has examined men's friendships, contrasted eighteenth-century Latvian and twentieth-century Canadian networks, and analyzed the network basis of various kinds of social support. He is now studying the ways in which those engaged in computer-supported cooperative work form virtual communities linked by new information technology. He is the founder of the International Network for Social Network Analysis and coeditor, with S. D. Berkowitz, of *Social Structures: A Network Approach* (Cambridge University Press, 1988). He is currently writing a book, *Personal Communities,* and editing another, *Networks in the Global Village,* to document the nature of personal communities in many countries.

STEVEN R. WILSON (Ph.D., Purdue University, 1989) is Associate Professor of Communication at Michigan State University. His research and teaching focus on the relationship between cognitive and communication processes in a variety of contexts, such as interpersonal influence, parenting, and conflict and negotiation. His work has appeared in several journals and edited books, including *Communication Monographs, Communication Research, Communication Yearbook, Human Communication Research, Management Communication Quarterly,* and *Research on Language and Social Interaction.* He currently serves on the editorial board for *Communication Studies.*

KIM WITTE (Ph.D., University of California, Irvine) is an Assistant Professor in the Department of Communication at Michigan State University. Her work examines how fear-arousing messages either motivate or inhibit health-promoting and/or disease-preventing behaviors. Recently, she has begun to investigate how members of different cultures respond to fear-arousing interpersonal and mass media messages. Her work has appeared in *Communication Monographs, Social Science & Medicine, International Quarterly of Community Health Education,* and elsewhere.